"As iron sharpens iron, so a man sharpens the countenance of his friend."-Proverbs 27:17 NKJV

Cover art by Randy Glass   www.randyglassstudio.com

i

Iron Sharpening Iron: A Biblical Guide for the God-Honoring
American Man
by Paul D. LeFavor

Copyright © 2014 by Blacksmith LLC

ISBN 978-0-9895513-1-1
Printed in the United States of America

Published by Blacksmith LLC
Fayetteville, NC

www.Blacksmithpublishing .com

Direct inquiries and/or orders to the above web address.

Table of Contents

Forward

America's greatest need is Jesus Christ. A not so distant second is the recovery of mature masculine servant leadership. Jesus Christ, the divine warrior, defined this type of leadership that is so badly needed in America today. Jesus Christ fought a mighty running battle against demonic forces in league with Satan, shook the powers of heaven and earth, and by the will and design of God the Father, died in climactic close combat at Golgotha, absorbing the penetrating wrath and punishment of God, and forever saving everyone who believes in Him. What a Savior! Jesus Christ came not to be served, but to serve and give His life as a ransom for many (Mt 20:28). This is leadership. Thinking of others as more important than yourself (Phil 2:3). Giving of yourself for the needs of others, defending the weak and defenseless, standing up against evil. America today is adrift in a sea of moral confusion and biblical illiteracy. America today desperately needs mature masculine servant-hearted leaders.

I have been privileged to command the finest, most elite units our nation has in its arsenal, from an Infantry platoon to the Special Forces Regiment. During my 36 year career in the US Army I spent 13 years in Delta Force, including two years as its commander. I had to make many difficult decisions as a commander in the Special Forces. And though I didn't initiate every action, I always felt responsible to provide guidance and initiative, so as to mobilize the strengths of others. In combat, I had to make sound and timely tactical decisions. And though I didn't always rely on all the advice given to me, I have always relied on the strength and guidance of my God, who was ever present, even in the most desperate of situations.

God desires for Christian men to be mature, masculine and responsible servant leaders in the home, at church, and at work. 1 Corinthians 16:13 reminds us to "Be on the alert, stand firm in the faith, act like men, be strong." Christian men hold it the highest honor to protect their families and defend their country. This book sounds a clarion call for the God-honoring men of America to take a stand for Christ and the written Word of God, and will be a valuable resource for years to come. This book is for American men. It's not meant to exclude women but seeks to bless them – immeasurably, by demonstrating biblically what it means to serve God as a man. The goal of this book is to recover biblical manhood and the disciplines that promote Christlikeness; to promote the principles that made our country free; to strengthen the family, defend life and advance true freedom that is found in Christ alone. This is a call to biblical mature masculine spiritual leadership. This is a call to repentance, responsibility, humility and risk-taking.

De Oppresso Liber
Lt General William G. Boykin, USA (Ret.)

Introduction

"He has shown you, O man, what is good; and what does the LORD require of you But to do justly, to love mercy, and to walk humbly with your God (Micah 6:8)?"

The prevalent attitudes and views of our society fluctuate like the wild waves of the sea.[1] The American values of relativism – there are no absolutes, pluralism – every system of thought is of equal value, toleration – everything is acceptable and individualism – every man is the captain of his own soul has resulted in a chaotic state of moral and spiritual anarchy. What we are experiencing in America today, as well as western civilization as a whole, is a disintegration of society's foundation. What we are seeing now is a near complete inversion of values. They call good evil and evil good. However, there can be only one foundation laid (Isaiah 5:20; Ephesians 2:20), "all other ground is sinking sand."

Repelled by moral absolutism, the tenets of traditional morality are being replaced by the dictates of the state. It is as though the effects of the Enlightenment and science have all but rendered Christianity intellectually untenable. To the effect that anyone holding to such naïveté as Christianity must be considered obtuse, medieval, and perhaps even hateful. Our society is in danger morally because binding and absolute norms are now seen as implausible.[2] Thus our society is repudiating biblical morality because it proceeds from supernatural truth but when you remove the foundation of any superstructure, the structure will most certainly collapse. The whole of western civilization was built on the foundation of biblical morality, which, as a whole, has ceased to exist.

Nietzsche, far from being a faithful adherent to Christianity, tellingly diagnoses the collapse of western civilization's biblical foundation by way of his parable of the madman. In his work, the *Gay Science*, Nietzsche's "madman" satirically prognosticates the plight of western man and exposes the sham hypocrisy of mere "Christian" pretenses. He writes:

---

[1] Isaiah the prophet tells us, "But the wicked are like the troubled sea, when it cannot rest, whose waters cast up mire and dirt. There is no peace, says my God, for the wicked." In the same vein Jude 13 tells us, "They are wild waves of the sea, foaming up their shame" (57:20-21), cf. James 1:6.

[2] Wells, God in the Wasteland, 156.

ix

Introduction

Have you not heard of that madman who lit a lantern in the bright morning hours, ran to the market-place, and cried incessantly: "I am looking for God! I am looking for God!" As many of those who did not believe in God were standing together there, he excited considerable laughter. Have you lost him, then? Said one. Did he lose his way like a child? Said another. Or is he hiding? Is he afraid of us? Has he gone on a voyage? Or emigrated? Thus they shouted and laughed. The madman sprang into their midst and pierced them with his glances.

"Where has God gone?" he cried. "I shall tell you. We have killed him – you and I. We are his murderers. But how have we done this? How were we able to drink up the sea? Who gave us the sponge to wipe away the entire horizon? What did we do when we unchained the earth from its sun? Whither is it moving now? Whither are we moving now? Away from all suns? Are we not perpetually falling? Backward, sideward, forward, in all directions? Is there any up or down left? Are we not straying as through an infinite nothing? Do we not feel the breath of empty space? Has it not become colder? Is it not more and more night coming on all the time? Must not lanterns be lit in the morning? Do we not hear anything yet of the noise of the gravediggers who are burying God? Do we not smell anything yet of God's decomposition? Gods too decompose. God is dead. God remains dead. And we have killed him. How shall we, murderers of all murderers, console ourselves? That which was the holiest and mightiest of all that the world has yet possessed has bled to death under our knives. Who will wipe this blood off us? With what water could we purify ourselves? What festivals of atonement, what sacred games shall we need to invent? Is not the greatness of this deed too great for us? Must we not ourselves become gods simply to be worthy of it? There has never been a greater deed; and whosoever shall be born after us – for the sake of this deed he shall be part of a higher history than all history hitherto."

Here the madman fell silent and again regarded his listeners; and they too were silent and stared at him in astonishment. At last he threw his lantern to the ground, and it broke and went out. "I have come too early," he said then; "my time has not come yet. The tremendous event is still on its way, still travelling – it has not yet reached the ears of men. Lightning and thunder require time, the light of the stars requires time, deeds require time even after they are done, before they can be seen and heard. This deed is still more distant from them than the distant stars – and yet they have done it themselves."

It has been further related that on that same day the madman entered divers churches and there sang a *requiem aeternam deo*. Led

Introduction

out and quieted, he is said to have retorted each time: "what are these churches now if they are not the tombs and sepulchers of God?"[3]

Although an atheist, when Nietzsche said God is dead, he wasn't saying there is no God, he was giving us in descriptive form the spiritual state of western Christendom. What he was saying is although western civilization was founded on the Christian faith, that foundation no longer exists because western man no longer believes in God. By and large, Western man still goes to church, takes part in Christian fellowship, albeit his idea of fellowship is drinking a cup of coffee and engaging in small talk, but to him God doesn't really exist anymore.

Nietzsche demonstrates the sheer hypocrisy of sham Christianity by way of the villagers in his parable. First, they mockingly deride the madman in a manner reminiscent of the false prophets of Baal (1 Kgs 18), but then their derision turns to shock and awe as the madman, by way of the phrase, "God is dead," reveals the deplorable spiritual condition of western man. What Nietzsche was concerned about relating to his own generation was the fact that God is dead in the hearts and minds of modern men; killed by an indifference that is directly related to a pronounced cultural shift away from faith and towards relativism and science. Nietzsche says, this is where Western Europe and western civilization as a whole is heading – atheism.

Though these words of Nietzsche may seem grotesque to Christian ears, he was correct in his deduction that God had become dead to a society, which although shared a defining set of traditional beliefs – biblical morality, it had ceased to acknowledge those foundational truths to originate in God and His word, and had relegated them to the creation of the state. Western man by and large no longer believes in God, hence the foundation is gone; the whole basis for social order, the Judeo-Christian ethic. And so, what is the projected end? Nihilism: life without purpose, meaning or intrinsic value. Once the foundation of western civilization has been completely undermined, removed, and eradicated, nothing will

---

[3] Nietzsche, The Gay Science, 119.

Introduction

remain but nihilism – values lose their value. And there simply is no virtue if there is no immortality.

Nihilism is a condition in which all values, such as marriage, family, decency, etc., lose their values. Values reflect our sense of right and wrong. Values generate behavior.[4] What we value exerts influence on our behavior so that our behavior becomes our character. The new values that are being developed are those that have nothing to do with the Bible or Jesus Christ. But what is this new framework of values to look like? It's as Dostoyevsky's character Ivan says, "If there is no God, then everything is permitted. Moreover nothing would be immoral, everything would be lawful, even cannibalism."[5]

The values being advanced today are in direct opposition to the Judeo-Christian framework which has guided and restrained our American society for more than two hundred years. America now seems bent on nothing short of creating a "brave new world" after its own image, unflinchingly charting a course into unexplored moral territory, jettisoning its unwanted cumbersome cargo, without rudder, without anchor, to wherever the gales lead on. Fellow voyagers on this Orphean odyssey are obliged to countenance the whole sportive enterprise, refrain from any rejoinder, or walk the plank. In fact, the whole drama is unfolding at such a pace that for any American with a biblical constitution to attempt a course correction would be likened to arranging deck chairs on the Titanic? One may ask like the apprehensive traveler, "is this ship really unsinkable?" To which the presumptuous reply is yet again, "God himself could not sink this ship."

Because the world rejects the Bible, in which God teaches us everything we need to know concerning Him as well as the duty He requires of us, the only morality it will recognize, advocate and foist is the one that furthers its own cause; a transvaluation of values. The impetus for which is really a subconscious desire to find some measure of peace by seeking to rid itself from a confused and agitated conscience. This is

---

[4] Rokeach, Understanding Human Values, 94.
[5] Dostoyevsky, The Brothers Karamazov, 72.

Introduction

the collective, prevailing woe of unregenerate fallen man; nothing is true and everything is permitted.

In America, at an appalling pace, a transvaluation of biblical values is underway. Values have been redefined according to convenience and preference. Some churches have found what they believe to be a biblical warrant for their alternative lifestyles while others have redrafted their bylaws so as to avoid any litigation. But isn't truth independent of human desire or preference? What are now becoming the standards of conduct are decidedly foreign to Holy Scripture as well as common sense.

As for the armed forces, due to policies that uniformed service members must acquiesce to, it is becoming increasingly difficult to be a Christian and serve; irrespective of their own conscience. Anyone who raises a moral objection to current dogmatic policy risks prosecution. Evangelical Christian service members are facing ever growing hostility toward their faith. Religious persecution is currently underway under the auspices of upholding the rights of others. It seems as though what is desired for Christian service members to do is to hide their faith in Christ as America continues to remove any and all vestiges of Christianity from the military. However, don't Christians serving in the military have a constitutional right to express their faith? This book will argue in the affirmative.

Looking at our current moral implosion in America begs the question, what's the driving force in all of this? Is it, as Schopenhauer proposed, a will to live? An all prevailing desire which all living creatures share to avoid death and procreate? Or, is it, as Freud postulated, a will to pleasure? An instinctual seeking of pleasure and avoiding of pain which satisfies psychological as well as biological needs? Or perhaps, as Nietzsche, the prophet of nihilism himself put it – the will to power? Which idea is perhaps best encapsulated with the words,

"Let us abolish the real world: and to be able to do this we first have to abolish the supreme value hitherto, morality. If the tyranny of former values is broken in this way, if we have abolished the "real world," then a new order of values must follow of its own accord,

Introduction

and the "real world," "truth," "God," this is what we have to abolish."[6]

Current societal trends evidence the insidious strategy that whatever brings affirmation to man's desire, be it a will to live, to pleasure, or to power, will be venerated; and we will become like what we revere.[7] And all this "political correctness," which is under the guise of freedom, is merely a reflection of mankind's fallen nature. For man is bent on audaciously and presumptuously carving out his existence without God and on his own terms. But when we defect from God's commands and forsake His Word, we freely lend our ears to the lies of Satan. Thus, the only morality the world will recognize is the one that will further their cause.[8] Thus, society's values are redefined according to political expedience and preference, which is, as Nietzsche predicted, decidedly nihilistic – valueless.

At this point there are two ways to go. The first is to call upon the faithful adherents of Christianity to repentance and faith thereby reestablishing the foundation – biblical morality. The second is to build a new system and a new foundation of values which is the work of a secular society. This book will argue for the first solution to our plight because there is such a thing as eternal, objective, and unchangeable truth which is the only foundation that is God-honoring, the only foundation that will last (Mt 7:24-27). Morality is not majority driven, morality is God driven. Besides with God, even one man is in the majority.

God's desire is for His people to become spiritually mature; conformed into the image of His Son Jesus Christ. This transformation requires God's corrective work. God's desire is for His people to want this conformity. This book will argue,

---

[6] Nietzsche, The Will to Power, 254. Nietzsche goes on to add, "This world, a monster of energy…transforms itself as a whole…as a becoming that knows no satiety, no disgust, no weariness: this, my Dionysian world of the eternally self-creating, the eternally self-destroying, this mystery world of the two-fold voluptuous delight, my "beyond good and evil,"…This world is the will to power – and nothing besides! And you yourselves are also this will to power – and nothing besides!

[7] Beale, We Become What We Worship, 307.

[8] Reagan, Speaking My Mind, 171.

Introduction

in a biblical-theological way, how God makes use of means in His corrective work of transformation; chastening every son He receives, and correcting those whom He loves (Heb 12:6). This book will emphasize the manner of God's transformative work which may be summarized by the following dictum: *God, making use of means, works to purify His saints.* This implies that sanctification is the work of God's purifying holiness in the life of one He has regenerated.

For this purpose, God intends to employ various means, both earthly and heavenly, both spatially and temporally. That is to say, God employs other men and women, along with supernatural spiritual beings, all both wicked and righteous to be the corrective, chastening instruments in the life of the saint, in order to conform him to the image of Christ (Gal 4:19). These corrective instruments, be they benevolent or malevolent, serve to bring about the desired change at every stage of God's developmental process. Detecting this transformative work of God, believers receive this corrective love as it were His, growing in grace and in the knowledge of God, becoming teachable, hearing and receiving God's correction from others (Pro 27:6).

The purpose of this book is to bring glory to God by promoting the Christian values that made America great – values such as biblical masculinity; biblical marriage and biblical family life; the God-honoring values that are directly under open and vile attack; to influence a generation of American men to live God-honoring lives worthy of the calling and appellation of *Christian*; to demonstrate the importance of male servant leadership in the home; to demonstrate the imperative of Christian fellowship and discipleship; to encourage believers to persevere in their verbal witness in spite of ostracism and/or legal action against them; and above all, to awaken Christian American men who are serving the nation to the realities of the conflict we are in, and what we stand to lose if we do nothing.

According to a USA Today poll, "Sixty percent of Americans cannot name five of the Ten Commandments."[9] The Ten Commandments form the overall structure of this

---

[9] Cureton, Ten Commandments: Foundation of American Society, 1.

Introduction

book. The first four commandments teach us to love God, while the last six teach us to love our neighbor (Ex 20:1-17). We may divide the Ten Commandments into one group of four, pertaining to our duty to God, and a group of six, describing our duty to man. With this understanding, the first half of this book, Part 1 and 2, mirror our duty to God, while the second half, Part 3 and 4, mirror our duty to man.

This book is intended to be an educational whetstone for Christian men who desire to live God-honoring, biblically moral lives while serving our country with distinction. As J.C. Ryle once said, "people will never set their faces decidedly towards heaven, and live like pilgrims, until they really feel that they are in danger of hell." Where there is no revelation the people cast off restraint (Pro 29:18). Can we help our fellow Americans see the writing on the wall? It's time for the God-honoring men of America to take a stand for Christ. The goal of this book is to sharpen the minds of men, causing men to dig deeper into God's inerrant Word, thereby promoting Christian growth, while living godly lives in the midst of moral depravity and cultural despair.

Along with Andrew Murray, my prayer is that if what I have written stirs you to go to the Master's Words and take His wondrous promises simply and literally as they stand, my purpose has been attained. Soli Deo Gloria.

Introduction

The Ten Commandments

Exodus 20:1-17

20 And God spoke all these words, saying:

[2] "I *am* the LORD your God, who brought you out of the land of Egypt, out of the house of bondage.

[3] "You shall have no other gods before Me.

[4] "You shall not make for yourself a carved image—any likeness *of anything* that *is* in heaven above, or that *is* in the earth beneath, or that *is* in the water under the earth; [5] you shall not bow down to them nor serve them. For I, the LORD your God, *am* a jealous God, visiting the iniquity of the fathers upon the children to the third and fourth *generations* of those who hate Me, [6] but showing mercy to thousands, to those who love Me and keep My commandments.

[7] "You shall not take the name of the LORD your God in vain, for the LORD will not hold *him* guiltless who takes His name in vain.

[8] "Remember the Sabbath day, to keep it holy. [9] Six days you shall labor and do all your work, [10] but the seventh day *is* the Sabbath of the LORD your God. *In it* you shall do no work: you, nor your son, nor your daughter, nor your male servant, nor your female servant, nor your cattle, nor your stranger who *is* within your gates. [11] For *in* six days the LORD made the heavens and the earth, the sea, and all that *is* in them, and rested the seventh day. Therefore the LORD blessed the Sabbath day and hallowed it.

[12] "Honor your father and your mother, that your days may be long upon the land which the LORD your God is giving you.

[13] "You shall not murder.

[14] "You shall not commit adultery.

[15] "You shall not steal.

[16] "You shall not bear false witness against your neighbor.

[17] "You shall not covet your neighbor's house; you shall not covet your neighbor's wife, nor his male servant, nor his female servant, nor his ox, nor his donkey, nor anything that *is* your neighbor's."

Part 1: Selfless Service

Signing of the Mayflower Compact 1620

³⁷ Jesus said to him, "'You shall love the LORD your God with all your heart, with all your soul, and with all your mind.' ³⁸ This is the first and great commandment. ³⁹ And the second is like it: 'You shall love your neighbor as yourself.' ⁴⁰ On these two commandments hang all the Law and the Prophets." (Matthew 22:37-40).

Chapter 1: The God-Honoring American Man

God desires for His saints to possess the character of His Son Jesus Christ and works at bringing transformation (Phil 1:6). This is the impetus behind the Messiah's declaration we read above. Jesus reduces the Law of Moses (613 distinct commandments) down to only two: the chief commandment, which harkens us back to Dt 6:4-5, love for God, and its counterpart from Lev 19:18, love for man. This first commandment is the Christian's foremost principle from which all duties and actions should flow, and the end to which all should be done. This first commandment is a summation of the first four commandments of the Decalogue, the Ten Commandments.[10] The second commandment is the

---

[10] The Ten Commandments are referred to as the Decalogue, or Ten Words or sayings. The word Decalogue comes to us from the Septuagint (LXX), which is a 3ʳᵈ Century BC Greek translation of the Hebrew Bible.

1

Chapter 1: The God-Honoring American Man

corresponding, reciprocal principle, which is only made possible by observing the first. This second commandment is a summation of the fifth to tenth commandments of the Decalogue. As mentioned before, the first four commandments teach us to love God, while the last six teach us to love our neighbor (Ex 20:1-17). Love for God comes first because we cannot love another person until we love God. Moreover, if we do not honor God, we will not truly honor one another.

The Scottish theologian Henry Scougal wrote: "The love of God is a delightful and affectionate sense of the divine perfections, which makes the soul resign and sacrifice itself completely unto Him, desiring above all things to please Him, and delights in nothing so much as in fellowship and communion with Him, and being ready to do or suffer anything for His sake, or at His pleasure."[11] Regarding the second greatest commandment Scougal writes, "A soul thus possessed with divine love must need be enlarged toward all mankind, in a sincere and unbounded affection, because of the relation they have to God."[12]

Jesus Christ, the Son of God, the Savior of all who believe in Him, lived out these commandments, as well as the entirety of the Law of Moses, perfectly; and remained obedient to the Father, even unto death, perfectly fulfilling the Father's will and plan. One of the goals of this book will be a practical working out of the two greatest commandments.

Two Criminals

Two criminals condemned, dying, cry out from their crosses adjacent the innocent Christ, one blasphemed, the other who had read the inscription on the cross, 'Jesus of Nazareth, the King of the Jews' (Jn 19:19), and no doubt moved by its truth, now conscious of his sins, cries out in his great need: "Lord, remember me when You come into Your kingdom" (Lk 23:42). In the response of Jesus, "Assuredly, I say to you, today you will be with me in Paradise" (Lk 23:43), we have

---

[11] Scougal, The Life of God in the Soul of Man, 46-47.
[12] Ibid.

the most profound truth a soul can have; divine assurance of sins forgiven and the promise of eternal life here and now!

The two criminals, who were crucified, along with the innocent Jesus, represent the two responses to the Gospel. Of the two criminals, both deserving of death (Rom 3:23-24; 5:12), one through faith was crucified along with Christ and included in Him, having his sins forever atoned for, and upon his last breath entered Paradise, eternal glory, and gained the beatific vision of God. The other, equally deserving of death, joins the mocking crowd in their blaspheming, breathes his last and enters hell; thus justly condemned and to be forever punished. The first man, by grace through faith was accounted righteous because the obedient and sinless Christ Jesus took upon Himself that man's sins; this is the life of God in the soul of man. The second, being blind, ignorant and obstinate, remained under God's condemning wrath and pays the penalty for his own sins, forever.

Space will not permit a full commentary on the texts used above but suffice it to say that: First, Christ's word to penitent criminals everywhere gives assurance of salvation. The dying thief saw in the face of Jesus, mankind's only Savior. Can you appropriate Christ's promise to yourself (Rom 10:9-10)? Second, Christ's word to penitent criminals throughout all time gives assurance of entrance into the kingdom of God. The *Scripture alone* gives us the only message that we may enter the kingdom of God because of *Christ alone*, by *grace alone*, through *faith alone*, for the *glory of God alone*.[13] Jesus had a lot to say about the kingdom of God. It was at the very heart of His message. He used many parables to describe it. Third, Christ's grace extends to all penitent criminals, from every tribe, tongue, people and nation. Our eternal life begins the moment we receive Jesus Christ as Lord and Savior (Jn 5:24, 25).

The believer will never be as saved as when he first believed, and though he may doubt his salvation and be

---

[13] *Sola Scriptura, Solus Christus, Sola Gratia, Sola Fide, Soli Deo Gloria.* These Five Solas represent a summary of historic Protestantism. Scripture tells us everything that God wants us to know "concerning all things necessary for His own glory, man's salvation, faith and life" (Westminster Confession of Faith, 1.6).

3

frustrated through various temptations and sins; yet the true believer is never left without the presence and provision of the Holy Ghost who keeps him from sinking into utter despair. It is hoped that the reader experiences the saving power of the risen Christ as these and other biblical concepts are developed throughout this book.

A Tale of Two Cities

The two criminals who were crucified along with Christ also represent the two cities of which mankind may belong; the City of God or the city of man. The difference between the two cities is the difference between the two loves. Those of mankind who are united together in their love of God and one another in Christ belong to the City of God. Those of the other city, not being united in any real sense, have one thing in common besides their opposition to God: each one of them is intent on the love of self above all else. In Augustine's timeless expression, "These two cities are made by two loves: the earthly city by the love of self, unto the contempt of God, and the heavenly city by the love of God, unto the contempt of self." The prophet Isaiah, in chapter 26, speaks about these two cities:

26 In that day shall this song be sung in the land of Judah; **we have a strong city; salvation will God appoint for walls and bulwarks.** [2] Open ye the gates, that the righteous nation which keepeth the truth may enter in. [3] Thou wilt keep him in perfect peace, whose mind is stayed on thee: because he trusteth in thee. [4] Trust ye in the LORD for ever: for in the LORD JEHOVAH is everlasting strength: [5] For he bringeth down them that dwell on high; the lofty city, he layeth it low; he layeth it low, even to the ground; he bringeth it even to the dust. [6] The foot shall tread it down, even the feet of the poor, and the steps of the needy (Is 26:1-6 KJV, emphasis added).

The earthly city glories in itself, the heavenly in the Lord.[14] The concept of the two cities will be developed throughout the

---

[14] Augustine, The City of God, 477. St. Augustine (354-430 AD), was the Bishop of Hippo in North Africa, in what is now Tunisia. He was one of the most influential of the early church fathers who framed the concepts of original sin and just war.

Chapter 1: The God-Honoring American Man

book, however in passing, let us consider that whereas those of faith enter through the narrow gate and rest within the walls of salvation, the proud and lofty are left outside and brought low to the dust.

The title of this chapter, "the God-honoring American man," presupposes a number of things, namely that, in addition to loving God with all one's heart, soul, strength and mind, as well as one's neighbor as one's self (Luke 10:27, cf. Dt 6:5; Lev 19:18), a God-honoring man, a Christian man, possesses certain attributes which mirror Christ's character. Additionally, the qualitative 'American' is added because one of the stated goals of this book is to recover what is presently being discarded in this country as chauvinistic, narrow-minded, old-fashioned, simplistic, bigoted, or even virulent.

What particular aspects characterize the God-honoring man? A man who loves the Lord with all that is in him and his neighbor as himself; a man who seeks to glorify God by his every thought, word and deed. In a nation that is rapidly throwing off restraint, and seeking to forget God, how do we go about recovering what formally made this nation great? It is believed that these following seven marks will distinguish what constitutes God-honoring behavior. The discussion of these marks will frame the entire chapter.

The following seven 'marks' caricature the God-honoring American man:

1. Faith in God.
2. Faithfulness to Christ's commandments.
3. Faithful family man.
4. Faithful member of a local Church.
5. Loyal patriot to State and Country.
6. Loyal member of an organization or unit.
7. Loyal comrade to my team mates.

Chapter 1: The God-Honoring American Man

First Mark of a God-Honoring American Man:
Faith in God

Pilgrims arriving in the New World

And God spoke all these words, saying: ² "I am the LORD your God, who brought you out of the land of Egypt, out of the house of bondage. ³ "You shall have no other gods before Me (Ex 20:1-3).

Augustine, in his book *Confessions* gives us timeless expressions. Two of which articulate man's greatest need: "Great are You, O Lord, and greatly to be praised; great is Your power, and infinite is Your wisdom. You have made us for Yourself and our hearts are restless until they rest in You."[15] And, "it was now a joy to put away what I formerly feared to lose."[16] These two assertions of Augustine approximate first, man is as anxious as he is confused before finding lasting solace in God, and second, this comes only by way of surrender.

God has made mankind for His own glory, as Pro 16:4 declares, "The LORD has made all for Himself, yes, even the wicked for the day of doom," and again in Romans 11:36, "For of him, and through him, and to him are all things." God therefore commands all men everywhere to seek Him in faith

---

[15] Augustine, Confessions, Book One, 5.
[16] Ibid, Book Nine, 162.

and repent of their sins (Acts 17:27). This is a commandment not a suggestion. Man's purpose in life or chief end is to glorify God and to enjoy Him forever.[17] To glorify God is man's foremost purpose; the enjoyment of God forever is wherein his chief happiness consists. Whereas only the man who has faith in God can ever hope to glorify Him, only the man whose heart rests in God can ever hope to enjoy Him. We must therefore know God personally if we are to ever hope to glorify Him.

Who is God?

The first mark of the God-honoring American man is faith in God, that is, the God of Israel, יְהֹוָה Yahweh, the Self-existent, Self-revealing God of the Bible. There have been many concepts of God throughout history. Some see God as everything – pantheism. This view envisions the world as being divine; others see God as *in* everything – panentheism; the whole is *in* God. Whereas pantheism identifies God and the world as identical, panentheism denies that God and the world are identical and suggests that God be thought of in the world much the way a mind is in a body. In fact, according to panentheism, the world may be thought of as the body of God.[18] What's important to note here is that both of these prominent views deny the biblical understanding of God on several important levels. First, the Creator-creature distinction; second, God is a Person, and third, God is Lord.

First, God is the Creator of all things and is separate from His creation. Therefore we must reject the pantheistic and panentheistic speculations about God. Likewise, God's creation doesn't become divine but remains creation.[19] In light of this, we must understand 2 Pet 1:4 which tells us that through the promises we may "partake of the divine nature," to refer not to the normative (essence) but ethical sense. In other words, God develops the image of Christ in us by faith. God is separate from His creation but transcends it in order to reveal Himself savingly to mankind.

---

[17] Westminster Confession of Faith, Shorter Catechism, Question 1, 287.
[18] Nash, The Concept of God, 23.
[19] For more on this point see chapter two.

Chapter 1: The God-Honoring American Man

Second, God is a Person. The word 'God' (*Elohim* אֱלֹהִים) functions as a proper name for Him. Though some world views, like Hinduism, envision millions of gods, the Bible however reveals only One living and true God (Dt 6:4).[20] Additionally, the Bible reveals God by His divine names and attributes. For instance, God reveals Himself as '*El-Shaddai*," which means 'God Almighty,' to Abraham, Isaac and Jacob (Ex 6:2-3); a name which not only signifies God's greatness, but a source of comfort and blessing as well. The greatest name of God is Yahweh (Jehovah). The name's origin and meaning are indicated in Ex 3:14-15. It expresses the fact that God is always the same, and especially that He is unchangeable in His covenant relationship, and is always faithful to His promises.[21]

God is a Person who reveals Himself in the Bible and teaches us that He is a Spirit, infinite, eternal, and unchangeable, in His being (self-existent), wisdom, power, holiness, justice, goodness, and truth.[22] Additionally, God is love personified (1 Jn 4:8). Moreover, God has eternally existed as Father, Son, and Holy Spirit, with distinct personal attributes, but without division of nature, essence, or being (1 Jn 5:7; Mt 28:19; 2 Cor 13:14). So, when we speak of faith in God, we mean the personal God of the Bible, whom we are able to know personally. Many deny the personality of God and conceive of Him as an impersonal force but God is a Person who thinks, feels, loves, speaks and acts in a completely holy manner. God is a Person with whom we may converse and trust, who helps us in our difficulties, and fills us with joy inexpressible (1 Peter 1:8).

---

[20] Everyone has a world view whether they have contemplated it or not. The major elements include: 1.Theology (God) is there a God? What is His nature? 2. Metaphysics (reality), did an eternal, omnipotent Being create the universe? If so, what is the relationship between God and the universe? Are miracles possible? 3. Epistemology (knowledge), how do we gain knowledge? What are the roles of reason and sense experience? 4. Ethics (morality), is morality relative? Is truth objective or subjective? 5. Anthropology (mankind), are human beings free? Is man dichotomous (body and soul/spirit) or trichotomous (body, soul and spirit) or perhaps (body, soul, and when he is regenerated – spirit)? Is there life after death? A person's world view functions as a sort an interpretive framework for life's ultimate questions.

[21] Berkhof, Summary of Christian Doctrine, 32.

[22] Westminster Confession of Faith, Shorter Catechism, Question 4, 287.

Chapter 1: The God-Honoring American Man

In the New Testament, the names of God are simply the Greek forms of those found in the Old Testament. For example, the name *Theos* θεὸς, the most commonly employed name for God in the New Testament, is simply the word used in place of the Hebrew word *Elohim* אֱלֹהִים. Additionally, the name *Kurios* κύριος, used over seven thousand times in the Bible, meaning 'Lord,' is applied not only to God but also to Christ (Phil 2:11; Rev 4:8). This name takes the place of both 'Adonai' and Yahweh.[23] God is a Person not an impersonal force. Yet, He is immanent (covenantally present) and reveals Himself in a personal form in Jesus Christ. God is Father, Son, and Holy Spirit. One God. Three Persons. God has eternally existed as the Father, the Son, and the Holy Spirit, and these three Persons are One God, being the same in substance, and equal in power and glory. God has eternally existed as three Persons within the unity of a single divine Being (Mt 28:19; Jn 8:24; 8:58; 17:5; Acts 5:3-4; Rom 9:5; 2 Cor 13:14; Tit 1:13; Heb 1:8).

Thirdly, as a Person, God is a completely holy Being who Himself is the source of moral obligation. As Lord, He is Head of a covenant community, which He has taken for Himself to be His own particular people (Tit 2:14). The heart of this covenant relationship is: "I will be your God, and you shall be My people" (Ex 6:7; Lev 26:12; Rev 21:3). Redeeming us from death, God brings us into His covenant community and demands certain behavior on our part, which He reveals to us in the Bible.

The Scripture

The final authority for the Christian is Scripture because it is the very Word of God. Scripture is directly binding on conscience. To go against conscience is "neither right nor safe." The Bible is perfect and complete, sufficient in all its parts. This view is known as biblical inerrancy. Having a low view of Scripture became a kind of stumbling block and method of entry for all sorts of biblically condemned practices that are now celebrated. J.C. Ryle put it best when he wrote,

---

[23] Berkhof, Summary of Christian Doctrine, 32.

9

Chapter 1: The God-Honoring American Man

"We corrupt the Word of God most dangerously, when we throw doubt on the plenary inspiration of any part of Holy Scripture."[24]

The Scriptures, the living oracle and revelation of God's mind and will, has been divinely composed through human agency. The doctrine of revelation states that God has chosen to give us information – propositional truths – that we could not gain on our own. The Bible reveals truth: truth about God, truth about the world, and truth about ourselves. "Truth," as R.C. Sproul puts it, "is reality as God sees it." This full and sufficient oracle of truth encapsulates all that must be believed concerning God, and the duty God requires of us.[25] Standing obstinately against this major premise is the spirit of the age. Man redefines terminology, in hopes of relieving his troubled conscience. To counter this trend, throughout this book we must: first, define our terms based upon what the Bible claims for itself; then, second we must answer objections to their terms and claims; and third, we must show the practical importance of believing in what the Bible claims for itself.

No amount of argument or evidence amassed by the human mind can convince the skeptic that God has spoken until God has permitted him to hear and understand. For the skeptic today, as always, it will be a journey of either doubt to faith or doubt to despair. In the final analysis, the one that comes to God must first believe that He exists; that He is the rewarder of those who diligently seek Him (Heb 11:6); that His Word is completely accurate in all matters, including science, mathematics, and history, and therefore accurate to the very letters and words (2 Tim 3:15-17) – thus plenary inspiration.

The Bible's authority is over the whole of creation much less one's own life (Lk 24:25), and is sufficient to give the means of salvation; knowing Christ as Savior (Jn 5:39-40; 10:27; Acts 4:12). This being at the very core of the Church's doctrine of Biblical inspiration was articulated by the magisterial Reformers with the words *Sola Scriptura*. Biblical inerrancy is thus the historic doctrinal assertion that the Bible, because it is the very Word of God, is perfect and complete,

---

[24] Ryle, Warning to the Churches, 25.
[25] Westminster Confession of Faith, Shorter Catechism, Question 3.

and sufficient in all its parts including the very words. This is the doctrine of verbal inspiration. The doctrine of verbal inspiration states that, the Bible is the revelation of God's mind and will written by men, who, under the influence and guidance of the Holy Spirit, wrote God's very words. Regarding the Church's doctrine of verbal inerrancy, Warfield writes,

> It has always recognized that this conception of co-authorship implies that the Spirit's superintendence extends to the choice of the words by the human authors (verbal inspiration), and preserves its product from everything inconsistent with divine authorship – thus securing, among other things, that entire truthfulness which is everywhere presupposed in and asserted for Scripture by the Biblical writers (inerrancy).[26]

Just how critical is the doctrine of plenary inspiration? As Warfield states, "Failing to espouse this view of Scripture can destroy all Biblical doctrines, because a low view of Scripture undermines our confidence in the trustworthiness of Scripture as a witness to doctrine."[27] The word plenary is derived from the Latin *plenus* meaning full and complete in every respect. Plenary inspiration serves as a column which buttresses the overarching roof of Biblical inerrancy. Along with the other columns of verbal inspiration, authority and sufficiency, these truths form a colonnade. If one were to remove any of these buttressing columns, the roof of Biblical inerrancy – along with the assurance with which it carries – collapses.

Plenary inspiration has been attacked from the beginning. As the apostolic writings were circulated, almost immediately we find the spirit of antichrist at work. Even before the canon was compiled men such as Marcion, and a horde of other textual critics, plied their trade of operating on the original manuscripts or sometimes wrote their own.[28] These men rejected plenary inspiration. They denied the unity of the

---

[26] Warfield, The Inspiration and Authority of the Bible 173.
[27] Ibid, 174.
[28] Eric F. Osborn, *Tertullian, The First Theologian of the West* (Peabody: Prince Press), 89.

whole of Scripture by viewing certain authors as uninspired. They viewed the words of Jesus as inspired while rejecting the words of some or all the apostles. Some even introduced spurious additions or made serious omissions to the gospels and to the apostle's epistles even in Peter's day. Peter writes about those who have altered Paul's writings as they do the other Scriptures (2 Pet 3:16). Peter in this way acknowledges Paul's writings as equal to the Old Testament canon. The apostles were conscious of the fact that what they were writing was Scripture.

Verbal inspiration, as the very term suggests, extends to the very words of Scripture. Our Lord echoing Isaiah 40:8 ascribes this very quality to the Scriptures, i.e., "the Scriptures cannot be broken" (Jn 10:35), and every jot and tittle, literally every word will be fulfilled (Mt 5:18). The minute details of God's plan will be carried out. The part of His plan He has revealed to us we have in Scripture (Dt 29:29). God has spoken. The very words He has used, every jot and tittle of the law are all equally important.

The doctrine of verbal inspiration has been denied on the grounds that there are numerous scientific and historic mistakes in the text. For example, the apparent disparity between the list of kings in the books of 1, 2 Kings and 1, 2 Chronicles has troubled many for centuries, and has proven to be the stumbling block for skeptics.[29] These seeming disparities in what textual critics have pointed out as apparent flaws in the Scripture have been worked out with other parts of Scripture to show the accuracy of the Bible in history. Seeming contradictions only seem to be contradictive. What we must do is harmonize these apparent contradictions by other parts of Scripture. We mustn't like Marcion and Bultmann deny the unity of the whole by approving some Scripture and rejected other parts based upon our own fallible assumptions.[30] *Scripture interprets Scripture.*

As to the apparent inconsistencies between the findings of science and the facts of the Bible, it must be stated that the Scripture does not contradict the findings of science; it

---

[29] However, I believe Edwin R. Thiele in his book *The Mysterious Numbers of the Hebrew Kings* finds a workable solution.

[30] James I. Packer, Fundamentalism and the Word of God, 110.

12

Chapter 1: The God-Honoring American Man

contradicts and opposes the godless Darwinian hypothesis of science – evolution. It's not the intent here to enter the debate between young and old earth creationists; however, the Bible speaks of a creative week, not a drawn-out evolutionary timeline. And contrary to the evolutionist theories, the Scripture speaks accurately and decisively about the origin of the universe (Gen 1:1, et al; Mt 19:4-6; Mk 10:5-9; Jn 5:17). And most importantly, if God didn't create Adam, as the Bible reveals in Genesis, and we evolved from apes, then the Adam-Christ parallel is dissolved, and the truth about redemption is destroyed (Rom 5:12-20; 8:23; 1 Cor 15:47-49; Phil 3:21).

The Scripture is Life-giving. It not merely contains the word of God; it is the Word of God. Verbal inspiration as such is the Biblical doctrine which espouses that every word of the Scripture is God-breathed and that the choices of these words by human authors were under the superintendence of the Holy Spirit. The Holy Spirit moved the authors along to write the very words of God while allowing these authors to retain their personal idiosyncrasies of culture, manners of speech while simultaneously preserving them from mistakes in teaching.[31]

For this reason, we cannot dismiss passages of the Bible we don't like, sloughing them aside as mere cultural idiosyncrasies because they fail to appeal to our sense of fairness and equality. For these passages are God-breathed commandments (1 Cor 14:34-37). B. B. Warfield writes,

When the Christian asserts his faith in the divine origin of his Bible, he does not mean to deny that it was composed and written by men or that it was given by men to the world. He believes that the marks of its human origin are ineradicably stamped on every page of the whole volume. He means to state only that it is not merely human in its origin.[32]

The words of Scripture are not infallible due to the holiness of the human authors but because the Holy Spirit's superintendence. The final authority for the Christian is Scripture because it is the very Word of God. The form critics of the mid 1800s rejected verbal and plenary inspiration and

---

[31] The Chicago Statement of Biblical Inerrancy, Article VIII.
[32] Warfield, The Divine Origin of the Bible, 1.

subsequently abandoned the formal principle of the Reformation *Sola Scriptura.* Form critics such as Bultmann, believing the Word of God to be divinely inspired, though mixed with mythology and other interpolated human inventions, dismissed plenary and verbal inspiration as untenable. This disregard for the Bible's authority and sufficiency brought many to the point of plummeting below the line of despair.[33] The purer the doctrine, the purer the flow of God's Holy Spirit. Anything short of the belief in the fullness of Scripture as a divine flow of grace is insufficient.

The Scripture is sufficient for salvation (Ps 119:97-104; Jn 5:39; 1 Tim 4:16; 2 Tim 3:14-17). All that need be known for life and godliness is clearly revealed in Scripture. Because Scripture is all sufficient for man's salvation, as well as every need in his walk of faith and practice, nothing is to be added.[34] Because the Holy Spirit makes the reading and especially the preaching of the word effectual unto salvation, we are not to tamper with God's Word. We are to proclaim it, especially the parts of Scripture that don't appeal to our flesh.

The biblical point being made here is this. Confusion and despair will be the only fruit of denying the inerrancy of the Bible. The current trends today are the fuller ramifications of the Renaissance and the Enlightenment. Today, in full bloom, liberalism displays its fruit of impenitence towards the authority of Scripture. It obstinately refuses to submit itself to the demands of God's Word. Seeking to ease their disparaging consciences, they gleefully carve up the text of Scripture, reducing it, and redefining, in hopes to render it voiceless and powerless. Higher criticism, a stratagem of liberals, is destructive to the composite unity of the whole of Scripture. Belief in Biblical inerrancy is affirming that all that God has spoken to us in His Word is entirely accurate, trustworthy, and authoritative. As Francis Schaeffer has so aptly pointed out, the rejection of the Bible's authority will lead only to despair.

Looking again at the Ten Commandments, we may divide them into one group of four, pertaining to our duty to God, and a group of six, describing our duty to man. The Ten

---

[33] Francis Schaeffer, The God Who is There, 8.
[34] The Westminster Confession of Faith , Chapter 1, Holy Scripture 22.

Chapter 1: The God-Honoring American Man

Commandments are the moral law. God's moral law reflects His holy character and imprints an indelible mark on man's soul. But must Christians obey the Law of Moses in order to be saved? No. Christians are not under the law but are under grace (Rom 6:14; 7:4, 6; 8:2; Gal 5:18). So how should Christians view the moral law?

The Moral Law

The law is holy, righteous, just, and good, as well as spiritual. It is the mirror of God's character and His nature. It was given to mankind for the purpose of not only revealing God's character and nature, so as to give mankind an ethical standard, but also to reveal sin. The law was given to teach sinners their sin. But what is sin? It's important we define our terms because in America, and society as a whole, we have redefined sin right out of existence. Sin is virtually missing from our vocabulary. What's more deplorable is the fact that sin is rarely spoken of from American pulpits. Yet, sin is very real. Its offense is rank and smells to high heaven.

Sin is any want of conformity unto or transgression of the law of God.[35] Sin hardens and blinds us but the gospel comes and we see our corruption. Seeing our sin is a revelation! This, revelation of our sin, is unto hardening obstinacy or willing surrender; and it comes to pass that mankind will harden themselves even under the means which God uses for the softening of others; by the same sun he softens wax and hardens clay.

In Bunyan's allegory, *The Pilgrim's Progress*, the main character, whose name is Christian, along with a would-be traveler on the *Way*, Pliable, leave the city of Destruction but soon afterward fall into a deep bog, known as the slough of despond. In the slough of despond, Christian and Pliable sink under the weight of sins and their sense of guilt for them. Pliable, offended and angry over this experience, turns back from his half-hearted venture and returns to the city of Destruction, exclaiming to Christian, "Is this the happiness

---

[35] Westminster Shorter Catechism, Question 14. Sin *hamartia* ἁμαρτία, is an archery term which means to miss the intended mark, that is, to miss the target; failing to hit the intended mark or goal of living.

you have told me all this while of?[36] If we have such ill speed at our first setting out, what may we expect between this and our journey's end? Christian, alone and endeavoring to make it through, is drawn out of the slough by Help, who sets him on solid ground and bids him go on the *Way*.

Like Christian in Bunyan's allegory, when we see our sin and own it, we're conducted by the Holy Spirit unto Christ for grace. What God demands in His law, He gives to us in His gospel. God the Father sent His Son Jesus to die for our sins or we would have been dead, defiled and damned forever (Jn 3:16).

The Puritan Thomas Watson wrote, "The moral law is the copy of God's will, our spiritual directory; it shows us what sins to avoid, what duties to pursue."[37] Jesus said, "If you love Me, obey my commandments" (John 14:15). The gospel of Jesus Christ therefore obligates us to keep the law of God (Mt 22:37-40). *We are not to keep the law of God so we may be saved, rather we keep the law of God because Christ has saved us.* Our salvation is by grace, through faith, unto good works which testify to what God through Christ did for us, not what we have done for ourselves. Christians are commanded to keep the law of God out of gratitude for what Christ has already done for us. There is a lot more we need to say regarding the Christian use of the law of God. This will be developed more throughout the book, but for now, let's look again at the first commandment.

The first commandment, "You shall have no other gods before Me" (Ex 20:3), God in effect is saying, "I have no rival." But if God is the only God, then why does the Bible

---

[36] Bunyan, The Pilgrim's Progress, 63. John Bunyan (28 November 1628 – 31 August 1688) was an English Puritan preacher and author of The Pilgrim's Progress, arguably the most famous Christian allegory. Bunyan, a dissenter, who was not ordained in the Church of England, was a minister of a Puritan Baptist congregation in Bedford, England. Not having a license to preach, he faced legal challenges in order to fulfill his calling but did not compromise to authorities. He preferred to face and endure twelve years of imprisonment at great sacrifice to himself and family, rather than resign himself to giving up preaching. Although he has been described both as a Baptist and as a Puritan, he himself preferred to be described simply as a Christian.

[37] Watson, The Ten Commandments, 14.

repeatedly speak of other *gods*? The apostle Paul tells us in 1 Cor 8:5, 6:

[5] For even if there are so-called gods, whether in heaven or on earth (as there are many gods and many lords), [6] yet for us *there is* one God, the Father, of whom *are* all things, and we for Him; and one Lord Jesus Christ, through whom *are* all things, and through whom we *live.*

Again the apostle Paul also tells us in 1 Cor 10:19-20,

[19] What am I saying then? That an idol is anything, or what is offered to idols is anything? [20] Rather, that the things which the Gentiles sacrifice they sacrifice to demons and not to God, and I do not want you to have fellowship with demons.

Furthermore, Psalm 96:5 tells us, "For all the gods of the peoples are worthless idols, but the LORD made the heavens."[38] There is only one true God, the rest are demons – fallen angels, who call for the worship of mankind, seeking to usurp the worship due God alone (Gal 4:8). The reason false gods (demons) have this enslaving power is because by demonic force they gain mastery over their worshippers. Thus the gods of Egypt held real spiritual power over the minds and hearts of the Egyptians, and also the Israelites.[39]

The first commandment therefore commands us to worship the only true God and not to worship any other so-called gods (1 Cor 8:5).[40] When God commands us to worship Him alone, He is commanding us to choose Him alone as true God, thus

---

[38] The LXX renders this verse, "For all the gods of the nations are demons, but the Lord made the heavens." See also Dt 32:8-9 and 17.

[39] Ryken, Written in Stone, 59-60.

[40] Question 104 of the Larger Catechism asks us: *What are the duties required in the first commandment?*
Answer. The duties required in the first commandment are, the knowing and acknowledging of God to be the only true God, and our God; and to worship and glorify him accordingly, by thinking, meditating, remembering, highly esteeming, honoring, adoring, choosing, loving, desiring, fearing of him; believing him; trusting, hoping, delighting, rejoicing in him; being zealous for him; calling upon him, giving all praise and thanks, and yielding all obedience and submission to him with the whole man; being careful in all things to please him, and sorrowful when in anything he is offended; and walking humbly with him.

Chapter 1: The God-Honoring American Man

enthroning Him as our only Lord. That what God forbids, is at no time to be done; what he commands, is always our duty.[41] The reformer John Calvin writes, "the first commandment requires us to contemplate, fear, and worship His majesty; to participate in His blessings; to seek His help at all times; to recognize, and by praises to celebrate, the greatness of His works, as the only goal of all the activities of life."[42]

What happens when we break the first commandment? The Bible tells us of King Solomon's great wisdom. How that no one in the ancient world rivaled him. This wisdom was in fact given to him from God as an answer to his prayer, so that he might rule Israel wisely (1 Kgs 3:5). The Bible tells us that Solomon judged his people rightly, and that he even served as a counselor to other kings and queens. The highlight of his tenure as king was his magnificent prayer he offered to God at the dedication of the temple in Jerusalem (1 Kgs 8). God answered Solomon's prayer by descending on His temple in glory, and in 1 Kgs 9:4-7 said to him,

[4]Now if you walk before Me as your father David walked, in integrity of heart and in uprightness, to do according to all that I have commanded you, *and* if you keep My statutes and My judgments, [5]then I will establish the throne of your kingdom over Israel forever, as I promised David your father, saying, 'You shall not fail to have a man on the throne of Israel.' [6]*But* if you or your sons at all turn from following Me, and do not keep My commandments *and* My statutes which I have set before you, but go and serve other gods and worship them, [7]then I will cut off Israel from the land which I have given them; and this house which I have consecrated for My name I will cast out of My sight.

Regrettably, Solomon failed to keep the first commandment by serving other gods. The Bible tells us that his many wives (700), and concubines (300) "turned his heart away," and he "went after Ashtoreth the goddess of the Sidonians, and after Milcom the abomination of the Ammonites" (1Kings 11:5). Yet, if we look at Solomon's life closely, we'll see that his heart began to turn away from God long before he ever bowed

---

[41] Westminster Larger Catechism Answer 99.5.
[42] Institutes of the Christian Religion, 2.8.16.

Chapter 1: The God-Honoring American Man

down to any idols.[43] The same thing happens to Christians when we are lured away from keeping the first commandment by our three enemies: the lust of the flesh, the lures of the world, and the lies of Satan, which tempt us to follow after other gods. This concept of a Christian's three enemies will be developed in chapter two.

Whereas the first commandment tells us *Who* to worship, the second commandment tells us *how* to worship. The second commandment urges us to worship only according to God's revelation of Himself.[44] The second commandment tells us:

> [4] "You shall not make for yourself a carved image—any likeness *of anything* that *is* in heaven above, or that *is* in the earth beneath, or that *is* in the water under the earth; [5] you shall not bow down to them nor serve them. For I, the LORD your God, *am* a jealous God, visiting the iniquity of the fathers upon the children to the third and fourth *generations* of those who hate Me, [6] but showing mercy to thousands, to those who love Me and keep My commandments.

God has a right to tell us how He wants to be worshipped. The second commandment forbids us to worship God by images, or any other way not appointed in His word.[45] Again, that which God forbids, is at no time to be done; what he commands, is always our duty. The Bible gives us an excellent example of the differences between the first and second commandments in the life of King Jehu of Israel (2 Kgs 9-10). King Jehu was a mighty man of war who God raised up to eliminate Baal worship from the life of Israel. Jehu put the wicked queen Jezebel and her Baal priests to the sword. He eliminated Baal worship. However, he "did not turn away from the sins of Jeroboam the son of Nebat, who had made Israel sin, that is, from the golden calves that were at Bethel and Dan" (2 Kgs 10:29).

Jehu had enforced the first commandment but broke the second commandment: he and his subjects continued to worship the golden calves. To Jehu and the people of Israel, the golden calves didn't represent false gods; to them they

---

[43] Ryken, Written in Stone, 63.
[44] Frame, The Doctrine of the Christian Life, 422.
[45] The Westminster Shorter Catechism, Answer 51.

represented the God of Israel. But God gave us the second commandment, forbidding us to worship Him that way; with an idol.

Historically, Christians have differed as to whether the second commandment forbids using pictures of Jesus. Packer writes, "There is no room for doubting that the commandment obliges us to dissociate our worship, both in public and private, from all pictures and statues of Christ, no less than pictures and statues of His Father."[46] Packer offers two reasons why the second commandment should be stressed so emphatically: (1) because images dishonor God, by obscuring His glory, and (2) because images mislead us, for they convey false ideas about God.[47] *The point being made here is God's purpose in giving us the second commandment is to compel us to take our thoughts of Him from His Holy Word alone.*

We've discussed the first and second commandments, how they define worship. The third commandment emphasizes worship also. Whereas the first commandment deals with the object of worship, and the second deals with the regulation of worship, the third deals with one's attitude toward worship. The third commandment states,

"You shall not take the name of the LORD your God in vain, for the LORD will not hold *him* guiltless who takes His name in vain" (Ex 20:7).

The third commandment forbids us from using God's name incorrectly; and the abuse of it in an ignorant, vain, irreverent, profane, superstitious, or wicked mentioning or otherwise using his titles, attributes, ordinances, or works, by blasphemy, perjury, and all sinful cursings.[48] Along with the other

---

[46] Packer, Knowing God, 45.

[47] Ibid, 45-47. Packer adds, "We were made in His image, but let's not think of Him as existing in ours."

[48] The Westminster Larger Catechism Answer 113. Additionally, the Catechism adds: all sinful oaths, vows, and lots; violating of our oaths and vows, if lawful; and fulfilling them, if of things unlawful; murmuring and quarreling at, curious prying into, and misapplying of God's decrees and providences; misinterpreting, misapplying, or any way perverting the word, or any part of it, to profane jests, curious or unprofitable questions, vain janglings, or the maintaining of false doctrines; abusing it, the creatures, or anything contained under the name of God, to charms, or sinful lusts and

commandments, the third commandment has many implications. This commandment regulates not only the speaking of God's name, but also the bearing of His name as well. This aspect will be developed in chapter four.

God's lordship is an extension of His personality. Those whom God has saved and brought into His covenant have an obligation to obey their Sovereign Lord (John 14:15). Therefore, to know God is to know at the same time the ultimate source of reality and the ultimate source of ethical obligation.[49] These concepts of the covenant community and Christian ethics will be developed throughout the book.

What is Faith?

The Bible has quite a lot to say about faith. To begin with, Hebrews 11:1 tells us that "faith is the substance of things hoped for, the evidence of things not seen." The two words, substance and evidence, used in this verse may further clarify the concept of faith. The first word 'substance' means essential nature, as well as assurance or reality. The second word, *evidence*, relates to conviction and proof of existence. We use these two words regularly in English to describe the saving response of the Christian: *belief* and *faith*.

In biblical Greek they are the same word, πίστις pistis, which is used 243 times. They are used in various ways which widen the scope and definition of belief and faith. Interestingly, the way we translate the words *belief* and *faith* reveals the various functions of faith. Here are ten biblical descriptions of faith:

- Faith or believing is a gift of God (Eph 2:8-10).
- Faith is the fruit of believing, it is the act of trusting in Jesus Christ alone for salvation (Jn 14:1).

---

practices; the maligning, scorning, reviling, or any wise opposing of God's truth, grace, and ways; making profession of religion in hypocrisy, or for sinister ends; being ashamed of it, or a shame to it, by unconformable, unwise, unfruitful, and offensive walking, or backsliding from it.

[49] Frame, *Greeks Bearing Gifts*, 45.

Chapter 1: The God-Honoring American Man

- Faith is a cognitive relationship to a reality beyond ourselves.[50]
- Faith is assured knowledge of the love of God. "It is a firm and certain knowledge of God's good will towards us, which being grounded on the truth of the free promise made in Christ, is both revealed to our minds and sealed upon our hearts by the Holy Spirit."[51]
- Faith is applicatory knowledge. "Faith is a wonderful grace of God by which a man doth apprehend and apply Christ and all His benefits unto himself."[52]
- Faith or believing is a relational response to God's promises. This involves knowing God personally (Jer 9:22-24; Jn 20:31; 1 Jn 5:13).
- Faith is obedience to the truth (Rom 16:26; 1 Pet 1:22). That is why repentance mustn't be separated from faith.
- Faith expresses itself in the Christian life *with* fruit of the Spirit: love, joy, peace, patience, kindness, goodness, faithfulness, gentleness, and self-control. These are the products of the Spirit (Gal 5:22) – Chapter 3.
- Faith is refined, like gold, in believers *through* tests and trials (1 Pet 1:6-7) – Chapter 8 – 10.
- Faith is what believers persevere *in* to the end (Mt 24:13; Rev 13:10) – Chapter 9 – 10.

The Scottish theologian Henry Scougal writes: "The root of the divine life is faith; the chief branches are love to God, love to man, purity, and humility; it extends itself unto all divine truths; but in our lapsed estate, it hath a peculiar relation to the declaration of God's mercy and reconcilableness to sinners through a Mediator; and therefore, receiving its denomination from that principal object, is ordinarily termed faith in Jesus Christ. This is the life of God in the soul of man."[53] Therefore,

---

[50] Horden, The Case for a New Reformation Theology, 35. This is expressed in Augustine's dictum *credo ut intelligam* I believe that I may understand, which is followed by Anselm's *fides quaerens intellectum* faith seeking understanding. This is why the Reformers emphasized faith as both a gift of God and a trust or decision.

[51] Calvin, Institutes of the Christian Religion, 3.2.7.

[52] Perkins, The Foundation of the Christian Religion gathered into Six Principles, the Fourth Principle Expounded.

[53] Scougal, The Life of God in the Soul of Man, 7.

Chapter 1: The God-Honoring American Man

faith in God is trusting in the One He has sent, Jesus Christ. Faith in God is faith in Christ (Jn 14:1).

Christians are saved by grace alone through faith (Eph 2:8-10). Grace is the life of God in the soul of man. Faith is the relational response to the promises of God; it is also the work of God in our hearts, which saves us (Luke 7:50), guides us (2 Cor 5:7), heals us (Luke 8:48) and transforms us (2 Pet 3:18). God brings us to Himself by faith, from first to last (Rom 1:17). *Faith, therefore regards not present things so much as the things it waits for; things beyond our understanding.* Hence, "Faith is the substance of things hoped for, the evidence of things not seen" (Heb 11:1), it advances beyond the intellect, and takes possession of the will and of the heart, to make us act with zeal and joyfully as the law of God commands.[54]

Senator John McCain, reflecting on what carried him through his harrowing ordeal as a prisoner of war during the Vietnam War writes,

The three essential keys to resistance…were faith in God, faith in country, and faith in your fellow prisoners. Were your faith in any of these three devotions seriously shaken, you became much more vulnerable to various pressure employed by the Vietnamese to break you. The purpose of our captors' inhumanity to us was nothing less than to force our descent into a world of total faithlessness; a world with no God, no country, no loyalty. Without faith, we would lose our dignity, and live among our enemies as animals lived among their human masters.[55]

Senator McCain goes on to say that during the worst moments in captivity, keeping faith in God, country, and one another was not only difficult but also imperative.[56] Let it be said that having faith in yourself will only go so far, and by itself leads to a complete loss of hope.

John Paton, the indefatigable missionary to the New Hebrides Islands in the South Pacific, labored for nearly fifty years to bring the gospel to cannibals at the cost of his wife and child. While he was translating the Bible into the

---

[54] Leibniz, Theodicy, 53.
[55] McCain, Faith of My Fathers, 252.
[56] Ibid, 253.

23

Chapter 1: The God-Honoring American Man

Polynesian language he was unable to find a word in their dialect for the *believing* or having *faith*. One day while he was working in his hut, a native came running into Paton's study and flopped into his chair, exhausted. He said, "It feels good to rest my whole weight in this chair." Instantly, John Paton knew he had his definition: Faith is resting your whole weight on God. That meaning helped bring a whole civilization to Christ.[57]

What we should also make abundantly clear is that salvation is of God; we cannot save ourselves. Titus 3:5-7 tells us:

[5] Not by works of righteousness which we have done, but according to His mercy He saved us, through the washing of regeneration and renewing of the Holy Spirit, [6] whom He poured out on us abundantly through Jesus Christ our Savior, [7] that having been justified by His grace we should become heirs according to the hope of eternal life.

Therefore, it must be clearly stated by the God-honoring man that though God commands righteous works to be done (Mt 5:16, 20), they will however never save us, but will serve God's purpose in holy living and evangelism when they are done in faith with the power God supplies. We cannot earn salvation by doing good works. The first Beatitude (Mt 5:3) tells us that the poor in spirit are blessed, which is the absence of self-aggrandizement or self-reliance.

By Grace through Faith

This important truth was once demonstrated by Jonathan Edwards. Edwards, an eighteenth century New England Christian pastor and theologian, arguably the ablest mind ever produced by America, once wrote to clarify how conversion to Christianity occurs. Edwards accounts in his *Faithful Narrative* examples of various conversions in his congregation.[58] Outlining several universal steps in

---

[57] MacArthur, How to Meet the Enemy, 111.

[58] Jonathan Edwards (1703-1758), was a New England Christian pastor and theologian, and widely held to be the pastor by which the Great Awakening got under way. His writings have been and remain very influential to the church. Some of his works include: *A Faithful Narrative of the Surprising Work of God* (1737); *Distinguishing Marks of A Work of the Spirit of God*

conversion, Edwards states: First, how conversion occurs when people with an interest in Christianity attempt to live righteously through their good works, and study their Bibles, in an attempt to avoid sin and hell and to "earn" salvation.[59]

Next, Edwards describes how these people inevitably fail to live up to the Old Testament legal standard, experience despair at their failures and inherent sinfulness, and often believe they have committed "unpardonable sin."[60] Then, Edwards describes how successful converts experience converting grace and awaken to see that forgiveness is available to all who have faith in Christ alone and that Jesus Christ's sacrifice atones for all sins. Finally, Edwards recounts how this revelation of saving grace is followed by a sense of joy or an internal new light from the Holy Spirit and a desire to spread the gospel and leave sin behind. Thus, salvation is impossible through works which are simply the evidence of faith.

Standing squarely over against Edwards is Emmanuel Kant. In Kant's view, it isn't important so much for us to know what God has done for our salvation but rather for us to know what we must do to be worthy of it.[61] Liberal theology, following Kant, translates grace into works righteousness. *However, we mock the mercy of the Giver if we seek to give as a work the thing we receive as a gift.*

Looking again at Bunyan's allegory, Christian, walking along the narrow path toward the City of God is lured out of the Way by Mr. Worldly Wiseman, who bids him take a less burdensome approach to ridding himself of his burden (the knowledge that he's a sinner needing a Savior) by seeking a judicious gentleman named Legality. By Mr. Worldly Wiseman's allurement, Christian turns out of the Way and seeks Legality, who lives in the village of Morality. As Christian went on, his burden grew heavier the further he went up the hill, Mount Sinai. "There came also flashes of fire, out

---

(1741); *Some Thoughts Concerning the Present Revival of Religion in New England* (1742); and *Religious Affections* (1746) to name a few.
[59] Edwards, A Faithful Narrative of the Surprising Work of God, 56
[60] Ibid.
[61] Kant, Religion within the Limits of Reason Alone, 83. In Kant's view, the essence of religion is the performance of all duties as divine commands.

of the hill, that made Christian afraid that he should be burnt: here therefore he did sweat and quake for fear. And now he began to be sorry that he had taken Mr. Worldly Wiseman's counsel."[62] However, Evangelist appears and reasoning with Christian sets him back on the Way to the Narrow Gate.

The proper mindset, as Bunyan's allegory shows us, is one which views faith as a gift of God (Eph 2:8); His Spirit enabling us to walk just as Christ walked (1 Jn 2:6). This is a narrow, difficult Way, which to the natural man is as unpleasant as it is offensive. Thomas Scott writes,

In the broad road every man may chose a path suited to his inclinations, shift about to avoid difficulties, or accommodate himself to circumstances; and he will be sure of company agreeable to his taste. But Christians must follow one another in the narrow way, along the same track, surmounting difficulties, facing enemies, and bearing hardships, without any room to evade them: nor is any indulgence given to different tastes, habits, or propensities.[63]

Jesus said, "I am the way, the truth, and the life. No one comes to the Father except through Me" (Jn 14:6). No other Way leads to the Celestial City and into the presence of the King. The point being made here is: we are God's work from beginning to end (Phil 1:6). He works in us that which is pleasing in His sight (Heb 13:20-21). Glorifying God is the chief end of all human activity. The good works Christians do are simply fruit of a lovely faith (Eph 2:8-10). Because our salvation is by grace through faith, good works testify to what God through Christ did for us, not what we have done for ourselves. This is the assurance a perfect atonement secures. God's wrath is forever extinguished by the atonement of the Lamb of God, who, for all that call upon Him in saving faith, accounts believing sinners with His spotless righteousness.

Colonial Christianity

We've talked about the meaning of faith and the object of faith. We've discussed how God forms faith in us to not only

---

[62] Bunyan, The Pilgrim's Progress, 69.
[63] Scott, Works of the Late Rev. Thomas Scott, Volume 3, 69.

save us but to guide us, heal us, and transform us into the image of Christ (2 Cor 3:18). We've discussed the personal nature of having faith in a transcendent, immanent, All-powerful, All-knowing, and All-present Being whom we call God. Our relationship with the personal God of the Bible is based on God's written revelation and the finished work of Jesus Christ in space-time history.

If you were as fortunate as I, you grew up in America hearing these truths from the cradle. Some argue I learned these truths merely because my father is a pastor and my mother is a godly woman but are these truths of the Christian faith foreign to America? Wasn't America founded on Christian principles and values? The weight and scope of discussions involving questions like these has been well established in other works, but for the sake of argument, even a casual glance at our history will reveal the truth that not only was America founded on biblical principles but was supplied with Christian values as well. Chief Justice Joseph Story writes in his great commentary on the U.S. Constitution,

Every colony, from its foundation down to the revolution, with the exception of Rhode Island, (if, indeed, that state be an exception,) did openly, by the whole course of its laws and institutions, support and sustain, in some form, the Christian religion; and almost invariably gave a peculiar sanction to some of its fundamental doctrines.[64]

The New England Puritans, who had experienced religious persecution first hand, sought refuge in the new world. Their founding of a commonwealth in Plymouth would foster a close church-state relationship in what would become Massachusetts. Before their landing, they drew up an original 'compact' in which they acknowledged themselves to be loyal subjects of the crown of England and on 11 November, 1620, wrote,

---

[64] Joseph Story, Commentaries on the Constitution, Document 69, 1867. Joseph Story, 1779-1845, was an American lawyer and jurist who served on the Supreme Court of the United States from 1811 to 1845. Story was appointed, at age 32, to be the youngest Justice on the U.S. Supreme Court, where he served 34 years and helped establish the illegality of the slave trade in the Amistad case. He later co-founded Harvard Law School.

Chapter 1: The God-Honoring American Man

Having undertaken, **for the Glory of God, and advancements of the Christian faith** and honor of our King and Country, a voyage to plant the first colony in the Northern parts of Virginia, do by these presents, solemnly and mutually, in the presence of God, and one another, covenant and combine ourselves together into a civil body politic; **for our better ordering, and preservation and furtherance of the ends aforesaid**; and by virtue hereof to enact, constitute, and frame, such just and equal laws, ordinances, acts, constitutions, and offices, from time to time, as shall be thought most meet and convenient for the general good of the colony; unto which we promise all due submission and obedience (emphasis added).[65]

Puritans making their landing in the New World

Later in 1630, John Winthrop, a prominent Puritan lawyer and leading figure in the founding of the Massachusetts Bay Colony, admonished his fellow pilgrims with these words:

We shall be as a city on a hill. The eyes of all the people are upon us, so that if we shall deal falsely with our God in this work we have undertaken and so cause Him to withdraw His present help from us, we shall be made a story and a byword through all the world.[66]

---

[65] Mayflower Compact, as quoted in Joseph Story, Commentaries on the Constitution of the United States, 38. Joseph Story goes on to write, "in pursuance of the compact, the colonists proceeded soon afterwards to organize the colonial government...they adopted the common law of jurisprudence as well as the universal obligation the Mosaic institutions," 39.
[66] Reagan, Speaking My Mind, 44.

Chapter 1: The God-Honoring American Man

Winthrop's intent was to prepare the people for the planting of a new society in the midst of a dangerous and uncertain environment. Whereas, his words tellingly represent a people who recognize that mankind is intrinsically bad, the prominent naïve view of most Americans in our society today would say that mankind is basically good. This contrast will be developed more in chapter two.

As the colonies experienced an influx of settlers, many of which sought freedom of religious expression, a wide scope of conceptions regarding the integration of politics and religion began to take shape. In Virginia, for example, the common faith of the colony was Anglicanism, the state church of England, which was legally protected by Virginia's governing body, the General Assembly.[67] Additionally, Presbyterianism was brought to America by those of Scots-Irish descent, but unlike their Anglican friends, they, along with the Baptists, entertained no such dreams of a union of church and state.

It would seem as if the multiplicity of religious groups in the American colonies served to prevent not only religious persecution from occurring but tended to preclude any one denomination from monopolizing church matters as well. Thus, ecumenical Christianity in early colonial America tended to stave off any religious persecutions that had plagued England and the rest of Europe for centuries. At variance with all the positive aspects of colonial ecumenicalism in America, the condition of the Church, even on both sides of the Atlantic, had become Laodicean – in dire need of revival.

Whereas, the first settlers had come to America with a devout faith and a vision of establishing a God-honoring nation, a *city on a hill*; within a scant hundred years their fervency had all but cooled. Now their progeny had become worldly, looking to mammon rather than the Kingdom of God and falling into a sleep of spiritual carnality. To further exacerbate their moral decline, the philosophical rationalism of the Enlightenment was beginning to spread its influence, ushering in a wave of religious skepticism and Deism.

---

[67] The Virginia General Assembly, established on July 30, 1619 in Jamestown, is the oldest legislative body in the Western Hemisphere.

Chapter 1: The God-Honoring American Man

The Great Awakening

In the early eighteenth century, a religious phenomenon swept through Europe and North America, one that revitalized Christianity. Early revival tremors[68] had been felt in New England during the 1730s but what has been coined the "Great Awakening" began in earnest with the preaching of Jonathan Edwards in Northampton, Massachusetts and continued on later with the arrival of George Whitefield.[69] The spiritual climate of the American colonies before the revival has been described as "a long season of coldness and indifference," into which the Great Awakening "broke like a thunderbolt out of a clear sky upon the slumbering churches."[70]

George Whitefield preaching in 1749.

---

[68] Solomon Stoddard (1643-1729), Jonathan Edwards' grandfather had ministered at Northampton, Massachusetts almost sixty years and during that time had seen five periods of revivals.

[69] George Whitefield (1714-1770), was an English Anglican preacher, a prominent leader in the Great Awakening, and co-founder of Methodism. As a leader in the Great Awakening he preached over 30,000 times in America and Britain, many times to thousands at once and without amplification. Dr. Ebenezer Pemperton said of him, "Perhaps no man since the apostolic age preached more often or with greater success." Whitefield's Protestant ecumenicalism viewed other traditions as part of the true Church.

[70] Sprague, Annals of the American Pulpit, I, 339.

Chapter 1: The God-Honoring American Man

The revival strengthened belief in all the fundamentals of the Christian faith emphasizing two themes: the necessity of spiritual rebirth and the demands for holy living; staples of pietistic preaching and teaching.[71] The Great Awakening brought America back to the Scriptures and the central doctrines of Christianity such as the inerrancy of Scripture, the Deity of Christ, His virgin birth, atoning death, literal resurrection, ascension, and His literal physical coming again.[72] Scholars have noted that Whitefield combined local sporadic revivals to form a generalized awakening, solidifying a new colonial identity. However, we would be remiss to credit Whitefield as the sole influence of the Great Awakening; his success was largely built upon the faithful ministries of Theodore Frelinghuysen, Jonathan Edwards, Gilbert Tennent and others.

The evangelical revival of the 1730s and 40s played a key role in the development of American democracy. First, it challenged the traditional social structure by preaching that all men are created equal; that man's true value lies in his moral behavior, not his class; and that all men can be saved if they repent and believe the gospel. This aspect of the revival did much to clear away social boundaries. Second, though the revival was not indifferent to denominational attachments it however emphasized the necessity of being born again and holy living thereby promoting above all a loyalty to the Gospel of Christ.

This aspect of the revival lowered the denominational walls and created a greater ecumenical spirit of American Christianity. Third, the revival ushered in key democratic developments by promoting beliefs in both free speech and free press. What may be seen therefore as the long-term effects of the Great Awakening, in addition to the great harvest of souls and increased church attendance, was that it dissolved socio-ethnic impediments and established conduits of communication which would be used to usher in a common

---

[71] Balmer, Protestantism in America, 43. As more young men prepared for service as Christian ministers, and a concern for higher education grew, colleges such as Princeton, Brown, and Dartmouth were all established as a direct result of the Great Awakening.

[72] Dallimore, II, 533.

Chapter 1: The God-Honoring American Man

American identity; hence the First Great Awakening may be seen as a major contributing precursor to the American Revolution.[73]

The Lockean Experiment and Common Sense

What gave America an identity was not so much a Declaration of Independence, albeit for all intents that did efficaciously render asunder our allegiance to England, but that we were a people, who contracted together in a unified belief in the authority of God's Word and a belief that each man, being made in the image of God, was entitled to life, liberty, and the pursuit of happiness. John Locke, the British Empiricist, had a profound impact on the political philosophy of the American Colonies.[74] Locke's version of the *social contract* placed citizens under a ruling "legitimate" government which had been elected by the people for the express purpose of protecting their natural rights.

According to Locke, natural rights are inalienable, and power resides from the consent of the governed. Hence, a morally legitimate government protects the fundamental moral rights of those it rules. If not, says Locke, the citizens are obliged to dissolve any government that becomes "illegitimate" and elect a new legislative body that will guarantee and maximize those inalienable rights.[75] It appears to be clear, that our Founding Fathers, thoroughly influenced by Lockean political philosophy, used Locke's social contract theory to not only justify the American revolution, but to

---

[73] In Colonial America there were ample opportunities to print; having some thirty-eight newspapers by 1775. Additionally, the many pamphlets, booklets, tracts, and letters, along with other mediums of communication broadcasted in widest form the increasing tension that was developing over Colonial issues.

[74] John Locke (1632-1704), was an English philosopher and physician, that was regarded as the foremost thinker in what became known as the Enlightenment. Locke's epistemology (theory of knowledge) was empirical, meaning he believed that the mind was a blank slate or tabula rasa. This was in contrast to the prevalent Cartesian (rational) philosophy of his day. Over against the rationalists, Locke maintained that we are born without innate ideas, and that knowledge is instead determined only by experience derived from sense perception.

[75] Locke, Second Treatise on Government, 370. Locke championed religious toleration and the freedom of the mind.

32

integrate his ideas into the Declaration of Independence and Constitution as well. Locke's influence extended beyond these foundations to sagaciously frame amendments which tackled thorny issues such as political and religious tolerance and separation of church and state.

This however says nothing of the united opposition to the new system of imperial taxation initiated by the British government in the 1760s. Awakened by a sense of individual liberty and the *inalienable rights of man*, America not only cast a vote of no confidence in what it perceived as an illegitimate government stemming from a collapse in the English constitutional rights of man, it additionally found biblical warrant in expressions like those of Thomas Paine.

Thomas Paine, considered a founding father, even though he had no hand in drafting the Declaration of Independence or Constitution, gave voice to the burgeoning demand for independence with his *Common Sense* and though his religious and constitutional views were not shared by all, he inspired the Colonies to declare and fight for independence from Britain.[76] Paine, calling for the American colonies to not only break with England but to form a new country, one with religious freedom, writes:

This new world hath been the asylum for the persecuted lovers of civil and religious liberty from every part of Europe…The reformation was preceded by the discovery of America, as if the Almighty graciously meant to open a sanctuary to the persecuted in future years, when home should afford neither friendship nor safety.[77]

America had truly become the new world and Paine's radical call for a decision on the part of the Thirteen American colonies in January 1776, played a major role in the Declaration of Independence being adopted by the Continental Congress on July 4, 1776. This was a dramatic step. Derek Davis states unequivocally, "it's important to realize that a majority of the American people would never have endorsed a

---

[76] Bailyn, The Ideological Origins of the American Revolution, 5. Bailyn goes on to say that Paine's *Common Sense* was not unanimously received and was in fact largely refuted by Tories who failed to share Paine's revolutionary sentiments.

[77] Paine, Common Sense, 24.

colonial separation from the mother country unless they believed that it had God's sanction."[78] Thus, the Declaration of Independence had to be theologically grounded in order to garner such popular weight with American Protestants as well as to ease any conscientious objection that would arise from any anarchical appearance to such developments. Pondering the intellectual origins of the War of Independence prompted John Adams to write,

What do we mean by the Revolution? The war? That was no part of the revolution; it was only an effect and consequence of it. The revolution was in the minds of the people, and this was effected from 1760-1775, in the course of fifteen years, before a drop of blood was shed at Lexington.[79]

The Continental Congress, from 1774 to 1789, served as the government of the thirteen American colonies and later the United States. In 1776, after the American Revolutionary War had been underway, it took the epochal step in declaring America's independence from Britain. In light of these momentous goings on, did Congress have a mind for God's Word? It is often argued by some that it did not; but that is patently false. In fact, for example, one of the first acts of the Continental Congress was a decision to print thousands of Christian Bibles.[80]

Additionally, Congress even went so far as to appoint chaplains not only for itself but for the armed forces as well. In 1777, Jacob Duché, Congress's first chaplain, defected to the British; soon after Congress appointed joint chaplains: William White, pastor of Christ Church, Philadelphia (Anglican), and George Duffield, pastor of the Third Presbyterian Church of Philadelphia. By appointing chaplains of different denominations, Congress established an ecumenical precedence in American religious practice, thereby

---

[78] Davis, Religion and the Continental Congress, 1774-1789, 95.

[79] John Adams, Letter to Thomas Jefferson (1815).

[80] Federer, America's God and Country, 25. Robert Aiken, publisher of *The Pennsylvania Magazine*, petitioned the Congress for permission to print Bibles, since there was a shortage due to the war with Britain. Congress approved the printing on September 10, 1782, and further recommended the Bible to the people.

expressing a desire to prevent any single denomination from monopolizing government benefaction. This policy was followed by the first Congress under the Constitution which on April 15, 1789, adopted a joint resolution requiring that the practice be continued.

Concerned about the moral condition of the American Army and Navy, Congress took steps to see that Christian morality prevailed in both organizations. For that purpose, Congress saw to it that the articles in Rules and Regulations of the Navy adopted on November 28, 1775, ordered all commanders to "discountenance and suppress all dissolute, immoral and disorderly practices." The second article required those same commanders "to take care, that divine services be performed twice a day on board, and a sermon be preached on Sundays." Can you imagine this happening today?

Second Continental Congress in prayer 1774.

As far as the Army, Congress drew up articles of war which included a recommendation to all officers and soldiers to attend divine services. Military Chaplains were appointed by Congress and received the equivalent to a major's pay, $8 dollars per month; more than what was paid a surgeon who was paid $4.60 per month! It would seem that Congress placed a high premium on morality as well as the spiritual welfare of their armed forces. Although, not officially authorized by the Articles of Confederation, Congress concerned itself with the advancement of the Christian faith.[81] American citizens did not object to these activities. Their lack of objection can only suggest that all considered it appropriate for the national government to promote a nondenominational Christianity. However, as far as arguing whether or not America is or ever was a Christian nation, Gary De Mar writes,

The proposal that America is a Christian nation does not mean that *every* American is now or ever was a Christian. Moreover, it does not mean that either the Church or the State should force people to profess belief in Christianity or attend religious services.[82]

The State governments also reflected the high premium that was placed on God's Word. For example, the constitution of the Commonwealth of Massachusetts, written in 1780, embodied the Christian principles of earlier American legislation and captured the unique American understanding of rights and their place in politics. Its principal author was John Adams. The first three articles state:

A Declaration of the Rights of the Inhabitants of the Commonwealth of Massachusetts.
Article I. All men are born free and equal, and have certain natural, essential, and unalienable rights; among which may be reckoned the right of enjoying and defending their lives and liberties; that of acquiring, possessing, and protecting property; in fine, that of seeking and obtaining their safety and happiness.
Art. II. It is the right as well as the duty of all men in society, publicly and at stated seasons, to worship the **Supreme Being, the great Creator and Preserver of the universe.** And no subject shall be hurt, molested, or restrained, in his person, liberty, or estate, for worshipping God in the manner and season **most agreeable to the dictates of his own conscience,** or for his religious profession or sentiments, provided he doth not disturb the public peace or obstruct others in their religious worship.
Art. III. As the happiness of a people and the good order and preservation of civil government essentially depend upon **piety, religion, and morality,** and as these cannot be generally diffused

---

[81] The Articles of Confederation was an agreement among the thirteen founding states that established the United States of America as a confederation of sovereign states and served as its first constitution.
[82] Gary De Mar, *America's Christian History*, 3.

through a community but by the institution of the **public worship of God** and of the public instructions in **piety, religion, and morality**...And every denomination of Christians, demeaning themselves peaceably and as good subjects of the commonwealth, shall be equally under the protection of the law; and no subordination of any sect or denomination to another shall ever be established by law (emphasis added).[83]

The point is our first national government, as well as our first state governments, believed that the essential principles of morality and civilization were only to be found in the doctrine of a supreme, intelligent, wise, Almighty Sovereign of the universe. Our first government thought it best to testify their gratitude to God for His goodness, and by a cheerful obedience to His laws, practice true and undefiled religion, which is the great foundation of public prosperity and national happiness (Jam 1:27). In a letter to Thomas Jefferson dated 28 June, 1813, President Adams wrote:

The general principles on which the fathers achieved independence, were...the general principles of Christianity, in which all those sects were united, and the general principles of English and American liberty, in which all those young men united, and which had united all parties in America, in majorities sufficient to assert and maintain her independence. Now I will avow, that I then believed and now believe that those general principles of Christianity are as eternal and immutable as the existence and attributes of God; and that those principles of liberty are as unalterable as human nature and our terrestrial, mundane system.[84]

In other words, the general principles on which the fathers achieved independence were the general principles of Christianity. Whether the founding fathers were Christian or not, you judge. What is clear to this discussion is that they understood not only the authority the Scripture has on governing the soul of man but on America as a nation as a

---

[83] Constitution of Massachusetts, 1780.

[84] John Adams (1735–1826) was the 2nd President of the United States, 1797–1801, established the Library of Congress and the Department of the Navy; Vice-President under George Washington, 1789–97; a member of the First and Second Continental Congress, 1774, 1775; a signer of the Declaration of Independence, 1776.

whole. If not, why else would Adams have called for a national day of humiliation, fasting and prayer? On March 6, 1799, President Adams issued the proclamation which said:

As no truth is more clearly taught in the Volume of Inspiration, nor any more fully demonstrated by the experience of all ages, than that a deep sense and a due acknowledgment of the growing providence of a Supreme Being and of the accountableness of men to Him as the searcher of hearts and righteous distributer of rewards and punishments are conducive equally to the happiness and rectitude of individuals and to the well-being of communities.

National days of thanksgiving and of "humiliation, fasting, and prayer" were proclaimed by Congress at least twice a year throughout the War of Independence. During James Madison's presidency he proclaimed, "To the same Divine Author of Every Good and Perfect Gift we are indebted for all those privileges and advantages, religious as well as civil, which are so richly enjoyed in this favored land." Congress was convinced that the prosperity of our society depended on living according to biblical principles.

America was founded on Christian values, directly from the Bible which has brought enormous blessings to the people of this land. The Constitution of the United States, bearing indelible marks of previous American colonial lawmaking, in Article I, section 7, recognizes Sunday as the day of rest, as well as stating that it was drafted in the year of our Lord one thousand seven hundred and eighty seven. If it was the desire of the framers to strip every vestige of Christianity from the Constitution, why did they include such obvious references to the observance of the Christian faith?[85]

Our constitutional liberties were founded on biblical values, and as John Adams said, "We have no Government armed with power capable of contending with human passions unbridled by Morality and Religion. Avarice, ambition, revenge, or gallantry, would break the strongest cords of our Constitution as a whale goes through a net. Our Constitution was made only for a moral and religious people. It is wholly

---

[85] Gary De Mar, America's Christian History, 92.

inadequate to the government of any other."[86] Congress declared to the American people that biblical principles would "make us holy, so that we may be a happy people!" Happy are the people whose God is the LORD (Ps 144:15)!

The First Amendment

Men like Thomas Jefferson and James Madison had witnessed firsthand the effects of religious persecution in Virginia where full citizenship privileges required being a part of a state church. Many of the colonies had done the same. Desirous of full religious freedom for all Virginians, Thomas Jefferson drafted in 1777 the 'Virginia Statute for Religious Freedom.' The statute, enacted in 1779 by the Virginia General Assembly, disestablished the Church of England in Virginia and granted freedom of religion to people of all faiths, including Catholics and Jews. It was a notable precursor to the Establishment Clause and Free Exercise Clause of the First Amendment to the United States Constitution which would follow suit. The First Amendment to the U.S. Constitution reads as follows:

Congress shall make no law respecting an establishment of religion, or prohibiting the free exercise thereof; or abridging the freedom of speech, or of the press; or the right of the people peaceably to assemble, and to petition the Government for a redress of grievances.

Of the first sixteen words; the first ten words are commonly called the Establishment clause, the following six are called the Free Exercise clause, and together these are frequently referred to as the religion clauses. It may be said that what the framers intended in both clauses was to protect religious liberty as well as prohibit religious coercion. The two clauses express a dual purpose: the prohibition of an "establishment of religion" and the "free exercise" of one's religion. The first clause was undoubtedly intended by the framers to eliminate the possibility of a state-church in America. The second clause, percipient to John Locke, intends to preserve the right of the citizen to believe free from civil coercion and

---

[86] Hannity, Deliver Us from Evil, 14.

"according to the dictates of his own conscience."[87] What exactly was the intent of Religious Clause of the First Amendment? Again Joseph Story writes,

The real object of the First Amendment was not to countenance, much less to advance Mohammedanism (Islam), or Judaism, or infidelity, by prostrating Christianity, but to exclude all rivalry among Christian sects and to prevent any national ecclesiastical establishment which should give to a hierarchy the exclusive patronage of the national government.[88]

The first line of the first amendment restricts lawmakers from making laws that would establish a state religion. What is to be prohibited is a restricting of "the free exercise" of religion. In other words, the first amendment, among other things, was passed in order to prevent problems that Europeans were quite familiar with; wars of religion. The First Amendment protects freedom of conscience and does not use the so often abused and misunderstood phrase, "separation of church and state."

The term is from the phrase, "wall of separation between church and state," which is found in a letter written by Thomas Jefferson to the Danbury Baptist Association in 1802. In that letter, referencing the First Amendment to the United States Constitution, Jefferson wrote:

Believing with you that religion is a matter which lies solely between Man & his God, that he owes account to none other for his faith or his worship, that the legitimate powers of government reach actions only, & not opinions, I contemplate with sovereign reverence that act of the whole American people which declared that their legislature should 'make no law respecting an establishment of religion, or prohibiting the free exercise thereof,' thus building a wall of separation between Church and State.

---

[87] Locke, A Letter Concerning Toleration, 51. Locke further influences this clause by saying, "Because the care of souls is not committed to the civil magistrate, any more than to other men. It is not committed unto him, I say, by God; because it appears not that God has ever given any such authority to one man over another, as to compel any one to his religion," Ibid, 49.

[88] Joseph Story, Commentaries on the Constitution, 1840.

Chapter 1: The God-Honoring American Man

Jefferson's intent was to insure the Danbury Baptists that in America one shall not be persecuted based on their religious beliefs. As we have seen, the Puritans, the Quakers, and other Protestants came to America to escape religious persecution for their beliefs. The First Amendment was framed to insure freedom of religion, that one shall not be persecuted based on their religious beliefs. In light of this fact, shouldn't those freedoms extend to our military personnel as well?

Some may ask, should Christians concern themselves with matters such as these? Does it really matter if America, which was founded as a Christian nation and has since become increasingly secular, does away with every vestige of the Christian faith? We think it does matter and so did Patrick Henry. In 1777 he wrote, "It cannot be emphasized too strongly or too often that this great nation was founded, not by religionists, but by Christians; not on religions, but on the gospel of Jesus Christ! For this very reason peoples of other faiths have been afforded asylum, prosperity, and freedom of worship here."

Our American society was founded on biblical principles and recognition of our God-given natural rights; the "unalienable rights" referred to in the Declaration of Independence (see appendix 2). Just how important is this? In 1954, Former Chief Justice Earl Warren gives an answer when he said,

I believe no one can read the history of our country without realizing that the Good Book and the spirit of the Savior have from the beginning been our guiding geniuses...Whether we look to the first charter of Virginia...or to the Charter of New England...or to the Charter of Massachusetts Bay...or to the Fundamental Orders of Connecticut...the same objective is present: a Christian land governed by Christian principles...I believe the entire Bill of Rights came into being because of the knowledge our forefathers had of the Bible and their belief in it: freedom of belief, of expression, of assembly, of petition, the dignity of the individual, the sanctity of the home, equal justice under law, and the reservation of powers to the people... I like to believe we are living today in the spirit of the Christian religion. I like also to believe that as long as we do so, no great harm can come to our country."[89]

---

[89] Gary De Mar, America's Christian History: The Untold Story, 1.

Chapter 1: The God-Honoring American Man

That's what prompted John Adams to say, "Without the morality of religion, our sinfulness would break the strongest cords of our Constitution as a whale goes through a net." Our morality, as a nation, is based squarely on the Word of God. President Reagan thought so, and flatly stated that America's greatness lay in her people, her families, her churches, her neighborhoods and communities – the institutions that promote traditional, not secular, values.[90] Antithetical to Reagan's view, there is overwhelming evidence to suggest that there is a conscious effort to renounce our Biblical heritage. America's founders were God-honoring men who desired America to be a God-honoring nation and believed that "all men are created equal, that they are endowed by their Creator with certain unalienable rights, which among these are life, liberty and the pursuit of happiness."

Can America truly be called a God-honoring nation now? According to a *Pew Research* study, more than ninety-percent of those living in the USA believe in God, eighty-one percent describe themselves as Christian, and eighty-five percent say their religion is an important part of their lives.[91] America has benefited greatly not only from the biblical heritage of our founding fathers but the continuing legacy of our American faith in God and His Word.

This line of thought must be developed further but suffice it to say that Christians are to care about what happens in government. America has an awesome heritage of faith. Those serving now, follow in the footsteps of God-honoring men, who were foremost believers in God, eternal truth, and freedom, and were prepared to give their lives in defense of "life, liberty, and the pursuit of happiness." True happiness is knowing God, personally.

Thus, the first mark of the God-honoring American man is faith in God. As Americans, when we exercise our faith in Christ, we are reminding ourselves of the godly heritage of the United States of America that was created to be "one Nation under God, indivisible, with liberty and justice for all."

---

[90] Reagan, Speaking My Mind, 168
[91] O'Reilly, A Fresh Piece of Humanity, 75.

Chapter 1: The God-Honoring American Man

Second Mark of a God-Honoring American Man:
Faithfulness to Christ's Commandments

Puritan Worship Service 1620s.

[15]"If you love Me, keep My commandments. [16]And I will pray the Father, and He will give you another Helper, that He may abide with you forever— [17]the Spirit of truth, whom the world cannot receive, because it neither sees Him nor knows Him; but you know Him, for He dwells with you and will be in you. [18]I will not leave you orphans; I will come to you (Jn 14:15-18).

Earlier we talked about how our forefather's faith in God shaped the very foundation of our great nation, establishing a godly heritage of biblically based laws. The faith of our founding fathers was a faith in the preeminence of Jesus Christ. The father of our nation, George Washington, thought so. Once, when he addressed a delegation from the Delaware Indian nation he said, "You do well to wish to learn our arts and ways of life, and above all, the religion of Jesus Christ. These will make you a greater and happier people than you are."[92]

Faith is the act of trusting in Christ's perfect, finished work. We must trust Jesus Christ was more than a mere man, He is the God-man, God the Son (Jn 20:28; Heb 1:8). We must

---

[92] John Fitzgerald, The Writings of George Washington, Vol XV, 55.

decide if He was crazy, or a deceiver, or telling the truth. Was He a lunatic? A liar? Or is He Lord? C.S. Lewis once wrote,

A man who was merely a man and said the sort of things Jesus said would not be a great moral teacher. He would either be a lunatic – on a level with the man who says he is a poached egg – or else he would be the Devil of hell. You must make your choice. Either this man was, and is, the Son of God: or else a madman or something worse. You can shut Him up for a fool, you can spit on Him and kill Him as a demon; or you fall at His feet and call Him Lord and God. But let us not come up with any patronizing nonsense about His being a great human teacher. He has not left that open to us. He did not intend to.[93]

Faith is not a mechanical process; it's the relational response to God's promises of salvation to all who receive Jesus Christ as Lord. Faith is 'obedience to the truth' (1 Pet 1:22), and so, the second mark of the God-honoring American man is faithfulness to Christ's commandments. Only he who believes is obedient, and only he who is obedient believes.[94] It's impossible to please God without faith (Heb 11:6). Faith is obeying God by repenting of our sins and throwing our lives on the mercy God has already provided for us in Christ Jesus. This is an exclusive Christian claim, for there is no other name by which we are saved (Acts 4:12). Salvation is therefore repentance towards God for our sins and faith in our Lord Jesus Christ. People often wonder what God's will is. The Bible tells us in Jn 6:37-40:

[37] All that the Father gives Me will come to Me, and the one who comes to Me I will by no means cast out. [38] For I have come down from heaven, not to do My own will, but the will of Him who sent Me. [39] This is the will of the Father who sent Me, that of all He has given Me I should lose nothing, but should raise it up at the last day. [40] And this is the will of Him who sent Me, that everyone who sees the Son and believes in Him may have everlasting life; and I will raise him up at the last day."

---

[93] Lewis, Mere Christianity, 56.
[94] Dietrich Bonhoeffer, The Cost of Discipleship, 69.

Chapter 1: The God-Honoring American Man

The Prophet, Priest, King

God's will is that everyone who looks to the Son and believes in Him will have (present tense) eternal life, to be raised up by Jesus on the last day. This is the revealed will of God. God's will is also that those who believe will be further sanctified; become more like Christ (1 Thess 4:3). God also has a secret will (Dt 29:29), which is His prerogative and for His glory to conceal, but what He requires of us is obedience to His revealed will. And the will of God is for us to believe on the One He has sent.[95]

The One God has sent fulfills a threefold office of *Prophet*, *Priest* and *King*. Christ perfectly fulfills the will of the Father by revealing God to men (Prophet), by redeeming men from sin (Priest) and by restoring man to God (King). Thus, Christ fulfills the covenant from the side of God as God and from the side of man as Man. God revealed Himself to Israel through Moses that in the fullness of time He would send them 'The Prophet.' Dt 18:15-19 tells us:

[15] "The LORD your God will raise up for you a Prophet like me from your midst, from your brethren. Him you shall hear, [16] according to all you desired of the LORD your God in Horeb in the day of the assembly, saying, 'Let me not hear again the voice of the LORD my God, nor let me see this great fire anymore, lest I die.' [17] "And the LORD said to me: 'What they have spoken is good. [18] I will raise up for them a Prophet like you from among their brethren, and will put My words in His mouth, and He shall speak to them all that I command Him. [19] And it shall be *that* whoever will not hear My words, which He speaks in My name, I will require *it* of him.

The Prophet spoken of here is not Joshua, David, Elijah, or Isaiah but Jesus Christ of Nazareth, the Messiah (Acts 3:19-26).[96] Jesus Christ, born of the virgin Mary, came and spoke the very words of God – the Gospel. Jesus said, "Repent, for

---

[95] See chapter four for a discussion on: what is the will of God?

[96] The Westminster Larger Catechism Question 43 asks us: *How does Christ execute the office of a prophet?*
Answer: Christ executes the office of a prophet, in his revealing to the church, in all ages, by his Spirit and word, in divers ways of administration, the whole will of God, in all things concerning their edification and salvation.

the kingdom of heaven is at hand (Mt 4:17)." All the teachings Jesus gave were not His own but his Father's, which he gave unto him, and put into his mouth, so that he should declare it to us. The coming of the Son of God brings a decision, a judgment. Jesus said, "He who rejects Me rejects Him who sent Me," and "He who rejects Me, and does not receive My words, has that which judges him—the word that I have spoken will judge him in the last day" (Lk 10:16).

The Bible tells us that Jesus Christ is the 'High Priest' of our confession (Heb 3:1), and the reason why He came into the world was to destroy the works of the devil (1 John 3:8).[97] God's Word tells us that Satan deceived our first parents (Gen 3:1-5), and the result is that mankind rebelled against God and broke His commandment, which we were free and able to obey and have incurred God's curse (death) and put ourselves under the dominion and control of demonic evil. The Bible characterizes Satan as the god of this world whose object it is to keep men under his control, thereby holding mankind in darkness and unbelief. The whole world, the Bible tells us in 1 Jn 5:19, is under the power of the evil one.

Christ destroys the works of the devil by redeeming men from sin. He did this at Calvary, once and for all. The Bible says, "For He made Him who knew no sin *to be* sin for us, that we might become the righteousness of God in Him (2 Cor 5:21)." As our Savior, Jesus is both the offering, the Lamb of God (Jn 1:29) and the Offerer, our faithful High Priest (Heb 5:5). Christian theology shows Jesus as the High Priest who stands between sinners and the Holy God. Christ mediates between fallen mankind who deserves God's wrath and the Judge, pleading for forgiveness on their behalf. In Christ, our sins have already been judged; what He restores in His crucifixion, He elevates in His resurrection; and as our Mediator, He is now enthroned at the right hand of God, making intercession for us (Heb 7:25), because of which we will never be lost.

---

[97] The Westminster Shorter Catechism Question 44 asks us: *How does Christ execute the office of a priest?*
Answer: Christ executes the office of a priest, in his once offering himself a sacrifice without spot to God, to be a reconciliation for the sins of the people; and in makipng continual intercession for them.

Chapter 1: The God-Honoring American Man

Follow Me

Christ, the King of kings (Lk 1:31-33), already possesses all authority in heaven and earth, restores man to God by conquering all of our enemies – sin, death, and the devil.[98] To Him we owe the highest love, reverence, and obedience. Jesus said "Follow Me (Mt 4:19)." Christians are first and foremost followers of Christ Jesus, who follow the Lamb wherever He goes (Rev 14:4). There are at least four fundamental imperatives regarding one's discipleship to the Lord Jesus Christ. These are:

1. Follow Christ. 2. Model (imitate) Christ.	Chapters 1-8
3. Suffer for/with Christ. 4. Conquer with Christ.	Chapter 9-10

These fundamental imperatives will serve to further frame our discussion in the remainder of this book, that is, how a man may live a God-honoring life in a pagan culture. The first two truths form the basis for our discussion from here to chapter eight. The last two truths we will discuss in chapters nine and ten.

For now, let's look at the first truth, following Him. Jesus Christ calls us to come to Him and experience *rest* for our souls (Mt 11:25-30) by being *yoked* to Him. To follow Jesus is to be yoked to Him. What does it mean to be yoked to Christ? The image of a yoke of oxen is employed. The oxen pull in only one direction while they plow the field or pull the cart. Using this analogy, Jesus tells us, following Him means going where He goes and bearing His burdens along with Him. This

---

[98] The Westminster Shorter Catechism Question 45 asks us: *How doth Christ execute the office of a king?*
Answer: Christ executes the office of a king, in calling out of the world a people to himself, and giving them officers, laws, and censures, by which he visibly governs them; in bestowing saving grace upon his elect, rewarding their obedience, and correcting them for their sins, preserving and supporting them under all their temptations and sufferings, restraining and overcoming all their enemies, and powerfully ordering all things for his own glory, and their good; and also in taking vengeance on the rest, who know not God, and obey not the gospel.

is also says much about evangelism, as we plow the field of the world along with Jesus – the Sower (Mt 13).

However, our part is *easy* and *light* compared to His. This is because if we are following Him correctly, we won't be doing the directing or the pulling. But we will suffer for His sake, and when we suffer, He will be right there with us. Our discipleship to Jesus Christ is a lifelong journey that begins when we are saved. These concepts will be developed further in the rest of the book.

Jesus said, "If you love Me, obey my commandments (Jn 14:15, 21)." Subjection to the authority of Scripture is subjection to the authority of Christ.[99] Jesus commanded many things in Scripture, the foremost commandments, as stated earlier, "Love the Lord your God with all you heart, soul, mind and strength" (Mk 12:30), and the second, "Love your neighbor as yourself." When we obey Christ's commandments we *model* Him, that is, live out His character. Jesus also commanded us to make disciples of all nations (Mt 28:18-20) and to love even our enemies (Mt 5:44). The Great Commission tells us to evangelize the world by telling people the gospel, baptizing them, and making disciples of Jesus by teaching them to obey everything He has commanded us. This is nothing short of a command to renew culture.[100]

Make Disciples

The expressed duty, when we are received into the body of Christ, is to profess the faith within us, to make ourselves known as followers of Christ on every proper occasion, and to lead others to Him by the influence of our testimony.[101] This is properly called discipleship. We will discuss this in depth in chapter eight. Of some 200 commands we have in Scripture from the Savior, I would like to focus on one of them, "make disciples of all nations" (Mt 28:19). Christ issues this

---

[99] James I. Packer, Fundamentalism and the Word of God (Grand Rapids: Eerdmans), 21.
[100] This will be covered in the fourth mark as well as the remainder of the book.
[101] Philip Schaff, The Creeds of Christendom, Volume 1, 4.

command before He is taken up in glory at His ascension. The apostle Matthew tells us,

> [18] And Jesus came and spoke to them, saying, "All authority has been given to Me in heaven and on earth. [19] Go therefore and make disciples of all the nations, baptizing them in the name of the Father and of the Son and of the Holy Spirit, [20] teaching them to observe all things that I have commanded you; and lo, I am with you always, *even* to the end of the age." Amen (Mt 28:18-20).

This is Christ's command to change the world! Love one another as I have loved you. Make disciples! Be salt! Be light! Share your faith! The Spirit of Christ in us is the empowerment of testimony (Rev 19:10). The Baptist Faith and Message puts it this way: It is the duty of every child of God to seek constantly to win the lost to Christ by verbal witness undergirded by a Christian lifestyle, and by other methods in harmony with the gospel of Christ.[102]

Having a *verbal witness* undergirded by a Christian lifestyle; this is the aspect of Christianity that has always been under attack. Our relationship with the personal God, based on God's written revelation and Christ's finished work in space-time history, is to be seen and heard. Because forgiveness of sins is based upon the vicarious righteousness of Christ imputed to the believing sinner, saving faith will inevitably be accompanied by good works, as sanctification proceeds on the prior basis of regeneration and faith.[103]

One of the most dangerous things in the Church today is the prevalent tendency to treat the gospel as something that is merely assumed. Many people say, "I believe the gospel!" but then focus on something other than the gospel as a certain kind of spiritual discipline. The gospel is not just something we need to understand and then move on, the gospel is something

---

[102] The Baptist Faith and Message, XI. Evangelism and Missions, 16.

[103] Sanctification is a work of God's grace, whereby they whom God hath, before the foundation of the world, chosen to be holy, are in time, through the powerful operation of His Spirit applying the death and resurrection of Christ unto them, renewed in their whole man after the image of God; having the seeds of repentance unto life, and all other saving graces, put into their hearts, and those graces so stirred up, increased, and strengthened, as that they more and more die unto sin, and rise unto newness of life. Westminster Larger Catechism, Answer 75. See also chapter 2, the three enemies of the saint.

we must go back to again and again. We must not try to master the gospel, the gospel must master us. Living a God-honoring life with a verbal witness is the Christian calling.

Two Kingdom Concept

Christians, says our Lord Jesus, are sons of the kingdom, and as such are to be primarily concerned with the coming and further expansion of that kingdom (Mt 6:9-13, 24-33). Christ Jesus, by conquering the powers of darkness in His incarnation, obedience, crucifixion, resurrection, and ascension is our present reigning King (Rom 1:4; Col 1:13-18); and the present "ruler over the kings of the earth" (Rev 1:5).

Believers are presently brought into Christ's kingdom by faith to be held in the divine grasp and endure to the end (Jn 5:25; 10:28). Believers now have a share in Christ's kingdom by obedient lives and bearing witness to His saving power (Rev 1:9; 12:11). We will discuss how believers are to relate to culture in chapter nine, but for now suffice it to say that although the Church is *in* the world; it is not to be *of* the world. And Christ's Kingdom has come, and is coming, and will come.[104] George Ladd has well written, "The age of fulfillment is not only near; it is actually present. Nevertheless, the time of apocalyptic consummation remains in the future."[105] This is the "now" and the "not yet" of the Kingdom of God.

The Kingdom of God is both a present reality and a future hope. Those who willingly surrender to Christ now, experience the saving power of His cross, a peace of conscience and spiritually enter His Kingdom (Mt 4:17; 11:28-30); those who reject Him experience a judicial hardening for their sins, an ever-increasing confused, agitated conscience until they face an angry God in judgment where they will be justly condemned for their sins, and will be punished with the everlasting torments of hell (Mt 22:13; 25:30). Man must respond to his overture of love, or face

---

[104] Compare Mt 4:17; Mk 1:15; Luke 11:20; 12:34; 16:16; 17:21; 23:43; Heb 12:22-24; 1 Pet 2:9 and Rev 1:9 with Mt 6:10; John 18:36, 37; Rev 21:1, 2.
[105] Ladd, The Presence of the Future, 120.

eternal condemnation. God Himself is not only the Author and Finisher of our faith but He is the very object of our faith, Christ Jesus. Faith is the obedience of Christ lived out in the life of the saint. We will discuss how that is so in the remainder of the book.

Third Mark of a God-Honoring American Man: Faithful Family Man

"You shall not commit adultery" (Ex 20:14).

In his book on Christian ethics, David F. Wells states that at one time there were three sinews that held our culture together: tradition, authority and power. They long served as essential garments, but of late they have been dropping away, leaving it exposed and indecent.[106]

Tradition, he said, was the way one generation passed on the values, beliefs and principles of our culture and society to the rising generation. It was the family who passed on tradition. He goes on to say that, "Our families and our schools have become so enamored of the ostensible virtues of pluralism – every system of thought is of equal value, that they no longer make a token effort to give the next generation moral instruction."[107] As for authority, at one time it lay mostly in the realm of the Church who spoke from the

---

[106] Wells, God in the Wasteland, 146.
[107] Ibid.

perspective of moral persuasion. Theism; "thus saith the Lord," "the Bible says," our creeds and confessions, etc. But now tradition is gone, moral authority is gone and only power remains.

Power lies primarily in the hands of the state. It has the right to the enforce the law. And now the state is tasked with the difficulty of making decisions where it is uninformed by tradition and unguarded by moral authority and has only power to make its own way. Wells goes on to add that now, in the absence of any consensus about what is right and wrong, we have to resort to lawyers to settle our disputes. In the absence of moral obligation, disputes are incredibly difficult to resolve and the duties that were once shouldered by a variety of other institutions like the family, the schools and the Church are now taken on by lawyers and bureaucrats.

The courts are deciding such issues as: when life begins in the womb; or which gender can marry the other gender but isn't that the decision of the Church? Sadly, not any more, it's the decision of the state. Because of our ethical confusion, we have forced our government to make decisions about everything ranging from stem cell research and the sale of embryos to euthanasia and surrogate parenting. Not to mention gender issues and same sex marriage because we have nothing but power left.

In this vein, Andreas Köstenberger makes clear, "The Judeo-Christian view of marriage and the family with its roots in the Hebrew Scriptures has to a significant extent been replaced with a set of values that prizes human rights, self-fulfillment, and pragmatic utility on an individual or societal level. It can rightly be said that marriage and the family are institutions under siege in our world today, and that with marriage and the family, our very civilization is in crisis."[108]

Marriage and the Family: God's Creation

In light of this analysis, what must be asserted with biblical clarity is the truth the Scriptures reveal regarding marriage and

---

[108] Köstenberger, God, Marriage, and Family: Rebuilding the Biblical Foundation, 15.

the family. With this in mind, this section seeks to discuss the practical aspects of being a faithful family man in the midst of a transvaluating society. For that, we will need to ask such questions as: What is marriage? What is the family? And what are the potential negative effects of disregarding the biblical standards of these? These questions were self-evident societal norms for centuries. However, as recent developments have shown, there is now more than ever a tremendous need to reassert biblical truth, thus defining these foundational terms.

The faithful family man is: one who commits to a loving, life-long, monogamous, marital relationship with one woman; who, in an attitude of sacrificial love, provides for his wife and children not only responsible spiritual leadership but cares for their physical, spiritual, and social well-being as well.

First, what is marriage? Marriage is the God-ordained institution on which the family, as well as society as a whole is founded. As it is the most ancient of all societies and the only natural one. Why did God create marriage? He created it for the mutual help of husband and wife, to provide mankind with a legitimate issue, and to give the Church a holy progeny, that is children that would grow up being nurtured by their mother and disciplined by their father while learning God's Word. Marriage is the bedrock on which the family is built, nourished and protected. Marriage is the uniting of one man and one woman in a covenant commitment for a lifetime (Mt 19:4-6).

Our government has also declared what marriage is. In 1996, President Clinton signed into law the federal Defense of Marriage Act (DOMA), which defines marriages as being a union of one man and one woman and allows individual states to deny recognition of same-sex marriages that may be performed in other states.

The Covenant, Sign, and Foundation

Marriage may be best described and understood by three principle truths: Marriage is a covenant, a sign, and the foundation for the family and society as a whole. As our country continues to redefine marriage, these principles are timeless and paramount for our day.

Chapter 1: The God-Honoring American Man

Marriage is a Covenant

First, marriage is a life-long covenant relationship between one man and one woman. Jesus Christ blessed the institution of marriage and sanctioned it by telling us in Matthew 19:

> [4] And He answered and said to them, "Have you not read that He who made *them* at the beginning '**made them male and female**,'[5] and said, 'For this reason a man shall leave his father and mother and be joined to his wife, and the two shall become one flesh'? [6] So then, they are no longer two but one flesh. Therefore what God has joined together, let not man separate" (emphasis added).

Using Genesis, Jesus demonstrates that just as Eve was taken out of Adam and was "bone of his bones, and flesh of his flesh," husband and wife constitute a unity that must not be divided by the caprice of mankind. Same-sex marriage apologists frequently claim that Jesus never taught against gay marriage, however, doesn't Jesus make it quite clear that marriage is to be between one male and one female (verse 4)? Additionally, our Lord states, in no uncertain terms, that the marriage bond is to be life-long. And this, He states, is in opposition to those who would allow divorce for nearly any reason.[109]

Man and woman were both created fully and equally in God's image. Man and woman were created to function covenantally. In other words, marriage represents Christ's relationship to His Bride – the Church. Man is personal and relational, being created to live relationally. God, thus created genders for His glory, and designed them to complement each other. God completed man by creating a helper out of the man to be his life-long companion. God created marriage and gave Eve to be Adam's helper with Adam as the head of the household (1 Cor 11:3, 8).

---

[109] During the First Century B.C., two opposing schools of thought known as the House of Hillel and the House of Shammai developed in Israel. Each house was led by two prominent rabbis. The House of Shammai (conservative) held that a man may only divorce his wife for a serious transgression, but the House of Hillel (liberal) allowed divorce for even trivial offenses, such as burning a meal.

Chapter 1: The God-Honoring American Man

Arnold Rhodes writes, "God's marriage arithmetic is a very extraordinary kind of mathematics: $1 + 1 = 1$. It entails a total psychophysical union: thinking together, feeling together, believing together, and working together. "I," "my," and "me" are replaced by "we," "our," and "us."[110] This is expressed by Thomas Adams who wrote, "As God by creation made two of one, so again by marriage He made one of two."[111]

Marriage, according to the Bible, is not merely a "committed interdependent partnership between consenting adults," marriage is a life-long covenant relationship before God between one man and one woman. Marriage is a covenant between one man and one woman. It is to be an unforced accord, to live together in love, with the prospect of procreating children (Ps 127:3). The man and woman, both created in the image of God, have gender specific roles according to God's design.[112] The man is to lovingly and sacrificially protect and provide for the needs of the wife, as well as the children; marriage makes the children who are procreated legitimate. Bearing the God-giving responsibility to *lead, protect and provide* for his family, the husband is charged as the familial head. This biblical truth will be developed in chapter five.

This explicit teaching of the Old Testament remains characteristic in the New Testament family (Eph 5:25-30; Col 3:18-25). The husband is therefore the defender of the family, including the unborn. Children, from the moment of conception are a blessing and heritage from the Lord. Therefore, fetuses are human beings created in God's image, and as such should be accorded the rights of humans from the moment of conception; any violent act to end their lives is immoral and should be prevented.[113] It is not the purpose here

---

[110] Rhodes, The Mighty Acts of God, 39.

[111] Adams, An Exposition Upon the Second Epistle General of St. Peter, 84.

[112] What does it mean to be created in the image of God? Among other things, it certainly means that: God gave mankind a mind, a will, and emotions; a mind to be rational, a will to be moral, and emotions to love the Creator reciprocally. In terms of mankind's God-giving rationality, he can find truth while his volition can make moral choices.

[113] The early Christians, following the lead of Jews, condemned abortion and exposure. The *Didache*, an ancient manual of Christian instruction, reads as

to enter the abortion debate, however, abortion must be considered as the unauthorized taking of a preborn human life, which is contrary to God's will (Ex 20: 6; Ex 21:22-25).

According to the World Health Organization, every year in the world there are an estimated 40-50 million abortions. That's roughly 125,000 abortions per day! And in our country, four out of every ten pregnancies are terminated by abortion.[114] Twenty-two percent of all pregnancies in the USA (excluding miscarriages) end in abortion.[115]

Additionally, the God-honoring American man is the priest of the home. All believers are priests, in that they serve as mediators between God and the unbelieving world.[116] God holds the head of the household responsible for the spiritual well-being of the whole family. The husband is held responsible by God whether or not he is a responsible man. Correspondingly, the wife, who is also made in the image of God and therefore equal to her husband, submits to the servant leadership of her husband and serves as his helper in managing the household as they both raise the next generation.[117]

Moreover, marriage is a covenant because it is a sacred bond instituted by and publically entered into before God; whether or not this is acknowledged by the married couple. The word for covenant in the Bible, *bereeth* בְּרִית, means a binding agreement. This Hebrew word derives from a root which means "to cut" hence a covenant is a "cutting." This is a reference to the ancient custom of cutting animals into two parts with the contracting parties passing between them, thus making a covenant (Jer 34:18-19). Essentially, the compacting partners in the covenant say "may I be torn apart like these animals if I fail to uphold my part of this covenant." The example par excellence in the Bible occurs when God brings Abraham into a covenant with Him. In Genesis 15 when

---

follows: "You shall not murder, you shall not procure abortion, nor commit infanticide," Did 2:2.

[114] Finer LB and Henshaw SK, Perspectives on Sexual and Reproductive Health, 2006, 38(2):90–96.

[115] Jones RK, Abortion in the United States: Incidence and access to services, 2005, Perspectives on Sexual and Reproductive Health, 2008, 40(1):6–16

[116] This will developed in chapter 4.

[117] Baptist faith and Message, XVIII, The Family, 21.

Chapter 1: The God-Honoring American Man

Abraham, who losing his physical strength in the tremendous presence of God, sleeps, as God alone passes between the slaughtered animals. Thus, emphasizing the one-sided nature of this covenant that Abraham and all his seed are privileged to be brought into.

Therefore, rather than being merely a contract for a limited amount of time, conditioned upon the performance of contractual obligations by the other partner, marriage is a life-long sacred bond that is characterized by permanence, sacredness, intimacy, mutuality, and exclusiveness.[118] Sexual intimacy, a gift of God to be enjoyed between a man and woman within the marriage covenant, is forbidden outside of marriage. The seventh commandment tells us,

"You shall not commit adultery" (Ex 20:14).

That the seventh commandment goes beyond mere physical contact is evident from Jesus' teaching in the Sermon on the Mount, where He corrects many misuses of the Law. For example, in Mt 5:27-28 He says, "You have heard that it was said to those of old, 'You shall not commit adultery.' But I say to you that whoever looks at a woman to lust for her has already committed adultery with her in his heart."

Whereas the Rabbinic tradition for the Law of Moses was noted for its externalistic interpretation, Jesus reestablishes the original intent of the Law. When properly interpreted, the Sermon on the Mount is for Christians today. This will be discussed further in chapter three.

Jesus went to the heart of every matter and as His followers, we should too. The following excerpts from the larger Catechism give us an extension of the seventh commandment:

Q. 138. *What are the duties required in the seventh commandment?*
A. The duties required in the seventh commandment are, chastity in body, mind, affections, words, and behavior; and the preservation of it in ourselves and others; watchfulness over the eyes and all the

---

[118] Köstenberger, God, Marriage, and Family: Rebuilding the Biblical Foundation, 78.

senses; temperance, keeping of chaste company, modesty in apparel; marriage by those that have not the gift of continency, conjugal love, and cohabitation; diligent labor in our callings; shunning all occasions of uncleanness, and resisting temptations thereunto.

Q. 139. *What are the sins forbidden in the seventh commandment?*

A. The sins forbidden in the seventh commandment, besides the neglect of the duties required, are, adultery, fornication, rape, incest, sodomy, and all unnatural lusts; all unclean imaginations, thoughts, purposes, and affections; all corrupt or filthy communications, or listening thereunto; wanton looks, impudent or light behavior, immodest apparel; prohibiting of lawful, and dispensing with unlawful marriages; allowing, tolerating, keeping of stews, and resorting to them; entangling vows of single life, undue delay of marriage; having more wives or husbands than one at the same time; unjust divorce, or desertion; idleness, gluttony, drunkenness, unchaste company; lascivious songs, books, pictures, dancings, stage plays; and all other provocations to, or acts of uncleanness, either in ourselves or others.

John Frame reminds us of how we may carry this line of thinking even further. He writes, "Scripture represents marriage as a reflection of our covenant relationship with God. To violate marriage is to violate that covenant, and unfaithfulness to God is adultery. All sin is unfaithfulness to God, spiritual adultery. So the seventh commandment, like the others, actually covers all of life in its particular perspective. Whenever we sin, we can think of it as marital unfaithfulness."[119]

Marriage is a Sign

Second, marriage is a sign that signifies the spiritual relationship between Christ (Bridegroom) and the Church (Bride). A sign in Scripture can be a visible, audible or sensible phenomenon that is meant to indicate something else, namely God's activity and power in the world; His kingdom. In the New Testament, we find that Jesus uses miraculous

---

[119] Frame, The Doctrine of the Christian Life, 747.

signs alongside the word He speaks, such as, His turning water into wine, His feeding of the five thousand, and His walking on the sea (Jn 2:7-11; 6:11; 6:19 respectively). In addition to meeting the immediate human need, each of these miracles had a corresponding supernatural equivalence. For example, Jesus' turning water into wine not only symbolically abrogates the Jewish ceremonial washings but portently anticipates the impending joy of the Messianic banquet – the Marriage Supper of the Lamb (Rev 19:6-11).

There are other signs in Scripture that, while visibly, audibly, or sensibly representing a corresponding spiritual reality, they are of a more natural occurrence. Such examples in Scripture include, the tree of life in the Garden of Eden, the rainbow after the Flood, and the Brazen Serpent (Gen 2:9; 9:12; Num 21:8 respectively). Likewise, Jesus leaves His Church such lasting signs; baptism and the Lord's Supper. These visible signs, that are also means of grace, relate the corresponding truth that they signify. Just as the Lord's Supper correlates to the Messianic banquet at the end of time, baptism shows, by sign, the manner in which believers are buried with Christ in His death and raised in His resurrection power to walk a new life, free from the guilt of sin and the condemning power of death.

Marriage, being a natural life-long committed relationship between one man and one woman is therefore a sign, a visible, audible, and sensible one, which correlates to a profound spiritual truth; the Bible calls "a great mystery" (Eph 5:32). Just as Eve derived her life from Adam, the Church derives its life from Christ because Christ and His people are one flesh and likewise share a common life (Gen 2:21-25; Mt 20:28; John 5:25). Moreover, as the woman is to submit to her husband in all things, the church is to submit to Christ. And just as Christ loves the church and gave Himself for her, husbands are to sacrificially love their wives. What God desires is for good marriages to portray the relationship between Christ and the church (Mt 22:1-14). Marriage is a total commitment and a total sharing of the total person with another person until death.[120]

---

[120] Mack, Strengthening Your Marriage, 6.

Chapter 1: The God-Honoring American Man

Marriage is the Foundation of Family and Society

Thirdly, marriage is the foundation for the family and society as a whole. The family has been the basic unit of society in all cultures since God first instituted it. What is the family? The French philosopher Jean Jacques Rousseau writes, "The most ancient of all societies and the only natural one, is that of the family. The family is therefore the prototype of society."[121] We would have to agree with Rousseau on biblical grounds that marriage is the oldest and most basic of God's institutions for mankind. *It takes a husband and wife in a committed life-long marital relationship to raise children; not a village.*

Currently, we are witnessing what is amounting to the disillusionment and destruction of the American family. In the past it would have been unthinkable to consider the marriage of two men or two women but in our present society this is a topic of debate. And the church, by and large, has backed away from making absolute statements out of fear of public opinion. Issues dealing with what constitutes marriage, and who can be ordained are currently up for debate in the established churches in America. And why are they up for debate instead of dismissed out right on the account of being condemned by Scripture? Because as John Wesley has aptly said, "What one generation tolerates, the next generation will embrace" (Rev 2:20).

When the church tolerates immorality, in all of its forms, it runs the danger of ceasing to exist as a church. Currently, there is much confusion over marriage because the attitudes and views in our society fluctuate like wild waves of the sea. But what does the Bible say about these issues? Isn't what God says in His Word the authority on moral issues?

Why did God create the family? Scripture reveals that God created the family in order to provide a framework for society, as well as legitimate means to procreate the human race. It is by God's design for the family to teach the next generation values and ethics. What are values? Values bind a society together and give it a sense of identity, dignity, security, and

---

[121] Rousseau, The Social Contract, 142.

continuity; whereas ethics is ideal behavior.[122] Values may therefore be seen as the what, to which ethics are the how. Values reflect what a people judge to be ultimately important. They reflect our sense of right and wrong. *Fundamentally, what we value exerts influence on our behavior so that our behavior becomes our character.* What God would have us do is value Him, His Word and the coming of His kingdom above all other values (Mt 6:33). And in doing this, our values shape us into the character of Christ (Gal 4:19).

The family is God's way of expressing His relationship to His covenant people in marital terms: Israel is the wife of Yahweh; the church is the bride of Christ; Israel is God's son; the church is God's son and daughters as well as the bride of Christ. Describing the closeness and intimacy into which God brings His people, He says, "I will set My tabernacle among you, and My soul shall not abhor you. I will be your God and you will be my people" (Lev 26:11).

Christian Bachelors

If marriage is the foundation for the family and society, than what about men and women who aren't married? The Word of God tells us that for some Christians avoiding marriage and sexual activity is a conscious issue, and for them to live the Christian life unmarried can be to God's glory. The Lord Jesus says in Mt 19:12, "For there are eunuchs who were born thus from *their* mother's womb, and there are eunuchs who were made eunuchs by men, and there are eunuchs who have made themselves eunuchs for the kingdom of heaven's sake. He who is able to accept *it,* let him accept *it.*"

We shouldn't take castration or sterilization (as Origen did) to mean any more than we should understand Jesus' admonition to "pluck out an eye or cut off a hand" to mean that we should physically disfigure ourselves. Still, we should understand Jesus' words to mean that He approves of Christians who abstain from marriage and sexual activity for the sake of serving Christ's kingdom. This is the life Paul chose for himself and presents to the church for us to consider.

---

[122] Frame, The Doctrine of the Christian Life, 856.

Chapter 1: The God-Honoring American Man

Paul tells us in 1 Cor 7:8-9, "But I say to the unmarried and to the widows: It is good for them if they remain even as I am; but if they cannot exercise self-control, let them marry. For it is better to marry than to burn *with passion.*"

D.A. Carson writes, "The apostle declares celibacy to be an excellent thing, provided one has the gift (both marriage and celibacy are labeled charismata, "grace gifts"), and provided it is for the sake of increased ministry (1 Cor 7). On the other hand, there is nothing that suggests celibacy is an intrinsically holier state, and absolutely nothing under the terms of the new covenant warrants withdrawing into cloisters of celibate monks or nuns who have physically retreated from the world to become more spiritual."[123] We must understand that the apostle Paul is not so much dissuading marriage, because it is honorable, as he is advising Christians to consider if God has called them to live celibate lives. And the reason he adds for consideration is, he would have us be ever mindful of who we are serving in this life, the Lord Christ (Col 3:17, 23).

A Secular View of Marriage

However, owing to mankind's insistent obstinacy in its unrelenting attack on biblical values, marriage risks being redefined out of existence. Here are some of the expressions today which pass as a definition of marriage: "Marriage is a committed interdependent partnership between consenting adults."[124] Andrew Sullivan, a prominent advocate of same-sex marriage, writes, "The essence of marriage is not breeding or even the romantic love that can blind us while it overwhelms us" but is instead "a unique and profound friendship." And, "marriage is merely a personal commitment that is intended to be permanent."[125]

Seeking to foster some measure of familial stability, our culture has created new family paradigms after its own image. But this is nothing novel. For example, it was Ludwig Feuerbach's highly influential work, *The Essence of*

---

[123] Carson, Spiritual Disciplines, Themelios, Volume 36, Issue 3, Nov 2011.
[124] Blankenhorn, The Future of Marriage, 1.
[125] Ibid.

Chapter 1: The God-Honoring American Man

Christianity that asserted "God is man self-alienated."[126] What Feuerbach meant is that God is the perversion of the idea of man. He believed that God is mankind's projection of the ideal being. Donald Palmer tells us, "For Feuerbach, as long as we humans continued to alienate our ideals into some non-human extraneous being we would never be able to achieve the fullness of our own being."[127] Feuerbach believed that God was merely a myth that collectively occupied man's conscious thought. "Those who have no desires," He wrote, "have no gods, gods are men's wishes in corporeal form."[128] Feuerbach's goal was for man to dissolve religion entirely, so as to remove the oppressive ideals he is unable to live up to, and so recover peace and happiness. The fiery brook of this line of thinking profoundly affected Karl Marx, who argued for what amounts to the abolition of marriage and the family.

In his *Theses on Feuerbach* Marx wrote, "Once the earthly family is discovered to be the secret of the holy family, the former must be theoretically criticized and radically changed in practice."[129] According to Feuerbach and later Marx, it is only by dissolving the image of God, and the ideal of the godly family that mankind will at last find rest for his soul. Because, as long as the image of God is before us, mankind will consider the earth merely a place of trial and punishment.[130]

What should be seen at the heart of arguments such as these is Satan. People make lofty claims that these 'meaningful relationships' are as good as or even better than biblical models. However, when we defect from God's commandments and forsake His Word, we are freely lending our ears to the lies of Satan; and what an insidious, demonic, Machiavellian plot? What better way to destroy a nation than to erode the very fabric of its societal infrastructure? Remember Nietzsche's parable? He diagnosed that God had

---

[126] Ludwig Andreas von Feuerbach (1804 - 1872) was a German philosopher who strongly influenced generations of later thinkers, including both Karl Marx and Frederich Engels. Feuerbach was himself strongly influenced by the thought of Hegel.

[127] Palmer, Looking At Philosophy, 266.

[128] Feuerbach, The Essence of Religion, 115-117.

[129] Marx, The German Ideology, Including Theses Against Feuerbach, 570.

[130] Palmer, Looking At Philosophy, 269.

become dead to western society because although it was built atop traditional beliefs and biblical morality, it had ceased to acquiesce to these foundational truths and instead turned to the state, which gives the majority of mankind what they really want; a life without God on their own terms. But Morality is not majority driven, it is God driven. Truth is eternal, unchangeable, and objective. How refreshingly absolute! God's Word never changes!

What Christian men must realize is we are involved in a cosmic spiritual war; one that pits God against the forces of darkness. As the Scripture tells us, "But, as he who was born according to the flesh then persecuted him who was born according to the Spirit, even so it is now"(Gal 4:29). The abolition of the family is not only the stated goal of communism but also the Beast (Rev 13:5-8). Is marriage merely the states' formal mechanism for recognizing adult partnerships? Or is marriage God's way of not only structuring society by enabling mankind to biblically fulfill His command of "Be fruitful and multiply; fill the earth and subdue it" (Gen 1:28). Marriage was created by God to channelize sexual expression in such a way that it creates intimate companionship as well as legitimate children.

Jane Drucker, a same-sex marriage advocate writes, "As a society we have made large strides in acknowledging the gay and lesbian community and the parents and their children within it, but there are clearly many challenges yet ahead of us before we are truly living the credo that "all (men) are created equal. For all of us, gay or straight, there are crucial decisions that need to be made about our future. Debating whether or not gay and lesbian families should exist is irrelevant. They're here. Disputing the ability of gay fathers and lesbian mothers to provide nurturing environments for their children ignores the facts. For the most part, they, like most parents, are doing so. What, then, are the questions that we need to be asking in order to take the next step on this journey? Do we even know where we want to go?"[131]

---

[131] Drucker, Lesbian and Gay Families Speak Out, 242. Parentheses are from the original quotation.

Chapter 1: The God-Honoring American Man

Drucker ends her paragraph with a most provocative question because once you have removed the ancient boundaries, having eradicated traditional familial values, nothing will remain but nihilism; values lose their value; and life becomes existence without purpose, meaning or intrinsic value.

Interestingly enough, same-sex activists say the real evil is using the Bible to declare homosexuality a sin! In their understanding, homosexuality is neither a sickness nor a sin but a gift of God.[132] Erasmus' remark regarding eisegetical pronouncements like these immediately comes to mind; "And how a happiness this is, think you? While as if Holy Writ were a nose of wax, they fashion and refashion it according to their pleasure."[133] These types of ideas come from people who are fooling themselves. They go to great lengths to explain away biblical warnings. However, homosexuality and same-sex marriage, along with other sins, are not only incompatible with biblical teaching but are soundly condemned by the Word of God. As Scripture tells us in 1 Cor 6:9-11:

[9] Do you not know that the unrighteous will not inherit the kingdom of God? Do not be deceived. Neither fornicators, nor idolaters, nor adulterers, nor homosexuals, nor sodomites, [10] nor thieves, nor covetous, nor drunkards, nor revilers, nor extortioners will inherit the kingdom of God. [11] And such were some of you. But you were washed, but you were sanctified, but you were justified in the name of the Lord Jesus and by the Spirit of our God.

What should be etched on every soul with an iron tool is the fact that if you are truly saved, washed in the blood of the Lamb, than you are to live free from the commanding bondage of sin, in all its forms (Rom 8:5-17): fornication (all sex outside of marriage, pornography, etc.), idolatry, adultery, homosexuality, thievery, alcoholism, vulgarism, and swindling, etc. If we are saved, born again, regenerated, converted (a rose by any other name would smell as sweet), than we are able, for the first time in our lives, to obey God's commandments. If we think we can live in unrepentant sin and

---

[132] Besen, Anything But Straight, ix.
[133] Erasmus, The Praise of Folly, 63.

be men who honor God, we fool ourselves. God will not bless sinful living. These issues will be covered more in chapter two.

But the Church by and large today either avoids these issues or embraces them. "What one generation tolerates, the next generation will embrace." With each shy away and indifference to such issues, with each shrink back from declaring the truth, our culture sinks deeper into a bog of confusion. And the greatest danger for Christians is compromise. *This is because the most intrinsic instinct is the desire to be accepted; to conform to established norms.* But we become uncritically open to the world's view when sin ceases to shock us. This is the subject of chapter four. Another issue we have not tackled here is divorce. This is a topic covered in chapter two.

Some say standing up for God's idea of marriage today is like trying to lock the gate after the horse has already bolted. But in every generation, "Where there is no revelation, the people cast off restraint" (Pro 29:18). As a nation, we not only court disaster when we dismiss God's Word, we welcome our own demise. Moreover, since God has provided the family and the church with male leadership, shouldn't God-honoring men stand up for what is biblically right?

God's plan for marriage and sexual intimacy is one man and one woman for life. The first society was the marriage God made; each marriage in turn is not only a reduplication of the first but an anticipation of the last. A wife is fitting proof that God loves a man and wants him to be happy. His Word tells us so; "A man who finds a wife finds a good thing and obtains favor from the LORD" (Pro 18:22). A woman may take her being from man, but man takes his well-being from woman.

The author of the Book of Hebrews tells us in 13:4, "Let marriage be held in honor among all, and let the marriage bed be undefiled, for God will judge the sexually immoral and adulterous." The first part of this verse tells us that God will judge those who dishonor marriage. At the time of writing this, fifteen U.S. states have legalized same-sex marriage. In Romans chapter one, the apostle Paul tells us that a society that progressively rejects God and His Word will progressively degenerate into homosexual activity. And, as people are given over by God more and more to a debase mind, they will be progressively forthright in making the case that homosexual activity be not only permitted, but approved.

The second part of this verse tells us that God will judge those who defile the marriage bed. "Let the marriage bed be undefiled; for God will judge the immoral and the adulterous." Two sinful acts are mentioned here, namely fornication and adultery. Both of these sins have the same evil source: having sex with someone other than your lawful spouse. This is called fornication if you aren't married and adultery if you are. John MacArthur tells us, "No sin that a person commits has more built-in pitfalls, problems and destructiveness than sexual sin. It has broken more marriages, shattered more homes, caused more heartache and disease, and destroyed more lives than alcohol and drugs combined. It causes lying, stealing, cheating and killing, as well as bitterness, hatred, slander, gossip and unforgivingness."[134]

God designed sexual activity and sanctions it only between one man and one woman who are lawfully married. God is going to judge fornicators and adulterers. Regarding sexual immorality Spurgeon writes, "This once brought hell out of heaven upon Sodom; God sent down fire and brimstone because of the lusts of the flesh that made Sodom to stink in his nostrils; the harlot and the adulterer, and the fornicator, shall know that they sin not without provoking God very terribly."[135]

But God provides forgiveness and healing for those who repent of these sins in the cross of Christ (1 Cor 6:9-11). John Newton was the captain of a slave trading ship before he became a pastor. To the end of his life, he was still marveling that he was saved and called to preach the gospel of grace. From his last will and testament we read:

I commit my soul to my gracious God and Savior, who mercifully spared and preserved me, when I was an apostate, a blasphemer, and an infidel, and delivered me from the state of misery on the coast of Africa into which my obstinate wickedness had plunged me; and who

---

[134] MacArthur, Commentary on 1 Corinthians, 147.
[135] Spurgeon, Sermon on Isaiah 54:1.

has been pleased to admit me (though most unworthy) to preach his glorious gospel.[136]

Newton's enduring expression to God's grace was, "I am not what I ought to be — ah, how imperfect and deficient! I am not what I wish to be — I abhor what is evil, and I would cleave to what is good! I am not what I hope to be — soon, soon shall I put off mortality, and with mortality all sin and imperfection. Yet, though I am not what I ought to be, nor what I wish to be, nor what I hope to be, I can truly say, I am not what I once was; a slave to sin and Satan; and I can heartily join with the apostle, and acknowledge, By the grace of God I am what I am."

There is escape from God's judgment for those who repent of their adultery and homosexuality, as well as other forms of what the Bible calls "lawlessness." Further, God will not only forgive adulterers and homosexuals – those who defile the marriage bed – but will heal them and remove the guilt of these particular sins. This might be a life-long battle for some who struggle with sexual sins such as these. But those who repent and believe the Gospel of Jesus Christ will experience God's saving grace and transforming power so they may avoid these entanglements (Heb 12:1).

Marriage is a life-long commitment between one man and one woman which coventally typifies the true marriage of Christ and His bride – the church. When a man finds a wife He finds what is good and receives favor from the Lord (Pro 18:22). William Penn puts it, "In marriage do thou be wise: prefer the person before money, virtue before beauty, the mind before the body; then thou hast a wife, a friend, a companion, a second self."[137] According to the Bible, the marriage act is more than a physical act. It is an act of sharing. It is an act of communion. It is an act of total self-giving wherein the husband gives himself completely to the wife, and the wife gives herself to the husband in such a way that the two actually become one flesh.[138]

---

[136] Piper, The Roots of Endurance, 45.
[137] Davies, The Quakers in English Society, 91.
[138] Mack, Strengthening Your Marriage, 120.

Chapter 1: The God-Honoring American Man

The Fourth Mark of a God-Honoring American Man:
Faithful Member of a Local Church

Puritans at Worship 1640s.

"Remember the Sabbath day, to keep it holy" (Ex 20:9).

So far we have discussed three marks or signatures of a God-honoring American man. First, he is a man who has a personal, saving, child-like trust in the God of the Bible. Second, that he is a man who loves the Lord with all his heart, soul, mind, and strength and his neighbor as himself, seeking to obey all Christ's commandments. Third, that if he is so blessed to find a wife, he is to be faithful to her and care for his children. Now we come to the fourth mark, a faithful member of a local church. But first let's discuss the meaning of the fourth commandment. What is God commanding us to do in it?

The Larger Catechism tells us, "the fourth commandment requires of all men the sanctifying or keeping holy to God such set times as he hath appointed in his word, expressly one whole day in seven; which was the seventh from the beginning of the world to the resurrection of Christ, and the first day of the week ever since, and so to continue to the end of the world; which is the Christian Sabbath, and in the New Testament called *The Lord's Day*."[139] The word *remember*

---

[139] The Westminster Larger Catechism Answer 116.

reminds us to hold sacred the Sabbath, it tells us to cease from work and worship the Lord. God intends the Sabbath to be a day of rest, both spiritual and physical, for His people. Jesus told us, "The Sabbath was made for man, not man for the Sabbath" (Mk 2:27). To all who are seeking to save themselves by their own supposed righteousness, Jesus says,

[28] Come to Me, all *you* who labor and are heavy laden, and I will give you rest. [29] Take My yoke upon you and learn from Me, for I am gentle and lowly in heart, and you will find rest for your souls. [30] For My yoke *is* easy and My burden is light" (Mt 11:28-30).

The rest Jesus is referring to is eternal – an eternal Sabbath. There are three significant truths we need to bring out of this text: (1) Christ has begun to build the true Temple of God with His resurrection (Jn 2:19; Eph 2:20-22); (2) the place of true worship has now been universalized to any place where the Spirit resides in true worshipers (Jn 4:21-24); and (3) Christ is the True Temple, and if we are in Him, than we are a part of it (1 Pet 2:4-5).

Greg Beale writes, "Christians begin now to enjoy existentially a Sabbath rest by virtue of our real inaugurated resurrection life, which has been communicated to us through the Holy Ghost. But our rest is still incomplete because our resurrection existence has begun only spiritually and has not been consummated bodily."[140] These concepts will need to be fleshed out further. The point we need to make here is as Philip Ryken tells us, "Jesus is the fulfillment of the fourth commandment, as he is of all the others. The Old Testament Sabbath pointed to the full and final rest that can only be found in Him."[141] Looking back on the first four commandments, we see the sum of the four commandments contains our duty to God, that is, to love the Lord our God with all our heart, and with all our soul, and with all our strength, and with all our mind.[142]

We will revisit the fourth commandment later in chapter four, but for now, the purpose of this section is to describe in a

---

[140] Beale, The Book of Revelation, 294.
[141] Ryken, Written in Stone, 110.
[142] The Westminster Larger Catechism Answer 102.

biblical manner what it means to be a faithful member of a local church. For that purpose, we must define a few things. First, what is the church? Second, how does the church relate to the world? Third, what does it mean to be a faithful member of the church?

An adequate system of Christian education is necessary to a complete spiritual program for Christ's people.[143] Where else are Christ's people to get fed with spiritual food than at a local church; we should not try to improve upon God's intended means of grace. The church is founded on the Person and work of Christ. Whereas Christ is the foundation for God's saving work, the church is the focus of Christ's saving activity. Outside of which there is no ordinary possibility of salvation (Acts 2:47).[144]

This expression doesn't mean that those who are visibly outside the church, that is non-members, are necessarily damned; likewise just because people are visibly a part of a local congregation will not ensure their salvation. What this means is outside the church there is no salvation because the church is the body of Christ (1 Cor 12:12-14). With this understanding, we may say the church is the redeemed of all the ages; believers from every tribe, tongue, people, and nation (Rev 5:9), that have been, are, or shall be gathered into one, under Christ, and is the bride (Eph 5:25-32), body, and fullness of Christ (Eph 1:22).

What is the Church?

Fallen in Adam – raised in Christ, the church is God's restoration program for the entire human race (Rom 5:12, 16; Rom 8:20). It is God's saving activity for His own glory. There are at least three reasons why God created the Church:

---

[143] Baptist Faith and Message, XII, 17.
[144] Westminster Confession of Faith, 25.2, 107. This expression comes from St. Cyprian's aphorism, *extra Ecclesiam nulla salus*, which means "outside the church there is no salvation." Down through the years there have been numerous explanations for this expression. The *Catechism of the Catholic Church* interprets this as, "all salvation comes from Christ the Head through the Church which is his Body," CCC, 846-848, 851.

Chapter 1: The God-Honoring American Man

First, to be His covenant community; Second, to be His visible witness; and Third, to be His instrument for the gospel.

God's Covenant Community

First, it may be said that God created the church to be His covenant community in which He Himself dwells with His adopted children (Lev 26:11; Eph 1:5; 2:19-22). The church is the 'called out' ones, from the Greek ekklésia ἐκκλησία, a conjugation of two words "ek" meaning "out from" and "kaleo" meaning "called." The Hebrew qahal קָהָל, an assembly gathered together for a solemn ceremony (Dt 9:10), is the Old Testament Masoretic Text equivalent to ekklésia.[145]

The story of the church, however, begins with Israel, the Old Testament people of God. James Montgomery Boice tells us, "Strictly speaking, the church is the creation of the historical Christ and therefore dates from the time of Christ. But the church has roots in the Old Testament and cannot be understood well without that background. This is true theologically because the idea of a called-out "people of God" obviously existed in the Old Testament period, just as in the New."[146]

According to the Bible, the church is the people of God, the assembly and the body of Christ, and the fellowship of the Holy Spirit.[147] God created everything that exists *ex nihilo,* that is out of nothing. He created mankind from one man and one woman while setting aside for Himself a particular people for His very own (Tit 2:14). A people, who the apostle Peter tells us, are not like those who rejected Jesus, the Messiah, to their own destruction, "But you *are* a chosen generation, a royal priesthood, a holy nation, His own special people, that you may proclaim the praises of Him who called you out of darkness into His marvelous light; who once *were* not a people

---

[145] The LXX, Septuagint, the 3rd Century BC Greek translation of the Hebrew Old Testament, always translates *qahal* as ekklésia which is used 80 times in the Canonical Septuagint Books. Dt 23:2 translates *qahal Yahweh* as ekklēsia Kyriou, the church of the Lord. The Masoretic Text is the God-breathed Hebrew text of the Old Testament.

[146] Boice, Foundations of the Christian Faith, 566.

[147] Clowney, The Church, 28.

but *are* now the people of God, who had not obtained mercy but now have obtained mercy."

Christians were indeed the recipients of the Apostle Peter's letter. But were they Jewish or Gentile Christians, or both? The answer lies in Peter's addresses: Peter, an apostle of Jesus Christ, to the pilgrims of the Dispersion in Pontus, Galatia, Cappadocia, Asia, and Bithynia, elect according to the foreknowledge of God the Father, in sanctification of the Spirit, for obedience and sprinkling of the blood of Jesus Christ: Grace to you and peace be multiplied" (1 Pet 1:1-2).

The Jewish people were driven out of their land many times in history in what is referred to as *diaspora* scattering.[148] Moreover, following the martyrdom of Stephen, Jewish Christians were scattered abroad and found themselves living as resident aliens. Likewise, Christians are strangers and pilgrims in the world because their citizenship is in heaven (Phil 3:20; Heb 11:13). When Peter says *pilgrims*, is he merely referring to Jewish Christians? Maybe, or perhaps we should understand the expression in a figurative way.

Remembering our earlier discussion of how marriage mirrors the way God relates Himself to His people should help us understand the verse quoted above. Israel is the wife of Yahweh; the church is the bride of Christ. It is not physical descent from Abraham that makes you part of the covenant people of God but faith in Christ. The presupposition here is that the New Testament church is the continuation of the Old Testament people of God, and as such, the *Ekklésia* or *Qahal* consists of all the redeemed of all the ages (Eph 2:19-22).

The prophet Ezekiel allegorically demonstrates God's relationship to His people in terms of a husband; Israel is presented as an unfaithful bride. "Yes, I swore an oath to you and entered into a covenant with you, and you became Mine," says the Lord God" (Ezek 16:8). But "You are an adulterous

---

[148] Diasporas begin with the Assyrian and Babylonian captivities in the 8th and 6th Centuries respectively. Additional diasporas include the one following the First Jewish-Roman War 66-73 AD, and the one after the failed Bar Kokhba Revolt of 132-136 AD. The word *diaspora* διασπορά is found in LXX Dt 28:25 and describes not only the Jewish exiles dispersed among the nations, but also relates to Christians who are "scattered abroad among the Gentiles."

wife, who takes strangers instead of her husband" (Ezek 16:32). Therefore "I will judge you as women who break wedlock" (Ezek 16:38). The relationship between God and His people is interrupted by sin, so that God calls Israel *Lo-Ammi*, 'not my people' (Hos 1:9; Mt 21:43); but the Scripture tells, "we once were not a people but now are the people of God" (1 Pet 2:10). By the grace of God, those who were, *Lo-Ammi* 'not my people,' whether they are covenant-breaking Jews or Gentiles outside the covenant, are made the people of God and receive mercy (Hos 1:10).[149]

What about Israel? Believing Jews will be grafted back into their own olive tree (Rom 11:24); and in this way all Israel will be saved (Rom 11:26). This is what the apostle Paul held firmly to and hoped for, that Jews, seeing the face of Jesus, the Messiah, as he is, and coming to Him in faith should, along with the Gentiles, become "fellow heirs of the same body, and partakers of His promise in Christ through the gospel" (Eph 3:6). What therefore consists of God's covenant community is everyone God *calls* out of darkness into His marvelous light (Dt 4:20, 34; 1 Pet 2:9).

The apostle Paul tells us in Eph 5:25, "Christ loved the church and gave Himself for her." According to this truth Wayne Grudem writes, "Here the term "the Church" is used to apply to all those whom Christ died to redeem, all those who are saved by the death of Christ. But that must include all true believers for all time, both believers in the New Testament age and believers in the Old Testament as well. So great is God's plan for the church that He has exalted Christ to a position of highest authority for the sake of the church: "He has put all things under His feet and has made Him the head over all things *for the church*, which is His body, the fullness of Him who fills all in all" (Eph 1:22-23).[150]

The church is the messianic community; the redeemed of all the ages. It includes believers from every tribe, tongue, people, and nation (Rev 5:9), that have been, are, or shall be gathered into one, under Christ, and is the bride (Eph 5:25-32), body, and fullness of Christ (Eph 1:22). The coming of the Spirit on

---

[149] Clowney, The Church, 29.
[150] Grudem, Systematic Theology, 853.

the Day of Pentecost didn't create the people of God but renewed them, fulfilling the promise to Abraham, that the Gentiles would be included in Abraham's seed (Gal 3:14, 29).

God's Visible Witness

God's people are to be salty and bright. As such, in the church, Christ's rule becomes visible as God's people submit to His lordship. This is to be in the totality of life. God's people are to model Christ in everything they think, say and do; reflecting Christ's character. This is the way the world should see Jesus in the church. Yet, however visible the people of God may be to the world at any particular time, it remains invisible, known only to God. Peter Craigie reminds us that, "whereas the old covenant had an external form in the nation state, the new covenant would be marked by an inner work of God in man's heart."[151]

This inner work on man's heart, "the answer of a good conscience toward God" (1 Pet 3:21), is made visible in both baptism and in the Lord's Supper.

These sacraments or ordinances are signs, symbols, and testaments. Signs point, symbols resemble, and testaments testify. Baptism is a sign showing that the true believer has been once-for-all incorporated into Christ.[152] That his sins have been forgiven. It shows our union with Christ in His death and our rising together with Him, by regeneration through His resurrection, to walk in newness of life (Rom 6:4; 1 Pet 1:3).

Baptism is a symbol resembling our death to the world and sin's dominion. It corresponds and relates in graphic form to Christ's sufferings and death for our redemption and righteousness. It is the visible gospel. Further, baptism is a testament, in that it bears witness or testifies to the believer's good conscience toward God (1 Pet 3:21) – removal of the guilt of sin through repentance and faith; love for Christ and his subjection to Him (lordship). John Calvin writes, "Baptism

---

[151] Craigie, The Problem of War in the Old Testament, 79.

[152] Biblical signs are physical and temporal phenomenon that have corresponding spiritual and eternal significance. Signs σημεῖον semeon produce faith in those who have ears to hear the gospel (Mt 13:10-17).

is a kind of entrance into the Church, an initiation into the faith, and the Lord's Supper the constant ailment by which Christ spiritually feeds his family of believers."[153] Thus, baptism reflects our once-for-all union with Christ, the Lord's Supper reflects our continuous participation in Him. Christ instituted the Eucharist or Communion so to help Christians grasp the reality of their union with Him in some measure.

The word "communion" κοινωνία koinonia means participation and fellowship. God's people are one body in Christ. Christ indwells His church in the fellowship of the Spirit.[154] Thus, Christians have fellowship with Christ and each other through the Holy Spirit. Perfected fellowship with God is the goal of human history.[155] The world should see this fellowship in the church. The Lord's Supper is a sign, symbol, and testament to this truth.

God's Instrument for the Gospel

So far in this fourth mark we've discussed that God has created a covenant community consisting of all believers from every tribe, tongue, people, and nation (Rev 5:9), and that this people are to be a visible witness, reflecting His glory. We now approach God's means for reaching the lost, which is a verbal witness for the saving power of the gospel.

Remember Christ's parable of the strong man (Mt 12:25-30)? Christ penetrates from the heavenly realm into the earthly, defeats Satan by the cross, and begins mankind's restoration with His resurrection. The City of God has come and will be victorious (Isaiah 26)! Christ didn't suggest we proclaim this, He commanded it (Mt 28:18-20). This is the church's message, salvation in Christ alone, by grace alone, through faith alone (Acts 4:12)!

One of the most fundamental truths of the Christian faith is the Incarnation was the coming of God to save us in the heart of our fallen and depraved humanity. God had to send His Son or mankind would be dead, defiled, and damned forever. If Adam's fall injured only himself, as Pelagius reasoned, and if

---

[153] Calvin, Institutes of the Christian Religion, Book IV, 19.

[154] Clowney, The Church, 29.

[155] Ibid, 173.

mankind can get their act together and merit God's eternal favor, then why did God send His Son to die for us? This is the prevailing woe of the social gospel, it's merely a help to morally shape culture. But God is renewing humanity in Christ. Mankind is fallen in Adam but raised in Christ (Rom 5:12, 18).

What demolishes Pelagian arguments is Scripture. The apostle Paul tells us in Gal 2:20-21:

> [20] I have been crucified with Christ; it is no longer I who live, but Christ lives in me; and the *life* which I now live in the flesh I live by faith in the Son of God, who loved me and gave Himself for me. [21] I do not set aside the grace of God; for if righteousness *comes* through the law, then Christ died in vain."

God's instrument for saving the lost is the gospel, and as we saw earlier, the gospel proclamation is like a sword; the very presence of Christ. The testimony of Jesus Christ, that is, a *verbal witness* to His saving power, reveals the truth of mankind's common standing in the sight of God; rebellious sinners that desperately need a Savior (Rom 3:23; 5:12). Christ builds His church through the verbal witness of His saints (Mt 16:17-19).

In our verbal witness, God is making His proclamation to a recalcitrant world. Christ speaks through us when we proclaim the gospel. Jesus said in Jn 5:24-25:

> [24] "Most assuredly, I say to you, he who hears My word and believes in Him who sent Me has everlasting life, and shall not come into judgment, but has passed from death into life. [25] Most assuredly, I say to you, the hour is coming, and now is, when the dead will hear the voice of the Son of God; and those who hear will live.

God's instrument for reclaiming lost sinners is Christ speaking through the church's verbal witness (Is 29:18; Mt 13:3-9; 18-23). The lost come to Christ and fellowship with His people. The church is the house of God, the body of Christ, and the temple of the Holy Spirit. It is therefore in this understanding that we can state with object certainty, "Outside the church there is no salvation," because everyone who is, was, or ever will be saved is included in the number of God's elect (Eph 1:11).[156] *There is only one flock and one Shepherd; God simply has no other saving program* (John 10:16).

The Kingdom has come, the Kingdom is coming, and the Kingdom will come. There is a pronounced tension in all of this which may be felt. George Ladd tells us, the tension between the future and the present is the tension between the Kingdom in complete fulfillment and the Kingdom in process of breaking in upon the present order.[157]

There is a now and not yet tension in all of this, but the Christian life is one of balance so we would do best to let the tension remain. God has established two kingdoms: the church and the state. One is temporary, one is eternal. One is of this world; the other is not of this world. He has given certain authority to each, and has placed certain limitations on each. Why did God establish the state? What is the purpose of the civil government? These are topics of discussion for our next section.

One final question we might ask. What does it mean to be a faithful member of the church? Most churches have constitutions and by-laws which reflect biblical doctrine. Here is an example of what most churches in the Protestant expression consider a faithful church member: "Members are expected to (1) be faithful in all duties of the church; (2) give regularly of their time, talents, and tithes for the support of the church and its causes, and (3) share in the work of its organization." While this seems reasonable, we would do well to remember the words of A.A. Hodge who said, "A church has no right to make anything a condition of membership which Christ has not made a condition of salvation."[158]

One of the goals of attending a local church is Christian maturity, which is fostered through faithful preaching, teaching, fellowship, and the discipline of God's Word. Some Christians demur from attending church; they forsake the assembly to their own hurt (Heb 10:24-25). Other issues that

---

[156] Election is the gracious purpose of God in the midst of Redemption-History by which God demonstrates His Sovereign acts of saving grace.

[157] Ladd, The Presence of the Future, 7.

[158] Hodge, A Commentary on the Confession of Faith: With Questions for Theological Students and Bible Classes, 21.

have not been addressed here, such as tithing and missions will be covered in chapter seven.

Being a member of a church involves many responsibilities, but is equally full of many privileges. "We must grasp once again," said Lloyd-Jones, "the idea of church membership as being the membership of the body of Christ and as the biggest honor which can come a man's way in this world."[159]

The God-honoring American man should value the great wealth of faithful teaching and spiritual insight that twenty centuries of the Christian church have to offer. But if this isn't enough to convince him, he should bear in mind that those who dismiss Christ's church as merely hypocrites and think they would do better on their own, have the words of Hebrews 10:23-25 to consider:

[23] Let us hold fast the confession of *our* hope without wavering, for He who promised *is* faithful. [24] And let us consider one another in order to stir up love and good works, [25] not forsaking the assembling of ourselves together, as *is* the manner of some, but exhorting *one another,* and so much the more as you see the Day approaching.

The author of the Book of Hebrews instructs us not to "forsake assembling together," and the reason is four-fold: First, in order to submit themselves to the teaching of the Holy Scriptures. Second, Christians share a common hope in the gospel and a common fellowship with God in the Spirit. Third, Christians are to regularly worship God and celebrate the Lord's Supper together, and fourth, Christians are to experience the presence and power of God with one another in prayer (Acts 2:42). And besides, for those to whom he is a Father, the church must also be a mother.[160] "Belonging to the church, as John MacArthur has said, is at the very heart of Christianity." For the church is the pillar and ground of the truth (1 Tim 3:15).

---

[159] Lloyd-Jones, Knowing the Times, 30.
[160] Calvin, Institutes of the Christian Religion, 4.1.1, 672.

Chapter 1: The God-Honoring American Man

The Fifth Mark of the God-Honoring American Man:
Loyal Patriot to State and Country

Reading of the Declaration of Independence 1776.

"You shall not murder" (Ex 20:13).

Since October 2001, some 2.5 million U.S. troops have deployed to Afghanistan and Iraq. Many have deployed more than once. Many who have deployed are Christians, and have killed insurgents. In light of our discussion, we must ask, should Christian men serve in war? How does a man serve in war, kill the enemies of his country, while keeping Christ's command of 'love your enemies'? This apparent antithesis presents a moral and theological dilemma of sorts, especially in light of history's atrocities and wanton acts of destruction. What should be the position of a Christian regarding war? Is the war in Afghanistan immoral? How about the war in Iraq? The war has raised questions such as these.

It is interesting to note that the question, 'is this war immoral?' had been raised in the Korean War, the Vietnam War and the wars in Iraq and Afghanistan, but it was not raised in WWII. No one questioned the legitimacy of WWII because of what President Roosevelt called our righteous indignation in response to that unwarranted act of terrorism perpetrated by the empire of Japan, as well as the evil regime known as National Socialism in Nazi Germany who was bent

80

on world conquest, the enslavement of what they deemed lesser peoples along with the attempted genocide of the race of the Jews. But nowadays there is confusion over this issue of profound importance.

What should be the position of a Christian regarding war? Let's narrow the focus to three questions in order to frame our discussion:

1. Is going to war ever right?
2. What should be the position of a Christian regarding war?
3. How can Christians serve in war, kill the enemies of their country, while keeping Christ's command of 'love your enemies'?

Is Going to War Ever Right?

The first question, is going to war ever right? Is best viewed from God's perspective. In Romans 13:1-7, God gives us His revealed purpose for the state. The apostle Paul writes:

13 Let every soul be subject to the governing authorities. For there is no authority except from God, and the authorities that exist are appointed by God. ² Therefore whoever resists the authority resists the ordinance of God, and those who resist will bring judgment on themselves. ³ For rulers are not a terror to good works, but to evil. Do you want to be unafraid of the authority? Do what is good, and you will have praise from the same. ⁴ For he is God's minister to you for good. But if you do evil, be afraid; for he does not bear the sword in vain; for he is God's minister, an avenger to *execute* wrath on him who practices evil. ⁵ Therefore *you* must be subject, not only because of wrath but also for conscience' sake. ⁶ For because of this you also pay taxes, for they are God's ministers attending continually to this very thing. ⁷ Render therefore to all their due: taxes to whom taxes *are due,* customs to whom customs, fear to whom fear, honor to whom honor.

The government was founded by God for a legitimate purpose: for there is no authority but of God and the authorities that exist are ordained of God.[161] The government

---

[161] The operative word in this verse is "authority." In the Greek, exousia ἐξουσία, which is used 102 times in the New Testament, means both authority

Chapter 1: The God-Honoring American Man

bears the sword and has a right to use it at its discretion to defend itself from what it perceives to be dangerous and destructive behavior on the part of those within or without the nation state. The nation state therefore not only has the right but the duty to protect its citizens, to correct or punish so as to bring to order its civilian population.

To narrow our focus even more, we should look closer at Romans 13:3-4. We are told here that the government bears the sword to restrain sin for three reasons:

1. It has the power to execute criminals.
2. It has the power to avenge wrong doing.
3. And has the power of the sword to wage war to protect its citizens and property from harm.

The state has the delegated authority from God to punish anyone who threatens the safety and the order of society whether those people are citizens involved in wrong doing or whether they are powers from outside society itself (Rom 13:3-5). The state has the power of the sword to defend itself through what is called a retributive or preventative war.[162]

Now it must be said at this point that the author is most decidedly not in favor of war. For war, as Sherman stated, is hell. War is hell on earth. It is one of the most dreadful evils that can be inflicted on a people. I wish there were no more war. I have been a soldier in war and have seen the raving madness of war. If there were no sin, there would be no war. War is indeed an extension of politics by other means, but it's also an expression of fallen man's nature.[163] But sometimes war is inevitable and must be waged by a legitimate government to defend its citizens and property.

---

and power; the right to do something and the power to back it up. When it is used of the government, it means conferred power, delegated power, authorization and empowerment from God Himself.

[162] Retributive war is fought in response to wanton acts of destruction perpetrated on its populace. Preventative war is begun in anticipation of, and not in response to aggression. Preventative war is waged in order to prevent an evil that has yet to have taken place but is believed will.

[163] Clausewitz, On War, Book I, Chapter 24, 99.

Chapter 1: The God-Honoring American Man

But some would ask, how can we say these things when the very next paragraph reads as follows, beginning in Romans 13:8-10:

> [8] Owe no one anything except to love one another, for he who loves another has fulfilled the law. [9] For the commandments, "You shall not commit adultery," "You shall not murder," "You shall not steal," "You shall not bear false witness," "You shall not covet," and if *there is* any other commandment, are *all* summed up in this saying, namely, "You shall love your neighbor as yourself." [10] Love does no harm to a neighbor; therefore love *is* the fulfillment of the law.

How can the state wage war and then say that it is not doing wrong to a neighbor? Isn't this antithetical? And how can a Christian kill in war and do no wrong to a neighbor? First, it is because Romans 13:1-7 speaks of the responsibilities of the state, and Romans 13:8-10 speaks of the responsibilities of an individual. Love and justice are not mutually exclusive concepts. For the state to execute justice is for the state to show love for its people. For it would be unjust and unloving for people in America to go around assaulting, raping, murdering others and have the government do nothing about it.

Injustice can be visited upon a people either by doing something that is oppressive and evil or by failing to do what is right to them when you have the power to do so (Pro 3:27; Jam 4:17). If all that is needed for evil to triumph is for good men to do nothing, force must therefore be used to hinder the evil-doer. It certainly would have be unloving and unjust for our government to have done nothing after a foreign power slammed into the twin towers and the pentagon, murdering nearly 3,000 people. Therefore, love and justice are not mutually exclusive concepts.

The theologian John Murray gives an interpretation of how we reconcile Romans 13:1-7 with Romans 13:8-14. Murray writes:

> Do no wrong to a neighbor and yet the state has the right to wage war even against our neighbors. The interpretation and application of these passages which would brand all war as sinful and participation in war as wrong proceed from the failure to make some necessary distinctions. The demand of love, unrelenting and all pervasive as it

is, does not abrogate the demand of justice. Love is not inconsistent with the infliction of punishment for wrong. Love is first of all love for God and must therefore love justice for God is just. Hence when we view the demand of love in the broader proportions, the demand for love and the demand for justice are really one and the same. A just war is simply a war undertaken and conducted in the defense and promotion of the dictates of justice; there can be no incompatibility between the demands of love and the conduct of such war. The wounding and killing involved are the use of the sword which God has put into the hands of the magistrate as an instrument of maintaining justice and punishing evil doers.

The sword is never intrinsically, and should never be practically, the instrument of vengeance and malicious hate. Whenever a nation, and especially a soldier on the field of battle, uses weapons of war as instruments of vindictive revenge rather than instruments of retributive justice than the dictates of both justice and love have been desecrated. That is to say that war is never just when it is the instrument of hate. It is hate that contradicts love, it always does. But war in the protection and vindication of justice is not prompted by hate but by the love of justice. And as such, such love never contradicts the love of our enemies which the Lord Himself always and unequivocally demands.[164]

How can the state wage war and then say that it is not doing wrong to a neighbor? Because God has delegated His authority, the power of the sword, to civil rulers to punish evil doers and avenge crimes and protect its citizens from threats to its welfare from those within and without, thereby preserving order and promoting lawfulness. Jesus Christ never condemned the Roman government for its military prowess, but did condemn it for its abuse of that power.

Likewise, in Luke 3:14 some soldiers are among those who come out to be baptized by John. The soldiers ask "what should we do"? The soldiers' question reflects a prevalent fear of many soldiers that they are beyond God's care because God seemingly disapproves of their occupation. Soldiers have ample opportunities to behave badly and get away with it. The words they use, "even us?" reflects this. John's reply in Luke 3:14 is threefold: So he said to them, "Do not intimidate anyone or accuse falsely, and be content with your wages."

---

[164] John Murray, Principles of Conduct: Aspects of Biblical Ethics, 179.

Chapter 1: The God-Honoring American Man

The response of John the Baptist is the following:

1. Don't intimidate others. Soldiers that are immature and unsure of themselves will often try to exert themselves to make up for their deficient qualities.
2. Don't accuse others falsely. This can lead to the imprisonment and/or wrongful death of the innocent.
3. Be content with your wages. Greedy soldiers loot.

Isn't it interesting that John the Baptist doesn't say if you want to be a Christian then stop soldiering? John the Baptist says, when you serve your country in the military don't abuse the power of the sword that has been delegated to you by doing evil simply because you have raw power. Use your sword for justice and not for evil. We have a similar instance in Matthew 8:5-11 when Jesus is approached by a Roman centurion, a commander of one hundred soldiers, and a representative of the occupying power in the nation of Israel. The centurion asks Jesus, "Lord, my servant is lying at home paralyzed, dreadfully tormented." And Jesus said to him, "I will come and heal him." The centurion answered and said, "Lord, I am not worthy that You should come under my roof. But only speak a word, and my servant will be healed. For I also am a man under authority, having soldiers under me. And I say to this one, 'Go,' and he goes; and to another, 'Come,' and he comes; and to my servant, 'Do this,' and he does it" (Mt 8:5-9).

Not only does Jesus not condemn the centurion for soldiering but Jesus says, "Assuredly, I say to you, I have not found such great faith, not even in Israel" (Mt 8:10)! If Jesus thought soldiering were wrong, than He would have condemned it. But God has delegated His authority, the power of the sword, to the government to punish evil doers and avenge crimes and protect its citizens from threats from within and without, thereby preserving order and promoting lawfulness.

If there were no sin in the world there would be no war, but the fact is there are some people so deeply committed to doing evil that they can only be restrained by force and not by reason and persuasion. Can we face the fact that as Christians there

Chapter 1: The God-Honoring American Man

are people in this world that are so evil that the only way that they can be stopped is they must be destroyed?[165] We don't have a problem with that when we think about such evil beings as Adolf Hitler, but we struggle to see it in other people. But the fact remains, there are some people who are so evil that the only way to restrain their evil is by superior force.

The church has developed its teaching on this issue and we find it by three principles taken from Romans 13:3-4 which tells us:

> [3] For rulers are not a terror to good works, but to evil. Do you want to be unafraid of the authority? Do what is good, and you will have praise from the same. [4] For he is God's minister to you for good. But if you do evil, be afraid; for he does not bear the sword in vain; for he is God's minister, an avenger to *execute* wrath on him who practices evil.

The state is given the power of the sword for three reasons:

1. To restrain evil both from within and without.
2. To preserve order and organize society.
3. To promote civil obedience.

What should be the position of a Christian regarding war?

The majority of the church has never argued against the three points listed above because that is what Romans 13 teaches us. However, someone may ask, this proves the state's role, but what should be the position of a Christian regarding war? There are three differing perspectives on war: The first is the view of *pacifism*; the second is the *crusader view*; and the third is the *just war view*.

The first view of *pacifism* is the view that war is never justifiable. This is the view of the minority of Christians and there are five reasons given for the pacifist's position. The first principle the pacifist applies is the turn the other cheek principle of Christ from the Sermon on the Mount in Matthew 5:38:

---

[165] Chapter ten will discuss this point further.

Chapter 1: The God-Honoring American Man

[38] "You have heard that it was said, 'An eye for an eye and a tooth for a tooth.' [39] But I tell you not to resist an evil person. But whoever slaps you on your right cheek, turn the other to him also. [40] If anyone wants to sue you and take away your tunic, let him have *your* cloak also. [41] And whoever compels you to go one mile, go with him two. [42] Give to him who asks you, and from him who wants to borrow from you do not turn away.

Pacifists conclude that the government should turn the other cheek. However, that is a faulty interpretation because this passage has nothing to do with a state's relationship to another state government but has everything to do with interpersonal relationships primarily as a person of the Kingdom of God who is being persecuted for the sake of the gospel. The government does not turn the other cheek. It has the responsibility to avenge wrong doing and the power of the sword to wage war to protect its citizens and property from harm. When Japan bombed Pearl Harbor, it was not the responsibility of the U.S. government to turn the other cheek and say to Japan: hit us somewhere else if you want to. Eventually America would have ceased to exist.

The second principle the pacifist applies is the love your neighbor principle found in Romans 13:10: "Love does no harm to a neighbor; therefore love *is* the fulfillment of the law." Again, it must be said that this passage has to do with personal conduct. However, war and capital punishment are loving duties because they are the just duties of a protective and righteous state. Love and justice are therefore not mutually exclusive concepts.

Thirdly, is their idea that war is murder and the Bible forbids murder. However, the word for murder in the Old Testament is רָצַח *ratzach*. The sixth commandment (Ex 20:13) states: "You shall not murder." *Ratzach* is used 49 times in the Old Testament but never of war. God commands us not to murder, but the word *ratzach* applies only to illegal killing, viz., premeditated murder or manslaughter, and is never used in the administration of justice or for killing in war. So the King James Version which has "thou shalt not *kill*" is too broad. The Hebrew language has eight different words for killing, and the one used here has been chosen carefully.[166]

The Bible makes a distinction between murder, which is the illegitimate taking of life and war which is the legitimate taking of life. Certainly the state can do evil and murder people and take life illegitimately against their own laws, against Scripture and the law of conscience. But war and murder are not synonymous.

Fourthly, pacifists say that war produces more wars but that is categorically false, for sometimes wars can end longer wars. For example, WWII ended Nazism and the Holocaust. For by the time we got rid of Hitler he had already murdered six million Jews! What would have happened to the rest of the world's Jews had we not gone to war with him? Wars can liberate people from terrible oppression such as Saddam Hussein's attempted genocide of the Kurdish people in Iraq.[167] War is most assuredly hell on earth but sometimes war can put an end to longer conflicts.

Finally, pacifists say that believers are forbidden by God to go to war and kill. And this is a mixed statement. When Christians enlist in the armed forces they are no longer private citizens but they are agents of the state and therefore they are given the responsibility, the privilege, and the power to execute the sword. Believers are not forbidden to go to war, in fact believers are commanded to be submissive to and obey the state, who has the right to send them to war unless their conscience dictates otherwise. And as long as soldiers fulfill

---

[166] Philip G. Ryken, Written in Stone, 136. The word *ratzach* רָצַח is never used in the legal system or in the military. The Bible uses seven additional words for killing, such as, *rahgam* רָגַם, the word used for stoning to death (Lev 20:27) - used 16 times in the Old Testament; *qetal* קְטַל is used seven times for slaying in war (Dan 2:13); *shachat* שָׁחַט, ceremonial slaughter is used 81 times (Ex 12:21); *harag* הָרַג, to slay or kill, as in the case of Cain killing Abel (Gen 4:8), is used 167 times, 26 of those in cases where God slays in judgment (Ex 22:23); *muth* מוּת, used 839 times in virtually every sense (Genesis 20:3 compare with 2 Kings 11:8); *tabach* חָטַב, to slaughter, used 11 times (Psalm 37:14); and *chalal* חָלַל, meaning to slay (Num 19:18).

[167] Saddam Hussein murdered as many as one million of his own people; he maimed, tortured, and imprisoned countless thousands. Estimates vary of the number of Kurds killed from 50,000 to 200,000. Staff Report to the U.S. Senate Committee on Foreign Relations, November 1991, p.14.

their duties in war without a spirit of vengeance and malice, they execute the sword of the government in a just manner.

If you are a pacifist, you must be consistent in your position and say that all force is wrong. Therefore, if you are about to be raped you must not resist. If someone wants to kill you or your wife and children, when they break into your home, then you mustn't resist. You cannot call the government to execute someone who has killed your loved ones. You cannot resist in any way to these crimes of kidnapping, physical abuse, or the molestation of your children. You can never use force to restrain an evil and greater force. When it comes down to it, I doubt a true pacifist exists anywhere on planet.

There are Christians who, being pacifists, are what we call *conscientious objectors* who choose not to go to war and we must honor them for their position; to live according to the dictates of their conscience.

The second position in war is what we call the crusader or holy war theory which prosecutes war by religious authority. This view accepts no compromises; it sets no limits on force and spares no prisoners. It ignores all odds, it villainizes its opponents, it distinguishes only between friend and foe, it never surrenders and never ceases as long as the opposition continues to exist. Its motto is "no quarter asked, no quarter given," and *Deus vult!*[168] And at one time in the 11th and 12th centuries, the Church took up holy crusades like that to get back the holy land. It proved to be a great travesty, a fool's errand, and a great blot on the reputation of Christianity.

The only legitimate crusade is the one that God initiates. In the book of Numbers in the Old Testament we find where God invokes a crusade. Speaking to Moses in Numbers 31:1-3:

31 And the LORD spoke to Moses, saying: [2]"Take vengeance on the Midianites for the children of Israel. Afterward you shall be gathered to your people." [3] So Moses spoke to the people, saying, "Arm some of yourselves for war, and let them go against the Midianites to take vengeance for the LORD on Midian.

---

[168] *Deus vult*, Latin for "God wills it," was the battle cry of Pope Urban II when he called for the First Crusade in the fall of 1095.

Chapter 1: The God-Honoring American Man

That was a crusade that God initiated, and the reason we no longer have crusades is because we no longer have a theocracy. Theocracy was the reign of God over the nation of Israel in the Old Testament. However, we no longer have a chosen nation where God is the King and the people are His chosen instruments to bring all people under His dominion by force of arms. Israel was like that in the Old Testament but when the New Testament time came, this theocracy ended and God now rules through His spiritual Kingdom which is headed by His Son Jesus Christ. Therefore, there is no longer any justification for a crusade-type war. God does not have crusaders in the Church. We don't kill for Christ. Christ's kingdom isn't advanced that way.

The third position is the just war position. It is the position of the majority of Christians in the Church. As the name implies, the just war position in the history of the Christian church holds that under some circumstances the Christian may participate in war for the preservation of justice. This position holds that some, but not all, wars are morally justifiable. The just war theory represents the dominant viewpoint of Catholic, Protestant, and Eastern Orthodox expressions of the Christian faith.

Augustine in a sermon on Luke 3:14 writes, "If the Christian Religion forbade war altogether, those who sought salutary advice in the Gospel would rather have been counseled to cast aside their arms, and to give up soldiering altogether. On the contrary, they were told: "Do not intimidate anyone or accuse falsely, and be content with your wages. If he commanded them to be content with their pay, he did not forbid soldiering."

Just War Theory

Later in history, Thomas Aquinas wrote in his Summa Theologiae that a just war is such when it meets three conditions:

1. The war is waged by a legitimate authority.
2. It is fought for a just cause, that is, the advancement of good, or the avoidance of evil.

90

3. The method of its conduct is proper, and in due proportion, at the beginning, during its prosecution and after victory.[169]

Aquinas goes on to say that when you have stopped the evil to go any further than that and gain an unfair advantage over them, to take more of their land, take more of their money, to punish them in greater excess than what is equitable and just; then you have stopped being the prosecutors of a just war. What is important about the third point is intent. Aquinas goes on to write, "It may happen that the war is declared by the legitimate authority, and for a just cause, and yet be rendered unlawful through a wicked intention. Hence, Augustine says (Contra Faust. xxii, 74): "The passion for inflicting harm, the cruel thirst for vengeance, an unpacific and relentless spirit, the fever of revolt, the lust of power, and such like things, all these are rightly condemned in war."[170]

Over the years, Christian theologians have expanded Aquinas' three conditions and made them into ten. A war is just:

1. If it's fought for a just cause.
2. If competent legitimate authority call us to war.
3. If the comparative righteous principle is present – in other words the war's cause is greater than the evil that it is confronting.
4. If there are proper motives for fighting the war.
5. If it is fought as a last resort.
6. If the probability of success and victory is good.
7. If the greater good is prosecuted – for example to end the holocaust and Nazism.
8. If there is the right spirit of justice and purpose on the part of those who fight (see Aquinas' third condition).
9. The least amount of force possible is used.
10. And when compassion and justice is shown to your defeated enemies.

---

[169] Aquinas, Summa Theologica, Part II, Question 40, On War.
[170] Ibid.

Chapter 1: The God-Honoring American Man

These ten conditions constitute the right to go to war and the right conduct in war. John Fienberg writes, "The just war theory recognizes that war is evil. The point at issue is not whether war is good but whether it is unavoidable in all cases and whether it can be conducted in a just and equitable manner."[171] War only exists because men, having fallen under the power of the devil, have fallen into depravity to such an extent that they will desecrate and destroy the image of God in another person for their own political and personal gain. There are few things in this life that are as evil as war. The issue we are faced with is not whether or not war is evil but is war necessary at times.

The goal in a just war is to secure a condition of peace that is either being threatened or has been lost. That's why the manner it is to be waged is so important. Again Aquinas tells us, "True religion looks upon as peaceful those wars that are waged not for motives of aggrandizement, or cruelty, but with the object of securing peace, of punishing evil-doers, and of uplifting the good."[172]

Phillip Ryken writes, "The bible teaches that it is not unlawful to kill enemies in war, provided that the war is just. Of course, the justice of a war needs to be considered carefully, especially by nations as heavily armed as the United States. Christians have long believed that a war is just only if it is waged by a legitimate government; for a worthy cause; with force proportional to the attack; against men who are soldiers not civilians; and when all other means of resolution have failed."[173] Now at this point you may be saying, well this is all fine but would Jesus Christ ever go to war? And the answer is yes; He would and He has.

When Philip said to Jesus Christ, show us the Father and it will be enough for us. What did Jesus say to him? He said to Philip, he that has seen me has seen the Father. I AM in the Father and the Father is in Me. I and the Father are One. In the Book of Exodus, chapter fifteen, God is called a Warrior.

---

[171] John Feinberg, Ethics for a Brave New World, 674.
[172] Aquinas, Summa Theologica, Part II, Question 40, On War.
[173] Ryken, Written in Stone, 137.

Chapter 1: The God-Honoring American Man

³ **The LORD *is* a man of war**; The LORD *is* His name. ⁴ Pharaoh's chariots and his army He has cast into the sea; His chosen captains also are drowned in the Red Sea. ⁵ The depths have covered them; They sank to the bottom like a stone (Ex 15:3-5, emphasis added).

And the last picture of the Son of God in the Bible comes to us from Rev 19:11-16:

¹¹ Now I saw heaven opened, and behold, a white horse. And He who sat on him *was* called Faithful and True, and in righteousness He judges and makes war. ¹² His eyes *were* like a flame of fire, and on His head *were* many crowns. He had a name written that no one knew except Himself. ¹³ He *was* clothed with a robe dipped in blood, and His name is called The Word of God. ¹⁴ And the armies in heaven, clothed in fine linen, white and clean, followed Him on white horses. ¹⁵ Now out of His mouth goes a sharp sword, that with it He should strike the nations. And He Himself will rule them with a rod of iron. He Himself treads the winepress of the fierceness and wrath of Almighty God. ¹⁶ And He has on *His* robe and on His thigh a name written:

KING OF KINGS AND LORD OF LORDS.

We could never love a God who was not a Judge of evil. The reason why we love God is because of His mercy for us in Christ on the cross. God is Love as well as Retributive Justice. God is a God of mercy but also of judgment. God's love and justice are compatible with His character, and so must the Christian's. Love and justice are therefore not mutually exclusive concepts. Love and justice should be compatible in the Christian life. And in the Christian state? If ever there will be one again.

How Can Christians Kill?

Let's look at our second question: How can Christians serve in war, kill the enemies of their country, while keeping Christ's command of 'love your enemies'? In the early Church, there was great disinclination to engage in military service because those that served gave themselves up to a power that persecuted Christians. As we stated earlier, the Bible makes a distinction between murder, which is the

93

illegitimate taking of life by an individual, and war which is the legitimate taking of life by the state. Certainly soldiers can and have committed evil and murdered people by taking life illegitimately against Scripture, the laws of land warfare, and their own conscience. But war and murder are not synonymous.

What is of primary importance for Christians serving in war is, they must follow the dictates of Scripture and their own conscience. Augustine demonstrates this point when he says, "What is required of the Christian is not bodily action, but inward disposition."[174] That is, one's motive. To illustrate this priority of inward motive, Augustine asked readers to consider a man hitting a boy and another man caressing a boy. The first case seems bad, but the man might be a father lovingly disciplining his son; the second case seems good, but the man might be a child molester. Thus, Augustine said, "We find a man by love made fierce; and by iniquity made to look pleasantly gentle."[175]

Harkening back to what has been said earlier, whenever a nation and especially a soldier on the field of battle, uses weapons of war as instruments of *vindictive revenge* rather than instruments of *retributive justice,* than the dictates of both justice and love have been desecrated. The Bible demonstrates many such incidents. For example, the first *murder* which is recorded in Gen 4:8, in which Cain murdered his brother Abel. There are many reduplications of this first murder in the Scriptures, but one in particular demonstrates the objective differences in killing and murdering.

In the Book of First Samuel we are introduced to David, the son of Jesse who replaced Saul and reigned as king in Israel. It was said that king "Saul had killed his thousands but David his tens of thousands" (1 Sam 18:7). David lawfully and honorably discharged the office delegated to him from the king of Israel and during his tenure as Saul's servant, he killed thousands of the enemies of Israel.

When David was a young man, he defended the honor of God, when no one else would face Israel's enemy, the

---

[174] Augustine, Against Faustus the Manichean, 22.76.
[175] Schaff, Nicene and Post-Nicene Fathers, Series 1, Volume VII, St. Augustine: Homilies on the Gospel of John, 8.

Chapter 1: The God-Honoring American Man

Philistine giant Goliath. The two armies had spent forty days in a standoff; every morning and night Goliath defied Israel's God. Determined to vindicate God's honor, David went down to encounter the giant without shield, armor or sword, gathered five stones from the brook and with a shepherd's sling, sank one of them into the giant's forehead; killing him where he stood and beheading Goliath with his own sword (1 Sam 17:40-51). That day, David became a national hero but it wasn't a desire for self-glory or renown that compelled David down into the valley to face the giant, but a love for God and to bring honor to God's great name. David killed the enemy of his country, not out of personal vengeance, but as a lesser magistrate, an extension of the state, a soldier defending his country.

Sometime later, after God had removed Saul from being king for want of obedience (1 Sam 31; Acts 13:22), David reigned as king over Israel. God's people prospered under David: Jerusalem was captured from the Jebusites and it was made the new capital; the Ark of the Covenant was brought into the city; and the nation experienced great blessings and peace all around. Then the Scriptures tell us in 2 Sam 11:1-5:

11 It happened in the spring of the year, at the time when kings go out *to battle,* that David sent Joab and his servants with him, and all Israel; and they destroyed the people of Ammon and besieged Rabbah. But David remained at Jerusalem. ² Then it happened one evening that David arose from his bed and walked on the roof of the king's house. And from the roof he saw a woman bathing, and the woman *was* very beautiful to behold. ³ So David sent and inquired about the woman. And *someone* said, "*Is* this not Bathsheba, the daughter of Eliam, the wife of Uriah the Hittite?" ⁴ Then David sent messengers, and took her; and she came to him, and he lay with her, for she was cleansed from her impurity; and she returned to her house. ⁵ And the woman conceived; so she sent and told David, and said, "I *am* with child."

David, remaining back in Jerusalem, commits adultery with Uriah's wife Bathsheba, impregnates her, and devises a plan to cover up his sin and guilt by calling her husband Uriah, a soldier, home from the siege of Ammon. David reasoned that Uriah, given this fortuitous opportunity, would undoubtedly sleep with his wife, and thereby think the child was his own and not David's. What a plot! And so, David recalls Uriah from the frontlines, inquires to the welfare of the army, and bids Uriah go home to wash and refresh himself. He even sends Uriah away with some food.

It seems David feigned to have Uriah return in the morning, presumably to deliver a dispatch from the king? But in the morning, David learned that his plan failed because Uriah, being an honorable man "slept at the door of the king's house with all the servants of his lord, and did not go down to his house" (1 Sam 11:9). It was because, as Uriah explains to David, "the ark and Israel and Judah are dwelling in tents, and my lord Joab and the servants of my lord are encamped in the open fields. Shall I then go to my house to eat and drink, and to lie with my wife? *As* you live, and *as* your soul lives, I will not do this thing." Uriah, being a faithful subject and a soldier of David's, would not allow himself the enjoyment of lawful pleasures, when his fellow soldiers were exposing their lives to danger for their country; and yet David under such circumstances indulged to sinful lusts and criminal pleasures.

So David bids Uriah, stay the night in his palace to sup with him, so that he may send him back with the army in the morning. Then David sins even more by getting Uriah drunk in order to make him forget his oath and vow, being inflamed with wine, so he might be excited to go home and lie with his wife, and cover over all of David's iniquity; but even this scheme did not succeed (2 Sam 11:12-13). And when David was informed that Uriah didn't go home, but remained in David's house with his servants, Satan put it into David's heart to take the wicked and cruel method of having Uriah die by the hand of the Ammonites, Israel's enemy. 2 Sam 11:14-17 tells us:

[14] In the morning it happened that David wrote a letter to Joab and sent *it* by the hand of Uriah. [15] And he wrote in the letter, saying, "Set Uriah in the forefront of the hottest battle, and retreat from him, that he may be struck down and die." [16] So it was, while Joab besieged the city, that he assigned Uriah to a place where he knew there *were* valiant men. [17] Then the men of the city came out and fought with Joab. And *some* of the people of the servants of David fell; and Uriah the Hittite died also.

Chapter 1: The God-Honoring American Man

Afterward, when David received news of Uriah's death, he brought Bathsheba into his house, made her his wife, and she bore a son. The plot had worked – or so it seemed. "But the thing that David had done displeased the LORD" (2 Sam 11:27). Soon afterward, God sent his prophet Nathan to David, who confronted the king's sin and drew out his confession with a parable. 2 Sam 12:1-15 tells us,

12 Then the LORD sent Nathan to David. And he came to him, and said to him: "There were two men in one city, one rich and the other poor. ²The rich *man* had exceedingly many flocks and herds. ³But the poor *man* had nothing, except one little ewe lamb which he had bought and nourished; and it grew up together with him and with his children. It ate of his own food and drank from his own cup and lay in his bosom; and it was like a daughter to him. ⁴And a traveler came to the rich man, who refused to take from his own flock and from his own herd to prepare one for the wayfaring man who had come to him; but he took the poor man's lamb and prepared it for the man who had come to him." ⁵So David's anger was greatly aroused against the man, and he said to Nathan, "*As* the LORD lives, the man who has done this shall surely die! ⁶And he shall restore fourfold for the lamb, because he did this thing and because he had no pity."

⁷Then Nathan said to David, "You *are* the man! Thus says the LORD God of Israel: 'I anointed you king over Israel, and I delivered you from the hand of Saul. ⁸I gave you your master's house and your master's wives into your keeping, and gave you the house of Israel and Judah. And if *that had been* too little, I also would have given you much more! ⁹Why have you despised the commandment of the LORD, to do evil in His sight? You have killed Uriah the Hittite with the sword; you have taken his wife *to be* your wife, and have killed him with the sword of the people of Ammon. ¹⁰Now therefore, the sword shall never depart from your house, because you have despised Me, and have taken the wife of Uriah the Hittite to be your wife.' ¹¹Thus says the LORD: 'Behold, I will raise up adversity against you from your own house; and I will take your wives before your eyes and give *them* to your neighbor, and he shall lie with your wives in the sight of this sun. ¹²For you did *it* secretly, but I will do this thing before all Israel, before the sun.'" ¹³So David said to Nathan, "I have sinned against the LORD." And Nathan said to David, "The LORD also has put away your sin; you shall not die. ¹⁴However, because by this deed you have given great occasion to the enemies of the LORD to blaspheme, the child also *who is* born to you shall surely die." ¹⁵Then Nathan departed to his house.

97

Chapter 1: The God-Honoring American Man

As time went by, it seems David was relieved that his scheme had worked. However, God revealed David's sins to the prophet Nathan, bringing conviction while drawing out David's confession and repentance. Psalm 51, one of the penitential psalms, gives us the setting of David's adultery with Bathsheba, his betrayal and murder of Uriah, along with the host of his other sins that were related to his attempted cover-up.[176] Among the victims of David's sin was his son who lived only seven days. A fitting reminder of how children may suffer for the sins of their fathers (cf. Num 16:27-33; Josh 7:22-25).

The point being made here is this, David was a mighty man of valor; he *killed* the enemies of his country by justly discharging the delegated power of the sword, but had *murdered* Uriah in the vain hope to cover up his sin. His motivation in both cases were antithetical; one to justice, selflessness and love, and the other to injustice, selfishness and self-love.

Soldiers, operating under the authority of the state which has been ordained by God, are an extension of the state and operate as representatives of the government and not as private citizens, and thereby discharge duties which include the killing of enemy combatants in war under the authority of state, in order to defend the state and its citizens and property against harm or loss. War is not opposed to the love of one's enemies; for whoever wages war honorably hates, not individuals, but the actions which he justly punishes.[177] The authority under which the soldier operates is derived from the state which is ordained by God (Rom 13:1). Similarly, Christian judges who have imposed the death penalty on criminals when representing the authority of the state have not committed murder, but have lawfully and justly used the power of the sword. God has delegated His authority to civil rulers and not to private citizens.

There are issues we haven't raised here, such as, the issue of women in combat, which the church has always opposed because war is for men; it is an evil that men must go through

---

[176] The penitential psalms include: Psalm 6, 38, 51, 102, 130, and 143.
[177] Suarez, quoted in Placher, Readings in the History of Christian Theology, Volume 2, 53.

and not our mothers, wives and daughters. One of the responsibilities of men is to protect women, not send them off to war!

Should Christians Serve in the Military?

Harkening back to what Augustine said about the two cities, should Christians serve in the armed forces? The answer to this question will depend on the dictates of one's conscience. John Feinberg asks,

Are the two kingdoms mutually exclusive? We think not. If the use of force is divinely entrusted to human governments, and if Christians receive benefits from the state, not the least of which is protection, it is unreasonable to think Christians should reject legitimate governmental use of force. Moreover, it does not seem inappropriate for government to expect Christians to participate in the use of force to protect all members of the society. Responsibilities accompany benefits! If such Christian participation is ruled out, it seems Christians would have to exclude themselves from the police force as well.[178]

The purpose of having an army is to preserve peace. The sword is a tool of political authority. Its purpose is to preserve the existence of the state it serves.[179] But God has not delegated the power of the sword to individuals. When we must go to war our objective should be, as Basil H. Liddell Hart's dictum states, "to achieve a better state of the peace."[180]

We may say, in all certainty, Christ's Kingdom is spiritual and it is advanced by the sword of the Spirit alone, not the antithetical material one. But if all that is needed for evil to triumph is for good men to do nothing, force must therefore be used to hinder the evil-doer so that the spiritual may have a free course. The Baptist Faith and Message helps us to keep things in perspective with the question of war by telling us:

It is the duty of Christians to seek peace with all men on principles of righteousness. In accordance with the spirit and teachings of Christ

---

[178] John Feinberg, Ethics for a Brave New World, 648.
[179] Clausewitz, On War, 1.1, 83.
[180] Snow, From Lexington to Desert Storm and Beyond, 11.

they should do all in their power to put an end to war. The true remedy for the war spirit is the gospel of our Lord. The supreme need of the world is the acceptance of His teachings in all the affairs of men and nations, and the practical application of His law of love. Christian people throughout the world should pray for the reign of the Prince of Peace.[181]

In this discussion, we are reminded of the biblical truth that the government was founded by God for a legitimate purpose: *to restrain sin; to preserve order and organize society; and to promote civil obedience.* However, the fact that governments are authorized by God doesn't guarantee that their actions will be just.[182] God has delegated His authority to civil rulers to punish evil doers and avenge crimes thereby preserving order.

How Should Christians Relate to Government?

Being under the lordship of Jesus Christ, how should Christians relate to the government? We are to render to Caesar that which is Caesar's (Mk 12:13-17; Rom 13:1-2; Tit 3:1). This is not an option but an obligation. The believer is both a citizen of the state and the kingdom of God. However, the state's authority over the believer is limited to the authority God has delegated to the state (Rom 13:1-7; cf. Rev 13:7).

In the Book of Daniel, world empires are likened to beasts rising out of the sea (Dan 7:1-8); likewise Revelation depicts pagan government as a Beast (Rev 13-14). A Christian's obedience to the state cannot be blind. If the state steps beyond that authority, and acts without legitimacy, then Christians are to resist.

We find an excellent example of this in the Book of Acts when God heals a lame man through the apostles Peter and John. In response, the civil authorities, who are fearful of losing their administrative positions, demand that the apostles cease speaking or teaching in the name of Jesus. Acts 4:19 tells us:

---

[181] The Baptist Faith and Message, XVI, Peace and War.
[182] Clowney, The Church, 190.

Chapter 1: The God-Honoring American Man

¹⁹ But Peter and John answered and said to them, "Whether it is right in the sight of God to listen to you more than to God, you judge. ²⁰ For we cannot but speak the things which we have seen and heard."

In other words, we are going to continue our verbal witness because this is the command of the Risen Christ and we will remain faithful to His commands; moreover we will continue in our *verbal witness* because we love people enough to warn them of the wrath to come. We must testify to what we have seen and heard. John Gill, commenting on the faithful witness of the apostles writes, "This shows their great fidelity and integrity, their inviolable attachment to Christ, and their fearlessness of the displeasure and wrath of men."[183] When the state commands what God forbids, or forbids what God commands, we are to obey God rather than men (Acts 5:29).

In light of Scripture, how should Christians respond to the laws of the state particularly those laws which require Christians to either break God's commands or prevent them from obeying them? What does God in His Word require in this instance? First, God requires that we obey legitimate civil authorities in their lawful and indifferent commands. Such as paying taxes, obeying the speed limit, and registering for selective service, etc. The Lord Jesus addresses this aspect of civil obedience when He said, "The teachers of the law and the Pharisees sit in Moses' seat. So you must be careful to do everything they tell you" (Mt 23:1-3).

Christians, as citizens of the state, are to obey the civil authorities because God has ordained them for the purposes of restraining sin and preserving order. Christians are commanded to obey lawful magistrates in their lawful and indifferent commands. The Bible tells us to "Be subject for the Lord's sake to every human institution, whether it be to the emperor as supreme, or to governors as sent by him to punish those who do evil and to praise those who do good" (1 Pet 2:13-14).

Furthermore, God has delegated authority to civil governments for the purpose of organizing and defending established societies. Again the Lord says in Matthew 22:21, "Render therefore to Caesar the things that are Caesar's, and

---

[183] Gill, Exposition of the Old and New Testaments, Acts 4.

Chapter 1: The God-Honoring American Man

to God the things that are God's." That is to say, give Caesar, i.e., the President, the state government, your unit commander, squad leader, etc., tribute, custom, honor and obedience, which are due to him. All of which is rendered knowing full well that all authority is derived from the Almighty. Thus, Christians honor God when they obey the authority He has delegated to legitimate governments. Obedience to civil magistrates is therefore not inconsistent with the reverence and fear of God. The God-honoring American man should give everyman his due as to not bring discredit upon the faith, "For there is no authority except that which God has established (Romans 13:1)."

The Conscience

Regarding indifferent commands, that is, things considered *amoral*? What is to be considered concerning these? This question brings to mind the role of the conscience. What is the conscience? The conscience either indicts you for wrong doing or exonerates you for doing right. Thus, Origen called it the chamber of justice, and Juvenal said, "By the verdict of his own breast no man is ever acquitted." Therefore, when we have done right, as Thomas a Kempis tells us, "He will easily be content and at peace," but if we have done wrong, "Suspicion always haunts the guilty mind; the thief doth fear each bush an officer."[184] This is why John Flavel wrote, "Conscience which should have been the sinner's curb here on earth becomes the sinner's whip that will lash his soul in hell. That which was the seat and center of all guilt now becomes the seat and center of all torment."[185] And Calvin observes, "The torture of a bad conscience is the hell of a living soul."

The English Puritan Richard Sibbes, writing some four hundred years ago tells us, "A man's conscience is his judgment of himself according to God's judgment of him." Sibbes describes man's conscience as a court, and as such enumerates the ways a conscience may arraign a man, as: 'a register, witnesses, a prosecutor, a judge, and an executioner.'

---

[184] Shakespeare, Henry VI, Part III, Act V, Scene VI.
[185] Flavel, The Whole Works of the Reverend Mr. John Flavel, 601.

"So," writes Sibbes, "upon accusation and judgment, there is punishment. And the first punishment is within a man before he comes to hell."[186] Only in Christ, by faith in His name, can we have peace with God and peace in our souls.

Regarding the power of the conscience Martin Luther famously said, "Unless I am convicted by Scripture and plain reason, I do not accept the authority of the popes and councils, which have so often contradicted themselves, my conscience is captive to the Word of God. I cannot and I will not recant anything, for to go against conscience is neither right nor safe. God help me. Amen."[187] The point in all this is God's law is directly binding on the conscience. And things indifferent, such as are either not covered in Scripture or are not against sound reason, are *adiaphorous*, that is to say, having no effect for either good or evil.[188]

Secondly, whereas Christians should obey the lawful and indifferent commands of civil authorities, they should refuse to obey unlawful or unrighteous commands to their own hurt. The best example of this I can think of comes from the Book of Daniel. Remember Sunday school? The Babylonian king Nebuchadnezzar erects an image of gold and requires all his subjects to worship it. All of the citizens comply except Shadrach, Meshach, and Abed-Nego, captive Hebrews. And when they are faced with certain death by being thrown into a fiery furnace they say to the king, "O Nebuchadnezzar, we have no need to answer you in this matter. If this be so, our God whom we serve is able to deliver us from the burning fiery furnace, and he will deliver us out of your hand, O king. But if not, be it known to you, O king, that we will not serve your gods or worship the golden image that you have set up" (Dan 3:16-18). Christians are commanded to obey lawful magistrates in their lawful and indifferent commands but

---

[186] Sibbes, Works III, 210. It would be beneficial to note that the word 'conscience' is derived from the two Latin words, *scientia* or science, meaning knowledge and *con* meaning with; together meaning something like, joint-knowledge.

[187] Martin Luther's response at the Imperial Diet of Worms, 18 April, 1521.

[188] Adiaphora, in Greek ἀδιάφορα "indifferent things" refers to matters that are not essential to faith. Thus, issues such as this are best left to conscience.

should refuse to obey unlawful or unrighteous commands to their own hurt.

Thirdly, Christians are to use lawful means to redress tyranny, by appealing to other magistrates. The church is to minister to the state; to be its conscience. It would be easy for Christians to assume that God isn't interested in politics and then just go on our merry way. Isn't it possible that the Almighty and omniscient God, the God who is concerned about even the fall of a sparrow and who has numbered the very hairs on our heads, does know what is going on in American politics and is interested in our affairs of state?[189]

The God-honoring American man is a citizen of the City of God who also lives and works within the city of man. While Christians are indeed citizens of God's kingdom, that does not mean they aren't citizens of this world as well. God has ordained the state for a purpose; to restrain sin; preserve order and organize society; and promote civil obedience. Christians are to live as people who are free, not using their freedom in Christ as a cover-up for evil, but living as servants of God, by honoring everyone: Loving the brotherhood, fearing God, and honoring the government (1 Pet 2:16-17).

The Sixth Mark of the God-Honoring American Man: Loyal Member of an Organization

"Honor your father and your mother, that your days may be long upon the land which the LORD your God is giving you" (Ex 20:12).

---

[189] John Eidsmoe, God and Caesar, x.

Chapter 1: The God-Honoring American Man

Before we discuss the manner in which Christians are to behave in a work setting, particularly a corporation or organization, we must define the fifth commandment. God's plan for preserving the family, one of His ordained institutions, as well as society, is the fifth commandment: "Honor your father and your mother, that your days may be long upon the land which the LORD your God is giving you" (Ex 20:12). We remember that what God forbids, is at no time to be done and what he commands, is always our duty. By *father* and *mother*, in the fifth commandment, are meant, not only natural parents, but all superiors in age and gifts; and especially such as, by God's ordinance, are over us in place of authority, whether in family, church, or commonwealth.[190] The Bible insists that mothers are to receive as much respect as fathers. This part of the fifth commandment obviously rules out same-sex parents.[191] The fifth commandment bids us to honor, not only our parents, but our superiors as well.

What we are trying to correlate is the sixth and seventh marks are in fact an elaboration of the fifth commandment. Remembering back to the last mark, the reason we are to behave honorably and respect authority is that "There is no authority except from God, and the authorities that exist are appointed by God" (Rom 13:1). John Frame tells us, "God has not left human beings to live as isolated individuals, but has placed them within communities. Over each community is a government, which the members of that community must honor. So there are structures of authority, in which "inferiors" must submit to "superiors."[192] The reference to inferiors and superiors here comes from the Westminster Larger Catechism. The following three questions exposit the Bible's teaching on respect:

Q. 126. *What is the general scope of the fifth commandment?* A. The general scope of the fifth commandment is, the performance of those duties which we mutually owe in our several relations, as inferiors, superiors or equals.

---

[190] The Westminster Larger Catechism Answer 124.
[191] Ryken, Written in Stone, 120.
[192] Frame, The Doctrine of the Christian Life, 593.

Chapter 1: The God-Honoring American Man

Q. 127. *What is the honor that inferiors owe to their superiors?*
A. The honor which inferiors owe to their superiors is, all due reverence in heart, word, and behavior; prayer and thanksgiving for them; imitation of their virtues and graces; willing obedience to their lawful commands and counsels; due submission to their corrections; fidelity to, defense, and maintenance of their persons and authority, according to their several ranks, and the nature of their places; bearing with their infirmities, and covering them in love, that so they may be an honor to them and to their government.

Q. 128. *What are the sins of inferiors against their superiors?*
A. The sins of inferiors against their superiors are, all neglect of the duties required toward them; envying at, contempt of, and rebellion against their persons and places, in their lawful counsels, commands, and corrections; cursing, mocking, and all such refractory and scandalous carriage, as proves a shame and dishonor to them and their government.[193]

Now that we have defined the fifth commandment, let's look at what we mean by a loyal member of an organization or unit. First, we need to define what we mean by organization. An organization is a structure through which people cooperate for the purposes of collective tasks. It is a social entity that has a collective goal. Legitimate organizations may include: corporations, governments, non-governmental, organizations, international organizations, armed forces, charities, not-for-profit corporations, partnerships, cooperatives, and universities, etc. There are also illegitimate organizations that may or may not operate in secret, such as secret societies, criminal organizations, and resistance movements. The goal of this section is in regards to the legitimate kind of organization, be it civilian or military.

Additionally, a Christian's understanding of two very important matters: the Ten Commandments and the two kingdom concept will determine how well he integrates with society and an organization. Why this is important will become evident. As we have said, the Ten Commandments are the summation of God's law. They demonstrate for us the absolute perfect character of Christ; God's standard of

---

[193] Larger Catechism Questions 126-128 are from the Westminster Confession of Faith, Free Presbyterian Publications edition, pp. 210-213.

excellence. God gave the law to reveal sin so mankind would be driven to Christ for grace (Rom 3:20). The law therefore shows us our need for the saving work of Christ. We will discuss the Christian's use of the law in chapter three, for now we need to say that the first four commandments teach us to love God, while the last six teach us to love our neighbor. Love for God comes first because we cannot love another person until we love God. If we do not honor God, we will not honor one another.

Of course, in some respects, human beings are equal: all are equal in the image of God, equally fallen, equally in need of redemption."[194] The reality is God has placed us all in communities, which will exert some measure of authority over us. This truth may be illustrated from Matthew chapter eight, when Jesus is confronted by a centurion who asks Jesus to heal his paralyzed servant. The centurion, a Roman commander of a hundred men, understood the cosmic truth that Jesus Christ has all authority (Mt 29:18). John Gill tells us, "The centurion did not say this to reject or despise Christ's presence or company, but is expressive of his great modesty and humility, and of his consciousness of his own vileness, and unworthiness of having so great a person in his house: it was too great a favor for him to enjoy.[195]

Christ has all authority, and is the Ruler of the kings of the earth (Mt 29:18; Rev 1:5), and our present reigning King. He will bring history to its consummation and bring all things under His feet (1 Cor 11:25). The biblical point being made here is, as Christian men, we have been placed by God in several communities that often overlap in their spheres of influence. And we are to render honor and respect to these authorities as if we were rendering it unto God Himself (Col 3:17, 23-24). Remember the two kingdom concept? Christians

---

[194] Frame, Doctrine of the Christian Life, 593. Frame lists three chief biblical communities we all live in: the family, the church, and the state.

[195] Gill, Exposition of the Whole Bible, Mt 8:8. Gill adds, And if such a man was unworthy, having been an idolater, and lived a profane course of life, that Christ should come into his house, and be, though but for a short time, under his roof; how much more unworthy are poor sinful creatures (and sensible sinners see themselves to be so unworthy), that Christ should come into their hearts, and dwell there by faith, as he does, in all true believers, however vile and sinful they have been?"

Chapter 1: The God-Honoring American Man

are citizens of two kingdoms: the city of God and the city of man. Spiritually, Christians live in the city of God that will one day be consummated fully, while physically they live in the city of man.

Because Christ has all authority, obedience rendered to our "superiors" is obedience rendered to God. A Christian's work is to be rendered to Christ and not to the world. The apostle Paul tells us in Col 3:23-25:

> [23] And whatever you do, do it heartily, as to the Lord and not to men, [24] knowing that from the Lord you will receive the reward of the inheritance; for you serve the Lord Christ. [25] But he who does wrong will be repaid for what he has done, and there is no partiality.

This is quite a liberating truth, especially to those who have wicked bosses. And as we will see later, this can also be a means of grace, a way for God to save your wicked boss (1 Pet 2:19-21).[196] A Christian's job earns him money that he needs to support himself and his family, and one's job may seem like absolute drudgery. But when we view our jobs from God's perspective, even the most tiresome, oppressive, thankless, or even boring job can become, as verse 24 tells us, service rendered to Christ. The Heidelberg Catechism is correct when it says that the fifth commandment requires "that I show honor, love, and faithfulness to my father and mother and to all who are set in authority over me; that I *submit myself with respectful obedience* to all their careful instruction and discipline; *and that I also bear patiently their failures, since it is God's will to govern us by their hand*" (emphasis added).[197]

How frequently do men despise the authority of their bosses; especially if their bosses are tyrants? But God's Word tells us to "Be submissive to our masters with all fear, not only to the good and gentle, but also to the harsh" (1 Pet 2:18). And the Bible tells us in Eph 6:5-8, to be obedient to our bosses,

In sincerity of heart, as to Christ; [6] not with eyeservice, as men-pleasers, but as bondservants of Christ, doing the will of God from

---

[196] See the *Grace of Patience* in chapter ten.
[197] Heidelberg Catechism, A. 104, italics added.

the heart, [7] with goodwill doing service, as to the Lord, and not to men, [8] knowing that whatever good anyone does, he will receive the same from the Lord , whether *he is* a slave or free. [9] And you, masters, do the same things to them, giving up threatening, knowing that your own Master also is in heaven, and there is no partiality with Him.

A Christian's obedience to his boss, commander, officer in charge or other authority figure is obedience rendered to God, Who Himself is the source of all authority. Whatever a Christian's vocation, he is to work as unto the Lord and not man. And his boss, whom a Christian is to respect, is to be treated as one having received authority from God. This is, as we saw earlier, an extension of the fifth commandment by which commands us to "Honor your father and your mother, that your days may be long upon the land which the LORD your God is giving you" (Ex 20:12).[198] The sum of the commandment is that we are to look up to those whom the Lord has set over us, yielding them *honor, gratitude,* and *obedience.* And it makes no difference whether our bosses are deserving of the honor we give them or not because God has conferred their station upon them and shows that he would have us honor them.[199]

What if our boss is undeserving of honor?

One of the best examples demonstrating how to give honor to those who don't deserve it comes to us from the life of David. If we remember, David had been chased by Saul for years. Saul was jealous and wanted David dead because he knew David had been anointed by God to replace him. At first, Saul sought to murder David indirectly. He offered David his daughter Michal's hand in marriage, only he would have to provide a 'dowry' consisting of two hundred Philistine foreskins (1 Sam 18:27)! Saul reasoned that David would get himself killed trying to get them; however, David succeeded and married Michal. David's honeymoon was short, and

---

[198] This is should bring home the point made in the third mark regarding the importance of a father's discipline of his children; if they don't learn it at home, where will they learn it?

[199] Calvin, Institutes of the Christian Religion, 2.8.35-36, pp 254-255.

Chapter 1: The God-Honoring American Man

Saul's fragile ego and fits of jealous rage sent David into the wilderness where he would be hunted by the army for about four years. Saul even took David's wife Michal and gave her in marriage to another man. In all this, David, knowing that God had forsaken Saul for disobedience (see 1 Sam 15), and haven been anointed by Israel's judge-prophet to be king in his place (see 1 Sam 16), continued to serve faithfully the very man who wanted him dead. Why? Because David understood this truth: "there is no *authority* except from God, and the *authorities* that exist are appointed by God. Therefore whoever resists the *authority* resists the ordinance of God, and those who resist will bring judgment on themselves" (Romans 13:1, 2). David departed Saul's company only after it was evident that an irreparable rift had come between them; Saul desiring him dead above all things.

Thus David began living like Robin Hood in the Judean wilderness, being hunted by Saul and his army. It was during this time that David spared Saul's life on two occasions (1 Sam 24 and 26). Both times, Saul, having accompanied his army in the field, is found vulnerable and assailable to David and his men. And despite the pleas of his mighty men to kill Saul, David spared Saul's life by restraining his men. David said, "I will not stretch out my hand against the Lord's anointed" (1 Sam 24:10). It is as if David had said, "If Saul dies it will not be by my hand or those under my authority."

Many of the Psalms were written by David and reflect not only his hardships but are also the many occasions of praise for deliverance. Of note Psalm 57, 59 and 63 relate to times when others sought David's life but God preserved him. David is hounded by Saul's army to such an extent; he finds refuge only by living within Philistine land! Finally, David's ordeal with Saul is brought to an end when Saul's army is annihilated by the Philistines at the Battle of Mount Gilboa (1 Sam 31). Following the death of Saul and his sons in battle, David is proclaimed king in Judea.

The point is, God has not left us to live as isolated individuals, but has placed us within organizations, over which is an authority of some type, under which the members of that organization must honor. Saul was the king of Israel; to whom David yielded honor, gratitude, and obedience by not

110

allowing his men to take Saul's life, even though Saul was clearly undeserving of David's respect, as well as acting as an illegitimate authority by ordering an illegal killing. If ever there was a king who failed to deserve the respect of his subjects, it was Saul.

As God-honoring men, like David, we are to recognize legitimate authority and obey their lawful and indifferent commands, but should refuse to obey unlawful or unrighteous commands and face the consequences. Additionally, as members of a particular organization (civilian or government), we understand that God has sovereignly placed us within that organization for a specific purpose. This can readily be demonstrated from the life of Joseph (Gen 37, 39-45).

Joseph, one of the sons of Jacob, the patriarch of Israel, had been exalted by God with visions of the future. Particularly, the manner in which God was going to deliver His chosen people (cf. Gen 15:13-16). The dreams God gives Joseph, along with his father Jacob's favor, cause him to incur the jealous wrath of his brothers, who promptly sell him as a slave. Joseph ends up in Egypt, where he spends about thirteen years of his young life as a slave and later a prisoner. But God had sovereignly placed Joseph there. And through God's *providence*, Joseph is exalted to be the prime minister of Egypt. It is from this position of influence, that God orchestrates a deliverance from a terrible seven year famine, of not only His chosen people but the known world as well.[200]

As a Christian husband and father I understand that God gives me my job in order to provide for my family's needs (Mt 6:25-34). I want to honor and show gratitude to God by obeying the authority He has placed over me. Additionally, with respect to the fifth commandment, Christians should

---

[200] God's providence is the working out of His own plan through the ordinary circumstances of life. One of the main messages of the Book of Ruth is that God is at work in the worst of times. What God did for Ruth and Naomi was to make provision for them by providing a means of sustenance, to provide protection for them by way of Boaz, and set them in the company of a God conscious praying people. This is what makes Naomi who says, "The Almighty has afflicted me" (Ruth 1:20), to later say, "Blessed be he of the Lord, who has not forsaken His kindness to the living and the dead" (Ruth 2:20).

honor and love their parents and appreciate them, by caring for them to the very end of their lives.

The Seventh Mark of the God-Honoring American Man:
Loyal Comrade to My Team Mates

[15] "You shall not steal. [16] "You shall not bear false witness against your neighbor. [17] "You shall not covet your neighbor's house; you shall not covet your neighbor's wife, nor his male servant, nor his female servant, nor his ox, nor his donkey, nor anything that *is* your neighbor's" (Ex 20:15-17).

This seventh mark of the God-honoring man accentuates the biblical principle that all good work honors God. What constitutes "good work?" A.W. Pink offers this advice, "If any occupation or association is found to hinder our communion with God or our enjoyment of spiritual things, then it must be abandoned."[201] As we have said, the Christian's goal should be to glorify God with a life that models the image of Christ. Work should be no different. George Whitefield once said, "It is very remarkable, that in the book of life, we find almost all kinds of occupations, who notwithstanding served God in their respective generations, and shone as so many lights in the

---

[201] Colkmire, *Evangelical Sunday School Lesson Commentary 2013-2014*, 237.

world."[202] All Christian work should be accomplished with the mindset that God Himself is receiving it (Col 3:23-24).

Whereas, in the fifth mark we discussed that God has all authority and in the sixth mark that He has placed everyone in several communities which range from family, church, and the state, as well as in organizations (civilian or government), that often overlap in their spheres of influence, to which we are to render honor and respect as if we were rendering it unto God Himself; this seventh mark seeks to discuss *how* we should do that, specifically in a team setting. What aids us in that endeavor is the second tablet of the Law: the fifth through tenth commandments.

Regarding the Decalogue, if you remember, the first four commandments teach us to love God, while the last six teach us to love our neighbor (Ex 20:1-17). The first group of four, pertaining to our duty to God, and a second group of six, describing our duty to man. Here we are focusing in on the last three commandments: the eighth, ninth, and tenth, which if we keep, we do no wrong to our neighbor whom we are required to love (Lev 19:18; Mt 22:37-40). We are not to steal, lie, or covet, because what God forbids is at no time to be done, and what He commands, is always our duty.

These commandments require us, along with the others, to certain duties we are not to neglect. Space will not permit a full explanation of all three (see chapter 4), but let's narrow our focus to define in such terms, what makes good team players in the workplace.

God-honoring living models Christ in the workplace. This is best accomplished when we work with an attitude that all work is unto the Lord (Col 3:17, 23-24). Good work in a good attitude while modeling Christ's image (thought, word, and deed), influences others in a way that will draw them to the gospel (1 Pet 2:19). This should be the primary motivation for the Christian work ethic.

Work is best when one strives for excellence, seeing God as the recipient one's labor. Work is even better when one can work with a team to effect that end, because as Ecc 4:9-12 tells us,

---

[202] Whitefield, Sermons on Important Subjects, Volume 1, 245.

Chapter 1: The God-Honoring American Man

[9] Two are better than one, because they have a good return for their labor: [10] If either of them falls down, one can help the other up. But pity anyone who falls and has no one to help them up. [11] Also, if two lie down together, they will keep warm. But how can one keep warm alone? [12] Though one may be overpowered, two can defend themselves. A cord of three strands is not quickly broken.

This seventh mark, a *loyal comrade to my team mates* caricatures principles of Christian teamwork in a small team/unit setting. This could range from any job in the civilian or military sector; from a military squad or platoon to a business partnership. The apostle Paul in Romans 12:9-21 gives us some guiding principles for Christian ethics. Essentially, ethics is proper behavior; morally correct speech and action. However, because the Bible goes to the heart of the issue, Christian ethics are proper, that is according to the Ten Commandments, thinking, speaking, and action. Jesus taught us that even our thoughts may constitute a sin, viz., looking at a woman with lustful intent (Mt 5:27-28). Christian ethics is encapsulated in Rom 12:17-21 which states,

17 Repay no one evil for evil. Have regard for good things in the sight of all men. 18 If it is possible, as much as depends on you, live peaceably with all men. 19 Beloved, do not avenge yourselves, but rather give place to wrath; for it is written, "Vengeance is Mine, I will repay," says the Lord. 20 Therefore "If your enemy is hungry, feed him; if he is thirsty, give him a drink; for in so doing you will heap coals of fire on his head." 21 Do not be overcome by evil, but overcome evil with good.

Being a team player is a both a highly prized personal attribute and an expected norm, however, with the degradation in moral standards comes a decrease in the prevalence of not only decency but selfless attributes. Being a team player is having the ability to work on a team for a purpose greater than yourself. It means being dependable and loyal. It means working selflessly with a sense of duty, giving respect to others. However, as Christians we should know that just doing the right thing in the workplace isn't always enough. In fact, simply being a Christian will incite ostracism, hate, and even physical violence against you. Lloyd-Jones explains, "A desire

114

to live a good life is not enough. Obviously we should all have that desire, but it will not guarantee success. So let me put it thus: Hold on to your principles of morality and ethics, use your willpower to the limit, pay great heed to every noble, uplifting desire that is in you; but realize that these things alone are not enough, that they will never bring you to the desired place. We have to realize that all our best is totally inadequate, that a spiritual battle must be fought in a spiritual manner."[203]

Having a good work ethic is one thing, but like Lloyd-Jones says it's not enough. We must model Christ. His character must be seen in us. Having the fruit of the Spirit, the result of the Holy Spirit's presence and work in our lives, is what Christian ethics is all about. This is the subject of chapter three.

The correct mindset in all of this is, that all our labor is unto Christ the Lord (Col 3:23-24). It means honoring others, working zealously, being amiable and as much as it depends on us – getting along. It means doing all things for the glory of God and the advancement of the gospel (Col 3:17). We must ever remember that what we value exerts influence on our behavior so that it becomes our character.

In light of this, the following acronym highlights nine biblical principles which, though not exhaustive in any sense, will serve to better our understanding of workplace ethics; with the glory of Christ and the advancement of the gospel as the goal: **CRAFTSMAN**

Committed – to team goals.
Reliable – professional.
Accountable – responsible, can be trusted.
Flexible – humble and respectful.
Technically and tactically proficient – knowing our job.
Spiritual gifts – a man's gifts are for others.
Maintain integrity.
Agile and initiative based.
Non carborundum illegitimi – indefatigable.

---

[203] Lloyd-Jones, The Christian Soldier, 20.

Chapter 1: The God-Honoring American Man

The first principle, *committed*, is under the auspices that God Himself receives all our labor (Col 3:23-24). Christians would do well to show an interest in team goals and genuinely seek the welfare of the team they work with (Rom 12:10-11). The apostle Paul tells us in 2 Tim 2:15, "Do your best to present yourself to God as one approved, a worker who has no need to be ashamed, rightly handling the word of truth." This Scripture's primary purpose is to remind those who are teachers of the Word of God to rightly handle the Scriptures.[204] However, it also reminds us to live in such a way as to not bring reproach on the name of Christ; to live out Christ's righteousness; a visible testimony to the saving power of God. True testimony always points away from the believer and points to Jesus Christ. Christians are called to testify in the workplace; to tell what he has seen and heard; to proclaim what he knows and has experienced; so as to express personal conviction and identification with the cause he defends.

What is testimony? Testimony is faithful words about the saving power of Jesus Christ which is empowered by the Holy Spirit. It is open, plain, and faithful. Thomas Watson writes, "Ministers are but the pipes and organs. It is the Holy Ghost breathing in them that makes their words effectual."[205] Whereas true testimony of Jesus Christ will incur rejection and the hatred of mankind, it will result in the glory of God by the salvation of sinners. Just how are Christians to bear witness in the workplace? This is becoming increasing difficult, especially in the military, nevertheless Christians are to be ambassadors for Christ wherever they live and work (2 Cor 5:20; 10:5), seeking to bring all things under the lordship of Christ (1 Pet 2:12).

In the 6th Century BC, the prophet Jeremiah wrote a letter to the first wave of exiles who were deported to Babylon. He admonished them with these words found in Jer 29:4-7:

---

[204] Literally a straight-cutting of the Scripture, a handling aright. The man who uses God's Word doesn't mutilate it, or pervert it, or even water it down, but he interprets Scripture aright in the light of Scripture; *Scriptura interpres Scriptura.*

[205] Watson, A Body of Practical Divinity, 385.

116

Chapter 1: The God-Honoring American Man

[4] Thus says the LORD of hosts, the God of Israel, to all who were carried away captive, whom I have caused to be carried away from Jerusalem to Babylon: [5] Build houses and dwell *in them;* plant gardens and eat their fruit. [6] Take wives and beget sons and daughters; and take wives for your sons and give your daughters to husbands, so that they may bear sons and daughters—that you may be increased there, and not diminished. [7] And seek the peace of the city where I have caused you to be carried away captive, and pray to the LORD for it; for in its peace you will have peace.

God would have us bloom where He has planted us. And seek the welfare of the culture He has placed us in, "for in its peace we will find peace" (Jer 29:7). Likewise, we should seek the welfare of the team God has placed us in, "for in its peace we will find our peace." As we have said, our faithful witness may bring ostracism, punishment, or even death, but God protects us spiritually so as to enable our witness. This brings God glory and sinners to Christ. The protection of the church in its witness is the subject for chapter 10.

The second principle, *reliable*, means we are professional, being consistent with our good performance. One of the prevailing woes of late is a marked decrease in work ethics. It seems hard to find a good work ethic these days. Americans seemed to be infected with an entitlement attitude; however, professionalism is still placed at a high premium in any vocation. By being reliable and professional, even if others slander you, because of your good conduct, they will be put to shame (1 Pet 3:16). Christian men must model a reliable work ethic and be consistent – following through with tasks. A good question to ask yourself is: The longer I am at a job, do things improve or get worse? If they get worse, why?

Further, our word should be our bond. Our word should be so reliable that a simple statement from us should ensure others of its credibility.

Accountable, the third principle of teamwork, highlights honesty and the trustworthiness of a team member. A Christian man should always take responsibility for his actions as well as seek additional responsibilities in order to grow as a leader. Responsibility is a forgotten word in America. America today is facing some tough challenges. According to recent statistics about conditions in the United States:

Chapter 1: The God-Honoring American Man

- Half of all marriages end in divorce.
- Two thirds of mothers with infants work outside the home.
- Two thirds of married women work outside the home compared to just 6% in 1900.
- One third of children are born to an unwed mother.

Who should we fault in all of this? As we search for an answer God Himself holds men responsible; whether they take responsibility or not (Gen 3:16-19; Mt 19:3-6; Eph 5:22-33). Men must take responsibility for their families, and the women they impregnate! The antithesis of responsibility is selfishness and self-love. A man who is self-absorbed and selfish will never be accountable. Accountability underscores the biblical concept of stewardship. This is a topic for latter discussion (see chapter five).

The fourth principle, *Flexible*, means Christians in the workplace are able to maintain their composure when they respond to problems. A good team player should be able to navigate socially within the team, and adjust himself if necessary to other personalities (Rom 12:16-21). Proverbs 12:16 tells us, "A fool shows his annoyance at once, but a prudent man overlooks an insult." Good team players are able to flexibly adjust to difficult situations and are humble enough to admit their faults. When we say flexible we are not meaning to suggest that Christians have to allow themselves to go along with sinful practices (see the fifth mark).

As Christians we are to obey those who are in authority over us, but we mustn't be blind, and we must resist evil even if it costs us our job. And when others won't reciprocate our Christian charity, we are not avenge ourselves but "leave room for God's wrath" (Rom 12:19), and overcome evil with good (Rom 12:21). The Christian who is mindful that it is God Himself Who provided them with the job in the first place need not worry. He need only "Seek first the kingdom of God and His righteousness" (Mt 6:33), while God Himself will provide "everything that pertains to life and godliness" (2 Pet 1:3).

Technically and tactically proficient, the fifth principle, reminds us that job expertise is a premium for men who want to hold on to one. Men must know their vocational specialty

Chapter 1: The God-Honoring American Man

well (Rom 12:11, 17), and "work well with their hands" (1 Thes 4:11), seeking to excel in every art and artifice of the job. For example, the apostle Paul was a tent maker. He made them while he spread the gospel so as not to become a financial burden on anyone (Acts 18:3). No one wants to work with a guy who doesn't care enough to understand his job! Christians should set the example at work by knowing their job description, parameters, and responsibilities. There is an old expression in the military, leave it better than you found it.

The sixth principle, *spiritual gifts*, reminds us that natural and spiritual gifts are gifts God gives us for others, not ourselves (Rom 12:11; 1 Pet 4:10); for the express purpose of building up the body of Christ (Eph 4:4-16). Christian men should seek and pray for spiritual gifts, so that they may serve the Lord by serving their wives, families, churches, corporations, units, and teams. Just how many spiritual gifts are there? Although Christians disagree as to the number, they are given sovereignly by the Holy Spirit, "for the equipping of the saints for the work of ministry, for the edifying of the body of Christ, till we all come to the unity of the faith and of the knowledge of the Son of God, to a perfect man, to the measure of the stature of the fullness of Christ" (Eph 4:12-13) For a list of spiritual gifts, see 1 Cor 12 and Romans 12:6-8.[206]

Maintain integrity, the seventh principle, reminds us to always do the hard right over the easy wrong. Even if no one is watching us, God is. Teamwork is built on trust. This is a reciprocal principle to being *reliable*, as we've mentioned the age-old expression "a man's word is his bond." Those of us who are older can remember when that meant something, perhaps it can again. Hughes writes, "Integrity characterizes the entire person, not just part of him. He is righteous and honest through and through. He is not only that inside, but also in outer action."[207] And Sam Storms notes, "The only reason integrity should be a burden to you is if you enjoy being dishonest."[208]

Agile and initiative based, the eighth principle, is the antithesis of laziness and indifference. An enduring definition

---

[206] For more on spiritual gifts see Chapter 6.
[207] Hughes, Disciplines of a Godly Man, 128.
[208] Storms, Pleasures Evermore, 236.

of leadership in the military is "the process of influencing people by providing purpose, direction, and motivation while operating to accomplish the mission and improve the organization."[209] Although not all Christians are leaders in the organizations they work in, that is, in the strictest sense, they are to be leaders in the broader sense, in that their work ethic should point away from themselves and model Christ, thus providing Christ-like influence. So even when everyone else is behaving poorly the God-honoring man is always looking for an opportunity to influence his unit in a positive way (Rom 12:11; Col 3:23): A way that will model Christ's righteousness, and point away from one's self and direct others attention to the saving power of Christ.

Non carborundum illegitimi is a Latin aphorism, which describes a particular character of a person who is indefatigable, who seemingly cannot be worn out with fatigue. It basically means, don't let the "illegitimate" people get you down – the obstinate rebels, who in their hating of God, turn on you. Endurance – staying power, is what Christians need in order to overcome (Heb 10:36). It is both a grace of God and a practical working out of the believer's faith (Rom 5:3-5). Suffering, afflictions, trials, tribulation and persecution manifests the grace of endurance. Endurance produces character – the character of Christ! The saints grow in grace and in the knowledge of God and loose nothing but their dross (Ps 119:67, 71, 119; Is 43:2).

What hinders testimony? Worldliness. Worldliness is what any particular culture does to make sin seem normal and make righteousness seem strange. This principle, *non carborundum illegitimi*, reminds us to stay the course and finish the race despite detractors and persecution on account of the Word (Mt 13:21; Gal 4:29; 2 Tim 4:7).[210] We are to work toward an end with commitment and resolve. That resolve is to be both the immediate good of the unit we work with and ultimately for God's glory (Col 3:23). Christians are called to bear up in persecution and "not be overcome by evil but overcome evil with good" (Rom 12:21). A worldly Christian has a watered-

---

[209] FM 6-22, 1-2.
[210] This is a topic for discussion in chapters 2 and 3.

down testimony. We become uncritically open to the world's view as we are fed the world's values.[211]

Colonel Joshua Chamberlin, the commander of the 20th Maine at the Battle of Gettysburg writes, "This is the great reward of service. To live, far out and on, in the life of others; this is the mystery of the Christ, to give life's best for such high sake that it shall be found again unto life eternal." Or, in other words, living for a purpose greater than yourself and seeing one's Christ-like influence take hold of others, so as to bring God glory in the salvation of sinners, what can be a better reward of one's service in this life? Chamberlin was a seminary trained US Army Infantry Colonel. What he wants us to understand is, *a man finds his worth not in the service of himself but in others.* And, as we will see later, *the saints cannot be perfected without rendering service to one another.*[212]

Jesus Christ told His disciples, "Greater love has no one than this, than to lay down one's life for his friends" (Jn 15:13). Jesus did lay His life down for all who believe in Him (Jn 3:16), and has called us to do the same.

Sergeant York

Every man wants his life to mean something, but what is the worth of a man? How much worth does a man's soul have? Alvin C. York, a native of Pall Mall, Tennessee, was a man who considered such questions. Although he was one of the most highly decorated soldiers of World War I, being awarded the Congressional Medal of Honor, as well as other awards, he was a conscientious objector, that is, he objected to serving in war because he believed killing in combat was a sin.[213] However, in 1917, York was drafted into the US Army, completed basic training in February 1918, and was assigned to G Company, 328th Infantry Battalion of the 82nd Infantry

---

[211] This is a topic for discussion in chapter 7.

[212] Chapter four develops this axiom further.

[213] See the fifth mark for further discussion of this point.

Division.[214] As a Christian, York had difficulties reconciling his loyalties to his unit and his belief that killing in war was a sin. He had even requested to be dismissed from the service on religious grounds, but his request was denied.

As his unit's deployment approached, York's Company commander allowed him a ten-day leave to think things over. What made up York's mind was an inner peace that God gave him regarding combat. He had discussed the whole issue over with his commander, CPT Danforth, who was very considerate to take the time to work with York over his troubled conscience. Additionally, York's Battalion commander, Major George E. Buxton, also a devout Christian weighed in with Scriptural support for the just war theory. Ultimately, York recounts, it was during his sabbatical at home that God gave him peace regarding service in war. "If a man can make peace by fighting," York said, "he is a peacemaker."[215]

By the summer of 1918, York's unit, the 328th, had moved up to the trenches of the frontline. And on October 8, 1918, during an attack by his battalion to capture German positions on Hill 223, near Chatel-Chéhéry, York took part in actions for which he would receive the Medal of Honor. York recounts, "The Germans got us, and they got us right smart. They just stopped us dead in our tracks. Their machine guns were up there on the heights overlooking us and well hidden, and we couldn't tell for certain where the terrible heavy fire was coming from. And I'm telling you they were shooting straight. Our boys just went down like the long grass before the mowing machine at home. Our attack just faded out. And there we were, lying down, about halfway across [the valley] and those German machine guns and big shells getting us hard."

Realizing the forward platoons of the 328th were trapped, Captain Danforth ordered a patrol to be sent out to see if anything could be done to silence those guns. Under the command of Corporal Bernard Early, four non-commissioned

---

[214] The 82nd Infantry Division, known as the "All-American Division, because of its proud claim to have soldiers from every state, was later redesignated the 82nd Airborne Division.
[215] Perry, Sergeant York, 35.

officers, including the recently promoted Corporal York and thirteen men infiltrated behind the German lines in an effort to relieve their beleaguered battalion. The patrol worked their way through the woods behind the Germans and overran the headquarters of a German unit, capturing a large group of German soldiers who were preparing a counter-attack against the U.S. troops. They happened to be eating breakfast at the time. After a few warning shots the Germans surrendered, but as the American patrol formed their POWs into a line, German machine gun fire from an upper ridge erupted killing six men and wounding three others, including Corporal Early.

This placed York in command of seven able bodied men. As York's men flattened themselves to the earth and held the prisoners at bay, York moved to take out the guns. The very essence of his life was compressed into the next few minutes. He recounts, "Those machine guns were spitting fire and cutting down the undergrowth all around me something awful. And the Germans were yelling orders. You never heard such a racket in all of your life. I didn't have time to dodge behind a tree or dive into the brush. As soon as the machine guns opened fire on me, I began to exchange shots with them. There were over thirty of them in continuous action, and all I could do was touch the Germans off just as fast as I could."

York yelled at the gunners to stop firing and surrender, but they kept shooting. York notes that the event reminded him of turkey shoots he'd taken part in back home in Tennessee, however the German's heads were a lot bigger than turkeys'. "In order to sight me in," says York, "the Germans had to show their heads. Whenever a head popped up, I just touched it off."[216] As York eliminated one machine gunner after the other, the shooting became less intense. "I didn't want to kill any more than I had to. But it was they or I." When York ran out of rifle ammunition, he transitioned to his Colt .45 pistol.

John Perry writes,

Then a German lieutenant led a bayonet charge against York with six men. York saw them coming and quickly thought of another Pall Mall shooting lesson. Hunting ducks, York had learned that if he shot the lead bird in a formation first, the others would scatter. But if he

---

[216] Perry, Sergeant York, 50.

shot the birds back to front, the others would keep flying and give him clean targets. Even though the bayonet charge was already dangerously close, York fired at the last man in the line first...and dropping them all in rapid succession, the first one last and nearly within a bayonet length.[217]

German Lieutenant Vollmer, commander of the First Battalion, 120th Infantry, emptied his pistol trying to kill York while he was contending with the machine guns. Failing to injure York, and witnessing the elimination of his unit, offered in English to surrender the unit to York, who accepted.[218] By the end of the engagement, York and his seven men marched 132 German prisoners back to the American lines. Later, Army investigators found twenty-five died Germans and counted thirty-five machine guns that York had put out of action. French Marshal Foch told York, "What you did was the greatest thing accomplished by any private soldier of all the armies of Europe."

According to Hollywood, York was knocked off a mule by a bolt of lightning. But York explained it differently: That weren't the right-down facts of it. "You see," said York, "I had met Miss Gracie and she said that she wouldn't let me come a-courting until I'd quit my drinking, fighting, and card flipping. So you see I was struck down by the power of love and the Great God Almighty all together."

York's life demonstrates a selfless sense of duty and a working toward a goal in which one's own cares are irrespective. Who can match an inspired marksman who believes that God is with him? These were the actions of Sergeant Alvin C. York, a Christian and an American war hero.

For God and Country

There is no better way of rounding out this chapter, which has been spent in earnest desire of recovering American values of former years; values of love for God, country and truth. Values, which it seems, are now suffering politically

---

[217] Perry, Sergeant York, 51.
[218] Lee, Sergeant York: An American Hero, 46.

expedient deaths. There was once a brave young man with a promising future, who had every prospect for a happy and fulfilling life; a man born into a Christian home and raised to live out these values.

Twenty-one year old Nathan Hale, known for his strong Christian faith, was a captain in the Continental Army. He was the son of a Congregational church deacon from Coventry, Connecticut. Volunteering for a dangerous intelligence gathering mission, and dressed as a Dutch farmer, Hale infiltrated British occupied New York City in the fall of 1776. Taking notes in Latin, he went through the entire British encampment, estimating their numbers and sketching their fortifications, when he was caught just a mile from the safety of American lines.

Captain Hale immediately acknowledged his true identity; the notes were found in his boot. Jailed that night, he was told he would hang in the morning. Hale asked for a chaplain and a Bible: both requests were denied. On the next morning, Hale was allowed to write a few letters and as he prepared to die, he remained calm. At the scaffold, he spoke briefly, urging the spectators to be prepared to die at any moment. His last words before the rope swung him into eternity were, "I only regret that I have but one life to lose for my country."

Nathan Hale was one heck of a model American. He loved the Lord and his country, had a promising life ahead of him, and traded all his tomorrows for his countrymen's sake. Hale's sacrifice typifies the greatest sacrifice of all time: Jesus Christ's sacrifice of Himself for everyone who believes in Him (Jn 3:16). Jesus Christ, mankind's only Savior, told us, "Greater love hath no man than this, that a man lay down his life for his friends." Death is not the end, but only an entrance into glory.

> Riches I heed not, nor man's empty praise,
> Thou mine inheritance, now and always:
> Thou and Thou only, first in my heart,
> High King of heaven, my treasure Thou art.[219]

---

[219] Byrne, Be Thou My Vision.

Chapter 1: The God-Honoring American Man

Chapter 1 Recommended Further Reading

1. John Bunyan, *Pilgrims Progress.*
2. J. I. Packer, *Knowing God.*
3. Gary De Mar, *America's Christian History.*
4. David F. Wells, *God in the Wasteland.*
5. John Piper, *What Jesus Demands from the World.*

Chapter 1 Review Questions

1. What did the framers of the First Amendment intend?
2. Why is it important for us as God-honoring men to stand up for marriage as God intended it?
3. How can you work for your boss as if working for the Lord?
4. What if you are commanded to do something unethical? Against God's Word? What would you do?
5. What other examples can you find in Scripture that teach us about team work?
6. Is it wrong for Christians to serve in war? To kill in combat?
7. What is the Bible's definition of marriage? Does it offer us one?
8. What did Jesus teach us regarding marriage?
9. Is there a biblical warrant for the just war theory?
10. What are the ramifications for society if biblical marriage is abandoned?

"Most assuredly, I say to you, whoever commits sin is a slave of sin. 35 And a slave does not abide in the house forever, but a son abides forever. 36 Therefore if the Son makes you free, you shall be free indeed" (Jn 8:34-36).

Chapter 2: The Three Enemies of the Saint

Making use of the basic redemptive-historical framework of the Bible; creation, fall, redemption, and restoration, this chapter will discuss the three enemies of the God-honoring man. To be forewarned is forearmed. Thus an understanding and awareness constitute a formidable defense against these three modes of attack on a righteous man's life. Before we proceed to discuss these, let's look at the Book of Genesis to consider some essential truths together. The Bible is the history of God's dealings with mankind. It is, in essence, a history of salvation through judgment. And chapter three of Genesis reveals to us how mankind fell from the good estate in which God had originally placed them.

Creation

God created man and placed him in paradise. Mankind is made in God's image. Man was created flesh out of God's

128

Chapter 2: The Three Enemies of the Saint

created dust. God actualized this flesh by His creative breath, creating man's invisible component, his soul. Man's soul is a direct creation of God, and is not pre-existent.[1] When we say that man is the image of God, we intend this to mean that man as *imago Dei* extends to the whole of his person or humanness, that is, man is pneumatic and somatic. Man inhabits the invisible realm by virtue of his soul, and the physical realm by virtue of his body. Man was created spiritually, physically, and morally perfect, being endued with a mind, will and emotions.

The Baptist Faith and Message tells us, "Man is the special creation of God, made in His own image. He created them male and female as the crowning work of His creation.[2] The gift of gender is thus part of the goodness of God's creation."[3] As we discussed in chapter one, God created everything *ex nihilo* (Heb 11:3), that is, out of nothing, and ordained marriage by creating the woman to be man's companion (Gen 2:21). Man and woman were both created fully and equally in God's image.

God created man, placed him in paradise, and was concerned for our first parent's needs, and so caused to grow many fruit producing trees in the garden, including the tree of life and the tree of the knowledge of good and evil. The tree of life would impart immortality to those who ate of its fruit. Adam and Eve were given permission to eat of any tree in the garden (including the tree of life), but were forbidding to, on pain of death, to eat of the tree of the knowledge of good and evil.

In mankind's original state, man and woman were *posse non peccare*,[4] that is, man had the ability to sin and the ability

---

[1] Origen, the early church father, following Plato (*Timaeus*) taught the pre-existence of souls. This view was condemned at the Second Council of Constantinople in 553 AD.

[2] The Bible tells us that God formed Adam, which in Hebrew means "man," out of the dust of the earth, "and breathed into his nostrils the breath of life: and man became a living being" (Gen 2:7). Eve in Hebrew means "life" or "living." The theory of evolution, which states that mankind is evolved from apes, is therefore incompatible with the Word of God, and should be rejected by Christians.

[3] Baptist Faith and Message, Section III, Man.

[4] Possible to not sin.

not to sin. Adam and Eve had the possibility of not sinning in the Garden. As Augustine helps us to understand, mankind's original estate involved both the *posse mori* and the *posse non mori*.[5] That is, Adam and Eve were created in such a way that it was possible for them to die if they sinned, while they retained the possibility before them of living forever based on their perfect obedience.

Fall

"Now we come into a realm," writes Lloyd-Jones, "that no one can possibly understand. And the Bible does not give us ultimate explanations. What it does tell us is that there is a world besides this one, a world that is spiritual, of world of spirits. It tells us that God not only made man but that He made creatures called angels, who are not physical but spiritual beings, and that God endued them with great and notable and remarkable powers and uses them as His servants. God made these great, powerful angelic beings. But one of them, we are told, rebelled against God and persuaded others to follow him (Rev 12:7-9). He defied God and stood against Him, and God smote him and he fell. And the Bible tells us that this terrible, dread spiritual power, called Satan and the Devil, entered into this world, into God's perfect creation, and by tempting the man and woman whom God had made brought about to pass everything bad that you and I know."[6]

The serpent deceived our first parents, and the result is that mankind rebelled against God and broke His commandment, which we were free and able to obey, and have incurred God's curse and put ourselves under the dominion and control of the Devil. We are told in the Word of God how the fall of mankind occurred:

3 Now the serpent was more cunning than any beast of the field which the LORD God had made. And he said to the woman, "Has God indeed said, 'You shall not eat of every tree of the garden'?" 2 And the woman said to the serpent, "We may eat the fruit of the trees of the garden; 3 but of the fruit of the tree which *is* in the midst of the

---

[5] Possible to die and not possible to die.
[6] Lloyd-Jones, The Gospel in Genesis: From Fig Leaves to Faith, 18.

garden, God has said, 'You shall not eat it, nor shall you touch it, lest you die.'" [4] Then the serpent said to the woman, "You will not surely die. [5] For God knows that in the day you eat of it your eyes will be opened, and you will be like God, knowing good and evil" [6] So when the woman saw that the tree was good for food, and that it was a delight to the eyes, and that the tree was to be desired to make one wise, she took of its fruit and ate, and she also gave some to her husband who was with her, and he ate. [7] Then the eyes of both were opened, and they knew that they were naked. And they sewed fig leaves together and made themselves loincloths. [8] And they heard the sound of the Lord God walking in the garden in the cool of the day, and Adam and his wife hid themselves from the presence of the Lord God among the trees of the garden. (Gen 3:1-8).

Satan enters the paradise of God and seductively insinuates a doubt regarding the goodness of God. In these first words of Satan there is an impugning of the character of God. Satan says in effect, "Isn't it ridiculous that you should regard the eating of the tree of the knowledge of good and evil to be forbidden you?" Satan says in effect, "if you eat of that tree you'll be just like Him, and God wants no competitor. Because God is insecure and afraid because if you eat of this fruit you and Adam will become gods like He is and then He won't have control of everything – you'll be equal with Him."

In Bunyan's allegory *The Holy War*, Diabolus alluringly proposes the question: "But if there was danger, what a slavery is it to live always in fear of the greatest of punishments, for doing so small and trivial a thing as eating a little fruit!"[7] Having insinuating doubt regarding God's commandment, Satan now, brazenly moves from doubt to outright lie. John Calvin observes, "He now, therefore, does not ask doubtingly, as before, whether or not the command of God, which he opposes, be true, but openly accuses God of falsehood."[8]

Satan flat out lies to the woman, "You will not surely die. For God knows that in the day you eat of it your eyes will be opened, and you will be like God, knowing good and evil"

---

[7] Bunyan, The Holy War, 37.
[8] Calvin, Genesis, 150. Calvin adds, "Moreover, it is not without some show of reason the he (Satan) makes the Divine glory, or equality with God, to consist in the perfect knowledge of good and evil."

Chapter 2: The Three Enemies of the Saint

(Gen 3:4-5). The first doctrine that Satan denied in Scripture was that sin results in death. *Death is separation from God.* The demonic lie states that God is trying to keep you down, that is, from participating in His glory. The unholy desire to be like God in power and authority originated in angelic sin.[9] And Eve erred by not regulating the measure of her knowledge by the will of God.[10] And when the woman saw: (1) "that the tree was *good for food*, and (2) that it was a *delight to the eyes*, and (3) that the tree was to be *desired to make one wise*, she took of its fruit and ate, and she also gave some to her husband who was with her, and he ate"(Gen 3:6).

Having entertained a doubt about God's Word, she was ready to deny it outright. Satan caused Eve to question the spiritual authority she was under; first God and then her husband. When God created marriage, He gave Eve to be Adam's helper with Adam as the head of the household (1 Cor 11:3, 8). Gerhardus Vos tells us, "The tempter addresses himself to the woman, probably not because she is more open to temptation and prone to sin, for that is hardly the conception of the Old Testament elsewhere. The reason may have lain in this, that the woman had not personally received the prohibition from God, as Adam had."[11]

The point is she may have received God's word through Adam. And perhaps Satan appealed to Eve because she was not only under God's authority, but also under her husband's authority and, therefore, more inclined to think God was withholding something from her. So, it appears without any further discussion she takes the forbidden fruit and ate it, and she gave it also to her husband and he ate it. And what we may learn from this is the natural inclination of a woman, apart from Christ, is to distrust authority and to always chaff against it. And the significant failure of the man is that he abdicated leadership.

---

[9] Likewise we don't become angels. See Luke 20:27-40 where Jesus teaches that all believers will be equal to the angels, specifically in spirituality, purity and immortality.

[10] Calvin, Genesis, 151. Calvin adds, "The principle point of wisdom is a well-regulated sobriety in obedience to God."

[11] Vos, Biblical Theology, 45.

Chapter 2: The Three Enemies of the Saint

When we look at this Scripture we see that it was Eve who circumvented the spiritual authority she was under and it was Adam who failed in his God-given responsibility to lead and protect Eve, as the head of the household, and allowed her to be led away and then followed her in the eating of the forbidden fruit. These are the fundamental failures in mankind; men fail because they abdicate spiritual leadership and women fail because they have trouble with authority. This is the heart of our problems in America!

Men have ceased to take responsibility for leading in the home! The major problem we have in our country is not women who demand to be in charge, it's men who have abdicated responsibility to lead their families. John Piper writes, "What women rightly long for is spiritual and moral initiative from a man, not spiritual and moral domination."[12] The sooner we face these failures of ours as men and women, the sooner we will experience peace and blessings in our marriages and families and in our nation!

Notice when God calls us to answer for problems in the marriage and family, He speaks to the man. Gen 3:9-13 tells us,

9 Then the Lord God called to Adam and said to him, "Where are you?" 10 So he said, "I heard Your voice in the garden, and I was afraid because I was naked; and I hid myself." 11 And He said, "Who told you that you were naked? Have you eaten from the tree of which I commanded you that you should not eat?" 12 Then the man said, "The woman whom You gave to be with me, she gave me of the tree, and I ate." 13 And the Lord God said to the woman, "What is this you have done?" The woman said, "The serpent deceived me, and I ate."

It's interesting to observe that when this sin is referred to throughout Scripture, it is not referred to as the sin of Eve – but rather as the sin of Adam! When Adam and Eve sinned in the garden and God came to call them to account, it didn't matter that Eve had sinned first. God said, "Adam, where are you?" (Gen 3:9). When God calls to Adam, "Where are you?" He is not trying to learn Adam's whereabouts, God knows all

---

[12] Piper, This Momentary Marriage - A Parable of Permanence, 89.

things and questions us to bring conviction of sin and bring out our confession. And what does Adam say? "The woman whom You gave to be with me, she gave me of the tree, and I ate." In other words, it's ultimately Your fault and her fault. I didn't do anything!

Adam was not an innocent bystander. He defected from God's command, which he was free and able to obey. He failed to protect his wife. He failed to take responsibility by not assuming his God-given role as the spiritual leader of the family.[13] Men may want to blame God for everything that's wrong in the world but the reality is it's our fault. Men think first of their own comfort before they think of spiritual good. Outside of Christ, men would rather watch TV, play video games, and drink beer all day rather than go to church, pray with their families, teach their children God's Word, and set spiritual priorities for their families. And Men at their worst are spiritual cowards and will always delay a decision as long as possible if it's controversial, and especially if their wives are upset.

The sad truth is that men will fistfight over nothing, but they will not get on their knees to fight for the souls of their family. Sadly, there are always fewer men in church than there are women. And by and large, men always care more about success and pretty women than about the Kingdom of God. This is the great failure of men! The sooner we face these truths about ourselves, and bring these realities to the feet of Jesus Christ, the better our marriages, our families, and our nation will be.

Then God disciplines or curses all of the parties involved in this fall: Satan, the woman, and the man. Gen 3:14-19 tells us,

14 So the Lord God said to the serpent: "Because you have done this, you are cursed more than all cattle, and more than every beast of the field; on your belly you shall go, and you shall eat dust all the days of your life. 15 And I will put enmity between you and the woman, and between your seed and her Seed; He shall bruise your head, and you shall bruise His heel." 16 To the woman He said: "I will greatly multiply your sorrow and your conception; in pain you shall bring forth children; your desire shall be for your husband, and he shall rule

---

[13] See chapter 5.

134

Chapter 2: The Three Enemies of the Saint

over you." 17 Then to Adam He said, "Because you have heeded the voice of your wife, and have eaten from the tree of which I commanded you, saying, 'You shall not eat of it': "Cursed is the ground for your sake; in toil you shall eat of it all the days of your life. 18 Both thorns and thistles it shall bring forth for you, and you shall eat the herb of the field. 19 In the sweat of your face you shall eat bread till you return to the ground, for out of it you were taken; for dust you are, and to dust you shall return."

God gives a judgment that is equal with the offense. But notice that God never asks Satan a question. He never asks why have you done this? That is because God knows that Satan would have said, "It's because I hate you so much, and I want to ruin your creation." God therefore judges Satan by way of the serpent, with the harshest condemnation of all. And God says that there will come from the woman One who will destroy everything that you are.

Then God turns to the woman and says here is your discipline (curse): "I will greatly multiply your sorrow and your conception; in pain you shall bring forth children; your desire shall be for your husband, and he shall rule over you" (Gen 3:16). With this pronouncement Eve and her daughters would experience increased pain bearing children.

There evidently would have been some pain in the process of bearing children before the Fall, but now womankind would experience increased pain. And women will *desire to control* their men (Gen 3:16). We know this is the proper meaning of this verse because of Gen 4:6-7 which says, "So the Lord said to Cain, "Why are you angry? And why has your countenance fallen? If you do well, will you not be accepted? And if you do not do well, sin lies at the door. And its *desire* is for you, but you should rule over it." Sin desires to master Cain, and Eve desires to master or dominate Adam.

"Your desire shall be for your husband, and he shall *rule* over you" (Gen 3:16). This is not a loving rule, for without Christ it is a domineering, harsh rule. Without the power of Christ a husband will only selfishly seek to dominate his wife instead of sacrificially loving her. Derek Kidner writes, "The words 'your desire shall be for your husband, and he shall rule over you,' portrays a marriage relation in which control has slipped from the fully personal realm to that of instinctive

135

urges passive and active."[14] So we might say to love and to cherish becomes to desire and dominate.

Headship and submission are not introduced in Genesis chapter three but are introduced back in chapter two. The wife was created for the husband.[15] Eve was created by God to be Adam's helper. God completed Adam by creating a wife out of him to be his companion. This is also what 1 Cor 11:3 tells us: "But I want you to know that the head of every man is Christ, the head of woman is man, and the head of Christ is God." Also 1 Cor 11:8 tells us "For man is not from woman, but woman from man. Nor was man created for the woman, but woman for the man." It was only after the Fall that the husband no longer leads easily; he must contend for his headship.

Sin has corrupted both the willing submission of the wife and the loving headship of the husband. The woman's desire without Christ is to control her husband, her divinely appointed leader in the marriage. And so "the rule of love founded in paradise is replaced by struggle, tyranny, domination, and manipulation."[16]

Then God turns to the man and says in effect, as the result of your disobedience, creation will suffer a curse and began to deteriorate. In Genesis chapter two Adam received the privilege of enjoying the garden, but this did not require strenuous labor. Now God tells Adam that he will have to toil hard to obtain a living from the ground. And that he will die rather than live forever experiencing physical immortality.

God says that because of the fall, mankind's natural inclination will be to worry excessively over where their next meal would come from. Without Christ, this will always be the plight of man. Again, God's punishments are commiserate. Gerhard von Rad observes, "The woman's punishment struck at the deepest root of her being as wife and mother. The man's strikes at the innermost nerve of his life; his work, his activity, and provision for sustenance."[17] And Allen Ross shows,

---

[14] Kidner, Genesis, 71.
[15] See the Third Mark for marriage (pages 47-64) and Chapter Five for the concepts of headship and submission (page 228).
[16] Westminster Theological Journal 37:3 (Spring 1975), 376-383.
[17] Von Rad, 94.

Chapter 2: The Three Enemies of the Saint

"These punishments represent retaliatory justice. Adam and Eve sinned by eating; they would suffer in order to eat. She manipulated her husband; she would be mastered by her husband."[18] And the serpent destroyed the man and woman; he will be destroyed by one who would come from the woman.

Adam, having indulged his lust, not being content with his present condition, despised God's command, became enslaved to the Devil, was justly condemned to die (Rom 5:12-21), and thrust out of paradise. Genesis 3:20-24 tells us,

20 And Adam called his wife's name Eve, because she was the mother of all living. 21 Also for Adam and his wife the Lord God made tunics of skin, and clothed them. 22 Then the Lord God said, "Behold, the man has become like one of Us, to know good and evil. And now, lest he put out his hand and take also of the tree of life, and eat, and live forever"— 23 therefore the Lord God sent him out of the garden of Eden to till the ground from which he was taken. 24 So He drove out the man; and He placed cherubim at the east of the garden of Eden, and a flaming sword which turned every way, to guard the way to the tree of life.

When Adam sinned, God passed the sentence of death on him and his posterity, that is, all of us (Rom 5:12). This is the doctrine the church calls original sin.[19] Regarding this doctrine C. S. Lewis writes,

The doctrine of original sin points to a sin against God, an act of disobedience, not a sin against the neighbor. This sin has been described by Augustine as the result of pride, of the movement whereby a creature, that is, an essentially dependent being whose principle of existence lies not in itself but in another, tries to set up on its own, to exist for itself. Such a sin requires no complex social conditions, not extended experience, and not great intellectual development. From the moment a creature becomes aware of God as God and of itself as self, the terrible alternative of choosing God or self for the center is open to it.[20]

---

[18] Ross, Genesis, 33.

[19] The Westminster Shorter Catechism Question 16 asks us: Did all mankind fall in Adam's first transgression? Answer: The covenant being made with Adam, not only for himself, but for his posterity; all mankind, descending from him by ordinary generation, sinned in him, and fell with him, in his first transgression.

[20] Lewis, The Problem of Pain, 70.

Chapter 2: The Three Enemies of the Saint

Adam, representing all mankind, has by his disobedience, brought the curse of death and condemnation on us all. Adam's sin and guilt have been imputed to all mankind, who remain under the curse of death and condemnation unless God in His grace saves them (Jn 3:36). This doctrine of the church, called original sin, is very unpopular. In fact, it has never been popular, because who wants to say we're sinners? This is what led Bertrand Russell to write, "When you hear people in church, debasing themselves and saying that they are miserable sinners, and all the rest of it, it seems contemptible and not worthy of self-respecting human beings."[21] But that is precisely what God demands (Jer 3:13; Acts 2:21; Rom 10:9-10, 13).

Redemption

After our first parents sinned, their "eyes were opened" (Gen 3:7); they saw they had been deceived by the serpent. A sinking horror like a thunder clap now fell on them. They saw their privileges vanish: communion with God, dominion over the creatures, and the purity and holiness of their nature gone in one instantaneous ruinous defection from God's command. God had said, concerning the tree of the knowledge of good and evil, "the day you eat of it you shall surely die" (Gen 2:17). Doubt opened the door to ambition, and ambition turned to pride, emboldening our first parents to cast aside the fear of God. Pride, the beginning of sin, is the movement whereby a creature tries to set up on its own to exist for itself.[22]

Adam's first sin was in effect, an attempt to have truth apart from subjection to the word of God. G. I. Williamson writes, by accepting what God had said about the tree of the knowledge of good and evil, without question, Adam could gain true understanding of its meaning and purpose. As soon as Adam sought to know, make an interpretation, apart from subjection to God's word, he was lost and completely in error. Now, what a miserable position had they found themselves to

---

[21] Russell, Why I am not a Christian: and Other Essays on Religion and Related Subjects, 23.
[22] Augustine, City of God, Book XIV, 460.

138

be in; exposed to the wrath of God and the curse of the law, and eternal death, along with their posterity.

But God, who is gracious and abundant in mercy, would not let the history of mankind end then and there. God summons the man and woman, hears their excuses, and decreed salvation through judgment (Gen 3:15); passing sentences on the serpent, the woman, and the man (Gen 3:14-19). In this very pronouncement of death and misery God proclaims the *protoevangelium*, first gospel in the Bible. Gen 3:15 tells us,

"And I will put enmity between you and the woman, and between your seed and her Seed; He shall bruise your head, and you shall bruise His heel."

The whole bible is the working out of this prophecy; justification is antithetical to condemnation. Condemnation is both the declaration of God, and the process of His judgment. And here in verse fifteen is a marvelous ray of light shining through all of this judgment. God said He would raise up a Seed to the woman, from the matrix of Israel (Rev 12:5), who would fight this foul tyrant who had made men and women his slaves (Eph 2:1-3; Col 1:13-14). Regarding this salvation through judgment John Hamilton writes,

The justice of God is put on display as He judges the serpent. The mercy of God is demonstrated as He announces – from no compulsion or constraint – a future salvation that humanity has neither merited not requested. God freely declares that the seed of the woman will crush the head of the seed of the serpent, and in this salvation that comes through judgment...Adam and Eve are responsible for their actions. They are guilty. They deserve death. God does not owe them mercy, and they have only sought to avoid justice by shifting blame (Gen 3:10-13)...This mercy, then, arises only from God. This is not something humans deserve, not even in part. Of His own goodness, displaying His own intrinsic character, God announces that the woman will have seed – which means that the promised punishment of death will not be immediately enacted on the physical bodies of the human couple. Not only will their physical lives continue, but they will have seed: offspring. Not only will they have seed, but their seed will triumph over the snake. Salvation comes through judgment, and God makes known His character in justice and mercy. His justice is as exacting as His mercy is surprising.[23]

Jesus Christ is the Seed of the woman, who in the "fullness of time" would fatally bruise the head of the serpent (Gal 4:4; Rev 12:5). God had to send His Son or mankind would be dead, defiled, and damned forever (Jn 3:16, 34-36). Thousands of years after this prophecy, the Son of God would invade the Devil's territory (Mt 12:28-29). This is the prophecy that the serpent would bite Him on the heel and inject his venom into Him and kill Him for three days but when Christ rises up He will crush the head of the serpent. This is as the apostle John says, "For this purpose the Son of God was manifested, that He might destroy the works of the devil" (1 Jn 3:8).

Cosmic D-Day

One of the best analogies of this is the one which pictures the Allied invasion of Normandy on June 6, 1944, also known as D-Day. It was the largest amphibious invasion in history. And on that day, Hitler's Wehrmacht was delivered a deathblow. But it came at a high price in blood; some 10,000 Allied lives. The invasion drove the Third Reich into a panicked retreat back across the Rhine. And although it took some very hard months of fighting on the part of the Allies to see the victory, for all intents and purposes the enemy's back had been broken at that pinnacle battle on the shores of Normandy.

So if the analogy holds (eastern front excluded), the Bible likens Satan to a despot who has conquered the whole world, holding mankind hostage as slaves to do his bidding. But the Son of God invades the strong man's occupied territory, and plunders his house (Mt 12:29), setting the captives free (Lk 4:18-19). So we may understand, whereas Christ's first coming was like D-Day, in that it was the decisive battle of the war, guaranteeing the enemy's final defeat, His second coming will be like VE-Day (Victory Europe Day), when the vanquished foe will finally lay down his arms and surrender.

---

[23] Hamilton, God's Glory in Salvation Through Judgment: A Biblical Theology, 78.

Chapter 2: The Three Enemies of the Saint

In these verses there is also an illusion to Christ's blood atonement (Gen 3:21). Adam and Eve had just told God that they were ashamed because they were naked (Gen 3:10). And rightfully so, for before they had sinned they were covered with an innocence. But now their glorious covering was removed. So God kills an animal. He makes a blood sacrifice and takes the animal's skin and covers their shame. This all points to the Lamb of God who would once for all take away the sins of the world at Calvary. His blood washes away our sins and His righteousness covers our guilt and shame.

God drove out the first family from Eden. And said lest we should eat of the tree of life and remain forever in the state of separation, He barred re-entry with a flaming sword (Gen 3:24). Only in Christ may we re-enter paradise.

Restoration

The gospel is God's restoration program for mankind, who are fallen in Adam's physical and spiritual death, but by grace through faith are raised in Christ's resurrection, first spiritually, then physically (Jn 5:25-29; 1 Pet 1:3; 2 Pet 3:10). Jesus Christ's sinless life and atoning death is an act of God in human nature fulfilling the covenant from the side of God as God and from the side of man as man. When a man is born again, he receives a renewed mind, will, and emotions. Conversion is the word we use to describe this action of God.

God's justification of a sinner is based upon the obedience and righteousness of Christ alone which He accounts to the believing sinner as his own. Whereas, in Adam all die because they receive his imputed sin, in Christ, all live, by grace through faith, and receive His imputed righteousness (Rom 4).[24] This righteousness of Christ, the believing sinner receives, and is accounted "just" or "righteous," in the sight of God. This is, as Luther put it, the article of a standing or falling church. Augustine writes, "Since in the first man, the whole human race fell under condemnation, those vessels which are made of it unto honor are not vessels of self-

---

[24] Romans 4 declares sinners justified before God on the basis of the imputed righteousness of Christ, and uses the word we translate "accounted" no less than 11 times.

Chapter 2: The Three Enemies of the Saint

righteousness, but divine mercy. When other vessels are made unto dishonor, it must be imputed not to injustice, but to judgment."[25]

God is Love incarnate. His solution to our predicament, is one in which He decrees to save by One whom He will raise up to David, the Lord our righteousness, Jesus Christ (Jer 23:5-6). *Justification is therefore, a legal, forensic declaration of God, and is used in Scripture to denote the acceptance of believers as righteous in the sight of God on account of the perfect finished work of God's Son, Jesus Christ.* The reformer John Calvin rightly called justification the principal hinge by which religion is supported, the soil out of which the Christian life develops, and the substance of piety. The righteousness of God is *God's incarnate obedience*, an act of God in human nature fulfilling the covenant from man's side.[26]

So any view which states that our faith is counted as righteousness is a misunderstanding of the whole council of God. For example, the apostle James demonstrates in James chapter two how believers are justified before observing men to be Christians, by saying that "a man is justified by works, and not by faith only" (Jam 2:24). But certainly this is not to be understood of one being justified in the sense as made in right standing with God, for this would contradict the apostle Paul, as well as the rest of Scripture, who states in no uncertain terms, that such righteousness is theoretically possible, though practically impossible (Rom 2:17-24). James' use of justified in verse 24 seems to go along with the "show

---

[25] Augustine, Epistle 106, *De Praedestinationae et Gratia*, as quoted in Institutes of the Christian Religion, III.23.11, 632.

[26] Conversely to this entire line of thought, the New Perspective on Paul (NPP) presents us with a revision of the historic Protestant understanding of justification by positing that justification is not an act but the sign that one is in the covenant. In other words, if one does good works he shows himself to be justified. The NPP scholars seek to support this idea by claiming that first century Judaism wasn't a works righteousness religion, but a law-keeping salvation religion, however, Second Temple Judaism did seek a righteousness by works (Luke 18:9-14). Some NPP adherents downplay the importance of the doctrine of original sin which is touching the very heart of the imputed righteousness issue. For a full refutation of the NPP see Carson, *Justification and Variegated Nomism: The Complexities of Second Temple Judaism*; Duncan, *Misunderstanding Paul: Responding To The New Perspectives*; Piper, *The Future of Justification: A Response to N. T. Wright*.

me", of verse 18. It seems James in chapter two is merely saying Abraham's works of faith demonstrated, among men, his justifying faith in God. John Gill writes, Abraham, in offering up his son, was a clear proof of the truth of his faith, there commended: by this it was made known what a strong faith he had in God, and what reason there was to believe that he was a justified person.[27]

The biblical point being made here is justification is the Father's legal decree, based on the Son's accomplished righteousness, as it is applied by the life-living Spirit. Our sins were the judicial ground of the sufferings of Christ, so that they were a satisfaction of justice; and his righteousness is the judicial ground of our acceptance with God, so that our pardon is an act of justice.[28]

God is Love incarnate, His solution to our predicament is Jesus Christ, the Lamb of God (Jn 1:29). God imputes righteousness to us and sees us in Christ. As Doug Kelly states, "The doctrine of justification by faith, is the article of a standing or falling church."[29] Justification constitutes the only escape from the wrath of God (Jn 3:36). Sinners escape the coming wrath of God by being accounted righteous by virtue of Christ's all-sufficient righteousness imputed to them (1 Thess 1:10). Thus, the righteousness of God is God's incarnate obedience.

Jesus uses a parable, the Pharisee and the tax collector, to demonstrate the impiety of self-righteousness in Luke 18:9-14. Jesus tells us, "Two men went up to the temple to pray, one a Pharisee and the other a tax collector" (Lk 18:11). The proud Pharisee's prayer, more of a pompous declaration, appealed to his own perceived self-righteousness by asserting, "God, I thank You that I am not like other men." The self-righteous Pharisee no doubt had the tax collector in mind, and "informs" God of his "righteous deeds," whereas the tax collector, painfully aware of his own unworthiness, bet his chest and cried "God, be merciful to me a sinner!" and appealed to God's sense of grace.

---

[27] Gill, Exposition of the Whole Bible, James 2:24.
[28] Hodge, An Exposition of the Second Letter to the Corinthians, 150.
[29] Kelly, The True Church, 11.

Chapter 2: The Three Enemies of the Saint

Jesus tells us that it was the tax collector, not the Pharisee, "who went down to his house justified" (Lk 18:14). Man will be vindicated, accounted "righteous" and justified solely on the grounds of his identification with Christ and His righteous. Any self-righteous is viewed as detestable in God's sight. Jesus told the Pharisees, "You are those who justify yourselves before men, but God knows your hearts. For what is highly esteemed among men is an abomination in the sight of God" (Lk 16:15).

Legalism is depending on one's own efforts toward righteousness rather than the righteousness that God accounts to us in Jesus Christ. The natural man desires to make himself acceptable before God by his fulfilling of the requirements of the law. The Bible tells us that this is an impossibility (Is 64:6; Rom 3:20; Gal 2:16; 3:11), however, God gives us the good news of the gospel that while we were yet sinners Christ died for us, so that whoever believes in Him might become the righteousness of God (Rom 5:8; 2 Cor 5:21).

John Wesley, the great evangelist and co-founder of the Methodist movement, before his 'Aldersgate experience' was a mere moralist.[30] He had been ordained as a minister in the Church of England but lacked saving faith. His religion consisted in earnestly striving to keep the commandments; it was void of the assurance of salvation that comes from relying on Christ's righteousness and not our own.[31] Then one evening at a prayer meeting on Aldersgate Street in London, while Wesley heard Luther's Preface to Romans being read, he recounts, "I felt strangely warmed, and I felt I did trust in Christ, Christ alone for salvation, and an assurance was given to me that He had taken away my sins, even mine, and saved me from the law of sin and death."[32] After his conversion Wesley's indefatigable evangelistic work began; work for which the world will never be the same.

---

[30] John Wesley (1703-1791) was an evangelist and theologian of the Church of England, who, along with George Whitefield, was instrumental in the First Great Awakening.

[31] Bloesch, Faith and It's Counterfeits, 107.

[32] Outler, John Wesley, 66.

Chapter 2: The Three Enemies of the Saint

No Condemnation in Christ

As Christians, we may look at the fall of man in light of Romans 8:1, which tells us "there is therefore now no condemnation for those who are in Christ Jesus." We were under a sentence of wrath, but in Christ, we have passed from death to life. And although as believers we are no longer under condemnation, will struggle with our sin nature until we pass into glory (Rom 7:13-25; Col 3:4).[33] We, as Christians understand that the old action of Adam is still being repeated today; there is none righteous (Rom 3:10). C. S. Lewis writes,

From the moment a creature becomes aware of God as God and of itself as self, the terrible alternative of choosing God or self for the center is open to it. This sin is committed daily by young children, ignorant peasants as well as by sophisticated persons, by solitaries no less than by those who live in society. It is the fall of every individual life, and in each day of each individual life, the basic sin behind all particular sins: at this very moment you and I are either committing, or about to commit it, or are repenting of it.[34]

The whole aim of the Bible is to bring mankind into submission to God. Whereas in justification all our sins are pardoned, in sanctification, God's ongoing program of restoration, our indwelling sin nature is subdued (Rom 8:12-17; 1 Cor 9:27).[35]

The Three Enemies of the Saint

Looking back now at Gen 3:6, the three ways by which our first parents were tempted, constitute the three enemies of the saint, or modes in which mankind is tempted and led into sin. These modes have a striking similarity with two other Scriptures: Matthew 4:1-11 and 1 John 2:15-17. Let's look at the similarity with 1 Jn 2:15-17 first, which says:

---

[33] See chapter 3.

[34] Lewis, The Problem of Pain, 70.

[35] See chapter 3 for the further development of this doctrine we call mortification of sin.

Chapter 2: The Three Enemies of the Saint

[15] Do not love the world or the things in the world. If anyone loves the world, the love of the Father is not in him. [16] For all that is in the world—the desires of the flesh and the desires of the eyes and pride of life—is not from the Father but is from the world. [17] And the world is passing away along with its desires, but whoever does the will of God abides forever.

The apostle John reminds us of the teaching of Jesus, we cannot love God and mammon (Mt 7:24).[36] We cannot have divided loyalties. John says in verse 16, everything *in* the world comes not from the Father but from the world. That which does not come from God is from the devil. Let's look at the three modes of temptation of 1 Jn 2:16 and correlate them with mankind's first temptation in Gen 3:6.

The first pitfall or mode of temptation, *the desires of the flesh* (1 Jn 2:16), corresponds to the first manner in which Eve was tempted, that is, she saw that the tree *was good for food*. The second mode, *the desires of the eyes*, corresponds to how the tree was a *delight to the eyes*. And lastly, *the pride of life*, the third mode of temptation, could correspond to the perception that the tree was to be *desired to make one wise*. The Hebrew word in Gen 3:6 for "wise," *lehaskil*, equates to a practical wisdom, a sagacious foresight, which would regulate one's actions, so as to be self-sufficient and free from anxiety.

The apostle John tells us, the desires of the flesh and the desires of the eyes and pride of life are from the world. These are the three enemies of the saint:

1. The lust of the flesh – *desires of the flesh* – filling one's immediate appetite (physical hunger, thirst, or sexual desire).
2. The lures of the world – *delight to the eyes* – keeping in step with the world (mere possessions).
3. The lies of Satan – *pride of life* – presumption to raise above one's station (physically, mentally, or vocationally).

The universal effects of our first parent's sin: penalty of death, ruin of mankind, and all creation, along with the accompanying shame and guilt, has tainted all aspects of man's life. The Bible portrays unregenerate (unconverted,

---

[36] Mammon is an Aramaic word meaning riches, material gain.

unsaved) man as spiritually dead. The Geneva Confession helps us to understand this truth. It says man by nature is "blind, darkened in understanding, and full of corruption and perversity of heart, so that of himself he has no power to be able to comprehend the true knowledge of God as is proper, nor to apply himself to good works. But on the contrary, if he is left by God to what he is by nature, he is only able to live in ignorance and to be abandoned to all iniquity." Further the Confession adds, "hence he has need to be illumined by God, so that he can come to the right knowledge of his salvation, and thus to be redirected in his affections and reformed to the obedience of the righteousness of God."[37]

Jesus once challenged a would-be disciple who was adamant on burying his father before following Him with the words, "Follow me, and let the dead bury their own dead" (Mt 8:22). Fallen man is completely corrupt in nature, and is *non posse non peccare*.[38] Meaning that he has lost the ability to not sin; born with a nature enslaved to sin. Apart from the saving work of Christ, mankind is defiled in conscience, self-absorbed, self-centered, and self-soothing; infected with the prideful sickness of egoism and a desire to be the center of the cosmos, to be his own god.

Now, in Christ, the believer is removed from the dominion of sin, and although he remains imperfect in this life, through the leading of the Holy Spirit, he grows in grace, being assisted by God's grace in the mortification of sin. Believers in Christ are, as Luther put it, *simil iustus et peccator* – at the same time justified and a sinner. Believers are *posse non peccare*, that is, it is possible for them to not sin, however we will, and when we do we have an Advocate in heaven who intercedes for us (1 Jn 2:1). For the apostle John tells us in 1 Jn 1:8-10, "If we say that we have no sin, we deceive ourselves, and the truth is not in us. If we confess our sins, He is faithful and just to forgive us our sins and to cleanse us from all unrighteousness. If we say that we have not sinned, we make Him a liar, and His word is not in us."

---

[37] The Geneva Confession of 1536, IV. Natural Man.
[38] Not possible to not sin.

Chapter 2: The Three Enemies of the Saint

Satan desires to bring all mankind under his own condemnation by tempting them to share in his rebellious apostasy. Not only did Adam neglect to punish the serpent, but he, along with his wife, subjected himself to it and become participators in the same apostasy. So when we sin, we are freely giving our ears to the lusts of our flesh, the lures of the world (remember Mr. Worldly Wiseman), and the lies of Satan.

As Christians, if we allow ourselves to be enticed by sin and be deceived to be lured away from God's commandments, we are in a dangerous position. There are many people in the church who are simply fooling themselves that they are really saved; they lack any fruit of conversion. When Christians sin, and they most certainly do, they may bring temporal judgments upon themselves, as God, seeking to bring them back to a repentant and watchful attitude against any future occasions of sins; disciplines them (1 Cor 11:32; Heb 12:7-11). God's fatherly discipline of His saints may take various forms. Believers may have their prayers hindered (1 Pet 3:7); be deprived of the joys of salvation (Ps 51:8; Rev 2:4).[39]

What is important to note in all of this is in justification, God pardons all our sins; all that we have done, are doing, and will do – forever, and in sanctification, sin is subdued. Sanctification is the work of God in the life of the saint. It is a life-long refining process. Sanctification, from the Greek hagiosmos ἁγιασμός, is God's process of making his saints like His Son Jesus. It is the process of being made holy and separate. It is an exfoliating but joyfully humbling experience, with spiritual highs and lows. Sanctification is the daily putting on of the new man in Christ and dying to ourselves (2 Cor 5:17; Eph 4:20-24; Col 3:8-11). It is a walk of faith (2 Cor 5:7), relying on the grace of God to strengthen us in our weaknesses.

When we fall, we get back up by the grace of God and learn from our failures. There is a deep desire within our spirit to become like Christ, and we engage daily in a battle against our three foes: *our flesh, the world, and Satan.* This we do through

---

[39] Westminster Confession of Faith, Chapter 17, Assurance of Grace and Salvation, 75 (Free Presbyterian Publications).

prayer, fellowship, worship, and studying His word. When we surrender our minds, wills, and emotions to Christ, we find ourselves able, through the indwelling Holy Spirit, to obey God's commandments and live lives worthy of our high calling. All this is solely because of Christ victory over Satan's devises; "if the Son has set you free, you are free indeed" (Jn 8:36)!

In Mark's gospel (Mk 1:12-13), Jesus, God's obedient Son, is driven (Greek *exballo* ἐκβάλλω) into the wilderness by the Spirit to be tempted by Satan for forty days. Longman tells us, "Old Testament imagery typology is alive here, recalling Israel in the desert." Jesus prevailed over temptation where Israel failed. And Longman adds, "Israel too was driven out of Egypt into the desert (note *ekballo* in the LXX Ex 12:33, 39), where she spent forty years and was tested (Ex 15:25; 16:4; Dt 4:34; 8:2) before marching into the land and driving out its occupants."[40]

In the wilderness Jesus fasted for forty days, just as Moses did, when he was about to deliver the law to the Israelites. Now before Jesus was to publish the gospel of grace, and bear witness to the truth, He was tempted by Satan.[41] Matthew's gospel tells us,

4 Then Jesus was led up by the Spirit into the wilderness to be tempted by the devil. 2 And when He had fasted forty days and forty nights, afterward He was hungry. 3 Now when the tempter came to Him, he said, "If You are the Son of God, command that these stones become bread." 4 But He answered and said, "It is written, 'Man shall not live by bread alone, but by every word that proceeds from the mouth of God.'" 5 Then the devil took Him up into the holy city, set Him on the pinnacle of the temple, 6 and said to Him, "If You are the Son of God, throw Yourself down. For it is written: 'He shall give His angels charge over you,' and, 'In their hands they shall bear you up, Lest you dash your foot against a stone.'" 7 Jesus said to him, "It is written again, 'You shall not tempt the Lord your God.'" 8 Again, the devil took Him up on an exceedingly high mountain, and showed Him all the kingdoms of the world and their glory. 9 And he said to Him, "All these things I will give You if You will fall down and

---

[40] Longman, God is a Warrior, 95.
[41] Satan in Hebrew שָׂטָן saw-tawn means adversary, or accuser. Satan is both the tempter and the accuser.

worship me." 10 Then Jesus said to him, "Away with you, Satan! For it is written, 'You shall worship the Lord your God, and Him only you shall serve.'" 11 Then the devil left Him, and behold, angels came and ministered to Him (Mt 4:1-11).

Jesus, faced with similar temptations as our first parents, and Israel in the wilderness wanderings, is obedient to God in every way in which we rebelled. Satan repeatedly tempts Jesus in His capacity as Son of God. First, touching on *provision*, in His hunger He is tempted to turn stone into bread; second, regarding *protection*, he is tempted to trust in the miraculous deliverance by angels; and third, regarding *position*, He is tempted to worship Satan in exchange for world sovereignty. These three modes of satanic temptation bear remarkable similarities with those used against our first parents. Longman writes, "Jesus answers with the words from Deuteronomy (Dt 8:3; 6:13, 16) and so proves Himself the faithful Son who has been called and tested, and who will be rewarded."[42]

What is Freedom?

In one of the most insightfully brilliant pieces of literature ever written, Fyodor Dostoyevsky drawing on this portion of Scripture (Jesus' refusal of Satan's three temptations), demonstrates a further meaning behind the encounter. In Dostoyevsky's *The Brothers Karamazov*, the self-avowed atheist Ivan Karamazov puts forth a story, the Grand Inquisitor, to his younger brother Alyosha, who is training to be a Christian priest. Ivan recounts to Alyosha a prose poem he has written, which is set in medieval Seville, Spain, during the most terrible time of the Inquisition.

In the poem, a funeral procession takes place outside Seville's cathedral when suddenly Christ appears and is recognized at once. The procession stops at precisely the same place where a hundred heretics were burnt the day prior by the Grand Inquisitor. There are cries of joy from the crowd as Jesus raises a little girl from the dead. At that moment, the Grand Inquisitor passes by the cathedral and grasps what is happening. His face darkens. Such is his power and the fear he

---

[42] Longman, God is a Warrior, 96.

inspires that the crowd suddenly falls silent and parts for him. He orders Jesus to be arrested and thrown into prison.

Later, the Grand Inquisitor enters the cell and silently watches Jesus from the doorway for quite a long time. Then the cardinal says, "Tomorrow, I shall condemn thee at the stake as the worst of heretics. And the people who today kissed Thy feet tomorrow at the faintest sign from me will rush to heap up the embers of Thy fire. Knowest Thou that? Yes, maybe Thou knowest it." He adds, "Why, then, art Thou come to hinder us?" Jesus says nothing.[43] Of all the questions the Grand Inquisitor puts forth to Jesus, the one regarding Christ's temptation in the wilderness is most fascinating. The Grand Inquisitor asks Jesus, "Why did you offer mankind freedom?" For the Grand Inquisitor, what Jesus brought into the world was freedom, specifically the freedom of faith: the truth that sets mankind free (Jn 8:31).

The Grand Inquisitor categorizes Satan's temptations of Jesus as *miracle, mystery and authority*. Recounting the temptations to Jesus he says, "Remember the first question?" If you are, as you say, the Son of God, then turn these stones into loaves of bread (Mt 4:3). Do this, not so much to feed yourself, starved as you are, but in order to feed those that might follow You. Turn these stones into loaves and people will follow you like sheep forever. Perform this *miracle* and people will happily become your slaves (Jn 6:26-27). Next the dread spirit brought You up to the roof of the temple in Jerusalem and invited You to throw Yourself down. For, he said, if You are the Son of God, then the armies of angels at Your command will save You from smashing Your feet against the rocks below.

Such an ostentatious display performed before the fickle crowd would appear to all to be an awesome *mystery* that would incite immediate devotion (Jn 6:15). Finally, the dread spirit takes You to an exceedingly high mountain and shows You all the kingdoms of the inhabited earth. He says to You, "To thee I will give *authority* and the glory of them, for such is my power and in my power to give. If You will but worship

---

[43] Dostoyevsky, The Brothers Karamazov, 277.

me, then I will give all the power and the glory to You. So as to unite all in one unanimous and harmonious ant-heap."[44]

Jesus refuses miracle, mystery and authority, as Satan would have it, and offers the world something radical, the freedom of conscience (Jn 8:31-36). What was it that the crowds desired after they had seen Jesus turn three loaves and two fish into a feast for over 5,000 people? Wasn't it Christ's power to feed them, so they reasoned, at whim (Jn 6:26-27)? Wasn't that among the reasons why they sought to take and make Him king by force (Jn 6:15)? And wasn't it the Pharisees, who forever seeking a sign, tempted Jesus while He was on the cross with the words, "Let the Christ, the King of Israel, descend now from the cross, that we may see and believe" (Mk 15:32).

Jesus came to offer us not mere worldly bread, or mere worldly peace, and He came not to unite all men together in the ways of the world, but Jesus offers us true freedom – peace with God and a purified conscience. Through Him we may experience guilt-free saving faith. Jesus, tempted to eat of the forbidden fruit, obeyed where we failed. He rejected the bread that merely fills one's immediate appetite, bidding us not to seek after a sign but only believe (Mt 8:12). And instead of the bread that perishes, Jesus offers us the bread of eternal life, God's Word, Himself the incarnation of it (Jn 6:53-68). For after all, what is freedom worth if it is bought with bread? He rejected a fading glory that capricious men could shower Him with, resolving rather for God to providentially direct and protect Him, preferring to see God glorified in the salvation of sinners which He came to die for by making Himself of no account (Phil 2:5-11).

Lastly, He rejected the prideful satanic temptation to rise above one's station preferring rather to be lifted up in due time by God's will and grace. If God were proud He would hardly have us on such terms: but He is not proud, He stoops to conquer.[45] By rejecting Satan's offers, He began the process of conquering the powers of darkness which culminated at Calvary – cosmic D-Day.

---

[44] Dostoyevsky, The Brothers Karamazov, 286.
[45] Lewis, The Problem of Pain, 96.

Chapter 2: The Three Enemies of the Saint

The Word of God tells us that God the Father made Jesus to be sin, who knew no sin, so that we might become the righteousness of God (2 Cor 5:21). In Christ we are presently blameless and righteous (Mt 12:7; Rom 5:17). And although we will remain imperfect in this life, we will grow in grace and in the knowledge of God. This is sanctification – becoming more like Jesus. And when we are low, we should remember that we cannot be anymore saved than when we first believed (Jn 10:28; Rom 8:31-39; Heb 7:25)!

Jesus has been tempted in every way we are, yet he never gave in (Heb 3:18; 4:15). This is comforting news for Christians because He helps us when we are tempted (Lk 22:31-32; 1 Cor 10:12-13; Heb 7:25) and by God's grace we overcome (Is 43:1-2; Rom 8:31-39). It's important for us to note here that a trial or temptation is not sinful in itself (remember how Christ was tempted), but may lead to sin if left unchecked (Jam 1:14-15). Through flood and through flame, the saints overcome through the power of the Holy Spirit, and lose nothing but their dross (Is 48:10).[46]

Sin is the result of following the suggestions of Satan. The God-honoring man would do well to be mindful of the three enemies of his soul: *the lust of the flesh, the lust of the eyes, and the pride of life* (1 Jn 2:15-17). The Puritan Thomas Brooks tells us, "Satan makes use of all his power and skill to bring all the sons of men into the same condition and condemnation as himself."[47] Brooks adds,

Whatever sin the heart of man is most prone to, that the devil will help forward. If David be proud of his people, Satan will provoke him to number them, that he may be yet prouder (2 Sam 24). If Peter be slavishly fearful, Satan will put him upon rebuking and denying of Christ, to save his own skin (Mt 16:22, 26). If Ananias will lie for advantage, Satan will fill his heart that he may lie, with a witness, to the Holy Ghost (Acts 5:3). Satan loves to sail with the wind, and to suit men's temptations to their conditions and inclinations. If they be in prosperity, he will tempt them to deny God (Pro 30:9); if they be in adversity, he will tempt them to distrust God; if their knowledge be weak, he will tempt them to have low thoughts of God; if their

---

[46] We have hinting at mortification, the daily dying to sin. This is a concept that will be developed in the next chapter.

[47] Brooks, Precious Remedies against Satan's Devices, 15.

conscience be tender, he will tempt to scrupulosity; if large, to carnal security; if bold spirited, he will tempt to presumption; if timorous, to desperation; if flexible, to inconstancy; if stiff, to impenitency.[48]

Jesus Christ brings us true freedom: freedom to live for God. Mankind is not only ruined but under a sentence of death, and will remain so unless he believes in Christ's once-for-all sacrifice. Without Him we are in bondage. What bondage you ask? Slavery to our own sin nature, slavery to the world's system, and slavery to Satan. Slavery which the old man had no freedom to not serve. Therefore "Be on the alert, stand firm in the faith, act like men, be strong" (1 Cor 16:13), and "Resist the devil and he will flee from you" (Jam 4:8). Let us heed the biblical counsel of the apostle Peter, "Be sober, be vigilant; because your adversary the devil walks about like a roaring lion, seeking whom he may devour. Resist him, steadfast in the faith, knowing that the same sufferings are experienced by your brotherhood in the world" (1 Pet 5:8-9).

My Shepherd will supply my need; Jehovah is His name;
In pastures fresh He makes me feed, beside the living stream.
He brings my wandering spirit back, when I forsake His ways;
And leads me, for His mercy's sake, in paths of truth and grace.[49]

---

[48] Brooks, Precious Remedies against Satan's Devices, 16-17.
[49] Watts, My Shepherd Will Supply My Need.

154

Chapter 2: The Three Enemies of the Saint

Recommended Further Reading

1. C.S. Lewis, *The Problem of Pain.*
2. Thomas Brooks, *Precious Remedies against Satan's Devices.*
3. Augustine, *The City of God.*
4. John Bunyan *The Holy War.*
5. John Piper *The Future of Justification.*

Chapter 2 Review Questions

1. What is the basic redemptive-historical framework of the Bible?

2. What are the three enemies of the saint?

3. How does the Bible describe righteousness?

4. What does the Bible teach us about original sin?

5. Is there a correlation between the modes of temptation used against our first parents with those employed by Satan when he tempted Christ in the wilderness?

6. Did Christ's atoning death on the cross purchase God's pardon from all sins: past, present and future?

7. How does the Book of James describe the way temptation can become sin?

8. Can Christians achieve sinless perfection in this life?

9. What is the difference between justification and sanctification?

10. Is the cosmic D-Day a fitting analogy for Christ's victory over the powers of darkness?

Part 2: Disciplined Service

Puritan Preaching 1670s.

"I have been crucified with Christ; it is no longer I who live, but Christ lives in me; and the life which I now live in the flesh I live by faith in the Son of God, who loved me and gave Himself for me. I do not set aside the grace of God; for if righteousness comes through the law, then Christ died in vain" (Gal 2:20-21).

Chapter 3: The Irreconcilable War

Use of the law, in Christian thought, perhaps unpopular and dismissed as legalism, orders the godly life while divine grace supplies the acting power. But this is no mere self-improvement program for saints. Let's look back at the last chapter. There we discussed that as Christians, though we were under a sentence of divine wrath (Jn 3:36), we have

Chapter 3: The Irreconcilable War

passed from death to life (Col 1:13-14), and are no longer
under condemnation (Rom 8:1). Before Christ saved us, we
had no power not to live in the flesh, but were slaves of the
devil (Eph 2:1-3). Now in the power that God supplies, we are
able to walk in the Spirit (Gal 5:16). This chapter will outline
the following:

- The Fruit of the Spirit.
- The Christian use of the Law.
- The Three Stages along Life's Way.
- The Two Paths.
- The Mortification of Sin in Believers.

The Christian life is one of balance. It is to be neither
legalistic nor antinomian (lawless). As Christians we are not
under the condemning power of the law, "For we are not
under law but under grace" (Rom 6:14). This is because Jesus
Christ has redeemed us from the curse of the law. All we need
do is receive His free gift of salvation (Gal 3:13-14; 2 Pet 1:3).
The Epistle to the Galatians makes this point very clear. In this
Epistle, the apostle Paul writes to the churches of Galatia. A
region of modern Turkey. The Galatians were pagan idolaters
who had received the gospel during Paul's first missionary
journey (45-46 AD).[1]

These Christians came under the spell of false teachers
(Judaizers), who corrupted the gospel by adding to it an
adherence to the Law of Moses (like circumcision, dietary
laws, etc.). The false teachers emphasized that the Law of
Moses must be followed in order for one to *earn* one's
salvation. Paul writes, "I marvel that you are turning away so
soon from Him who called you in the grace of Christ, to a
different gospel" (Gal 1:6). The Judaizers promoted another
Jesus, a different spirit, and a different message from the one
Paul had preached to them. Paul asks them, "This only I want
to learn from you: Did you receive the Spirit by the works of
the law, or by the hearing of faith? Are you so foolish? Having
begun in the Spirit, are you now being made perfect by the

---

[1] Galatians was probably written by Paul during his 18 months in Corinth 51-
52 AD. So William Hendriksen, Galatians, 16.

flesh" (Gal 3:2-3)? In other words, if you received salvation by grace alone through faith in Christ alone without the works of the law, then why are you working in vain to save yourselves through the law (Gal 2:21; 3:3)?

The Reformer Martin Luther considered Galatians the battle cry of the Reformation because of its denouncement of legalism. In deed it is. The theme of the letter is unmistakable: a man is justified (declared righteous) not by works of the law but only through faith in Christ alone. The apostle hammers away this truth no less than seven times in Gal 2:16; 2:21; 3:9; 3:11; 4:2-6; 5:2-6; and 6:14-16. What is foremost in Paul's mind is not an *outward act* but an *inward attitude*. Paul teaches us that love is the law's fulfillment (Gal 5:13-14; Rom 13:8-10), as well as an expression of faith (Gal 5:6). Then the apostle tells us,

I say then: Walk in the Spirit, and you shall not fulfill the lust of the flesh. 17 For the flesh lusts against the Spirit, and the Spirit against the flesh; and these are contrary to one another, so that you do not do the things that you wish. 18 But if you are led by the Spirit, you are not under the law. 19 Now the works of the flesh are evident, which are: adultery, fornication, uncleanness, lewdness, 20 idolatry, sorcery, hatred, contentions, jealousies, outbursts of wrath, selfish ambitions, dissensions, heresies, 21 envy, murders, drunkenness, revelries, and the like; of which I tell you beforehand, just as I also told you in time past, that those who practice such things will not inherit the kingdom of God. 22 But the fruit of the Spirit is love, joy, peace, longsuffering, kindness, goodness, faithfulness, 23 gentleness, self-control. Against such there is no law. 24 And those who are Christ's have crucified the flesh with its passions and desires. 25 If we live in the Spirit, let us also walk in the Spirit. 26 Let us not become conceited, provoking one another, envying one another (Gal 5:16-26).

The Fruit of the Spirit

The fruit of the Spirit is the result of the Holy Spirit's presence and work in the lives of believers that are yielding themselves to God. It grows like a well-watered plant that is rooted and grounded in love. The nine fruit of the Spirit are communicable attributes of God; a natural result of the exercise of love:

Chapter 3: The Irreconcilable War

- Love (1 Cor 13; Gal 5:6, 22; Eph 5:2; Col 3:14; 1 Jn 4:7-8).
- Joy (Neh 8:10; Mt 25:21; Jn 16:20-21, 24; 17:13; 1 Pet 1:8).
- Peace (Ps 119:165; Mt 5:9; Rom 5:1; Eph 4:3).
- Longsuffering-*Patience* (Rom 2:4; Col 3:12; 1 Tim 1:16).
- Kindness (Mt 5:43-48; Jn 19:25-27; 2 Cor 6:6; Rom 11:22).
- Goodness (Lk 8:15; Eph 5:9; Acts 23:1; Jms 1:17).
- Faithfulness (Mt 25:21; Jn 20:27; Heb 3:5; Rev 13:10).
- Gentleness (Mt 5:5; 11:29; 2 Cor 10:1; Eph 4:2; 1 Pet 3:4).
- Self-control (Acts 24:25; 2 Cor 10:5; 2 Pet 1:6).

This fruit is possible only because of the saint's union with God in Christ through the Holy Spirit. The Bible reveals three great unions which are most relevant to this discussion: (1) the union of the Persons of the Trinity (Gen 1:26; 3:22; 11:7; Num 6:22-26; Mt 3:16-17; 28:18-20; Cor 13:14, et al.); (2) the union of the two natures of Christ in One Person (Jn 3:13; 17:5; 20:28); and (3) the union of Christ and believers in the Holy Spirit (Mt 28:20; Jn 14:17-18; Rom 8:9; Col 1:27; Heb 13:15). The Galatian churches are admonished to yield themselves to the Holy Spirit so that the Spirit's work may be demonstrated in their lives, and bring glory to God – a product of the third union in Scripture. This is what Jesus told His disciples – to bear much fruit so as to glorify the Father (Jn 15:8). But this fruit comes not from themselves but from God – the life of God in the soul of man.

God is love incarnate in Jesus Christ. And "Greater love have no man than this," John's gospel tell us, "that a man lay down his life for his friends: (Jn 15:13). Love (agape) is the fruit of the Spirit, in which Christians are commanded to do everything (Mt 22:37-39; Gal 5:13-14). And yet this command is impossible to obey without the power to do it. But God Himself supplies the acting power which the believer graciously receives and fulfills the law's demands. Regarding this marvelous exchange, Augustine wrote, "Lord give what Thou command, and command what Thou will."[2]

---

[2] Augustine, Confessions, Book 9, Chapter 29.

Chapter 3: The Irreconcilable War

The fruit of the Spirit, the visible attributes of the Christian life may be viewed from the triadic structure of mind-will-emotions:

- **Mind:** Love – self-sacrificing affection for others.
  Joy – gladness regardless of circumstances.
  Peace – inner quietness.

- **Will:** Longsuffering – forbearance even provoked.
  Kindness – graciousness and benevolence.
  Goodness – generosity of spirit.

- **Emotions:** Faithfulness – loyalty and trustworthiness.
  Gentleness – acquiescence to authority.
  Self-control – ability to master oneself.

We are to surrender our minds, wills, and emotions to God, so to be controlled by the love of Christ, Who compels us to have compassion on our neighbor. Thus, divine grace supplies the acting power. This concept is known to theologians as the *indicative-imperative paradigm*. This concept states that the indicative is the accomplished reality, that is, what has been accomplished by Jesus Christ in His incarnation, life, death, resurrection, ascension, and present intercession gives us the power to do the enabled commandment – the imperative. Herman Ridderbos writes, "The imperative manifests the indicative. The indicative represents the "already" as well as the "not yet." Thus, every indicative is an actualizing of the imperative." The apostle Paul uses the indicative-imperative paradigm quite often, for example in Gal 5:25, he writes, "If we live in the Spirit, let us also walk in the Spirit." That is if the Spirit is the source of our life, let the Spirit also direct our course. This is the Pauline interplay between the indicative and imperative. Another example is Col 3:1-4 which tells us,

If then you were raised with Christ, seek those things which are above, where Christ is, sitting at the right hand of God. 2 Set your mind on things above, not on things on the earth. 3 For you died, and your life is hidden with Christ in God. 4 When Christ who is our life appears, then you also will appear with Him in glory.

160

Chapter 3: The Irreconcilable War

In this passage, the indicative (accomplished reality), "If then you were raised with Christ," empowers the imperative (enabled command) "seek those things which are above, where Christ is, sitting at the right hand of God." Thus, what God commands, as Augustine said, He first gives. Perhaps the clearest expression of this paradigm is found in Phil 2:12-13, "work out your own salvation with fear and trembling; for it is God who works in you both to will and to do for His good pleasure." The word 'for' in the second clause furnishes the ground for the appeal in the first.

Simply stated, this means because Christ has already accomplished everything, I need to live a God-honoring life (2 Pet 1:3), a reality I apprehend only by faith, I have been made free to live a holy life for the glory of God. It is as John the Baptist put it, "He must increase, and I must decrease."

With an understanding of this concept we may see that all of these fruit of the Spirit the believer is commanded and enabled to bear (Jn 15:4-5). And when we do, in the Spirit's supplied endowment, then we'll be actively fulfilling the law of God (Jn 13:34-35; Rom 13:8; 1 Cor 13; 2 Cor 5:14; Gal 5:14; Phil 1:8). According to F. F. Bruce, "The fruit of the Spirit is the lifestyle of those who are indwelt and energized by the Spirit."[3]

The antithesis to the Spirit's fruit is the flesh. The flesh is the power that opposes God. Flesh is not your body. It is a craving of the human heart to express itself subtly or ostentatiously. Flesh is the saint's first enemy. It hates the Spirit and wages war against it. The flesh is rooted in rebellion which expresses itself in the form of self-righteousness. As in the case of the Pharisees who "trusted in themselves that they were righteous, and despised others" (Lk 18:9).[4] They in fact are blind and unable to receive the things of the Spirit (Jn 9:40-41; 1 Cor 2:14).

F. F. Bruce observes,

"To be 'led by the Spirit' is to walk by the Spirit – to have the power to rebut the desire of the flesh, to be increasingly conformed to the

---

[3] Bruce, Commentary on Galatians: New International Greek Testament Commentary, 251.
[4] See also Lk 5:32; 10:29; 16:15 and Mt 6:2, 5, 16.

likeness of Christ (2 Cor 3:18), to cease to be under law. To be under the law affords no protection against the desire of the flesh. 'Spirit' is equally opposed to 'law' as to 'flesh.' To be led by the Spirit brings simultaneous deliverance from the desire of the flesh, the bondage of the law, and the power of sin: 'sin will have no dominion over you, since you are not under law but under grace' (Rom 6:14). To be 'under grace' is to be 'led by the Spirit.'[5]

In Jeremiah 24, the prophet is shown a sign consisting of two baskets of figs (Jer 24:1-10). "One basket had very good figs, like the figs that are first ripe; and the other basket had very bad figs which could not be eaten, they were so bad" (Jer 24:2). God said to Jeremiah, "Like these good figs, so will I acknowledge those who are carried away captive from Judah, whom I have sent out of this place for their own good, into the land of the Chaldeans. For I will set My eyes on them for good, and I will bring them back to this land; I will build them and not pull them down, and I will plant them and not pluck them up" (Jer 24:5-6). Then God said, "I will give them a heart to know Me, that I am the Lord; and they shall be My people, and I will be their God, for they shall return to Me with their whole heart" (Jer 24:7). The good figs represent those who have received a new heart, and are obedient to God's commands. These are the righteous who have the root of divine love in them, enabling them to love God and His word (Ps 119:97; Jer 31:33-34). The prophet Jeremiah declares, "They shall be My people, and I will be their God; then I will give them one heart and one way, that they may fear Me forever, for the good of them and their children after them. And I will make an everlasting covenant with them, that I will not turn away from doing them good; but I will put My fear in their hearts so that they will not depart from Me (Jer 32:38-40).

Regarding the bad figs, which represent the wicked, God says, "I will deliver them to trouble into all the kingdoms of the earth, for their harm, to be a reproach and a byword, a taunt and a curse, in all places where I shall drive them. And I will send the sword, the famine, and the pestilence among

---

[5] Bruce, Commentary on Galatians: New International Greek Testament Commentary, 245.

them, till they are consumed from the land that I gave to them and their fathers" (Jer 24:8-10). This is the common destiny for everyone who despises God and His Word (Job 18:5-21). They desire to live without God on their own terms and when they die they get it forever! Jesus told us we would know them by their fruit (Mt 7:16-20), and "If you keep my commandments, you abide in My love" (Jn 15:10).

So what is the Christian to make of the law? We remember from chapter one, we do not keep God's law in order to be saved, but we keep God's law because we are saved. And we were saved to glorify God and to enjoy Him forever. As heirs of the promise, we are made free by Christ. Those outside the covenant of grace remain in bondage to the law (Gal 4:21-26). Furthermore, as Christians we glorify God by keeping His commandments (Jn 15:8-10); joyfully living out Christ's righteousness; serving others, allowing our conduct to be directed by the Spirit (Gal 5:25). As Gal 5:13 teaches us, "Through love serve one another."

The law reminds me of why Christ had to die – so I would no longer be a slave of sin and the devil, but so I could live a righteous life for Him, obeying His commandments. Genuine liberty is therefore neither legalism nor a license to sin. As Christians we are not under the condemning power of the law, "For we are not under law but under grace," yet we are under the commanding power of the law, unto the glory of Christ, that in all things He may be preeminent (Rom 6:14; Col 1:18).

The Christian Use of the Law

Christians are at war: with the flesh, the world, and the devil. In this irreconcilable war, Christians need guidelines to frame their lives, as they go from strength to strength, growing in grace and in the knowledge of God. The law, given by God to teach sinners their sin, is both the Christian's joyful service to Christ and the force that drives the sinner to Christ. John Bunyan tells us, "The man who does not know the nature of the law cannot know the nature of sin. And he who does not know the nature of sin cannot know the nature of the Savior."

J.I. Packer tells us, "Unless we see our shortcomings in the light of the Law and holiness of God, we do not see them as sin at all."[6] We remember from chapter one, that the law is holy, righteous, just and good, and is the mirror of God's nature and character. The Bible gives three principle uses of the law: (1) to restrain the spread of lawlessness. This is sometimes referred to as the civil use of the law; (2) to bring all mankind under conviction of sin. This is known as the pedagogical use of the law; and (3) to serve as a guide for Christians to live holy lives. This is known as the didactic use of the law (See figure 3-1 below).

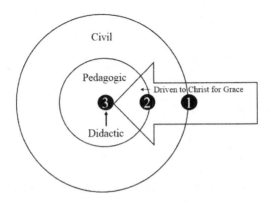

The Three Uses of the Law.

When Christ receives repentant, believing men and women, He forgives them, grants them His righteousness, and gives them the Holy Spirit. He writes His law on their new hearts and empowers them to follow Him in obedient discipleship. John Murray writes, "Christ as the vicar of his people came under the curse and condemnation due to sin and he also fulfilled the law of God in all its positive requirements. In other words, he took care of the guilt of sin and perfectly fulfilled the demands of righteousness. He perfectly met both the penal and the preceptive requirements of God's law. The passive obedience refers to the former and the active obedience to the latter."[7] God accepts repentant sinners and

---

[6] Packer, Evangelism and the Sovereignty of God, 62.
[7] Murray, Redemption Accomplished and Applied, 22.

receives His Son's righteousness in their place. He further works to purify His saints, thereby sending them to His law to frame their lives, thus living out Christ's righteousness. Doctrine is grace and obedience is gratitude.

Remembering the fifth mark, the first use of the law restrains lawlessness. Romans 13:5 tells us that the civil laws also bind the conscience. We will discuss the conscience later but for now we need to see how God's law restrains wickedness.

Across the Texas border in Mexico lies the city of Nuevo Laredo. The town has lost its civil authority and is ruled by rival drug cartels. The drug-violence in Nuevo Laredo began back in 2003, when the city came under the control of the Gulf Cartel. The streets are virtually empty during the day, and the city's residents rarely venture outside their homes after dark for fear of being raped or murdered. In June 2005, Alejandro Dominguez, the only person brave enough to be police chief, was gunned down by thugs only hours after he assumed office. In 2012, dismembered remains of 14 men were found in several plastic bags inside a parked car. On 24 April, 2012 a car bomb exploded outside the city's police department. When the Mexican military arrived at the scene they were engaged in a firefight with cartel members. Not even the national army was respected. The people of Nuevo Laredo feel defenseless and view the drug cartels as being better organized than the civil and national authorities.

This is a picture of what the world would look like without the restraining power of God's civil authority. The state is given the power of the sword for three reasons: (1) to restrain evil both from within and without; (2) to preserve order and organize society; and (3) to promote civil obedience. Let us praise the Lord for His wisdom and the restraining power of His authority without which the whole world would be an enormous Nuevo Laredo.

The exercise of authority is measured morally in terms of its divine origin; the Law of God restrains sin and promotes righteousness in the church and society. It further prevents both from lapsing into chaos.[8] As Christians, what motivates

---

[8] Calvin, Institutes of the Christian Religion, Book Two, Chapter 7, 222-228.

Chapter 3: The Irreconcilable War

us to obey civil authority? Are we motivated merely for the sake of avoiding punishment? The loss of time and money that could result from an infraction? That is hypocritical, contrived, and artificial obedience. The biblical model of obedience is obeying authority in the realization that all authority is in God's hands and He develops that authority for His holy, wise, and just ends. We must submit ourselves to all authority and obey out of an inward love and reverence for the holy law of God. We must genuinely and sincerely submit to all authority. We must submit out of godly fear, a fear which is consistent with the exercise of love and respect.

What about when the state is wrong? Sometimes the state functions as it should, i.e. restrains lawlessness, however, when it's dysfunctional, it misuses God's delegated authority. Sometimes it functions in even a demonic way, like it did under National Socialism. Under normal circumstances the church is to be thankful to God for providing the state and show our thankfulness to God by obeying the state's delegated authority. On the other hand, the church as the state's conscience must be ready to challenge the state for its immoral laws and even disobey the state when its laws contradict the law of God (see page 103).

When considering these matters there are two extremes to avoid: First, a refusal to pray for or obey rulers with whose policies we disagree with (1 Tim 2:1-4), and second, an absolute subjection to the state whether it is right or wrong. The Christian is loyal to his government but not subservient. He is a patriot, but not a slave. We are to be bond servants only to Christ.

The pedagogic or second use of the law, exposes sinfulness. Charles Spurgeon once said, "I do not believe that any man can preach the gospel who does not preach the Law. The Law cuts into the core of the evil, it reveals the seat of the malady, and informs us that the leprosy lies deep within. They must be slain by the law before they can be made alive by the gospel." And A. W. Tozer writes, "No one can know the true grace of God who has not first known the fear of God."

The second use of the law has an evangelical power, it exposes and convicts of sin, driving one to Christ for grace. We are not merely imperfect creatures who must be improved:

we are rebels who must lay down our arms; we must be re-created in Christ, born again.

This convicting use of the law is also critical in the life of the believer, for it serves to prevent the resurrection of self-righteousness which is always prone to reassert itself even in the holiest of saints. As Luther once said, the Christian life is a life of repentance. The law of God disciplines, educates, and convicts us, driving us out of ourselves to Jesus Christ and keeps us ever so near His cross. Whereas the law sends us to the gospel for justification, the gospel sends us back to the law to frame our way of life. Its chastening work doesn't imply that a believer's justification is ever diminished or annulled, because from the moment of regeneration, the believer's state before God is fixed and irrevocable. He is a new creation in Christ Jesus (2 Corinthians 5:17), and is accounted righteous by God because of what Christ has already done at Golgotha (Rom 4).

Although the believer can never be under the condemning power of the law again, he remains under the commanding power of it, and the Holy Spirit uses it as a mirror to show us our guilt and brings us to repentance. "The Moral Law tells us the tune we have to play: our instincts are merely the keys."[9] Those who believe that Christians can lose their salvation show they are still trusting in themselves for salvation. They would have to affirm that what Christ accomplished on the cross was insufficient to save completely, that it did not cover all our sin. What assurance can ever be enjoyed by Christians who believe this? Believing this way amounts to being born again, but if one falls away or "back slides" (apostatizes), one loses one's salvation, and if one repents then they become born again "again?"

According to this reasoning, just how much sinning constitutes losing one's salvation anyway? There is a big difference between being convicted and being condemned. However, God's justification of a sinner is based upon the obedience and righteousness of Christ alone which He accounts to the believing sinner as his own. Our salvation is

---

[9] Lewis, Mere Christianity, 10.

the work of God from beginning to end (Jn 10:28; Rom 8:28-30; Eph 2:8-10; Phil 1:6; 2:12-13; 2 Thess 2:13-14).

Raised for Our Justification

The resurrection of Christ, so often unconsidered during debates of this sort, is an essential part of God's act of justification. As the apostle Paul tells us in 1 Corinthians 15:17, "And if Christ is not risen, your faith is futile; you are still in your sins." And again in Rom 4:25 the apostle Paul tells us, Christ "was delivered up for our offenses, and was raised for our justification." The resurrection of Christ not only accomplishes our justification, as the Spirit applies Christ's death as an all-sufficient price for our sins, but also brings us into relational right standing, into a "new humanity" in Christ. Thus, the Holy Spirit regenerates all those whom Christ died for. One cannot be "regenerated," then because of a certain measure of sinful behavior become "unregenerated," because regeneration is a one-for-all act of God's redemptive power.

The Spirit applies the decree of God to save everyone who believes in Christ; forensic enables pneumatic. And this all is by virtue of the finished, perfect redemptive work of the Son. So we may clearly see that the biblical definition of justification is one in which "God who gives life to the dead and calls those things which do not exist as though they did" (Roman 4:17). This is based solely on the work of the Son, "so as to create in Himself one new man from the two (both Jew and Gentile), thus making peace, and that He might reconcile them both to God in one body through the cross, thereby putting to death the enmity" (Ephesians 2:15, 16; 1 Corinthians 15:47).

The biblical point being made here is Jesus is more than just a perfect example of how we should live our lives to the glory of God, God saves us through Christ's physical resurrection from the dead. Salvation is an utter impossibility so long as man is obliged to obtain merit for himself on his own. Justification is God's act by which He accounts the believing sinner as righteous in His sight solely for the perfect righteousness of Jesus Christ alone. Additionally, God's law, being a mirror showing us His character and nature, so as to convict the believer of sin, orders the conduct of saints aright, and so daily transforms them into Christ's image.

The third use of the law, the didactic use, is the rule of life for the believer, a guide for holy living. The Geneva Catechism asks us, "What is the rule of life which he (God) has given us? The answer is the law of God which is summarily comprehended in the Ten Commandments. What Christian men must realize is we are involved in a cosmic spiritual war. The enemy of our soul wants Christian men to be irresponsible, immature, and effeminate lusty beasts. America is clearly under a demonic attack. One that will stop at nothing to annihilate the biblical understanding of marriage, the family, morality, masculinity, femininity, right, wrong, etc., *ad infinitum*. It is as the Scripture tells us, "But, as he who was born according to the flesh then persecuted him who was born according to the Spirit, even so it is now"(Gal 4:29).

The conflict is not only between the unbelieving world and Satan, the conflict is deeper than that. It goes even to the very heart of the believer. There is a war within the saint, between the flesh and the Spirit, so that when he would do good, evil is present with him. The apostle Paul tells us in Rom 7:15-25,

15 For what I am doing, I do not understand. For what I will to do, that I do not practice; but what I hate, that I do. 16 If, then, I do what I will not to do, I agree with the law that it is good. 17 But now, it is no longer I who do it, but sin that dwells in me. 18 For I know that in me (that is, in my flesh) nothing good dwells; for to will is present with me, but how to perform what is good I do not find. 19 For the good that I will to do, I do not do; but the evil I will not to do, that I practice. 20 Now if I do what I will not to do, it is no longer I who do it, but sin that dwells in me. 21 I find then a law, that evil is present with me, the one who wills to do good. 22 For I delight in the law of God according to the inward man. 23 But I see another law in my members, warring against the law of my mind, and bringing me into captivity to the law of sin which is in my members. 24 O wretched man that I am! Who will deliver me from this body of death? 25 I thank God—through Jesus Christ our Lord! So then, with the mind I myself serve the law of God, but with the flesh the law of sin.

Chapter 3: The Irreconcilable War

John Gill tells us, "The distinctions between flesh and spirit, the inward and the outward man, and the struggle there is between them, are to be found in none but regenerate persons." This is because in the unregenerate man (unsaved), there is no struggle because, as a slave of Satan, he utterly lies under the dominating power of sinful flesh. He is a slave of sin (Jn 8:31-36; Rom 6:20). The Scriptures tell us the mind of natural (unregenerate) man is at enmity with God, and cannot submit to God's law (Rom 8:5-8). Those who are unregenerate cannot please God (Rom 8:8; Heb 11:6). Thus the third use of the law is for the holy life of the saint, doing what God commands and avoiding what He condemns. The only way we can know whether we are sinning is by knowing God's Moral Law. And living holy lives as saints in a depraved world is not easy but it's possible, only in the power of the Holy Spirit, remaining near the cross.

God works to effect renewal in the whole of man. Though we are born again, there remains an 'old man' that we must contend with all our days this side of heaven (Rom 8:12-13). Man, being made in the image of God, has a mind, will, and emotions, or a rational, volitional, and emotive faculty. Regarding these correlative powers in man's soul, Peter Kreeft offers the following: the intellect is the soul's navigator but the will is its captain. The intellect is its Mr. Spock, the will is its Captain Kirk, and the feelings are its Dr. McCoy. The soul is an Enterprise. The will can command the intellect to think but the intellect cannot command the will to will, only inform it. Yet the will cannot make you believe. It cannot force the intellect to believe what appears to be false, or to disbelieve what seems to be true.[10]

When a man is converted he receives a renewed mind, his will is conformed and bent back to God, and his emotions are made responsive to the move of the Spirit. The whole aim of the word of God is to bring the soul of man into submission to God's mind, God's will, and God's affection (love). Conversion is the word we use to describe this divine action. Godly sorrow turns our hearts, minds, and wills toward God. How well you have understood with your mind, and how

---

[10] Kreeft, Handbook of Christian Apologetics, 31.

genuinely you have responded with your emotions, will be
tested by the decisions of your will. The biblical point being
made here is, a life of self-discipline and devotion to God is
the practical outworking of the new birth, not its cause.[11]

Three Stages on Life's Way

Søren Kierkegaard, the Danish philosopher presents us with
three stages or spheres of existence along life's way: the
aesthetic, ethical, and religious conscious stages.[12] These
stages roughly correlate to the three uses of the law. The
following diagram illustrates Kierkegaard's approach:

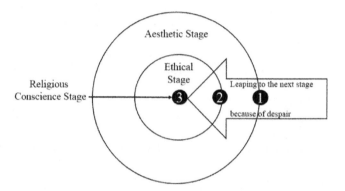

Kierkegaard's Three Stages on Life's Way.

Kierkegaard's *aesthetic stage*, characterized by immediacy
and hedonism, is a sphere of Kierkegaardian existence in
which men are concerned merely for the present moment. The
greatest threat to the aesthetic man's world is boredom and
responsibility. The worst that can confront the aesthete, a man
trapped in the aesthetic stage, is duty because duty limits
freedom. *Responsibility* is a word that strikes fear in the heart
of the aesthetic man. The aesthete runs from any tethering
duty or responsibility. He is a man who is characterized as one

---

[11] The concept of biblical self-discipline is developed further in chapter four.
[12] Søren Kierkegaard (1813-1855) was a Danish philosopher, theologian, and
author who is widely held to be the first existentialist philosopher.

having an infinite variety of options requiring realization. The aesthetic existence demands sensual stimulation. Kierkegaard gives us several examples of the aesthetic man. In *Don Juan*, he shows us a man who seeks pleasure in the quantity of sexual experiences. The more experiences the better. Don Juan is the consummate womanizer. He is a slave to his lustful appetite. And aesthetes of this type are indifferent to the suffering they cause. For Don Juan types, the prospect of marriage is to be avoided like the plague.

The *Seducer*, another one of Kierkegaard's aesthetic types, seeks pleasure rather not in the amount of sexual experiences, but in the quality of a single drawn out seduction culminating in a sexual experience which brings to closure the whole game.[13] The Seducer tirelessly works on his intended victim, wearing them down with overtures. He takes more pleasure in the chase than in the end result. In both caricatures, Kierkegaard demonstrates the manner in which boredom is dealt with and responsibility is avoided.

The *rotation method*, a Kierkegaardian concept, is one which is used to describe the manner in which advanced aesthetes avoid boredom. Kierkegaard likens the rotation method to the way in which farmers rotate their crops so as to maintain the nourishing value of the soil. Kierkegaard says most aesthetic individuals practice the rotation method so as to avoid commitment and boredom and to maximize their pleasure they derive from any given activity. The aesthete employing the rotation method flips from one activity to another so as to avoid boredom in pursuit of empty hedonistic pursuits.

Without being conscious of all of this, the aesthete flees anything that would perhaps give meaning to his life. Kierkegaard uses a character named Judge Wilhelm who points out that the "happy" life of an aesthete will eventually turn to despair as the aesthete runs out of new sensations as well as money to procure them. How does one free himself from this stage of life? Kierkegaard tells us we can't reason our way out of the aesthetic stage of life. He believed rather

---

[13] Kierkegaard, Stages on Life's Way, 76. The Seducer knows when to break off the relationship at the consummation so he may go on to still further conquests.

that a person came to the end of themselves. Suffering a sense of overwhelming psychological feelings of inadequacy and despair, one would make a "leap" to another stage of life.

During his university years Kierkegaard led a life of a destitute aesthete. A journal entry of his during this stage of his life reveals a deeply melancholy and shocking entry. He writes, "I have just now come from a party where I was its life and soul; witticisms streamed from my lips, everyone laughed and admired me, but I went away — yes, the dash should be as long as the radius of the earth's orbit ————————and wanted to shoot myself." Kierkegaard, tired of his hedonism, in desperation undergoes an ethical 'conversion,' which he himself recounts as not being a Christian conversion, but one in which he reached a stage of his life when he found the end of himself. He grew tired of meaningless pursuits and commits himself to a different kind of life, one in which there is responsibility and obligation.[14]

This man, in desperation enters the *ethical stage* of life. Socrates, Kierkegaard's representative of the ethical stage of life, is a man who commits himself to a life of principle and purpose, and takes on duties and responsibilities. But in the end, he says the ethical stage of life is empty, because we simply don't have the power in us to live up to this ethical stage of life. We can't live up to its demands so we are driven again to a sense of hopelessness and despair. This dissatisfaction which drives men to "leap to" religious consciousness, Kierkegaard tells us is God Himself. Kierkegaard believes this is God's way of helping us reach the end of ourselves. When we have come to the end of ourselves we are compelled either to revert back to our old hedonistic habits or, as Kierkegaard puts it, we "leap" to the *religious conscious stage* of life, that is, we are driven to Christ for grace, and enter the religious conscience stage by repentance and faith. According to Kierkegaard, there are only two ways in life: either the aesthetic-ethical, which leads to despair, or the religious leading to a genuine faith in God.

Vincent Miceli tells us, "In his life and writings Kierkegaard vehemently rejected the smug complacency and

---

[14] Kierkegaard, Either/Or, 2:169.

sham sanctity of the secularized Christianity of his day."[15] Kierkegaard's concern was for a personal encounter with the living Christ; a living faith as opposed to mere intellectual ascent.

The Two Paths

There are two paths laid out before men, one to the city of God, and the other to the house of death. The Book of Proverbs is all about wisdom and how to get it. In it God lays the entrance to the two paths before all men. Proverbs begins with the express purpose of imparting wisdom to the simple (Pro 1:2-6), and states unequivocally that wisdom is the beginning of knowledge (Pro 1:7).[16] This is the reoccurring theme of Proverbs, "get wisdom, it's supreme." And "He who finds me finds life, and obtains favor from the Lord; But he who sins against me wrongs his own soul; All those who hate me love death" (Pro 8:35-36).

Regarding the fear of the Lord, John Gill observes,

By "the fear of the Lord" is not meant a servile fear, a fear of punishment, of hell, wrath, and damnation, which is the effect of the first work of the law upon the conscience; but a filial fear, and supposes knowledge of God as a father, of his love and grace in Christ, particularly of his forgiving love, from whence it arises, Psalm 130:4; it is a holy, humble, fiducial (L. trustful) fear of God; a reverential affection for him, and devotion to him; it includes the whole of religious worship, both internal and external; all that is contained in the first table of the law, and the manner of performing it, and principle of acting: this is the first of all sciences to be learned, and it is the principal one; it is the basis and foundation of all the rest, on which they depend; and it is the head, the fountain, the root an source, from whence they spring; and unless a man knows God, knows God in Christ, and worships him in his fear, in spirit and in truth, according to his revealed will, he knows nothing as he ought to know; and all his knowledge will be of no avail and profit to him; this

---

[15] Miceli, The Gods of Atheism, 187.

[16] The following is an outline of the Book of Proverbs: 1:1-7 Preamble; 1:8-9:18 Extended discourse on wisdom; 10:1-22:16 Solomonic Proverbs; 22:17-24:34 Sayings of the wise; 25:1-29:27 Additional Solomonic proverbs; 30 Sayings of Agur; 31:1-9 Sayings of Lemuel; and 31:10-31 Poem to the virtuous woman.

Chapter 3: The Irreconcilable War

is the first and chief thing in spiritual and evangelical knowledge, and without which all natural knowledge will signify nothing.[17]

Proverbs provides us with divine help in understanding human personality and behavior. But it all begins with the fear of the Lord. Proverbs 8:13 tells us, "The fear of the Lord is to hate evil; Pride and arrogance and the evil way." The fear of the Lord is the beginning of wisdom (Pro 9:10). What is wisdom? Augustine said that wisdom is the intellectual apprehension of things eternal. This was in comparison to knowledge, which he termed the rational apprehension of things temporal. Wisdom is not only speaking but also doing what is appropriate at any given moment. It is experiential knowledge, knowing what to do and how to do it. This is the wisdom of God which is unattainable for those who reject Christ. The apostle Paul tells us in 1 Cor 1:18-31,

18 For the message of the cross is foolishness to those who are perishing, but to us who are being saved it is the power of God. 19 For it is written: "I will destroy the wisdom of the wise, and bring to nothing the understanding of the prudent." 20 Where is the wise? Where is the scribe? Where is the disputer of this age? Has not God made foolish the wisdom of this world? 21 For since, in the wisdom of God, the world through wisdom did not know God, it pleased God through the foolishness of the message preached to save those who believe. 22 For Jews request a sign, and Greeks seek after wisdom; 23 but we preach Christ crucified, to the Jews a stumbling block and to the Greeks foolishness, 24 but to those who are called, both Jews and Greeks, Christ the power of God and the wisdom of God. 25 Because the foolishness of God is wiser than men, and the weakness of God is stronger than men.

Over against the wisdom of this world that apostle Paul tells us "true wisdom" is knowing Jesus Christ as savior, Who is Himself the power of God and the wisdom of God (verse 24). True wisdom is experiential knowledge of God through His Son Jesus Christ. True wisdom is knowing God personally.

Wisdom is personified as the virtuous woman, Lady Wisdom. She is presented to us over against the foolish woman, lady folly. In chapters 1-9 of Proverbs Solomon says,

---

[17] Gill, Exposition of the Whole Bible, Proverbs.

my son get wisdom. Lady Wisdom's house is the house of God (Ps 84; Eph 2:19-22). She calls for all to the banquet inside, to the marriage feast of the King's Son (Mt 22:1-14). Everyone is invited, provided he wears the King's garment – Christ's righteousness (Mt 22:12; Rev 19:6-9).

On the other hand, lady folly is loud and clamorous. Those who follow her lack understanding. Solomon tells us there will be a number of ways in which you will be tempted to hear the voice of lady folly but you must continue to listen to the voice of Lady Wisdom, who perhaps at times is speaking softly,. These two woman are calling out to the simple from the highest point of the city (Pro 8:2; 9:1-3, 13-14). This is a figurative way of describing the religious and philosophical centers of life. In ancient times, pagan temples were built on the highest part of each town so as to be the most prominent. Lady's Wisdom's is also to be heard from the highest parts of each town, perhaps not in respect to mere physical locale, but more so in regard to interaction with religion and philosophy. Lady Wisdom is to be heard in these institutions, wisdom is justified by her children.

Solomon says in chapter 7 that if you listen to the lady folly, she will continuously draw you out of the way until you will be like an ox that leads himself to slaughter (7:22). Solomon then goes beyond the temporal and shows us that Lady Wisdom is eternal, she was with God in the beginning, and so she takes precedence, while lady folly, being evil will last for a time and no more.

What is important to note here is wisdom is not a *hypostasis* or person all its own. Wisdom is a personification of a divine attribute. Solomon says follow Lady Wisdom because she is from the beginning and by her God made everything. In chapter 9, the two woman, Lady Wisdom and lady folly are pictured calling out to the simple. Lady Wisdom calls those who have ears to hear into the house that is eternal, founded on the Rock. In contrast, lady folly, loud and proud, lures wayward simpletons to their eternal doom, to forever remain in the abode of the dead. While on life's way, says Solomon, guard your heart, for out of it is the wellspring from which you flow (Pro 4:24). Don't allow yourself to become contaminated, get wisdom and follow after her voice. Proverbs

Chapter 3: The Irreconcilable War

4:18-19 tells us, "But the path of the just is like the shining sun, that shines ever brighter unto the perfect day. The way of the wicked is like darkness; they do not know what makes them stumble."

There are a number of pitfalls or ways lady folly employs to entice simpletons out of the Way. Some of these pitfalls have been mentioned in the two previous chapters albeit not in an extensive list. The Medieval church categorized sins in seven ways, i.e., the *seven deadly sins*: pride, wrath, envy, impurity (lust), gluttony, slothfulness (laziness), and avarice (greed). What's important to note here is temptations to sin are not sins in themselves. Given in to temptation becomes sin. The apostle James tells us,

12 Blessed is the man who endures temptation; for when he has been approved, he will receive the crown of life which the Lord has promised to those who love Him. 13 Let no one say when he is tempted, "I am tempted by God"; for God cannot be tempted by evil, nor does He Himself tempt anyone. 14 But each one is tempted when he is drawn away by his own desires and enticed. 15 Then, when desire has conceived, it gives birth to sin; and sin, when it is full-grown, brings forth death.

The biblical point being made here is this, the fact that a Christian is struggling is not a sign that he or she is not very spiritual or maybe not even saved, to the contrary, the fact that a man or woman is struggling is the sign of the new birth. A struggle within the believer is good news. For the flesh struggles against the spirit and the spirit against the flesh; the struggle therefore is evidence of the new life. Remember our Lord Jesus was tempted in every way we are, yet didn't sin (Heb 4:15).

Solomon's Seven Deadly Sins

Solomon sets before us seven deadly sins that are an abomination to God. Proverbs 6:16-19 tells us,

16 These six things the Lord hates, Yes, seven are an abomination to Him: 17 A proud look, A lying tongue, Hands that shed innocent blood, 18 A heart that devises wicked plans, Feet that are swift in

running to evil, 19 A false witness who speaks lies, And one who sows discord among brethren.

These seven things are abominable to God. These seven actions of man illicit hate in God's holy heart. These are the pitfalls the lady folly employs to draw simpletons out of the Way and into the house of Sheol:

1. A proud look (verse 17): the prideful look of arrogance.
2. A lying tongue (verse 17): the perverting or ignoring of truth.
3. Hands that shed innocent blood (verse 17): violence against the innocent or defenseless.
4. A heart that devises wicked plans (verse 18): the planning of sinful ideas.
5. Feet that are swift in running to evil (verse 18): the lust for and the love of doing things in rebellion against God, family, church, and state.
6. A false witness, a perjurer who breathes out lies (verse 19): corruption of the legal process of justice in the court via perjury.
7. And one who sows discord among brothers (verse 19): promotion of disunity, schism and conflict which causes both disruption of peace and disorder to society.

In a similar list, the apostle Paul enumerates to us the works of the flesh:

19 Now the works of the flesh are evident, which are: adultery, fornication, uncleanness, lewdness, 20 idolatry, sorcery, hatred, contentions, jealousies, outbursts of wrath, selfish ambitions, dissensions, heresies, 21 envy, murders, drunkenness, revelries, and the like (Gal 5:19-21).

When we compare these two lists we find that Galatians 5:19-21 is a practical exposition of Proverbs 6:16-19. These Scriptures provide us with the things God cannot stand or tolerate, that are an abomination to Him. Let's look at these again in light of Gal 5:19-21 with a relevance for today. There are six things that God hates, even seven that are abominable to Him (Pro 6:16):

Chapter 3: The Irreconcilable War

The first deadly sin, is a *proud look* from a conceited man. A man who makes a lot of money or the man who thinks he knows everything or perhaps even the man who thinks he's God's gift to women. These are the narcissists (2 Tim 3:1). In the Book of Proverbs there are three prominent types of fools: the khesel, a thick-headed man who won't listen; an aveel, a morally deficient man with no self-control; and a nabal, a disgraceful, crude, perverse man who has no respect for anyone or anything. A proud look comes from one of these three fools.

The only thing that matters to people like this is 'self.' They are consumed with the sickness of self: self-love, self-righteous, and self-centered. The Word of God tells us that pride comes before destruction, and a haughty (conceited) spirit before a fall (Pro 6:17; 16:18). Akin to the sin of pride is selfish ambition (Gal 5:20). This is the chief sin and entrance to all other sins (Ex 20:1-7; Is 14:13; Ezek 28:15). When God reveals Himself to a man, that man is undone, and as Calvin said, "knowledge of God comes before knowledge of self." C.S. Lewis describes this experience as follows:

In God you come up against something which is in every respect immeasurably superior to yourself. Unless you know God as that – and, therefore, know yourself as nothing in comparison — you do not know God at all. As long as you are proud you cannot know God. A proud man is always looking down on things and people: and, of course, as long as you are looking down, you cannot see something that is above you.[18]

The second deadly sin, is a *lying tongue* that twists the facts to suit one's own purposes, one that manipulates others to get their way (Pro 6:17; 1 Tim 1:10). This is the gossiper, and slanderer. A practitioner of this sin eventually will find his home in the lake of fire (Rev 21:8).

The third deadly sin, are the *hands that shed innocent blood* like when they take part in an immoral killing in combat or at an abortion clinic. This is the sin of failing to hold life in reverence (Gen 9:5-7; Ex 1 Tim 1:9; Rev 21:8).[19]

---

[18] Lewis, Mere Christianity, 124.
[19] See the fifth mark in chapter one for a discussion of this particular sin.

Chapter 3: The Irreconcilable War

A *heart that devises wicked plans*, the fourth deadly sin, uses creative energy to event ways of evil, ways to disobey God's Word, and convince others to do the same (Rom 1:28). The collective mass of unregenerate humanity are given a voice by their rulers and say, "Let us break Their bonds in pieces and cast away Their cords from us" (Ps 2:3). Their mouth reveals the plans of their collective heart, to throw off God's law and create their own morality. Psalm 2:1 asks us the rhetorical question, "Why do the nations rage, and the people plot a vain thing?" It's because fallen man claims deity for itself and violates God's will by rejecting His King.

The fifth deadly sin, are *feet that are swift in running to evil.* They run after the "cool" things that are in vogue. These feet are swift in running to fornication, drugs, porn, vandalism, and being disrespectful and undermining their boss' authority. The man entangled with this pitfall is likened to the dog in the old adage of Cleanthes of Assos. Cleanthes tells us that a wicked man is like a dog tied to a cart that is compelled to go wherever the cart leads on. The Bible relating a similar truth to us, tells us that a man who allows himself to be enticed by a lust is like an ox who leads itself to the slaughter (Pro 7:22). Porn is a deadly evil. Like other sins, porn seems to be harmless at first, but becomes a deadly trap to the men and women who have given full vent to it.

The biggest internet money maker in America by far is the porn industry! Americans spend more on porn every year than anything else. About 13 billion dollars is spent on pornography every year! According to Mark Kastleman, there are over 4 million separate and independent porn sites on the internet.[20] All of which may be accessed in the privacy of your own home. What is that doing to the men of this country? Porn destroys marriages by cheapening and distorting sacred marital intimacy and creates sexual deviants. This is grievous evil. King David writes, "I will set nothing wicked before my eyes; I hate the work of those who fall away; It shall not cling to me" (Ps 101:3). Porn is another sin that may be triumphed over in the Cross of Jesus Christ.[21]

---

[20] For a thorough discussion on this subject see Mark Kastleman's *Drug of the New Millennium: Pornography 500mg.*

[21] This is a topic for discussion in chapter four.

Chapter 3: The Irreconcilable War

A *false witness who speaks lies*, the sixth deadly sin, is a perjurer who says things against the boss, pastor, and those in a position of authority, in order to misrepresent them and make them look incompetent or otherwise unfit for their position. What is the difference between Proverbs 6:17 and 19 or more precisely between liars and perjurers? 1 Tim 1:8-10 makes a distinction between the two when it tells us," The law is not made for a righteous person, but for the lawless and insubordinate, for the ungodly and for sinners, for the unholy and profane, for murderers of fathers and murderers of mothers, for manslayers, for fornicators, for sodomites, for kidnappers, for *liars*, for *perjurers*, and if there is any other thing that is contrary to sound doctrine."

The distinction may be seen by the story of Naboth in 1 Kings 21. The wicked king of Israel Ahab wanted Naboth's vineyard but Naboth was unwilling to sell. In order to take Naboth's property Ahab's wicked queen Jezebel devises an evil scheme. She has false witnesses testify, perjure themselves, against Naboth (they falsely accused him of breaking the Law of Moses), for which Naboth is stoned to death, leaving the property to Ahab.[22]

The seventh and last deadly sin, *one who sows discord among brethren*, is committed by those who stir up dissention and schism. This type of sin keeps things stirred up so that godly goals and spiritual order become more difficult. A biblical example is Korah's rebellion found in Numbers 16. Korah stirred up the people of Israel against Moses, but God judged him and everyone with him by causing the earth to devour and cover them up.

Looking back at these seven deadly sins of Proverbs, Leibniz writes, "One sees numbers of people despising the entreaties of their friends, the counsels of their neighbors, the reproaches of their conscience, discomforts, tortures, death, the wrath of God, hell itself, for the sake of running after follies which have no claim to be good or tolerable, save as being freely chosen by such people."[23] God commands all men everywhere to repent of these sins and all others. We learned

---

[22] See 1 Kings 21:1-22:40.
[23] Leibniz, Theodicy, 268.

in chapter one that sin is any want of conformity unto or transgression of the law of God. God has appointed a day on which He will judge the world in righteousness by the Man whom He has ordained (Acts 17:30).

The Christian life is one of balance. And due to the remnants of our indwelling sin nature, the lures of the world, and the lies of the devil, we are "hindered in all our spiritual services, and our best works are imperfect and defiled in the sight of God."[24] The Christian grows in grace and in the knowledge of God, but the flesh continues to lust against the Spirit, and the Spirit against the flesh (Gal 5:17). The God-honoring man is living in the second half of Romans 7, and is bound in an irreconcilable war against the three enemies of his soul: his own sin nature, the world, and the devil.

Idolatry

The chief pitfall Christian men should be ever mindful of is the root of all other pitfalls – covetousness. The apostle Paul tells us, "Therefore put to death your members which are on the earth: fornication, uncleanness, passion, evil desire, and covetousness, which is idolatry. Because of these things the wrath of God is coming upon the sons of disobedience, in which you yourselves once walked when you lived in them" (Col 3:5-7). What is idolatry? An idol can be anything that claims the loyalty that belongs to God alone. Idolatry can be whatever your heart clings to for ultimate security.[25]

Christopher Wright tells us, "The primal problem with idolatry is that it blurs the distinction between the Creator God and His creation. This both damages creation (including ourselves) and diminishes the glory of the Creator." Wright goes on to say, "Since God's mission is to restore creation to its full original purpose of bringing all glory to God Himself and thereby to enable all creation to enjoy the fullness of the blessings that He desires for it, God battles against all forms of idolatry and calls us to join Him in that conflict."[26]

---

[24] WCF Larger Catechism Answer 78.
[25] Beale, We Become What We Worship, 17.
[26] Wright, The Mission of God, 187-188.

Chapter 3: The Irreconcilable War

Perhaps you can see that idolatry is more than bowing down to idols. As Christians we are to be ever watchful against covetousness (idolatry), and reflect the image of Christ, living out His righteousness. Greg Beale writes, what we revere, we resemble, either for ruin or restoration. Thus, we become like what we worship.[27] And William Tyndale writes, "To have a faith, therefore, or a trust in anything, where God hath not promised, is plain idolatry, and a worshipping of thine own imagination instead of God."[28]

The tenth commandment encapsulates the entirety of the Decalogue. Have you ever considered that the Ten Commandments begin and end with virtually the same commandment? "You shall have no other gods before me" (Exodus 20:3) and "You shall not covet" (Exodus 20:17) are almost equivalent commands. Coveting is not being content with God's blessings; our family, our jobs, our cars, etc. Covetousness is not being satisfied in God. Covetousness is a heart divided between two gods. That is why it is called idolatry (Col 3:5). The apostle Paul tells us in 1 Tim 6:6-10,

6 Now godliness with contentment is great gain. 7 For we brought nothing into this world, and it is certain[c] we can carry nothing out. 8 And having food and clothing, with these we shall be content. 9 But those who desire to be rich fall into temptation and a snare, and into many foolish and harmful lusts which drown men in destruction and perdition. 10 For the love of money is a root of all kinds of evil, for which some have strayed from the faith in their greediness, and pierced themselves through with many sorrows.

The word "covetousness" isn't used here, but the reality is what this text is all about, verse six says, "godliness with contentment is great gain." This gives us the key to the definition of covetousness. Covetousness is desiring something so much that you lose your contentment in God. "Godliness with contentment is great gain." The opposite of covetousness is contentment in God. When we decrease our contentment in God, covetousness for gain increases. That's why Paul says in Colossians 3:5 that covetousness is idolatry.

---

[27] Beale, We Become What We Worship, 16.
[28] Tyndale, The Works of William Tyndale, 317.

Chapter 3: The Irreconcilable War

"Put to death what is earthly in you: immorality, impurity, passion, evil desire, and covetousness which is idolatry." It's idolatry because the contentment that the heart should be getting from God, it starts to get from something else. God is our ultimate security.

John Piper writes, "All human relational problems—from marriage and family to friendship to neighbors to classmates to colleagues—all of them are rooted in various forms of idolatry, that is, wanting things other than God in wrong ways." The Christian is at war! As Christians we need to become increasingly aware of the pitfalls that lead to sin (1 Jn 5:21). We should realize that Christians are more injured by the deceitful and insidious enemy that lulls them into a sleep of carnal security than open and vile assaults.[29] Watchfulness is a Christian virtue.

In this irreconcilable war, may not true believers, by reason of their imperfections, and the many temptations and sins they are overtaken with, fall away from the state of grace? The Larger catechism tells us,

> True believers, by reason of the unchangeable love of God, and his decree and covenant to give them perseverance, their inseparable union with Christ, his continual intercession for them, and the Spirit and seed of God abiding in them, can neither totally nor finally fall away from the state of grace, but are kept by the power of God through faith unto salvation.[30]

The reason believers can live lives worthy of God is solely for the sacrifice of Christ alone (Gal 2:20-21; Rom 4). Believers live out Christ's righteousness. Christ's incarnation, life, crucifixion, and resurrection brought about a renewing of the creation. Lewis writes, "Our whole being by its very nature is one vast need; incomplete, preparatory, empty yet cluttered, crying out for Him who can untie things that are now knotted together and tie up things that are still dangling loose."

Sin was judged in our assumed, fallen, and depraved nature. Through His incarnation the Son of God appropriated our

---

[29] Alexander, Thoughts on Religious Experience, 158.
[30] WCF Larger Catechism Answer 79.

Chapter 3: The Irreconcilable War

fallen humanity under the judgment of God. The unassumed in unredeemed. The resurrection is therefore God's process of new creation (Mk 14:58; Jn 2:19-22; 1 Pet 1:3-5). We see in the resurrection a reversal of the work that introduced death, i.e., destroy the works of the devil (1 Jn 3:8). Jesus Christ's one-for-all sacrifice restored humanity, fellowship, and worship. Christ's resurrection established the Kingdom of God spiritually which will be consummated physically (Mt 4:17; Mk 1:15; Lk 13:29-30; 17:20-21; 2 Thess 1:5-10; Rev 21, 22).

Jesus is resurrection life, He is new humanity. His resurrection life is the cause, pledge, and security of ours. Certainty of the resurrection of believers is the fact that Christ arose just as He said. Proof of the resurrection is Christ's abiding presence. In His abiding presence we are able to overcome the three enemies of our soul, to the glory of God.

What we have tried to make abundantly clear in this chapter is the Christian is at war! And becoming like Jesus Christ requires commitment and effort on our part.

Mortification of Sin in Believers

The will of God is our sanctification (1 Thess 4:3).[31] God desires for His saints to have a mind for truth and a heart for Him. How well we have understood with our mind and how genuinely we have responded with our hearts will be tested by the decisions of our will. And unless we behave a certain way, we raise serious questions regarding the depth of our understanding of the gospel.

Christians are at war against the three enemies of their souls: their indwelling sin nature (flesh), the world, and the devil. *Mortification* is the life-long battle against the first enemy – the flesh. There are two texts from the Bible that are essential in this fight: "Mortify therefore your members which are upon the earth; fornication, uncleanness, inordinate affection, evil concupiscence, and covetousness, which is idolatry: For which things' sake the wrath of God cometh on the children of disobedience" (Col 3:5-6 KJV); "For if you live according to the flesh you will die; but if by the Spirit you

---

[31] See chapter four for a discussion on the will of God.

put to death the deeds of the body, you will live" (Rom 8:13). The word 'mortify' means put to death. J. I. Packer informs us that the verb 'mortify' in Rom 8:13 is in the aorist tense, implying that mortification, once commenced, will be successfully accomplished.[32]

Looking back from earlier in this chapter, we stated, that the fruit of the Spirit is the result of the Holy Spirit's presence and work in the lives of believers that are yielding themselves to God. As the believer yields more and more to the Spirit, the flesh is sacked and strangled while the new man of the Spirit, growing like a well-watered plant, bears fruit – visible marks of Christian maturity, showing that he is rooted and grounded in love. This is how indwelling sin is killed. We are to be killing sin or it will be killing us.[33]

The Spirit is willing but the flesh is weak (Mt 26:41). The Spirit is willing to uproot all manner of demonic strongholds in our lives: alcoholism, adultery, pornography, homosexuality, and the like, if we surrender our minds, wills, and emotions to Christ. Christ is willing to bear our burdens. He has already paid the penalty for our sins.

Martin Luther once said, "Original sin is in us, like the beard. We are shaved today and look clean, and have a smooth chin; tomorrow our beard has grown again, nor does it cease growing while we remain on earth." But how do we mortify (kill) sin in our flesh? How do we put to death our desires to look at pornography? How do we put to death our willingness to have an affair? How do we put to death our desire to get drunk? Or use drugs? How about our outbursts of wrath? What is the instrument for killing these inclinations? These works of the flesh?

In the Gospel of John, Jesus teaches us a vital lesson regarding sanctification and mortification.

15 "I am the true vine, and My Father is the vinedresser. 2 Every branch in Me that does not bear fruit He takes away; **and every branch that bears fruit He prunes, that it may bear more fruit.** 3 You are already clean because of the word which I have spoken to you. 4 Abide in Me, and I in you. As the branch cannot bear fruit of

---

[32] Packer, God's Words, 181.
[33] Owen, The Mortification of Sin in Believers, 9.

itself, unless it abides in the vine, neither can you, unless you abide in Me. 5 "I am the vine, you are the branches. He who abides in Me, and I in him, bears much fruit; for without Me you can do nothing. 6 If anyone does not abide in Me, he is cast out as a branch and is withered; and they gather them and throw them into the fire, and they are burned. 7 If you abide in Me, and My words abide in you, you will ask what you desire, and it shall be done for you. 8 By this My Father is glorified, that you bear much fruit; so you will be My disciples (emphasis added).

By saying "I am the true vine" Jesus is saying, "I am true Israel" (Is 5:7), as is everyone who is in Him (Rom 2:28-29; Phil 3:3). Whereas those who reject Christ are like the evil tenants in the parable of the wicked vinedressers (Mt 21:33-44), who beat and killed every prophet sent to them and when the Son and Heir appeared they reasoned they could kill Him and take possession of the vineyard. However, they will be ground to powder while the vineyard is given to a nation that will bear the fruits of the kingdom (Mt 21:43). Those who reject Jesus as the Messiah are void of the Spirit and so 'fruitless.' But those who receive Him as Savior are clean because the gospel takes root in them (Mt 13:23; Jn 15:3), and the Spirit produces fruit in their lives (Gal 5:22, 25). Grace is the life of God in the soul of man.

Regarding sanctification, God's work of purifying His saints, Jesus says that those who abide (remain) in Him will bear fruit. And will be 'pruned' so as to bear more fruit (Jn 15:2). Pruned so as to be refined. John the Baptist put it this way, "He must increase but I must decrease." As we are led by the Spirit, God the Father prunes us – moving us to cast into the fire of His presence all thoughts, words, and deeds that He condemns by His Word. Eliminating what is fruitless. So the Spirit can grow more fruit in place of the works of the flesh that have been eradicated. John Piper says, "A Christian is not a person who experiences no bad desires. He is a person who is at war with those desires by the power of the Spirit." So I ask, can anyone who is engrafted into Christ be without fruit?

The Scripture tells us in Romans 6:1-4, "What shall we say then? Shall we continue in sin that grace may abound? Certainly not! How shall we who died to sin live any longer in it? Or do you not know that as many of us as were baptized into Christ Jesus were baptized into His death? Therefore we were buried with Him through baptism into death, that just as Christ was raised from the dead by the glory of the Father, even so we also should walk in newness of life.

Whereas, mortification from a self-strength, carried on by ways of self-invention, unto the end of a self-righteousness is the soul and substance of all false religion in the world.[34] What cuts down the works of the flesh is the mighty sword of the Spirit – the Word of God (Eph 6:17). When we are tempted to sin we must remind ourselves of the Scripture that condemns it. And triumph over temptations like Christ did when He was tempted in the wilderness (Mt 4:1-11). As blood-bought Christians, we are to live as we are called, not as who we were (Gal 5:13, 16; 2 Tim 2:19). That is, we must kill sin in our path. We must be relentless in our pursuit to starve sin and everything that feeds it. We must, as John Owen said, 'be killing sin or it will be killing us.' For all other ways of mortification are vain, all helps leave us helpless, it must be done by the Spirit.[35]

Mortification of sin is evidence of one's salvation not the cause of it. And the vigor and power and comfort of our spiritual life depends on our mortification of deeds of the flesh.[36] This is how a young man keeps his way pure. By guarding it according to your word (Ps 119:09). If we have been crucified with Christ (Gal 2:20), then let us put to death what remains in our old self – our sin nature (Col 3:5). And if we were raised with Christ to walk in newness of life (Rom 6:4), then let us be led by the Spirit (Gal 5:25), and seek heavenly things (Col 3:1), namely how we may please our heavenly father (Rom 12:2; Eph 5:8-10). And in so doing let us not set aside the grace of God, for apart from Christ we can do nothing (Jn 15:4-5), for if righteousness were through the law then Christ died for no purpose (Gal 2:21). This subject is the topic for discussion in the following chapter.

---

[34] Owen, On Temptation and the Mortification of Sin in Believers, 149.
[35] Ibid, 149.
[36] Ibid, 152.

Chapter 3: The Irreconcilable War

Long my imprisoned spirit lay
Fast bound in sin and nature's night;
Thine eye diffused a quickning ray,
I woke, the dungeon flamed with light;
My chains fell off, my heart was free;
I rose, went forth and followed Thee.
Amazing love! How can it be,
That thou my God, should die for me![37]

Christian in the Valley of the Shadow of Death.

---

[37] C. Wesley, And Can it Be.

Chapter 3: The Irreconcilable War

Recommended Further Reading

1. John Owen *The Mortification of Sin in Believers*.
2. J. C. Ryle *Holiness*.
3. C. S. Lewis *Mere Christianity*.
4. Greg Beale *We Become What We Worship*.
5. Augustine, *Confessions*.

Chapter 3 Review Questions

1. What is the relationship between Christ's resurrection and man's salvation?
2. Is there biblical relevance to Kierkegaard's *Three Stages*?
3. What are the three uses of the Law?
4. What is justification?
5. What is the significance of Christ's righteous life?
6. What does the Book of Proverbs teach us?
7. What is the correlation between idolatry and covetousness?
8. What are the dangers of pornography? How can pornography affect the marriage relationship?
9. What is mortification?
10. What is the fruit of the Spirit?

Pilgrims Moving to Connecticut

"I appeal to you therefore, brothers, by the mercies of God, to present your bodies as a living sacrifice, holy and acceptable to God, which is your spiritual worship. Do not be conformed to this world, but be transformed by the renewal of your mind, that by testing you may discern what is the will of God, what is good and acceptable and perfect" (Rom 12:1-2).

Chapter 4: Distinguished Service

Of all the concepts we've discussed so far, those we'll cover in this chapter are perhaps the most formative for disciplined Christian living. Our proof and assurance of our conversion is the fruit of the Spirit, Christ's character radiating out of us; living out Christ's righteousness. Or better yet, Christ living in us (Gal 2:20-21). In this chapter we'll discuss the five following topics:

- The Priesthood of Believers.
- The Ethics of the Kingdom.
- Growing in Grace – 10 Christian disciplines.
- The Kingdom of Priests.
- The Pilgrim-Indigenous Paradigm.

Chapter 4: Distinguished Service

The Priesthood of Believers

All of life is spiritual worship, and every believer is a priest.[1] Every Christian is a priest who is to offer himself as a sacrifice "holy and acceptable to God," according to the pattern laid down by Christ (Rom 12:1; Jn 17:19). The priesthood of believers or universal priesthood is the Christian doctrine that states that all believers have direct access to God through the mediation of Jesus Christ – our great High Priest (1 Tim 2:5-6). The apostle Peter writing in 1 Peter 2 tells us, "But you are a chosen generation, a royal priesthood, a holy nation, His own special people, that you may proclaim the praises of Him who called you out of darkness into His marvelous light." And the apostle John in the Apocalypse tells us we have been made a kingdom of priests (Rev 1:6).

Martin Luther pointed out in his *Babylonian Captivity of the Church* that "all we who are Christians are priests," and no believer has greater access to the Creator than any other.[2] Beale writes, "From one perspective, all believers are priests and they function as priests by offering up prayers in the sphere of the spiritual temple.[3] Affirming the priesthood of believers doesn't negate the necessity of ordained ministry. Pastors, elders, and deacons are appointed to teach the church the will of God from His Word (1 Tim. 3:1–7), but they do not represent us before the heavenly throne like the Levitical priests did under the administration of the old covenant.[4] Before Luther, this was a biblical concept that was revived by John Wycliffe.[5]

John Wycliffe, believing the church should be patterned after the New Testament, opposed various medieval traditions

---

[1] Ridderbos, Paul: An Outline of His Theology, 481.

[2] Luther, Weimar Ausgabe, Vol. 6, 407.

[3] Beale, The Temple and the Church's Mission, 397.

[4] See Chapter 6 for discussion on the distinctions in the priesthood.

[5] John Wycliffe (1320-1364) was a lecturer at Oxford, the rector at Lutterworth, and an early reformer in the Church of England. Through Wycliffe the church witnessed a revival of Augustinian studies. His great desire was to pattern the church after the New Testament. Although Wycliffe's lasting contribution to the church wouldn't find lasting expression until Jan Huss and Luther, his immediate contribution was his translation of the Bible into English.

that had passed into observance. Some of his views include:
(1) Christ, not the pope, is head of the church – *solus Christus*,
(2) the Scripture, not the church, is the rule of authority – *sola Scriptura*, (3) Christ's work, not our own, gains God's favor – *sola gratia,* (4) the priest's main vocation is to preach the Word of God, not act as a church appointed mediator between God and His people – *sola fide*, and (5) entrance into the church of God is controlled, not by the clergy, but by God Himself, that is salvation doesn't depend upon one's connection with the visible church or the mediation of the priest, but on one's faith in Christ alone – *soli Deo gloria*.[6]

The focus of this chapter is the practical living out of the new life in Christ. Because Christ dwells in our hearts by faith, He roots and grounds us to Himself in love, so that we may endure to the end (Phil 1:6), and live out His righteousness (Phil 2:12-13). This is what the Bible calls our 'living sacrifice.' It is our life-long selfless service to God in light of Christ's once-for-all sacrifice. This offering up of ourselves has been both granted unto us to do and commanded of us to give. Through this offering up of ourselves as a living sacrifice: (1) God makes His appeal to a dying world through us, (2) we are Christ's hands and feet – His body, and (3) we bring the presence of the Holy Spirit.

Looking back at the chapter, we introduced the *indicative-imperative* paradigm. This concept states that the *indicative* is the accomplished reality, that is, what has been accomplished by Jesus Christ in His incarnation, life, death, resurrection, ascension, and present intercession gives us the power to do the enabled commandment, that is, the *imperative*.

Regarding our discussion of the 'living sacrifice,' the next thing we should bear in mind is the new life. The new life begins when we receive Jesus Christ as Savior and Lord. The new life comes into being by the Holy Spirit and its realization

---

[6] Although the five solas, *sola Scriptura*, etc., come to us from the Magisterial Reformers, their embryonic form may be found in the five views of Wycliffe shown above. Additionally, Wycliffe opposed transubstantiation, the cult of saints, relics, and pilgrimages, and papal infallibility. His views were condemned by the pope in 1377, and his body was later exhumed in 1415, following the council of Constance, which also condemned and burned Jan Huss at the stake for similar beliefs.

is new creation. The realization of this mighty work is regeneration – death to life (Rom 4:17). The new life in Christ brings regeneration and obedience. We are now talking about the new life and the new life is in reference to the old life.

In chapter two we saw that the old life is dead, defiled, and damned. It cannot submit to God's will, God's Word, or God's Spirit. The old life is self-willed, self-ruled, and self-indulgent. It cares only for itself. The old self is, to name a few more dubious characteristics, lawless, murderous, lecherous, adulterous, idolatrous, lustful, vengeful, and effeminate. The old self hates others and is hated by others, and most of all the old self hates God. The only future the old self will know is hell, which the old self now experiences by a horror of conscience and a fearful expectation of the coming judgment. But thanks be to God through Jesus Christ our Lord for while we were God-haters, Christ died for us. The Just for the unjust (Rom 5:8).

In chapter three we saw that there are three enemies of the saint who battles against them in an irreconcilable war; the flesh fighting the Spirit, and the Spirit fight against the flesh (Gal 5:17). When Christ saves a man, He enables him to live a life of holiness unto God – this is a 'living sacrifice.' The apostle Paul introduces us to this concept in Romans 12:1-2:

12 I appeal to you therefore, brothers, by the mercies of God, to present your bodies as a living sacrifice, holy and acceptable to God, which is your spiritual worship. 2 Do not be conformed to this world, but be transformed by the renewal of your mind, that by testing you may discern what is the will of God, what is good and acceptable and perfect.

Paul appeals to believers "by the mercies of God." If God were to deal with us as we deserve, exacting our full debt to Him, we would be prostrated by the horrors of our conscience and cast into outer darkness. In light of this, Paul tells us, "Present your bodies as a living sacrifice." The word 'present' used in verse one is *parastemi* παρίστημι which is translated "offer," and can mean in the biblical sense 'to be at hand for service.' The apostle Paul uses the aorist tense to demonstrate that this presenting is something we do and continue to do. We are to continuously offer ourselves as a living sacrifice to God.

Chapter 4: Distinguished Service

This is the sense in a parallel verse found in 1 Peter 2:4-5, "Coming to Him as to a living stone, rejected indeed by men, but chosen by God and precious, you also, as living stones, are being built up a spiritual house, a holy priesthood, to offer up (parastemi) spiritual sacrifices acceptable to God through Jesus Christ."

This presenting of ourselves is to be whole-hearted. This presentation of ourselves as a living sacrifice resembles Christ's once-for-all dying sacrifice of Himself for our debt of sin. To present ourselves as a 'living sacrifice' requires confidence to enter the Holy places by the blood of Jesus, through His flesh. Christ in this way presents Himself to the Father through the lives of His redeemed servants, interceding for us. Only in this way can our living sacrifice be holy and acceptable to God (Heb 7:25; 10:19-25). This, as the apostle says, is our 'reasonable service.' The word reasonable *logiken* λογικὴν when combined with λατρείαν service means priestly service, i.e., worship, that is rendered from the whole man: mind, will, and emotions.

Paul says, "Present your bodies as a living sacrifice." This sacrifice to God is to be a living one not a dead one. In the Levitical sacrifice, prefiguring Christ's sacrifice, the high priest offered (λατρείαν) a pure, spotless lamb. The fire consumed the dead sacrifice as well as that of our Lord's sacrifice which cost Him His life for ours. However we are to present (*parastemi*) ourselves as a living sacrifice as we are purged and refined in the fires of the Holy Spirit's sanctifying work. Thus, the believer's body (mind, will, and emotions) is a holy and acceptable sacrifice as it is morally and spiritually presented to God.

The biblical point being made here the new life in Christ, in its moral manifestation, is proclaimed and lived out as the fruit of the redemptive work of God through the powerful operation of the Holy Spirit. Thus the believer, as a new creation is made willing and obedient, and is enabled to die to indwelling sin more and more, and to present his body as an instrument of righteousness (Rom 6:13-14). The new man has been set free from bondage which the old man had no freedom to not serve.

Then in verse two, Paul says, "And do not be conformed to this world, but be transformed by the renewing of your mind, that you may prove what is that good and acceptable and perfect will of God." In the first verse the apostle shows us what to do. In the second verse he shows us how to do it. For what to do he says, "do not be conformed to this world." Paul uses the verb *suschématizó* συσχηματίζω which is a compilation of the two words: fashion and together. *Suschématizó* is the derivation of our word for schematic, and in the biblical sense *suschématizó* means to fashion oneself together to the pattern of this age, that is to participate in the ways of the world, value what the world values, etc. This is conformity. An act of matching attitudes, beliefs, and behaviors to group norms.

The human tendency is to conform to the pressures of small groups and to society as a whole. These pressures may come as a subtle influence, or as a direct and overt force. Unwillingness to conform carries the risk of social and economic ostracism. The point the apostle makes when he says, "But be transformed by the renewing of your mind," is don't allow yourself to be fashioned by the pressures and influences of the world, either by acquaintances at work, or friends, or even family! We must live as who we are now and not who we were (indicative-imperative).

"We must be transformed by the renewing of our minds" (Rom 12:2). The word used here *metamorphao* μεταμορφόω is the derivation of the word metamorphosis, that is, transfigured into another form, that of the image of Christ. We are not to yield to the temptation to compromise with the world – to be conformed to the world's image. We are to allow ourselves to be continuously transformed by God's Word. This inner transformation is the work of God in us, but we are responsible for submitting to God's Word in all things (Phil 2:12-13). We are commanded and enabled to do this.

"That you may prove what is that good and acceptable and perfect will of God" (Rom 12:2). This is the stated purpose of Scripture to glorify God by doing what He demands. The Scriptures principally teach what man is to believe concerning God and what duty God requires of man.[7] This is what God

---

[7] WCF Shorter Catechism Answer 3.

Chapter 4: Distinguished Service

requires of us – obedience to His revealed will. And what is the will of God?

The Will of God

Regarding the will of God, the Christian tradition has understood it in two senses: the secret or decretive will of God, and the revealed or preceptive will. These are understood as two aspects of God's divine will. First, God's *decretive will* is the rule which governs His own actions in creation (Rev 4:11), in providence (Dan 4:35), and in grace (Rom 9:15).[8] Second, God's *revealed will* is the truth He makes known to us for what we are to believe concerning Him and what He requires of us. The correlation between these two aspects of the divine will be discussed further in chapter ten.

For now we may ask, what is the revealed will of God? To believe in the One He has sent, Jesus Christ – mankind's only Savior, to be further sanctified and set apart for His great work (Jn 6:40; 1 Thess 4:3). The verb Paul uses here is dokimazo δοκιμάζω which means: to test, examine, and to prove. This verse shows a few things namely: (1) If we have the mind of Christ, by being born again, we are able to test and discern what is pleasing to the Lord. And (2) we are able to judge ourselves, that is, our thoughts, speech, and actions to see if whether they are approved of God or not. We are always to prayerfully consider what God's will is in each situation. We are to test, examine, and prove all things. We may surmise three biblical points from all of this: (1) we are commanded and enabled to continuously present our lives as a living sacrifice. Christ saved us from eternal death and separation in hell, not so we could live for ourselves but so we could live for God. (2) We are commanded and enabled to be transformed by the continuous renewing of our minds by God's Holy Scripture.

Our wills are activated by the Spirit but we don't transform ourselves, we surrender to Christ, Who by the Spirit transforms us. We must look to God's Word for conformity not the world. The imperative action is from our will, while

---

[8] Kelly, If God Already Knows – Why Pray?, 65-66.

197

the transformative action is by God. Further, (3) we are commanded and enabled to persevere while doing God's will, that is, what is the good, acceptable and perfect will of God. We are to live to Christ but die to the world daily as we live out His righteousness. A life of self-discipline and devotion to God is the practical outworking of the new birth, not its cause. Our expectable priestly service to God is accomplished when we do all things unto the glory of God (1 Cor 10:31; Col 3:23).

The Ethics of the Kingdom

Those called by the Father, saved by the Son, and regenerated by the Spirit, are brought from death to life – translated into the kingdom of Christ, to be further sanctified (Jn 6:37-40; Col 1:13; 1 Pet 1:3). This section discusses Christ's Sermon on the Mount, which Augustine called, "the perfect pattern of the Christian life." It is indeed that, for in it, Jesus gives His disciples His ethical demands for Kingdom-living. Rightly has William Perkins called it "the key to the whole Bible." John Stott tells us, "The Sermon on the Mount is probably the best known part of the teaching of Jesus, though arguably it is the least understood, and certainly it is the least obeyed."[9] The following is the basic structure of the Sermon on the Mount:

Beatitudes	(5:3-12)
Task of those in the Kingdom – Witness	(5:13-16)
Jesus Christ, the fulfillment of the Law	(5:17-20)
Christ's correction of theological errors	(5:21-48)
Christ's correction of piety errors	(6:1-18)
Living in the Kingdom	(6:19-7:12)
Christ's eschatological warnings	(7:13-27)

The Beatitudes

In the Beatitudes, Mt 5:1-12, Jesus describes to His followers the character of the Christian:

---

[9] Stott, *Sermon on the Mount*, 5.

Chapter 4: Distinguished Service

5 And seeing the multitudes, He went up on a mountain, and when He was seated His disciples came to Him. 2 Then He opened His mouth and taught them, saying:

3 "Blessed are the poor in spirit, For theirs is the kingdom of heaven.
4 Blessed are those who mourn, For they shall be comforted.
5 Blessed are the meek, For they shall inherit the earth.
6 Blessed are those who hunger and thirst for righteousness, For they shall be filled.
7 Blessed are the merciful, For they shall obtain mercy.
8 Blessed are the pure in heart, For they shall see God.
9 Blessed are the peacemakers, For they shall be called sons of God.
10 Blessed are those who are persecuted for righteousness' sake, For theirs is the kingdom of heaven.

11 "Blessed are you when they revile and persecute you, and say all kinds of evil against you falsely for My sake. 12 Rejoice and be exceedingly glad, for great is your reward in heaven, for so they persecuted the prophets who were before you.

Jesus doesn't say to us live like this and you'll be saved, but because you're saved, live like this. Jesus does not describe to us how we are to be saved but describes the character of those whom He saves. The character Jesus depicts in the Beatitudes leads to conduct in the rest of the Sermon on the Mount. Character leads to conduct. Before we go on to examine some spiritual disciplines we should consider the character that Christians are to evidence in their lives.

The first Beatitude tells us we must be poor in spirit, which is the absence of self-aggrandizement or self-reliance. No one who has not felt spiritual poverty enters the kingdom of heaven. This first beatitude, "Blessed are the poor in spirit, for theirs is the kingdom of heaven," declares to us that in order to be *full* we first must be *empty* (Mt 5:3). Martyn Lloyd-Jones tells us, "If anyone feels anything in the presence of God save an utter poverty of spirit, it ultimately means that you have never faced Him. That is the meaning of this Beatitude."[10]

The Beatitudes describe the signs and evidences of the work of God's saving grace upon the soul. They are not entrance

---

[10] Lloyd-Jones, Studies in the Sermon on the Mount, 36.

requirements but are a description of Christ's character in us. They are an absolute anti-thesis of the worldly standard. "Blessed are those who mourn, for they shall be comforted," the second Beatitude, relates the truth that a real sense of sin must precede conversion. Our relationship with the Personal God is based on: God's written Self-revelation to man – the Bible; Christ's finished work in space-time history; and the Spirit's application of both in us. Our mourning for sin is comforted by an assurance of God's forgiveness in Christ. Godly sorrow produces repentance unto life (2 Cor 7:8-10).

The third Beatitude, "Blessed are the meek, for they shall inherit the earth," relates to us the truth that meekness is evidence of the life of God in the soul of man. This Beatitude shows us that meekness is not a mere moral quality but a fruit of the Spirit (gentleness – Gal 5:23). Thus meekness is not weakness but rather the exercising of God's strength under His control, enduring injury with patience and without resentment. As the Beatitudes progress they become more difficult, hence the more we become like Jesus, the more the world will hate us, the more they will persecute us.

The natural man, the man dead in his trespasses and sins is a proud fellow, he is fond of his own righteousness, and is ignorant of Christ's. We cannot merit the pardon of our sins by even our best works. Those who try show they are void of faith. "Blessed are those who hunger and thirst for righteousness, for they shall be filled," the fourth beatitude, relates to us that those who have saving knowledge of God in Christ possess a deep consciousness of their need for a righteousness apart from themselves.

This righteousness we hunger and thirst for is something the world cannot give us. It's not mere happiness. Jesus did not say happy are those who hunger and thirst after happiness. This is the error of the health, wealth, and prosperity gospel. To say we are 'Kingdom kids' and we are going to be happy and rich in this life because God wants us to be happy and rich in this life, is the devil's ancient lure. Lloyd-Jones writes, "The man who hungers and thirsts for righteousness has come to see that the world in which he lives in is controlled by sin and Satan. The righteousness we hunger and thirst for is Christ Himself and His righteousness."[11]

The point we are making is what we value exerts influence on our behavior so that it becomes our character. In this way we may see how values shape our character. Beale tells us,

"God has made all people to reflect, to be imaging beings. People will always reflect something, whether it be God's character or some feature of the world. If people are committed to God, they will become like Him; if they are committed to something other than God, they will become like that thing, always spiritually inanimate and empty like the lifeless and vain aspects of creation to which they have committed themselves."[12]

The fifth Beatitude, "Blessed are the merciful, for they shall obtain mercy," relates to us the truth that mercy flows from a heart that has first felt its spiritual bankruptcy. The truth is all men are dead, defiled, and damned and will remain so unless Christ in His power saves them; to be further sanctified by the Holy Spirit moving them to show the mercy they have experienced. To be further glorified with Him and all His saints when He returns to resurrect all flesh and judge the world in righteousness (Acts 17:31). When Christ calls a man, He gives him life – His life, and righteousness – His righteousness, and vicariously lives and triumphs through that man, bringing him to heaven to Himself to be with Him forever (Jn 6:37-40).

Can a Christian be unforgiving? Certainly. However his prayers are hindered, his testimony is weakened and tarnished, his joy and peace fade, and he grieves the Holy Spirit. When a Christian is unforgiving, he presumes to stand as judge over the offense and exact a payment due so as to make the offending person feel resentment, anger and pain for the wrong they've caused you. We show the mercy of God by the way Christ moves us in His compassion for the lost, pitiable, and the afflicted. Christ Jesus enlarges our heart to embrace

---

[11] Lloyd-Jones, Studies in the Sermon on the Mount, 65-67.
[12] Beale, We Become What We Worship: A Biblical Theology of Idolatry, 284.

the whole world of pitiable men who remain under the domain of the devil.

"Blessed are the pure in heart, for they shall see God," the sixth Beatitude, brings us to the very heart of the gospel. What we learn from this Beatitude is that Jesus is concerned with our heart. The aim of Christ in the world is not merely to clean up society to a higher moral standard, the aim of Christ is to transform a world's worth of people into His image and bring them to Himself (Jn 6:37-40). What does pure in heart mean?

Two things pure in heart is not: (1) legalism, (2) asceticism. As Christ's denouncement of the Pharisees shows, pure in heart is not a mere outward religiosity – churchianity. This is hypocrisy at worst and a living a sham at best. Additionally, pure in heart is not mere asceticism, in other words it's not mere rigorous self-denial. We cannot help our souls by hurting our bodies. We can't make ourselves pure in heart; this was the error of monasticism. A Christian should and must practice self-restraint, but this practice will not make us pure in heart, because it's based upon the false assumption that by torturing our body we can earn heaven.

Three things Pure in Heart is: (1) conscious allegiance to Christ. Consciously submitting to the Lordship of Jesus Christ, and obeying His commandments (Jn 14:15); (2) the surrender of one's will to that of God's; to say in all instances, not my will but Thy will be done on earth as it is in heaven (Mt 6:10); (3) the sensitive humility to the convicting, guiding, and directing of God the Spirit. Hence, being pure in heart is a condition of our whole person, our mind, will, and emotions and a direction of them toward one goal; the glory of God in the salvation of sinners.

The Beatitudes are not a prescription for making the world a better place. The Beatitudes describe the way to heaven. The pilgrim pathway – the Calvary road. This is a further manifestation of the Christian's character. There is a logical progression, and the seventh Beatitude, "Blessed are the peacemakers, for they shall be called sons of God," relates the truth that those who have been called out of darkness into light desire to share the love of Christ by proclaiming the gospel to everyone. Those who take up this work are acknowledged by God as sons and daughters. Peacemakers are those who have experienced the releasing power of God's peace in Christ, and are made sons and daughters of God (Heb 2:14-15).

If we are saved, born-again, converted, quickened, regenerated, Spirit-filled (a rose by any other name would smell as sweet), then Jesus says, we will desire to see God glorified in the salvation of sinners by bringing the offending message of the gospel (Mt 5:9). And two things will result, peace or division (Mt 10:34). Peacemakers are those whose message of peace with God through our Lord Jesus Christ is rejected by the world – rejected and hated! They bring the message of peace and are killed for it (Rev 6:10). One of two things will occur when the gospel is proclaimed: peace or conflict. Peace when men and women hear the gospel and surrender their lives to Christ, but irreconcilable war, when the gospel is rejected. Dietrich Bonhoeffer writes, "The peace of Jesus is the cross. But the cross is the sword God wields on earth. It creates division."[13] Without a merciful, pure, peacemaking heart one cannot be called a son of God at the judgment day. No Jesus, no peace – know Jesus, know peace (Is 26:1-8); if you don't know Jesus Christ as Savior; you'll know Him as Judge (Jn 3:35-36). Carson writes, "Jesus does not limit the peacemaking to only one kind, and neither will his disciples. In light of the gospel, Jesus Himself is the supreme Peacemaker, making peace between God and man, and man and man. Our peacemaking will include the promulgation of the gospel."[14]

It's God's will, for everyone who looks to the Son and believes in Him, to not only have eternal life, but to be further sanctified unto purifying holiness and to endure to the end in the power He supplies (Jn 3:16; 6:37-40; 8:35-36; 10:28-30; 16:33). The gospel is like a drawn sword thrust forth into the world by the living oracle of God (Mt 10:32-42). The incarnation of the Son of God brings a crisis. Believers are saved because Jesus paid their penalty, and unbelievers suffer the wrath Jesus bore. They refused God, so they pay their own penalty. Persecution is the inevitable result when the gospel comes.

---

[13] Bonhoeffer, The Cost of Discipleship, 219.
[14] Carson, Commentary on Matthew 5:13-16.

Chapter 4: Distinguished Service

"Blessed are those who are persecuted for righteousness' sake, for theirs is the kingdom of heaven," the eighth Beatitude, relates the truth that sufferings and persecution for the sake of Christ is the inevitable result for those who obey the gospel (Mt 5:10-13). Jesus tells us the more you are like Me, the more the world will hate you, and persecute you but the more you are like Me the more blessed you will be and will glorify your heavenly Father. God ordains suffering as the price and means of finishing the Great Commission (Mt 24:9). Through flood and flame, the gospel will be proclaimed throughout the world as a testimony to all nations, and then the end will come (Mt 24:14).[15]

The Puritan Thomas Watson regarding Christian suffering writes,

"God has never promised us a charter of exemption from trouble, but he has promised to be with us in trouble. No vessel can be made of gold without fire; so it is impossible that we can be made vessels of honor, unless we are melted and refined in the furnace of affliction. God's chastening rod draws Christ's image more distinctly upon us. It is good for there to be symmetry between the Head and the members: to be part of Christ's body; "He was a man of sorrows, acquainted with grief. Hence, it is good to be like Christ, albeit by sufferings."[16]

Christ indeed bore the punishment for our sins so that our sufferings are never punishment from God but a call to suffer with Christ, not to bear our sins, but to love the way He loved and be ready to suffer for doing the will of God the way He did (Mt 20:28; Phil 2:5-11; 1 Pet 4:17-19; Rev 1:9).

As we look at each Beatitude, we see one after the other that the blessings of eternity will be given only to those who have become new creatures in Christ. Blessed are the merciful, for they shall obtain mercy. Blessed are the pure in heart, for they shall see God. Blessed are the peacemakers, for they shall be called the sons of God. If we don't obtain mercy, we receive judgment. If we don't see God, we are not in heaven. If we aren't called the sons of God, we are outside the family. These

---

[15] This subject is the topic for chapter 10.
[16] Watson, Puritan Gems, 2-9.

are all descriptions of Christian character (Mt 5:3-10), and the character of the Christian as proved by the world's reaction to him (Mt 5:11-12). In other words these are all descriptions of final salvation. And it is promised only to the merciful, the pure in heart, and the peacemakers. The glory outstrips the sufferings! We learn endurance in the school of holy experience! The cross before the crown! Blessed are those who are Christ-like (Mt 5:3-12)!

Growing in Grace – 10 Christian Disciplines

At the close of His sermon on the mount, Jesus spoke about two differing foundations for living: the Rock, and the sifting sand (Mt 7:24-27; 16:17-19). The thrust of His entire sermon was an admonition to build one's life on Christ and His righteousness alone – the Rock (2 Sam 22:32). This section will present us with some Christian disciplines that are essential for growth in the Christian life, in order for us to imitate Jesus, to model His life and ministry, thereby living out His righteousness (Mt 5:13-16). This is a life built on the Rock, the good confession (1 Tim 6:12), over against a vain life of valueless nihilism. This life built on the Rock is possible only when Christ, Who receives repentant, believing men and women, forgives them, grants them His righteousness, and gives them the Holy Spirit Who enables them to live lives for the glory of God. Christ therefore writes His law on their new hearts and empowers them to follow Him in obedient discipleship (Jer 31:33-34; Heb 8:10-12; 10:16). Doctrine is grace and ethics is gratitude; for love awakens love in return; and love, once awakened, desires to give pleasure to God.[17]

In the Sermon on the Mount, Christ re-establishes the original intent of the Law: "Love the Lord your God with all your heart, soul, mind and strength," and "Love your neighbor as yourself" (Mark 12:30). When interpreted correctly, the Sermon on the Mount is for Christians today.

If what I think, say, and do, proceeds from a heart purified by faith in Christ then it is acceptable to God – this is

---

[17] Packer, Knowing God, 137.

Chapter 4: Distinguished Service

Christian ethics. The following disciplines from Christ's Sermon on the Mount (Mt 5-7) present us with what constitutes the ethics of the Kingdom, the Bible's "essentials" for Christian growth:[18]

1. Witness (Mt 5:13-16).
2. Scripture reading and meditation (Mt 5:17-20).
3. Long-suffering (Mt 5:21-26; 38-48; 7:1-6; 12; 15-23).
4. Purity (Mt 5:27-32; 7:13-14)
5. Integrity (Mt 5:33-37).
6. Ministry (Mt 6:1-4; 7:24-29).
7. Prayer (Mt 6:5-15; 7:7-11).
8. Fasting (Mt 6:16-18).
9. Giving (Mt 6:19-34).
10. Worship Mt 6:24; 5:23-24; 7:13-14).

The Discipline of Witness

Witness, the first discipline, is to cover the totality of life.[19] All preaching and witnessing is a testimony announcing the advent of salvation. Christ demands nothing less than our lives as we receive Him and follow Him. For Christ's present authority and power in His present kingdom begins in us and continues in us only as we faithfully endure tribulation. We are called to defend the faith against error by witnessing to the fact that ruin follows the corruption of truth. Sunday Christians, those who attend worship services once a week but fail to live consistent Christian lives, have a difficult time staying salty. Jesus commands His disciples to be salt and light, so as to be a city on a hill that cannot be hidden (Mt 5:13-16).

We are to watch our lives and doctrine closely, persevering in them. But if Christians return to wallow in the mire how can they be faithful witnesses of the gospel (1 Tim 4:16)? The Church in America faces its greatest threat ever – it is falling into a deep sleep of carnal security. Churches in America are

---

[18] Additional Christian disciplines such as fatherhood, leadership, and fellowship will be discussed in subsequent chapters.

[19] Being a witness for the gospel of Jesus Christ is the central topic of chapter nine.

falling prey to the lies of Satan by permitting things that are condemned by Scripture to be practiced openly. The church in America has misdiagnosed itself as being "rich, having become wealthy, and having need of nothing," when in reality she is "wretched, miserable, poor, blind, and naked" (Rev 3:17). More accurately, the church in America is like Sardis than Laodicea: enjoying the peace of a cemetery. To this church Jesus says, "Be watchful, and strengthen the things which remain, that are ready to die, for I have not found your works perfect before God" (Rev 3:2). There is to be a difference between light and darkness (2 Cor 6:14). What we value exerts influence on our behavior so that it becomes our character.

How can Christians who live just like the world expect to witness the truth of the gospel without watering down the message so to make it less offensive? Ruin follows corruption of the truth! Christians are to love the Lord so much as they willingly accept the ostracism, hatred of the world, even death, conquering as lampstands of witness (Rev 12:11). The new life in Christ is to be proclaimed and lived out as the fruit of the redemptive work of God. Conversion is justification by faith alone yet is followed by the discipline of sanctification. This is the believer's reasonable service (Rom 12:1). The Spirit is the "Lamp" within the people of God, Who shines the light of the gospel wherever He sends God's mediating-minister priests throughout the world as the testimony to all nations (Mt 24:14; Rev 11:3; 12:6, 14). By following Christ's model, believers are to faithfully witness by mediating Christ's priestly and royal authority to the world.[20] We must confront the world with the gospel and not try to remove its offensive elements. Our testimony is an announcement of the advent of salvation. Can't we tell others how much Jesus means to us?

The Discipline of Scripture Reading and Meditation

The second discipline, *Scripture reading and meditation,* is paramount to living a godly life in Christ. It cannot be

---

[20] Beale, Revelation, 193.

marginalized without suffering great loss, least of all an effective Christian witness. The chief discipline and means of grace is the preaching and hearing of God's Word (Acts 2:42), along with a dependence for the daily nourishing of one's soul with Scripture reading and meditation (Dt 8:3; Mt 4:4). Psalm 119:9 provides us with a perfect catechism question when it asks us, "How can a young man cleanse his way? By taking heed according to Your word." Commenting on this Psalm, Augustine writes, "This, after all, is the reason why a young man corrects his way of life: because he meditates upon the words of God as he ought to meditate upon them, observes them because he meditates upon them, and lives correctly because he observes them."

Why is immorality rampant in the church? Why are souls starved? Why are homes mismanaged? Why are men irresponsible? Because God's Word isn't being read and heeded! The Word of God transforms the mind (Rom 12:2). Theonas, the third century bishop of Alexandria writes, "Let no day pass by without reading some portion of the Sacred Scriptures, at such convenient hour as offers, and giving some space to meditation. And never cast off the habit of reading in the Holy Scriptures; for nothing feeds the soul and enriches the mind so well as those sacred studies do." This is how Christians for twenty centuries have grown in grace and in the knowledge of God, by reading and meditating on the Scripture. For through the disciplined practice of the daily reading and meditation of God's Word we come to know God more. We don't become more justified, but we learn more about what God desires of us, and what He loves and hates.

The first Psalm tells us, "Blessed is the man who walks not in the counsel of the ungodly, nor stands in the path of sinners, nor sits in the seat of the scornful; but his delight is in the law of the Lord, and in His law he meditates day and night" (Ps 1:1-2). The promise which is appended to this discipline is spiritual vitality; "he shall be like a tree planted by the rivers of water, that brings forth its fruit in its season, whose leaf also shall not wither; and whatever he does shall prosper" (Ps 1:3, cf. Rev 1:3).

For this reason Jesus tells His disciples, "Whoever therefore breaks one of the least of these commandments, and teaches

Chapter 4: Distinguished Service

men so, shall be called least in the kingdom of heaven; but whoever does and teaches them, he shall be called great in the kingdom of heaven" (Mt 5:19). The word disciple literally means 'a learner.' Christians are called to follow Christ, to be His disciples, to be 'learners' of Jesus. Jesus said to disciples: "If you abide in My word, you are My disciples indeed. And you shall know the truth and the truth shall make you free" (Jn 8:31-32).

William Bridge correctly states, "As meditation is a great help to knowledge, so it is a great friend to memory."[21] In other words, Scripture meditation helps us get God's truth firmly set into our minds, so we may recall them in time of need. Therefore, careful study of the Bible is necessary for true discipleship. The Lord calls for our minds to be continually renewed by an application of His Word to every facet of life (Rom 12:2). This continual renewal by God's Word will never be a reality unless be have been born-again (Jn 3:3; 1 Cor 12:3). For unless we are 'first poor in spirit' and thereby indwelt by the Holy Spirit, we can never submit to His transforming instruction and power. D. A. Carson writes, "the truly transformative element is not the discipline itself, but the worthiness of the task undertaken: the value of reading God's Word." Bible reading is therefore an imperative, for by it we were born-again (James 1:18), and by it we grow (1 Pet 2:2). A man will never exceed the righteousness of the scribes and Pharisees without being born-again; a miracle which will be further demonstrated by a desire to feast on God's Word as often as time will allow (Mt 5: 20). God delights in obedience. Let us seek to do His will in all situations.

Jesus Christ fulfills the Law of God. During Jesus' earthly ministry, all the Old Testament prophecies concerning His first coming had been fulfilled. These include: His miraculous conception and birth from the Virgin Mary, His inauguration of the Kingdom of God as witnessed by the preaching of the Gospel, the healings and mighty works of His ministry, the persecution and sufferings that followed, His death by crucifixion, the place of His burial, and His resurrection. Still many prophecies in the whole of Scripture regarding Christ's

---

[21] Bridge, The Works of the Reverend William Bridge, 130.

second coming have yet to be fulfilled. These will be fulfilled in the time appointed by the Father (Acts 1:7). Jesus said concerning the Scriptures: "For assuredly, I say to you, till heaven and earth pass away, one jot or one tittle will by no means pass from the law till all is fulfilled" (Mt 5:18). Those in Him live out His righteous fulfillment by loving God and man with the totality of one's self (Mk 12:29-31; Jn 5:39).

What will undermine everything that has been said about the Bible so far is a denial of the inerrancy of the Scriptures. Confusion and despair will be the only fruit of denying the inerrancy of the Bible. The current trends today of Liberalism are the fuller ramifications of the Renaissance and the Enlightenment. Today in full bloom Liberalism displays its fruit of impenitence towards the authority of Scripture. It obstinately refuses to submit itself to the demands of God's word. Seeking to ease their disparaging consciences they gleefully carve up the text of Scripture, reducing it, and redefining, in hopes to render it voiceless and powerless.

A stratagem of Liberals, Higher criticism, is destructive to the composite unity of the whole of Scripture. Belief in Biblical inerrancy is affirming that all that God has spoken to us in His word is entirely accurate, trustworthy, and authoritative. In the words of Francis Schaeffer, redefining definitions right out of existence, the rejection of the Bible's authority will lead only to despair.

The next three disciplines are within the context where Christ corrects various misuses of the Law (Mt 5:21-48). The Pharisees placed man-made tradition over the Word of God in a casuistic attempt to avoid the law (Mk 7:13). They were guilty of reducing the meaning and even the demands of the Law.[22] Their worship was in vain because they neither knew God nor were their hearts properly oriented (Mt 22:29). In these antithetical pronouncements, Jesus not only corrects their misuse regarding murder, adultery, oaths, retaliation, and loving others, but demonstrates the full meaning and intent of the Law.

---

[22] Lloyd-Jones, Studies in the Sermon on the Mount, 194.

Chapter 4: Distinguished Service

The Disciple of Long-suffering

Long-suffering (patience), the third discipline, which is also a fruit of the Spirit (Gal 5:22), is a grace of God by which believers are able to genuinely bear with the failings of others, forgiving them and loving them in spite of themselves and their behavior (Mt 5:44-45). This is a Christian discipline and fruit of the Christian existence that will not only keep one out of trouble but will glorify God (Mt 5:25-26; 48). A mere pretense of long-suffering, the counterfeit, pride-based kind, will take one only so far, but the genuine long-suffering, a living out of Christ's righteousness, can endure anything by the power God supplies (Mt 5:38-42). When Christ corrects these misuses of the Law, in this instance murder, He demonstrates that the Ten Commandments are not restricted to outward actions but apply also to the dispositions of the mind and heart.[23] Murder lies within malicious anger. Lloyd-Jones writes, "Anger in the heart of toward any human being, and especially to those who belong to the household of faith, is, according to our Lord, something that is as reprehensible in the sight of God as murder."

The point being made here is, our anger must only be against sin, and not against those who have wronged us or caused us great loss and pain. The apostle Paul tells us "Be angry, and do not sin" (Eph 4:26). And the apostle James tells us "Be slow to anger, for the anger of man does not work the righteousness of God" (Jam 1:19-20). Additionally, the Scripture tells us to "Put away anger and malice" (Eph 4:31; Col 3:8). Jesus demonstrated righteous anger that is anger against the people's sin of unbelief (Mk 3:5).

Long-suffering or patience is the self-restraint which does not hastily retaliate a wrong. In Alexander Dumas' *Les Misérables*, Bishop Myriel, has a man named Jean Valjean show up at his door, asking for a place to stay for the night. The bishop graciously accepts him, feeds him, and gives him a bed. However, Valjean takes most of the bishop's silver and runs off in the night. The police capture Valjean and take him back to face the bishop. When the police inform the bishop

---

[23] Boice, Foundations of the Christian Faith, 227.

211

Chapter 4: Distinguished Service

they have found the silver in Valjean's knapsack, Myriel tells the police that he had given the silverware to Valjean as a gift. And the bishop says to Valjean, "Ah, there you are! I gave you the candlesticks too. Why did you not take them along with the plates?" With this the police release Valjean and depart. And the bishop says to Valjean, "Take this silver and become an honest man. Jean Valjean, my brother: you belong no longer to evil, but to good. It is your soul that I am buying for you. I withdraw it from darkness and perdition, and I give it to God!"[24] The bishop's long-suffering made forgiveness a reality.

At the Lemberg Concentration Camp in 1943, Simon Wiesenthal, a Jewish prisoner, is summoned to the bedside of a dying Nazi soldier. The soldier, Karl Seidl, tells Wiesenthal he is seeking a Jew's forgiveness for a crime that has haunted him his entire life. Seidl confesses that he destroyed a house full of Jews – some three hundred, men, women, and children. He recounts to Wiesenthal how he gunned down everyone who tried to escape the flames by leaping out of windows.

After Seidl finishes his story, he asks if Wiesenthal can forgive him. But Weisenthal gets up and leaves the room without saying a word. In his book *the Sunflower*, Wiesenthal poses an ethical dilemma to the reader, asking if whether or not he was right; should he have forgiven the dying soldier? Wiesenthal says, forgiveness is an act of the will; only the sufferer is qualified to make that decision, it is only the one offended who can finally pronounce forgiveness. Wiesenthal was right about one thing. Only the one most offended can finally pronounce forgiveness. And God is the One Who is most offended by sin.

The story of Joseph is well known. He is favored by his father Jacob and God favors him with dreams (Gen 37). For this, He is sold into slavery by his jealous brothers. He becomes the slave of Potiphar, the captain of Pharaoh's palace guard, but things go bad for him when he refuses the sexual advances of his master's wife. Joseph says, "How then can I do this great wickedness, and sin against God" (Gen 39:9). And the false accusations of his master's wife sends him to

---

[24] Dumas, Les Misérables, 27-28.

212

prison. While there he interprets the dreams of Pharaoh's servants (Gen 40). Then after some thirteen years as either a slave or a prisoner, Joseph interprets Pharaoh's dreams and is exalted to become the prime minister of Egypt (Gen 41). Joseph interprets Pharaoh's dreams to reveal a great famine that will plague the whole earth for seven years. Later, when his brothers come down to Egypt to buy grain, Joseph refuses the opportunity for revenge, but instead forgives them. Later, all of Joseph's family comes to Egypt and escapes the famine. Joseph says, "Do not be afraid, for am I in the place of God? But as for you, you meant evil against me; but God meant it for good, in order to bring it about as it is this day, to save many people alive." (Gen 45:7).

God is the One Who is most offended by sin. Patience is genuinely bearing the faults of others and forgiving them as God has forgiven us (Mt 5:44-45; 6:14-15; 18:21-35). As Christians, we are God's representatives in showing the divine characteristic of pardoning grace (Ps 130:3-4).

The Discipline of Purity

The fourth discipline, *purity*, is essentially the daily summons to "be holy, for I am holy" (1 Pet 1:16). The fine, bright and clean linen with which Christ's bride clothes herself consists of: remaining pure by not being conformed to the idolatrous aspects of pagan culture (Rev 19:7-8). Impure lifestyles make one's Christian witness innocuous. God's people are commanded to be pure and undefiled from the world (2 Cor 6:14-7:1; Jam 1:27). To be in the world but not of it (Jn 17:16-18). Holy living based on God's inerrant Word is to be the daily discipline of Christians (Mt 5:27-32; 7:13-14). R. Kent Hughes writes, "Sensuality is easily the biggest obstacle to godliness among men today and is wreaking havoc in the Church. If we are to 'discipline ourselves for the purpose of godliness' (1 Tim 4:7), we must begin with the discipline of purity."

God's people march to the beat of a different drum and perfect holiness in the fear of the Lord (2 Cor 7:1). Godly men are to live lives free of degrading impurities, such as: drunkenness, pornography, sex outside of marriage, rage, verbally abusing one's family, and the like. They live pure lives in the grace God supplies, without a hypocritical spirit, for the glory of God. Pure living glorifies God (Mt 5:16).[25]

A big part of the discipline of purity involves the tongue. It's a tiny member that can be used graciously to bring the saving power of the gospel (Rom 10:14-15) or vanity at best and destructive speech at worst as Proverbs 18:21 tells us, "Death and life are in the power of the tongue, and those who love it will eat its fruit." And the apostle James tells us, the tongue is a little member and boasts great things. See how great a forest a little fire kindles! (Jam 3:5).

The Bible tells us if a Christian does not bridle his tongue his religion dishonors God (Jam 1:26). That is, Christians who give no thought to their gossiping, coarse jesting, slandering, abuse, innuendos, flattery, cursing, criticism and the like, dishonor Christ and wreak havoc on the church. But rather Christians are to refrain from speaking evil of one another (Jam 4:11) and build each other up in our most holy faith (1 Thess 5:11; Jud 1:20), practicing true Christianity as James 1:27 tells us, "Pure and undefiled religion before God and the Father is this: to visit orphans and widows in their trouble, and to keep oneself unspotted from the world."

A sobering word regarding the purity of the tongue is given to us by the Lord Jesus who says, "I say to you that for every idle word men may speak, they will give account of it in the day of judgment. For by your words you will be justified, and by your words you will be condemned" (Mt 12:36-37). And the apostle Paul tells us,

29 Let no corrupt word proceed out of your mouth, but what is good for necessary edification, that it may impart grace to the hearers. 30 And do not grieve the Holy Spirit of God, by whom you were sealed for the day of redemption. 31 Let all bitterness, wrath, anger, clamor, and evil speaking be put away from you, with all malice. 32 And be kind to one another, tenderhearted, forgiving one another, even as God in Christ forgave you (Eph 4:29-32).

---

[25] Chapter 8 discusses practical godly living assisted by holding each other accountable to God's inerrant Word.

Chapter 4: Distinguished Service

Many men feel it necessary to curse in order to appear macho but this has no place in the kingdom of God. But godly men are to ensure their speech is wholesome because unwholesome, foul mouthed speech grieves the Holy Spirit. We are to 'discipline ourselves for the purpose of godliness' (1 Tim 4:7). As believers we are individually and corporately the temple of the Holy Spirit. We must be careful to honor the Lord with the totality of our lives, including our tongues.

The Discipline of Integrity

The fifth discipline, *integrity*, is both an essential Christian character and a discipline which flows from a heart made pure by saving faith in Christ. *Integrity* or incorruptibility is the quality of being truthful as well as having strong moral principles, giving one moral uprightness. Titus 2:6-8 (ESV) tells us, "Likewise, urge the younger men to be self-controlled. Show yourself in all respects to be a model of good works, and in your teaching show integrity, dignity, and sound speech that cannot be condemned, so that an opponent may be put to shame, having nothing evil to say about us."

Paul uses the word ἀφθορίαν aphthorion, meaning lacking a capacity to decay, unable to experience deterioration. *Integrity* is speaking the truth even to one's own hurt. Doing the hard right over the easy wrong, because God sees everything. Martin Niemöller, a German pastor, withstood the evils of the Third Reich by refusing to acquiesce to their immoral demands. In the early 1930s, Niemöller was an anti-communist and supported Adolf Hitler's rise to power. But soon afterward, when Hitler showed his true colors and insisted on the nazification of German Protestant churches, Niemöller became the leader of a group of German clergymen that opposed Hitler.

In 1937, he was arrested and sent to concentration camps in Sachsenhausen and Dachau. He remained in Dachau until he was liberated by the Allies in 1945. He then went on to continue ministering as a pastor to the German people. Not only is his life a great example of living out the discipline of integrity, it is also one that highlights the dangers of political apathy. Niemöller witnessed many in the church of Germany give in to Nazi demands. For example, the Cross of Christ was replaced with the swastika (the crooked cross), and only two items were permitted on the communion table: a sword and Hitler's *Mein Kampf.*

Niemöller is famous for his expression, "First they came for the Socialists, and I did not speak out – because I was not a Socialist. Then they came for the Trade Unionists, and I did not speak out – because I was not a Trade Unionist. Then they came for the Jews, and I did not speak out – because I was not a Jew. Then they came for me – and there was no one left to speak for me."

How import is integrity? Jesus tells us a Christian man's word is to be his bond: "let your yes be yes and your no be no" (Mt 5:33-36). Truth is eternal, objective, and unchangeable. It is the only foundation that is God-honoring, the only foundation that will last (Matthew 7:24-27). Christians that hold to the truth have integrity. And 1 Peter 3:10-12 tells us,

"For he who would love life and see good days, let him refrain his tongue from evil, and his lips from speaking deceit. Let him turn away from evil and do good; let him seek peace and pursue it. For the eyes of the Lord are on the righteous, and His ears are open to their prayers; but the face of the Lord is against those who do evil."

According to recent statistics, the estimated number of people who cheat on their taxes in America in 2012 was 1.6 million people. These million and a half people cost the government a staggering $270 billion. What these figures don't include are tax returns that are fudged. Perhaps so many cheat because they reason, "hey everybody else is doing it. Why can't I?"

Thomas Brooks writes, "Hold fast your integrity, and rather let all go than let that go. A man had better let liberty, estate, relations, and life go, than let his integrity go. Integrity maintained in the soul will be a feast of fat things in the worst of days; but let a man lose his integrity. And it is not in the power of all the world to make a feast of fat things in that soul."[26] Integrity is hard won and easily lost.

---

[26] Brooks, The Legacies of Thomas Brooks, 8.

Chapter 4: Distinguished Service

Ebenezer Erskine, commenting on the church in Sardis (Rev 3) writes, "By their zeal, uprightness, integrity, and their honest appearance for God, in that degenerate day and place, they had distinguished themselves from others, and so purchased a name to themselves; and they were known to men as well as unto God: 'The Lord knows the righteous;' and he knows them by name, they are marked out among others."[27] Like the faithful remnant in Sardis, the faithful of the church in America, like Job, maintain their integrity, and keep their garments clean and undefiled, fearing God and shuns evil (Job 1:8; 2:3; Tit 2:7; Rev 3:4-6). G. K. Chesterton wrote, "Morality, like art, consists in drawing a line somewhere."[28] And morality is not majority driven, it is God driven. And it is God's Word that is to draw the line, not culture.[29] Can we share Job's determination, "Till I die I will not put away my integrity from me" (Job 27:5)?

Christ dwells in our hearts by faith and He roots and grounds us to Himself in love, so that we may endure to the end (Phil 1:6), and live out His righteousness (Phil 2:12-13). True Christian ministry is actuated, empowered, and lead by the Spirit. Jesus told us that although we should practice good works publicly (Mt 5:16), we should not draw special attention to them. What Christ forbids is ostentation seeking our own honor and applause. Like Ananias and Sapphira did, who wanting recognition and praise from the church in Jerusalem lied to God. What Christ forbids is seeking honor and applause from men. Otherwise you have no reward.

The Discipline of Ministry

The sixth discipline, *ministry*, is what Christ demands – obedient performance of our duty without fanfare (Mt 6:1-4; 7:24-29). Jesus says, "Beware of practicing your righteousness (piety) before other people in order to be seen by them, for then you will have no reward from your Father who is in heaven (Mt 6:1 ESV). Jesus also tells us, "Do not let your left

---

[27] Erskine, God's Little Remnant Keeping their Garments Clean in an Evil Day, 38-40.

[28] Henry Fairlie, The Seven Deadly Sins Today, 36.

[29] Hughes, Disciplines of a Godly Man, 131.

hand know what your right hand is doing, that your charitable deed may be in secret; and your Father who sees in secret will Himself reward you openly" (Mt 6:3-4). By this expression Jesus means, that we ought to be satisfied with having God for our only witness, and to be so earnestly desirous to obey him, that we shall not be carried away by any vanity. Our 'living sacrifice' is our life-long selfless service to God in light of Christ's once-for-all sacrifice of Himself. This offering up of ourselves has been both granted unto us to do and commanded of us to give (Rom 12:1-2).

God has ordained some of His saints to serve His people as under shepherds, leaders of His household, for the building up of the body of Christ (Eph 4:11-13). But He has ordained all His people to serve Him in the true temple as mediating-ministering priests, to make God's appeal to a dead world (2 Cor 5:19-21), to be Christ's hands and feet (Rom 12:12-31), and to bring the presence of the Holy Spirit; the scent of life unto life, or death unto death (2 Cor 2:14-17). Greg Beale writes, "The mark of the true church is an expanding witness to the presence of God: first to our families, then to others in the church, then to our neighborhood, then to our city, then the country and ultimately the whole earth."[30]

Cast adrift in the Java Sea after the Japanese sank his ship, the USS Houston, Chaplain (Commander) George S. Rentz led survivors in prayer. Castaway sailors from the Houston clung to whatever would float. Among the castaways, Houston's chaplain, George Rentz, a fifty-nine year old WWI veteran, made his rounds to all the sailors he could reach, in the black night with the strong current and oil that burned their eyes and face. The chaplain appeared in high spirits. The overcrowded pontoon was slowly sinking, taking on water through a gaping hole in its side. It couldn't remain afloat much longer with all the bodies clinging to it. Rentz led the men in prayer and a hymn. The refrain of amazing grace was never rendered with such raw and poignant emotion.

Grueling hours passed. Most of the men had life jackets but Seaman Walter Beeson, hanging on to the float next to chaplain Rentz didn't. Weakened by his wounds, his hands

---

[30] Beale, The Temple and the Church's Mission, 401.

stiffening, he kept sinking into the sea. His neighbors kept pulling him back to the pontoon. Finally, chaplain Rentz said, "You men are young, with your lives ahead of you. I am old and have lived my life and I'm ready to be with God." With that, he removed his life jacket and thrust it at Beeson. Put it on he ordered. Beeson protested weakly but reluctantly put it on. Waves washed over the surface of the pontoon as it began to take on more water. It wouldn't be long before it sank, leaving the men with only their life jackets to keep them afloat. In exhaustion Rentz prayed for the men one last time then vanished beneath the black waves of the Sundra Strait.[31]

Colonel Joshua Chamberlin, the commander of the 20th Maine at the Battle of Gettysburg writes, "This is the great reward of service. To live, far out and on, in the life of others; this is the mystery of the Christ, to give life's best for such high sake that it shall be found again unto life eternal." Or, in other words, living for a purpose greater than yourself and seeing one's Christ-like influence take hold of others, so as to bring God glory in the salvation of sinners, what can be a better reward of one's service in this life?

As Christians, we owe love to everyone, and love always serves. Serving is an essential quality of love. The true standard of greatness is service. Our life does not consist in the abundance of our possessions, our wisdom, or our strength, but what we do with our life, which is the real test of character. Our Lord taught this truth when he said, "Whoever wants to become great among you must be your servant, and whoever wants to be first must be slave of all" (Mk 10:43-44). Regarding service, John Newton remarked that, "If two angels were sent down from heaven, one to conduct an empire, and the other to sweep a street, they would feel no inclination to change employments."[32] He who serves the most fully and the most unselfishly, is the greatest in the kingdom of heaven.[33] What God demands He gives, He does, and He completes (Phil 1:6).

---

[31] Sasser, God in the Foxhole, 140-142.
[32] Newton, The Works of Reverend John Newton, 60.
[33] Miller, The Building of Character, 68.

Chapter 4: Distinguished Service

The Discipline of Prayer

Prayer, the seventh discipline, is a means of grace and our connectivity with the eternal God. Prayer is God's way of stirring up the hearts of His saints, whereby they petition Him for: (1) protection from wickedness, (2) purifying holiness, and (3) punishing imprecation upon the enemies of God's Kingdom. God's people are priests who minister-mediate before Him in the true temple to the unbelieving world. The world either receives their mediating witness or rejects it and persecutes the saints whereby they incur God's talionic judgment which is mediated by saintly prayers for justice. By prayers, God not only delivers His people from their enemies, but works to further purify them while mediating through their prayers His judgment on a recalcitrant world.[34]

What is prayer? Prayer is not eloquence, but earnestness; not the confession of helplessness, but the feeling of it; not figures of speech, but compunction of soul.[35] John Bunyan writes, "Prayer is sincere, sensible, affectionate pouring out of the heart or soul to God, through Christ, in the strength and assistance of the Holy Spirit, for such things as God has promised, or according to the Word of God, for the good of the church, with submission in faith to the will of God."[36] Prayer is the pouring out of our hearts by the Spirit unto God. How many Christians have weak spiritual lives for lack of prayer?

True, effective prayer is God-willed, God-centered, and God-glorifying, like the greatest prayer, "Father, forgive them, for they do not know what they do" (Lk 23:34). There are at least four aspects of effective prayer:

1. We must learn to pray in the strength and assistance of the Holy Spirit.
2. We must learn to pray continuously.
3. We must learn to pray persistently.
4. We must learn to pray for others.

---

[34] This aspect of prayer, imprecation, will be discussed in chapters 9 and 10.

[35] More, Practical Piety, 102.

[36] The Works of Bunyan, 623.

Chapter 4: Distinguished Service

The effective, fervent prayer of a righteous man avails much (Jam 5:16). First, Christians must learn to pray in the strength and assistance of the Holy Spirit. Kent Hughes writes,

The Holy Spirit tells us what we ought to pray for. Apart from the Spirit's assistance, our prayers are limited by our own reason and intuition. But with the Holy Spirit's help they become informed by heaven. As we seek the Spirit's help, He will speak to us through His Word, which conveys His mind regarding every matter of principle. Thus, in Spirit-directed prayer we will think God's thoughts after Him. His desires will become our desires, His motives our motives, His ends our ends.[37]

Prayer changes things: it changes us and it changes the world getting things done according to God's will. There are two types of prayer: there is prayer that is made by virtue of a gift of knowledge and utterance, and there is prayer that is made by virtue of the Holy Spirit. Though prayer proceeds from the Holy Spirit within the Christian. The Holy Spirit literally prays within us, so that true prayer starts from the mediatorial throne of Christ, comes into the believer, and then goes back up to that throne with divine acceptance and power. Doug Kelly writes,

When we are stuck in some hard situation and are begging God for His revealed will to be brought to pass, we are actually praying that way because God has put us in the position where we will feel the need to pray! Our praying is, in fact, a preparation for the release of the blessings of God.[38]

Secondly, Christians must learn to pray continuously, but one may ask, is continuous prayer possible? Yes and no because it's impossible to carry on a dialogue with God at all times, for example when we are sleeping or working. However, what Paul is telling is that continuous prayer is not so much the articulation of the mouth as it is the attitude of the heart. The medieval monk Brother Lawrence writes, "The time of business does not differ with me from the time of prayer; and in the noise and clatter of my kitchen, while

---

[37] Hughes, Disciplines of a Godly Man, 96.
[38] Kelly, If God Already Knows Why Pray, 58.

several persons are at the same time calling for different things, I possess God in as great tranquility as if I were on my knees."[39]

Thirdly, Christians must learn to pray persistently. Jesus tells us in Jn 15:7, "If you abide in Me, and My words abide in you, you will ask what you desire, and it shall be done for you." Jesus says, the promises of Scripture are to abide in us, so that we petition God with His very Words. In Christ's parable of the persistent widow, He teaches us to not loose heart in prayer, for He says, "shall God not avenge His own elect who cry out day and night to Him, though He bears long with them" (Lk 18:7)?

Fourthly, Christians must learn to pray for others. God's special rule of direction for prayer is the Lord's Prayer (Mt 6:9-13). In the Lord's Prayer there are three requests: (1) give us our daily bread, (2) forgive us our debts as we forgive our debtors, and (3) lead us not into temptation but deliver us from evil. In the first petition, we are asking God to provide for our physical needs. In the second petition, we are asking God to remove any resentment and bitterness from offenses (Heb 12:15), so as to free ourselves from any hindrance to our own prayers (Mt 6:14-15; 1 Pet 3:7). In the third petition, we are asking God to keep us "from getting into situations of trial or temptation which would be stronger than we could resist."[40]

Calvin writes, "As we cannot distinguish between the elect and the reprobate, it is our duty to pray for all who trouble us; to desire the salvation of all men; and even to be careful for the welfare of every individual. At the same time, if our hearts are pure and peaceful, this will not prevent us from freely appealing to God's judgment that He may cut off finally the impenitent."[41] When we pray for deliverance from our enemies, we are essentially praying for Christ to come and consummate his kingdom (Mt 6:8-13).

Whatever may be the cause pressing us to pray unto the Lord, we must realize our need for Him, and let God the Holy Spirit move us to earnest, consistent prayer. Doug Kelly writes,

---

[39] Brother Lawrence, The Practice of the Presence of God, 19.
[40] Kelly, If God Already Knows Why Pray, 93.
[41] John Calvin, The John Calvin Bible Commentaries, Ps 109:16.

Chapter 4: Distinguished Service

Although the main emphasis in our prayers must be on the clearly revealed will of God in Scripture, this does not mean that His secret will has no connection with our praying. On the contrary, when we pray on the basis of the revealed will, we are lining ourselves up with the person of God and thus with the secret purposes of God. His secret purposes are carried out through the praying of His saints on the basis of His revealed will in Scripture.[42]

When we interact with the transcendent, sovereign, personal, God, our purpose in prayer is not to inform Him or change His plan in some way but our purpose in prayer is to be a channel through which His ordained plan comes to pass (Rev 5:8-11; 6:10; 8:1-5). We pray to align ourselves with God's will and we pray because God has ordained prayer as one of the means by which He will accomplish His plan. God has received these prayers which have been met with divine acceptance and power (Rev 5:8-11; 8:1-5).

"Right praying," writes Thomas Boston, "is praying in the Spirit. It is a gale blowing from heaven, the breathing of the Spirit in the saints, that carries them out in the prayer, and which comes the length of the throne."[43] God is effectively working by the Spirit through the lives of His saints to consummate His Kingdom; draw out of it all causes of evil (141:5b-6, 10; Mt 13:41). And he is doing it in answer to those prayers.

Pray for the deliverance that God has promised will come at the end of this age. Pray with confidence for Christ to come. God loves it, Satan hates it, and every true Christian values it. Your prayers will arise as incense to the throne room of Heaven, and at the appointed time, God will answer.

> Adoration is the noblest employment of created beings;
> Confession is the natural language of guilty creatures;
> Gratitude is the spontaneous expression of pardoned sinners.[44]

---

[42] Kelly, If God Already Knows Why Pray, 56-57.
[43] Boston, How the Spirit Enables Us to Pray.
[44] More, Practical Piety, 102.

Chapter 4: Distinguished Service

The Discipline of Fasting

Fasting, the eighth discipline, is an ancillary to devotion and to the mortification of sin. *Fasting* is a willing act of abstinence or reduction from certain or all food, drink, or both, for a period of time. Fasts are either partial or total. In the history of the Church, believers have normally fasted for two reasons: repentance and spiritual development. The Book of Daniel describes a partial fast and its effects on the health of its observers (Dan 1:12-15). When Jonah preached to the Ninevites, they repented, and tasted neither bread nor water for three whole days (Jon 3:3-10). This was a total fast. Additionally, the Book of Daniel tells us that Daniel fasted for twenty-one days; but this was not a total abstinence, for he says, "I ate no pleasant food, no meat or wine came into my mouth, nor did I anoint myself at all, till three whole weeks were fulfilled" (Dan 10:3). And Peter's fast, when he saw the vision of the sheet let down, was only until three o'clock (Act 10:9-16).

Regarding *fasting*, the Lord Jesus says, "Moreover, when you fast, do not be like the hypocrites, with a sad countenance. For they disfigure their faces that they may appear to men to be fasting. Assuredly, I say to you, they have their reward. But you, when you fast, anoint your head and wash your face, so that you do not appear to men to be fasting, but to your Father who is in the secret place; and your Father who sees in secret will reward you openly" (Mt 6:16-18). Jesus tells us that *fasting* without a corresponding penitence and humiliation is hypocrisy. Such fasting is vain and censored by the Word of God.

Archibald Alexander writes, "One special occasion on which the apostles and their companions were accustomed to fast, was when ministers were to be ordained and sent forth." Thus we read in Acts 13:2-3, "As they ministered to the Lord and fasted, the Holy Spirit said, "Now separate to Me Barnabas and Saul for the work to which I have called them." Then, having fasted and prayed, and laid hands on them, they sent them away." And again in Acts 14:23 we read, "So when they had appointed elders in every church, and prayed with fasting, they commended them to the Lord in whom they had believed."

How are we to *fast*? Are we to practice *fasting* when we ordain ministers of the gospel? A few general observations seem to be needed. First, fasting is to be a private matter between the Christian and God (Mt 6:16-17). The Scriptures nowhere command believers to fast but Jesus gave some principles regarding it. Jesus is not commanding us to fast, He is assuming we will fast and teaches us how to do it and how not to do it. Jesus says that fasting is to be without making a show so as to look 'spiritual' (Mt 6:16). Hypocrites are people who do their spiritual disciplines so as "to be seen by men." This is the 'reward' the hypocrites are after – the praise of men. They fast in order to be "seen" fasting. This is a reward Christians are to avoid like the plague, "For what is highly esteemed among men is an abomination in the sight of God" (Lk 16:15).

In fact, Jesus says when you fast, look as though you are not (Mt 6:17-18). We are not to draw attention to ourselves, so as to say "look I'm spiritual, I'm fasting." The whole point of fasting is to be "seen" by God, so as to say "my heart burns for more of You Lord." What is at the heart of fasting is our heart not our appearance. Second, an appropriate fast, however long, is one at the direction of the Spirit for the mortification of the flesh, and to seek a closer intimacy with God – the 'reward' of fasting (Mt 6:18). Here's a picture of an appropriate fast from Joel 2:12-13:

12 "Now, therefore," says the Lord, "Turn to Me with all your heart, With fasting, with weeping, and with mourning." 13 So rend your heart, and not your garments; Return to the Lord your God, For He is gracious and merciful, Slow to anger, and of great kindness; And He relents from doing harm.

The Reformers believed that Christians may choose to fast individually as a spiritual exercise to discipline their own flesh (mortification of sin), but the collective diet rules and prohibitions imposed by the canon law was rejected outright. Calvin and Zwingli believed that collective fasting was only appropriate in times of calamity and grief for the community. And Martin Luther wrote in his Small Catechism "Fasting and bodily preparation are certainly fine outward training, but a person who has faith in these words, 'given for you' and 'shed for you for the forgiveness of sin' is really worthy and well prepared."[45] The point of all this is well made by John MacArthur, "A fast is always meaningless if it is performed from habit and does not result from deep concern and mourning over some spiritual need."[46]

Third, fasting is to be done with the Christians health in view. As fasting renders some people sick, so that it hinders their devotion. Such believers should adopt a partial fast; for the Lord will have mercy, and not sacrifice (Hos 6:6; Mt 12:7). God's wants our hearts to burn with desire for Him and His approval, to hear God say, "Well done, good and faithful servant" (Mt 25:21). The Scriptures encourage us to set aside time for prayer and fasting, in order to seek a closer intimacy with God, as well as an act of petition. For example, the Rev. Robert Murray M'Cheyne set aside time for special prayer and fasting which in his own words "brought him nearer to God."[47] George Whitefield also practiced fasting as a regular discipline. The point being made here is, let the Christian who fasts, do so privately, and out of a sincere spiritual need, then we will have meat to eat that others know not of" (Jn 4:32).

This is why Andrew Murray writes, "Because of the often negative effect of the body upon the spirit, payer needs fasting for its full growth. Prayer is the one hand with which we grasp the invisible. Fasting is the other hand, the one with which we let go of the visible. In nothing are we more closely connected with the world of sense than in our need and enjoyment of food. It was with fruit the woman and man were tempted and fell in the Garden of Eden. It was with bread that Jesus was tempted in the wilderness. But He triumphed in fasting."[48]

---

[45] An Explanation of Luther's Small Catechism: The Sacrament of the Eucharist, section IV: Who receives the Sacrament worthily?

[46] MacArthur, New Testament Commentary, Matthew 8-15, 69.

[47] The Life and Remains, Letters, Lectures, and Poems of the Rev. Robert Murray M'Cheyne, 84.

[48] Murray, With Christ in the School of Prayer, 111.

Chapter 4: Distinguished Service

The Discipline of Giving

Giving, the ninth discipline, like fasting is to be done so as to avoid ostentation. For Jesus says, "Beware of practicing your righteousness (piety) before other people in order to be seen by them, for then you will have no reward from your Father who is in heaven (Mt 6:1 ESV)." None of these disciplines will be possible for us to do genuinely without our love for the Father, our full surrender to Christ and the Holy Spirit's power and direction. For if theses disciplines: serving, prayer, fasting, giving and the like proceed from a heart purified by faith then they are acceptable to God. However, if they are done out of a desire to be noticed so as to look 'spiritual' and to be praised by others than they are worthless and contemptible to God (Mt 6:5; Lk 6:24). Rather, the Lord Jesus wants us to give for the right reasons – the glory of God.

God makes use of means to produce in His saints the character of Jesus Christ so they may witness the gospel of His grace and bring Him glory in the salvation of sinners. And giving is a discipline where saints freely render to the cause Christ died for. "For where your treasure is, there your heart will be also" (Mt 6:21). But some Christians say that giving was mandated in the Old Testament it is now optional. However, the Lord Jesus expects and requires us to give. Jesus said to His disciples, "when you give" not "if you give" (Matthew 6:2). The point is Christian giving is not optional, but rather essential.

The Bible teaches us that Christian giving is worship. The apostle Paul tells us, "On the first day of every week each one of you is to put aside and save" (1 Corinthians 16:2 ESV). Paul here teaches the Corinthian church that their taking up of the collection is an act of worship. When we put money in the plate, we are worshiping God in accordance with His Word.

In Randy Alcorn's excellent little book, *The Treasure Principle,* he reckons that "15 percent of everything Christ said relates to money and possessions which is more than His teachings on heaven and hell combined. Just why did Jesus place such an emphasis on money and possessions?" Asks Alcorn, "because there's a fundamental connection between

Chapter 4: Distinguished Service

our spiritual lives and how we think about and handle money."[49]

The Lord's teaching is we are to value the eternal, heavenly treasure over the mere temporal and earthy. Jesus' central teaching on giving is found in Matthew 6:19-21, Jesus says,

19 "Do not lay up for yourselves treasures on earth, where moth and rust destroy and where thieves break in and steal; 20 but lay up for yourselves treasures in heaven, where neither moth nor rust destroys and where thieves do not break in and steal. 21 For where your treasure is, there your heart will be also.

Jesus warns us not to store up treasures on earth because they are temporally and will always be lost. They either leave us while we live, or we leave them when we die. There are no U-hauls behind hearses. Jesus spoke of a man who spent all his wealth to live sumptuously. In order to horde his great fortune and live leisurely he planned to tear down his barns so to build bigger ones. But God calls the man a fool, saying, "This very night your life will be demanded from you. Then who will get what you have prepared for yourself" (Lk 12:20? This is the man who is merely rich toward himself and not God.

Everything belongs to God. Job 41:11 tells us, "Everything under heaven is Mine," Your house, car, children, all of your money, God even owns us (1 Cor 6:19-20). God is the Owner and we are the managers of all that He has blessed us with. God wants us to adopt a stewardship mentality. One that envisions all things as belonging to God – for indeed they do. As stewards of God's possessions, we are to carry no sense of entitlement to the things we manage.[50] Our loyalties mustn't be divided, Jesus tells us, "No one can serve two masters; for either he will hate the one and love the other, or else he will be loyal to the one and despise the other. You cannot serve God and mammon" (Mt 5:24; Lk 16:13).

Mammon is the Aramaic word for money or possessions. What Jesus is saying is one cannot serve δουλεύειν douleuein (as a slave) two masters, God or the god mammon, who

---

[49] Alcorn, The Treasure Principle, 8.
[50] Ibid, 25.

Chapter 4: Distinguished Service

receives the worship of worldly men. But Jesus says His disciples are not to let money or possessions master them, they are to steward both holding on to them loosely enough so as to avoid entanglements, praising God for His daily blessings. We are to trust in God's provision (Mt 6:25, 30-33):

25 "Therefore I say to you, do not worry about your life, what you will eat or what you will drink; nor about your body, what you will put on. Is not life more than food and the body more than clothing? 30 Now if God so clothes the grass of the field, which today is, and tomorrow is thrown into the oven, will He not much more clothe you, O you of little faith? 31 "Therefore do not worry, saying, 'What shall we eat?' or 'What shall we drink?' or 'What shall we wear?' 32 For after all these things the Gentiles seek. For your heavenly Father knows that you need all these things. 33 But seek first the kingdom of God and His righteousness, and all these things shall be added to you. 34 Therefore do not worry about tomorrow, for tomorrow will worry about its own things. Sufficient for the day is its own trouble.

Christians are not to worry (Mt 6:31), for this is the slavery of worldlings who worship the god mammon. Rather trusting in God's daily provision no matter what is the condition of the heart by which we break free from our addiction to temporal earthly treasure and give ourselves with passion to eternal heavenly treasure. An attitude of trust looks away from one's self to God.[51] Faith in God's promises frees us from the slavery of anxiety, removing from the craving of mere earthly treasures on earth anymore.

The Book of Numbers tells us that Israelites out of love for God offered the firstfruits of their crops or livestock to Him (Num 18:11-13). Kent Hughes writes, "The beautiful thing about this was that he did so when he had not yet harvested the rest of the crop and did not know what he would ultimately reap. He gave the best to God, trusting He would bring in the rest. It was faith giving and was totally voluntary."[52] Tithing is "grace giving" or non-required offerings.

Although the New Testament does not explicitly require the tithe, it does however, as we have seen, say much about giving. The Bible tells us in 2 Corinthians chapters eight and

---

[51] Belcher, The Messiah and the Psalms, 90.
[52] Hughes, Disciplines of a Godly Man, 194.

nine that giving should be voluntary, cheerful and generous, as 2 Cor 8:12 tells us "For if there is first a willing mind, it is accepted according to what one has, and not according to what he does not have." The readiness is all. Christ wants giving not out of drudging servitude but out of joyful exhilaration.

Regarding whether Christians should tithe or not John Frame writes,

"It might be argued, therefore, that the tithe is not appropriate in the new covenant, in which the promise of Canaan fades away into the greater promise of the new heavens and the new earth. We note, however, that Abraham, who owned no land in Canaan, paid a tithe to Melchizedek, the mysterious priest-king who in Hebrews foreshadows Christ (Gen 14:20; Heb 7:4-10), indicating that tithes were sometimes appropriate even apart from Israel's ownership of the Promised Land. Can we give anything less to the Christ who fulfills the priesthood of Melchizedek?"[53]

Tithing is grace giving, from a free offering not out of drudgery. "Each one must do just as he has purposed in his heart, not grudgingly or under compulsion; for God loves a cheerful giver" (2 Cor 9:7). God wants our hearts not our money – He already owns everything. God hates legalism, besides all the examples of giving in the New Testament go beyond the tithe (Acts 4:34-37). The tithe is a good start.

But if we remember that God commands us to give – giving isn't an option, isn't that a contradiction to "the Lord loves a cheerful giver?" No. because giving is both mandatory and voluntary. It is required by God, but always willingly given by the believer. As Augustine says "what I formally feared to loose I freely give away." And Augustine was referring to his life. Pro 3:9 tells us, "Honor the Lord with your possessions, and with the firstfruits of all your increase." We are to give to God our "first" not our "last." Not to mention how God asks us to test Him in giving the tithe. Malachi 3:8-11 tells us,

8 "Will a man rob God? Yet you have robbed Me! But you say, 'In what way have we robbed You?' In tithes and offerings. 9 You are cursed with a curse, For you have robbed Me, Even this whole nation. 10 Bring all the tithes into the storehouse, That there may be

---

[53] Frame, The Doctrine of the Christian Life, 801.

food in My house, And try Me now in this," Says the Lord of hosts, "If I will not open for you the windows of heaven And pour out for you such blessing That there will not be room enough to receive it. 11 "And I will rebuke the devourer for your sakes, So that he will not destroy the fruit of your ground, Nor shall the vine fail to bear fruit for you in the field," Says the Lord of hosts; 12 "And all nations will call you blessed, For you will be a delightful land," Says the Lord of hosts.

Sadly, according to statics in America only 12% of Christians tithed their income to churches in 2012, which is on par with the average for the past decade. If American Christians were to focus on the simple obedience of giving back to God what is really His, the church would have the resources to do great things. The Bible teaches that Christian giving ought to be cheerful, voluntary, and generous (2 Cor 8:12; 2 Cor 9:7; Pro 11:25). God wants us to adopt a stewardship mentality. One that envisions all things as belonging to God – for indeed they do. And as stewards of God's possessions, we will be merely giving back to God what is already His. When the Bible tells us that "God loves a cheerful giver," it shows that the Lord takes a special delight in those who are joyful givers. Are we cheerful givers? We will never give joyously or cheerfully if we love money and possessions more than God.

The Discipline of Worship

The purpose for which we were made by the power of God is to worship Him and to give Him glory forever. God does not need us, but we need Him. The Bible tells us that God is independent and Self-existent (Ex 3:14). John Owen asks, "What does God require of us in our dependence on him, that He may be glorified by us, and we accepted with Him?" And he answers, "That we may worship Him in and by the ways of His own appointment."[54] John Owen lays out the biblical principles that regulate our worship of God: (1) that we are to worship God, and (2) that we are to worship God in the way that He chooses. The tenth discipline, *worship*, is both the

---

[54] Owen, A Brief Introduction to the Worship of God, Catechism Question 1.

Chapter 4: Distinguished Service

Christian's chief joy and highest aim in this life and in the next.

First, worshiping God is the duty of every human being. In John's Apocalypse, he is overawed by the surpassing greatness of the many visions, and in confusion he bows to an angel, who lightly rebukes him by saying, "See that you do not do that! I am your fellow servant, and of your brethren who have the testimony of Jesus. Worship God! For the testimony of Jesus is the spirit of prophecy" (Rev 19:10). Whatever John's motive was, the prohibition is a warning to Christians not merely against the worship of angels, but all forms of idolatry.[55] We are to worship God only.

All of life is spiritual worship, and every believer is a priest.[56] The Church is the temple of God's dwelling place (1 Cor 6:19-20). An important distinction in this discussion is our motivation in the worship of God. Our worship of God is not a meritorious work but a gracious participation with the one High Priesthood of Christ (Rom 12:1-2; Col 1:24; Heb 12:22-24; Jud 1:22-23; Rev 11:3). We are all through God's grace made priests, in order that we may dedicate ourselves and all we have to the glory of God. In our worship no sacrifice of expiation is wanted; and none can be set up, without casting a manifest reproach on the cross of Christ.[57] The new life comes into being by the Holy Spirit and its realization is new creation. God satisfies His saints with His presence and the only appropriate response is praise. As John Piper puts it, "God is most glorified in us when we are most satisfied in Him." We mock the mercy of the Giver if we seek to give as a work the thing we receive as a gift. Worship is true when it flows out of a heart made pure by God's grace.

This leads us to our second point, God is to be worshipped in the manner He prescribes – in spirit and in truth. Jesus said to the Samaritan woman at the well,

"Woman, believe Me, the hour is coming when you will neither on this mountain, nor in Jerusalem, worship the Father. 22 You worship what you do not know; we know what we worship, for salvation is of

---

[55] Beale, Revelation, 946.
[56] Ridderbos, Paul: An Outline of His Theology, 481.
[57] Calvin, Commentary on Romans 12:1.

the Jews. 23 But the hour is coming, and now is, when the true worshipers will worship the Father in spirit and truth; for the Father is seeking such to worship Him. 24 God is Spirit, and those who worship Him must worship in spirit and truth" (Jn 4:21-24).

Jesus tells us we must "worship in spirit and in truth." Worshipping "in spirit," refers to our human spirit, our inner person. That's why the small "s" is used. Genuine worship flows from our hearts, and is therefore not an external activity. Our worship of God is not a meritorious work. In our local churches we worship through reading God's Word, singing God's Word, preaching God's Word, and seeing God's Word in the Sacraments. Our worship is all about Christ and His once-for-all sacrifice of Himself for us so that we might become the righteousness of God (2 Cor 5:21). Worship of the Almighty is to be "in spirit and in truth" (Jn 4:24). This single consideration which relates to the worship of God, ought to be sufficient for restraining the wantonness of our minds.[58]

When Jesus tells us we must worship the Father "in spirit and in truth," He is telling us at least two things: first, that the Father is a spiritual rather than a corporeal being, and that those who worship Him must do so in a spiritual rather than a material way. And two, a spiritual birth, regeneration is prerequisite for spiritual worship (Jn 3:5). Therefore, those who worship Him must worship "in spirit" over against what the Bible calls hypocritical worship. Mark quoting Isaiah tells us, "Well did Isaiah prophesy of you hypocrites, as it is written: 'This people honors Me with their lips, but their heart is far from Me. And in vain they worship Me, teaching as doctrines the commandments of men" (Mk 7:6-7). Acceptable worship to God is also "in truth." Kent Hughes writes, "Worshipping in truth means that we come informed by the objective revelation of God's Word about the great God we serve and the precepts He has spoken."[59] Heb 12:28-29 tells us, "Therefore, since we are receiving a kingdom which cannot be shaken, let us have grace, by which we may *serve* God acceptably with reverence and godly fear. For our God is a consuming fire" (emphasis mine).

---

[58] Calvin, Commentary on John 4:24.
[59] Hughes, Disciplines of a Godly Man, 114.

Chapter 4: Distinguished Service

The highlighted word means "priestly service" latreon λατρείαν is worship that is rendered from the whole man – a living sacrifice, by the Spirit. The believer's body (mind, will, and emotions) is a holy and acceptable sacrifice as it is morally and spiritually presented to God. As a result of Christ's resurrection, God's people as mediating-witnessing priests extend His tabernacling presence throughout the whole earth, and serve as the building materials for God's end-time temple (1 Pet 1:4-5). Worship, is therefore, is not primarily self-expression, but rather the groaning, praising, and interceding of the Holy Spirit within us (Rom 8:15-17, 22-27), moving us to pray for God's kingdom to be extended and consummated by Christ's return. It's as Lewis says, "It is in the process of being worshipped that God communicates His presence to men."[60] How can those who have experienced His covenant blessings not praise His name?[61] All of our worship points to the perfect sacrifice of Jesus at Calvary, which forever removed the necessity of the sacrificial system. Christ's sacrifice of Himself on the cross confirmed that the sacrificial system of the Old Testament was not the final solution, but that through the sacrifice of Jesus we would be accepted.

When we look back at all of these disciplines, we see that none will be possible for us to do without the Holy Spirit's power and direction. We are advised like Augustine to pray, "Lord, give what you command, and command what you will." What God demands He gives, He does, and He completes (Phil 1:6). Grace is the life of God in the soul of man, and holiness, a communicable attribute of God, is at once a demand of God and a quality He gives to His people; what God demands He first gives.

Kingdom of Priests

Further, as priests in Christ's Kingdom, we are to make it our goal to test everything in order to do God's will in every situation. What God commands is for us to do God's will not

---

[60] Lewis, Reflections on the Psalms, 93.
[61] Belcher, The Messiah and the Psalms, 47.

in a disingenuous way but in a sacrificial way from the heart unto Him and not unto anyone or anything. The apostle John identifies himself with fellow Christians as actively being in Christ's Kingdom. Rev 1:9 tells us,

9 I, John, both your brother and companion in the tribulation and kingdom and patience of Jesus Christ, was on the island that is called Patmos for the word of God and for the testimony of Jesus Christ.

The three words "the tribulation and kingdom and patience" mutually interpret one another, in that they have a single article. Regarding this Greg Beale writes, John and his community are people who even now reign together in Jesus' kingdom. The exercise of rule in this kingdom begins and continues only as one faithfully endures tribulation. This is a formula for kingship: faithful endurance through tribulation is the means by which one reigns in the present with Jesus. Such kingship will be intensified at death and consummated at Jesus' final Parousia (Rev 21:1-22:5).[62]

God demands nothing less than our lives as we receive Christ and follow Him. For Christ's present authority and power in His present kingdom begins in us and continues in us only as we faithfully endure tribulation. What seeks to withhold our living sacrifice is tribulation. This is the subject of chapters 7 through 10. The biblical point being made here is, holiness, a communicable attribute of God, is at once a demand of God and a quality He gives to His people; what God demands He first gives. And the people of God are the new place of worship which replaced the Temple. As fellow workers with Christ we are building God's temple, as Jesus ministers though us. We extend the holy sphere over all the earth.[63] In this way, God's tabernacling presence expands spiritually through us as we minister to the world. Beale writes, "All Christians are now spiritual Levitical priests (in fulfillment of Isaiah (66:21). Our ongoing task is to serve God in His temple in which we always dwell and of which we are a part. Our continual priestly tasks are what the first Adam's were to be: to keep the order and peace of the spiritual

---

[62] Beale, Revelation, 201.
[63] Beale, The Temple and the Church's Mission, 79.

sanctuary by learning and teaching God's word, by praying always, and by being vigilant in keeping out unclean moral and spiritual things."[64]

Indigenous-Pilgrim Paradigm

Practically how Christians should interface with culture is a topic for further discussion (see chapter 7). For now there are two principles that help illustrate overall how we are to transform culture, or better still, how we are to submit to Christ in all things, seeking to find what is pleasing to Him, as we do all things to God's glory. First, God would have us be *in* the world, so as to win the lost for Christ. This is called the indigenous principle.[65] The apostle Paul gives us this is 1 Cor 5:9-11:

[9] I wrote to you in my epistle not to keep company with sexually immoral people. [10] Yet *I* certainly *did* not *mean* with the sexually immoral people of this world, or with the covetous, or extortioners, or idolaters, since then you would need to go out of the world. [11] But now I have written to you not to keep company with anyone named a brother, who is sexually immoral, or covetous, or an idolater, or a reviler, or a drunkard, or an extortioner—not even to eat with such a person.

In a negative sense, the principle laid out in verse 10 states that Christians are not to keep company with people who are merely calling themselves Christians, that is, people who either are secretly making inroads into Christian fellowship for the purposes of introducing destructive heresies or sexual perversions (Acts 20:28-31; Rev 2:20-26). Both of which are ways Satan has ransacked congregations in history. In the positive sense of the indigenous principle, Christians are to make inroads into the culture, seeking to positively shape it to reflect Christian values while developing relationships with people in order to win them for Christ. This aspect of the indigenous principle may be found two chapters later in 1 Cor 9:19-23,

---

[64] Beale, The Temple and the Church's Mission, 398.
[65] Walls, The Missionary Movement in Christian History, 9.

Chapter 4: Distinguished Service

[19] For though I am free from all *men*, I have made myself a servant to all, that I might win the more; [20] and to the Jews I became as a Jew, that I might win Jews; to those *who are* under the law, as under the law, that I might win those *who are* under the law; [21] to those *who are* without law, as without law (not being without law toward God, but under law toward Christ), that I might win those *who are* without law; [22] to the weak I became as weak, that I might win the weak. I have become all things to all *men*, that I might by all means save some. [23] Now this I do for the gospel's sake, that I may be partaker of it with *you*.

The apostle Paul tells us in these verses that he accommodates himself to other cultures for the gospel's sake. Additionally, Andrew Walls tells us, Christians should maintain a certain cultural awareness and ability to interact with the culture they live in. He writes, "The fact, then, that if any man is in Christ he is a new creation does not mean that he starts or continues his life in a vacuum, or that his mind is a blank table. It has been formed by his own culture and history, and since God has accepted him as he is, his Christian mind will continue to be influenced by what was in it before. And this is true for groups as for persons. All churches are culture churches – including our own."[66] Again, in 1 Cor 10:32-33, the apostle Paul teaches us,

[32] Give no offense, either to the Jews or to the Greeks or to the church of God, [33] just as I also please all *men* in all *things*, not seeking my own profit, but the *profit* of many, that they may be saved.

The Bible also represents Christians as strangers and pilgrims in this world. The pilgrim principle, the counterpart to the indigenous principle, instructs Christians to separate themselves from immorality so as not to be yoked with the unbelieving world. The apostle Paul tells us in 2 Cor 6:14-7:1:

[14] Do not be unequally yoked together with unbelievers. For what fellowship has righteousness with lawlessness? And what communion has light with darkness? [15] And what accord has Christ with Belial? Or what part has a believer with an unbeliever? [16] And

---

[66] Walls, The Missionary Movement in Christian History, 8.

what agreement has the temple of God with idols? For you are the temple of the living God. As God has said: "I will dwell in them and walk among them. I will be their God, and they shall be My people." [17] Therefore "Come out from among them and be separate, says the Lord. Do not touch what is unclean, and I will receive you." [18] "I will be a Father to you, and you shall be My sons and daughters, says the LORD Almighty."

7 Therefore, having these promises, beloved, let us cleanse ourselves from all filthiness of the flesh and spirit, perfecting holiness in the fear of God.

For God has called His people to be *in* the world but not *of* it, or better yet, not *of* the world but sent *into* it. Christ, in His High Priestly prayer makes this distinction in John 17:14-19,

[14] I have given them Your word; and the world has hated them because they are not of the world, just as I am not of the world. [15] I do not pray that You should take them out of the world, but that You should keep them from the evil one. [16] They are not of the world, just as I am not of the world. [17] Sanctify them by Your truth. Your word is truth. [18] As You sent Me into the world, I also have sent them into the world. [19] And for their sakes I sanctify Myself, that they also may be sanctified by the truth.

The people of God are not of this world, meaning by virtue of their regeneration they are born from above (Is 26:19; Ezek 11:19-20; 36:26-27; John 3:3; 2 Cor 5:17; 1 Pet 1:3).[67] They march to the beat of a different drum. Their status as being "born again" should manifest itself visibly and audibly to the culture they live in. Their presence in the world should be as pronounced as salt is to bland food and light is to a pitch black room as Jesus described in Mt 5:13-16.

There is a tension in the Christian life between this life and the next, between the city of man and the city of God. We are not to take part in the unfruitful works of darkness, because of

---

[67] The term "born again" in New Testament Greek γεννηθῇ genethe ἄνωθεν anothin means both "born anew" and "born from above." The tense used in the Greek is the aorist subjunctive passive. The aorist expresses an action that has occurred in the past without indicating its completion, whereas the subjunctive mood shows contingency, so "Unless one is born again/from above, he cannot see the kingdom of God" (John 3:3).

Chapter 4: Distinguished Service

which the wrath of God is coming (Eph 5:6-11), but rather we are to expose evil and withdrawal ourselves from immoral company (2 Cor 6:17).

So, just to sum up these two principles:

1. Christians are to be *in* the world but not *of* it (Jn 17:15-16).
2. Christians are to *separate* from the world (1 Cor 6:9-7:1) but in some ways *participate* in it (1 Cor 5:9-11).
3. Christians are to *adapt* to their particular culture (1 Pet 2:12) while *exposing* evil (Eph 5:11).
4. Christians are to refuse *conformity* with the world (Rom 12:1-2) but *contextualize* life situations to save others (1 Cor 9:22; 10:32-33).

The challenge to these principles is to keep oneself unspotted from the world (Jam 1:27), not allowing oneself to be entangled in someone else's sins, and avoiding even an appearance of evil (1 Thess 5:22), while working to bring the gospel to everyone, seeking that in all things Christ might be preeminent (Col 1:18). Godly wisdom is paramount for this task. Here we have no lasting city and we seek that city which is to come (Heb 13:15-16). Let us work to redeem even the time, for the days are evil (Eph 5:16).

The rise of a city, which swelled into an empire, may deserve, as a singular prodigy, the reflection of a philosophic mind. But the decline of Rome was the natural and inevitable effect of immoderate greatness. Excess of liberty, whether in states of individuals, seems only to pass into excess of slavery – Edward Gibbons.[68]

In All Things – In All Circumstances

What God demands He gives, He does, and He completes (Phil 1:6). We are God's work from beginning to end. We are not passive in the sense that we idly wait, in an oblivious sense, but we are passive in the sense that we are waiting and actively seeking God's direction and the fulfillment of His will in all things.

---

[68] Gibbons, History of the Decline and Fall of the Roman Empire, Volume 4, 119.

Chapter 4: Distinguished Service

The filling and control of the Holy Spirit will lead us to a spirit of humility, a desire to seek the welfare of others before our own and be mutually submissive. We are to live to Christ but die to the world daily as we live out His righteousness. As we do this the two extremes to avoid are: (1) an arid pharisaical intellectualism devoid of spiritual life on one end of the spectrum and, (2) a hysterical theologically obtuse emotionalism devoid of doctrinal structure on the other.

Philippians, one of the apostle Paul's prison epistles, was probably written around 60 AD, during the reign of Nero. When the church at Philippi heard that Paul was imprisoned they sent their pastor Epaphroditus to him. If you remember, the apostle Paul was the first to bring the Philippians the gospel on his second missionary journey recorded for us in Acts 16. Epaphroditus visited Paul and gave him support under his afflicted circumstances, and related to Paul the spiritual state of the church in Philippi.

Paul sent the letter, known to us as the Book of Philippians, to the church at Philippi along with pastor Epaphraditus. In this letter, Paul express his love and affection for them; gives them an account of his bonds, and the usefulness of them, and how he was supported by them; to encourage them under all the afflictions and persecutions, they endured for the sake of Christ; to excite them to love, unity, and peace, among themselves; to caution them against false teachers, Judaizing Christians, that were for reverting to Judaism in order to be saved.

After Paul thanks the church for their spiritual gift, he relates to us a great spiritual axiom of immense depth and usefulness. He tells us in 4:12, "I know how to behave when I have little and when I have much." Paul says, I know how to be low, to be treated with indignity and contempt, to be trampled upon by man, to suffer hardships and distress, to work with my own hands, and minister to his own and the necessities of others in that way; to be in hunger and thirst, to be cold and nakedness, and have no certain dwelling place; and, Paul says, I know how to behave under all this; not to be depressed and cast down, or to fret, be anxious, or grumble.

I know how to abound, to behave in the midst of plenty; so as not to be lifted up, so as not to be proud and haughty, and injurious. To use what I have to the glory of God, and for the good of my fellow man, and fellow Christians.

Paul says, "Everything I treasured, I now find worthless compared to the surpassing greatness of knowing Jesus Christ my Lord, for whose sake I have lost all things" (Phil 3:8).

> Ye servants of God, your Master proclaim,
> And publish abroad His wonderful name;
> The name all victorious of Jesus extol;
> His kingdom is glorious and rules over all.[69]

---

[69] C. Wesley, Ye Servants of God.

Chapter 4: Distinguished Service

Recommended Further Reading

1. Andrew Murray, *With Christ in the School of Prayer.*
2. Greg Beale, *The Temple and the Church's Mission.*
3. Randy Alcorn, *The Treasure Principle.*
4. James M. Boice, *Foundations of the Christian Faith.*
5. John Piper, *Seeing and Savoring Jesus Christ.*

Chapter 4 Review Questions

1. What is prayer? Is it important?

2. What do you treasure most?

3. What is the indigenous-pilgrim principle? Is it important?

4. How does prayer change things? Does it change God's mind?

5. What is ministry? Are all Christians ministers?

6. What is worship? Can we worship God in any way?

7. How important is long-suffering (patience), integrity, and purity to the Christian life?

8. What does it mean to "let your light so shine?"

9. In what sense are Christians priests?

10. How are we to understand Christ's kingdom?

Part 3: Spiritual Leadership

And the Lord said, "Who then is that faithful and wise steward, whom his master will make ruler over his household, to give them their portion of food in due season? Blessed is that servant whom his master will find so doing when he comes" (Lk 12:42-43).

Chapter 5: The Spiritual Leader of the Family

Is America the better for having systematically removed God's Word from her institutions? How did we get to this point? Since the late 1940s, the Bible has been systematically removed from our country. First, biblical teaching was removed from the public classrooms, followed by prayer in 1962. Next, the Bible itself was removed in 1963. Additionally, the Sabbath was targeted by partial or wholesale removal of Blue Laws. Following hard upon the heels of such tragic defamation of God's Word was the 1973 legalization of abortion; legalized murder which has taken the innocent lives of over 57 million human beings. Since the Bible was removed from the public classrooms the number of teen pregnancies, divorces, suicides, and violent crimes have increased exponentially!

Is it any wonder that children are shooting each other in our schools? Now that many denominations have held Biblical inerrancy in contempt is it so shocking they have ordained practicing homosexuals? Since we are dismantling our moral

Chapter 5: The Spiritual Leader of the Family

foundation, should we be so perplexed at the level of gender confusion? Is it so shocking that our nation no longer knows what constitutes marriage? That more and more evangelicals are approving of woman's ordination? That pornography has reached epic proportions? And the definitive controversy on our generation – gender and sexuality, has taken center stage? These issues we encounter are the symptoms of the spiritual deterioration of our country. How did America become so confused?

America has fallen prey to spiritual and social decline. The Bible reveals to us how such a decline occurs. In Romans 1:18-32 we learn of rebellion in four stages:

18 For the wrath of God is revealed from heaven against all ungodliness and unrighteousness of men, who suppress the truth in unrighteousness, 19 because what may be known of God is manifest in them, for God has shown it to them. 20 For since the creation of the world His invisible attributes are clearly seen, being understood by the things that are made, even His eternal power and Godhead, so that they are without excuse, 21 because, although they knew God, they did not glorify Him as God, nor were thankful, but became futile in their thoughts, and their foolish hearts were darkened. 22 Professing to be wise, they became fools, 23 and changed the glory of the incorruptible God into an image made like corruptible man— and birds and four-footed animals and creeping things. 24 Therefore God also gave them up to uncleanness, in the lusts of their hearts, to dishonor their bodies among themselves, 25 who exchanged the truth of God for the lie, and worshiped and served the creature rather than the Creator, who is blessed forever. Amen.

26 For this reason God gave them up to vile passions. For even their women exchanged the natural use for what is against nature. 27 Likewise also the men, leaving the natural use of the woman, burned in their lust for one another, men with men committing what is shameful, and receiving in themselves the penalty of their error which was due. 28 And even as they did not like to retain God in their knowledge, God gave them over to a debased mind, to do those things which are not fitting; 29 being filled with all unrighteousness, sexual immorality, wickedness, covetousness, maliciousness; full of envy, murder, strife, deceit, evil-mindedness; they are whisperers, 30 backbiters, haters of God, violent, proud, boasters, inventors of evil things, disobedient to parents, 31 undiscerning, untrustworthy, unloving, unforgiving, unmerciful; 32 who, knowing the righteous

Chapter 5: The Spiritual Leader of the Family

judgment of God, that those who practice such things are deserving of death, not only do the same but also approve of those who practice them.

As man departs from God's Word he invites disaster. Notice the four stages of rebellion in the above passage: First, there is a theological rejection of God and His revelation (Rom 1:20-21). Second, there is a philosophical construction which amounts to a Godless world view (Rom 1:22-23). Third, there is sociological pressure to legislate what is immoral (Rom 1:25), and fourth, there is legalization of what God condemns (Rom 1:32). *America has departed theologically from the Bible, has legislated what is immoral, and now values what God hates.*

Few things are more broken today than marriages. We are adrift in a sea of moral confusion and the price of that brokenness has been costly. What is at stake is not just the fabric of society and the endurance of civilization, but the revelation of the covenant-keeping Christ and his covenant-keeping church. What we are witnessing in America today is a disintegration of society's foundation, a near complete inversion of values. Collective unregenerate mankind, alienated from their Creator, and suffering from an agonizing conscience, tireless aims at casting off the restraining power of God's Law (Ps 2:1-3). Ultimately, mankind desires to live on their own terms and worship a god made in their own image – themselves (Rev 13:8).

The values being advanced today are in direct opposition to the Judeo-Christian framework which has guided and restrained our American society for nearly four hundred years. America is simply confused morally and sexually!

In his book *Our Dance Has Turned to Death*, Carl W. Wilson identifies the common pattern of family decline in ancient Greece and the Roman Empire. Wilson demonstrates how these seven stages parallel what is happening in America today. In the first stage, men ceased to lead their families in spiritual matters. Spiritual and moral development became secondary. Their view of God became naturalistic and scientific. In the second stage, men selfishly neglected care of their wives and children to pursue material wealth, political

245

and military power, and cultural development. Material values began to dominate thought, and the man began to exalt his own role as an individual.

The third stage involved a change in men's sexual values. Men who were preoccupied with business or war either neglected their wives sexually or became involved with lower-class women or with homosexuality. Ultimately, a double standard of morality developed. The fourth stage affected women. The role of women at home and with children lost value and status. Women were neglected and their roles devalued. Soon they revolted to gain access to material wealth and also freedom for sex outside marriage. Women also began to minimize having sex to conceive children, and sought sex for pleasure. And marriage laws were changed to make divorce easy.

In the fifth stage, husbands and wives competed against each other for money, home leadership, and the affection of their children. This resulted in hostility and frustration and possible homosexuality in the children. Many marriages ended in separation and divorce. Many children were unwanted, aborted, abandoned, molested, and undisciplined. The more undisciplined children became, the more social pressure there was not to have children. *The breakdown of the home produced anarchy.*

In the sixth stage, selfish individualism grew and carried over into society, fragmenting it into smaller and smaller group loyalties. The nation was thus weakened by internal conflict. The decrease in the birthrate produced an older population that had less ability to defend itself and less will to do so, making the nation more vulnerable to its enemies. *Finally, as unbelief in God became more complete, parental authority diminished, and ethical and moral principles disappeared, affecting the economy and government.* Thus, by internal weakness and fragmentation, the societies came apart. There was no way to save them except by a dictator who arose from within or by barbarians who invaded from without.[1]

And what exactly was the catalyst for this destruction? Carl W. Wilson states, "This chain of events began by men turning

---

[1] Wilson, Our Dance Has Turned to Death, 84-85.

Chapter 5: The Spiritual Leader of the Family

from God to pursue material wealth, and each successive step occurred automatically. The first step was to abandon the worship of God for the worship of mammon (idolatry = covetousness). What follows is devaluation of marriage, which leads to immorality, gender confusion, homosexuality, abortion, and ultimately the destruction of the state. *When the family is dissolved, so will the state.*

Looking back at Romans 1:18-32, we may see that the pattern of spiritual and social decline follows four steps:

The first stage of our alienation from God is our rejection of God and His revelation – the Bible. This has lead our nation to redefine and devalue everything. Because as a nation we have rejected God, He has given us over to depravity. And now we value what God despises, and have passed laws legalizing what He hates. But those civilizations that have gone the way of Sodom and Gomorra haven't survived.

Marriage has been greatly devalued. Studies show that nearly 75 % of women ages 30 or younger live with a partner outside of marriage, compared to 70 % in 2002, and 62 % in 1995. The trend reflects that marriage is increasingly thought to be "optional." Following this trend, 73 % of all Black babies are born to unwed mothers. Native Americans, Hispanics, and Whites are close behind with percentages at 70%, 53%, and 30% respectively.

Our devaluation of marriage has progressed along with our devaluation of life. At present, one of every five babies are aborted! What we are witnessing is the wholesale destruction of the family. Who is at fault? Men. American men are abdicating their responsibility to care for the women and children that God has given them. The only way to avoid the systematic destruction of our country is to repent of our sins and build godly homes on the Word of God (Mt 7:24-25). What America desperately needs is spiritual leadership in the home, church and nation.

Spiritual Leadership

Before we discuss spiritual leadership we must ask, what is leadership? Leadership serves as the catalyst that creates conditions for success. If leadership is to be defined in one

247

Chapter 5: The Spiritual Leader of the Family

word, then that word is "influence." Leaders inspire others to succeed.[2] However, as Christopher Kolenda informs us, "This concept hinges on the notion of influence. If by influence we mean to get someone to do what we want them to do, then we are left with the very significant problem of legitimizing coercion as an appropriate method of leadership."[3] So we must qualify our definition of leadership to be one that views influence as inspirational and not coercive. The US Army defines leadership as "the process of influencing people by providing *purpose, direction*, and *motivation* while operating to accomplish the mission and improving the organization."[4] God made the man to be the leader of the home, to inspire and influence his family to accomplish the godly goal of doing everything for the glory of God (Mt 6:33; Col 3:17, 23).

So the question now is what is spiritual leadership? J.R. Miller tells us, "There is no memorial that any man can make for himself in this world so lasting and so satisfying, as that which a life of unselfishness and beneficence builds up." A man's lasting contribution is a godly family. He must build well with God's Word. Thomas Boston reminds us, "As when men find a well-ordered family that tells what a man the leader of it is." Spiritual leadership in the home is the godly influence a man exercises over his family as husband and father. And finally, John Piper offers this excellent definition of spiritual leadership: "Spiritual leadership is knowing where God wants people to be and taking the initiative to get them there by God's means in reliance on God's power."[5]

The tendency in America today is to stress the equality of men and women by minimizing the unique significance of our maleness and femaleness. But, as Piper and Grudem tell us, "This deprecation of male and female personhood is a great loss. It is taking a tremendous toll on generations of young men and women who do not know what it means to be a man or woman. Confusion over the meaning of sexual personhood today is epidemic. The consequence of this confusion is not a free and happy harmony among gender-free persons relating

---

[2] LeFavor, U S Army Special Forces Small Unit Tactics Handbook, 157.
[3] Kolenda, Leadership: The Warrior's Art, xviii.
[4] FM 6-22 Leadership, 1-2.
[5] Piper, Brothers, We Are Not Professionals, 11.

on the basis of abstract competencies. The consequence rather is more divorce, more homosexuality, more sexual abuse, more promiscuity, more social awkwardness, and more emotional distress and suicide that come with the loss of God-given identity."[6]

Before we go, on let's review some of the ground we've covered. In chapter one we discussed how marriage is a sign and a covenant, one of God's ordinances – one of the ways He manages mankind. The other two being the church and the civil government. In marriage, God delegates authority to the man, to *lead, protect,* and *provide* for the physical and spiritual needs of his household, for the glory of God and the good of His people. In like manner, God's blessings flow to His people through His two other ordinances: the church and the civil government. As we discussed in chapter one (third mark, pages 47-64) God ordained marriage, and blessed it to operate with the man being the representative head of the household (1 Cor 11:3, 8; Eph 5:21-33).

There are two concepts which bear much weight in this discussion: *headship* and *submission.* The Bible gives us the definitive teaching on these concepts in Ephesians 5:21-33:

21 Submitting to one another in the fear of God. 22 Wives, submit to your own husbands, as to the Lord. 23 For the husband is head of the wife, as also Christ is head of the church; and He is the Savior of the body. 24 Therefore, just as the church is subject to Christ, so let the wives be to their own husbands in everything.

25 Husbands, love your wives, just as Christ also loved the church and gave Himself for her, 26 that He might sanctify and cleanse her with the washing of water by the word, 27 that He might present her to Himself a glorious church, not having spot or wrinkle or any such thing, but that she should be holy and without blemish. 28 So husbands ought to love their own wives as their own bodies; he who loves his wife loves himself. 29 For no one ever hated his own flesh, but nourishes and cherishes it, just as the Lord does the church. 30 For we are members of His body, of His flesh and of His bones. 31 "For this reason a man shall leave his father and mother and be joined to his wife, and the two shall become one flesh." 32 This is a great mystery, but I speak concerning Christ and the church. 33

---

[6] Piper and Grudem, Recovering Biblical Manhood and Womanhood, 26.

Chapter 5: The Spiritual Leader of the Family

Nevertheless let each one of you in particular so love his own wife as himself, and let the wife see that she respects her husband.

Wives, Submit – Husbands, Love

This Scripture is one of several "house-rule" lists in the New Testament (cf. Ephesians 5:22 to Ephesians 6:9; 1 Timothy 2:8-15; 1 Timothy 6:1-2; Titus 2:1-10; 1 Peter 2:18 to 1 Peter 3:7). In Ephesians 5:21-6:5 the apostle Paul addresses six groups: wives and husbands (Ephesians 5:22-33), children and parents (Ephesians 6:1-4), and then slaves and masters (Ephesians 6:5-9). In each the first is responsible to be submissive or obedient, however, the second is also to show a humble spirit. And all are to relate to one another as unto the Lord.

Submitting to one another is therefore an expression of one's being filled with the Holy Spirit. John Stott tells us, "What is beyond question is that the three paragraphs which follow (Eph 5:21-6:5) are given as examples of Christian submission, and that the emphasis throughout is on submission."[7] Husband and wife humble themselves in order to lift the other up. And as much as they are able they are to relegate their own desires and preferences, aspiring to love and serve one another. This can be as simple as letting your wife chose where the family will eat dinner. (This is always a good start). Wayne Mack writes, "When two people know, accept, and fulfill their varying but complementary responsibilities, oneness in marriage is promoted."[8]

If leadership may be summed up by the word *influence*, headship may be summed up by the word *responsibility*. Headship also implies leadership. For the husband is head of the wife, as Christ is head of the church (Eph 5:23). God has so designed marriage to reflect Christ's relationship with His people. This is how marriage is a living parable (Eph 5:32). Headship is not a right to be tyrannical, controlling or abusive, headship is sacrificial. God makes the husband the head of the wife, and calls him to love her like Christ loves the church – His bride. Husbands, we must learn to love our wives as Christ

---

[7] Stott, The Message of Ephesians, 214.
[8] Mack, Strengthening Your Marriage, 16.

loves the church. Christ's sacrifice is the pattern for headship. This is impossible without the Holy Spirit's presence and power and is a check to any propensity to arrogance and tyranny.

Likewise, wives are to submit to their own husbands, as to the Lord (Eph 5:22). The husband's authority is not his own but it is delegated to him. Therefore, God's desire for wives to submit to the delegated authority of their husbands, is His desire that they do so unto Him; the husband being his representative in the family. This submission of the wife is not slavish or coerced but willing, and genuine. This is the way God desires for His people to respond to Christ, God's Son, the Bridegroom. Jay Adams writes, "Husbands, do you love your wives enough to die for them? Wives, do you love your husbands enough to live for them? That is what the latter part of Ephesians 5 is all about. The husband must learn to love his wife as Jesus Christ loves His church. A husband, if need be, should be willing to give up his life for his wife. On the other hand, a wife should so love her husband that she is willing to live for him. She must be willing to pour her life into being his helper. This involves living for him, just as the church is required to live for Jesus Christ."[9]

Headship and submission are reciprocal concepts, that is, they are complementary. John Piper writes, "Headship is the divine calling of a husband to take primary responsibility for Christ-like, servant-leadership, protection and provision in the home." And, "submission is the divine calling of a wife to honor and affirm her husband's leadership and help carry it through according to her gifts."[10]

Principles of Spiritual Leadership

What every wife desires is for her husband to be faithful to her, to love her and the children she gave him, to protect their lives, to provide for their physical needs, to guide them spiritually by building their home on the Bible, and to lead them in prayer, Scripture reading, and worship. Likewise,

---

[9] Adams, Christian Living in the Home, 70-71.
[10] Piper, Affirming the Goodness of Manhood and Womanhood in All of Life, 1.

what every husband desires is for his wife to respect him, to love and be faithful to him, to be his helper in everything, to nurture and care for his children that she gave him, and to assist him in providing for the physical and spiritual needs of the family. Our problem is not women who demand to be in charge, rather its men who have abdicated responsibility to lead their families. We must agree with Carl W. Wilson when he writes, "The root of the problem is men's spiritual failure. Instead of leading their families in the worship of God and caring about their wives and children, they have neglected these responsibilities in pursuit of wealth and worldly status."[11]

God has called men to be the responsible leaders of their families. The following five principles outline the husband and father's spiritual leadership: SHARP – Headship implies leadership.

> **S** – Stewardship (Responsibility).
> **H** – Humility (Sacrificial love).
> **A** – Awareness (Protection).
> **R** – Respect (Leading by example).
> **P** – Provision (Primary bread-winner).

S – Stewardship (Responsibility).

The first principle is *stewardship*. Stewardship is the responsibility for you to manage things that are not your own. Everyone is a steward in some sense, and everyone will give an account to God for the manner in which they stewarded God's possessions (Mt 25:14-30). The Bible teaches us that everything is God's. Scripture emphasizes the fact that we are not owners of anything, we are simply managers (Lk 19:11-27). We have been entrusted with everything that belongs to God: our very lives, our wives we love, our children, our money, our time, et al, and we will give account for how we have managed it. When a man finds a wife, he finds what is good and receives favor from the Lord (Pro 18:22). If he is doubly blessed, God adds to that marriage children. These and

---

[11] Wilson, Our Dance has Turned to Death, 230.

all things God entrusts to the man, His delegated leader in the family.

In the parable of the servant in authority (Mt 24:45-51: Lk 12:42-48), the Master entrusts one of His servants with a stewardship over His household. With this parable Jesus teaches us the importance of faithfulness and watchfulness. The main emphasis of the parable involves how the servant who is entrusted with the Master's household treats his fellow servants. Jesus responds to a question of Peter with a question and says,

42 And the Lord said, "Who then is that faithful and wise steward, whom his master will make ruler over his household, to give them their portion of food in due season? 43 Blessed is that servant whom his master will find so doing when he comes. 44 Truly, I say to you that he will make him ruler over all that he has. 45 But if that servant says in his heart, 'My master is delaying his coming,' and begins to beat the male and female servants, and to eat and drink and be drunk, 46 the master of that servant will come on a day when he is not looking for him, and at an hour when he is not aware, and will cut him in two and appoint him his portion with the unbelievers. 47 And that servant who knew his master's will, and did not prepare himself or do according to his will, shall be beaten with many stripes. 48 But he who did not know, yet committed things deserving of stripes, shall be beaten with few. For everyone to whom much is given, from him much will be required; and to whom much has been committed, of him they will ask the more (Lk 12:42-48).

The principle of stewardship reminds us that as head of the house, the man is responsible of all that is God's, which is everything. And he is answerable to God for the manner in which he manages God's possessions. For as the parable makes clear the home is part of God's household, and the man is God's representative. This is stewardship. The husband is to be:

1. The steward of God's possessions (Luke 19:11-27).
2. The priest of the home (Eph 5:25-29).
3. The principle teacher of God's Word (1 Tim 4:16).
4. The principle disciplinarian of the children (Eph 6:4).

253

Chapter 5: The Spiritual Leader of the Family

Every home is to be a miniature church with the husband and father the leader of it. The head of the household bears the chief responsibility for everything the home does or fails to do. The head of the household is the priest of the home. He is responsible for what the family believes and how the family lives (Dt 4:9; 6:1-9; Eph 6:4; 1 Tim 4:16). Additionally, the managers of God's church are to be men; viz., a man "who rules his own house well, having his children in submission with all reverence (for if a man does not know how to rule his own house, how will he take care of the church of God (1 Tim 3:4-5)? Obedience to God is to be first learned at home (Pro 22:6; Eph 6:4).

The man as the steward of God's possessions is to lead his family according to Scripture and not worldly principles. Husbands are to steward time, creating margin for the reading of God's Word, prayer, and worship. The husband is head (responsible steward) of the home and is to be the family priest (Eph 5:25-29). The biblical precept is for the father to teach the commandments of God to his children. The Book of Deuteronomy tells us,

4 "Hear, O Israel: The Lord our God, the Lord is one! 5 You shall love the Lord your God with all your heart, with all your soul, and with all your strength. 6 "And these words which I command you today shall be in your heart. 7 You shall teach them diligently to your children, and shall talk of them when you sit in your house, when you walk by the way, when you lie down, and when you rise up. 8 You shall bind them as a sign on your hand, and they shall be as frontlets between your eyes. 9 You shall write them on the doorposts of your house and on your gates (Dt 6:4-9).

The man is to be the priest of the home. He is to teach his family God's Word and commandments. And as priest, because he represents his wife and children to God, he spends time in prayer everyday mindful of the needs and concerns of his family. He prays for God's will to be accomplished in his home. He prays for the salvation of his children. And like Job, he asks the Lord to forgive the sins of his children (Job 1:5). The Puritan Richard Baxter writes, "The husband must be the principal teacher of the family. He must instruct, examine, and rule them about the matters of God as well as his own service

Chapter 5: The Spiritual Leader of the Family

and see that the Lord's Day and worship be observed by all who are within his gates."[12]

As stewards, husbands are to seek the will of God for their families. Men are to base their decisions not on the influences of the world, but on biblical truth (Mt 7:24-25). James Dobson writes, "A Christian man is obligated to lead his family to the best of his ability. If his family has purchased too many items on credit, then the financial crunch is ultimately his fault. If the family never reads the Bible or seldom goes to church on Sunday, God holds the man to blame. If the children are disrespectful and disobedient, the primary responsibility lies with the father not his wife. In my view, America's greatest need is for husbands to begin guiding their families, rather than pouring every physical and emotional resource into the mere acquisition of money."[13]

Withhold Not Correction

The privilege of receiving children from the Lord accompanies the responsibility of stewardship. An additional responsibility God has placed on the man of the house is the discipline of the children. The apostle Paul in Ephesians 6:1-4 tells us,

Children, obey your parents in the Lord, for this is right. 2 "Honor your father and mother," which is the first commandment with promise: 3 "that it may be well with you and you may live long on the earth." 4 And you, fathers, do not provoke your children to wrath, but bring them up in the training and admonition of the Lord.

Fathers are to teach their children the Word of God and discipline them so they obey it. The Bible teaches us if we love our children we will spank them. But fathers today are half apologetic for having brought their children into the world, afraid to restrain them lest he should create inhibitions or even to instruct them lest he should interfere with their

---

[12] Baxter, The Godly Home, 153.
[13] Dobson, Straight Talk to Men and Their Wives, 64.

independence of mind. As C.S. Lewis tells us, "this is a most misleading symbol of Divine Fatherhood."[14]

However, Proverbs 23:13-14 tells us "Do not withhold correction from a child, for if you beat him with a rod, he will not die. You shall beat him with a rod, and deliver his soul from hell (Pro 23:13-14)." Regarding the physical discipline of our children, there are at least three pillars in the foundation for our approach: knowledge of God's Word, patience, and consistency. Piper tells us, "Mature masculinity expresses itself in a family, but taking the initiative in disciplining the children when both parents are present and a family standard has been broken."[15] The man is to be the primary disciplinarian. Our children, like us, have fallen natures, and must be brought up in the training and admonition of the Lord" (Eph 6:4). They must be taught God's Word, obedience to it, and self-control.

The following principles outline a biblical approach to correction:

1. Must empress upon the child God's Word and authority.
2. Must be administered in love.
3. Must be proportionate to the offense.
4. Must be accompanied by verbal reproof.
5. Must be attended with prayer.
6. Must be finished and forgotten.
7. Must be consistent.

1. Must empress upon the child God's Word and authority.

Obedience to God is to be first learned at home. Spanking is moral correction that prepares children for godly service. Spanking teaches a child to control himself, to obey authority, and to fear and love God. Ultimately, the aim of physical discipline is to witness the salvation of the child. In the words of Charles Hodge, "God's authority should be brought into constant and immediate contact with the mind, heart and

---

[14] Lewis, The Problem of Pain, 37.
[15] Piper, Recovering Biblical Manhood and Womanhood, 40.

conscience of the child." Our authority as parents is delegated to us from God (Rom 13). We must empress upon the minds of our children that when they obey us, they are obeying God, in whose authority we are operating under. And we must start while they are young before it's too late.

Richard Baxter informs us to, "Labor much to possess their hearts with the fear of God, and a reverence of the holy Scriptures; and then whatsoever duty you command them, or whatsoever sin you forbid them, show them some plain and urgent texts of Scripture for it; and cause them to learn them and oft repeat them; that so they may find reason and divine authority in your commands; till their obedience begin to be rational and divine, it will be but formal and hypocritical."[16] Fathers must inculcate trust in God's Word.

2. Must be administered in love.

Everything the saint does in life is to be rooted and grounded in love (1 Cor 13; Gal 5:22, 25; Eph 3:17) – no less the discipline of our children. Proverbs 13:24 tells us, "He who spares his rod hates his son, but he who loves him disciplines him promptly." God says in His Word, "My son, do not despise the chastening of the Lord, nor be discouraged when you are rebuked by Him; for whom the Lord loves He chastens, and scourges every son whom He receives" (Heb 12:5-6). Hebrews goes on to ask, "God deals with you as with sons; for what son is there whom a father does not chasten" (Heb 12:7)? If we love our children, then we spank them in order to correct them so as to teach them to obey us as they would the Lord. We spank our children because we love them and don't want them to grow up to be miscreants. And spanking may be painful at the time, but afterward it yields the peaceable fruit of righteousness to those who have been trained by it" (Heb 12:11).

Chip Ingram tells us, "The Bible never implies that the rod of discipline should be violent. It offers no specifics about how hard a spanking should be, and there's no reason to

---

[16] Baxter, Practical Works, Vol. 1, A Christian Directory, Part II, Christian Economics, Chapter X, Direction 5.

assume that it's talking about a brutal form of punishment. Just the opposite, in fact. A parent who reaches back and swings hard is acting out of anger and frustration, not out of love and desire for the child's welfare. That's unbiblical by anyone's definition." And Baxter tells us, "Correct them not in passion, but stay till they perceive that you are calmed; for they will think else, that your anger rather than your reason is the cause."[17]

Additionally, if at all possible, we should not use the hand to spank. The hand should be used for comfort following a spanking. Then what should we use for spanking? Perhaps best is the belt or paddle. Growing up my Father used his belt which he knew just how much power to put into it. I'd hate to think of how spoiled and rotten or perhaps how many times I would have been in and out of prison if he hadn't. My father and mother spanked me because they wanted me to learn discipline and ultimately to fear and love God. Thanks Mom and Dad.

3. Must be proportionate to the offense.

Spanking is not the only form of discipline advocated in the Bible. Other forms of discipline such as, temporary isolation or "grounding," may be more appropriate in some situations with children of differing ages and temperaments. Likewise, children should be disciplined unless they are legitimately sick. When I was a child and tried to "fake it" my Mom and Dad could always tell. And they spanked me. But when I was sick they sent me to my room to sleep if I acted up.

Additionally, when we spank our children it should be sufficiently firm, that is, it should bring tears or it will have no effect. Prov. 19:18 tells us, "Chasten your son while there is hope, and do not set your heart on his destruction." A child who is spanked while wearing a diaper will not get disciplined. And may think it's a joke. As a child, when my father and mother spanked me, it was over the underwear only. No pants allowed, no matter how much I tried to barter.

---

[17] Ibid, Direction 17.4.

Chapter 5: The Spiritual Leader of the Family

4. Must be accompanied by verbal reproof.

Foolishness is bound up in the heart of a child; the rod of correction will drive it far from him (Pro 22:15). When we spank our children it's important for us as parents to impress open the child's mind that they have erred from God's Word and broken His commandments. Spanking must be accompanied by verbal reproof. That is, we must tell the child what they did was wrong according to the Word of God. Spanking without words is useless. Again Richard Baxter tells us, "Before children come to have any distinct understanding of particulars, it is a hopeful beginning to have their hearts possessed with a general reverence and high esteem of holy matters."[18]

Dt 6:6-7 says "And these words which I command you today shall be in your heart. You shall teach them diligently to your children." Our children must never be spanked for 'making Daddy or Mommy angry' but for not honoring God's Word by talking back to Mom and Dad. This is why it is important for parents to teach their children the Ten Commandments and the Scriptures.

They must learn that they have offended God by disregarding His Word. Parents spank their children in faith, believing that they're preparing them for a disciplined life of service to God. This is the motive, to bring our children to a submissive relationship with God and His authority. However, we should not raise our voice because this teaches children to obey only after you are frustrated.

Additionally, as parents, we should never issue a warning without following through with the consequence or we may lose the respect of our children. Many parent say, "Alright Johnny, I'm going to count to three and you'd better straighten up or I'm going to spank you." One, two...then the child complies, but the child has been rebellious by not obeying immediately. Warnings teach children to obey only after the second or third time but obedience should be immediate.

---

[18] Baxter, Practical Works, Vol. 1, A Christian Directory, Part II, Christian Economics, Chapter X, Direction 6.

Chapter 5: The Spiritual Leader of the Family

5. Must be attended with prayer.

My wife and I have two grown daughters, Liane and Collette. When they were young, Becky and I made a lot of mistakes in parenting – especially when it came to spanking. Liane, our oldest, broke us in as parents. It took a lot of prayer to get through all the temper tantrums, and the 'no, I won't do it' episodes (she would even hide the spank spoon) but through the continuous supply of God's strength we made it through (Phil 4:13). We didn't always do everything right but we sure loved Liane, and wanted so much for God to save her. Now Liane is a godly woman who loves the Lord. My wife and I were privileged to lead her to Christ. Collette, on the other hand, proved to be easier to discipline than our first daughter. We had to spank her significantly less. And they both know the Lord.

Spanking must be attended with prayer. A practice we used when spanking went something like this. We would ask our children:

- What did you do?
- What does God's Word say about that?
- What happens when you disobey?
- What do Mommy and I have to do?

Then I would spank them, or if I was absent, my wife would. And afterward, we would pray, "Dear Lord, please forgive _____ for disobeying Your Word by _____. Help her to obey You by helping her to obey Mom and Dad. In Jesus name we pray. Amen." Then we would console them as much as we could.

It's vital, as Charles Hodge says, that "God's authority should be brought into constant and immediate contact with the mind, heart and conscience of the child." The goal of physical discipline is to witness the salvation of the child.

6. Must be finished and forgotten.

After we discipline our children we are to forgive them and move on with life. No bringing up their failures again and again. The apostle Paul tells us, "And you, fathers, do not provoke your children to wrath, but bring them up in the training and admonition of the Lord" (Eph 6:1-4). And Col 3:21 tells us, "Fathers, do not provoke your children, lest they become discouraged." If we were to continually bring up all of our child's past faults they will become discouraged. It will have a profound impact on them psychologically. When God forgives us, He forgets. This is what we are admonished to do to our fellow man (Mt 6:14-15). If we truly want our children to follow us as we follow Christ, then we will forgive and forget (1 Cor 11:1). Richard Baxter tells us, "Always show them the tenderness of your love, and how unwilling you are to correct them, if they could be reformed any easier way; and convince them that you do it for their good."[19]

7. Must be consistent.

This is perhaps the hardest of all – being consistent. We are going to need patience (perhaps of Job) in order to follow through every time in discipline. If we are tempted to overlook a small act of disobedience because we are tired, J. C. Ryle warns us, "Beware of letting small faults pass unnoticed under the idea that it is a little one. There are no little things in training children; all are important. Little weeds need plucking up as much as any. Leave them alone and they will soon be great." Men, if you are discouraged remember, the first important fact about a Christian home is that sinners live there.[20]

Every home is to be a miniature church and the father is to be the leader and priest of it. He is responsible for what the family believes and how the family lives (Dt 4:9; 6:1-9; Eph 6:4; 1 Tim 4:16). A man must rule his own house well, having his children in submission with all reverence to him and his wife (1 Tim 3:4-5). Above all, fathers are to lovingly steward their children, bringing them up in the training and admonition of the Lord (Eph 6:4). The oft quoted Proverbs 22:6 is not a promise to parents that their child will be saved if they

---

[19] Baxter, Practical Works, Vol. 1, A Christian Directory, Part II, Christian Economics, Chapter X, Direction 17.5.
[20] Adams, Christian Living in the Home, 10.

discipline them, but it's a promise for parents who discipline that their labor of love will have a permanent effect on their child for good; for Christ must save them. Once again Baxter bids us,

"Let your own example teach your children that holiness, and heavenliness, and blamelessness of tongue and life, which you desire them and to learn and practice. The example of parents is most powerful with children, both for good and evil. If they see you live in the fear of God, it will do much to persuade them, that it is the most necessary and excellent course of life, and that they must do so too; and if they see you live a carnal, voluptuous, and ungodly life, and hear you curse or swear, or talk filthily or railingly, it will greatly embolden them to imitate you. If you speak never so well to them, they will sooner believe your bad lives, than your good words."[21]

H – Humility (Sacrificial love).

The head of the household is to be motivated by the love of God (1 Cor 13). The spirit of love requires a husband to honor his wife. Richard Baxter tells us, "The husband must so unite authority and love that neither of them may be omitted or concealed, but both will be exercised and maintained."[22] J. R. Miller writes, "In the spirit of this love every husband should be a large-hearted man. He should never be a tyrant, playing the petty despot in his home. A manly man has a generous spirit which shows itself in all his life—but nowhere so richly as within his own doors."[23]

Husbands, what our wives desire is to be included in every aspect of our lives. In fact, men rob themselves of the benefit of their wives lovely counsel when they shut them out. The influence of one gentle and unselfish life softens rudeness and melts selfishness. This is how wives win their husbands to the Lord, and this is how wives sweeten the home. Likewise, every husband should seek to be worthy of the wife he has won. As the priest of the home, he sacrificially loves his wife and children, and would willingly give his life for their safety.

---

[21] Baxter, Practical Works, Vol. 1, A Christian Directory, Part II, Christian Economics, Chapter X, Direction 18.
[22] Baxter, The Godly Home, 152.
[23] Miller, Home-Making, 52.

Chapter 5: The Spiritual Leader of the Family

Husbands are to include their wives in the ruling of their homes. The wife is the husband's helper. Together they raise the next godly generation. Dennis Rainey tells us, "The core role of a husband is to be a servant-leader, leading as Christ leads and loving as Christ loves. The wife's core response to this leadership is submission. The core role for a wife is to be a helper-homemaker, filling the gaps in her husband's life and prioritizing her life around home and family. The husband's core response to his wife is praise and honor."[24]

He must admit when he's wrong and listen to the advice of his wife. John Maxwell tells us that godly leaders are to be "big enough to admit their mistakes, smart enough to benefit from them and strong enough to correct them."

A – Awareness (Protect).

The primary responsibility of the husband and father is to image Christ by shepherding his family. He must be aware of all the influences that are trying to invade his home. He is to be the first to stand in between danger and his family. Because the Godly man seeks to honor God and build a godly home based on God's Word, he disciplines his children. He must place a high premium on obedience to God's Word. God expects parents to discipline their children. And when both parents are present, the father is to be the primary disciplinarian. The Bible tells us that "He who spares his rod hates his son, but he who loves him disciplines him promptly" (Pro 13:24). And "Chasten your son while there is hope, and do not set your heart on his destruction" (Pro 19:18).

Children are a gift from the Lord (Ps 127:3). And they come with the responsibility to "bring them up in the training and admonition of the Lord" (Eph 6:4). Without discipline in the home the parents risk the destruction of their children. This is precisely what happened to Eli's sons. Eli was a priest and judge of Israel before the reign of Saul, about 1100 BC. His sons, Hophni and Phineas, although priests, didn't know the Lord and were wicked. Their disregard for the Lord and His commandments grieved the people greatly.

---

[24] Rainey, Ministering to Twenty-First Century Families, 3.

Chapter 5: The Spiritual Leader of the Family

The Book of First Samuel informs us that Eli's sons took more than their allotted share because they abhorred the offering of the Lord (1 Sam 2:12-17). And to add to their delinquencies, they thumbed their noses at God by debauching women in the tabernacle. Eli was a good man but he failed as a father. He failed in the moral and religious training of his family. Jamieson-Fausset-Brown tell us, "He erred on the side of parental indulgence; and though he reprimanded them, yet, from fear or indolence, he shrank from laying on them the restraints, or subjecting them to the discipline, their gross delinquencies called for. In his judicial capacity, he winked at their flagrant acts of maladministration and suffered them to make reckless encroachments on the constitution, by which the most serious injuries were inflicted both on the rights of the people and the laws of God."[25]

Eli was far too gentle in the reproof of his sons. In Charles H. Spurgeon's opinion, Eli was afraid of his own sons.[26] This seems to be true. And the Scripture tells us that Eli's sons had gone so far in their wicked contempt of God, that the Lord saw it fit to destroy them. Spurgeon writes, "They had transgressed so foully that He would permit them to go on in sin until they perished in it (1 Sam 2:25). And when Israel went out to battle the Philistines, the Ark of the Covenant was captured and Hophni and Phineas were slain (1 Sam 4:1-11).

As fathers, we should take warning from the faults of Eli. In this vein, Richard Baxter writes, "Consider also that an ungoverned, ungodly family is a powerful means to the damnation of all the members of it; it is the common boat or ship that hurries souls to hell and is bound for the devouring gulf. Whoever is the Devil's coach or boat is likely to go with the rest, as the driver or the boatman pleases. But a well-governed family is an excellent help to the saving of all the souls who are in it."[27]

---

[25] Jamieson-Fausset-Brown Bible Commentary, 1 Samuel 2:22-24.
[26] Spurgeon's Expository Encyclopedia, Volume 13, 493.
[27] Baxter, The Godly Home, 106.

Chapter 5: The Spiritual Leader of the Family

R – Respect (Lead by example).

An effective leader evaluates his strengths and weaknesses in light of the Word of God. An accurate and clear understanding of yourself and an understanding of human nature will help you determine the best way to deal with any given situation. Leaders must know and understand those being led. A man of the home is to be above reproach to as to not lose his families trust. A man's children must respect him.

Godly men aren't to frustrate their wives and children, but gain their trust and confidence by strength and honor. What is manhood? Jesus who is the Lion of Judah (Revelation 5:5) and the Lamb of God (Revelation 5:6)—he was lionhearted and lamblike, strong and meek, tough and tender, aggressive and responsive, bold and brokenhearted. He sets the pattern for manhood. Men earn the respect of their wives by mature masculine leadership. Husbands rob their wives when they prevent them from sharing in the whole of their lives. Piper tells us, "Mature masculinity expresses itself not in the demand to be served, but in the strength to serve and to sacrifice for the good of woman."[28]

Complementing the God-honoring man, the God-honoring woman strengthens the strength she receives, and refines and extends the leadership she looks for. Piper and Grudem write, "At the heart of mature femininity is a freeing disposition to affirm, receive and nurture strength and leadership from worthy men in ways appropriate to a woman's differing relationships.[29]

Men, our children need to know we respect our wives and that we expect that they do the same on the authority of the Word of God. Godly men never let their children get away with sassing their mother. Richard Baxter writes, "It is the duty of husbands to preserve the authority of their wives over their children. They are joint governors with them over their children. The infirmities of women are apt many times to expose them to contempt, so that children will be likely to

---

[28] Piper, Recovering Biblical Manhood and Womanhood, 38.
[29] Ibid, 46.

slight and disobey them if the husband does not interpose to preserve their honor and authority."[30]

Like children who are disciplined, more and more after conversion, a believer's motivation should move from a desire to escape the threat of punishment to a desire to please the Lord who loved them and gave His life for them. This is what the God-honoring man should seek to model more in the home than anything else. This is the attitude we are to have in leading our families.

P – Provision (The man is the primary bread - winner).

By God's design, the head of the house is to be the primary bread winner. 1 Tim 5:8 tells us, "But if anyone does not provide for his own, and especially for those of his household, he has denied the faith and is worse than an unbeliever." Andreas Kostenberger writes, "The roles and responsibilities in a household according to Scripture – Fathers: Provide for family/children (2 Cor. 12:14) and ensure proper nurture and discipline (Eph. 6:4; Col. 3:21; Heb. 12:6). Mothers: Raising of children/motherhood (1 Tim. 2:15) and managing the home (1 Tim. 5:14). Children: Obedience to parents (Eph. 6:1-3; Col. 3:20) and care for parents in old age (1 Tim. 5:8)."[31]

As Robert Dabney observes,

It was essential to the welfare of both husband and wife and of the offspring that there must be an ultimate human head of the family. Now let reason decide, was it necessary that the man be head over the woman, or the woman over the man? Was it right that he for whom woman was created should be subjected to her who was created for him; that he who was stronger physically should be subjected to the weaker; that the natural protector should be the servant of the dependent; that the divinely ordained bread-winner should be controlled by the bread-dispenser? Every honest woman admits that this would have been unnatural and unjust. Hence God, acting, so to speak, under an unavoidable moral necessity, assigned to the male the domestic government, regulated and tempered, indeed, by the strict laws of God, by self-interest and by the most tender affection; and to the female the obedience of love. On this order all other social order

---

[30] Piper, Recovering Biblical Manhood and Womanhood, 152.

[31] Kostenberger, God, Marriage and Family, 123.

Chapter 5: The Spiritual Leader of the Family

depends. It was not the design of Christianity to subvert it, but only to perfect and refine it.[32]

What if your father failed to demonstrate this manner of leadership in the family you grew up in? You have a heavenly Father, who lives in you, and will teach you how to lead your family. Homes in America are falling apart at an alarming rate. Carl Wilson writes, "The renewal of the family and nations rests on renewing the spiritual leadership of men. While cooperation and assistance of women is needed, this will most readily take place after men's commitment to God occurs. Therefore, the main need is to call men away from idolatrous pursuit of business and wealth and back to the worship of God and the priority of building the kingdom of God through the home, which is the germ cell of the church and society."[33]

It's time for men to stand up and be men. To take responsibility for their actions and for their families that God gave them to steward. This will take repentance and humility on our part because we are failing. Every home is to be a miniature church. Yet, for the most part, men have ceased to lead their families in the worship of God. Men have abdicated their role as priest of the home. Our families get fed their values from television and the media – America's intellectual popes. The God-honoring man must set standards in the home that reflect what is most important in this life: to glorify God and to enjoy Him forever; to value God and His Word. For what we as men value will exert influence on our family's behavior so that it will eventually become our nation's character.

When considering the behavior of a good husband and father, a good analogy would be what we are told when we fly on commercial airlines. Do you remember sitting in your seat shortly before takeoff while the flight attendant is providing instructions in case of an emergency? We are instructed that if the cabin loses pressure and the oxygen masks fall from the overhead compartment, to place the mask first on ourselves,

---

[32] Dabney, The Public Preaching of Women, The Southern Presbyterian Review October, 1879.
[33] Wilson, Our Dance Has Turned to Death, 230.

and then assist our children with their masks. For some, this seems selfish and neglectful. How could any man look after himself prior to ensuring the safety of his own children? There is, of course a good reason for doing exactly as we're instructed. What if while we're neglecting ourselves of oxygen, struggling to properly fit masks on our children, we were to pass out, especially considering the fact that our children may simply remove what we've struggled so hard to fit, leaving us no choice but to repeat the entire process from the beginning. We may never get them to realize the importance of the life giving oxygen flowing through those masks. On the other hand, if we simply lead by example, demonstrating to our children that we are to wear the masks, and they won't hurt them, they are all the more willing to comply with our wishes and receive our assistance. Being a good husband and father works the same way. We aren't to use excuses for our own shortcomings. We can't blame our wives or children for falling short if we ourselves aren't leading by example, showing them the way to behave and live a righteous life.

J. R. Miller praises the divine institution of marriage by stating, "United, then, on earth in a common faith in Christ, their mutual love mingling and blending in the love of God— they shall be united also in heaven in eternal fellowship! Why should hearts spend years on earth in growing into one, knitting life to life, blending soul in soul—for a union that is not to reach beyond the valley of shadows? Why not weave for all eternity?" Though we will relate to our wives differently in heaven, we will never stop knowing and loving them but will share in the divine fellowship with them forever.[34]

What are the duties of the husband? "How does the Word of God define his duties? What is involved in his part in the marriage relation? What does he owe his wife? One word covers it all – love. "Husbands, love your wives" (Eph 5:25)! What are the duties of the father? How does God's Word define his role? One word covers it all – train. "Bring them up in the training and admonition of the Lord" (Eph 6:4).

---

[34] Miller, The Home Beautiful, 36.

268

Chapter 5: The Spiritual Leader of the Family

"Who then is that faithful and wise steward, whom his master will make ruler over his household, to give them their portion of food in due season? Blessed is that servant whom his master will find so doing when he comes" (Lk 12:42-43).

Happy the home where God's strong love is starting to appear,
Where all the children hear His fame and parents hold Him dear.[35]

The Priest of the Home Reads God's Word.

"But as for me and my house, we will serve the Lord" (Josh 24:15).

---

[35] Ware, Happy the Home When God is There.

Chapter 5: The Spiritual Leader of the Family

Recommended Further Reading

1. Carl W. Wilson, *Our Dance Has Turned to Death*.
2. John Piper and Wayne Grudem, *Recovering Biblical Manhood and Womanhood*.
3. Richard Baxter, *The Godly Home*.
4. Stu Weber, *The Christian Husband: God's Job Description for a Man's Most Challenging Assignment*.
5. Jerry Boykin, *Never Surrender*.

Chapter 5 Review Questions

1. What does 'God-honoring' mean?
2. Has God created marriage? What is marriage?
3. According to the Word of God, what is the family?
4. Should Christian parents spank their children?
5. How important is discipline for children?
6. What is spiritual leadership?
7. Has God designed the family to be led by the husband/father?
8. Regarding marriage and the family, what are some of the challenges we are facing as Christians in America?
9. How important is respect in a marriage? In a family?
10. What are the ramifications for disregarding God's intent for marriage and the family?

"You know that those who are considered rulers over the Gentiles lord it over them, and their great ones exercise authority over them. Yet it shall not be so among you; but whoever desires to become great among you shall be your servant. And whoever of you desires to be first shall be slave of all. For even the Son of Man did not come to be served, but to serve, and to give His life a ransom for many" (Mark 10:42-45).

Chapter 6: The Spiritual Leader

Works done in an attitude that envisions God as the recipient, with the power God supplies; this is what the apostle Paul meant when he said, "To this end I also labor, striving according to His working which works in me mightily" (Col 1:29). When God calls men to lead His people, He is not looking for those who feel sufficient to the task but for those who are faithful. This chapter is about spiritual leadership – leading God's people by His Spirit. In this chapter we'll discuss the following nine topics:

- Christian Calling and the Providence of God.
- Distinctions within the Priesthood.
- Spiritual Gifts.
- Who Qualifies to Lead Christ's Church?
- Calling to the Ordained Ministry.

Chapter 6: The Spiritual Leader

- The Art of Prophesying.
- The Leader's Self-Watch

Christian Calling and the Providence of God

Before we discuss spiritual leadership we need to consider to what end spiritual leadership serves, namely Christ's kingdom. In the Gospel of Matthew, Jesus asks the question, "Who do you say that I am" (Mt 16:15)? One's answer to that question will determine one's eternal destiny. And when Peter declared that Jesus was the "Christ, the Son of the living God," he meant that Jesus was the long awaited Messiah, the Anointed One, Who, as Mediator between God and man, (Himself being both God and man) was ordained by the Father and anointed by the Holy Spirit to be His people's chief Prophet (Dt 18:15; Acts 7:37); only High Priest (Ps 110:4; Heb 6:20; 7:24); and eternal King (Ps 2:6; Eph 1:20-26; Rev 11:15; 19:6). In response to Peter's confession of faith, Jesus replied,

"Blessed are you, Simon Bar-Jonah, for flesh and blood has not revealed this to you, but My Father who is in heaven. 18 And I also say to you that you are Peter, and on this rock I will build My church, and the gates of Hades shall not prevail against it. 19 And I will give you the keys of the kingdom of heaven, and whatever you bind on earth will be bound in heaven, and whatever you loose on earth will be loosed in heaven."

The literature regarding the interpretation of these verses is vast, but most importantly, our understanding of the words "and on this rock," determines a lot. Petra is Greek for *rock* meaning a *bedrock* or a group of *little stones*. For example, it is used metaphorically in Matthew 7:24 to refer to Christ's teaching or Christ Himself. Some argue that *rock* in Matthew 16:18 refers to Peter while others prefer it to signify Christ Himself.

So, what does "you are Peter, and on this rock I will build My church" supposed to mean? First, we may understand the *rock* to refer to Peter the apostle with some qualifications. (1) Peter is a leader among equals, (2) he is a man that has just confessed Jesus as Lord, and (3) we cannot separate the man

272

Chapter 6: The Spiritual Leader

from his words. Secondly, employing a pun, Jesus drew attention to Peter's name and said in effect, "Peter, you are a *rock* (living stone), and upon this confession of yours – Jesus is the Christ, the Son of the Living God – which testifies to Me as the divine Messiah, the church's One Foundation – upon your testimony I will build My church.

So whereas, in the first sense, we understand that the church, which is to begin after Jesus' death and resurrection, is to be the work of Peter, along with the other apostles (Eph 2:20). In the second, we see the manner in which Christ builds the church – the testimony of Jesus Christ – the apostolic proclamation (Acts 2:42; 1 Cor 3:10; Rev 21:14) – both the confession of it and witness to it (1 Tim 6:12; 1 Jn 4:15; 5:11; Rev 12:11). Having said that, let's qualify the first statement. In the words of Herman Ridderbos, "The building of the church upon Peter can hardly mean anything else than Peter's future apostolic activity."[1] And I would add, it is Christ who builds His church (Mt 16:18). But He does so through those whom He has called and gifted. Christ builds His church first through His apostles and their apostolic proclamation (Eph 2:20). Every teaching in the church can only consist in a repetition of the apostolic teaching.

The church is therefore built upon the apostolic proclamation – Jesus of Nazareth is both Lord and Christ (Acts 2:36). Men are to repent of their sins and believe in Him. The church is built on the one sure foundation of Christ – the testimony of His saving work on the cross. For no other foundation can be laid (1 Cor 3:11). And the church is a living building that consists of living stones which grows by the direction set by the Cornerstone (1 Pet 2:5). Little by little the church is built up with the certainty of a master Builder. Christ Himself builds His church (Mt 16:18), and all the powers of darkness cannot overpower it. His church pushes back the domain of spiritual death, rescuing redeemed prisoners, and exercising the power of the keys (Mt 16:19).

Christ's authority is delegated to His church to bind and loose. Ridderbos has rightly said, "This entitles them to draw a line of demarcation already on earth between those who will

---

[1] Ridderbos, The Coming of the Kingdom, 359.

enter the kingdom and those who will not."[2] The terms *bind* and *loose* were technical terms used by the rabbis meaning to decide with authority. *Binding* means to forbid – to declare something as unlawful, and *loosing* means to permit – to declare something as lawful. In another sense these terms mean to place under a ban (bind) and to relieve the ban (loose). These terms were used by the rabbis to refer to the expulsion from or reinstatement into the synagogue. Ultimately, bind and loosing may have the general meaning of "consigning to divine judgment" and "acquitting" from it.

Again, Ridderbos explains,

> In the case of Mt 16:19, the safest method will be to interpret these words in close connection with what has been said above, namely, to make pronouncements of condemnation or acquittal with respect to entry into the kingdom of heaven. And a heavenly reality will correspond with this in that he who is promised entry into heaven by Peter will ultimately go in, whereas he who is told that the kingdom is shut to him will actually find it shut. So the general point at issue here is the judicial power given to Peter with reference to admission to or exclusion from the kingdom of heaven.[3]

As representative for the other apostles, Peter used these keys at Pentecost when he *loosed* three thousand out of the kingdom of darkness, admitting them into the kingdom of Christ (Acts 2:41). Likewise, as in the case of Cornelius, Peter admitted Gentiles into the Messianic community. As to binding, perhaps the most demonstrative example is the case of Ananias and Saphira. These Peter shut out (Acts 5:1-11), thereby excluding them, at least in the physical sense, from the church's fellowship. This pronouncement of Peter no doubt corresponded to the heavenly counterpart. Additionally, the authority Peter is entrusted with in Matthew 16:19, binding and loosing, is given to the other apostles in Matthew 18:18-20.

---

[2] Ridderbos, The Coming of the Kingdom, 367.
[3] Ibid, 361.

Chapter 6: The Spiritual Leader

The Stone

In Mt 16:19, Jesus declares that He will forcibly rescue His church from the powers of death (hades). Satan is a despot, who, through malice, conquered the whole world, holding mankind hostage as slaves to do his bidding (Eph 2:1-3; 1 Jn 5:19).[4] But the Son of God invades the strong man's occupied territory, and plunders his house (Mt 12:29; Jn 12:31), setting the captives free (Lk 4:18-19; 2 Cor 3:16). The demons considered His coming as their destruction (Mk 1:24; Lk 4:34).

Christ is the Stone that invades (strikes – as with a sword) the world empires – the city of man, which is under the sway of Satan, and crushes it like chaff (Ps 2; Is 26:5-6; Dan 2:34-35, 44; Mt 10:34-39; Rev 19:15). The words of Prophet Daniel envision a stone cut out of a mountain without human hand. The stone violently strikes an image which symbolizes the composite whole of all the world's empires which lie under the power of Satan. The stone, falling upon the city of man, pulverizes it into powder, which is carried away like chaff born on the wind of the summer threshing floors. Further Daniel tells us, "And the stone becomes a great mountain and fills the whole earth" (Dan 2:35).

The Bride

Another way to look at this is: the Father gave the Son a people (Jn 6:37; Tit 2:14). From heaven, Christ came and sought her to be His holy bride (Jer 3:14-15; Mt 22:2; Jn 3:29). And He gathers and strengthens her but He does so through those He has called and gifted for the express purpose of building – gathering and strengthening – her (2 Cor 11:2; Eph 5:25-27). Christ accomplishes this through the Spirit, by His servant's readiness to listen to His Word. Christ's servants continue to build upon the foundation laid by the apostles (Eph 2:20; 1 Cor 3:11), gathering and strengthening Christ's bride through the authoritative apostolic proclamation (Acts 2:42; Eph 2:20; 4:16; 1 Pet 2:4-5).

---

[4] See Chapter 3.

Chapter 6: The Spiritual Leader

Regarding the 'parable' of the stone (within the parable of the tenants – Mt 21:33-44), when the religious leaders of Israel rejected Christ, He said to them, "I say to you, the kingdom of God will be taken from you and given to a nation bearing the fruits of it. And whoever falls on this stone will be broken; but on whomever it falls, it will grind him to powder" (Mt 21:43-44). With the rejection of the Son comes God's swift retribution. Whereas, those who reject Christ, judging themselves unworthy of eternal life (Acts 13:46), stumbling at the gospel (Mt 13:21; 1 Pet 2:8), forfeiting God's grace (Jonah 2:8), pervert the gospel (Acts 13:10; 1 Tim 4:1; 2 Pet 2), persecute believers (Gen 3:15; Acts 14:19-22; Gal 4:29; Rev 13:7), bear evil fruit (Jer 24:2, 8-10; Mt 7:15-23; 12:33; Jn 15:2), and ultimately become like chaff (Dan 2:34-35, 44; Mt 13:40-42; 21:44; Rev 20:14-15); those who have saving faith in Christ (Rom 1:16-17), receiving God's mercy (Acts 17:11; Lk 18:13-14), and bear the continuous spiritual fruit of the gospel proclamation (Jer 24:2, 4-7; Mt 3:8; 7:17; 12:33; 21:43; Mt 28:18-20; Jn 15:2; Gal 5:22), and will ultimately (if I may be able to mix the parables) shine forth in the kingdom of their Father (Mt 13:43).

The Kingdom

God has a plan for history. God's kingdom comes from heaven and enters this world. The kingdom has begun with Jesus' activity, as Matthew tells us "But if I cast out demons by the Spirit of God, surely the kingdom of God has come upon you" (Mt 12:28). The kingdom of God is not a state or a society created and promoted by men (social gospel), the kingdom of God includes the realm of salvation – the reign of Christ. The Baptist Faith and Message addresses the kingdom this way:

The Kingdom of God includes both His general sovereignty over the universe and His particular Kingship over men who willfully acknowledge Him as King. Particularly the Kingdom is the realm of salvation into which men enter by trustful, childlike commitment to Jesus Christ. Christians ought to pray and labor that the Kingdom may come and God's will be done on earth. The full consummation of the Kingdom awaits the return of Jesus Christ and the end of this age.[5]

This excellent definition demonstrates that the church is not exclusively the kingdom but is included within God's kingdom. George E. Ladd clarifies the issue by writing, "The church is the community of the kingdom but never the kingdom itself."[6] That is why Christ tells us in the parable of the wheat and tares that "The Son of Man will send his angels, and they will *gather out of his kingdom* all causes of sin and all law-breakers, and throw them into the fiery furnace (Mt 13:41-42 emphasis mine). When we consider the kingdom of God, particularly as the realm of salvation under Christ the King, we would do best to see it as *having come* (Mt 12:28-29; Heb 1:8; Rev 1:6), *coming* (Mt 21:43-44; Lk 17:20-21; Heb 12:22-28; Rev 1:9), and *will come* (Mt 6:10; 1 Cor 15:24-27; Heb 2:8-9; Rev 2:26-27). The kingdom *has come*, the kingdom is *coming*, the kingdom *will come*. This is the now and not yet of the Christian understanding of the kingdom of God.

But the question remains, is the kingdom of God a reign or a realm? George E. Ladd, when asking us to consider this question, gives us four considerations. He writes, (1) "The most notable sayings are Mk 10:15 where the kingdom is something men must *now receive*; (2) Mt 6:33 = Lk 12:31 where the kingdom is *something to be sought*; (3) Mt 11:12 and 12:28 where the kingdom *is a power active in the world* and Lk 17:21 where the kingdom is plainly asserted to be *present within or among men*. (4) In a fourth group, the kingdom is represented as a present realm or sphere *into which men are now entering*" (Mt 11:11 = Lk 16:16; Mt 12:31; 23:13; cf. Lk 11:52).[7]

Now that we have discussed the realities of the kingdom of God, here are some important points to consider:

1. The kingdom of God is His universal sovereign rule which was inaugurated and made manifest in the Person and mission

---

[5] Baptist Faith and Message, IX, The Kingdom.
[6] Ladd, The Presence of the Future, 262.
[7] Ibid, 123.

of Jesus Christ, was proclaimed by His apostles, is continuously proclaimed by His servants, and will be consummated by Christ's return at the end of the age. The kingdom of God is the sphere in which His reign is experienced.

2. The kingdom creates the church.[8] The ascended Christ, presently reigning over all mankind, calls for men everywhere to repent and surrender to His Lordship with the promise of forgiveness, eternal life and fellowship.

3. The mission of the church is to witness (testify) to the saving power of Christ – the gospel of the kingdom (Mt 24:14; 28:18-20; Act 1:8; 2 Cor 4:5-12; 5:20; 2 Tim 4:2). The Church exists to worship and glorify God. The church worships and glorifies God best by proclaiming the gospel to all (Mt 24:14; Jn 15:8). The proclamation of the gospel in this world is the testimony of Christ's present reign (Acts 2:22-36; Rev 1:5).

The reality of Jesus Christ's present reign as King of the universe, not to mention the ruler of the kings of the earth, is well reflected in the words of the great commission (Mt 28:18-20):

18 And Jesus came and spoke to them, saying, "All authority has been given to Me in heaven and on earth. 19 Go therefore and make disciples of all the nations, baptizing them in the name of the Father and of the Son and of the Holy Spirit, 20 teaching them to observe all things that I have commanded you; and lo, I am with you always, even to the end of the age." Amen.

We will consider the Great Commission more in depth in the following chapters. For now, we should note that presently Christ has "all authority" in heaven and on earth (Mt 28:18). The apostle Paul teaches us, that by virtue of Christ's resurrection, He is "declared to be the Son of God with power" (Rom 1:4), "having disarmed principalities and powers" (Col 2:15), 'triumphing over them in the cross," and

---

[8] Ladd, The Presence of the Future, 265.

is the present reigning Almighty King "over the kings of the earth" (Rev 1:5-8). Jesus is Lord!

Christ builds His church and preserves it despite the satanic onslaught (Mt 16:18). He proclaims the gospel through His servants (Mt 13:3-9, 18-23). All gospel activity is directed toward the *pleroma* – the fullness of Christ – the full number intended by God from all nations, tribes, peoples, and tongues – a prospect in which all history coincides (Rom 11:12, 25-26; Rev 7:9).[9]

Priesthood of Believers

It is not the intent to cover what has been said in previous chapters (see chapter 4), but suffice it to say, that all believers have direct access to God through the mediation of Jesus Christ – our great High Priest (1 Tim 2:5-6). Christ builds His church in the world by calling His own sheep by name and leading them out of the world, where they, having undergone the Spirit's regenerative work, constitute the one house of God (Heb 3:5-6). Christ qualifies all of His saints to serve God through Him as priests. As He builds His church His building materials are His saints. Christ builds the church and commissions all of His saints to proclaim the gospel of His grace (Mt 28:18-20).

All who are saved are priests and servants *diakonos* of God under Jesus, the High Priest of our confession (Heb 3:1). As a member of the royal priesthood, each Christian has access to God through the mediatorship of Christ (1 Tim 2:5-6; Heb 10:19-25). "Each Christian is a consecrated priest, offering himself as a sacrifice 'holy and acceptable to God,' according to the pattern laid down by Christ "(Jn 17:19; Rom 12:1). The apostle Peter tells us so in his first epistle,

Coming to Him as to a living stone, rejected indeed by men, but chosen by God and precious, you also, as living stones, are being built up a spiritual house, a holy priesthood, to offer up spiritual sacrifices acceptable to God through Jesus Christ (1 Pet 2:4-5).

---

[9] This is the subject of Chapter 9 and 10.

Chapter 6: The Spiritual Leader

Distinctions within the Priesthood

In his *Appeal to the German Nobility* the great Reformer Martin Luther taught that all Christians were priests by virtue of their faith and wrote, "There is no true difference between lay people, priests, princes and bishops, between the spiritual and the secular, except for their office and work and not on the basis of their status."[10] In other words, all Christians share the same status – saints (priesthood of believers). God further sets apart some men to serve Him in a particular office or work of ministry within the church. According to Calvin, if God Himself were to speak from heaven, then,

It were no wonder if His sacred oracles were received by all ears and minds reverently and without delay. For who would not dread His present power? Who would not fall prostrate at the first view of His great majesty? Who would not be overpowered by that immeasurable splendor? But when a feeble man, sprung from the dust, speaks in the name of God, we give the best proof of our piety and obedience by listening with docility to His servant, though not in any respect our superior. Accordingly, He hides the treasure of His heavenly wisdom in frail earthen vessels (2 Cor 4:7), that He may have a more certain proof of the estimation in which it is held by us.[11]

As we've discussed earlier, affirming the priesthood of believers doesn't negate the necessity of the ordained ministry. God saves us and calls us into one fellowship.[12] God appoints men to teach the church the will of God from His Word (1 Tim. 3:1–7). God appoints some of His saints to serve Him in the ordained ministry, equipping them with gifts commensurate to the task. God tells us in His Word, "I will take you, one from a city and two from a family, and I will bring you to Zion. And I will give you shepherds according to My heart, who will feed you with knowledge and understanding" (Jer 3:14-15).

At Pentecost, the ascended Christ began to pour out gifts He had received from the Father. The apostle Peter proclaimed,

---

[10] Luther, Appeal to the German Nobility, Kritische Gesamtausgabe, vol 6, 406.21-408.30.

[11] Calvin, Institutes of the Christian religion, 3.1.1.

[12] This is the subject of Chapter seven.

Chapter 6: The Spiritual Leader

"This Jesus God has raised up, of which we are all witnesses. Therefore being exalted to the right hand of God, and having received from the Father the promise of the Holy Spirit, He poured out this which you now see and hear" (Acts 2:32-33). God calls some of His saints to serve Him in the ordained ministry and equips them with gifts commensurate to the task. Thus, Christ bestows spiritual gifts to build a spiritual house (Mt 16:18-19).

The ascended Christ apportions gifts to men for the express purpose of building (gathering and strengthening) His church (Mt 16:18-19; 1 Cor 3:11). The purpose of the outpouring at Pentecost was to equip the church to preach the gospel. As a result of Christ's resurrection and ascension, God's people as mediating-witnessing priests extend His tabernacling presence throughout the whole earth – so that Christ might "fill all things, as the waters cover the sea" (Hab 2:14; Eph 4:10). God's people serve as the building materials for Christ's end-time temple (Is 26:1-4; Jn 2:19-22; Gal 4:26; 1 Cor 3:9, 16; 2 Cor 6:16; Heb 12:22-23; 1 Pet 1:4-5; Rev 11:1; Rev 21:22).

Spiritual Gifts

Christ bestows spiritual gifts on His church. Peter Wagner defines a spiritual gift as "a special attribute given by the Holy Spirit to every member of the body of Christ according to God's grace for use within the context of the body."[13] A spiritual gift is given to every member of the body of Christ. It is an expression of the Holy Spirit in the life of the believer which empowers believers to gather and strengthen (build) the body of Christ – the church. The Holy Spirit sovereignly distributes gifts as He wills (1 Cor 12:11).

It's not the intent to treat the subject of spiritual gifts in an exhaustive sense, however, at a minimum let us say that the gifts which Christ bestows on His church may be divided into two categories: (1) ministers of the Word; and (2) ministers of practical service. Among the first group are apostles, prophets, and teachers, as well as those who speak in tongues, interpret tongues, give words of wisdom and knowledge, and discern

---

[13] Wagner, Your Spiritual Gifts Can Help Your Church Grow, 42.

various spirits. This first group may be viewed by what the apostle Peter calls the gift of speaking (1 Pet 4:11). The second group are those who perform more practical functions such as contributing, helping, administrating, those who perform acts of mercy, healing, and work wonders. This second group the apostle Peter refers to as gifts of service (1 Pet 4:11).

As far as spiritual gifts are concerned, the apostle Paul provides no systemization but, emphasizing diversity, he lists them in four groupings of Scripture: Rom 12:6-8; 1 Cor 12:8-10; 1 Cor 12:28-30; and Eph 4:11.

The following is a list of New Testament spiritual gifts:

1. Apostles (1 Cor 12:28; Eph 4:11).
2. Prophets (Rom 12:6; 1 Cor 12:10; Eph 4:11).
3. Evangelists (Eph 4:11; cf. 2 Tim 4:5).
4. Pastor-Teacher (Rom 12:7; 1 Cor 12:28; Eph 4:11).
5. Service (Rom 12:8).
6. Helps (1 Cor 12:28).
7. Administration (1 Cor 12:28).
8. Exhortation (Rom 12:8).
9. Giving (Rom 12:8).
10. Leadership (Rom 12:8).
11. Showing mercy (Rom 12:8).
12. Word of Wisdom (1 Cor 12:8).
13. Word of Knowledge (1 Cor 12:8).
14. Faith (1 Cor 12:9; 13:2).
15. Healings (1 Cor 12:9, 28).
16. Miracles (1 Cor 12:10, 28).
17. Discernment of spirits (1 Cor 12:10).
18. Tongues (1 Cor 12:10, 28).
19. Interpretation of tongues (1 Cor 12:10).[14]

For a local congregation to function correctly, all believers must exercise their gifts of helping (1 Cor 12:28), discerning of spirits (1 Cor 12:10), knowledge (1 Cor 12:8) or whatever

---

[14] Some refer to marriage and celibacy as spiritual gifts bringing the total number of gifts to twenty one. See Grudem, Systematic Theology, 1020.

gift the Holy Spirit has graced them with. The diversity of gifts is intended by God to promote interdependence – fellowship.

Apostles (1 Cor 12:28; Eph 4:11)

The apostle Paul tells us that God has appointed in the church first apostles *apostoloi*, meaning one who is sent. The apostles were the first to be sent by the risen Christ to proclaim the gospel. "They were the first architects of the church, to lay its foundations throughout the world."[15] The apostles were first men who had been with Jesus during His earthly ministry and had been witnesses to His resurrection (Acts 1:21-22; 1 Cor 9:1), and second had been personally commissioned by Him as an apostle (Acts 9:15; Rom 11:13; Gal 2:8). These two reasons constitute the qualifying marks of an apostle. The apostles had the authority to write words which became words of Scripture (2 Cor 13:10; 2 Pet 1:21). For example, Peter refers to Paul's letters as Scripture (2 Pet 3:15-16). To disbelieve or disobey the apostles is to disbelieve or disobey God.[16] The apostles founded churches where there were none. And once a church had been established, the apostle appoint elders and aid the congregation by giving counsel (Acts 14:23;

In this sense of the word there are no more apostles, nor are we to expect any. However, the Bible does use the word apostle in a broader sense. For example, the apostle Paul called Epaphroditus an *apostolos,* a messenger of a congregation (Phil 2:25). Likewise, Paul's agents can also be designated "apostles" (2 Cor 8:22-23). And in this broader sense, some are referred to by the word apostle. For example, William Carey was known as the apostle to India, and before him, George Whitefield was known as the apostle to the English. These men, and others before and after them, fulfilled an apostolic role by their effective missions and church planting.

---

[15] Calvin, Institutes of the Christian Religion, Bk 4.3.4, 702.
[16] Grudem, Systematic Theology, 906.

Chapter 6: The Spiritual Leader

According to the gifts Christ gave His church – to gather and strengthen her, of those who preside over the government of the church "some to be apostles, some prophets, some evangelists, and some pastors and teachers," only the last two have an ordinary office in the church. Calvin writes, "The Lord raised up the other three (apostles, prophets, and evangelists) at the beginning of His Kingdom," and he says, however, "and still occasionally raises them up when the necessity of the times requires." For the express purposes of forming the church "where none previously existed."[17] These words of Calvin agree with our earlier point that God raises up men to work in His church apostolically, such as missions and church planting, like Carey and Whitefield.

We may refer to men like these in this way, but it is worth noting, writes Grudem, "That no major leader in the history of the church – not Athanasius or Augustine, not Luther or Calvin, not Wesley or Whitefield – has taken to himself the title of 'apostle' or let himself be called an apostle." Wayne Grudem goes on to write, "If any in modern times want to take the title 'apostle' to themselves, they immediately raise the suspicion that they may be motivated by inappropriate pride and desires for self-exaltation, along with excessive ambition and a desire for much more authority in the church than any one person should rightfully have."[18]

Prophets (Rom 12:6; 1 Cor 12:10, 28-29; Eph 4:11)

The apostles were followed by the prophets. While the apostles laid the foundation for the church and wrote Scripture, the prophets worked mainly within the congregations (Acts 11:27-28; 15:12; 21:10). But like the apostle, the prophet held no office in the church. They would edify the local congregation in which they were members. Some traveled from church to church strengthening the body by exhorting Christian character and holy living.

As the church grew, false prophets appeared to lead the church astray into errant doctrine and heresy as the apostles

---

[17] Calvin, Institutes of the Christian Religion, Bk 4.3.4, 702-703.
[18] Grudem, Systematic Theology, 911-912.

Chapter 6: The Spiritual Leader

Paul and Peter warned (Acts 20:29-32; 1 Cor 10:15; 2 Tim 4:3-4; 2 Pet 2; 1 Jn 4:1). This raises the question, what is prophecy? Wayne Grudem offers an excellent definition by telling us: "prophecy is the reception and subsequent transmission of spontaneous, divinely originating revelation."[19]

The Word of God tells us in the Book of Deuteronomy, "But the prophet who presumes to speak a word in My name, which I have not commanded him to speak, or who speaks in the name of other gods, that prophet shall die. And if you say in your heart, 'How shall we know the word which the Lord has not spoken?'— when a prophet speaks in the name of the Lord, if the thing does not happen or come to pass, that is the thing which the Lord has not spoken; the prophet has spoken it presumptuously; you shall not be afraid of him" (Dt 18:20-22).

Prophecy is a special form of the Spirit given to and working in the church. Prophets are the Spirit-impelled proclaimers of the Word of God. It's important here to make a clear distinction between apostolic testimony (prophecy), which was inspired by the Holy Spirit, with let's say the testimony in the church today. Theirs was a prophetic testimony infallibly inspired by the Holy Spirit (Rev 19:10). Ours today is quite fallible. The apostolic testimony was protected by the Holy Spirit and inscripturated for the church (Rom 15:4; 2 Pet 3:16).

The apostles were conscious of the fact they were writing Scripture. The Holy Scripture is inerrant, verbally inspired, and closed. Every teaching in the church today can only consist in a repetition of the apostolic teaching. Now, having said that, there are a few concessions regarding testimony. Although not to be inscripturated, modern testimony bears weight so long as it is a faithful repetition of the apostolic declaration; as it were a forth-telling of the Scriptures. Regarding this Wayne Grudem tells us,

On the one hand, there is "apostolic" prophecy, with absolute divine authority in the actual words used. Any instances of prophecy with this kind of absolute divine authority seemed to be regularly

---

[19] Grudem, The Gift of Prophecy in the New Testament and Today,

associated with the apostles, as in Mt 10:19-20 (and parallels), Eph 2:20 and 3:5, and the Book of Revelation. On the other hand, there is "ordinary congregational prophecy," prophecy for which no absolute divine authority is indicated. Christian men and women who experience this ordinary functioning of the prophetic gift are found in several New testament congregations and would include the prophets in the church at Corinth (1 Cor 14:29-30, 36-38; 11:5), and the disciples at Tyre (Acts 21:4), the prophets at Thessalonica (1 Thess 5:19-21), Philip's four daughters (Acts 21:9), the disciples at Ephesus (Acts 19:6), and probably Agabus in Acts 11:28 and 21:10-11.[20]

Gift – Office Distinction

It's important at this point to make a distinction between a spiritual gift and a church office. We said a spiritual gift is an expression of the Holy Spirit in the life of the believer which empowers believers to gather and strengthen (build) the body of Christ – the church. An office, on the other hand, is a function in the local church, such as, pastor, elder, and deacon. These three normally constitute the church offices that require ordination. A church officer is a man who has been "publically recognized as having the right and responsibility to perform certain functions for the benefit of the whole church."[21] Gifts enable ministry. For example, a pastor is given, among other things, the gift of *teacher* (Rom 12:7; 1 Cor 12:28; Eph 4:11); and a deacon is given the gift of *service diakonos* – from which we derive the word deacon (Acts 6:1-6; Rom 12:8). These gifts enable God's servant to function in a particular ministry.

All Christians are priests, however, God further sets apart some men to serve Him in a particular office within the church. To these He bestows gifts enabling the ministry He calls them into. In church parlance, this is referred to as the *inward call* (to ministry, not salvation) to which God's people authenticate by their *outward call*. About this we must discuss further. Whereas the first three offices in the government of the church – apostles, prophets, and evangelists – were extraordinary, having laid the foundation (Scripture and

---

[20] Grudem, The Gift of Prophecy in the New Testament and Today, 90.
[21] Grudem, Systematic Theology, 905.

organization), the last two are ordinary and are instituted to be of continuous duration until the return of the Lord (1 Cor 13:10).

Christ gifts and calls particular men to serve as pastors, elders and deacons in the church. These men receive delegated authority from Christ to shepherd the church. Through these representatives, Christ Himself rules His church. Thus all church power, whether exercised by the body in general, or by representation (pastors, elders, and deacons), is only ministerial and declarative since the Holy Scriptures are the only rule of faith and practice.[22]

Who Qualifies to Lead Christ's Church?

Like the Marine Corps, the church today is looking for a few good men. America, in her spiritual and moral depression, is floundering while the church seems to grow effeminate. America is adrift in a sea of moral confusion and biblical illiteracy. Where are the men? Where are the George Whitefields? Where are the Edwards? The Wesley's? The Spurgeons? The Girardeaus? When we consider the present appalling state of our nation it would be easy to be discouraged, however, as John Owen reminds us, "It is a promise relating to the New Testament that God would give unto his church pastors according to his own heart, which should feed His church in knowledge and understanding." [23]

Additionally, it would be good for congregations to not just accept any volunteer who steps up to the plate. The church needs leaders but they must be godly men. The church needs mature masculine spiritual leadership. What follows is a discussion regarding the character and qualifications that are required of spiritual leaders in the church, specifically those who serve in the ordained offices of pastor, elder, and deacon.

---

[22] PCA Book of Church Order, Preface, Preliminary Principles, 7.
[23] John Owen, The True Nature of a Gospel Church, 75.

Chapter 6: The Spiritual Leader

Pastor and Elders

In the early church, the apostles would proclaim the gospel, gather God's people together, thereby establishing the church in every city to which they were sent. Then they would ordain pastors or elders from among the local believers to carry on the work of shepherding the people (Acts 14:21-23; Tit 1:5). MacArthur writes, "The twelve apostles led the early church until it spread out and elders and deacons were trained to lead and serve in other congregations. Because everyone was a new convert in the early church, God left the Twelve with the Jerusalem church for at least seven years."[24]

The apostle Paul tells us "If a man desires the position of a bishop (elder), he desires a good work. The terms elder, pastor-teacher, and over-seer (translated bishop or presbyter) refer to the same office. These terms are used to describe various aspects of the same ministry.[25] Some consider the office of elder to be the same as "pastor," while others choose a group of men to serve as presbyters (session), often with the lead elder (preaching elder) ministering the Word and ordinances. The apostle Peter brings all three terms together in 1 Pet 5:1-2:

The elders who are among you I exhort, I who am a fellow elder (*presbuteros*) and a witness of the sufferings of Christ, and also a partaker of the glory that will be revealed: Shepherd (*poimaino*) the flock of God which is among you, serving as overseers (*episkopeo*), not by compulsion but willingly.

God gifts and calls men to serve as elders in the local church which confirms and ordains them to the task of leading and teaching. The Bible furnishes no provision for women to serve as elders. The Bible says, "Let a woman learn in silence with all submission. And I do not permit a woman to teach or to have authority over a man, but to be in silence" (1 Tim 2:11-12; cf. 1 Cor 14:34-38). The reasons for this is not because Paul was prejudiced against women, as many claim, or because the Bible was written in a first century cultural

---

[24] MacArthur, The Master's Plan for the Church, 87.
[25] See also Acts 20:17, 28; Phil 1:1; 1 Tim 3:1; 5:17; Tit 1:5-9).

context, rather the reasons are rooted in the creation order: "For Adam was formed first, then Eve" (1 Tim 2:13).[26]

Christ rules His church through a plurality of godly men. He qualifies these men by giving them spiritual gifts and prepares them to serve in the local congregation. This may take years or even decades, four of them to be precise, as in the case of Moses. It took God time to prepare him for the service He had in mind for him. The same could be said of Joseph, Joshua, David, Paul, et al. In God's time, He releases these leaders to shepherd His people. Like Calvin put it, God "uses the ministry of men, by making them, as it were, His substitutes, not by transferring His right and honor to them, but only doing His own work by their lips, just as an artificer (skilled craftsman) uses a tool for any purpose."[27]

Elders lead God's people. The men who serve as elders in the church should be commensurately gifted for that end – to lead. Earlier, we remarked that leadership is "the process of influencing people by providing purpose, direction, and motivation while operating to accomplish the mission and improve the organization." We might add to that expression, in addition to an elder's leadership being influential, it is also inspirational. An elder manages God's household. It is as Thomas Boston said, "As when men find a well-ordered family that tells what a man the leader of it is."

The principle task of the elder is three-fold:

1. Teach and explain sound doctrine (Eph 4:11-12; 1 Tim 4:6-11; 13, 16; 2 Tim 4:2-4; Tit 1:9; 2:1). The elder feeds Christ's lambs on the pure Word of truth (Jn 21:15; 1 Jn 2:12), equipping the sheep by expounding the apostolic doctrines (Jn 21:17; 1 Jn 2:13-14), strengthening and guiding them as under shepherds (1 Pet 5:2), demonstrating a Christ-like example to follow and emulate (1 Cor 4:16; 11:1; Heb 13:7). Additionally, an elder's method of instructing his congregation in the Word should extend beyond the walls of

---

[26] For an excellent defense of the complementarian view being espoused here see - Piper and Grudem, *Recovering Biblical Manhood and Womanhood.*
[27] Calvin, Institutes of the Christian Religion, Book Four, Chapter 3.1, 700.

the church building, to include private admonitions in what is commonly referred to as pastoral visitation.

2. <u>Rule the church with a servant's heart</u> (Mt 18:15-17; 1 Tim 5:17; 2 Tim 2:14-26; Tit 3:9-11; Heb 13:17; 1 Pet 5:1-3). The elder maintains order and discipline in a local congregation much like a father would in his own household. Expounding Hebrews 13:7, "Remember those who rule over you," John MacArthur rightly comments, "In other words, the congregation is spiritually accountable to the elders, and the elders are accountable to God. The congregation should submit to the elders' leadership and let the elders be concerned with their accountability before the Lord. And if the congregation is submissive and obedient, the elders will be able to lead with joy and not grief, which is ultimately unprofitable for everyone." On occasion, the elder may have to discipline erring brethren who are living in unrepentant sin.

3. <u>Protect the church from false doctrine</u> (Acts 20: 17, 28-30; 1 Tim 1:3-4; 6:20-21; 2 Tim 4:1-5; Tit 1:9-16). The elder guards the purity of the flock by discerning and shielding them from pernicious teachings and influences (Acts 20: 28-31).

The apostle Paul speaks of those who have erred doctrinally. He writes, "And their message will spread like cancer. Hymenaeus and Philetus are of this sort, who have strayed concerning the truth, saying that the resurrection is already past; and they overthrow the faith of some (2 Tim 2:17-18). 1 Tim 1:19-20 records how Paul dealt with this issue. He says, "Some having rejected, concerning the faith have suffered shipwreck, of whom are Hymenaeus and Alexander, whom I delivered to Satan that they may learn not to blaspheme." Paul as an apostle, used the power of the keys (Mt 16:19) to bind and loose. The Book of Church Order for the Presbyterian Church of America (PCA) states, "Our blessed Savior, for the edification of the visible Church, which is His body, has appointed officers not only to preach the

Gospel and administer the Sacraments, but also to exercise discipline for the preservation both of truth and duty."[28]

The following qualifications are God's requirements for elders and pastors (preaching elders). The principle texts are: 1 Tim 3:1-7 and Tit 1:6-9.

1. He is blameless (1 Tim 3:2, 10; Tit 1:6, 7).
2. He is the husband of one wife (1 Tim 3:2; Tit 1:6).
3. He is temperate (1 Tim 3:2; Tit 2:1).
4. He is sober-minded (1 Tim 3:2; Tit 1:8).
5. He is of good behavior (1 Tim 3:2).
6. He is hospitable (1 Tim 3:2; Tit 1:8).
7. He is able to teach (1 Tim 3:2).
8. He is not addicted to wine (1 Tim 3:3, 8; Titus 1:7).
9. He is not violent (1 Tim 3:3; Tit 1:7).
10. He is not greedy for money (1 Tim 3:3; Tit 1:7).
11. He is gentle (1 Tim 3:3).
12. He is not covetous (1 Tim 3:3).
13. He rules his own house well (1 Tim 3:4).
14. He has believing children that are under control (1 Tim 3:4; Tit 1:6).
15. He is not a new convert (1 Tim 3:6).
16. He has a good reputation outside the church (1 Tim 3:7).
17. He is not self-willed (Tit 1:7).
18. He is not quick-tempered (Tit 1:7).
19. He loves what is good (Tit 1:8).
20. He is just (Tit 1:8).
21. He is holy (Tit 1:8).
22. He is self-controlled (Tit 1:8).
23. He holds to the faithful word (Titus 1:9).[29]
24. He is able to exhort with sound doctrine and refute those who contradict (Tit 1:9).

Deacons

The early church was faced with the need to provide men who could assume the leading role of serving and caring for

---

[28] PCA Book of Church Order, Preface, Preliminary Principles, 3.
[29] To hold fast to the Word means to trust God regardless of the circumstances.

Chapter 6: The Spiritual Leader

the people, specifically the widows and orphans. The term deacon comes to us from the Greek word meaning 'servant,' 'or one who serves.' Acts chapter six tells us that seven men who were "full of the Spirit" were selected among the congregation so the apostles would be free to minister in the Word and prayer. Likewise, the Book of Acts shows us that as local churches were established and grew, deacons were elected among the congregation to assist the elders so they could give themselves to teaching and prayer.

God gifts and calls men to serve as deacons in the local church which confirms and ordains them to the task of administrating and caring for the flock. Some deacons also serve as 'trustees.' The only passage that mentions the qualifications for deacons is 1 Tim 3:8-13. Here are the nine that are listed:

1. Reverent (v. 8): They must have dignity and be worthy of respect. Never treating serious things lightly.

2. Not double-tongued (v. 8): Those who are double-tongued are two-faced and insincere. Their words cannot be trusted, so they lack credibility.

3. Not given to much wine (v. 8): deacons must be self-controlled and disciplined, so as to not give themselves over to addiction to wine or other strong drink.

4. Not greedy for money (v. 8): This is especially important because deacons are normally responsible for handling funds. A man who has a pervasive desire for financial gain is disqualified.

5. Hold the Mystery of the Faith with a clear conscience (v. 9): He must hold conviction from solid biblical truth and apply it daily.

6. Blameless (v. 10): Paul writes that deacons must "be tested first; then let them serve as deacons if they prove themselves blameless" (v. 10). "Blameless" is a general term referring to a person's overall character. Although Paul does not specify

what type of testing is to take place, at a minimum, the candidate's personal background, reputation, and theological positions should be examined.

7. Godly wife (v. 11): According to Paul, deacons' wives must "be reverent, not slanderers, but temperate, faithful in all things" (v. 11). Like her husband, the wife must be dignified or respectable. Secondly, she must not be a slanderer or a person who goes around spreading gossip. A deacon's wife must also be sober-minded or temperate. That is, she must be able to make good judgments and must not be involved in things that might hinder such judgment. Finally, she must be "faithful in all things" (cf. 1 Tim. 5:10).

8. Husband of one wife (v. 12): He must be a "one-woman man." That is, there must be no other woman in his life to whom he relates in an intimate way either emotionally or physically.

9. Manage children and household well (v. 12): A deacon must be the spiritual leader of his wife and children. This qualification affirms the consistent biblical teaching on male leadership in the home.[30]

The demands made of deacons are more of a general variety. Deacons are to administrate, shepherd, and care for the local church. Ridderbos writes, "It is to be gathered from the remainder of the New Testament that the office of deacon especially provided for (the direction of) mutual assistance in the church and will therefore have had reference in particular to what Paul describes in Romans 12 as the charisma of serving, sharing, showing mercy (vv. 6-8), and in 1 Corinthians 12:28 as the gift given by God to the church of the "capacity to help" (*antilempseis*)."[31]

---

[30] MacArthur, The Master's Plan for the Church, 257.
[31] Ridderbos, Paul: An Outline of His Theology, 459.

Chapter 6: The Spiritual Leader

Calling to the Ordained Ministry

Within Christ's 'general calling' to be His servants, is a 'particular calling' to serve Him as minister of the Word. The nature of one's ministry is determined by the gift received. Christ bestows gifts (pastor, elder, deacon, evangelist, et al) to His church for "the equipping of the saints for the work of ministry, for the edifying of the body of Christ, till we all come to the unity of the faith and of the knowledge of the Son of God, to a perfect man, to the measure of the stature of the fullness of Christ; that we should no longer be children, tossed to and fro and carried about with every wind of doctrine, by the trickery of men, in the cunning craftiness of deceitful plotting" (Eph 4:12-14).

As Spurgeon has aptly stated, "No one may intrude into the sheepfold as an under-shepherd; he must have an eye to the chief Shepherd, and await His beck and command."[32] Likewise, in the parable of the places of honor at the table, Jesus teaches us a lesson in self-abasement (Lk 14:7-14). We are not to presume to take a choice seat but humbly wait for the King to call us forward to serve Him.

The scriptural calling comes not only through the heart of the candidate, but also from the Church itself; for the call is never complete until the church has confirmed it. The call comes from God through his people. The sheep must hear the voice of the Shepherd through the under-shepherd. Ligon Duncan remarks, "Without this defining characteristic of the call, the intruder will be found guilty of the sin of Uzzah. He was wrong in presuming to serve God in a way that God had not prescribed." Jeremiah the prophet, demonstrating the genuine call over against the presumptuous, says,

"I have not sent these prophets, yet they ran. I have not spoken to them, yet they prophesied. But if they had stood in My counsel, and had caused My people to hear My words, then they would have turned them from their evil way and from the evil of their doings" (Jer 23:21-22).

---

[32] Charles H. Spurgeon, Lectures to My Students, 25.

Chapter 6: The Spiritual Leader

All are not called to labor in the Word and doctrine, or be deacons but if a man desires the position of an elder, he desires a good work (1 Tim 3:1). It is clearly evident to us from Scripture (Eph 4:11) that Christ Himself gifts and calls men to serve His church. Christ governs His church through His appointed officers. And "Those who profess to be called of God," writes Spurgeon, are "selected to their positions by the free choice of believers."[33]

Regarding the inward call - how do we know if we are called? We must have an intense, all-absorbing desire for the work. We must feel, "woe unto me for I must preach the gospel." As Isaiah (Is 6:8), Jeremiah (Jer 1:4-10), and Ezekiel (Ezek 2:1-3; 3:1-4) did. How can we justify our calling if we don't have a similar call (Acts 20:17-32)? If you are called of God to preach the Word, the passion will bear the test of time. Christ's gifts confirm your calling; what God requires: He gives.

And regarding the outward call – the confirmation of the church, requires the prayerful judgment of the church (see qualifications above). Along with the candidate's aptitude for preaching, and long consent of the flock, Spurgeon writes, "That which finally evidences a proper call, is a correspondent opening in providence, by a gradual train of circumstances pointing out the means, the time, the place of actually entering upon the work."[34]

The Art of Prophesying

Preaching the Word is prophesying in the name and on behalf of Christ. Through preaching, those who hear are called into the state of grace, and preserved in it.[35] The Preacher must break up the fallow ground. According to the Puritan William Perkins, there are four axioms of preaching:

1. Primacy of the intellect. "Everyman's first duty in relation to the Word of God is to understand it; and every preacher's

---

[33] Spurgeon, Lectures to My Students, 85. See also Perkins, The Art of Prophesying, 188-190.
[34] Charles H. Spurgeon, Lectures to My Students, 36.
[35] William Perkins, The Art of Prophesying, 7.

first duty is to explain it." [36] Likewise, Perkins spoke of three aims to every sermon: (1) humble the sinner; (2) exalt the Savior; and (3) promote holiness.

2. Belief in the supreme importance of preaching. "Nothing honors God more than the faithful declaration and obedient hearing of his truth." [37]

3. Belief in the life-giving power of the Holy Scripture. "Better not preach at all than preach beyond the Bible." [38]

4. Belief in the Sovereignty of the Holy Spirit. "Man's task is simply to be faithful in teaching the Word; it is God's work to convince of its truth and write it on the heart." [39]

Preaching is theology from a man who is on fire! A preacher should crave the unction of the Holy Ghost so as to preach as he has never preached before, as a dying man to dying men! It's not difficult for a preacher to distinguish between mere pulpit eloquence and spiritual unction. The first will lift him up; the second will humble him in awe.

Here are some helpful gems I've learned preaching. The sermon must be theological and not merely a lecture on theology, nor merely a class. We are called to preach the gospel not about it. The sermon should be derived from the Scripture and always be textual. A sermon is comparative to a symphony. It mustn't deal with any text in isolation, the greatest care should be made to keep the text within its context. Because good teaching requires driving home biblical truth, repetition in a sermon is good. The sermon should always be expositional. Additionally, the sermon should be derived from the whole counsel of God and include doctrinal content. The sheep need food. As Lloyd-Jones put it, "Feed the sheep; don't entertain the goats." The sermon is no mere essay. It's not merely a display of the preacher's knowledge,

---

[36] J.I Packer, A Quest for Godliness, 281.
[37] Ibid.
[38] Ibid, 282.
[39] Ibid, 73.

as Perkins put it "The preaching of the Word is the testimony of God, not human wisdom."

According to William Perkins, there are four interrogative questions we may ask of any particular scripture passage:

1. What does this particular scripture teach?
2. How does this apply to us today?
3. What are we to do in response?
4. How does scripture teach us to do it?

As we approach Scripture for the purposes of exposition, we should not interpret any verse in the light of our experiences, but we should examine our experiences in the light of the teaching of the scriptures.[40]

True preaching is centered squarely on the cross. The cross of Christ is so central to the gospel that the apostle Paul referred to it as the word or message of the cross. The preaching of the cross is "foolish ness to those who are perishing, but to us who are being saved it is the power of God" (1 Cor 1:18). The cross is so central that when the apostle Paul came to Corinth, a center for pagan thought, he didn't engage them along philosophical lines but said that he "determined not to know anything among you except Jesus Christ and him crucified" (1 Cor 2:2).

Ralph Turnbull writes, "The preaching which calls for no sacrifice, no cross or resurrection, no kingdom demands, will entertain and amuse some bit it will not secure disciples."[41]

And lastly, you should have a main thrust in the sermon and arrive at a particular doctrine(s). You should be careful to consider the relevance of it and demonstrate its importance. If possible, following Perkins, indicate the main theme and its various divisions in the introduction: (1) explain the context; (2) examine important words; and (3) extrapolate (draw out) the lesson(s) – E3. Above all, faithful preaching of the gospel is Christ centered, structured by Scripture, and urgent.

What America desperately needs is a recovery of biblically sound Christ-centered preaching. J.I. Packer writes, "To

---

[40] Lloyd-Jones, Joy Unspeakable, 17.
[41] Turnbull, The Preacher's Heritage, Task, and Resources, 76.

recover the old, authentic, biblical gospel, and to bring our preaching and practice back into line with it, is perhaps our most pressing present need."[42] "The preacher's task, in other words, is to display Christ; to explain man's need of Him, His sufficiency to save, and His offer of Himself in the promises as Savior to all who truly turn to Him."[43]

The Leader's Self-Watch

We must ensure that the work of grace be thoroughly accomplished in your own soul, as Paul writes to "work out your own salvation with fear and trembling; for it is God who works in you both to will and to do for His good pleasure" (Phil 2:12-13). We are God's work from beginning to end. God makes use of means to mold us into the instruments for His glory. Preachers are no different. And there is nothing juicier to the devil that to destroy the ministry of one of Christ's under shepherds. Leaders, we must ensure that we are not only in a state of grace, but daily vigorously exercise that grace.

We must ensure that your example doesn't contradict our doctrine. The doctrines we preach must first have worked their power in our own lives. As Owen put it, "If it doesn't dwell with power in us, it will not pass with power from us."

We ensure that you don't live in the very sins you preach against lest when we've preached to others, we should become disqualified (1 Cor 9:27). We must watch our lives and doctrine closely. Persevering in them, because if we do, we will save both ourselves and our hearers (1 Tim 4:16). As Baxter put it, "If we would be skillful in governing others, we must learn first to command ourselves."

The most radical social teaching of Jesus was His total reversal of the contemporary notion of greatness. Leadership is found in becoming the servant of all. Power is discovered in submission, the foremost symbol of this radical servanthood is the cross. Jesus flatly rejected the cultural givens of position and power when He said "You are not to be called Rabbi...

---

[42] Owen, The Death of Death in the Death of Christ, 2.
[43] Ibid, 16.

neither called masters."[44] Biblical leadership is influencing others by providing purpose, direction, and motivation to live obedient lives for Christ. When God calls men to lead His people, He is not looking for those who feel sufficient to the task but for those who are faithful.

> See, the streams of living waters, springing from eternal love,
> Well supply thy sons and daughters, and all fear of want remove:
> Who can faint, while such a river ever does their thirst assuage?
> Grace which, like the Lord, the giver, never fails from age to age.[45]

George Whitefield Preaching

---

[44] Foster, Celebration of Discipline, 101.
[45] Newton, Glorious Things of Thee Are Spoken.

Chapter 6: The Spiritual Leader

Recommended Further Reading

1. J. C. Ryle, *Thoughts for Young Men.*
2. J. Oswald Sanders, *Spiritual Leadership.*
3. Charles H. Spurgeon, *Lectures to My Students.*
4. John MacArthur, *The Master's Plan for the Church.*
5. David Martyn Lloyd-Jones, *Preaching and Preachers.*

Chapter 6 Review Questions

1. What is leadership? What is spiritual leadership?
2. What is a pastor? What is an elder? What is a deacon? What is an apostle? Are there apostles today?
3. Do you find in Scripture a gift-office distinction?
4. What is prophesy?
5. What are personal revelations? With an understanding that the Canon of Scripture is closed, is it possible that God may make new revelations to particular persons about their duties which He requires of them?
6. What is unction?
7. What are the duties of a pastor? What are the duties of an elder? What are the duties of deacons?
8. How do we know if we have been called of God into the ordained ministry?
9. In the ministry, how important is accountability?
10. What is authority? How important is it to the church?

Part 4: Iron Sharpening Iron

"Behold, how good and how pleasant it is for brethren to dwell together in unity! It is like the precious oil upon the head, running down on the beard, the beard of Aaron, running down on the edge of his garments. It is like the dew of Hermon, descending upon the mountains of Zion; for there the Lord commanded the blessing—Life forevermore" (Psalm 133).

Chapter 7: Biblical Fellowship

To live life as a Christian, is to live within a redeemed covenant community consisting of God's people who enjoy the fellowship of His presence – eternal life (Ps 133:3). This is fellowship. Fellowship with God is the starting point that shapes and defines how we are to view everything else. The goal of our fellowship is the corporate worship of God – to glorify God and to enjoy Him forever (Jn 4:23-24). Let's review where we've been so far. In chapter one we discussed that God's covenant community consists of everyone God calls out of darkness into His marvelous light (Dt 4:20, 34; 1 Pet 2:9). We said that God's covenant community is the Ekklésia - the called out ones. We discussed that the New Testament church is the continuation of the Old Testament

Chapter 7: Biblical Fellowship

people of God, and as such, the Ekklésia or Qahal consists of all the redeemed of all the ages (Eph 2:19-22).

Regarding the church we said that there are three significant truths: (1) Christ has begun to build the true Temple of God with His resurrection (Jn 2:19; Eph 2:20-22); (2) the place of true worship has now been universalized to any place where the Spirit resides in true worshipers (Jn 4:21-24); and (3) Christ is the True Temple, and if we are in Him, than we are a part of it (Mt 12:6-8; 1 Pet 2:4-5). We discussed that God created the church to be *His covenant community*, to be *His visible witness*, and to be *His instrument for the gospel*. Later, in chapter nine we will discuss how the church is to relate to the world. This chapter will discuss the following seven topics:

- The Definition of Fellowship.
- How do we enter Fellowship?
- The Purpose of Fellowship.
- The Test of Fellowship.
- 6-8-10 Principle.
- Iron Sharpens Iron: Imperatives of Fellowship.
- Renewed Fellowship.

The Definition of Fellowship

Fellowship was created when the Son of God was incarnated in the Man Jesus – Emmanuel. God calls us out of darkness and into the glorious light of Jesus Christ not so we can go at it alone but so we can experience fellowship with Christ and each other through the Holy Spirit (Jn 17:21; Eph 2:5; Col 1:13, 22; 2 Tim 1:9; Heb 10:25; 1 Jn 1:7). The Bible uses the word "communion" κοινωνία koinonia meaning 'common' to describe the union believers have with the risen Christ and each other.[1] The Scriptures tell us that God's people are one body in Christ (Jn 10:16; 1 Cor 12:13; Eph 2:14-18; 3:6; 4:4). And Christ indwells His church in the

---

[1] Koinonia in the biblical sense is used largely to refer to the enterprise people share together, by way of resources, in order to work together toward a common goal. With this in mind, Christians share a common life with God and each other.

Chapter 7: Biblical Fellowship

fellowship or communion of the Spirit (2 Cor 13:14). In this way Christians have fellowship with Christ and each other through the Holy Spirit.

Fellowship with God is the starting point that shapes and defines how we are to view everything else. Looking back to chapter three we saw how there are three great unions in Scripture: (1) the union of the Persons of the Trinity (Gen 1:26; 3:22; 11:7; Num 6:22-26; Mt 3:16-17; 28:18-20; 2 Cor 13:14, et al.); (2) the union of the two natures of Christ in One Person (Jn 3:13; 17:5; 20:28); and (3) the union of Christ and believers in the Holy Spirit (Mt 28:20; Jn 14:17-18; Rom 8:9; Col 1:27; Heb 13:15; 1 Jn 1:3, 6-7). This chapter regards the third great union. As God's people we are the house of God, the body of Christ, and the temple of the Holy Spirit.

Fellowship is the participation and common life that believers enjoy in Christ. Fellowship entails sharing our lives with one another. Stepping out in the covenant community to share the new life we've received. There are essentially three basic elements to a Christian's fellowship with God: (1) The Scriptures – God speaks to us by His Word; (2) prayer – God speaks to us in prayer; and (3) fellowship – God speaks to us through His people. In these three ways, God draws us nearer to Himself.

How do we enter Fellowship?

When the Lord appeared to Abraham, He said, "Do not be afraid, Abram. I am your shield, your exceedingly great reward" (Gen 15:1). As Calvin states, "Here we see that the Lord is the final reward promised to Abraham, that he might not seek a fleeting and evanescent reward in the elements of this world, but look to one that was incorruptible. A promise of the land is afterward added for no other reason than that it might be a symbol of the divine benevolence, and a type of the heavenly inheritance."[2] The author of Hebrews tells us, "By faith Abraham obeyed when he was called to go out to the place which he would receive as an inheritance. And he went out, not knowing where he was going. 9 By faith he dwelt in

---

[2] Calvin, Institutes of the Christian Religion, 2.11.2, 289.

the land of promise as in a foreign country, dwelling in tents
with Isaac and Jacob, the heirs with him of the same promise;
10 for he waited for the city which has foundations, whose
builder and maker is God" (Heb 11:8-10).

Abraham's commitment to what he was to receive
afterward was demonstrated, as John Owen tells us, by the
way he sojourned as a stranger:

> He built no house in it, purchased no inheritance, but only a burying
> place. He entered, indeed, into leagues of peace and amity with some,
> as with Aner, Eshcol, and Mamre (Gen 14:13); but it was as a
> stranger, and not as one that had anything of his own in the land. He
> reckoned that land at present no more his own than any other land in
> the world – no more than Egypt was the land of his posterity when
> they sojourned there, which God had said was not theirs, nor was so
> to be (Gen 15:13). The manner of sojourning in this land was, that he
> "dwelt in tabernacles;" These tents were pitched, fixed, and erected
> only with stakes and cords, so as that they had no foundation in the
> earth; And with respect unto their fitting condition in these movable
> houses, God in an especial manner was said to be their dwelling-
> place (Ps 90:1).[3]

Owen adds, "This place whereunto he went is described by
his future relation unto it and interest in it; he was 'afterwards
to receive it for an inheritance.' At present he received it not,
but only in right and title, nor during his life." The point being
made here is Abraham's call is a pattern of the call of every
Christian. We, like Abraham, are called out of the world, to
live as pilgrims on the Way (Ps 84:5-7; Is 26:7; 35:8; Act 9:2;
Jn 10:4; 1 Pet 2:11); And, like Abraham, not having a
permanent residence here, "confess that we are strangers and
pilgrims on the earth," as we look to the "heavenly country,"
the heavenly Jerusalem – the city of God (Ps 48; Is 26; Gal
4:26; Heb 11:13-16; 12:22; Rev 21).

All of these titles, "heavenly country," city of God," etc.
represent the future state of blessedness and rest which the
saints are permitted to enjoy now in part. For the rest God
promised to the patriarchs was far more than just a secure life
in an earthly land of promise. The promise of the land typified
the eternal inheritance they were to receive – God Himself

---

[3] Owen, An Exposition of Hebrews, Vol 7, 67.

Chapter 7: Biblical Fellowship

(Gen 15:1; Eph 1:11, 18; 3:6). The author of Hebrews makes this point abundantly clear when he writes, "For if Joshua had given them rest, then He would not afterward have spoken of another day. There remains therefore a rest for the people of God. For he who has entered His rest has himself also ceased from his works as God did from His" (Heb 4:8-10).

The point is this, long after the conquest of the Promised Land under Joshua was achieved, David spoke of a rest that might be entered or forfeited.[4] For, "Thus says the Lord: 'Heaven is My throne, and earth is My footstool. Where is the house that you will build Me? And where is the place of My rest' (Is 66:1). And in the fullness of time Jesus comes and declares, "Come to Me, all you who labor and are heavy laden, and I will give you rest. Take My yoke upon you and learn from Me, for I am gentle and lowly in heart, and you will find rest for your souls. For My yoke is easy and My burden is light" (Mt 11:28-30). Jesus is Emmanuel, God with us. He is the place of eternal Sabbath rest. But a sword guards the way to that rest (Gen 3:24; Mt 10:34; Heb 4:12). Jesus is the True Temple, the place of God's eternal rest. But the only entrance into the Temple is through the narrow gate (Mt 7:13-14; Acts 4:24).

According to Greg Beale, in Christ we have a positional rest in which we await a future consummated practical rest. Beale writes, "Christians begin now to enjoy existentially a Sabbath rest by virtue of our real inaugurated resurrection life which has been communicated to us through the life-giving Spirit. But our rest is still incomplete because our resurrection existence has begun only spiritually and has not been consummated bodily."[5] Then as Augustine said, "Our flesh will be renewed by being made exempt from decay, just as our soul is renewed by faith."[6]

The point being made here is the Sabbath rest, the rest Christians enjoy because of Christ's perfect atonement, is both a personal and corporate dimension. Christians begin now to

---

[4] The author of Hebrews uses the word rest no less than eleven times in twenty verses (Heb 3:11, 18; 4:1, 3 (2x), 4, 5, 8, 9 (Sabbath rest), 10, and 11). That rest *katapausin* is a positional one which awaits a future consummated one.

[5] Beale, The Temple and the Church's Mission, 293-312.

[6] Augustine, City of God, Book XX, Chapter 5, 715.

share Christ's resurrection life (Life – forevermore) together in covenant fellowship. They enter that fellowship with God in Christ and with each other by the Spirit.

A Perfect Atonement

A further word on the atonement of Christ will not go amiss. An important question inquisitive Christians have asked down for the last twenty centuries is: Who received Christ's ransom payment? This question has baffled theologians for centuries. It was Origen's belief the ransom was paid to Satan. This was probably believed by most medieval scholastics, however Anselm of Canterbury's *Cur Deus Homo* (Why the God-man?) changed all that. In this book, Anselm postulates the satisfaction theory of atonement which is first, that satisfaction is necessary on account of God's honor and justice; second, that such satisfaction can be given only by the mediatorial work of the God-man Jesus; and, third, that such satisfaction is really given by this God-man's voluntary death.

Anselm's theory, as opposed to Origen's, was God honoring. In chapter eighteen Anselm writes, "He (Christ) offered Himself to Himself, that is He offered his humanity to his divinity, which is one and the same divinity common to three persons. Nevertheless, in order to say more clearly what we mean, while still abiding within this truth, let us say that the Son freely offered himself to the Father."

Anselm further relates that the ransom payment is not to the devil. In chapter nineteen: "God did not owe anything to the devil except punishment, but man owed to God, not to the devil, whatever was required of him." Luther and Calvin later developed Anselm's theory into the penal substitutionary atonement theory commonly held in most Protestant churches today. Anselm purporting Christ having obeyed where we should have obeyed, Calvin postulating Christ was punished where we should have been punished. Francis Turretin cogently writes, "Christ gives the payment as Mediator and receives it as Judge."

The capacity for fellowship was given by God to all men but was mutilated by sin. John White tells us that "Sin has damaged our capacity to know one another because it damaged our capacity to know God. Therefore any attempt to mend the broken fragments of humanity, however exciting or apparently successful, will be illusory and doomed to ultimate failure unless humanity's relationship with God is restored. I cannot have true fellowship with you unless both of us have fellowship with God."[7] That is why the author of the Book of Hebrews in chapter four culminates his teaching on the Sabbath rest with these words:

11 Let us therefore be diligent to enter that rest, lest anyone fall according to the same example of disobedience. 12 For the word of God is living and powerful, and sharper than any two-edged sword, piercing even to the division of soul and spirit, and of joints and marrow, and is a discerner of the thoughts and intents of the heart. 13 And there is no creature hidden from His sight, but all things are naked and open to the eyes of Him to whom we must give account.

The Word of God spoken of here is the Person of Christ – the incarnate Word of God (Heb 4:12); the pronouncement of truth to which we must either receive or reject. To Him we must give account (Heb 4:13). Christ knows and searches all hearts. His words penetrate into our very souls and deal directly with our consciences, discerning who is regenerate or not. He is like the flaming sword that guards the way to paradise. Our words regarding Him will either justify or condemn us (Mt 10:32; 12:33-37; 16:15; Lk 19:22).

In chapter four of the Book of Hebrews, the inspired apostle admonishes us with these words: "Therefore, since a promise remains of entering His rest, let us fear lest any of you seem to have come short of it. For indeed the gospel was preached to us as well as to them; but the word which they heard did not profit them, not being mixed with faith in those who heard it" (Heb 4:1-2). God led Israel out of bondage in Egypt to serve *latreon* Him in the desert.[8] They had the gospel preached to them (Gal 3:9), but virtually *en masse* the visible assembly proved unfaithful to Yahweh, forfeiting the Sabbath rest because of unbelief (1 Cor 10:1-22; Heb 3:19) – the

---

[7] White, The Fight, 141.
[8] See Chapter four – page 224 for this concept of priestly service.

unpardonable sin. By virtue of their being part of the visible assembly, the Israelites reckoned they had eternal security.

How many in the church today are guilty of the same presumption? We cannot go to heaven on our father's coat tails. Or perhaps they think they are saved because of some outward acts they've done – they went up forward, raised their hand, or filled out a decision card. And those actions might accompany saving faith, the point is we have to know Christ personally! It is to Him we must give an account. So, how do we enter fellowship? Christ calls us into it (1 Cor 1:9). As a result of Christ's resurrection, God's people, as mediating-witnessing priests are to extend His tabernacling presence throughout the whole earth, themselves serving as God's building materials for His end-time temple (1 Pet 1:4-5).

What we have discussed so far is fellowship with God and each other is grounded solely on the Word of God (Heb 4:1-16). The proof our regeneration is that we submit to the authority of the Scriptures. And because our corporate faith rests on the conviction of God's revealed truth, the belief in biblical infallibility is an imperative. It is the great sin of modern times that many deny this. If we deny the infallibility of the Bible what do we stand on (Mt 7:24-25)?

For the church is the pillar and ground of truth (1 Tim 3:15). A second important aspect of fellowship is it's only on the basis of Christ perfect atonement (1 Jn 1:3-4). Of this much has already been said. A third aspect is our fellowship with God is evidenced by our obedience to the gospel (1 Pet 1:22). With these points in mind we may see that God's purpose in Christian fellowship has two goals: first, is so the church may be a visible witness to the saving power of Jesus Christ. And, second, that through His established means of grace, He may build His church.

Where do we Fellowship?

Everyone who professes Christ as Savior and Lord is to join themselves to a Bible-believing, gospel-preaching, Christ-centered congregation (1 Cor 1:9; Heb 10:24-25). Because the world cannot detect the invisible church, it's imperative that those who profess to be Christians gather together to be a

Chapter 7: Biblical Fellowship

visible witness to the saving power of Jesus. Some are saying today that we don't need any church structure or buildings to meet in. However, Christ has said that He builds His church on an apostolic foundation, and equips her with spiritual gifts for the work of ministry (Eph 4:11-16). Christ provides ministry and leadership. His sheep must submit themselves to those Christ has authorized to lead His church. As MacArthur cogently puts it,

In Matthew 18, for example, He (Christ) implied that the church would have form since it would meet together in a given place: "If your brother sins, go and show him his fault in private; if he listens to you, you have won your brother. But if he does not listen to you, take one or two more with you, so that by the mouth of two or three witnesses every fact may be confirmed. If he refuses to listen to them, *tell it to the church*" (vv. 15-17, emphasis added).[9]

The Purpose of Fellowship

Christ builds His church through what the Bible reveals as the four means of grace. The purpose of fellowship is to make disciples. On the Day of Pentecost, Peter preached the gospel and 3,000 became disciples (Acts 2:41). Now that's unction! Then Acts 2:42-47 declares to us God's pattern for the church,

42 And they continued steadfastly in the apostles' doctrine and fellowship, in the breaking of bread, and in prayers. 43 Then fear came upon every soul, and many wonders and signs were done through the apostles. 44 Now all who believed were together, and had all things in common, 45 and sold their possessions and goods, and divided them among all, as anyone had need. 46 So continuing daily with one accord in the temple, and breaking bread from house to house, they ate their food with gladness and simplicity of heart, 47 praising God and having favor with all the people. And the Lord added to the church daily those who were being saved.

These verses give us God's established means of grace, which are: (1) the apostle's doctrine – the fundamental teachings of the Christian faith; (2) fellowship – the sharing of the common life of grace; (3) communion – partaking of the

---

[9] MacArthur, The Master's Plan for the Church, 86.

Lord's Supper; and (4) prayer – the pouring out of our needs to God. These four means of grace are the ways in which God saves us, brings us into His fellowship, sanctifies us, and spiritually feeds us along the Way (Ps 84:5-7; Is 35:8; Acts 9:2; 24:14). This is Christ's disciple making program for the world.

In addition to what has been stated already, *fellowship is also God's instituted way of making a public profession of the faith and hope of the gospel.* The apostle Paul, encouraging Timothy, admonishes him to "Fight the good fight of faith, lay hold of eternal life, to which you were called and have confessed the good confession in the presence of many witnesses" (1 Tim 6:12). It is by our true profession of faith that we enter into fellowship with the saints (Rom 10:9-13).

Fellowship is also the visible bond of our union with the disciples of Jesus. When we meet with other Christians we are bearing testimony to the saving power of Christ. We begin to share the common life of the saints. Regarding the way Christians are to share the common life together the Baptist Faith and Message tells us,

God is the source of all blessings, temporal and spiritual; all that we have and are we owe to Him. Christians have a spiritual debtorship to the whole world, a holy trusteeship in the gospel, and a binding stewardship in their possessions. They are therefore under obligation to serve Him with their time, talents, and material possessions; and should recognize all these as entrusted to them to use for the glory of God and for helping others. According to the Scriptures, Christians should contribute of their means cheerfully, regularly, systematically, proportionately, and liberally for the advancement of the Redeemer's cause on earth.[10]

When Christ saves us it's not so we can go at it alone, we are in this together. We are at war against the corruptions of our flesh, the world and the devil. We can't win the war alone. Fellowship is the visible bond of our union together. The church is God's visible witness. We are in effect declaring that we are on the Lord's side (Ex 32:26). And our Christian fellowship is in itself an indictment to the world (2 Cor 6:14; 1

---

[10] Baptist Faith and Message, XIII. Stewardship, 17.

Pet 4:4). This is what Moses is commended for in the Book of Hebrews. Rather than enjoy the passing pleasures of sin, he chose to "suffer affliction with the people of God." Because the Scripture says, he esteemed "the reproach of Christ greater riches than the treasures in Egypt; for he looked to the reward" (Heb 11:25-26).

Fellowship must be genuine. Kierkegaard spoke out against the shame "Christendom" of his day. He called attention to the stark difference between the 'state church' of Denmark and the Christianity of the New Testament. He remarked that everyone in Denmark is saved because they all have been baptized! Kierkegaard's point is well taken. Fellowship is not merely membership. That is hypocrisy.

Often times in the church we mistake mere social activities, such as a pot luck or coffee before worship service as fellowship. But is this the full meaning of fellowship? Hardly. Fellowship is much more and vital for the church's spiritual well-being. Fellowship involves the giving of our time, talents, and tithes to the cause that Christ died for. Fellowship is participating in the common life of the saints as we make our pilgrimage to the city of God (Ps 84; Is 35). The Bible teaches us that fellowship is a means of grace. Because in true Christian fellowship one cannot but hear the testimony of God's mighty work in the lives of His saints (Rev 12:11). In this sense, it is a means that God uses for the converting and sanctifying of His people. Thus, God, making use of means, works to purify His saints.

A vital aspect of fellowship is that it is a spiritual imperative. The apostle Paul writes to the church at Corinth, and pleads with them to put away any schismatic activity caused by elitist attitudes among them for the sake of Christ. He writes, "Now I plead with you, brethren, by the name of our Lord Jesus Christ, that you all speak the same thing, and that there be no divisions among you, but that you be perfectly joined together in the same mind and in the same judgment" (1 Cor 1:10). Paul appeals to the fact that they are all one in Christ regardless of who baptized them! We are to preserve unity and not forsake the assembly (Heb 10:23-25).

J.I. Packer writes, "Fellowship with God, then, is the source from which fellowship among Christians springs; and fellowship with God is the end to which Christian fellowship is a means." Further he states, "God has made us in such a way that our fellowship with Himself is fed by our fellowship with fellow-Christians, and requires to be so fed constantly for its own deepening and enrichment." When I ask people why they don't attend a local church they often reply "I don't go because the church is full of hypocrites!" Well, I say, that's because the church is full of sinners. We may not all act as perfect as those outside would like but we are forgiven! Christians who demur from attending church forsake the assembly to their own hurt. Besides, can we truly love God if we despise His people?

Fellowship is also a declaration of ours, determining to submit to one another and to the government and discipline of the church. Ephesian 5:21 instructs us to "submit to one another in the fear of the Lord," as we "esteem others better than ourselves" (Phil 2:3). And the apostle Peter exhorts younger people to "submit to their elders," and for everyone to "be submissive to one another, and be clothed with humility" (1 Pet 5:5). Likewise, the author of the Book of Hebrews exhorts us to "Remember those who rule over you," and "obey those who rule over you, and be submissive, for they watch out for your souls, as those who must give account" (Heb 13:7, 17). When we submit to the authority of the church, we are submitting to God who gave that authority (Ps 133; Rom 13:1). This touches on discipline as one of the marks of a gospel church. Christians submitting to the leadership of the church. This is very unpopular these days. Imagine young people everywhere honoring their elders!

So who needs fellowship? Every true Christian needs to participate with the body of Christ in order to grow in grace and in the knowledge of God. Many never consider that their lack of fellowship stagnates their spiritual lives. Fellowship is shared life – life in the Spirit (Jn 17:21). We are to not let the world press us into its mold but through God's Word and the fellowship of the saints, we are to be continuously transformed (Rom 12:2). There aren't to be any "Lone Ranger" Christians. We need each other. And we should never try to improve on God's established means of grace.

Chapter 7: Biblical Fellowship

The Test of Fellowship

In Christ's parable of the Sower, He details the characteristics of four soil types. Each of these soils are a picture of what is in our hearts that creates distance in fellowship. Matthew 13 tells us,

18 "Therefore hear the parable of the sower: 19 When anyone hears the word of the kingdom, and does not understand it, then the wicked one comes and snatches away what was sown in his heart. This is he who received seed by the wayside. 20 But he who received the seed on stony places, this is he who hears the word and immediately receives it with joy; 21 yet he has no root in himself, but endures only for a while. For when tribulation or persecution arises because of the word, immediately he stumbles. 22 Now he who received seed among the thorns is he who hears the word, and the cares of this world and the deceitfulness of riches choke the word, and he becomes unfruitful. 23 But he who received seed on the good ground is he who hears the word and understands it, who indeed bears fruit and produces: some a hundredfold, some sixty, some thirty."

The first soil is the hard heart (Mt 13:19). This is the person who is completely self-centered. And so he is unable to respond to God's love, and doesn't know how to love others. This is a person who is unconverted, who fails to see the surpassing worth of Christ and the fellowship with His saints. This type fails the test of life and never knows the communion of the saints. The second soil is rocky (Mt 13:20-21). When the seed lands, is grows quickly but it doesn't develop deep roots and when troubles come and life stops being fun, the enthusiasm wanes. This is the type of person who leaves fellowship because of a supposed injustice against them. Their zeal seemed genuine during the good times, but they didn't sign up for trouble. As soon as trouble or disappointment appears they disappear. Perhaps this is the person who couldn't stand for any constructive criticism or discipline the church saw fit to give them. Immediately they stumble. Fellowship for them meant only what they could get out of it. These fail the test because they had no root.

The third soil grows into a plant, but then it's choked by thorns. Faith in Christ can be choked not by actual thorns but by "the cares of this world and the deceitfulness of riches." The same is true for fellowship if one allows a preoccupation with material things or a root of bitterness to choke it. 1 Timothy 6:9 warns us that "those who desire to be rich fall into temptation and a snare." The apostle Paul tells us that Demas had forsaken him "having loved this present world" (2 Tim 4:9). And Hebrews 12:15 warns us against the trouble a root of bitterness can cause. Bitterness is often caused by wounded pride or a sense of injustice. These pitfalls seek to rob us of the grace of fellowship. Our souls should turn to God and the fellowship of the saints when we encounter trouble (Ps 46; Ps 48; Is 26:1-4).

Additionally, this soil type is like a person who is self-sufficient, a lone Ranger who doesn't see the worth of Christian fellowship. Regarding this type, Packer writes, "This self-sufficient attitude may reflect the deadness of the unconverted, to whom the whole realm of spiritual things seems unreal; or it may reflect the purblindness of sluggish Christians (Heb 5:12; Rom 12:1-3) – who may be mature in years, and have been Christians of sorts for many of those years; or it may be the rationalized stance of one who through pride or guilt or conscious hypocrisy or all three is not willing to share his spiritual needs and ask for others' help. But whatever the source, self-sufficiency excludes fellowship from the start."[11]

The fourth soil produces fruit. This soil stands for the good heart that understands God's Word, receives it, applies it, and seeks to live within the covenant fellowship with God and His people. This is the person who has seen the surpassing worth of knowing Christ as Savior and the saints as fellow adopted sons and daughters. This is the man that passes the test of fellowship, who has a personal relationship with Christ and His people, and relies on that relationship for the power and perseverance he needs to love for the long haul.

"On the other hand," Maurice Roberts tells us, "the unconverted have no spiritual access to God in the time of distress but are commonly swallowed up with despair like Saul and Judas; or else they harden themselves against God

---

[11] Packer, God's Words: Studies of Key Bible Themes, 198.

like Pharaoh, till they become reckless. Afflictions, therefore, are a fan in God's hand to separate between good and evil men. All men are good company in fair weather but the storms of life prove character."[12] Ultimately, those who reject the fellowship of the church show 'a will most incorrect to heaven,' and should take to heart the words of 1 John 2:19: "They went out from us, but they were not of us; for if they had been of us, they would have continued with us; but they went out that they might be made manifest, that none of them were of us."

The 6-8-10 Principle

Fellowship is the participation and common life that believers share in Christ. Christians need each other. And because our relationship with God is fed by our fellowship with fellow believers how we treat each other matter immensely. There is a group of principles in the Pauline corpus known as the 6-8-10 principle because they are found in 1 Corinthians chapters 6, 8, and 10. They form a sort of paradigm when we consider our interaction in fellowship. The first is found in 1 Cor 6:12. Because we are not under the law but under grace (Rom 6:14) the apostle Paul tells us, "All things are lawful for me, but all things are not helpful. All things are lawful for me, but I will not be brought under the power of any." The apostle is saying that because we belong to the Lord and because we are joined to Him (the Temple of the Holy Spirit) we should consider how our actions will affect the body (1 Cor 6:17-20).

On the basis of this Scripture we may ask: Is the action I'm considering condemned by Scripture? Or if it is adiaphorous, will it be beneficial to myself and Christ's body? We should think this way because the Scripture tells us that individually and corporately believers constitute the Temple of God (1 Cor 6:19; 2 Cor 6:16). The 8 principle builds on the 6 principle and asks us to consider: will the perceived action cause our fellow believing brother or sister to stumble? Paul writes in the context of eating meat that has been offered in pagan temples,

---

[12] Roberts, The Thought of God, 4.

says, "If food makes my brother stumble, I will never again eat meat, lest I make my brother stumble" (1 Cor 8:13). Christians are to consider their fellows believers when they feel they have the liberty to drink or eat certain foods. However, when we read Scripture like 1 Cor 6:12 can we consciously say that cigarettes, alcohol, and drugs can't enslave us? Won't these destroy our temple?

The third in this paradigm which asks us to consider our fellow believer is the 10 principle. This is found in 1 Corinthians 10:23-24 and sums it all up by saying: "All things are lawful for me, but not all things are helpful; all things are lawful for me, but not all things edify. Let no one seek his own, but each one the other's well-being." This is followed by the Scripture which states, "Therefore, whether you eat or drink, or whatever you do, do all to the glory of God" (1 Cor 10:31). The apostle would have us consider: Does this perceived action glorify God? Will it serve to further gather and strengthen Christ's body? Will it cause my brother or sister to stumble (1 Cor 10:29)? And all of this is to be understood in the context of fellowship. Because our relationship with God is fed by our fellowship with fellow believers (1 Cor 10:16-17).

Iron Sharpening Iron

We have discussed what fellowship is: life within a redeemed covenant community consisting of God's people who enjoy the fellowship of His presence – eternal life (Ps 133:3). We've discussed God's purpose in fellowship: to make Disciples of Christ. We've discussed the tests of fellowship: having the root of the divine Life in us. And we've discussed the 6-8-10 principle which reminds us we are to do everything for the glory of God. What we need to discuss now is at the heart of fellowship – the imperatives of fellowship. The foremost imperative is we must share faith in Christ. There must be a unity in faith: one Lord, one faith, and baptism; one God and Father of all (Eph 4:4-5). Without the apostolic doctrine there can be no fellowship. For what fellowship has righteousness with lawlessness? And what communion has light with darkness? And what accord has Christ with Belial?

Or what part has a believer with an unbeliever (2 Cor 6:14-15). The foremost imperative of fellowship is we must be of like faith.

My grandfather, Bonnie Underhill, was a mighty preacher of the gospel. He was also a butcher by trade. And when someone came to his butcher's shop and selected a portion of meat to buy, the first thing he would do is unsheathe his butcher's knife, which was fastened to his side, and reach for his file that hang on the wall. Then he would take his knife and with great dexterity he would work the file over the knife's blade edge. He would make the knife sharper than it was. Only after that action would he slice through the specified portion of meat.

All Christian ministry is like the sharpening of dull knives. This is the action that is being referred to in Proverbs 27:17, "As iron sharpens iron, so a man sharpens the countenance of his friend." As the edge of my grandfather's file would sharpen the knife edge of his butcher's knife so does the bright countenance of a godly man sharpen that of his friend. A blade requires sharpening on occasion. Jonathan sharpened the countenance of his friend David. When David was discouraged, Jonathan would say, "The Lord is with you." They encouraged one another in the things of God. They shared a lively faith in God. They were as iron sharpening iron. Godly friendship strengthens our walk with God.

There are great advantages to godly company. In the Book of Malachi, the godly of the land of Judah strengthened one another during a time of spiritual and moral decline. And the Scripture tells us, "Then those who feared the Lord spoke to one another, and the Lord listened and heard them; so a book of remembrance was written before Him for those who fear the Lord and who meditate on His name" (Mal 3:16). The hearts of those who feared the Lord considered others. They considered how to build one another up. Christian fellowship is essential to Christian growth. Know fellowship – know growth; no fellowship – no growth.

"As iron sharpens iron, so a man sharpens the countenance of his friend" (Pro 27:17). There are a number of observations we may make from this verse. We are strengthened by

317

Chapter 7: Biblical Fellowship

Christian *company, conversation, and prayer*. Ecclesiastes 4:9-12 tells us, "

9 Two are better than one, because they have a good reward for their labor. 10 For if they fall, one will lift up his companion. But woe to him who is alone when he falls, for he has no one to help him up. 11 Again, if two lie down together, they will keep warm; but how can one be warm alone? 12 Though one may be overpowered by another, two can withstand him. And a threefold cord is not quickly broken.

Two are better than one. Jesus sent out His disciples by twos. Paul was sent to the mission field first with Barnabas then with Silas. Together they made more of an impact for Christ. Christians become dull by forsaking the assembly. Our minds are made sharp by God's Word. The apostle Paul, writing to Timothy, the young pastor he had ordained to minister to the church in Ephesus, says:

14 But you must continue in the things which you have learned and been assured of, knowing from whom you have learned them, 15 and that from childhood you have known the Holy Scriptures, which are able to make you wise for salvation through faith which is in Christ Jesus. 16 All Scripture is given by inspiration of God, and is profitable for doctrine, for reproof, for correction, for instruction in righteousness, 17 that the man of God may be complete, thoroughly equipped for every good work.

The context for this Scripture, found in verses 14-15 is, within godly fellowship. Paul is admonishing Timothy to draw strength from the Scriptures he has learned from childhood. Timothy had learned to appreciate the Word of God while in fellowship. Christian fellowship facilitates the learning of God's Word. And we are to learn God's Word in the church of the living God, the pillar and ground of truth (1 Tim 3:15). It is in church that we learn what the Scriptures teach us. The Scriptures principally teach us what man is to believe concerning God, and the duty God requires of man.[13]

In church we learn the apostolic doctrines. We learn what the Bible approves of and condemns. We learn of what promises we may claim; what sins to avoid; what commands

---

[13] Westminster Confession of Faith, Shorter Catechism Question 3.

to obey; what lessons to take to heart; and what examples to follow – on and off the pages of Scriptures. Particularly, we learn from the living letters we congregate with – fellow Christians whom God is using as a means of grace in our lives. It takes a church to make disciples. Thus, God, making use of means, works to purify His saints. Two are better than one. We are strengthened, become more like Christ through Christian company and conversation. "As iron sharpens iron, so a man sharpens the countenance of his friend" (Pro 27:17). Thus fellowship is essential to become more like Christ.

As we have said, Christians are more injured by their insidious invisible enemy than all other enemies combined. We must remember that we are at war! Against our three enemies; the flesh, the world, and the devil. The Bible teaches us, "The devil prowls about like a roaring lion, seeking whom he may devour" (1 Pet 5:8). The greatest danger the church faces is compromise. We need Christian fellowship to remain faithful witnesses to the saving power of Christ.

The apostle Paul was often encouraged by his fellow believers, and in Romans chapter one he says, "I long to see you, that I may impart to you some spiritual gift, so that you may be established – that is, that I may be encouraged together with you by the mutual faith both of you and me. Even the apostle Paul needed Christian fellowship. He asked the churches to pray for him so that he may preach as he ought (Eph 6:18-20). The apostle Paul recognized his need for Christian fellowship and prayer – do we?

There is nothing so disappointing as trying to slice through a rope when the knife won't cut through butter. Thus, the idea of a lone ranger Christian is completely unbiblical. We need each other to remain sharp and effective for Christ. Paul reminds Timothy and us to "Be diligent to present yourself approved to God, a worker who does not need to be ashamed, rightly dividing the word of truth" (2 Tim 2:15). Paul exhorts gospel ministers to "cut straight" with God's Word. He employs the word *orthotomeó* which is a combination of the words cut *temno* and straight *ortho* (as in orthodontist = straight teeth). The apostle's concern is for ministers to handle the Word of God correctly. The Word of God is "living and powerful, and sharper than any two-edged sword," and we

Chapter 7: Biblical Fellowship

must handle it correctly to bring down the strongholds of the enemy as we advance truth against darkness (Eph 6:17).[14]

Christians need each other's prayers. The churches out of their poverty greatly assisted Paul both with prayer and practical means. Paul recognized his need to be encouraged by the mutual faith of his fellow believers. God moves us to pray for our fellow believers when He causes us to consciously feel their needs. Following this foremost imperative – the sharing of saving faith in Christ alone – there are some additional imperatives for fellowship. There are more, but at a minimum consider these:

1. We must love one another (Jn 13:31-35; Rom 12:9; 1 Cor 13; Gal 5:14, 22; 1 Jn 4:7-8; et al). This is the first and foremost mark of our regeneration – love for others. This we cannot do until we have experienced the love of God (Rom 5:8). Remembering what Henry Scougal wrote: "This is the life of God in the soul of man. A soul thus possessed with divine love must need be enlarged toward all mankind, in a sincere and unbounded affection, because of the relation they have to God."[15] In Luther's words, "The whole being of any Christian is faith and love – faith brings the man to God, love brings him to men. God commands a blessing in fellowship. Perfected fellowship with God is the goal of human history. Fellowship is impossible without love (1 Cor 13). The love of Christ is to control us (2 Cor 5:14). Let love be genuine (Rom 12:9).

2. We must serve one another (Mt 25:31-46; Rom 12:10-13; Eph 5:21; 1 Jn 2:29; 3:18; 1 Pet 4:10). The good works which the righteous perform are not the root but rather the fruit of grace.[16] Christians need each other! Dietrich Bonhoeffer was a German pastor during WWII who suffered for the cause of Christ. He spent nearly two years of his life in prison.

Bonhoeffer illuminates fellowship when he writes, "The physical presence of other Christians is a source of incomparable joy and strength to the believer. Longingly, the

---

[14] This is the topic for discussion in Chapters 9 and 10.
[15] See Chapter 1 – page 1.
[16] Hendriksen, Matthew, 888.

imprisoned apostle Paul calls his 'dearly beloved son in the faith,' Timothy, to come to him in prison in the last days of his life; he would see him again and have him near. Paul has not forgotten the tears Timothy shed when last they parted (2 Tim 1:4). Remembering the congregation in Thessalonica, Paul prays 'night and day exceedingly that we might see your face' (1 Thess 3:10). The aged John knows that his joy will not be full until he can come to his own people and speak face to face instead of writing with ink (2 John 12).[17]

We are to "Be kindly affectionate to one another with brotherly love, in honor giving preference to one another (Rom 12:10). When we as Christians serve one another we serve Christ (Rom 12:11; Gal 5:13). On the last day, all the nations of the world will stand before the Son of Man and are judged on the basis for how they cared for the people Christ identified Himself with (Mt 25:31-46).

3. We must bear one another's burdens (Mt 18:15-17; Rom 12:13-14, 17-21; 1 Cor 12:25-26; Gal 6:1-5; Col 3:13; Jude 20-23). Whereas, Job's friends chose the right time to visit, they failed to take the right course of improving their visit; the time they spent praying for him was used in hot disputes with him. Had they come "to suffer along with" Job they would have profited him and pleased God more (1 Cor 12:26).

John Piper tells us "Gal 6:1-5 is a warning against the danger of pride in those of us who take on the burden of correcting and restoring a fellow believer." But he says, "It is not a warning against correcting and admonishing and restoring a person; it is a warning against doing it arrogantly." We must speak the truth in love if God directs us to correct an erring brother or sister (Eph 4:15). We must help each other practice the truth.

4. We must forgive one another (Mt 6:14-15; Mt 18; Rom 12:14, 17-21; Col 3:3). We are to be God's representatives in showing the divine characteristic of pardoning grace. Col 3:12-13 tells us, "Therefore, as the elect of God, holy and beloved, put on tender mercies, kindness, humility, meekness,

---

[17] Bonhoeffer, Life Together, 29.

longsuffering; bearing with one another, and forgiving one another, if anyone has a complaint against another; even as Christ forgave you, so you also must do." Forgiving others is a commandment not a suggestion.

Just how often should we forgive our brother? Jesus' answer to Peter conveys the idea of infinity (Mt 18:22). Faithful are the wounds of a friend (Pro 27:6). The Book of Proverbs certainly teaches doctrine but the main aim of the Book is to teach us how to live our lives in a practical way. Proverbs 17:9 teaches us, "He who covers a transgression seeks love, but he who repeats a matter separates friends." This proverbs teaches us two important truths: we are to allow the love of Christ to control us and deflate our egos, so that we may forgive and forget the perceived injustices of others.

And second, we are not to gossip. The Bible specifically commands us to avoid the temptation of highlighting the faults of others for the purposes of defaming them making ourselves look more spiritual in the process (Rom 1:29; 1 Tim 5:13). Gossip betrays a trust (Pro 11:13), and often leads to bitterness, strife and even schism. The Bible encourages us to build one another up in faith not tear each other down in gossip. Besides, our mercy for others is the evidence of God's mercy in us.

5. We must confess our sins to one another (James 5:16). Fear prevents Christians from opening their lives to each other, but the Bible tells us, "perfect love casts out fear (1 Jn 4:18). God's promise is that when we confess our sins to one another He will bring healing in whatever capacity – emotional, physical or spiritual. If we want to grow in grace and in the knowledge of God we will confess our sins to one another. They who confess their sins more grow more (1 Jn 1:8-2:2).

Sometimes God will withhold His blessings so He may teach us humility. This is how God delivered me from alcoholism and pornography. I know Christ died for those sins at Calvary but they certainly had a crippling effect on me at that time in my life. I sought God in the Scriptures, in prayer but not in fellowship. I had resolved to battle my indwelling sins alone. It wasn't until I humbled myself and sought the comfort of a fellow Christian brother that God blessed me by demolishing those strongholds.

When someone raises a question or concern regarding our Christian walk the first response we usually have (at least I have), is to defend ourselves and explain things. Proud people minimize sins. But this is when we need to be humble. We cannot practice those things that the Scriptures condemn and claim to be in fellowship with God. God causes us to consider the sin in our lives and seek the prayerful assistance of a brother. Thanks brother! We are to walk with fellow sinners who share with one another to make progress – to be more like Jesus. This is the iron sharpening iron process (Pro 27:17).

6. <u>We must instruct one another</u> (Rom 15:4; Col 3:16; Heb 3:13; Jude 1:20). God saves us and calls us into a fellowship together with Him and His saints in a local church (1 Cor 1:9). There Christian discipleship takes place.

Once someone brought to my attention the fact that I wasn't fathering my daughter correctly. She had been creating a lot of problems in the youth ministry of the church by squabbling with other girls. My immediate response was to defend my parenting and make excuses for my daughter's behavior. The matter was resolved but only half-heartedly. I left the church angry, feeling attacked. But this served as a catalyst. It began a journey for me. I began to see my responsibilities more as a father. I began to care more about my daughter, more about the effects of my parenting (good or bad), and more about my interaction with the church.

Bringing these types of observations takes a high degree of courage and love from a fellow brother. I had to grow as a father and leader of my family. My oldest daughter today is a fine young Christian woman in a Christian university. God makes use of means. Fellowship is about helping others practice the truth. Thanks brother.

7. <u>We must suffer together</u> (Is 63:9; Rom 12:15; 1 Cor 12:26; Phil 1:8). If we are in Christ, the very things which seek to destroy us are the things that will bring us closer to Him. God would have us not focus on the circumstances but look to Him for grace. This is another imperative of fellowship, we must be

genuinely concerned for God's people. If we truly love God, we will love the brotherhood (1 Pet 2:17; 1 Jn 4:11). And this is how people will know that we are Christ's disciples (Jn 13:34-35).

We learn a lot about the co-suffering among saints when we read about the most famous conversion in history. When the risen Christ appeared to the apostle Paul on the road to Damascus, who was at that time the church's greatest opponent, Christ said to him, "Saul, Saul, why are you persecuting Me?" And he said, "Who are You, Lord?" Then the Lord said, "I am Jesus, whom you are persecuting" (Acts 9:4-5). Christ says, when anyone who believes in Me suffers I suffer, as Isaiah the prophet reveals, "So He became their Savior. In all their affliction He was afflicted" (Is 63:8-9).

And the Scripture reminds us that we are saved into one body – Christ's. "And if one member suffers, all the members suffer with it; or if one member is honored, all the members rejoice with it" (Rom 12:15; 1 Cor 12:26). The promise of fellowship is therefore the covenant presence of God which is eternal life in Christ. This is the shared common life of the saints – the regenerated life we enjoy together because of the sacrifice of Christ (Jn 17:21; Rom 4:25; 6:4). We are to allow ourselves to be continually renewed by God's means of grace. As Christians, I need you and you need me. We need fellowship. As Bonhoeffer put it "We belong to one another through and in Jesus Christ."[18] Our corporate worship of the triune God is a foretaste of heaven, where we inherit God Himself (Is 57:13).

Renewed Fellowship

What if we have fallen out of fellowship for whatever reason? How are we to recover our first love? How are we to rekindle our affection for God's people? When the risen Christ bid His apostle John to write to the church at Laodicea, He gave those in the church an opportunity to demonstrate their faith in Him by way of renewed repentance. Christ's words to Laodicea, along with all smugly complacent Christians is

---

[18] Bonhoeffer, Life Together, 21.

arresting – "I know your works, that you are neither cold nor hot. I could wish you were cold or hot. So then, because you are lukewarm, and neither cold nor hot, *I will vomit you out of My mouth.*" Further Jesus says, "As many as I love, I rebuke and chasten. Therefore be zealous and repent. Behold, I stand at the door and knock. If anyone hears My voice and opens the door, I will come in to him and dine with him, and he with Me (Rev 3:15-16, 19-20, emphasis added).

Christ's message to Laodicea is an invitation not for the readers to be converted but to renew their relationships with Christ. Those who refuse to repent manifest themselves as unbelievers. If they cannot endure such chastening then they show themselves as illegitimate children and not sons of God (Heb 12:3-11). So to answer our earlier questions: How are we to recover our first love?

Christ Himself comes to us and commands us to repent lest we demonstrate we were never a part of His body. William Gurnall puts it this way, "Oh, it is sad for a poor Christian to stand at the door of the promise, in the dark night of affliction, afraid to draw the latch, whereas he should then come boldly for shelter as a child into his father's house." Jesus Christ's sinless life and atoning death is an act of God in human nature fulfilling the covenant from man's side. Justification is God's incarnate obedience. The deity of Christ Jesus is the guarantee that the work of revelation and reconciliation is not hollow or unreal but is real and final. When we stray from Christ's fold He recovers us and brings us first to renew our relationship with Him which enables our renewed fellowship with the church.

This is the sense of Christ's parable of the lost sheep which ends with a celebration amongst Christ's friends as well as the angels of God (Lk 15:4-7). This is how we rekindle our affection for God's people, it all begins with a rekindling of our love for God. Only God can repair the past and redeem the time. The more we surrender to Christ the more our fellowship with God's people will grow. It is as Luther puts it, "the Christian life is one of repentance." And God will forgive as long as we repent.

As our nation succumbs to organized atheism, the church, as the conscience of the state, must continue to testify to the saving power of Jesus Christ, and the repentance that is freely offered through Him. The biblical way to do this is fellowship. A vital aspect of fellowship we have yet to discuss is surmised in an Augustinian dictum: "In essentials unity, in non-essentials liberty, and in all things charity." This reminds us that in order to maintain the unity of the Spirit in the bond of peace we should "keep the main thing, the main thing." Doctrine matters. Christians share "one Lord, one faith, one baptism, and one God and Father of all" (Eph 4:5-6).

If Christians can share the fundamental tenets of the Christian faith, such as those that are encapsulated in the Apostle's and Nicene creeds – the essentials, than they can share the common faith. "Though the terror upon our adversary would be greater if we all were more uniform, we follow the same colors. And though not clothed alike, and differing in things less significant, against the common enemy, Christians march as soldiers all under the same Captain."[19]

However, once there is doctrinal apostasy, moral and ethical decline are an absolute certainty. This is occurring because we are turning away from the authority of the Scriptures. "All Scripture is given by inspiration of God, and is profitable for doctrine, for reproof, for correction, for instruction in righteousness, that the man of God may be complete, thoroughly equipped for every good work" (2 Tim 3:16). The Word of God is inerrant!

All Christians are disciples who, by Christ's design, are to be equipped for service within the fellowship of the local church. This is the benefit of being within a Christian fellowship. When Christians meet together they enable one another to practice the truth, they sharpen one another's countenance – the entirety of the person (mind, will, and emotions of the person); their very soul. What we will discuss in the next chapter is how the church makes disciples.

> Ye chosen seed of Israel's race,
> Ye ransomed from the fall,
> Hail him who saves you by his grace,
> And crown him Lord of all.[20]

---

[19] Burroughs, Irenicum: To the Lover of Truth and Peace, 101.
[20] Perronet, All hail the Power of Jesus' Name.

Chapter 7: Biblical Fellowship

Recommended Further Reading

1. Bonhoeffer, Dietrich *Life Together*.
2. Packer, J.I. *God's Words*.
3. Bridge, William *A Lifting Up for the Downcast*.
4. Calvin, John *Institutes of the Christian Religion*.
5. Clowney, Edmund *The Church*.

Chapter 7 Review Questions

1. What is fellowship?
2. Is it important? Why?
3. What is the correlation between fellowship and evangelism?
4. What is the correlation between fellowship and sanctification?
5. How do Christians bear one another's burdens?
6. What does the 6-8-10 principle teach us? Is it important?
7. What is the purpose of fellowship?
8. Are there any *tests* of fellowship that you are failing?
9. Can fellowship be lost? How is fellowship renewed?
10. What is the importance of fellowship in regards to the Lord's Supper?

11 For the grace of God that brings salvation has appeared to all men, 12 teaching us that, denying ungodliness and worldly lusts, we should live soberly, righteously, and godly in the present age, 13 looking for the blessed hope and glorious appearing of our great God and Savior Jesus Christ, 14 who gave Himself for us, that He might redeem us from every lawless deed and purify for Himself His own special people, zealous for good works (Titus 2:11-14).

Chapter 8: Biblical Discipleship

"Purify my heart, O God." This is concurrently an unfeigned petition flowing out of a heart made pure by faith as it is evidence and proper fruit of repentance (Mt 3:8). Christ is purifying for Himself His own special people who are made zealous for good works (Tit 2:14). God is bringing many sons to glory out of every tribe and tongue and people and nation (Heb 2:10; Rev 5:9). He has been gathering His own since history began, calling them to live in a covenant fellowship with Himself and His people – the church, which is the pillar and ground of truth (1 Cor 1:9; 1 Tim 3:15). The place where the saving truths of the gospel are conveyed to the next generation by Christ's design. The place where Christ gathers, cleanses, and refines all the sons of Levi, so they may present right offerings to God – true worship (Mal 3:3; Jn 4:24).

This chapter is about biblical discipleship and will focus on the following:

- The Great Commission.
- Refiner's Fire.
- Tests to Discipleship.
- Principles for Discipleship.
- Accountability.

In the previous chapter we concluded that all Christians are disciples who, by Christ's design, are to be equipped for service within the fellowship of the local church. Christ said, "I will build My church" (Mt 16:18). The church is God's plan and strategy for discipleship. Christ emphasizes this when He commissioned His church with the words, "All authority has been given to Me in heaven and on earth. Go therefore and *make disciples* of all the nations, *baptizing* them in the name of the Father and of the Son and of the Holy Spirit, *teaching* them to observe all things that I have commanded you; and lo, I am with you always, even to the end of the age." Amen (Mt 28:18-20, emphasis mine).

The chief end of man is to glorify God and to enjoy Him forever (SCQ 1). This was the very reason God created mankind. As has been said, God has made mankind for His own glory, as Proverbs 16:4 declares, "The Lord has made all for Himself, yes, even the wicked for the day of doom," and again in Romans 11:36, "For of him, and through him, and to him are all things." The chief end of all human activity should therefore be to glorify God. But another important distinction should be made involving the use of the word "glorify."

As the Puritan Thomas Boston stated, "to glorify, is either to make glorious, or to declare to be glorious," however, "man cannot make God glorious, for He is not capable of any additional glory, being in Himself infinitely glorious, as Job 35:7 states, "If you are righteous, what do you give Him? Or what does He receive from your hand?"[1] Boston goes on to

---

[1] Thomas Boston, Of Man's Chief End and Happiness, 1.

state that "God is glorified, then, only declaratively; He is glorified when His glory is declared."[2] So it is the duty and chief joy of the God-honoring man to glorify God by declaring His glory through thought, word and deed.

Therefore, *glorify* does not mean make glorious. It means to reflect or display as glorious. This is the impetus behind the Great Commission – "For the earth will be filled with the knowledge of the glory of the Lord, as the waters cover the sea" (Hab 2:14).[3] Christians are to declare the glorious saving work of Christ to all nations, thereby making disciples, baptizing them in God's three-fold name, and teaching the apostolic doctrines of the church (whole counsel of God). As John Frame succinctly puts it,

As God's image, we are made to reflect God's glory back to Him. In one sense, we do that by virtue of our creation. In another sense, to reflect that glory is a deliberate choice that we make or refuse to make. In one sense, we cannot increase God's glory. But when our lives image God, others see the presence of God in us. So we ourselves become part of that light from God that goes forth over the earth."[4]

The Great Commission

The Great Commission is explicitly about making disciples. It is of course about world evangelism and missions but it is first and foremost about discipleship.[5] The way Bonhoeffer put it is, "Christianity without discipleship is always Christianity without Christ." Christ created the church and builds it by gathering His sheep into one body, where He teaches them His Word through those who are led by His Spirit. Christ's purpose in discipleship is spiritual maturity, that He may be formed in us all, until the new spiritual life be

---

[2] Thomas Boston, Of Man's Chief End and Happiness, 1.

[3] The Great Commission is essentially an amplification of Adam's cultural mandate of Gen 1:28. God commanded Adam, as the representative of the human race, to fill, subdue, and rule over the earth. Likewise, the church is now commanded by the risen Christ to make disciples, baptize and teach God's Word. In the Great Commission, Jesus Christ renews God's original purpose to fill the earth with worshipers of God.

[4] Frame, The Doctrine of the Christian Life, 303.

[5] Evangelism and world missions is the topic for chapters 9 and 10.

shaped anew in His image (Gal 4:19). The Spirit implants the very life of Christ within us and enables us to live out His righteous character. The character of Christ within us is to be lived out in righteous conduct. Christ calls us to live in fellowship so we may cultivate purity with fellow saints.

A quick glance back at the means of grace will prove beneficial. As Acts 2:42 teaches us they are, "the apostles' doctrine and fellowship, in the breaking of bread, and in prayers." It has been well said that all true fellowship is predicated on apostolic doctrine. There can be no genuine Christian fellowship without the ground of biblical truth. Likewise, there can be no discipleship (disciple making) without fellowship; fellowship in the local church. The word 'disciple' *mathetes* μαθητής according to Merrill Unger is, "one who professes to have learned certain principles from another and maintains them on that other's authority."[6] And Christ determined the place of discipleship was to be with the place of baptism that is in the gathered community of believers. The point being made here is, discipleship is to be within the context of fellowship in the local church, because you cannot make a disciple without God's means of grace. And let's not try to go beyond or improve His means of grace. Additionally, it takes a church to make disciples.

In the last chapter, we made the point to say that, in addition to other things, fellowship is a determination of ours to submit to one another and to the government and discipline of the church (Eph 5:21; Heb 10:24-25; 13:17). Those who forsake the assembly, forsake spiritual maturity.

But why is disciple-making to be accomplished in the local church? Can't we just meet with some like-minded friends, drink coffee and discuss the important issues in our lives? That may be beneficial but that does not equate with the biblical conception of fellowship. Crucial aspects are missing of which we must now discuss. In light of this, it is essential to the Great commission that disciple making be undertaken in the local church for two essential reasons:

First, so that those Christ has gifted and assigned to equip may be accountable for the work they are doing (Heb 13:7,

---

[6] Unger's Bible Dictionary, 265.

17). Christ has gifted and called His under shepherds: His pastors, elders, and deacons to equip His sheep for the work of service (Eph 4:11-12). And He holds them accountable, "for they watch out for your souls." One important reason for belonging to a local church.[7] We are to therefore submit to our spiritual leaders. They not only teach us God's Word but they watch out for our souls.

And second, so that the fellow saints, those who are walking on the Pilgrim pathway with us, may teach us with their living and breathing example what it means to be a 'learner' of Jesus Christ. So that they may encourage us (1 Thess 5:11), bear our burdens and restore us, that is, correct us when we are living in open sin (Gal 5:25-6:2). We are to submit to one another (Eph 5:21). Further, and more exfoliating I might add, is the discipline of accountability – the reciprocal to discipleship.

Refiner's Fire

When our fathers disciplined us, assuming they did it in love, it was to teach us that we are to be held accountable for our words and actions. Obedience to God is to be first learned in the home. Likewise, the author of Hebrews tells us that the object of God's chastening (discipline) is so that we will become spiritually mature so as to be conformed to the image of His Son. Hebrews 12:5-11 teaches us,

5 And you have forgotten the exhortation which speaks to you as to sons: "My son, do not despise the chastening of the Lord, nor be discouraged when you are rebuked by Him; 6 For whom the Lord loves He chastens, and scourges every son whom He receives." 7 If you endure chastening, God deals with you as with sons; for what son is there whom a father does not chasten? 8 But if you are without chastening, of which all have become partakers, then you are

---

[7] Calvin says, "Church officers do by duty what all Christians are to do by love." The officers of the church: the pastor, teachers, elders, and deacons have an obligation to serve Christ and His people, for, as Gill tells us, "the ministry of the word is designed for the completing the number of these in the effectual calling; and for the perfecting of the whole body of the church, by gathering in all that belong to it, and of every particular saint, who is regenerated and sanctified by the Spirit of God."

illegitimate and not sons. 9 Furthermore, we have had human fathers who corrected us, and we paid them respect. Shall we not much more readily be in subjection to the Father of spirits and live? 10 For they indeed for a few days chastened us as seemed best to them, but He for our profit, that we may be partakers of His holiness. 11 Now no chastening seems to be joyful for the present, but painful; nevertheless, afterward it yields the peaceable fruit of righteousness to those who have been trained by it.

The author of Hebrews reminds Christians that their sufferings are tokens of God's fatherly love and care. Those adopted into Christ's household must endure God's Fatherly chastening. This is part and parcel of God's refining work in the life of one He has regenerated and called to live within His covenant community. God's refining process is so that His Son will be more clearly displayed in us. Refinement is not acceptance by God but fellowship with Him. The work of His Son has already made us acceptable – if we can apprehend that by faith. Hebrews 12:10 teaches us that our earthly fathers "chastened us as seemed best to them, but He for our profit, that we may be partakers of His holiness." Therefore, God's refinement process, which we call sanctification, is the work of God, which we must yield to and endure so that we may glorify God by bearing the fruit of the Spirit – the character of Christ. Whereas there is no sanctification without greater conformity to the truth, there is no greater conformity to the truth without knowledge to the word.

The Scriptures characterize God's presence as a consuming fire (Dt 4:14; Heb 12:29). As God is a consuming fire, what might we ask is consumed by Him? All causes of sin and what may proceed from sin, what may be figuratively called wood, hay or stubble (1 Cor 3:13). And the prophet Isaiah poses for us a similar question when he asks: "Who among us shall dwell with the devouring fire? Who among us shall dwell with everlasting burnings" (Is 33:14)? And David answers, all men whose hearts have been purified by faith in the Redeemer; whose hands are kept clean from sin and every form of idolatry (Ps 24:3-6, cf. Ps 15). Men to whom this characterizes are the adopted sons of God, who live in mount Zion, His holy tabernacle and undergo the fiery refinement of God's love (Ps 15:1; 24:3).[8]

In Malachi, God gives an answer to the wearisome words of the people, as spoken by the prophet Malachi who said, "Where is the God of justice" (Mal 2:17)? And God replies,

"Behold, I send My messenger, and he will prepare the way before Me. And the Lord, whom you seek, will suddenly come to His temple, even the Messenger of the covenant, in whom you delight. Behold, He is coming," Says the Lord of hosts (Mal 3:1).

This Messenger of the covenant, Jesus Christ, will bring God's justice, as Isaiah says, "Behold! My Servant whom I uphold, My Elect One in whom My soul delights! I have put My Spirit upon Him; He will bring forth *justice* to the nations" (Is 42:1, emphasis added, cf. Mt 12:18). The word *justice*, in Hebrew מִשְׁפָּט *mishpat* is also translated *judgment*, meaning a verdict, a decision rendered, a separating, a trial, a contest, along with a well-ordered state. Calvin's comments on John 12:31, "Now is the judgment of this world; now the ruler of this world will be cast out," is quite beneficial at this point. He writes,

Now we know, that out (outside) of Christ there is nothing but confusion in the world; and though Christ had already begun to erect the kingdom of God, yet his death was the commencement of a well-regulated condition, and the full restoration of the world. Yet it must also be observed, that this proper arrangement cannot be established in the world, until the kingdom of Satan be first destroyed, until the flesh, and everything opposed to the righteousness of God, be reduced to nothing. Lastly, the renovation of the world must be preceded by mortification. Accordingly, Christ declares: Now shall the prince of this world be cast out; for the confusion and deformity arise from this, that while Satan usurps tyrannical dominion, iniquity everywhere abounds. When Satan has been cast out, therefore, the world is brought back from its revolt, and placed under obedience to the government of God. It may be asked, how was Satan cast out by the death of Christ, since he does not cease to make war continually? I reply, this casting out must not be limited to any short period of

---

[8] Tabernacle, hill and mountain are used interchangeably.

time, but is a description of that remarkable effect of the death of Christ which is daily manifested.[9]

Jesus Christ, God's Messenger of the covenant, brings God's judgment on Satan's kingdom and establishes God's just order (justice), in the kingdom of God (Mt 12:28-29; 1 Jn 3:8). Christ's coming affects a separation (Mt 10:34); a sifting (Hag 2:6-7), and winnowing (Is 41:15-16; Mt 3:12) trial. This is the now and the not yet of the kingdom.[10] God is a consuming fire. "Behold, He is coming, says the Lord of hosts" (Mal 3:1). And Malachi asks us, "But who can endure the day of His coming? And who can stand when He appears? For He is like a refiner's fire and like launderers' soap" (Mal 3:2).

Jesus, the Messenger of the covenant, enacts judgment on Satan and his kingdom, bringing true life, light, order out of chaos (kingdom of God), through His incarnation, life, ministry, death, resurrection, ascension, and intercession. "For Christ was manifested to destroy the works of the devil," so that "through death He might destroy him who had the power of death, that is, the devil, and release those who through fear of death were all their lifetime subject to bondage" (1 Jn 3:8; Heb 2:14-15). Satan was dealt a mortal blow by Christ's death and resurrection. And though the devil has been defeated, he can still oppress the saints.[11]

The biblical point being made here is, Jesus Christ, the Messenger of the covenant, delivers everyone who believes in Him from God's wrath (1 Thess 1:10). God, adopting them into His family (Eph 1:5), brings them into covenant fellowship with Him and His Son (1 Jn 1:3), where they endure God's Fatherly chastening (if they are indeed genuine believers), so that they may glorify God by bearing the fruit of the Spirit – the character of Christ. "Christ gave Himself for us, that He might redeem us from every lawless deed and

---

[9] Calvin, Commentary on John 12:31.

[10] See concept will be developed more in the next two chapters but let a word now be said. The kingdom of God is God's present reign Christians experience in this world and more fully in the next. It includes God's rule in the individual soul. It is both a present reality and future hope.

[11] Beale, Revelation, 680.

Chapter 8: Biblical Discipleship

purify for Himself His own special people, zealous for good works" (Tit 2:11-14, emphasis added). This about being made holy. This is all about discipleship. Jesus said, "If anyone desires to come after Me (be My disciple), let him deny himself, and take up his cross, and follow Me" (Mt 16:24). "The peace of Jesus is the cross. But the cross is the sword God wields on earth. It creates division."[12]

At this point, it may be beneficial to say a word about afflictions. God's purpose in afflictions is two-fold: either a (1) refining chastisement unto purifying holiness and obedience for believers, or (2) a punishing prejudgment unto hardening obstinacy for unbelievers. These concepts will be further developed throughout the remainder of the book. Ultimately, the purpose for all Christian discipline, suffering, afflictions, and persecutions is to glorify God and to witness the saving power of Christ's cross.

Now when we look back at Malachi, we will see that Jesus is the Refiner of the saints. Malachi tells us,

"But who can endure the day of His coming? And who can stand when He appears? For He is like a *refiner's fire* and like *launderers' soap*. 3 He will sit as a *refiner* and a *purifier* of silver; He will *purify* the sons of Levi, and *purge* them as gold and silver, *that they may offer to the Lord an offering in righteousness.* 4 "Then the offering of Judah and Jerusalem will be pleasant to the Lord, as in the days of old, as in former years. 5 *And I will come near you for judgment;* I will be a swift witness against sorcerers, against adulterers, against perjurers, against those who exploit wage earners and widows and orphans, and against those who turn away an alien—because they do not fear Me," Says the Lord of hosts. 6 "For I am the Lord, I do not change; therefore you are not consumed, O sons of Jacob" (Mal 3:2-6, emphasis added).

God is a consuming fire! Christ says, now is the judgment of this world (Jn 12:31). Now is the judgment, the decision, the sentence of condemnation for this world. Now the ruler of this world will be cast out. *Condemnation is both the declaration of God, and the process of His judgment.*[13] Christ

---

[12] Bonhoeffer, The Cost of Discipleship, 219.
[13] See page 139.

brings salvation through judgment.[14] Christ says "I will come near you for judgment" (Mal 3:5). In light of this Scripture we also understand two important truths: (1) Christ has already absorbed the wrath of God for everyone that believes in Him (Jn 3:16, 34-35); and (2) there remains yet a future judgment where everyone who is not included in Christ will suffer an eternal punishment. If we know not Christ as Savior, we will know Him as Judge.

For He is also like launderers' soap. Christ washes every believer white as snow with His own blood, cleansing us from all unrighteousness (Is 1:18; 1 Jn 1:9). It is for this reason only that we may stand in His fiery presence, enduring His refining fire (Mal 3:6). The judgment of God comes upon believers in order to test and refine their faith, never for condemnation (1 Pet 1:3).

Before Malachi, Isaiah the prophet similarly prophesies the work of God's Messenger of the covenant. Isaiah laments that the faithful city had become a harlot (Is 1:21)! The people of Israel had turned to idolatry; the worship of whatever human beings can make with their hearts and hands.[15] Silver represents worship as gold represents faith. And because idolatry claims the loyalty that belongs to God alone, God battles against all forms of it, and calls us to join Him in that conflict. Isaiah metaphorically refers to idolatry as dross (Is 1:22). Dross is a particular scum that forms on the surface of molten metal. And the Lord declares, "I will turn My hand against you, and *thoroughly purge away your dross*, and take away all your alloy. I will restore your judges as at the first, and your counselors as at the beginning. Afterward you shall be called *the city of righteousness, the faithful city*" (Is 1:25-26, emphasis added). Both passages in Malachi 3 and Isaiah 1 refer to the refining work of the Son of God, Who brings salvation through judgment; purifying us from dead works (Is 64:6; Heb 9:14).

Consider also Psalm 12 which states, "The words of the Lord are pure words, like silver tried in a furnace of earth, purified seven times. You shall keep them, O Lord, You shall

---

[14] This is James M. Hamilton Jr.'s thesis from his excellent book *God's Glory in Salvation Through Judgment.*

[15] See page 168.

preserve them from this generation forever" (Ps 12:6-7). In other words, we are a furnace of earth, being made out of the dust of the ground. And God's holy Word refines us from the inside out until completion (seven times). And just what is the purpose for God's refining? It is as Malachi 3:3 declares, "He will purify the sons of Levi, and purge them as gold and silver, *that they may offer to the Lord an offering in righteousness* (emphasis added).

Israel's worship of God had degenerated into idolatrous traditions of men.[16] Jesus comes and restores true worship by: gathering the outcasts of Israel by redeeming them from death and establishing them as a kingdom of priests, who, as they are continuously being refined, are enabled to offer up themselves as living sacrifice – spiritual sacrifices acceptable to God through Jesus Christ, so that they may proclaim the praises of Him who called them out of darkness into His marvelous light, which saves the lost and glorifies God (Is 56:3-8; Jn 3:16, 34-35; 6:37-40; Rom 12:1-2; 1 Pet 2:5; 9).

A great word of comfort in all this talk about fire is found in Malachi 3:6, "For I am the Lord, I do not change; therefore you are not *consumed*, O sons of Jacob." Likewise, Psalm 12 we quoted earlier says, "You shall keep them, O Lord, *You shall preserve them* from this generation forever" (Ps 12:7, emphasis added). And the reason why we are not destroyed is because Jesus Christ is the same yesterday, today, and forever (Heb 1:8; 13:8). His promises do not change. Jesus said, "My sheep hear My voice, and I know them, and they follow Me. And I give them eternal life, *and they shall never perish*; neither shall anyone snatch them out of My hand. (Jn 10:27-28, emphasis added). God says, "When you walk through the fire, you shall not be burned, nor shall the flame scorch you" (Is 43:2).

God's refining fire is an expression of his love, never His wrath. His judgment begins with his own people, and then consumes unbelievers (1 Pet 4:17). And only the man who can endure the refining fire of God's holy presence can remain in God's house forever (Jn 8:35). As Thomas Watson put it, "No

---

[16] Isaiah 29:13; Mark 7:7-13; Matthew 15:9; Acts 7:37-53. See the discipline of worship pp. 216-219.

vessel can be made of gold without fire; so it is impossible that we can be made vessels of honor, unless we are melted and refined in the furnace of affliction."[17]

The following anonymous story draws some insightful reflections upon this subject:

Some time ago, a few ladies met to study the Scriptures. While reading the third chapter of Malachi, they came upon a remarkable expression in the third verse: "And He shall sit as a refiner and purifier of silver" (Mal 3:3). One lady decided to visit a silversmith, and report to the others on what he said about the subject. She went accordingly, and without telling him the reason for her visit, begged the silversmith to tell her about the process of refining silver. After he had fully described it to her, she asked, "Sir, do you sit while the work of refining is going on?" "Oh, yes ma'am," replied the silversmith; "I must sit and watch the furnace constantly, for, if the time necessary for refining is exceeded in the slightest degree, the silver will be injured." The lady at once saw the beauty and comfort of the expression, "He shall sit as a refiner and purifier of silver." God sees it necessary to put His children into the furnace; but His eye is steadily intent on the work of purifying, and His wisdom and love are both engaged in the best manner for us. Our trials do not come at random, and He will not let us be tested beyond what we can endure. Before she left, the lady asked one final question, "How do you know when the process is complete?" "That's quite simple," replied the silversmith. "When I can see my own image in the silver, the refining process is finished."

And God's Word says, "Take away the dross from silver, and it will go to the silversmith for jewelry. Take away the wicked from before the king, and his throne will be established in righteousness" (Pro 25:4-5).

Everything we have discussed so far regarding God's Messenger of the covenant bringing salvation through judgment, refining chastisement unto purifying holiness and obedience or punishing prejudgment unto hardening obstinacy is vividly portrayed by Zechariah the prophet. He declares,

7 "Awake, O sword, against My Shepherd, against the Man who is My Companion," says the Lord of hosts. "Strike the Shepherd, and the sheep will be scattered; then I will turn My hand against the little

---

[17] Watson, All Things For Good, 26.

ones. 8 And it shall come to pass in all the land," says the Lord, "That two-thirds in it shall be cut off and die, but one–third shall be left in it: 9 *I will bring the one–third through the fire, will refine them as silver is refined, and test them as gold is tested.* They will call on My name, and I will answer them. I will say, 'This is My people'; and each one will say, 'The Lord is my God'" (Zech 13:7-9, cf. Mt 26:31, emphasis added).

God refines His people. His purpose is so His Son will be more clearly displayed in us. Therefore He prunes, if I may mix metaphors, and beatifies His people so He may present a pure spotless bride to Christ (Eph 5:27; Rev 19:7). And the local church is the place He has prescribed for this work. As has been said, it takes a church to make a disciple.

Tests to Discipleship

God is a consuming fire – He tests the genuineness of our faith. To remain in His fiery presence we must endure His sanctifying work. The test is whether or not you can endure God's discipline. His discipline benefits us so that we may share His holiness in a moral sense. In Scripture I find three tests of discipleship. We should discuss these so as to gain an appreciation for the manner in which God recovers wondering sheep. Here are the three tests:

1. Can we endure the Refiner's fire?
2. Can we endure God's correction by way of His leaders?
3. Can we endure God's correction by way of fellow believers?

The believer lives, in a way, between two paradoxical bookends: the first, which declares, "Whoever has been born of God does not sin, for His seed remains in him; and he cannot sin, because he has been born of God" (1 Jn 3:9), and the other that states, "If we say that we have no sin, we deceive ourselves, and the truth is not in us. If we confess our sins, He is faithful and just to forgive us our sins and to cleanse us from all unrighteousness. If we say that we have not sinned, we make Him a liar, and His word is not in us" (1 Jn 1:8-10). Whereas, in the first Scripture, by virtue of regeneration, believers are no longer under the condemning power and dominion of sin, and so will not make a practice of sinning – though they daily commit sin (Rom 7:14-25). The point being, those who are born again do not live in unconfessed sin. However, let me be quick to point out, the moment we first repent of our sins and trust in Christ for salvation is the moment we are saved. A man can never be, as Spurgeon put it, any more justified, than when we first believed.

The second, declares that those who are united with Christ through faith, having fellowship with Him and fellow believers will freely and willingly demonstrate that reality by confessing their sin to God and one another (Jms 5:16). Believers in Christ are, as Luther put it, *simil iustus et peccator* – at the same time justified and a sinner.

The biblical point being made here is this: the fact that God has removed the penalty for our sins at conversion (Eph 1:7; 4:32; Col 2:13) does not remove the necessity of confessing our sins frequently (1 Jn 1:1:8-10). Again, the issue is not acceptance by God but fellowship with Him. Christ's perfect finished work, which we may apprehend by repentance and faith in His name, makes us acceptable as members of God's family. And because of our sin nature, we will continue to sin but repentance enables us to experience intimate fellowship as sons within God's family (1 Jn 1:3-2:2; Heb 7:25); the Spirit Himself restraining the lusting of sin (Jms 4:5).

In God's house we learn from Christ as He is presented to us through God's appointed means of grace. According to John Calvin, God "uses the ministry of men, by making them, as it were, His substitutes, not by transferring His right and honor to them, but only doing His own work by their lips, just as an artificer (skilled craftsman) uses a tool for any purpose."[18] Christians are taught, ruled, and protected by Christ through the plurality of His chosen servants, which we in the local churches recognize and ordain to the ministry.[19]

God's judgment is mediated through human means. Sin, in whatever form, is not to be tolerated within the covenant

---

[18] Calvin, Institutes of the Christian Religion, Book Four, Chapter 3.1, 700.
[19] See chapter 6.

community. Christ, by way of His under shepherds, *disciplines* us, requiring of us to respond positively to their corrective word as it were His. *Thus, God, making use of means, works to purify His saints.* As a father teaches a child to control himself, obey authority, and to fear and love God, so does our Heavenly Father when He adopts us and allows us to live in His household.

As was said earlier, God's desire is for His people to want holiness; to be like Jesus. And that it is why it is absolutely imperative that discipleship take place in the local church because it's in the church where we are to be equipped and taught (means of grace). *The first and foremost test of discipleship is whether or not we can endure the Refiner's fire?* Can we endure God's fiery presence? If not, we fail the test and demonstrate by our disobedience our sham discipleship. If men assume the title of the people of God, without being so in deed and in truth, they gain nothing by their self-delusion.[20] And we will see that God makes use of others to mediate discipline. Christ leaves the ninety-nine sheep and recovers the one who goes astray (Mt18:10-14).

Augustine, when reflecting on the folly of going astray writes,

> But at that time, in my wretchedness, I loved to grieve; and I sought for things to grieve about. In another man's misery, even though it was feigned and impersonated on the stage, that performance of the actor pleased me best and attracted me most powerfully which moved me to tears. What marvel then was it that an unhappy sheep, straying from thy flock and impatient of thy care, I became infected with a foul disease?[21]

Augustine had grown impatient and left Christ's flock, only to suffer God's chastising temporal judgments. These are God's way of allowing believers to experience fiery trials and afflictions in order to bring them back to repentant obedience and fellowship. The word temporal is derived from Latin and has to do with time as opposed to eternity; with earthly life as opposed to heavenly existence. Christ brings temporal

---

[20] Calvin, Commentary on Psalm 15.
[21] Augustine, The Confessions, Book Three, Chapter 2, 39.

judgments upon churches and even individuals, but when we undergo temporal judgment we are chastened by the Lord, so that we will not be condemned along with the world (1 Cor 11:32, cf. Rev 2:22). Christ corrects us as He is our Lord. And this correction shows that we are His legitimate children (Heb 12:11).

It's interesting to note that Augustine's conscience was so deeply troubled by his sin that he saw it wherever he went, being constantly reminded of it – "In another man's misery."[22] It's as Calvin says, "the reprobate, as they know not that they are governed by God's hand, for the most part think that afflictions come by chance," but, "everyone who knows and is persuaded that he is chastised by God, must immediately be led to this thought, that he is chastised because he is loved by God." God's corrections are parental when we obediently submit to them.

This brings us to consider our second test: *can we endure God's correction by way of His leaders?* Most of these ideas have been covered in previous chapters but it would be good to highlight some examples.[23] We are now discussing the lost holy practice of church discipline. And we must bear in mind its purpose – the restoration of a sinning brother. MacArthur skillfully frames the parameters by writing, "The goal of church discipline is not to throw people out, embarrass them, be self-righteous, play God, or exercise authority and power in some unbiblical manner. The purpose of discipline is to bring people back into pure fellowship with God and others in the assembly."[24]

In Psalm 141, David's plea is that his words not dishonor God, or make others stumble (Ps 119:165; Lk 17:1). That he may not, through his own fallen nature, and the continuous provocations of his enemies, sin by speaking anything distrustful of God's preserving providence; anything that might be envious or impenitent. David knows full well that the mouth speaks what the heart is full of (Pro 4:23; Lk 6:45). His petitioning prayer in verse four turns inward, beseeching God

---

[22] See conscience on pp 93-94.
[23] See Spiritual Leaders chapter 6.
[24] MacArthur, The Master's Plan for the Church, 267.

for the restraining power of His Spirit, so that his heart may not be inclined to any evil.

David's desire is for God to restrain the power of his sin nature, thereby giving the Spirit lease to use his mind, speech, and actions for God's glory. The effect of his prayer in verses one through four is to say, my whole life is an offering to You. Whatever it takes for You to make me holy in thought, word, and deed (protection from inner wickedness) – God do it.

David is so committed to God, and desirous of holiness that he prays, I want to be conformed to your perfect nature, even if it means being rebuked by a friend (Ps 141:5). God's desire is for His people to want this conformity. God makes use of means in His corrective work of transformation, chastening every son He receives, correcting those whom He loves (Pro 3:11-12; Heb 12:3-11). In His transformative work, as has been said, God makes use of other men and women to be corrective, chastening instruments in the life of the saint.

Therefore, David welcomes a righteous man's rebuke as he would a holy kiss but rejects the kisses of the wicked (Ps 141:5). While Satan tempts the wicked by his allurements, they, at the same time, deceive one another by flattery, which leads David to declare, that he would much rather be awakened to his duty by the severe rod of reproof, than be seduced through pleasing falsehoods.[25] David is welcome to God's Fatherly correction at the hands of a righteous man, but in the same breath calls upon God for justice.[26]

And who can forget how Nathan the prophet drew out David's confession with a parable (2 Sam 12:1-15). God expects those who call themselves believers to demonstrate it by submitting to the leaders in the church (Heb 13:17). This is for our good.

And this brings us to our third test of discipleship: *can we endure God's correction by means of fellow believers*? This is perhaps the more difficult of the three. Why? Probably because most feel it's the responsibility of the elders and deacons to address issues of sin in the church. And they're

---

[25] Calvin, Commentary on Psalm 141.
[26] The topic of imprecation will be discussed in chapter 10.

right. It is the primary responsibility for the leaders of the church to do so. That is why an elder is called an over-seer.[27]

As has been said, the authority Peter is entrusted with in Matthew 16:19, binding and loosing, is given to the other apostles in Matthew 18:18-20. Likewise, "As to the exercise of this authority," writes Hendriksen, "the local congregation must not be ignored" (Mt 18:17). The power of the keys, the task of binding and loosing, has from the outset been committed to the entire church and not just Peter or the other apostles (confer Mt 16:19 with Mt 18:18-20; 1 Cor 5:1-5; 1 Cor 5:12-13; 2 Cor 2:6-8; 1 Tim 1:20).

In Matthew 18, Jesus teaches His disciples how to act when a brother or sister has wandered from the Shepherd and the fold. In the preceding discourse (Mt 18:1-14), Jesus establishes the kingdom principles of the least is the greatest (Mt 18:3-4), and especially important: the humble disciple will be careful not to put a stumbling block in the path of another disciple (Mt 18: 6-7).

Matthew 18:15-17 is the central governing passage for church discipline. It states, "Moreover if your brother sins against you, go and tell him his fault between you and him alone. If he hears you, *you have gained your brother*. "But if he will not hear, take with you one or two more, that 'by the mouth of two or three witnesses every word may be established.' And if he refuses to hear them, tell it to the church. But if he refuses even to hear the church, let him be to you like a heathen and a tax collector" (Mt 18:16-17, emphasis added). Regarding the two ways our brother may sin: (1) directly – they have committed a sin against us personally, such as, they have lied to us, stole from us, etc.; and (2) in indirectly – they have brought reproach on the assembly. Both require of us to forgive as long as our brother repents (Mt 18:22).

Observe how in Matthew 18:15 if our brother hears us we have "gained" him. The Greek word *kerdaino* refers to acquiring wealth, revealing the treasure we have recovered – our brother. James 5:19-20 teaches us, "Brethren, if anyone among you wanders from the truth, and someone turns him

---

[27] See pastors and elders pp 288-291.

back, let him know that he who turns a sinner from the error of his way will save a soul from death and cover a multitude of sins." And Galatians 6:1 tells us, "Brethren, if a man is overtaken in any trespass, you who are spiritual restore such a one in a spirit of gentleness, considering yourself lest you also be tempted."

Sin is not to be tolerated within the local church. And if it goes unchecked, God will hold the whole local church accountable (Heb 13:17; Rev 2:22). But just how this is to be dealt with when noticed is with sensitivity, the minimal amount of publicity, and the recovery of the sinning believer as the goal.

Regarding the recovery of an erring brother, there are mainly two things which are occurring: God is afflicting the sinning brother in some way (by way of his troubled conscience and perhaps temporal judgments), and the church is providing a voice (in love) to how God disapproves of the erring brother's sin. And in this way, the erring brother, detecting this transformative work of God, receives this corrective love, grows in grace and in the knowledge of God, by receiving God's correction from others (Pro 27:6). The whole enterprise can prove difficult, but if we love them we'll do it. It's as Carson puts it, "if it is hard to accept a rebuke, even a private one, it is harder still to administer one in loving humility." [28]

Let's look at how this plays out in a 'congregational' setting. Chapter nine of the Book of Proverbs presents us with two rival banquets: wisdom and folly (Pro 9:1-18).

9 Wisdom has built her house,
She has hewn out her seven pillars;
2 She has slaughtered her meat,
She has mixed her wine,
She has also furnished her table.
3 She has sent out her maidens,
She cries out from the highest places of the city,
4 *"Whoever is simple, let him turn in here!"*
As for him who lacks understanding, she says to him,
5 "Come, eat of my bread

---

[28] Carson, Matthew, 402.

Chapter 8: Biblical Discipleship

And drink of the wine I have mixed.
6 Forsake foolishness and live,
And go in the way of understanding.

7 *"He who corrects a scoffer gets shame for himself,*
And he who rebukes a wicked man only harms himself.
8 *Do not correct a scoffer, lest he hate you;*
Rebuke a wise man, and he will love you.
9 *Give instruction to a wise man, and he will be still wiser;*
Teach a just man, and he will increase in learning.

10 "The fear of the Lord is the beginning of wisdom,
And the knowledge of the Holy One is understanding.
11 For by me your days will be multiplied,
And years of life will be added to you.
12 If you are wise, you are wise for yourself,
And if you scoff, you will bear it alone."

13 A foolish woman is clamorous;
She is simple, and knows nothing.
14 For she sits at the door of her house,
On a seat by the highest places of the city,
15 To call to those who pass by,
Who go straight on their way:
16 "Whoever is simple, let him turn in here";
And as for him who lacks understanding, she says to him,
17 "Stolen water is sweet,
And bread eaten in secret is pleasant."
18 But he does not know that the dead are there,
That her guests are in the depths of hell (emphasis added).

Without embarking on a full-scale exposition of this passage, it is nonetheless beneficial for us to stop and note several weighty matters: First, the similarity and relevance to Christ's parable of the wedding feast is unmistakable (Mt 22:1-14). Only those who "turn" *ekklino* (as in 1 Pet 3:11), "away from evil" entering the King's palace on His terms may remain, viz., having on a wedding garment – the righteousness of Christ (Mt 22:11-14). Second, there are numerous similarities between the two women in the proverb.[29]

---

[29] (1) They both give speeches from the highest point of the city (vv. 3, 14); (2) they both speak to the same audience (vv. 4, 16); (3) they both offer food (vv. 5, 17); and (4) they both make promises (vv. 5-6, 17). Verses 5-6

Chapter 8: Biblical Discipleship

And third, verses 7-9 present us with two responses to a loving rebuke. Wisdom bids us rightly apply spiritual discernment regarding the over-arching aim of doing everything decently and in order, so as to recover an erring brother. In doing this, we are to make a correct assessment of the person as to whether they exhibit the character of the wise or the wicked; mocker or scoffer are synonyms for the wicked (Pro 9:7, cf. Ps 1:1). Pro 9:8 tells us, "Do not correct a scoffer, lest he hate you." A scoffer or mocker, is characterized by pride and arrogance (Pro 21:24). Bruce Walke astutely writes,

Wisdom admonishes the gullible, for they are still impressionable and even credulous, but a mocker (scoffer) is so full of himself and contemptuous of others that he will not humble himself under any authority, not even that of the Lord. Consequently, the disciplinarian of the mocker gets shame or insults. This opprobrium comes either from imprudently wasting time and energy on a futile cause or, more probably, to judge from verse 8, from the mocker himself, who, because of his hatred has been aroused, verbally attacks and publically humiliates the wise.[30]

So, we are to avoid applying biblical correction in the church? By no means! Proverbs 9:7-9 is not saying that the wicked should not be rebuked, but that we should not be surprised by receiving hate in return for a loving rebuke, and little to no genuine reparation. Jesus teaches us how to act when a brother or sister has wandered from the fold of God. Every man that experiences the saving power of God should be open to God's fatherly disciplines when it comes at the hands of those he shares fellowship with. Thus, when the secrets of the wise man's heart is made manifest to his brethren, it will result in repentance and renewed fellowship (1 Cor 14:25; Heb 4:11-13).

I have always been struck by the poetic polarity in Proverbs 9:8, Do not correct a scoffer, lest he hate you; rebuke a wise

---

represent Christ's promise that He will sup forever with those who enter at the narrow gate (Mt 7:13; Rev 3:20). This juxtaposes the choice mankind must make between good and evil, the straight and crooked paths, true and false religion, the worship of the One true God and idolatry.

[30] Walke, The Book of proverbs, Chapters 1-15, 440. This is an excellent resource for the Book of Proverbs.

man, and he will love you. Though loving correction is offered to the wicked, they reject the overture, and despise you (Lk 14:15-24). Even something like, "please don't allow your child to bring their cellphone to children's church, it's distracting to others." If wisdom is rejected this will not be acquiesced to; Love's Labor's Lost. Even if grace is shown to the wicked, they will not learn righteousness, they will fail the test of discipleship because they cannot accept God's discipline by the hand of His people (Is 26:10). It is for this reason we must distance ourselves from holding on to bitterness. If we cannot endure God's Fatherly chastisements, then we demonstrate to all our sham religion.

On the contrary, "rebuke" a wise man, and he will love you. And verse 9 adds, "Give instruction to a wise man, and he will be still wiser; teach a just man, and he will increase in learning." The man who accepts the rebuke of wisdom shows himself to be wise. The man who loves the Lord, delights in His discipline, and can say along with David, Let the bones You have broken rejoice" (Ps 51:8). For God's discipline "yields the peaceable fruit of righteousness to those who have been trained by it" (Heb 12:11).

As a congregation, Christians are called to be submissive to each other: younger people to the older men in the church (1 Pet 5:5), women to their husbands (1 Pet 3:1), younger women to older women (Tit 2:3-4), and children to their parents and those older (Eph 6:1-3). And all Christians, regardless of age, should put on humility as a garment. These are the basic qualities of a sound church (Tit 2:1-10). It is in this atmosphere of mutual submission to Christ and others that discipleship becomes a reality.

Judge not?

But what about judging? Aren't Christians to avoid that sort of thing? Jesus told us to "judge not lest we be judged," but likewise He said, "Do not give what is holy to the dogs; nor cast your pearls before swine, lest they trample them under their feet, and turn and tear you in pieces (Mt 7:1, 6). So what would Christ have us do? As Lloyd-Jones writes, "Merely to look at the word 'judge' cannot satisfy us at this point. It has

349

many different meanings so it cannot be decided that way."[31]
This whole matter is a study of its own. The key to what Jesus
means comes to us from the Gospel of John. Jesus says, "Do
not *judge* according to appearance, but *judge* with righteous
judgment" (Jn 7:24, emphasis added). Meaning, we are not to
pronounce damnatory sentences on people, that's God's
prerogative for people who reject Christ. Instead, we are to
make a right assessment of a person's heart, and if need be call
them to repentance (Mt 18:15-20). "Do not judge according to
appearance, but judge with righteous judgment" (Jn 7:24).

D.A. Carson cogently explains this Scripture,

In an age when Matthew 7:1('Do not judge or you too will be
judged') has displaced John 3:16 as the only verse in the Bible the
man in the street is likely to know, it is probably worth adding that
Matthew 7:1 forbids judgmentalism, not moral discernment. By
contrast, John 7:24 demands moral and theological discernment in the
context of obedient faith (7:17), while excoriating self-righteous
legalism and offering no sanction for censorious heresy-hunting.[32]

Christian's aren't to be judgmental Pharisees but they are to
make judgment calls. They are to be humble Christ-loving
fruit inspectors not prideful self-righteous mote-hunters. This
is what the risen Christ commanded the church at Thyatira to
do because of sexual immorality and false prophecy that they
were allowing to go on unchecked (Rev 2:20-25). Christ
warned the church at Thyatira, and all of His churches, that if
they didn't do something about it He would. To love someone
enough to admonish them for sinning isn't easy, it's a labor of
love. We cannot let sin go unchecked in the church. A failure
to do so brings the guilt of sin on the whole church.

The Corinthian Church Example

There is a well-known example we have in 1 Corinthians
chapter five regarding ongoing impenitent immorality – much
like that in Thyatira. The apostle Paul writes, "It is actually

---

[31] Lloyd-Jones, Studies in the Sermon on the Mount, 427.
[32] Carson, The Gospel According to John, 317. This is by far one of the best
commentaries on John's Gospel.

reported that there is sexual immorality among you, and such sexual immorality as is not even named among the Gentiles— that a man has his father's wife! And you are puffed up, and have not rather mourned, that he who has done this deed might be taken away from among you" (1 Cor 5:1-2). Paul says, a man in your congregation is sleeping with his step mother and you are allowing this to go on unchecked! And this sort of debauchery isn't even committed by the unsaved!

Here is a large church content to say in effect, "Christ died for our sins, therefore we can sin and grace will abound" (Rom 6:1). The Corinthian church lacked a passion for truth, holiness and humility. But eternal life is the outcome of Christ's work from beginning to end (Rom 6:1, 22; 8:29-30; Phil 2:12-13). The proof of God's pardon of our sins, is a life that is passionate for the purity of holiness. The time for church discipline has come. Paul calls on the church to make a judgment regarding this case of unrepentant immorality, and says, "Deliver such a one to Satan for the destruction of the flesh, that his spirit may be saved in the day of the Lord Jesus" (1 Cor 5:5).

We mustn't fail to remember the goal of church discipline – a spiritual act so that something good may come, namely the recovery of an erring brother. A pulling of them as it were out of the fire (Jude 1:22). The Bible tells us that we are to discipline in love in the hope of saving the impenitent brothers soul (1 Cor 5:5). Paul's intent is to avoid the chastening hand of the Lord, which will indeed fall upon the whole congregation unless this case of brazen rebelliousness is removed. Paul's command to "deliver such a one to Satan" is an act of excommunication. This has a parallel in the pastoral epistle of 1 Timothy when Paul writes, "Of whom are Hymenaeus and Alexander, whom I delivered to Satan that they may learn not to blaspheme" (1 Tim 1:20). The phrase "deliver such a one to Satan" probably indicates that the realm outside the fellowship of the church is regarded as Satan's sphere, and the immoral man must be consigned to that by a solemn act of the congregation."[33] The unrepentant man was

---

[33] Jackman, Let's Study 1 Corinthians, 85.

handed back to the world, where Satan rules and deals death.[34]
And Gordon Fee writes, "What the grammar suggests is, then,
is that the 'destruction of his flesh' is the anticipated result of
the man's being (sic) put back out into Satan's domain, while
the express purpose of the action is his redemption."[35] What
must not be overlooked in all this is the goal which is not to
punish but to restore. When the church exercises discipline, it
is not to function like an inquisition. As to the purpose of
discipline, Bonhoeffer observes,

Is not to establish a community of the perfect, but a community
consisting of men who really live under the forgiving mercy of God.
Discipline in a congregation is a servant of the precious grace of God.
If a member of the Church falls into sin, he must be admonished and
punished, lest he forfeit his own salvation and the gospel be
discredited.[36]

The biblical point being made here is: it is more loving to
send a man out of fellowship, so that he might be brought to
his senses, than for the church to tolerate his unrepentant sin.
For the church is to be a community of those who readily
admit sin, who seek "what is that good and acceptable and
perfect will of God" (Rom 12:2). Because the Christian life is
defined by sincerity and truth (1 Cor 5:8), we are to no longer
live in sin but become a purified and holy people. God is a
consuming fire! He brought premature death on other
Corinthians for their improper conduct during the Lord's
Supper (1 Cor 11:30).

Paul's argument in the fifth chapter of 1 Corinthians is this:
Everyone who calls himself a believing brother, because he
fears God and knows what he has been saved from – eternal
destruction – will demonstrate his love for God in the manner
in which he willingly and whole-heartily, joyously obeys
God's commandments. And those who are living like the
world – unrepentant rebels – and call themselves believing
brothers he says to have no dealings with – not even a meal (1

---

[34] Bonhoeffer, The Cost of Discipleship, 329.
[35] Fee, The First Epistle to the Corinthians, 209.
[36] Bonhoeffer, The Cost of Discipleship, 325.

Chapter 8: Biblical Discipleship

Cor 5: 9-11). For outside are the dogs, the unrepentant rebels who scoff at God's commandments.

The apostle Paul says, "For what have I to do with judging those also who are outside? *Do you not judge those who are inside?* But those who are outside God judges. Therefore "put away from yourselves the evil person" (1 Cor 5:12-13, emphasis added). The answer to Paul's rhetorical question is yes. As Paul Kretzman tells us,

He that knows of the sin that has been committed should first approach the sinner and should try to gain his brother. If all his efforts fail, then he should take one or two witnesses along with him and repeat his attempt. Loving patience is essential at this point. But if every endeavor meets with the same obstinate resistance, then the matter must finally be brought to the attention of the congregation. And here again, all long-suffering must be employed, as long as there is any hope whatsoever of gaining the erring member. It is only when every effort proves futile that the resolution of excommunication should be passed.[37]

And like Bonhoeffer puts it, "excommunication is really nothing more than the recognition of a state of affairs which already exists, for the unrepentant sinner has condemned himself already (Tit 3:10), before the community had to exclude him. The sinner is ejected from the fellowship of the Body of Christ because he has already separated himself from it."[38]

The aim of such discipline is the recovery of erring brethren who, despite previous overtures of loving rebukes, failed to repent (Mt 18:15-17). The goal of church discipline is repentance, restoration, and readmittance. We find an example of this when we come to Paul's Second Epistle to the Corinthians, "This punishment which was inflicted by the majority is sufficient for such a man, so that, on the contrary, you ought rather to forgive and comfort him, lest perhaps such a one be swallowed up with too much sorrow. Therefore I urge you to reaffirm your love to him" (2 Cor 2:6-8).

---

[37] Kretzman, 1 Corinthians 5:9-13.
[38] Bonhoeffer, The Cost of Discipleship, 329.

Chapter 8: Biblical Discipleship

With pastoral delicacy, Paul, referring to the immoral man that was excommunicated by the church, now calls for a halt; enough has been done, and the object has been attained. Whether or not the immoral man accepted the discipline of the congregation we are not told. But it would seem that the erring brother had borne some measure of punishing sorrow for his sin (2 Cor 2:7). Paul now asks the church at Corinth to reaffirm their love to him lest with excessive sorrow such a one be swallowed up (2 Cor 2:8).

The biblical pattern of church discipline here states that as soon as a full and willing confession of sins has been made on the part of the erring brother or sister, they are to be readmitted to the congregation with the love of its members reaffirmed to them. For, unless the repentant sinner is given a full assurance of divine grace and pardon, he may give up all hope of salvation and turn from the Gospel with a heart forever embittered against Christ and the Christian Church.[39]

The fact that the church as a whole is shying away from this important part of what Jesus commands argues for the increasing worldliness of the Church, and is, to a large degree, an indication of disintegration. And a cause for demonic exuberance for the devil and his angels who would say that "a moderated religion is as good for us as no religion at all—and more amusing."[40]

"You shall not hate your brother in your heart. You shall surely rebuke your neighbor, and not bear sin because of him" (Lev 19:17). Even when the church must exercise the power of the keys in this way, it should be done in sorrow and in the hope that, the soul of the offender may yet be saved in the day of the Lord Jesus (Mt 18:18; 1Cor 5:4-5). For "in righteousness you shall judge your neighbor" (Lev 19:15).[41]

Personally, what keeps me from acting like a complete buffoon is not so much that I don't want to look idiotic but

---

[39] Kretzman, 1 Corinthians 5:9-13.

[40] Lewis, The Screwtape Letters, 41.

[41] If it be objected, that in this way God is made a sort of petty judge, who concurs in the sentence of mortal men, the reply is at hand. For when Christ maintains the authority of his Church, he does not diminish his own power or that of his Father, but, on the contrary, supports the majesty of his word (Calvin).

354

Chapter 8: Biblical Discipleship

because I know Christ saved me and I no longer live for myself but for Him (2 Cor 5:14-15). Learning to be like Jesus requires us to live with those He has saved. *God, making use of means, works to purify His saints.* This implies that sanctification is the work of God's purifying holiness in the life of one He has regenerated. The church is absolutely essential for discipleship because it is in the local church that we are equipped and taught. You cannot make a disciple without God's means of grace. Know fellowship – know discipleship; no fellowship – no discipleship.

It's as John White tells us, "Both fire and drought are part of God's disciplinary process. He trains, disciplines, shapes you as a runner in the race of faith, as a fighter in the warfare of faith. The training involves correction and pain. Your faith will increase or decrease according to how you respond to His intervention."[42]

We have already seen how God employs various means, both earthly and heavenly, both spatial and temporal. That is, He employs other men and women, along with supernatural spiritual beings, either evil or holy to be the corrective, chastening instruments in the life of the saint, in order to conform him to the image of Christ (Gal 4:19). These corrective instruments, be they benevolent or malevolent, serve to bring about the desired change at every stage of God's developmental process. Even if it's done in the wrong spirit, as when Shimei cursed David (2 Sam 16:5-8), God uses trials to shock believers back into the reality of their faith. Since Christ holds sway over the power of salvation and judgment,

Christ desires for discipleship to Him to encompass the totality of life. As such, our lives serve both as God's indictment on lawlessness, and the instrument for the gospel to be propagated (2 Cor 4-5). None of the spiritual disciplines we've discussed in previous chapters, (namely chapter four), can be accomplished alone; at least if they are to be genuine. We are in this together.

When it comes to obedience, there are generally speaking three types of people: the first person, whether it can be said they're obedient or not, will refrain from breaking the rules or

---

[42] White, The Fight, 112.

Chapter 8: Biblical Discipleship

laws for fear they will get caught and punished, costing them money and/or time. The second, refrain from breaking the rules or laws mainly out of pride, because they are above that sort of thing, and doing such a thing might jeopardize their social standing, along with of course, the accompanying penalties already mentioned. The third, and I might add much less common type, is the one, who, having experienced divine grace, desires to glorify God for Whom the rules and laws originate from (Rom 13:1-7).

Whereas, the first obeys, if we may use that term, out of fear, and while the second, obeys out of pride, the third obeys out of love – the reason why my parents disciplined me.

Principles for Discipleship

According to our first president, we should carefully select our friends. He bids us to "Be courteous to all, but intimate with few, and let those few be well tried before you give them your confidence. True friendship is a plant of slow growth, and must undergo and withstand the shocks of adversity before it is entitled to the appellation." In Christian fellowship we affect others. What you do affects me and vice versa. As has been said in the previous chapter, those in fellowship with one another and God enable each other to practice the truth, sharpening, as it were, one another's countenance – the totality of the person, their mind, will, and emotions, for the glory of God (Pro 27:17). We discussed how fellowship is imperative for Christian growth. Here, the emphasis is on the practical method of cultivating a life that is God-honoring.

William Gurnall writes in his classic *The Christian in Complete Armour,*

Get some Christian friend, whom thou mayest trust above others, to be thy faithful monitor. O, that man hath a great help for the maintaining the power of godliness, that has an open-hearted friend that dare speak his heart to him! A stander-by sees more sometimes by a man, than an actor can do by himself, and is more fit to judge of his actions than he of his own. Sometimes self-love blinds us in our cause, that we see not ourselves so bad as we are; and sometimes we are over-suspicious of the worst by ourselves, which makes us appear to ourselves worse than we are. Now, that thou mayest not deprive thyself of so great a help from thy friend, be sure to keep thy heart ready with meekness to receive, yea, with thankfulness to embrace, a reproof from his mouth. Those that cannot bear pain dealing hurt themselves most; for by this they seldom hear the truth. He that hath not love enough to give a reproof seasonably to his brother, nor humility enough to bear a reproof from him, is not worthy to be called a Christian: by the first he shows himself a 'hater of his brother' (Lev 19:17); by the second he proves himself a scorner (scoffer) – Proverbs 9.[43]

This is the very quintessence of iron sharpening iron – we are to be our brother's keeper. We are, as Scougal put it to be so possessed with divine love that our heart must be enlarged toward our brother, in a sincere and unbounded affection, that we would resent any evil that befalls him as it happened to ourselves.[44] God desires us to so crave a life of holiness that we would say along with David, "Let the righteous strike me; it shall be a kindness. And let him rebuke me; it shall be as excellent oil; let my head not refuse it" (Ps 141:5). And "Purge me with hyssop, and I shall be clean; wash me, and I shall be whiter than snow. Make me hear joy and gladness, that the bones You have broken may rejoice" (Ps 51:7-8).

Our desire as Christian men should be for God to restrain the power of our sin nature so that the Spirit may be free to use the totality of our being for God's glory (Col 3:17, 23). As we fall short, God disciplines us so that we will become spiritually mature, being conformed to the image of His Son, so that light of the Son will be more clearly displayed in those who desire the holy Life they have been brought into (Rom 7:13-25).

In light of the fact that a disciple is a follower of Christ, a person who has experienced the quickening power of the Holy Spirit, I find in the Bible at least three essential elements for discipleship: a disciple is *humble, hungry and honest.*

Humble (mind) – This is the quality of a God-honoring man who is capable of being shown he is wrong and admitting it. He is able to accept correction. A man who has this quality is

---

[43] Gurnall, The Christian in Complete Armour, 325.
[44] Scougal, The Life of God in the Soul of Man, 22, 46-47.

teachable and willing to learn (Pro 9:8-9; 2 Tim 2:24-26; 2 Thess 3:14-15; 1 Pet 1:13-16). In order to become spiritually mature in Christ a man must be vulnerable and teachable.

Hungry (emotion) – This is the quality of a God-honoring man who has a deep consciousness of his own need for personal purity. He willingly responds to loving rebuke because he senses in it the love of God. Above all, he desires to be holy; he desires to be like Jesus (Mt 5:6; 2 Cor 7:1).

Honest (will) – This is the quality of a God-honoring man who is committed to the truth. He is able to admit the truth no matter how painful or humiliating it may be. This is a man who wants to see the truth triumph (Eph 4:15).

Accountability

What these three principles are built upon is accountability. Accountability is the reciprocal principle to discipleship. It's the imperative to holy living. As we have seen, we are to be accountable to God's Word, His spiritual leaders, and each other in the local congregation. Christians must be accountable to each other if there is to be any genuine move toward spiritual maturity. I can say unquantifiably that everyone I know who has fallen in their Christian walk has failed to be accountable in some way.

Many a landmine has been stepped on by an unaccountable Christian man, who, confident of their own *spiritual arrivedness*, have fallen in extra-marital affairs or financial conundrum, et al. Without accountability, a fall is not far off. Wayne Mack states, "The plain, unvarnished truth is, that every one of us needs the accountability that comes from formal, regular, intimate relationships with other godly people."[45]

As Alfred North Whitehead put it, "Apart from blunt truth, our lives sink decadently amid the perfume of hints and suggestions." This is essentially the message of Proverbs 27:6 which tells us, "Faithful are the wounds of a friend, but the

---

[45] Mack, To Be or Not To Be a Church Member, 64.

kisses of an enemy are deceitful." In other words, trustworthy are the bruises caused by the wounding of one who loves you, but deceitful are the kisses of the one who hates you. This is tough love. Loving someone enough to rebuke them for their sin in the hope that they will repent (Mt 18:15). The principle of accountability states that as we are responsible to point out to our brother his sins, we must do it from a stand-point of first dealing with our own (Mt 7:1-6).

Stu Weber cogently writes, "The thrust of accountability is not meant to be punitive, but preventative. It's not to yell after your brother as he plummets over the cliff, "See what you get, you jerk?" It's to say, "I'm committed to your good. When you need me, I'll act as a human guardrail for you. I'm not made of steel, but I cannot watch you go over the cliff without warning you. And I want to warn you right at the road's edge where you still have an opportunity to regain control."[46] It's as they say in the Army, prevention is the best cure.

Christian men must have an open-hearted friend to, as Gurnall put it, "maintain the power of godliness." Someone who is well tried to receive our confidence with which we may mutually sharpen each other into instruments for God's glory (Pro 27:17). A friend, who will love us in spite of our shortcomings; for a brother is born for adversity (Pro 17:17). We are to be so committed to God and desirous of holiness that we pray, "Lord I want to be conformed to your perfect nature, even if it means being rebuked by a friend" (Ps 141:5). Faithful are the wounds of a friend (Pro 27:6), meaning, our friend, in the earnest concern for our welfare, may at times be compelled to give us a sharp reproof (2 Cor 5:14-15).

But what does this look like practically speaking? In short, we are to find other men who are as humble, hungry and honest for holiness as we are. We are to make an investment of our lives into someone else, as it was done for us. We can't win the war alone. This could all start by simply finding someone else who knows more about God and His Word than we do and be humble, hungry and honest enough for them to teach us. The biblical model for discipleship is to teach as we are taught. This is precisely the reason why discipleship must

---

[46] Weber, Locking Arms: God's Design for Masculine Friendships, 162.

be done in the local church – the visible community of Christian faith.

We can learn a lot about discipleship from the great evangelist John Wesley. As Whitefield is remembered for his evangelistic zeal, Wesley is remembered for his zeal for holiness and discipleship. Mark Shaw is correct in saying that Wesley is reminding the church of a simple truth: "The church changes the world not by making converts but by making disciples." According to Mark Shaw, Wesley's concept of discipleship encompasses four convictions: (1) *the necessity of discipleship*: it's the church's responsibility to follow-up and disciple new converts to bring them to maturity; (2) *the necessity of small groups for discipleship*: this facilitates spiritual maturity (3) the necessity of lay leadership for discipleship: this facilitates leadership training and; (4) the necessity of making holiness and service the double goal of discipleship: this invigorates the life of the church.[47]

The biblical example of this process is found in 1 Cor 11:1 where Paul says, "Imitate me, just as I also imitate Christ." The man we disciple is to follow our imperfect example. Discipleship brings spiritual maturity, as John MacArthur writes, "Discipleship is nothing more than building a true friendship with a spiritual basis. It's not being friends with someone because you both like the same sport, the same music, the same hobbies, or work at the same place. At the core of your friendship should be openness about spiritual issues, which will carry your discipling relationship along."[48]

In this way, God-honoring men are to forge ahead, sharpening each other, holding each other accountable, refining each other's faith, perfecting holiness in the fear of the Lord (2 Cor 7:1; 1 Pet 1:6-7). Again Stu Weber writes,

Accountability is not a restricting thing, it's freeing. When you're accountable, you have a brother to stand beside you, someone to call when temptation is really rough, an affirming friend who will praise your progress as you become more like Christ. Keep your arms locked with a brother. Don't let go of your Ranger buddy – except in

---

[47] Shaw, Ten Great Ideas from Church History: A Decision-Maker's Guide to Shaping Your Church, 136.
[48] MacArthur, The Master's Plan for the Church, 67-68.

the most unusual of situations. And I need to explain that one. Sometimes, in extreme cases, it is necessary to pull away from someone who consistently and blatantly violates God's principles. To them your backing off may feel like rejection and disapproval. But if a friend shows utter disrespect and contempt for God and His Word you really don't have much left in common. Your partner has deliberately broken through every guardrail you could offer, and it's quite likely that the relationship will grow apart. And both of you will know the reason for the distance. It's okay. You've done your best. [49]

God's desire is for His people to be zealous for conformity to His Son. God's promise in this matter is sure, "Delight yourself also in the Lord, and He shall give you the desires of your heart. Commit your way to the Lord, trust also in Him, and He shall bring it to pass. He shall bring forth your righteousness as the light, and your justice as the noonday" (Ps 37:4-6).

> Am I a soldier of the cross,
> A follower of the Lamb?
> And shall I fear to own His cause,
> Or blush to speak His name?[50]

---

[49] Weber, Locking Arms: God's Design for Masculine Friendships, 164.
[50] Watts, Am I a Soldier of the Cross?

Chapter 8: Biblical Discipleship

Recommended Further Reading

1. Willem VanGemeren, *The Progress of Redemption.*
2. Stu Weber, *Locking Arms: God's Design for Masculine Friendships.*
3. John White, *The Fight.*
4. Dietrich Bonhoeffer, *The Cost of Discipleship.*
5. C.S. Lewis, *The Screwtape Letters.*

Chapter 8 Review Questions

1. What is discipleship?
2. Why is the church important for discipleship?
3. How should Christians disciple one another?
4. What does, "you have gained your brother" mean?
5. What does enduring correction have to do with discipleship?
6. What do discipleship and fellowship have in common?
7. Are there any *tests* of discipleship that you are failing?
8. What is the correlation between discipleship and sanctification?
9. Why is accountability important?
10. Does the church make judgments concerning sin?

Whitefield Preaching in America 1740s

"And this is the will of Him who sent Me, that everyone who sees the Son and believes in Him may have everlasting life; and I will raise him up at the last day" (John 6:40).

Chapter 9: Biblical Evangelism

His glorious gospel will cover the earth like the waters cover the sea (Hab 2:14). This is the way prophet Habakkuk envisioned the efficacy of the gospel of the kingdom. And the means for this glorious truth is the church – God's bride. The church is God's instrument for bringing in the full number of God's people (2 Tim 2:19). This chapter will survey the biblical doctrine of evangelism – the proclamation of Christ's accomplished deliverance, and will discuss the following topics:

- Delayed Judgment.
- The Suffering Servant.
- The Suffering Servants.
- Faith-Hope-Love Triad.
- Tribulation-Kingdom-Endurance Triad.
- Christ and Culture.
- Revival.

Chapter 9: Biblical Evangelism

Delayed Judgment

At the beginning of Christ's earthly ministry, following His triumph over Satan in the wilderness, and His blessing of the covenant of marriage with the miracle at Cana, He attended Sabbath worship at the synagogue in Nazareth. As was custom for visiting rabbis, Jesus rose and read from the scroll handed to Him. And from the prophecy of Isaiah He read these words:

18 "The Spirit of the Lord is upon Me, because He has anointed Me to preach the gospel to the poor; He has sent Me to heal the brokenhearted, to proclaim liberty to the captives and recovery of sight to the blind, to set at liberty those who are oppressed; 19 To proclaim the acceptable year of the Lord" (Lk 4:18-19).

Then Jesus rolled-up the scroll, gave it back to the attendant and sat down. And with everyone waiting with baited breath He said to them, "Today this Scripture is fulfilled in your hearing" (Lk 4:21). Our understanding of the Great Commission begins with these words. What Jesus was saying in the synagogue at Nazareth was that the day of the Messiah had arrived. The hoped-for king, the Son of David, the liberator, the Savior, the bringer of justice and peace—the Messiah had finally come. To the poor He preaches the gospel, to those who feel their conscious need for forgiving grace. With these, the gospel will trade their spiritual poverty with true riches (Lk 4:18, cf. Mt 5:3).

Jesus was sent by the Father to heal those whose hearts are broken by the gospel, those who mourn for righteousness (Lk 4:18, cf. Mt 5:4). To preach to the captives, those who are held by the power of sin and Satan and their fear of death (Is 29:18; Lk 4:18; Heb 2:14-15), the liberating message of the gospel (Lk 1:74, 77). Giving spiritual eyes to see the surpassing worth of Christ (Lk 2:32; 4:18) to those who, by their spiritual blindness, were slaves of their own lusts and Satan, like the rest of the unsaved mass of mankind (Jn 9:39-41; Eph 2:1-3; Rev 13:8). This was often literally fulfilled as a type of acted out parable (Mt 11:5 and esp. Jn 9:11). However, the deliverance Christ brings is not primarily from physical hardship, for He does that as well, but from supernatural spiritual demonic bondage. And to "set at liberty," to free those from their consciousness of condemning sin (Lk 4:18).

And all of this together points to the 'acceptable year of the Lord (Lk 4:19).' The time which God willed and fixed for the redemption of his people (Mt 1:21); everyone that has saving faith in Jesus. Regarding the "acceptable year of the Lord" Albert Barnes writes,

There is, perhaps, here, an allusion to the year of jubilee - the fiftieth year, when the trumpet was blown, and through the whole land proclamation was made of the liberty of Hebrew slaves, of the remission of debts, and of the restoration of possessions to their original families (Lev 25:8-13). The phrase 'the acceptable year' means the time when it would be acceptable to God to proclaim such a message, or agreeable to him - to wit, under the gospel."[1]

But the way Jesus quotes Isaiah 61 reveals a mystery. Jesus breaks it off in the middle of a verse. Jesus says in Lk 4:19 that He has been sent "to proclaim the acceptable year of the Lord" and He stops. However, Isaiah 61:2 says: "to proclaim the acceptable year of the Lord, and the day of vengeance of our God." Why didn't Jesus finish the sentence? Jesus didn't finish the sentence because there is a mystery about his coming, namely, that it is a two-act drama. The Old Testament prophets, like Isaiah, saw the whole drama together and didn't separate the two acts by many centuries. This is because they saw salvation and judgment together. The acceptable year of the Lord and the day of vengeance were all one.

The first coming of Jesus Christ ushered in the acceptable year of the Lord—a year (i.e., a space of time) for salvation not judgment. The time we currently live in is a day of God's gracious patience. The apostle Paul says in 2 Corinthians 6:2, "Behold, now is the acceptable time; behold, now is the day of salvation." While this acceptable year lasts, God withholds His judgment, offering full amnesty through the cross of Christ.

Therefore, Jesus says in Luke 4:18-19 at the beginning of His ministry, now is the 'acceptable year.' Now is the time of the Lord's favor. For now the day of vengeance is postponed. God warns with his wrath and woos with his kindness. God

---

[1] Barnes, Exposition of Luke 4:18-19.

never promises salvation for believers in Christ without on the other hand pronouncing vengeance on unbelievers, who, by rejecting Christ, bring eternal destruction on themselves. By and large this is what befell the Israel of Jesus' day (Jn 1:11). Regarding this Beale writes, "Perhaps one of the most striking features of Jesus's Kingdom is that it appears not to be the kind of kingdom prophesied in the OT and expected by Judaism."[2] What the people of Nazareth greatly longed for, and were eagerly in expectation for, was an earthly conqueror, a mighty king that they hoped would vanquish Rome and restore Israel and usher in a physical millennial kingdom. But what they really needed desperately was a Savior to deliver them not from earthly physical hardship but from supernatural demonic bondage.

God delay's His final judgment until the full number of His people are brought in. As the great deliverance at the Exodus from Egypt was a visitation unto salvation for Israel and judgment upon Egypt and the gods of Egypt, so is the New Exodus from the world which Christ accomplished unto salvation for all who believe in Him and judgment upon an unbelieving world behind which the god of this world and his demonic powers lurk. But when the year of Jubilee is over, and the time appointed by the Father has come, then the day of vengeance will arrive and the prophecy of Isaiah 61:2 will be completed. As the apostle Paul declares to us, "the Lord Jesus will be revealed from heaven with his mighty angels in flaming fire, inflicting vengeance upon those who do not know God and upon those who do not obey the gospel of our Lord Jesus Christ" (2 Thess 1:7-8).

The Suffering Servant

The coming of the Son of Man brings a decision – a judgment (Jn 3:19; 12:31). The Apostle John tells us that the reason the Son of God was manifested was so He might destroy the works of the devil. This is precisely how we are to understand the words of Jesus from the synagogue in

---

[2] Beale, *Revelation*, 341. Beale adds, "Part of the reason for the unexpectedness is that the Kingdom had begun but was not consummated, and this lack of consummation was to continue until Christ's second coming."

Chapter 9: Biblical Evangelism

Nazareth. Jesus is God's suffering Servant, Who, in His mediatorial work settles a true judgment, a verdict, a decision rendered which brings separation (Mt 10:34-39). We may look at Christ's work as the Suffering Servant in three essential ways. As we have discussed in chapter one, the One God has sent fulfills a threefold office of Prophet, Priest and King. Christ perfectly fulfills the will of the Father by *revealing God to men* (Prophet), *by redeeming men from sin* (Priest) and by *restoring man to God* (King). Thus, Christ fulfills the covenant from the side of God as God and from the side of man as Man.

First, Christ as the Prophet, reveals God's will for the salvation of men (Jn 6:40), therefore rendering a judgment that God alone is to be worshipped, and not these so-called gods to whom the nations worship (Dt 18:15-19; 32:17; Ps 106:36-37; 1 Cor 10:20). There remains however, a future judgment in which Christ shall judge all men in righteousness (Acts 17:31; Rev 20:11-15). Second, Christ as High Priest, reveals the character and nature of God by sacrificing Himself for His people; Himself being both the Offerer and the Offering (Heb 2:17; 4:14-5:4; 7:26-28; 8:3-10:18). Third, Christ as King, restores the covenant by inaugurating His Kingdom (Dan 2:34-35, 44; 7:14; Rev 1:5). Christ in His three-fold work of mediation *calls*, *gathers*, and *strengthens* His church. Jesus, as the Mediator, brings us justifying grace, the effective working out of God's decree which is: "everyone who sees the Son and believes in Him may have everlasting life; and I will raise him up at the last day" (Jn 6:40).

Justification is the electing, judicial declaration of God the Father, which is solely by virtue of God the Son's righteous life, death, and resurrection, as it is applied by God the Holy Spirit. This forensic decree of God, being based on the promise of the Son to live and die, and rise again in our place, is made effectual to believers by the Spirit, Who, in time, actually applies the righteous life, propitious death, and life-giving resurrection to them. *Thus the righteousness of God is God's incarnate obedience* (Is 49:4; 59:15-16). This Christ Jesus accomplished for us while we were dead in our trespasses and sins (Rom 5:8).

Chapter 9: Biblical Evangelism

Jesus is the One through whom God's righteous purpose is finally accomplished – to raise up the ruined posterity of Adam (Gen 3:15; Rom 5:12-21; 1 Cor 15:45). It was necessary for the Father to send the Son in time or mankind would be dead, defiled, and damned forever (Jn 3:16; 34-36).

Thus, the incarnation of the Son of God brings a crisis. The gospel is like a drawn sword thrust forth into the world by the living oracle of God (Dt 32:41; Heb 4:12). In Matthew 10, Christ describes the effect of the gospel:

> [34] "Do not think that I came to bring peace on earth. I did not come to bring peace but a sword. [35] For I have come to 'set a man against his father, a daughter against her mother, and a daughter-in-law against her mother-in-law'; [36] and 'a man's enemies *will be* those of his *own* household.'[37] He who loves father or mother more than Me is not worthy of Me. And he who loves son or daughter more than Me is not worthy of Me. [38] And he who does not take his cross and follow after Me is not worthy of Me. [39] He who finds his life will lose it, and he who loses his life for My sake will find it.

In the Scripture quoted above, Christ sends out His disciples on a missionary tour, gives them His authority and explicit instructions for their conduct. Before sending them out in "buddy teams," Jesus warns them of persecution that is sure to come for proclaiming the gospel. He exhorts them to persevere, for a good part of the world would be at variance against them and they would be hated by all for His sake. And why would the world hate them? Because of the offending message of the gospel. The gospel is the proclamation that all mankind are dead, defiled and damned, and are desperately in need of a Savior.

The sword is therefore the proclamation of the gospel; the very presence of Christ. Hence, the testimony of Jesus Christ, that is, a *verbal witness* to His saving power, reveals the truth of mankind's common standing in the sight of God; rebellious sinners (Rom 3:23; 5:12). And as such, carries with it a heavy, trepidacious effect which the Bible calls "godly fear" (Pro 1:7). There are only two responses to this two-edged sword: a godly sorrow leading to repentance (2 Cor 7:10), forgiveness of sins and salvation or a rebellious, incorrigible obstinacy leading to further hardening. Whereas, for those who humbly, yet unmeritoriously experience the first effect, enjoy the love of God, a peace of conscience, and a marvelously waxing joy in the Holy Spirit (Rom 5:1, 5; 2 Cor 1:22); those of the second, viewing God in light of their own envious and selfish nature, justly experience a horror of conscience, and a fearful expectation of judgment, which is merely a foretaste of the punishment they will endure after death (Mt 3:12; 7:19; 13:41, 42; 22:13; 25:46).

Christ pictures a sword hurling to the earth where peace was expected. Christ's very presence, in the verbal witness of the gospel, brings the animosity of the world. This is not opposed to the peace that Jesus brings into the world according to those who have surrendered to Him because that peace is a heavenly one, which is peace with God, not of the world.[3] The peace on earth men enjoy is for those on whom his favor rests (Luke 2:14).

Christ, echoing Micah 7:6, "a man's enemies are the men of his own household," in verses 35-36 of Matthew 10, demonstrates the gospel's depth of penetrating division to be even within one's own immediate family and relatives. Such is the effect produced by the knowledge of the truth. For it is necessary that, for the sake of salvation, the one who has received the word of truth be separated from his unbelieving parents. This love for Christ is to be so far surpassing in quality that the love for others will seem in comparison like hatred. Further Jesus addresses how His followers must live as those who deny themselves, that is take up their cross (an instrument of death), undergo suffering, and be given over to death for His sake.

George Ladd writes, "Suffering, persecution, and martyrdom must be the expectation of Jesus' disciples."[4] Jesus Christ never promises His disciples a "primrose path" of easy living, however, He tells us "in the world you will have tribulation; but be of good cheer, I have overcome the world" (Jn 16:33). Jesus says it's enough for a disciple to be like His teacher, and a servant to be like His master (Mt 10:25). These truths will be discussed more in chapter ten, but suffice it to

---

[3] Turretin, Institutes of Elenctic Theology, Vol II, 298.
[4] Ladd, A Theology of the New Testament, 202.

say for now, the gospel is glorious and sweet, though its proclamation be ever followed by tribulation. Nevertheless, tribulation itself furnishes us with an opportunity to testify (Mt 24:9-14; Lk 21:13). The Christian must experience both the gospel's sweetness and suffering (Rev 10:9-11).

The gospel presentation is life and peace for those who receive Christ; a damnatory sentence for those who reject Him. The sword Christ brings in the Christian verbal witness may be further understood in light of the sword which God placed to guard the way into the garden; for it is only in Christ that we can ever hope to regain paradise lost (Gen 3:24). The sword guards the way to eternal life, and the coming of the Kingdom of God into the world causes separation. The gospel of the Kingdom brings peace with God, not peace to the world. The sword Christ brings is spiritual, differing dramatically from that of man (Mt 26:52). The sword of man will not bring about the Kingdom of God, and those merely living off the earthly one will perish by it.

The coming of the Son of Man brings a crisis. In the second "Song of the Suffering Servant," the Messiah proclaims through the mouth of His prophet Isaiah, "He has made My mouth like a sharp sword" (Is 49:2).[5] Jesus Christ is the One through whom God's righteous purpose is finally accomplished. Isaiah 49:2 tells us Christ's words are likened to a sharp two-edged sword. Christ specifies that he has come: to fulfill the Law (Mt 5:17), call sinners to repentance[6] (Mt 9:13), bring division (Mt 10:34), to gather the lost sheep of Israel (Mt 15:24), and to seek and save the lost (Mt 18:11). Of these so-called 'elthon' ἤλθον (coming) sayings in Matthew, the demon's question in 8:29 sheds much light on Christ's earthly mission. And behold, they cried out, "What have you to do with us, O Son of God? Have you come here to torment us before the time?" Demons know that Jesus is the 'Son of God' who has come to earth from heaven. They also knew that

---

[5] There are traditionally five *Songs of the Suffering Servant,* all of which are in the Book of Isaiah. In order they are: (1) Isaiah 42:1-4; (2) 49:1-6; (3) 50:4-9; (4) 52:13-53:12; (5) 61:1-3.

[6] Repentance is a grace of God's Spirit whereby a sinner is inwardly humbled and visibly reformed. Christians, remaining close to the cross, are called to a life of repentance.

they will be tormented by Him, but they don't know quite when that will be.

There is an illusion in Matthew 8:29 which draws upon the imagery of Dt 32:8-9. The gods and idols of other nations are in reality demons (Dt 32:17; 1 Cor 10:10), who are to be judged by the Judge of all the earth.[7] Thus the demons do shudder and know that Jesus is the Judge who brings a sword to the earth. Thus Christ has come in order to execute judgment upon Satan's demonic kingdom (Mt 25:41), and release those who through fear of death were all their lifetime subject to bondage (Heb 2:15).

While casting out a demon, Jesus reveals His heavenly mission in Mt 12:28-29,

[28] But if I cast out demons by the Spirit of God, surely the kingdom of God has come upon you. [29] Or how can one enter a strong man's house and plunder his goods, unless he first binds the strong man? And then he will plunder his house. [30] He who is not with Me is against Me, and he who does not gather with Me scatters abroad.

In a parabolic way Jesus demonstrates His heavenly mission, which is one that invades the earthly city of man, ruled by his powerful adversary Satan, defeats him through the cross, and begins to plunder his house by liberating Satan's oppressed captives (Lk 4:18-19).

Parable of the Sword

In Richard Wagner's opera *Siegfried*, the main character of the same name forges a sword which he names Nothung. Siegfried skillfully hammers away at the sword, folding the metal of the blade upon a large anvil into razor sharp perfection. The sword is forged for the death of the great dragon, Fafner. At length Siegfried proves the power of the sword by cutting the anvil in two. Similarly, Christ brings a sword not of steel but of truth and light.

In a sense, the people of God are like a sword. Gathered into one by the Spirit, tempered through fiery orders, and

---

[7] Longman, God is a Warrior, 142.

sharpened by hammer blows of the Word, so as to bear the character of Christ, it is the very instrument of God in bringing a judiciary sentence on an unbelieving world and a toppling and abasing of the strongholds of the devil. In the divine grasp, God's people endure the hammering of the Word while the world itself serves as its anvil. As the dragon makes war on the seed of the woman, the Lord with his glittering sword will cut to pieces the fleeing serpent (Gen 3:15; Dt 32:31; Isaiah 27:1; Rev 12; Rev 19:15).

Christ's two-edged sword incites a response as its truth pierces the conscience of man. The cross is the peace of Christ but it is also the sword God wields on the earth.[8] The sword of the Lord finds its way to the very soul of every man (Heb 4:12-13); God, in judging man, takes the sinner's conscience as his accuser; and in this way Christ brings judgment to the conscience of a man; either for redemption and restoration or ruin. Greg Beale, expounding on this concept writes, "Jesus, Who holds sway over the power of salvation and judgment, exerts this power through His followers (so Mt 16:18)."[9]

Doug Kelly, describing this action of the Spirit tells us, "God doesn't come to manipulate man but to save him personally, in such a way that while He judges sin and exposes man's heart with all its evil, He forgives him and draws out his heart in surrender and love to Himself." Whereas, those who repent and believe the gospel are brought through judgment to salvation to the praise of God, those who reject the gospel harden themselves against it to their own eternal destruction.

But this hardening is also the purpose for the preaching of the Gospel; namely a judiciary sentence.[10] *Those who reject the Gospel harden themselves under the same means God employs for the softening of others.* The judgment at the end of time will complement all the previous visitations of divine recompense: warning either heeded or unheeded (John 12:47-48). Those made willing, humbly receive the righteousness of Christ as it is freely offered in the Gospel. In this way, and

---

[8] Bonhoeffer, *The Cost of Discipleship*, 69.
[9] Beale, *Revelation*, 287.
[10] Ribberbos, *The Coming of the Kingdom*, 127.

only this way, will anyone be saved through judgment for the glory of God. Thus, God is love as well as talionic justice.[11]

The Suffering Servants

The Spirit of Christ ruling in His servants empowers their testimony (Acts 16:7; Rom 8:11; Rev 12:11; 19:10). The gospel proclamation brings life and peace for those who receive Christ; a damnatory sentence for those who reject it. The Book of Acts clearly demonstrates this in Paul's message to the synagogue at Antioch (Pisidia). On the Sabbath, Paul presented the gospel (bringing the sword) which divided the hearers; those who received it and those who rejected it. The Holy Spirit then speaks through Paul, demonstrating how the mission of the Suffering Servant is now being undertaken by Christ's followers.

Paul declares, "It was necessary that the word of God should be spoken to you first; but since you reject it, and judge yourselves unworthy of everlasting life, behold, we turn to the Gentiles. For so the Lord has commanded us: 'I have set you as a light to the Gentiles, that you should be for salvation to the ends of the earth'" (Acts 13:47). Christ is set for the fall and rising of many (Lk 2:34). Then Luke writes, "Now when the Gentiles heard this, they were glad and glorified the word of the Lord. And as many as had been appointed to eternal life believed" (Acts 13:48).

God's purpose of raising up the ruined posterity of Adam is now being accomplished through the followers of Jesus. This is in fulfillment to what Jesus had said; "But when they deliver you up, do not worry about how or what you should speak. For it will be given to you in that hour what you should speak; *for it is not you who speak, but the Spirit of your Father who speaks in you* (Mt 10:19-20, emphasis mine).[12] Jesus told His disciples, "you shall receive power when the Holy Spirit has come upon you; and you shall be witnesses to Me in Jerusalem, and in all Judea and Samaria, and to the end of the

---

[11] The concept of Talionic Justice will be discussed in chapter 10.
[12] See also Mark 13:11 and Luke 12:11-12.

earth" (Acts 1:8). Jesus said, you will testify to My saving work.

Looking back at Christ's promise to His disciples, we may say that the Spirit will give us the words we need to bear testimony (Mt 10:20. Commenting on this Scripture, Calvin writes,

> Frequently does it happen that the Lord leaves believers destitute of the gift of eloquence, so long as he does not require that they give him a testimony, but, when the necessity for it arrives, those who formerly appeared to be dumb are endued by him with more than ordinary eloquence. Thus, in our own time, we have seen some martyrs, who seemed to be almost devoid of talent, and yet were no sooner called to make a public profession of their faith, than they exhibited a command of appropriate and graceful language altogether miraculous.[13]

The biblical point being made here is, Christ builds His church on the testimony of His saving work at Calvary (Mt 16:18). Evangelism is the mission of the church (Mt 28:18-20). It's important to define our terms: evangelism and gospel. The word evangelism comes to us from the Latin *evangelium*, itself derived from the Greek *euaggelizo* which means "I bring good news." And the derivation of "gospel" is the old English *godspel* from gōd good + spell tale – good news.[14] Evangelism is the proclamation of the saving truths of the Gospel of Jesus Christ – the message of the cross. It's the verbalizing of the great things we have come to know personally of God for the purpose of gathering and strengthening the church – the body of Christ. This is the prophetic role for the entire church. As it is written, "How then shall they call on Him in whom they have not believed? And how shall they believe in Him of whom they have not heard? And how shall they hear without a preacher? And how shall they preach unless they are sent? As it is written: "How beautiful are the feet of those who preach the gospel of peace, who bring glad tidings of good things" (Rom 10:14-15)!

---

[13] Calvin, Commentary on Mathew 10:20.

[14] The derivation of the word "gospel" may also suggest an etymological construct from the old German *Godspel* (God + tale = God's tale, tell or God's play).

Chapter 9: Biblical Evangelism

This is the prophetic role for the entire church – evangelism: first by the infallible apostles who spoke "thus saith the Lord," and throughout the church age by the prophetic work of the church who brings the revelation of Christ's saving work on the cross to all peoples, which will end at Christ's Second Coming.

The church evangelizes those outside with the intent of witnessing the saving efficacy of Jesus Christ to the glory of God. In short, Christians proclaim the saving power of Jesus so that others may be saved to the glorify God. This is the *kerygma*, the apostolic proclamation (Acts 2:42; 1 Cor 3:10; Rev 21:14). Christ gathers and strengthens His church on both the confession of it and witness to it (1 Tim 6:12; 1 Jn 4:15; 5:11; Rev 12:11). The church is therefore built upon the apostolic proclamation – Jesus of Nazareth is both Lord and Christ (Acts 2:36).

The Kerygma

The preaching of the early church consisted not in arguments for the existence of God, or easy messages carefully crafted so as not to wound anyone's conscience. The preaching of the early church consisted of "a simple recital of the great events connected with the historical appearance of Jesus Christ"[15] and a testimony to His saving work in the lives of His Messianic community. When we review the great messages the apostles preached in the New Testament we may find the essential elements of the *kerygma* or apostolic proclamation.[16] The word kerygma is related to the Greek verb *kerusso*, meaning to proclaim as a herald, as it is famously used in 1 Cor 1:21, "For since, in the wisdom of God, the world through wisdom did not know God, it pleased God through the foolishness of the message *preached* to save those who believe" (emphasis mine). In the original Greek there is only one word that stands in for message preached –

---

[15] Niebuhr, The Meaning of Revelation, 23.
[16] For example see Acts 2:14-39; 3:12-26; 4:8-12; 10:35-44; 1 Cor. 15:1-5; Phil. 2:5-11, etc.

proclamation). According to Dodd, the kerygma is "the public proclamation of Christianity to the non-Christian world."[17]

The following enumerates the essential elements of the kerygmatic proclamation which were summarized by C. H. Dodd:

1. The age of fulfillment has dawned. The Messianic age for which the people of God had waited so long has come.
2. This age has been ushered in by the ministry of Jesus, particularly by His death and resurrection.
3. God has exalted this Jesus to His right hand, so that He is the risen Lord in glory.
4. The Holy Spirit in the Church is the sign of the present power and glory of Christ.
5. The Messianic age will shortly reach its consummation in Christ's return.
6. Because of these things, believers are to repent, be baptized and received in the fellowship of the Church.

Here is an acronym that might prove helpful in memorizing the kerygmatic (apostolic) proclamation: **POETIC**

Promise (point 1): The promises of God in the OT have been fulfilled with the coming of Jesus the Messiah.

Ordained (point 2): It was the Father's eternal plan to send His only Son Jesus in order to ransom us from the coming wrath.

Exalted (point 3): By virtue of His resurrection, Jesus Christ has been exalted to the right hand of the Father as the Head of the church, His own body.

True (point 4): The Holy Spirit in the church is the true sign of Christ's present power and glory.

Imminent (point 5): Christ's return is imminent.

Command (point 6): Repent and believe the gospel. This is a divine command not a suggestion.

---

[17] Dodd, The Apostolic preaching and It's Developments, 7.

Chapter 9: Biblical Evangelism

The mission of the church is to witness (testify) to the saving power of Christ – the gospel of the kingdom (Mt 24:14; 28:18-20; Act 1:8; 2 Cor 4:5-12; 5:20; 2 Tim 4:2). How significant is that! The church is the divinely appointed means for spreading the gospel, and to further gather and strengthen God's elect. And the message of the church is not the social gospel or the seven steps to being the perfect parent, the message is the gospel – the announcement of salvation accomplished by Jesus Christ. This is biblical evangelism – the appeal to and awakening of those outside the church.

J.I. Packer explains, "According to Scripture, preaching the gospel is entirely a matter of proclaiming to men, as truth from God which all are bound to believe and act on, the following four facts:

(1) That all men are sinners, and cannot do anything to save themselves;
(2) That Jesus Christ, God's Son, is a perfect Saviour for sinners, even the worst;
(3) That the Father and the Son have promised that all who know themselves to be sinners and put their faith in Christ as Saviour shall be received into favour, and none cast out;
(4) That God has made repentance and faith a duty, requiring of every man who hears the gospel "a serious full recumbency and rolling of the soul upon Christ in the promise of the gospel, as an all-sufficient Saviour, able to deliver and save to the utmost them that come to God by Him;

Biblical evangelism is displaying Christ; explaining man's need of Him, His sufficiency to save, and His offer of Himself in the promises as Savior to all who truly turn to Him."[18] The gospel is to be proclaimed, not edited. The proclamation of the gospel in this world is the testimony of Christ's present reign (Acts 2:22-36; Rev 1:5). Christ builds His church on both the confession and testimony of His saving work at Calvary (1 Tim 6:12; Rev 12:11). The word testify, from the Greek *marturia*, is where we derive the word martyr. Martyr means "witness." The terms testimony and witness are synonymous.

---

[18] Owen, The Death of Death in the Death of Christ, 16.

Chapter 9: Biblical Evangelism

The Spirit of Christ in us is the empowerment of the testimony to bring the revelation of Christ's saving work on the cross to all peoples. And finishing the Great Commission is going to cost some of us our lives as it already has, and which it always has. As C.S. Lewis puts it, "The sacrifice of Christ is repeated, or re-echoed, among His followers in varying degrees, from the cruelest martyrdom down to a self-submission of intention."[19] And eighteen centuries ago Tertullian said, "We (Christians) multiply whenever we are mown down by you; the blood of Christians is seed."[20] And 200 years later St. Jerome said, "The Church of Christ has been founded by shedding its own blood, not that of others; by enduring outrage, not by inflicting it. Persecutions have made it grow; martyrdoms have crowned it."[21]

The point being made here is God's purpose of raising up the ruined posterity of Adam is now being accomplished through the followers of Jesus, who, taking on the role of the suffering servant, bear witness *marturia* to the saving power of Jesus Christ, preparing the way of the Lord by ushering in the kingdom of Christ, resulting in salvation through judgment for believers. Likewise, this brings the enmity of the world as unbelievers are further hardened in rebelliousness, bringing tribulation upon believers. These tribulations come upon Christ by way of His followers (Jn 16:33; Col 1:24; 2 Tim 3:12).

The Kingship Formula

When considering this, there are two biblical structures which will enable us to conceptualize the church's evangelistic mission in the presence of the tribulation: the *faith-hope-love*, and the *tribulation-kingdom-endurance* triads. The triad of faith, hope and love is the quintessence of the God-given life in Christ.[22] The Scripture reveals the faith-hope-love triad; the three cardinal Christian virtues; a kind of gracious triumvirate which governs the Christian life. For

---

[19] Lewis, The Problem of Pain, 104.
[20] Tertullian, Apology, 50.
[21] Jerome, Letter 82.
[22] Bornkamm, Paul, 219.

example 1 Thess 1:3 tells us, "We give thanks to God always for you all, making mention of you in our prayers, remembering without ceasing your *work of faith, labor of love,* and *patience of hope* in our Lord Jesus Christ in the sight of our God and Father" (emphasis added). And 1 Cor 13:13 famously tells us, "And now abide faith, hope, love, these three; but the greatest of these is love."

In John's Apocalypse, he identifies himself with fellow Christians and with Jesus as "your brother and fellow partaker" in the *tribulation* and *kingdom* and *patient endurance* of Jesus Christ (Rev 1:9, emphasis added). What this verse tells us is John and all believers are brothers and fellow partakers of: the *tribulation* (persecution, affliction, distress which comes on account of the gospel witness);[23] and *kingdom* (the exercise of rule in the present and future kingdom of Christ); and *patient endurance* (the remaining faithful to Christ despite persecution). Greg Beale informs us,

John and his community are people who even now reign together in Jesus' kingdom. The exercise of rule in this kingdom begins and continues only as one faithfully endures tribulation. This is a formula for kingship: faithful endurance through tribulation is the means by which one reigns in the present with Jesus. Their endurance is part of the process of "conquering."[24]

An amalgamation may be made between the triads we've discussed, *tribulation-kingdom-endurance* and the *faith-hope-love* triad as follows: (1) Tribulation (work of faith) – our faith in Christ and the preaching of the gospel brings tribulation; (2) kingdom (labor of love) – our love for our fellow man compels us to tell others about Jesus Christ; and (3) endurance (patience of hope) – patience defines our character – it's essential to steadfastness. The trial makes the man.

So what does this all mean? *Faith* lays hold of the promises of God in Christ and breaks forth into action – telling people about the saving power of Jesus Christ. But this work of faith

---

[23] Tribulation is distress or suffering resulting from oppression or persecution. The tribulation we are referring to here occurs on account of the gospel message that is proclaimed and lived out.

[24] Beale, The Book of Revelation, 201-202.

brings with it the world's hatred (Gen 3:15). And so *tribulation* ensues, ushering in its train a progressive pressure and maddening violence which seeks to eradicate the offending witness that brought the threat of destruction – repent and believe the gospel or suffer the fires of hell forever (Mt 3:7-12). The truths of the gospel of the kingdom are hidden by a judicial act of God, from those who, in their own estimation, are the wise and prudent. They cannot see the light of the gospel because they trust their own dim light, and will not accept the light of God.[25] The gospel enlightens some but blinds others (Jn 9:39-41). In spite of it all, *love* labors long, guiding the work of faith, enabling believers, as mediating priests, to be self-squanders in Christ service, seeking the recovery of the lost (2 Cor 5:14, 20). And Christ enlarges our hearts to include others so that we might by all means save some (1 Cor 9:22). And the continuing loyalty to Christ despite persecution serves to define our character and produces *endurance* by which we may *hope* large in our inheritance – God Himself, at our coming resurrection with the personal physical visible return of Christ.

We may conceptualize the triad as follows:

- *Faith in Christ* (New Passover) – Evangelistic works of faith brings tribulation.
- *Love for our fellow man* (New Exodus) – Love laboring through us wins the lost, bringing them into the kingdom.
- *Hope in the resurrection* (New Promised Land) – The steadfastness of hope, like iron bred in his soul, engenders staying power for the citizens of the heavenly city; those who look to the new heavens and new earth, to the city of God.

Together, Christians are brothers and fellow partakers in the *tribulation* and *kingdom* and *patient endurance* of Jesus Christ (Rev 1:9). As we minister in Christ's kingdom, we are compelled by the love of Christ to witness to His saving power, which is assured the world's hatred and brings tribulation, through which we are enabled to endure to the end

---

[25] Spurgeon, Commentary on Matthew, 141.

by His presence. The kingdom is present in Jesus. And God is making His appeal to the world through His church to be reconciled to Him (2 Cor 5:20-21).

All of this is brought together by Jesus in His Olivet Discourse (Mt 24). When answering the disciples' questions regarding: (1) when will be the destruction of the temple? (2) when will be the sign of His coming? And (3) when will be the consummation of the age? Jesus told them some things relating to the destruction of Jerusalem, some things about His second coming, and some things which would immediately precede the end of the world. It would seem Jesus makes a point to answer the last two questions before the first. Namely, there will be a delay characterized by persecution and tribulation for His followers before His return (Mt 24:4-14). As for the first question, Jesus describes in vivid detail how Jerusalem will undergo, in the near future, a violent destruction, which will stand as a type signifying the manner in which a world-full of obstinate rebels shall in the end likewise perish (Mt 24:15-28).[26]

As to the other two questions, Jesus describes for His disciples the inter-advent period in Matthew 24:4-14. Jesus characterizes the period of time between His first and second comings as a time of false prophets, wars, famines, pestilences, and earthquakes. And in Mt 24:9-14 He says,

9 "Then they will deliver you up to *tribulation* and kill you, and you will be hated by all nations for My name's sake. 10 And then many will be offended, will betray one another, and will hate one another. 11 Then many false prophets will rise up and deceive many. 12 And because lawlessness will abound, the love of many will grow cold. 13 But he who *endures* to the end shall be saved. 14 *And this gospel of the kingdom will be preached in all the world as a witness to all the nations, and then the end will come* (emphasis added).

These words of Jesus give us the express purpose of preaching – a witness to all nations. The goal of preaching the "gospel of the kingdom" is for "every tribe and tongue and people and nation" to hear the glorious saving power of

---

[26] Jerusalem and the temple were sacked and destroyed by Roman legionnaires under Titus in the summer of 70 AD.

Christ's cross. So that they might by faith surrender to King Jesus and love and obey Him.

I find in these words of Jesus a *command*, a *cost*, and *confidence* which is ultimately buttressed with the Great Commission (Mt 28:18-20). "This gospel of the kingdom will be preached in all the world as a witness to all the nations," is a command, not a suggestion (Mt 24:14). "They will deliver you up to tribulation and kill you, and you will be hated by all nations for My name's sake," is the cost for the completion of the Great Commission (Mt 24:9). And "He who endures to the end shall be saved," is the confidence which a perfect atonement secures (Mt 24:13). As Christians, we are enabled to do this because we have been crucified with Christ, Who now dwells in our hearts by *faith* with which He roots and grounds Himself to us in *love*, which is the power that compels us to minister in His kingdom, as we proclaim the gospel; mankind's only *hope* for forgiveness and salvation and the resurrection.

Christians are brothers and fellow partakers in the tribulation and kingdom and patient endurance of Jesus Christ (Rev 1:9). We are enabled to persevere in faith through a period of time (between Christ's First and Second Advents) which is characterized by persecution and tribulation for His followers (Mt 24:4-14, cf. Heb 7:25). During this period, believers serve God as a kingdom of ministering-witnessing priests, who proclaim the saving truths of the gospel of the kingdom. D.A. Carson cogently writes, "If all of God's sovereignty is even now mediated through Jesus, Jesus is reigning – but He is doing so in the teeth of sustained opposition: He reigns until He has put all enemies under His feet, and utterly destroyed the last enemy, death itself" (1 Cor 15:25).[27]

Tribulation

In the first century of the Christian era, Rome leveled ten accusations against the church. Christians were held worthy of death because: (1) they were *anti-social* – they refused to take

---

[27] Carson, How Long O Lord: Reflections on Suffering and Evil, 119.

part in pagan festivals which honored the gods of Rome; (2) for *novelty* – because they rejected the traditional religion of Rome and worshipped Jesus Christ, the God-man; (3) for *cannibalism* – because they ate the body and blood of their Savior; (4) for *gross immorality*, including incest – because they loved one another and called each other "brother" and "sister;" (5) for their *lack of patriotism* – because they refused to burn incense and 'Swear by the genius of Caesar,' thus saying Caesar is lord; (6) for *atheism* – because Christians worshiped a God that could not be seen; (7) for *economic disruption* – because they refused to work on the Lord's Day;[28] (8) for their *anti-family behavior* – because Christianity caused division;[29] (9), for their *promotion of poverty* – because they welcomed those who were unemployed, as well as slaves and foreigners while they failed to cater to the rich and affluent; and (10) for *natural disasters* – because Christians would not honor the Roman gods.

Following the sack of Rome in 410, Augustine, Bishop of Hippo, wrote the *City of God* in part to defend Christianity against the tenth accusation which blamed Christianity for the scourge of the Roman gods.[30] In his beginning chapters he writes:

Are your minds bereft of reason? You are not merely mistaken; this is madness. Here are people in the East bewailing Rome's humiliation, and great states in remote regions of the earth holding public mourning and lamentation – and you Romans are searching for theaters, pouring into them, filling them, behaving more irresponsibly than ever before. It is this spiritual disease, degeneration, decline into immorality and indecency that Scipio feared when he opposed the erection of theaters. He saw how easily ease and plenty would soften and ruin you. He did not wish you to be free from fear. He did not think that the republic could be happy while walls were standing, yet morals were collapsing. But, you were more attached to the seductions of foul spirits than the wisdom of men with foresight. That

---

[28] In some areas the church radically altered pagan society by causing sales of idols to plummet (Acts 19:19-41).

[29] See Matthew 10:34-39.

[30] Tertullian (160-220 AD) arguing in a similar vein said, "If the Tiber reaches the walls, if the Nile does not rise to the fields, if the sky doesn't move or the earth does, if there is famine, if there is plague, the cry is at once: 'The Christians to the lion.' What, all of them to the lion" (Apology 40:2)?

is why you take no blame for the evil you do, but blame Christianity for the evil you suffer. **Depraved by prosperity and unchastened by adversity, you desire, in your security, not the peace of the State but liberty for license.** Scipio wanted you to have a salutary fear of the enemy, lest you should rot in debauchery. Though crushed by the enemy, you put no check on immorality, you learned no lessons from calamity; in the depths of sorrows you still wallow in sin (emphasis added).[31]

History shows that those civilizations that have gone the way of Sodom and Gomorra haven't survived. America seems bent on carving out its own existence without God. But when we defect from God's commands and forsake His Word, we freely lend our ears to the lies of Satan. And Like Rome, America is failing to detect God's chastening hand. May we observe this in what appears to be the removal of His blessing?

Vincent Miceli writes, "When atheism takes the form of a social conspiracy to dethrone God, it takes as its communal mission the messianic goal of secularizing every cell of society until the whole body is militantly atheistic."[32] And again Augustine asks, "For why in your calamities do you complain of Christianity, *unless because you desire to enjoy your luxurious license unrestrained,* and to lead an abandoned and profligate life without the interruption of any uneasiness or disaster" (emphasis added)?[33]

The point being made here is the church is the conscience of the nation. As M.L. King wrote "The church must be reminded that it is not the master or the servant of the state, but rather the conscience of the state. It must be the guide and the critic of the state, and never its tool. If the church does not recapture its prophetic zeal, it will become an irrelevant social club without moral or spiritual authority."[34] *The church is the conscience of the nation and the pulpit is the voice of that conscience.* We cannot be silent. It is easy to talk about what is popular but the church is called to witness and warn the nation of what it doesn't want to hear.

---

[31] Augustine, City of God, Book I, Chapter 33.

[32] Miceli, The Gods of Atheism, 41.

[33] Augustine, City of God, Book I, Chapter 30.

[34] King, Strength to Love.

Chapter 9: Biblical Evangelism

In His parable of the children in the marketplace, Jesus demonstrates fickle responses to the gospel. Jesus says, "But to what shall I liken this generation? It is like children sitting in the marketplaces and calling to their companions, and saying: 'We played the flute for you, and you did not dance; we mourned to you, and you did not lament.' For John came neither eating nor drinking, and they say, 'He has a demon.' The Son of Man came eating and drinking, and they say, 'Look, a glutton and a winebibber, a friend of tax collectors and sinners!' But wisdom is justified by her children" (Mt 11:16-19).

This perverse generation has its representatives on earth today. The world wants nothing of either conviction of sin and repentance (John) or the joy of salvation and faith (the Son of Man). It's as Kretzman tells us, "The preaching of the Law, of repentance, hurts their fine sensibilities, but the Gospel of free grace and mercy in Christ Jesus is still less to their liking."[35]

In this vein, Kierkegaard asks, what happens to those who try to warn the present age? He writes, "It happened that a fire broke out backstage in a theater. The clown came out to inform the public. They thought it was just a jest and applauded. He repeated his warning, they shouted even louder. So I think the world will come to an end amid general applause from all the wits, who believe that it is a joke." [36] But wisdom, (the personification of a divine communicable attribute), is justified by her children (Mt 11:19). The wisdom of God, which is foolishness to the world, is freely offered in the gospel of the kingdom. It's like Spurgeon put it, "Those who perish with salvation sounding in their ears perish with a vengeance."[37]

Kingdom

We read in the first three chapters of the Book of Revelation how Christ commands the Seven Churches of Asia to remain steadfast under attack. The Book of Revelation, though it transcends our finite minds, communicates to us by various

---

[35] Kretzman, Matthew 11:18-19.

[36] Kierkegaard, Either/Or, I, 30.

[37] Spurgeon, Commentary on Matthew, 139.

symbols that the ultimate victory of God's people is already assured.[38] These seven historical churches of Asia Minor tackled difficult and complex issues, both in life and in doctrine, both within the pale of the church and without. And the conditions in which they lived occur not in one particular age of church history but cover all history as they function representatively for the whole of history between Christ's first and second coming.

Christ's message to the Seven Churches, and by extension the church of all ages, is meant to shock Christians into the reality of their faith by giving a heavenly perspective of the cosmic spiritual conflict of which the church finds herself in, thereby heightening their sense of awareness; encouraging them to persevere in their faithful witness. Christ addresses the church, calling for repentance and watchfulness, and commands her to faithfully maintain her verbal witness to Him. The point of all this is, as a kingdom of priests (Rev 1:6), Christians are to be eager to emulate the faithfulness of the Seven Churches and vigilant to prayerfully avoid their failings.[39] For Jesus Christ expects obedience from everyone He has cleansed of sin.

As has been said, the Kingdom has come, the Kingdom is coming, and the Kingdom will come. The Baptist Faith and Message succinctly puts it,

The Kingdom of God includes both His general sovereignty over the universe and His particular Kingship over men who willfully acknowledge Him as King. Particularly the Kingdom is the realm of salvation into which men enter by trustful, childlike commitment to Jesus Christ. Christians ought to pray and labor that the Kingdom may come and God's will be done on earth. The full consummation of the Kingdom awaits the return of Jesus Christ and the end of this age.[40]

---

[38] Rev 1:1 tells us "The Revelation of Jesus Christ, which God gave Him to *show* His servants—things which must shortly take place" (emphasis added). Show in the Greek is *semaino* meaning to 'signify.' In other words, Jesus communicated through symbols what was shorty to take place.

[39] There are five churches who are falling away and only two who are remaining faithful. These will be discussed in these last two chapters.

[40] Baptist Faith and Message, IX The Kingdom, 15.

Chapter 9: Biblical Evangelism

Christians enter Christ's kingdom now spiritually, and are called to remain faithful to Christ and engage their culture, seeking to win the lost. The church must take its cues from God's Word not the world, and not give in to the pressure of watering down biblical doctrines in order to present a less offensive more tolerating gospel. As Martin Luther writes,

> Also it does not help that one of you would say: 'I will gladly confess Christ and His Word on every detail, except that I may keep silent about one or two things which may not (be) tolerated...For whoever denies Christ in one detail or word has denied the same Christ...in all the details.[41]

The biblical point being made here, is the church is called to remain faithful to Christ by maintaining doctrinal purity, which in turn governs morality. Christ calls His church individually and corporately to testify – bear witness to the truth of the gospel. A testimony expresses personal conviction and identifies with the cause one defends (1 Pet 3:15). Christians are called to tell others what they have seen and heard – to proclaim the saving power of Christ they have experienced. All preaching and witnessing is a testimony announcing the advent of salvation. In proclaiming the Lordship of Jesus, one makes public confession of faith. Works of faith may accompany the spoken testimony. And the ultimate testimony, leaving no room for discussion, is the testimony of the self, martyrdom.[42]

Endurance

The church, God's instrument of evangelism, is to go out, charged with this command: "And this gospel of the kingdom

---

[41] Luther's Works, Weimar Edition, Letters, Volume 3, 81. This sentiment of Luther is similarly described in the following quote that is attributed to him: "If I profess with the loudest voice and clearest exposition every portion of the Word of God except precisely that little point which the world and the devil are at that moment attacking, I am not confessing Christ, however boldly I may be professing Him. Where the battle rages there the loyalty of the soldier is proved; and to be steady on all the battle front besides, is mere flight and disgrace if he flinches at that point."

[42] This topic will be discussed more in chapter ten.

will be preached in all the world as a witness to all the nations, and then the end will come" (Mt 24:14). This is both the manner in which the full number of God's people will be brought in, and the event that will usher in the climactic return of the King. This is the specific reason why the church at Ephesus is rebuked – they had lost their first love (Rev 2:4).

It would be beneficial in passing to note at least four purposes of the letters to the Churches (Rev 2:1-3:22):

1. To give us an eternal trans-historical perspective of the One Who is, and Who was, and Who is to come, in order to enable understanding and motivate obedience.
2. To give us a heightened sense of awareness as to the reality of spiritual warfare – the cosmic battle that we are in.
3. To shock us into reality by way of the warnings.
4. To encourage us to continue to persevere in the faithful witness that we are maintaining.

Ephesus

It's not the aim here to enter into a full commentary of the Seven Churches of Asia, nevertheless it is worth pausing to note several weighty matters bearing on this topic. The first church addressed, Ephesus, was called upon to repent because she had "left" her first love (Rev 2:4). The church who could boast of such pastors as Paul, Timothy, and John had lost their evangelistic zeal to win the lost for Christ. The church at Ephesus is admonished to repent or cease to exist as a church of Christ (Rev 2:5).

Ephesus, like the other churches of Asia, were facing tribulation ranging from ostracism to martyrdom, as in the case of Antipas, the faithful witness (Rev 2:15). The pagan Greek culture placed intense pressure on the Christians of Asia Minor to compromise the purity of apostolic doctrine as well as the accompanying verbal and moral witness to Christ's Lordship. For this reason, Jesus admonishes them to "Remember therefore from where you have fallen; repent and do the first works" (Rev 2:5). Their first works, their works of faith, a summary phrase attests to the Spirit's transforming power in their living witness, which ranges from their confession and baptism to their continuous witness to the gospel. "Where there is no revelation, the people cast off restraint" (Pro 29:18).

Smyrna

Smyrna was a center for the worship of Dionysus, who was originally a god of fruitfulness and vegetation; later god of wine. Caesar worship was compulsory, and once a year a citizen had to burn a pinch of incense on the altar to the godhead of Caesar. Once he performed this duty he was given a certificate, a *libellus*, declaring him to be a citizen in good standing with Rome. All a Christian had to do, to insure that they would be left in peace, was burn a pinch of incense and say "Caesar is Lord."

Polycarp, who studied at the feet of the apostle John, a leader in the church at Smyrna in later years, refused to make this sacrifice. And as a result, he was burned at the stake during the Olympic Games held in the city on Saturday, February 23, 155 A.D. Eusebius, in his Ecclesiastical History recounts Polycarp's martyrdom:

Now, as Polycarp was entering into the stadium, there came to him a voice from heaven, saying, "Be strong, and show yourself a man, O Polycarp!" No one saw who it was that spoke to him; but those of our brethren who were present heard the voice. And as he was brought forward, the tumult became great when they heard that Polycarp was taken. And when he came near, the proconsul asked him whether he was Polycarp. On his confessing that he was, the proconsul sought to persuade him to deny Christ, saying, "Have respect to your old age," and other similar things, according to their custom, such as, "Swear by the genius of Cæsar; repent, and say, Away with those that deny the gods." But Polycarp, gazing with a stern countenance on all the multitude of the wicked heathen then in the stadium, and waving his hand towards them, while with groans he looked up to heaven, said, "Away with the impious." Then, the proconsul urging him, and saying, "Swear, and I will set you at liberty, curse Christ;" Polycarp declared, "Eighty and six years have I served Him, and He never did me any injury: how then can I blaspheme my King and my Saviour?"

And when the proconsul yet again pressed him, and said, "Swear by the fortune of Cæsar," he answered, since you are vainly urgent that,

389

as you say, I should swear by the fortune of Cæsar, and pretend not to know who and what I am, hear me declare with boldness, I am a Christian. And if you wish to learn what the doctrines of Christianity are, appoint me a day, and you shall hear them. The proconsul replied, "Persuade the people." But Polycarp said, to you I have thought it right to offer an account of my faith; for we are taught to give all due honor (which entails no injury upon ourselves) to the powers and authorities which are ordained of God. But as for these, I do not deem them worthy of receiving any account from me.

The proconsul then said to him, "I have wild beasts at hand; to these will I cast you, unless you repent." But he answered, "Call them then, for we are not accustomed to repent of what is good in order to adopt that which is evil; and it is well for me to be changed from what is evil to what is righteous." But again the proconsul said to him, "I will cause you to be consumed by fire, seeing you despise the wild beasts, if you will not repent." But Polycarp said, "You threaten me with fire which burns for an hour, and after a little is extinguished, but are ignorant of the fire of the coming judgment and of eternal punishment, reserved for the ungodly. But why do you tarry? Bring forth what you will."[43]

One cannot read *Foxe's Book of Martyrs* without reflecting on the presence and staying power of God given to His saints at the time of their ultimate testimony. This is endurance – remaining faithful to Christ despite persecution.[44] Interestingly, Smyrna was located by Mt. Pagus, the top of which was girded with temples, glittering like a crown. It actually resembled a crown when viewed from the city. It came to be known as "the Crown of Smyrna." And Smyrna was also known as "the Crown City." But Jesus said to the church there, "Be faithful until death, and I will give you the crown of life" (Rev. 2:10).

Pergamum

Pergamum or Pergamos, was built on a huge conical hill in the fertile Caicus river valley some 20 miles north of Smyrna. The city gained the coveted title Thrice Neokorus, signifying

---

[43] Eusebius, Ecclesiastical History, 145-146, cf. the Martyrdom of Polycarp.
[44] This is the subject of Chapter 10.

that it contained three separate temples dedicated to Roman emperors in which these men were worshipped as gods. This is one of the additional reasons Christ referred to this city as the site of Satan's throne (Rev 2:13). Hemer listed a number of possible historical allusions to "Satan's throne" in Pergamum, the most likely being: the throne-like altar of Zeus Soter; the Serpent symbol of Asklepios Soter; and the center of the emperor cult in Asia Minor. He opts for the latter.[45]

Christ's rebuke of the church at Pergamum is they are compromising with evil institutions and practices in order to maintain a low profile so as to avoid persecution. Regarding the Christians in Pergamum, Greg Beale writes,

In such an atmosphere it would be more difficult for Christians to maintain a high profile about their faith without also running into conflict with those committed to the officially accepted pagan religions, behind all of which Satan stood as king. This is highlighted by the fact that in most Greek cities, like Pergamum, citizens were typically expected to sacrifice to the gods that had been long honored in the area because of local religious tradition. Often when Christians were coerced to sacrifice to the Emperor it was because they had already refused to recognize the locally venerated gods and were consequently called to account by the Roman authorities.[46]

The church in Pergamum had resisted external pressures to compromise with paganism but had permitted a subtle form of compromise to develop. And it is indicted for harboring a group of compromisers, named here as the sect of the Nicolaitans (Rev 2:15). It is remembered that Balaam devised a plan in which some Moabite women would entice the Israelite men to defect from the Lord by joining them in worship of their pagan gods and fornicating with them (Num 25:1-3; cf. 2 Pet 2). Thus what this Nicolaitans are doing in the church of Pergamum is spiritual adultery with the world. Behind this defection are demons who are calling for the worship of men (1 Cor 10:20).

Doctrine matters! A deemphasizing of doctrinal purity leads to an over identification with the world. As has been said, the

---

[45] Hemer, The Letters to the Seven Churches of Asia in Their Local Setting, 68.
[46] Beale, The Book of Revelation, 246-247.

church must engage the culture, seeking to win the lost. The church must not give in to the pressure of watering down biblical doctrines in order to make them less offensive. Paul likewise admonishes Timothy and all of us with these words, "Take heed to yourself and to the doctrine. Continue in them, for in doing this you will save both yourself and those who hear you" (1 Tim 4:16).

Thyatira

Thyatira was not nearly as important or as large as the other cities mentioned in Revelation, but it was still a busy and wealthy commercial center located in the northern part of Lydia, near the border of Mysia, on the Lycas River. Thyatira was especially well-known for its trade guilds, namely that of the wool, linen, and dyers guild, and best known for its dyed fabrics, particularly for its purple dye (Acts 16:14).[47] Several demons were worshipped in Pergamum: Aesculapius, Baachus, and Artemis. The most important, however, was Apollo Tyrimnos where the temple of the Chaldean sibyl was also located. At this shrine was a prophetess (well known in the city) who claimed to receive knowledge from this goddess. She then imparted this information to the worshippers who came to the temple. She seems to have had her "Christian" counterpart in the congregation in the church at Thyatira whose actions were much like that of the Jezebel of the OT (Rev 2:20-23).

Christ begins the letter to Thyatira with His description of Himself as the divine Judge (Rev 2:18). He commends the Christians at Thyatira for their works of witness (Rev 2:19), but chastises them for their permissive spirit of idolatrous doctrinal compromise (Rev 2:20). The church at Thyatira characterizes as it were all Christian churches that lack doctrinal purity. Regarding this, James Packer writes,

---

[47] There is no evidence of how the church was started in Pergamum. Some think Lydia may have returned home and shared the good news with those of her native city. Others point to Acts 19:10 and the time of Paul's work in Ephesus.

Chapter 9: Biblical Evangelism

For over a century now, belief in the devil has seemed to be on the way out. The toothy red imp with the tail and the trident has become a secular figure of fun, while Protestant theologians generally have banished the personal devil of the Bible to the lumber-room for broken-down myths. No doubt this state of affairs is just what the devil has been working for, since it allows him to operate now on the grandest scale without being detected or opposed. Nor has he wasted his chances. During the past hundred years, he has engineered a world-wide collapse of evangelicalism in all the old Protestant denominations. The present spineless, powerless, unevangelical state of these churches, as compared with what they were a century ago, gives heart-breaking proof of the skill and thoroughness with which the devil has done his job. The Bible is no longer fully believed, the gospel is no longer thoroughly preached, and post-Christian paganism sweeps through the world like wildfire. Not for centuries has Satan won such a victory.[48]

Jezebel was probably a prophetess of the Gnostic-Nicolaitan faction in the church. And while Ephesus hated the deeds of the Nicolaitans (Rev 2:6), the church at Thyatira tolerated flagrant immorality (Rev 2:20). Here in the message to Thyatira, Christ says He brings temporal judgments upon churches and even individuals.[49] Believers will repent – false believers will continue in their sin. Correct doctrine is paramount to living a godly life in Christ, because you will live out what you believe.

One of Satan's chief aims is to destroy the doctrinal purity of the church. For example, Archibald Alexander writes, "Christians are more injured in this warfare, by the insidious and secret influence of their enemies lulling them into the sleep of carnal security, than by all their open and violent assaults."[50] Paul, in admonishing the elders of Ephesus says "Therefore take heed to yourselves and to all the flock, among which the Holy Spirit has made you overseers, to shepherd the church of God which He purchased with His own blood. For I know this, that after my departure *savage wolves* will come in among you, not sparing the flock. *Also from among yourselves men will rise up, speaking perverse things, to draw away the*

---

[48] Packer, God's Words: Studies of Key Bible Themes, 83.
[49] See chapter nine.
[50] Alexander, Thoughts on Religious Experience, 158.

disciples after themselves. Therefore watch, and remember that for three years I did not cease to warn everyone night and day with tears. (Acts 20:28-31; 2 Tim 3:1-9; 4:3-4; 2 Pet 2, cf. 1 Tim 4:16, emphasis added).

Augustine paradoxically writes, "But the devil seeing the temples of demons deserted, and the human race running to the name of the liberating Mediator, has moved the heretics under the Christian name to resist the Christian doctrine, as if they could be kept in the city of God without any correction."[51] *Thus, it may be said that to a large extent heresy strengthens the church.* As again, Augustine put it, "For even thus they profit by their wickedness those true catholic members of Christ, since God makes a good use even of the wicked, and all things work together for good to them that love Him."[52]

A holy spur necessitates the defense of orthodoxy. Through succeeding waves of heresy, the church has exercised the Spirit's wisdom by *rejecting error* and *confirming truth.* First, the connectivity of the Old and New Testaments were defended, viz., one God, the Father Almighty. Polemic works like Tertullian's *Adversus Marcionem*, were written to refute the error of Marcion, the Ebionites, and the Gnostics. Second, in regards to God the Son, being of one substance with the Father, heresies such as Arianism, Docetism, and Apollinarianism shaped the faith of the church by forcing her to mine deep into the Scriptures to defend the truth of Christ's full divinity and humanity. Third, errors such as Modalistic Monarchianism brought the defense of the divinity of God the Holy Spirit, the Lord and giver of life, and the Trinity. The church formulated the creeds in response to heretical errors. Philip Schaff states, "the Bible is God's Word to man; the Creed is man's answer to God." And, "the Creed states the truth in the logical form of the doctrine."[53]

There was then as will be now voluntary separations in the visible church between those who profess and teach the true Christian faith, and those, who lacking the Spirit's saving illumination, are not able to bear up under the teaching of

---

[51] Augustine, The City of God, 661.

[52] Ibid, 662.

[53] Schaff, Creeds of Christendom, Vol II, 3.

truth. They went out from us, but they were not of us (1 John 2:19), as if they could be kept in the city of God indifferently without any correction. They brought us a different spirit, a different gospel, and a different Jesus. They who were not of us hardened themselves against the gospel truth. This hardening is also the purpose of preaching the gospel, yet none of the elect are lost.

Heresy, in large measure, has also served as discipline for the Church. For God makes a good use even of the wicked (Pro 16:4), and He will thoroughly purge His threshing floor (Mt 3:12). Then as now, factions are inevitable and true believers become evident as the church earnestly contends for the faith that has once and for all delivered to the saints (1 Cor 11:19; Jude 3).

God called His church into existence to be a visible witness of the kingdom of God on earth, and to be His instrument for spreading the gospel of the kingdom throughout the world (Mt 24:9-14). Like, the church of Thyatira, we must trust in God alone for our economic welfare. In order to survive economically, some of the Christians at Thyatira were fornicating with pagan culture. In some measure they rationalized the veneration of the local Roman gods so as to avoid persecution. Likewise, we must resist giving in to cultural pressures even if that means losing our tax exempt status if we don't. We can't water down the doctrinal truths of the gospel in order to soften its rough edges. The gospel is to be proclaimed not edited.

Sardis

Sardis was the capital of the kingdom of Lydia, and was one of the most ancient and renowned cities of Asia Minor. Ancient Sardis was built on top of a 1000 foot high hill which projected from the northern side of Mt. Timolus. The sides of this hill were smooth, perpendicular rock which provided a natural citadel. Because of their feeling of security, the people of Sardis had always had a tendency to become soft and complacent. They lived in luxury and splendor, and were a proud, arrogant, and overconfident people. This was a city with a great past, but at the time of the writing of Revelation it was only a third rate city (in time, it ceased to exist altogether).

History shows that Sardis was complacent and found napping. Although considered impregnable, it was captured twice: First, in 549 B.C. by Cyrus, king of Persia. During the siege of Cyrus, a Persian soldier observed a Sardian descending the southern winding path to retrieve his fallen helmet. Unknown to the soldier and the city, the Persians followed his path back up to the summit and captured the whole city, taking them completely by surprise. And in 218 B.C., Sardis was surprised again, this time by Antiochus the Great. After a similar occurrence was reduplicated, Sardis was captured again by surprise during the night.

The risen Christ is calling the church at Sardis and all churches to remain spiritually alert: this is paramount to maintaining a faithful Christian witness. And in light of the history of Sardis, the Lord's warning to the congregation becomes a little more meaningful: "If therefore you will not wake up, I will come like a thief, and you will not know at what hour I will come upon you" (Rev. 3:3). And to the faithful in churches like Sardis Jesus says, "You have a few names even in Sardis who have not defiled their garments; and they shall walk with Me in white, for they are worthy" (Rev 3:4).

Soiling or defiling one's garments seems to be a symbol for mingling with pagan life and thus defiling the purity of one's relation to Christ. The Sardian Christians were suppressing their witness by assuming a low profile as to avoid ostracism and persecution. They are to repent of this, wake up and be watchful against their three enemies: (1) the prevailing lust of the flesh; (2) the lures of the world system; and (3) the lies of Satan.

Philadelphia

Like the church at Smyrna, Jesus finds nothing to condemn in this congregation, but offers only praise. Philadelphia was founded by colonists from Pergamum during the reign of King Attalus II. This king was given the nickname "Philadelphos" (Greek for "brother-lover") because of his great love for his brother King Eumenes II of Lydia. Christ commends the church at Philadelphia for its persevering witness and He promises to empower them even more (Rev 3:8-9). The open door refers not only to the church's salvation but also to their witness to that salvation (Rev 3:8). Further, the risen Lord encourages them to continue to remain faithful by persevering in their witness and inherit eternal fellowship with Him (Rev 3:12).

Christ's message to the church of Philadelphia teaches us that Jesus holds sovereignty over the sphere of life and death (Rev 3:7). And trials serve as punishments to unbelievers but tests to strengthen the faith of God's people (Rev 3:10-11). This is either punishment unto hardness of heart or chastening purgation unto holiness of heart. Additionally, the risen Lord Jesus Christ encourages believers that they can have peace in Him in the midst of the world's tribulation, because He has overcome the world. It's important to note that Jesus denies a physical removal from tribulation and affirms a spiritual protection from the devil (Rev 3:12, cf. Jn 16:20-24, 31-33; 17:1-26; 1 Thess 3:4; 2 Tim 3:12, et al).

The biblical point being made here is, our staying power (patient-endurance) is demonstrated by the keeping of Jesus Christ's word in faithful testimony in thought, word, and deed, and by not denying His name, i.e., not being ashamed of Him. For Jesus promises peace in Him alone in the midst of the world's tribulation because He has overcome (conquered) the world. And like the Philadelphian Christians, we must remain heavenly-minded and focused on the final reward or we will be tempted to conform ourselves to the world spirit and compromise our witness because of persecution (Rev 3:12, cf. 2 Cor 4:16-18; Phil 3:17-21).

Laodicea

Laodicea was located some 100 miles east of Ephesus on the Lycas River. It was founded by Antiochus II, a Seleucid king who named the city after his wife, Laodice, who later poisoned him. In the year 361 A.D. a Council was held here which established the canon of the New Testament. It became a great, wealthy center of industry, and was especially famous for its high-grade black wool. It was the veritable Wall Street of Asia Minor, a financial Mecca. There were many luxuries in the city such as theaters, a stadium, a gymnasium equipped with baths, etc. Laodicea was situated in the area of some hot springs which emitted lukewarm water that was used in their baths. There was also a famous school of medicine here, which was noted for its production of a remedy for weak eyes called "Phrygian powder."

It was such a wealthy and self-sufficient city that after an earthquake in 60 A.D. they refused any assistance from the Roman Empire, and as Tacitus informs us: "The same year Laodicea, one of the most famous cities of Asia, having been prostrate by an earthquake, recovered herself by her own resources, and without any relief from us." The people of the city were so rich and self-reliant that they were all but unbearable; an attitude which carried over into the church located there. The church at Laodicea believed their economic prosperity indicated their spiritual welfare but their self-evaluation couldn't have been more wrong. The effect Laodicea's conduct on Christ was like the effect of their own water – lime laden, sickly and nauseatingly tepid (Rev 3:16).

Christ's indictment against the church of Laodicea, and the church in America today is that they are half-hearted in their relationship with him. They lack their former zeal and love that they had for Him. Prosperity having found its home in them, they have grown to wane spiritually to the extent that they live in some halfway existence between being fully committed to Christ and having no mind to Him at all. Regarding the spiritual torpidity of the church of Laodicea, John Piper says, "Christ has a moderate influence on their lives. They are not uninfluenced by the Lord; but neither do they go overboard nor get very excited about the Creator of all. In relation to prayer, it would be safe to say that they probably pray at meals and pause for two or three minutes at bedtime. But they do not burn with a desire for more of God. They do not go hard after him in the secret place. They do not fling the door wide and welcome him into the innermost places of their emotions. But they keep him just outside the door and do their business with him coolly, lukewarmly, through the mail-slot." Therefore Jesus says,

16 So then, because you are lukewarm, and neither cold nor hot, I will vomit you out of My mouth. 17 Because you say, 'I am rich, have become wealthy, and have need of nothing'—and do not know that you are wretched, miserable, poor, blind, and naked— 18 I counsel you to buy from Me gold refined in the fire, that you may be rich; and white garments, that you may be clothed, that the shame of your nakedness may not be revealed; and anoint your eyes with eye salve, that you may see. 19 As many as I love, I rebuke and chasten. Therefore be zealous and repent (Rev 3:16-19).

Jesus says to the Laodicean church throughout history, self-sufficiency is spittle to Me, be rich toward God, bearing gold refined in fire (Rev 3:18), that is faith that is tested in trials (1 Pet 1:6-7, cf. Is 48:10). Laodicean Christianity is too comfortable in the world. What Christ demands is genuineness and openness. It's as C.S. Lewis put it, "Prosperity knits a man to the world. He feels that he is finding his place in it, while really it is finding its place in him."[54] The Laodicean church is always faced with the danger of being lukewarm. The church is to faithfully proclaim the gospel (the work of faith), however, faithful preaching of the Word of God always brings tribulation (Jn 16:33), something which the Laodicean church seeks to avoid by taking a low profile. A sort of *non rockaboatus Ecclesiasticus*? But God has not called the church to a low profile but a lofty one – like a city on a hill that cannot be hidden (Mt 5:14). Christians shouldn't think it something strange when persecution follows hard on the heels of her evangelistic efforts (1 Pet 4:12), as the true *work of faith* is sure to bring *tribulation* (1 Thess 2:15; 2 Thess 1:4; 2 Tim 3:12, cf. Is 26:12).

Also, as we have seen, Christians are called to appeal to the world, on behalf of God, the urgent message of reconciliation (2 Cor 5:20). This is the church's *labor of love*; loving others in spite of themselves; demonstrating in actions our love for our fellow man. And this is because the love of Christ compels us to tell others about Jesus Christ – the gospel of the *kingdom*.

---

[54] Lewis, The Screwtape Letters, 144.

Chapter 9: Biblical Evangelism

The *command* of Christ to His church is "This gospel of the kingdom will be preached in all the world as a witness to all the nations" (Mt 24:14). As for the *cost* for the completion of the Great Commission, "They will deliver you up to tribulation and kill you, and you will be hated by all nations for My name's sake," (Mt 24:9). And "He who endures to the end shall be saved" (Mt 24:13). This is the *confidence* a perfect atonement secures, for not even death can separate us from the love of Christ (Rom 8:31-39). In the power of Christ, we will endure to the end and be saved while we preach like self-squanderers the gospel of the kingdom. *Endurance* means remaining faithful to Christ despite persecution. This grace of patience we will discuss further in chapter ten, but for now, suffice it to say that endurance – staying power, is granted to us at the time of need. For as Christians, we are enabled to endure all things because we have been crucified with Christ, Who now dwells in our hearts by faith with which He roots and grounds Himself to us in love. Divine Love is both the power that compels us to proclaim the good news of the gospel of the kingdom, and our chief joy, for we no longer live for ourselves but for Him who died for us (2 Cor 5:15).

As has been said, Christ's message to the Seven Churches, and by extension the church of all ages, is meant to jolt Christians back into the reality of their faith by giving a heavenly perspective of the cosmic spiritual conflict of which the church finds herself in, thereby heightening their sense of awareness; encouraging them to persevere in their faithful witness. Here were the salient truths involving the churches:

1. Ephesus: rediscovery of our first love – Jesus.
2. Smyrna: commended for faithfulness under persecution.
3. Pergamum: importance of doctrinal purity and devotion to truth.
4. Thyatira: importance of ethical purity and true worship.
5. Sardis: importance of an awakened orthodoxy.
6. Philadelphia: commended for courage in missions and outreach.
7. Laodicea: repentance from lukewarm worldliness and pride.

Christ and Culture

As we consider evangelism, a question remains as to how we are to relate to the world we are to evangelize. How are

400

Chapter 9: Biblical Evangelism

Christians to understand culture? How is the church to relate to culture? And how should the church approach culture? We should first define culture. Etymologically, the term "culture" has its roots in antiquity, from the Latin word *colere*, which refers to tilling the ground in order to grow crops. Cicero, applying the word philosophically, expands its meaning to include things that aren't grown in the soil, viz., what we make, both with our minds and our hands.[55] In this way, we may understand culture to include everything that mankind works at to achieve. Culture includes every system of thought, all languages, customs, businesses, political systems. Culture includes literature, music, cuisine, and fashions. Is culture everything? No, it isn't. There is a difference between creation and culture.

John Frame helps us make an important distinction between the two. He writes,

Creation is what God makes; culture is what we make. Now of course God is sovereign, so everything we make is also His in one sense. Or, somewhat better: creation is what God makes by Himself, and culture is what He makes through us. The sun, moon, and stars are not culture. The light and darkness are not culture. The basic chemistry of the earth, and the original genetic structure of life forms are not culture; they are God's creation.[56]

Given an understanding of what culture is, the next question we should pose is how are Christians to relate to it? Any discussion regarding this topic is libel to include H. Richard Niebuhr's work *Christ and Culture*. In it he famously outlined five ways that Christians might relate to culture. These are: (1) Christ against culture, (2) the Christ of culture, (3) Christ above culture, (4) Christ and culture in paradox, and (5) Christ the transformer of culture. Let's briefly investigate each one and draw some important inferences in the process.

---

[55] Cicero's, in his *Tusculan Disputations*, wrote of a cultivation "*cultura*" of the soul employing an agricultural metaphor to describe the development of mankind.

[56] Frame, The Doctrine of the Christian Life, 854-855. Frame adds that "culture is both what human society is and what it ought to be, both real and ideal. Culture is what a society has made of God's creation, together with its ideals of what it ought to make of it," p. 857.

Chapter 9: Biblical Evangelism

The first view, *Christ against culture* may be argued by Christians who might fail to make a distinction between culture and the world. The Bible defines "world" in more than one sense. For example, in John's Gospel the "world" kosmos is used 78 times with various meanings; ranging from a world full of people God's Son came to save in John 3:16, to the ungodly multitude of fallen man who are slaves of the devil in John 7:7.[57] However, we must understand that before we are saved by Christ we are all slaves of Satan (Eph 2:1-10). In this way we may understand "world" to mean the collective mass of unregenerate humanity. But should we equate culture (everything mankind makes with his mind and hands) with the world?

The *Christ against culture* view equates culture purely in an evil sense. The Latin Church father Tertullian, argued for Christians to take this view. He asked, "What indeed has Athens to do with Jerusalem?" And called for faithful Christians to remain completely separate from secular society, staying out of politics, the military, and trade; virtually all secular life. Perhaps what motivated Tertullian to make this appeal was because during his life time Rome made open attacks on Christianity.[58] However, this view became less common after Rome officially made Christianity a legal religion.

Modern adherents to this view renounce all participation in culture, i.e., politics, military service, education, etc., and make their own distinct culture. This view may be conceptualized by the following diagram:

---

[57] The word kosmos κόσμος is used 186 times in the NT and can also refer to the universe, as in John 21:25, the earth itself, as in 1 Tim 6:7, as well as a general collection of things, as in Jam 3:6, or even to adornments, as in 1 Pet 3:3. Usually the word "world" is used in a negative sense in the Bible and refers to the kingdom of the Evil One, as well as the unregenerate "sea of humanity" held under his captive will. See John 8:43-47.

[58] Tertullian, who considered Greek philosophy to be incompatible with Christian wisdom said, "What has Athens to do with Jerusalem?" The oft misquoted, Tertullian made strong lasting contributions to the Church by what amounts to the first articulation of the Trinity, as well as the Person of the Son of God. Paradoxically, he rescued the Church from the heresy of Sabellianism because he was a Montanist. A good book demonstrating Tertullian's contribution to the Church is Eric Osborne's *Tertullian, First Theologian of the West*.

Chapter 9: Biblical Evangelism

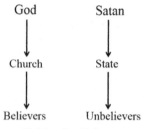

Christ against Culture

An argument made earlier was that culture consists of both good and evil. Remember Nietzsche's parable? The very foundation of Western society (culture) was built squarely on the Word of God. Yes, the world (unsaved mankind) is under the power of the devil, however, culture is mixed with both good and evil effects. As was said earlier, Christ has called us to be *in* the world but not *of* it.[59] 1 John 2:15-17 tells us:

[15] Do not love the world or the things in the world. If anyone loves the world, the love of the Father is not in him. [16] For all that *is* in the world—the lust of the flesh, the lust of the eyes, and the pride of life—is not of the Father but is of the world. [17] And the world is passing away, and the lust of it; but he who does the will of God abides forever.

The world, says Jesus, will hate you as it hates Me (John 15:18). In the world, Christians will be persecuted but Christ has conquered the world (John 16:33). And the apostle Paul tell us that in Christ, the world is crucified to us and we are crucified to the world (Gal 6:14). So, should we take the *Christ against culture* view and adopt it? The Bible says no. Remember Christ's High Priestly prayer for all Christians in John 17:15? Jesus prays to the Father, "I do not pray that You should take them out of the world, but that You should keep them from the evil one." And as the Father has sent His Son Jesus into the world, so does Jesus Christ send His disciples into the world.

---

[59] See chapter 4.

Chapter 9: Biblical Evangelism

Similarly, the apostle Paul accommodates his behavior to the customs of various cultures so that he may win them to Christ.[60] This will be discussed in more detail later, but suffice it to say, Christians are to concern themselves about what goes on in this world and work to cultivate God-honoring values in their respective cultures they live in.

It is interesting to note that not even Tertullian was consistent with this view. Defending Christianity in his *Apology* about 195 AD, he writes,

We sojourn with you in the world, abjuring neither forum, nor shambles, nor bath, nor booth, nor workshop, nor inn, nor weekly market, nor any other places of commerce. We sail with you, and fight with you, and till the ground with you; and in like manner we unite with you in your traffickings – even in the various arts we make public property of our works for your benefit.[61]

However, while Tertullian defends Christianity in this way he admonishes Christians to withdrawal from secular culture. This stance, as D. A. Carson tells us, "is both inevitable and inadequate." Because he says, "the most radical Christians inevitably make use of the culture, or parts of the culture."[62]

The second view, *the Christ of culture*, nearly antithetical to the first one, blurs the distinction between culture and Christianity. This position is perhaps best represented by such early church fathers as Justin Martyr, Clement of Alexandria, and Origen who viewed Christianity as the fulfillment of Greek philosophy. According to Justin, God makes the world from pre-existing substance. He got this idea from Plato. Justin thought Plato got the idea from Moses, and Clement viewed philosophy as God's covenant with the Greeks. Later theologians, like Peter Abelard and Ulrich Zwingli, and to some extent Desiderius Erasmus, shared this view. For example, Ulrich Zwingli wrote,

Then you may hope to see [in heaven] the whole company and assemblage of all the saints, the wise, the faithful, brave, and good who have lived since the world began. Here you will see the two Adams, the redeemed and the redeemer, Abel, Enoch, Noah,

---

[60] Frame, The Doctrine of the Christian Life, 866.
[61] Tertullian, Apology, 42.
[62] Carson, Christ and Culture Revisited, 15.

Chapter 9: Biblical Evangelism

Abraham, Isaac, Jacob, Judah, Moses, Joshua, Gideon, Samuel, Phineas, Elijah, Elisha, Isaiah, and the Virgin Mother of God of whom he prophesied, David, Hezekiah, Josiah, the Baptist, Peter, Paul; here too, Hercules, Theseus, Socrates, Aristides, Antigonus, Numa, Camillus, the Catos and Scipios; here Louis the Pious, and your predecessors, the Louis, Philips, Pepins, and all your ancestors who have gone hence in faith. In short there has not been a good man and will not be a holy heart or faithful soul from the beginning of the world to the end thereof that you will not see in heaven with God.[63]

This position presents Christianity as the crown of the particular culture it is making inroads into. It may be called the accommodationistic approach.

But we must make a distinction between human reason and divine revelation, between the perceived goodness in human culture and biblical principles. This view seems less likely to present culture with the revelation of sin. The danger with this view is the tendency to downplay sin and lob off the rough edges of biblical truth in order to make the gospel more palpable. However, we can't water down the meaningful truths in order to be less offensive to the world. The gospel of the kingdom is a sword. For, where there is no revelation, the people (culture) cast off restraint (Pro 29:18). *The Christ of culture* view point may be conceptualized in the following diagram.

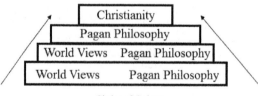

Christ of Culture

Perhaps the best modern examples of this view came from the German theologians of the Enlightenment such as Albrecht Ritschl and Rudolf Bultmann, who viewed Jesus as a great

---

[63] Zwingli, Exposition of the Christ Faith, 16. Erasmus may have shared this view. In his "Enchiridion Militis Christiani" Handbook of the Christian Knight, Chapter 4, he writes, "Which things Plato perceiving by inspiration of God, wrote in his book called *Timeus.*"

moral teacher. The essence of Bultmann's view is perhaps best stated as, "It doesn't matter what you believe (Bultmann advocated demythologizing the Bible to find historic Christianity) but how you live that counts." But Christ is no mere moral teacher, He is the Lord of heaven and earth, He died to save us from the wrath of God, and to give us eternal life so that we might live godly lives and win the lost for Him.

As stated earlier, this particular view blurs the distinction between Christ and culture. It is perhaps most likely due to the prevalence of liberal theology and non-Christian philosophy. But because non-Christian philosophy draws only from the mind of man to answer questions about: ultimate reality (metaphysics), how we come to know things (epistemology), and how we should live (ethics), it's therefore a rather mixed bag; ranging from being a valuable tool for Christian apologetic and theological use on one end of the spectrum, to being a quite misled, depraved, or even demonic exercise on the other.

God is pleased to reveal some measure of the truth even to pagans. In this way, non-Christian philosophy may be therefore useful to Christians (Ps 19) as the apostle Paul shows us (Acts 17), however, because Scripture alone is the Christian's ultimate authority, being God's Self-revelation to His covenant people, far surpassing the mind of man, Christian philosophy is to be the servant of theology.[64] Besides, Christ's wisdom is far greater than any Greek philosopher or modern moralist ever dreamed.[65]

There are two biblical points being made here: (1) whereas our culture seeks answers apart from biblical revelation,

---

[64] We might add here that philosophy enables the human mind to think on a level that penetrates to the deeper significance of things; assisting us to organize our thoughts about God, the world and ourselves. Also, philosophy enables the human mind to think critically, enabling Christians to better arrange and systematize facts, and provides a thinking man with conceptual tools and a frame of reference so as to enable pattern and form recognition. This will aid the Christian to better discover and answer the inconsistencies of competing world views. In these ways, Christians may better visualize, organize and defend Christianity, while working to uncover and answer non-Christian world views. Thus, in a manner of speaking, Christians redeem the culture they live in.

[65] Frame, The Doctrine of the Christian Life, 868.

holding the mind of man (reason) as the sounding board, Christians are to be restrained and guided by God's Word and Spirit alone, seeking to make Christ preeminent in everything (Col 1:18); and (2) Christianity's exclusive claim is salvation by grace alone through faith in Christ alone. Any other message, including the social gospel, simply isn't Christian.

Christ above culture, the third view, the synthesist's viewpoint according to Niebuhr, is best understood if we view the church as "synthesizing" divine revelation with the natural revelation of human culture. Niebuhr tells us, "Thomas Aquinas represents a Christianity that has achieved or accepted full social responsibility for all the great institutions."[66] Aquinas believed man could prove the existence of God by reason alone but required God's grace to be saved from our sins. This view posits an inherent quality in culture, such as values and morals, which only require a little guidance from the church in order to rise to the level God has established it to be. This position, which the medieval church held, envisions Christ reigning sovereignly above culture as He does the church. The following diagram represents the *Christ above culture* view.

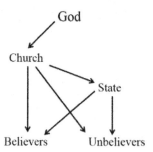

Christ above Culture (Synthesist)

John Frame explains Aquinas' view, "Generally speaking, culture is man's development of nature. Christ supplements nature with something higher. The higher then mingles easily

---

[66] Niebuhr, *Christ and Culture*, 128.

with the lower, in a synthesis."[67] Should we take the *Christ above culture* view and adopt it? The Bible says no. The Word of God presents unregenerate mankind as defiled in mind and conscience (Tit 1:15). Mankind doesn't merely need a little help so that culture may achieve a higher level, mankind is dead in its trespasses and sins (Rom 3:23). Therefore, whereas the church is not an instrument of the state, *Christ of culture,* the state is not an instrument of the church, *Christ above culture.*

The fourth view, *Christ and culture in paradox*, the dualist perspective of Christ above Culture, has traditionally been associated with the Lutheran tradition, as well as many Reformed people today. This view envisions God exercising two kingdoms: the church and the world. Gene Veith explains,

In the church, God reigns through the work of Christ and the giving of the Holy Spirit, expressing His love and grace through forgiveness of sins and the life of faith. In the world, God exercises His authority and providential control through natural laws. Similarly, God rules the nations – even those who do not acknowledge Him – making human beings to be social creatures, in need of governments, laws, and cultures to mitigate the self-destructive tendencies of sin and to enable human beings to survive.[68]

The following diagram conceptualizes the *Christ and culture in paradox* view.

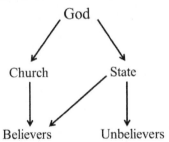

Christ and Culture in Paradox (Christ above Culture –Dualist)

---

[67] Frame, The Doctrine of the Christian Life, 869.
[68] Veith, Christianity and Culture: God's Double Sovereignty.

As stated, this view posits two spheres by which God's sovereignty is exercised. As Veith states, "A Christian is thus a citizen of two kingdoms-the kingdom of heaven and the kingdom of this world. These spheres have different demands and operate in different ways. But God is the King of both." However, despite Dr. Veith's excellent argument, history seems to demonstrate the patent weakness of this view in light of the Nazification of the German church. Should we take the *Christ and culture in paradox* view and adopt it? That's to be determined.

Lastly, *Christ, the Transformer of culture*, the third subcategory under the Christ above culture pattern envisions Christ transforming culture by the power of the gospel. The previous two where the synthesist and dualist; this one is the conversionist. Regarding this view Niebuhr writes, "Christ is the transformer of culture...in the sense that He redirects, reinvigorates, and regenerates that life of man, expressed in all human works, which in present actuality is the perverted and corrupted exercise of a fundamentally good nature."[69]

The Christian life is all about balance. The *Christ, the Transformer of Culture* view seems to be most within both God's cultural mandate for man, as well as the Great Commission. The *Christ, the Transformer of Culture* view may be conceptualized as follows.

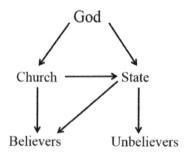

Christ, the Transformer of Culture (Christ above Culture – Conversionist)

---

[69] Niebuhr, Christ and Culture, 209.

Chapter 9: Biblical Evangelism

God has called the church to transform culture according to biblical standards. God's plan for the church is to transform culture by calling upon the men and women of all nations to repent and believe the gospel, ushering in Christ's lordship not only in their individual lives, but in their families, and societies as well. Thus, by the Great Commission, Christ extends His reign from individuals, to marriages, families, societies (culture), states, and nations. As Niebuhr writes, "We are not dealing with human progress in culture, but with the divine conversion of the spirit of man from which all culture rises."[70]

The Christian life is all about balance. As has been said, God would have us be *in* the world, so as to win the lost for Christ – the Great Commission. This we referred to as the indigenous principle.[71] And equally important as the counterpart to the indigenous principle, the pilgrim principle taught us to remain separate from immorality so as not to be yoked with the unbelieving world. We summed up these two principles with the following points:

1. Christians are to be *in* the world but not *of* it (Jn 17:15-16).
2. Christians are to *separate* from the world (1 Cor 6:9-7:1) but in some ways *participate* in it (1 Cor 5:9-11).
3. Christians are to *adapt* to their particular culture (1 Pet 2:12) while *exposing* evil (Eph 5:11).
4. Christians are to refuse *conformity* with the world (Rom 12:1-2) but *contextualize* life situations to save others (1 Cor 9:22; 10:32-33).

David Kinnaman states in *unChristian*, "Being salt and light demands two things: we practice purity in the midst of a fallen world and yet we live in proximity to this fallen world. If you don't hold up both truths in tension, you invariably become useless and separated from the world God loves. For example, if you only practice purity apart from proximity to the culture, you inevitably become pietistic, separatist, and conceited. If you live in close proximity to the culture without also living in

---

[70] Ibid, 228.
[71] See chapter 4.

a holy manner, you become indistinguishable from fallen culture and useless in God's kingdom."[72]

Revival

As said before, evangelism is the proclamation of the saving truths of the Gospel of Jesus Christ. It's the verbalizing of the great things we have come to know personally for the purpose of gathering and strengthening the church. Evangelism is the prophetic role for the entire church. Whereas, evangelism is the appeal to and awakening of people outside the church, revival is the renewal and reawakening of the church from within.[73] Psalm 85 voices our plea for revival:

Restore us, O God of our salvation, and cause Your anger toward us to cease. Will You be angry with us forever? Will You prolong Your anger to all generations? **Will You not revive us again**, that Your people may rejoice in You? Show us Your mercy, Lord, and grant us Your salvation (Psalm 85:4-7, emphasis added).

Revivals are God's way of restoring spiritual life to the church after a period of decline. The great revivals of history have contained the following elements: (1) the revelation of Jesus Christ through sound gospel preaching, teaching and witnessing – the Church's increased zeal is instrumental in the conversion of sinners; (2) conviction of sin, as having wronged God and offended Him; and (3) people so moved to take their minds and hearts off of the cares of this world and on to Christ Jesus.

The Greatest Revival in History

In 612 BC Nineveh, the capitol of Assyria was mercilessly sacked and laid waste by the combined armies of the Medes and the Babylonians. There were few who mourned Nineveh's passing. As the prophet Nahum prophesied (3:18-19), "Your shepherds slumber, O king of Assyria; Your nobles rest in the dust. Your people are scattered on the mountains, and no one

---

[72] Kinnaman, unChristian, 133.
[73] Turnbull, The Preacher's Heritage, Task, and Resources, 33.

gathers them. Your injury has no healing, your wound is severe. All who hear news of you will clap their hands over you, for upon whom has not your wickedness passed continually?" Assyria's policy was to dissuade opposition to their rule by setting violent examples which potential rebels might expect. As such, entire male populations of select cities were slaughtered without mercy. The Assyrian army was quite formidable and would commit atrocities so as to discourage resistance, and so cause their enemies to come to terms quickly.

And one hundred and fifty years prior to the destruction of Nineveh, God sent them a prophet to call them to repentance, and the world witnessed what has been called the greatest revival in history. Jonah, the prophet of this great revival lived in Israel during troubled times. We learn from the Book of 2 Kings that Jonah, the son of Amittai (Jonah 1:1), of the tribe of Zebulon, was a prophet in the court of Jeroboam II, a wicked king of Israel, during the 820s - 780s BC, in a time when Assyria had previously made rapacious incursions into Israel. Assyria was both feared and hated by the people of Israel. In this setting we learn that Jonah is sent by God to bring a message of judgment to his national enemy Assyria. He preaches judgment and the greatest revival in history begins.

But the greatest revival didn't happen because of Jonah himself. We may surmise this for at least three reasons: first, it wasn't Jonah's fine oratory, or his articulate message. For as Jonah 3:4 tells us, it was short and edgy, "Yet forty days and Nineveh shall be overthrown." The word overthrown is the same word used to describe what happened to Sodom and Gomorrah. Hearing these words of judgment, the king of Nineveh even calls for the animals to wear sackcloth (Jonah 3: 8). The king says, "Let neither man nor beast, herd nor flock, taste anything; do not let them eat, or drink water. But let man and beast be covered with sackcloth, and cry mightily to God; yes, let everyone turn from his evil way and from the violence that is in his hands. Who can tell if God will turn and relent, and turn away from His fierce anger, so that we may not perish?"

Chapter 9: Biblical Evangelism

The king of Nineveh admits that the Lord is right and that Nineveh is wicked and violent and deserving of destruction. In the words of Jonah, the people of Nineveh recognized the authentic demand of God and repented. It was therefore not Jonah's rhetorical ability but God's power that was responsible for the Ninevites' repentance.

Secondly, it wasn't Jonah's great preaching that brought about Nineveh's repentance because if you remember that only a third of the city heard his message on the first day. Jonah 3:3-4 tells us, "So Jonah arose and went to Nineveh, according to the word of the Lord. Now Nineveh was an exceedingly great city, a three-day journey in extent. And Jonah began to enter the city on the first day's walk. Then he cried out and said, "Yet forty days, and Nineveh shall be overthrown!" So it wasn't Jonah's great preaching ability that transformed a city, but the power of God's Word. And the people's repentance was immediate!

And thirdly, it wasn't Jonah's desire for the lost to be saved either, and knowing the beginning of this story it's amazing to consider back in chapter one we read, "Now the word of the Lord came to Jonah the son of Amittai, saying, "Arise, go to Nineveh, that great city, and cry out against it; for their wickedness has come up before Me." But Jonah arose to flee to Tarshish from the presence of the Lord. He went down to Joppa, and found a ship going to Tarshish; so he paid the fare, and went down into it, to go with them to Tarshish from the presence of the Lord." Jonah boards a ship and sails in the opposite direction to avoid preaching in Nineveh. It is clear from chapter four that Jonah greatly disliked the Ninevites and thought it best that they be judged by God rather than receive His grace. Jonah 4:1-3 tells us,

"But it displeased Jonah exceedingly, and he became angry. 2 So he prayed to the Lord, and said, "Ah, Lord, was not this what I said when I was still in my country? Therefore I fled previously to Tarshish; for I know that You are a gracious and merciful God, slow to anger and abundant in lovingkindness, One who relents from doing harm. 3 Therefore now, O Lord, please take my life from me, for it is better for me to die than to live!"

413

Chapter 9: Biblical Evangelism

The man God uses to bring the greatest revival in history boards a ship going the opposite direction to where he is sent, and would rather die along with innocent sailors than obey God. Amazingly, God does not remove Jonah from his prophetic office, even though he blatantly disobeyed the Lord's call when it was first given. Instead, God rescues His messenger from falling into Sheol (Jonah 1:17) and delivers the prophet back onto the dry land so that he may finish his appointed task (Jonah 2:10).

God desires us to have a heart like His for the lost. Before we can be used for God's work of winning the lost for Christ, we as Christians must first be renewed in heart. God needed to enlarge Jonah's heart to include the lost. Jonah forgot that God's covenant with Israel was to be a blessing for all the nations. In Gen 12:1-3, God tells Abraham, "Get out of your country, from your family and from your father's house, to a land that I will show you. I will make you a great nation; I will bless you and make your name great; and you shall be a blessing. I will bless those who bless you, and I will curse him who curses you; and in you all the families of the earth shall be blessed."

Israel was blessed in order to be a blessing. What God was doing in Jonah was leaving the ninety-nine to go after the lost (Lk 15:4). Jonah says in effect, why are you saving these people? They are too wicked! They are too violent! They are socially unjust. They are beyond recovery. They have committed such atrocities! But God has love for the worst sinners. Oswald Chambers reminds us,

The entrance into the kingdom of God is through the sharp, sudden pains of repentance colliding with man's respectable "goodness." Then the Holy Spirit, who produces these struggles, begins the formation of the Son of God in the person's life (see Gal 4:19). This new life will reveal itself in conscious repentance followed by unconscious holiness, never the other way around. The foundation of Christianity is repentance. Strictly speaking, a person cannot repent when he chooses— repentance is a gift of God. The old Puritans used to pray for "the gift of tears." If you ever cease to understand the value of repentance, you allow yourself to remain in sin. Examine yourself to see if you have forgotten how to be truly repentant.[74]

God relents from the calamity He said He would bring upon Nineveh. Regarding this R C Sproul writes, "God is free to alter His announced judgments when we repent (Jer 18:1-10). Despite His knowing whether we will trust Him before we do so, He still condescends to respond to our trust, and thus our actions are significant. Though we must not take this truth for granted, our Father will always freely forgive those who turn to Him. His lordship does not abolish the real impact of our choices; instead, it establishes them as part of His overall decree (WCF 3.1)."[75] By warning of judgment to come, God intends by prophecy to excite those threatened with it to take proper measures for averting them.[76]

The Commission is not fulfilled yet. The Gospel enlarges our heart for the world! Can't God forgive murders on death row? Do you believe God can save people like Jeffrey Dahmer? Revival is about renewal, regeneration, and revocation. When God renews and enlarges the hearts of His people to be as big as His for the lost, He sends them out and the lost are saved, they are regenerated, born again to the glory of God! As Peter declares, "in every nation whoever fears Him and works righteousness is accepted by Him" (Acts 10:35).

God's purpose in revival is to impress upon the hearts of His people the fact that people are perishing. God would have us be a church that burns with holy zeal for winning the lost for Christ. Jonah was a sign. After spending three days and nights inside the belly of a great fish whose stomach made him look like something out of a science fiction novel, Jonah gets vomited up on the shore and goes to Nineveh and preaches, and the greatest revival occurs.

It was a miraculous appearance of a man thought to be dead. Jesus said that the sign of Jonah was the only sign to be given to the people (Mt 12: 38-41). Regarding this G. B. Caird relates that,

---

[74] Chambers, My Utmost for His Highest, Dec 7.
[75] The idea here of God's sovereignty and human responsibility will be discussed more in the next chapter.
[76] Von Rad, Genesis, 376.

Chapter 9: Biblical Evangelism

Those who asked for a sign wanted some peculiar proof that Jesus was the emissary of God he claimed to be. He replied that the only proof of His credentials he was prepared to give was that which Jonah offered to the Ninevites; Jonah called them to repentance, and in his words they recognized the authentic demand of God. The same demand was present in the preaching of Jesus, and those who were deaf to it were not likely to be convinced by any other form of authentication. They were an evil generation who had proved by their lack of response that, for all their religiosity, they could not recognize the voice of God when they heard it. The Queen of Sheba and the city of Nineveh had responded to the best revelation of God available in their day; and those foreigners would compare favorably on the Day of Judgment with the chosen people of God who had turned their backs on the greatest of all opportunities.[77]

God desires us to have a heart like His for the lost, and He will do what He must for us to have it. Anyone can be saved! Peter tells us, "The Lord is not slack concerning His promise, as some count slackness, but is longsuffering toward us, not willing that any should perish but that all should come to repentance" (2 Pet 3:9). And God speaking through His prophet Ezekiel tells us, "Say to them: 'As I live,' says the Lord God, 'I have no pleasure in the death of the wicked, but that the wicked turn from his way and live. Turn, turn from your evil ways" (Ezek 33:11).

Everyone is equally lost! Paul tells us, "There is none righteous, no, not one; there is none who understands; there is none who seeks after God" (Rom 3:10-11). Everyone is equally as lost and hopeless apart from Christ. It is hardly complimentary to God that we should choose Him as an alternative to Hell; yet even this He accepts.[78] God desires us to have a heart like His for the lost. We have been blessed in order to be a blessing.

Like Treasure Hidden in a Field

God desires for us to have a heart like His for the lost; He wants us to treasure what He treasures. And what does God

---

[77] Caird, The Gospel of Luke, 156.
[78] Lewis, The Problem of Pain, 96.

treasure? His people. Here's a few verses that speak about it: In Exodus 19:5-6 God says, "Now therefore, if you will indeed obey My voice and keep My covenant, then you shall be a *special treasure* to Me above all people; for all the earth is Mine. And you shall be to Me *a kingdom of priests and a holy nation.*" Likewise, through the apostle Peter God says, "But you are a *chosen generation, a royal priesthood, a holy nation, His own special people,* that you may proclaim the praises of Him who called you out of darkness into His marvelous light (1 Pet 2:9); and again in Titus 2:13-14 through the apostle Paul God says, "Looking for the blessed hope and glorious appearing of *our great God and Savior Jesus Christ,* who gave Himself for us, that He might redeem us from every lawless deed and purify for Himself *His own special people,* zealous for good works." God treasures His people. And who are God's people? Everyone who has faith in Christ?

Oskar Schindler, a German industrialist, and member of the Nazi party, renowned for saving over a thousand Jewish lives during the Holocaust, began by seeing the value of making easy money from free labor. For so Schindler thought, they were going to die anyway. Why not make a profit? In 1939, Schindler obtained an enamelware factory in Krakow, Poland, where he employed some 1,700 workers, of whom a thousand were Jews. Initially, Schindler was interested in the money-making potential of the business. But when Schindler had a change of heart, everything changed. He saw the value of those people's lives, and through his connections, Schindler protected his Jewish workers from deportation and death in Nazi concentration camps. Ultimately, he bankrupt himself to save those people. For Schindler, losing everything he had to gain their lives was all worth it.

And that's the point of the parable in Matthew 13:44. Jesus says, "Again, the kingdom of heaven is like treasure hidden in a field, which a man found and hid; and for joy over it he goes and sells all that he has and buys that field. The Kingdom of heaven is so valuable, that losing everything in life, including life itself, and gaining it, is a joyous exchange. Jesus tells us in Mt 6:33, "Seek first the kingdom of God and His righteousness." God's desire is for His people to seek the furtherance of Christ's kingdom and His righteousness. God wants us to treasure what He treasures. In other words, having the omnipotent, saving reign of Christ in our lives and seeking the lost for Christ, is the greatest treasure in this life.

A man is walking home from business in the city. He veers off the road into a field to cut the corner. The field is uneven and in order to keep his balance the man thrusts his staff into the dirt. And thunk. His staff strikes something hard. So he bends down and scraps away the dirt to find a treasure chest. And opening it, he discovers something that's worth more than the universe. From the moment of his discovery, the traveler's life changes. The treasure captures his heart and fills his mind with dreams. Within seconds he makes a plan. He quickly puts the treasure back in its place, covers it up, and goes home. He knows the present owner of the field has no idea of the treasure being there. And he sells everything he has in order to buy the field. And in that way, he gains the treasure. *He buys the field in order to gain the treasure.*

The man's covering of the treasure is not necessarily bad morality. If it was a shrewd piece of work, that's not the point of the parable. The point of the parable is – the surpassing wealth of the Kingdom, for which any sacrifice – all that one has, is not too great a price to pay. The apostle Paul expresses this very thing in Philippians 3:7-8, "Whatever gain I had, I counted as loss for the sake of Christ. Indeed, I count everything as loss because of the surpassing worth of knowing Christ Jesus my Lord. For His sake I have suffered the loss of all things and count them as rubbish, in order that I may gain Christ." Paul suffers the loss of all things that he may gain Christ. And for joy over the treasure the man went and counted everything rubbish because he wanted it so bad. The object of the man's desire costs him his life. God wants us to treasure what He treasures.

Just how should we relate to earthly riches? In the Parable of the Unjust Steward (Luke 16:1-13), Jesus demonstrates the nature of using true riches, and how we should use temporal wealth to gain eternal riches. Of all we could discuss concerning this parable, let's just look at verse 9: "And I say to you, make friends for yourselves by unrighteous mammon, that when you fail, they may receive you into an everlasting home." What exactly does this mean? It means at least this:

just as worldly people are wise to use their earthly wealth for material gains, God's people must be spiritually wise to use earthly wealth for eternal gains. We buy the field in order to gain the treasure (Mt 13:44). Jesus says in effect, use money and worldly goods, tainted as they are, to make friends for yourselves, so that when it comes to an end they may welcome you into eternal habitations. What does Jesus mean by friends? Jesus says, when you are Mine then you are no longer a slave but a friend – "Greater love has no one than this, than to lay down one's life for his friends. You are My friends if you do whatever I command you. No longer do I call you servants, for a servant does not know what his master is doing; but I have called you friends, for all things that I heard from My Father I have made known to you" (Jn 15:13-15).

Just as Abraham was called the friend of God, so is everyone who is won for Christ. They become our brother and sister in Christ. Those whom we have reached with the gospel's power are drawn into an intimate, abiding fellowship with God and His people. "And I say to you, make friends for yourselves by unrighteous mammon, that when you fail, they may receive you into an everlasting home" (Luke 16:9).

The biblical point being made here is, you can't buy or negotiate for the kingdom; if it cost you everything for the kingdom, it's a great deal. Because the kingdom of God is received without pay. Bankrupt people get the Kingdom (Mt 5:3). Blessed are the spiritually bankrupt for they know they have nothing with which to buy the kingdom! Jesus said, "You received without paying; give without pay" (Mt 10:8). So, you don't get the kingdom because you buy it, you get it because you want it more than anything. The Lord Jesus tells us in Luke 12:32-34:

32 "Do not fear, little flock, for it is your Father's good pleasure to give you the kingdom. 33 Sell what you have and give alms; provide yourselves money bags which do not grow old, a treasure in the heavens that does not fail, where no thief approaches nor moth destroys. 34 **For where your treasure is, there your heart will be also** (emphasis added).

What does it mean to lay up treasures in heaven? It means using all that we have for the glory of God. But we might ask,

how can earthly treasures become heavenly ones? William
Borden was born in 1887. He graduated from Yale, and was
heir to great fortune. To his father's disappointment, however,
Borden entered Princeton Theological Seminary, aspiring to
preach the gospel to the nations. What made William Borden
special was that he rejected a life of ease in order to bring the
gospel to Muslims.

Borden gave away hundreds of thousands of dollars to
missions. And after only four months of zealous ministry in
Egypt, he contracted spinal meningitis and died at the age of
twenty-four.[79] Precious in the sight of the Lord are the death of
His saints (Ps 116:15). Apart from Christ there is no
explanation for such a life. A.W. Tozer tells us:

As base a thing as money is, it yet can be transmitted into everlasting
treasure. It can be converted into food for the hungry and clothing for
the poor; it can keep a missionary actively winning lost men to the
light of the gospel and thus transmute itself into heavenly values. Any
temporal possession can be turned into everlasting wealth. Whatever
is given to Christ is immediately touched with immortality.[80]

Borden used mammon for heavenly treasure. He was laying
up treasures in heaven. For Borden, those whom he reached
with the gospel became a crown of joy for him as he entered
the reward of his Master (Mt 25:21; Phil 4:1).

The Kingdom is free but it's costly. It's free for all who
receive it but it cost Jesus everything. And like Borden, Jesus,
at the utmost cost, bought the field of the world to gain His
church, which is the treasure He sought. Whereas we buy
eternal things with temporal wealth – Jesus bought eternal
treasure with the most costly worth – His own life's blood.
Jesus purchased a treasure – God's people. He saw the value
of our lives and He bankrupt Himself to purchase us. For Jesus
Christ, losing everything He had to gain our lives was all
worth it. As we have seen, God renews and enlarges the hearts
of His people to be as big as His for the lost. And we buy the
field in order to gain the treasure.

---

[79] Alcorn, The Treasure Principle, 34-36.
[80] Tozer, The Transmutation of Wealth, 107. Cited in Alcorn, The Treasure
Principle, 55.

Chapter 9: Biblical Evangelism

Distinguishing Marks

Revival is the renewal and reawakening of the church from within. Thus, revivals begin with God's own people. In the words of J.I. Packer, "Revival is an extraordinary work of God the Holy Spirit reinvigorating and propagating Christian piety in a community. *Revival is an extraordinary work because it marks the abrupt reversal of an established trend and state of things among those who profess to be God's people.*"[81] As we have seen, God's purpose in revival is to impress upon the hearts of His people the fact that people are perishing. Revival renews God's people and regenerates sinners. However, when revival comes, the true work of God is always mixed with false works. When revival falls, "A great deal of noise and tumult, confusion and uproar, darkness mixed with light, and evil with good," writes Jonathan Edwards, "is always to be expected in the beginning of something very glorious in the state of things in human society, or the church of God."[82]

As we have discussed earlier, the Great Awakening was a series of religious revivals that swept over the American colonies about the middle of the 18th century. It began in the 1720s with the evangelistic efforts of Theodorus Frelinghuysen and Gilbert Tennent. The revival then swept through New England around 1734 with the preaching of Jonathan Edwards, and as Richard Hofstadter wrote, "it was nothing less than a second and milder Reformation."[83] The colonists of New England had experienced revival before. Edwards identified five earlier revivals he termed *harvests* which, as he said, some were more remarkable than others, and the ingathering of souls was plentiful.

Edwards described this first wave of revival in his *A Faithful Narrative of the Surprising Work of God* which was published between 1737 and 1739.[84] Edwards was asked to

---

[81] Packer, A Quest for Godliness, 318.

[82] Edwards, Some Thoughts Concerning the Present Revival of Religion, Part I, Section III.

[83] Richard Hofstadter, America at 1750: A Social Portrait, 217-218.

[84] The full title is: *A Faithful Narrative of the Surprising Work of God in the Conversion of many hundred souls in Northampton, and the Neighboring Towns and Villages of the County of Hampshire, in the Province of Massachusetts-Bay in New England.*

write this more detailed account in response to an earlier letter he had written to Dr. Benjamin Colman, the pastor of Brattle Street Church in Boston. Needless to say, it raised much interest. This was the first wave of the Spirit's movement during Edward's tenure as pastor of Northampton. Later, in 1740, the second wave arrived largely through the preaching of George Whitefield and lasted until 1742.[85]

What about the revival was so controversial? For one, it was intense. Edwards writes, "God has also seemed to have gone out of His usual way, in the quickness of His work, and the swift progress His Spirit has made in His operations on the hearts of many. It is wonderful that persons should be so suddenly and yet so greatly changed."[86] Many recovered their former zeal for the Lord, and many experienced God's converting grace. Edwards, describing some of the effects of the revival in his *Faithful Narrative*, writes:

Many have spoken much of their hearts being drawn out in love to God and Christ; and of their minds being wrapt up in delightful contemplation of the glory and wonderful grace of God, the excellency and dying love of Jesus Christ; some persons having had such longing desires after Christ, or which have risen to such degree, *as to take away their natural strength*. Some have been so overcome with a sense of the dying love of Christ to such poor, wretched, and unworthy creatures, *as to weaken the body*...And they have talked, *when able to speak*, of the glory of God's perfections, the wonderfulness of His grace in Christ, and their own unworthiness, in such a manner as cannot be perfectly expressed after them...Many, while their minds have been filled with spiritual delights, *have as it were forgot their food*; their bodily appetite has failed, *while their minds have been entertained with meat to eat that others knew not of*.[87]

As the revival was coming to an end, Edwards noted that "In the latter part of May, it began to be very sensible that the Spirit of God was gradually withdrawing from us, and after this time Satan seemed to be more let loose, and raged in a

---

[85] The Great Awakening itself was part of a move of God in the North Atlantic regions, as is evidenced by outbreaks of revival in England (Wesley and Whitefield), Scotland (Whitefield), and Wales (Daniel Rowland, William Williams, and Howell Harris).

[86] Edwards, A Faithful Narrative of the Surprising Work of God, 21.

[87] Ibid, 45-46.

Chapter 9: Biblical Evangelism

dreadful manner." Edwards recounts that his uncle, Joseph Hawley, who suffered from depression, killed himself by cutting his throat. Nevertheless, Edwards believed that the many who had been converted generally seemed to have had an abiding change wrought on them.

The revival was spread further by a tour of the evangelist George Whitefield in 1740-1742. This "Great Awakening" stirred up a tremendous amount of religious activity and controversy and witnessed the conversion of countless thousands along with the birth of hundreds of new churches. The revival also resulted in missionary work among Native Americans. Notable in this missionary work was David Brainerd, who labored tirelessly to bring the gospel to the Delaware Indians. Additionally, it witnessed the founding of new educational institutions, such as Harvard and Yale, which were founded with the express purpose of training clergy.

Conversely, it led to bitter doctrinal disputes, in fact, a schism in the Presbyterian and Congregational denominations resulted in 1741 on account of it. Why? The revival carried with it a significant amount of excess. For, many who got caught up in religious zeal, fell prey to wandering evangelists, having them believe they had experienced something genuine, when in fact, it was quite often phony. As such, the revival received mixed feelings. Some saw it as spurious, however, Edwards, who supported it, affirmed it was a genuine work of God.

Edwards' congregation found themselves in the center of it all. Therefore, Edwards was faced with the task of examining the effects of the revival. And in a biblical-theological manner, Edwards had to ascertain, what are the distinguishing marks of a true work of the Spirit? Edwards had to answer, was the revival a true work of God's Spirit? Or was it a satanic counterfeit? And how could one tell the difference? Are there signs or criteria that the Word of God gives us to gage whether something is a true move of God or not? Edwards believed we can know with some measure of confidence that a person has truly experienced the saving activity of the Spirit over against the counterfeit works.

So in 1741, Edwards published *The Distinguishing Marks of a Work of the Spirit of God.* In this work, Edwards's purpose was to defend the awakening by showing what are "the true, certain, and distinguishing evidences of a work of the Spirit of God, by which we may safely proceed in judging of any operation we find in ourselves, or see in others."[88] Edwards's approach was to demonstrate in nine ways, "negative signs" that don't positively prove either way if a work is genuine or not; followed by five ways or certain evidence in which a true work of God may be definitely known. When an outpouring of God's Spirit occurs, deadened saints are revitalized, sinners are brought to new birth, and with this intensity comes excess. A revival becomes an epicenter for spiritual warfare as God's grace is opposed by both satanic opposition and fleshly excess. This is why Edwards devoted so much time to combating extremes.

Negative Signs

Negative signs, according to Edwards, may be the fruit of the Holy Spirit's work or human weakness. These signs prove nothing either way:

1. *Therefore it is not reasonable to determine that a work is not from God's Holy Spirit because of the extraordinary degree in which the minds of persons are influenced.* Edwards asks us to consider the extraordinary manner of the Holy Spirit's work in the world. The very nature of the work of the Spirit is intense, and we should expect to see God's extraordinary work to influence people in extraordinary ways.

J.I. Packer writes, "A revival, accordingly, is always a *disfigured* work of God, and the more powerful the revival, the more scandalizing disfigurements we may expect to see." Packer goes on to say, "No; revival, though in itself a purging and purifying work of God, is never free from attendant disfigurements. We need not read beyond the New Testament to appreciate that."[89] Therefore, we shouldn't dismiss a work as not being of God's Spirit just because it's intense. Besides, Scripture is full of evidences of the saints becoming

---

[88] Edwards, Distinguishing Marks of a Work of the Spirit of God, Section 1.
[89] Packer, A Quest for Godliness, 318.

overwhelmed in mind and body at the presence of God. God's presence is intense. And in revival what God gives to His saints is a foretaste of the heavenly happiness they will enjoy (Ps 42; 84:2).

2. A work is not to be judged of by any effects on the bodies of men; such as tears, trembling, groans, loud outcries, agonies of body, or the failing of bodily strength. This was Edwards' most controversial issue in his defense of the awakening. One of the preachers of the Great Awakening was James Davenport. Labeled an "enthusiast," Davenport believed that bodily effects were "sure evidences" and was responsible for many of the excesses that characterized the revival. Davenport argued that unless one has experienced some type of visible, physical or otherwise physiological bodily effect, such as convulsions or weeping, or laughing, or falling down, then one has not experience the power of the Spirit. Sam Storms writes,

Many, such as Davenport and his followers, claimed that they were recipients of the Spirit's grace because they experienced a wide range of physical phenomena, whether shaking or shouting, laughing or weeping, or other overt displays of what they considered genuine religious zeal. Edwards himself was witness to folk who "lost their bodily strength" (i.e., fell to the ground), including his own wife, Sarah. Others testified to seeing visions, hearing voices, or otherwise feeling "impressions" on the "imagination." At times, some would fall into a trance-like state and would remain therein for twenty-four hours or longer. Were such physical manifestations and convulsions a sure sign of the Spirit's work? Or were they in every instance the product of manipulative ministers who excelled in unleashing the emotions of unsuspecting sheep? Neither, said Edwards. Such physical phenomena may be the result of the Spirit's encounter with the frailty of human nature. But maybe not. In any case they are insufficient grounds on which to base one's argument of salvation and by no means constitute the essence of the religious life.[90]

Edwards considered "bodily effects" incidental to the real work of God, but likewise believed that the Holy Spirit's operation may overpower the body. Edwards writes,

---

[90] Storms, *Signs of the Spirit: An Interpretation of Jonathan Edwards' Religious Affections*, 34.

Chapter 9: Biblical Evangelism

If it was not unaccountable that the queen of Sheba fainted, and had her bodily strength taken away, when she came to see the glory of Solomon, much less is it unaccountable that she who is the antitype of the queen of Sheba, (viz.) the Church, that is brought, as it were, from the utmost ends of the earth, from being an alien and stranger, far off, in a state of sin and misery, should faint when she comes to see the glory of Christ, who is the antitype of Solomon; and especially will be so in that prosperous, peaceful, glorious kingdom, which he will set up in the world in its latter age.[91]

During the revival, Edwards' wife, Sarah, also experienced bodily effects, and Edwards recorded them. Regarding his wife's experience, he states, "If such things are enthusiasm and the offspring of a distempered brain, let my brain be possessed evermore of that happy distemper. If this be distraction, I pray God that the world of mankind may all be seized with this benign, meek, beneficent, beatific, glorious distraction."[92]

Edwards, states that revival ushers us into the presence of God: "The glory of the divine power and grace are set off with the greater lustre by what appears at the same time the weakness of the earthen vessel." In other words, if heaven and earth cannot contain God, much less an earthly temple, why would we think that the awesome, holy, majestic presence of God would not lead the frailty of mankind to tremble, weep, or even loose bodily power (Job 32:18-20; Ps 119:120; Jer 20:9; Dan 10:8; Hab 3:16; Rev 1:7). By this negative sign, Edwards reminds us that a work is not to be judged of by any effects on the bodies of men. For, this does not prove nor disprove either way.

3. *It is no argument that an operation on the minds of people is not the work of the Spirit of God, that it occasions a great deal of noise about religion.* Edwards here draws our attention to the fact that on the Day of Pentecost "it occasioned a great stir everywhere. What a mighty opposition was there in Jerusalem, on occasion of that great effusion of the Spirit! And

---

[91] Edwards, Distinguishing Marks of a Work of the Spirit of God, Section 1.2.
[92] Works, I:cxi.

so in Samaria, Antioch, Ephesus, Corinth, and other places! The affair filled the world with noise, and gave occasion to some to say of the apostles, that they had turned the world upside down (Acts 17:6)."[93]

4. *It is no argument that an operation on the minds of a people, is not the work of the Spirit of God, that many who are the subjects of it, have great impressions made on their imaginations.* Edwards argues here that it is perfectly natural for people who are experiencing the power of God to have an extraordinary sense of His holiness and majesty. He writes,

It is no argument that a work is not of the Spirit of God, that some who are the subjects of it have been in a kind of ecstasy, wherein they have been carried beyond themselves, and have had their minds transported into a train of strong and pleasing imaginations, and a kind of visions, as though they were rapt up even to heaven, and there saw glorious sights. I have been acquainted with some such instances, and I see no need of bringing in the help of the devil into the account that we give of these things, nor yet of supposing them to be of the same nature with the visions of the prophets, or St. Paul's rapture into paradise. Human nature, under these intense exercises and affections, is all that need be brought into the account. If it may be well accounted for, that persons under a true sense of the glorious and wonderful greatness and excellency of divine things, and soul-ravishing views of the beauty and love of Christ, should have the strength of nature overpowered.[94]

5. *It is no sign that a work is not from the Spirit of God, that example is a great means of it.* Edwards argues here that a work can neither be judged true nor false based on the effect a person who is experiencing the power of God has on others. However, he states, that there was never a time in the operations of the Spirit when personal examples were not important. He writes, "So it was at the reformation, and in the apostles' days, in Jerusalem and Samaria, and Ephesus, and other parts of the world, as will be most manifest to any one that attends to the accounts we have in the Acts of the

---

[93] Edwards, Distinguishing Marks of a Work of the Spirit of God, Section 1.3.
[94] Ibid, Section 1.4.

Apostles."[95] Further, Edwards states that it's not a valid objection against personal examples being used, because the Scripture tells us that personal testimony is the principal means of carrying on God's work.

6. *It is no sign that a work is not from the Spirit of God, that many, who seem to be the subjects of it, are guilty of great imprudences and irregularities in their conduct.* In other words, just because "enthusiasts" like Davenport are carrying on as they do does not prove the work is false. Again, this is insufficient grounds on which to base an argument either way.

The revival was met with opposition from some conservative Congregationalist ministers, such as Charles Chauncy, the pastor of First Church of Boston. Chauncy was a leader in the Old Lights. The Old Lights were those who distrusted emotionalism and opposed revival. The other extreme party were the New Lights. The New Lights' intemperate excesses were characterized by preachers like Davenport. The point Edwards made in his writings on revival is that both extremes are wrong. In the estimate of Mark Shaw,

It is possible to view the church-growth movement around the world (which is charismatic in character) as another great awakening. Some reject this interpretation because they dislike the theological anemia or the extremist behavior that attends this global movement. But Edwards warns us against a knee-jerk reaction to excesses and problems. We might find ourselves becoming Spirit-quenching critics of spiritual outpourings because they are filled with carnality and corruption. Our task is to perfect and reform the imperfections of revival, much as Edwards sought to do (through teaching, writing, and prayer) and find the middle way between Old Light cynics and New Light fanatics.[96]

In 1743, Chauncy wrote a book entitled *Seasonable Thoughts on the State of Religion in New England.* In it he wrote, "People have scarce heard of such a thing as the outpouring of the Spirit of God...that the outpouring of the Spirit should introduce such a state of things, as that those

---

[95] Ibid, Section, 1.5.
[96] Shaw, Ten Great Ideas from Church History: A Decision-Maker's Guide to Shaping Your Church, 124.

upon whom he has been poured out, should not know how to behave, will, I think, admit of no good plea in its defense."[97] Chauncy believed that any display of what appeared to be an emotional, passionate, physical, visible, or vocal display was, in Chauncy's language, "the effect of enthusiastic heat."[98]

Chauncy writes, "For myself I am among those who are clearly in the opinion that there never was such a spirit of superstition and enthusiasm reigning in the land before, never such great disorders and barefaced affronts to common decency, never such scandalous reproaches on the Blessed Spirit, making him the author of the greatest irregularities and confusions."[99]

In the last analysis, Chauncy was as interested in opposing the revival as Edwards was in defending it. As Gaustad has observed, "both men were trying to separate the wheat from the chaff but Chauncy was interested in the chaff while Edwards was concerned with the wheat."[100] Edwards would have us understand that whenever revival occurs, the devil mimics and mingles false works with it. However, as Edwards states, "a work of God without stumbling-blocks is never to be expected."[101]

7. *Nor are many errors in judgment, and some delusions of Satan intermixed with the work, any argument that the work in general is not of the Spirit of God.* Edwards argues here, that a revival is a mixed work. He insists that revivals never occur without the devil perverting and caricaturing all that the Holy Spirit is doing.

Edwards writes, "if many delusions of Satan appear, at the same time that a great religious concern prevails, it is not an argument that the work in general is not the work of God, any more than it was an argument in Egypt, that there were no true miracles wrought there, by the hand of God, because Jannes

---

[97] Chauncy, Seasonable Thoughts, 320.
[98] Ibid.
[99] Palfrey, History of New England, 40.
[100] Gaustad, The Great Awakening in New England, 81.
[101] Works, II, 273.

and Jambres wrought false miracles at the same time by the hand of the devil."[102]

Regarding this point, J.I. Packer elaborates, "God is content to allow human weakness and sin to obtrude itself in times of revival, in order to make it evident beyond all peradventure that the spiritual fruits of the movement spring, not from any goodness in the persons concerned, but solely from his own work of grace."[103]

Even in a revival, Satan is at work employing various tactics to carry revived believers away to commit excesses. We have discussed James Davenport. It is recounted that he once exhibited a most bizarre act. In an act reminiscent of Savonarola, Davenport led a crowd to burn a large pile of books he felt opposed his radical views. The following day, in order to further prove their commitment to God, he called them to throw their expensive and fancy clothing onto the fire. Leading by example, Davenport removed his pants and cast them into the bonfire. One woman in the crowd quickly grabbed his pants out of the blaze, and threw them in his face, admonishing him to get a hold of himself. And this woke Davenport up to the excess he'd been carried away to.[104]

8. *If some, who were thought to be wrought upon, fall away into gross errors, or scandalous practices, it is no argument that the work in general is not the work of the Spirit of God.* Edwards argues here, that because there are counterfeit works, we should not be surprised when false professors, who formally felt that they had experienced some *religious affections* fall away from Christ. Edwards gives an example by way of Nicolas, who was one the seven deacons in Acts 6. Edwards tells us, Nicolas,

Who was looked upon by the Christians in Jerusalem, in the time of that extraordinary pouring out of the Spirit, as a man full of the Holy Ghost, and was chosen out of the multitude of Christians to that office, for that reason; as you may see in Acts vi. 3, 5. Yet he

---

[102] Edwards, Distinguishing Marks of a Work of the Spirit of God, Section 1.7.
[103] Packer, A Quest for Godliness, 324.
[104] Kidd, The Great Awakening, 153-154.

afterwards fell away and became the head of a sect of vile heretics, of gross practices, called from his name the sect of the Nicolaitans, Rev. ii. 6, and 15.[105]

9. *It is no argument that a work is not from the Spirit of God, that it seems to be promoted by ministers insisting very much on the terrors of God's holy law, and that with a great deal of pathos and earnestness.* For this last point, Edwards remarks, "If there be really a hell of such dreadful and never-ending torments, as is generally supposed, of which multitudes are in great danger – and into which the greater part of men in Christian countries do actually from generation to generation fall, for want of a sense of its terribleness, and so for want of taking due care to avoid it – then why is it not proper for those who have the care of souls to take great pains to make men sensible of it?"[106]

As we look at Edwards "negative signs," he reminds us that the Christian life is one of balance. In the words of Sam Storms, "we can only conclude that they are in great error who condemn people as fanatical and deluded merely because their affections are intense and powerful. On the other hand, it is equally important to note that the intensity of spiritual affections is not infallible proof that they are of saving and gracious nature."[107]

Sure Marks

So, how may we know what are true works of the Spirit? Following the negative signs, Edwards goes on to state positively, what are "the sure, distinguishing scripture evidences and marks of a work of the Spirit of God, by which we may proceed in judging of any operation we find in ourselves, or see among a people, without danger of being misled."[108] We are to test the spirits to see if they are of God,

---

[105] Edwards, Distinguishing Marks of a Work of the Spirit of God, Section 1.8.
[106] Ibid, Section 1.9.
[107] Storms, Signs of the Spirit: An Interpretation of Jonathan Edwards' Religious Affections, 61.
[108] Edwards, Distinguishing Marks of a Work of the Spirit of God, Section II.

431

so we aren't lead stray from Christ; because many antichrists have gone out into the world (1 Jn 2:18; 2 Jn 1:7-8).

For Edwards, the essence of revival is the Spirit's work of producing or renewing faith in Christ.[109] Edwards lists five sure evidences of a true work of the Spirit. I have outlined them according to the following acronym which may be of use to help us keep them in mind: **CREDO**. Credo means "I believe" in Latin.

C – Conducts us to Scripture.
R – Results in Love for God and man.
E – Elevates the Truth.
D – Declares Jesus Christ as Lord and Christ.
O – Opposes the work of Satan.

The following five sure signs of a true work of the Spirit of God (Edwards's order is in parenthesis):

C – <u>Conducts us to Scripture</u>: (3) *The spirit that operates in such a manner, as to cause in men a greater regard to the Holy Scriptures, and establishes them more in their truth and divinity, is certainly the Spirit of God.* Edwards argues here that the spirit that causes people to have a greater regard for the God's Word and establishes them more in the truth is certainly the Spirit of God.

Edwards writes, "A spirit of delusion will not incline persons to seek direction at the mouth of God. To the law and to the testimony, is never the cry of those evil spirits that have no light in them; for it is God's own direction to discover their delusions (Is 8:19-20)."[110] This is as the apostle John tells us in 1 Jn 4:6, "We are of God. He who knows God hears us; he who is not of God does not hear us. By this we know the spirit of truth and the spirit of error."

R – <u>Results in Love for God and man</u>: (5) *If the spirit that is at work among a people operates as a spirit of love to God and man, it is a sure sign that it is the Spirit of God.* Edwards

---

[109] Shaw, Ten Great Ideas from Church History: A Decision-Maker's Guide to Shaping Your Church, 125.
[110] Edwards, Distinguishing Marks of a Work of the Spirit of God, Section II.

argues here that if the spirit that is at work among a people operates as a spirit of love to God and man, then it's a sure sign that it is the Spirit of God. Because grace is the life of God in the soul of man, it results in a love for God and our fellow man. As the apostle John states in 1 Jn 4:7-11:

7 Beloved, let us love one another, for love is of God; and everyone who loves is born of God and knows God. 8 He who does not love does not know God, for God is love. 9 In this the love of God was manifested toward us, that God has sent His only begotten Son into the world, that we might live through Him. 10 In this is love, not that we loved God, but that He loved us and sent His Son to be the propitiation for our sins. 11 Beloved, if God so loved us, we also ought to love one another.

E – Elevates the Truth: (4) *Another rule to judge of spirits may be drawn from those compellations given to the opposite spirits, in the last words of the 6th verse, "The spirit of truth and the spirit of error."* Edwards argues here that the spirit that leads people to the truth, and convinces them of those things that are true, is a sure sign that it's of the Spirit of God. Because the devil and his demons are called the rulers of darkness, then whatever spirit removes our darkness, and brings us to the light, thus "undeceives us" by convincing us of the truth, Edwards argues, does us a kindness. "If I am brought to a sight of truth, and am made sensible of things as they really are, my duty is immediately to thank God for it, without standing first to inquire by what means I have such a benefit."[111]

D – Declares Jesus as Lord and Christ: (1) *When the operation is such as to raise their esteem of that Jesus who was born of the Virgin, and was crucified without the gates of Jerusalem; and seems more to confirm and establish their minds in the truth of what the gospel declares to us of his being the Son of God, and the Saviour of men; is a sure sign that it is from the Spirit of God.*

Edwards reminds us that the devil has the most bitter hatred against Christ, and hates the gospel so much that he would

---

[111] Edwards, Distinguishing Marks of a Work of the Spirit of God, Section II.

never go about stressing its truths. Therefore, we may be sure that it's a sure work of the Spirit of God if it directs us to the Savior Jesus Christ. This is what John tells us in 1 Jn 4:2-3: "By this you know the Spirit of God: Every spirit that confesses that Jesus Christ has come in the flesh is of God, and every spirit that does not confess that Jesus Christ has come in the flesh is not of God. And this is the spirit of the Antichrist, which you have heard was coming, and is now already in the world."

O – Opposes the work of Satan: (2) *When the spirit that is at work operates against the interests of Satan's kingdom, which lies in encouraging and establishing sin, and cherishing men's worldly lusts; this is a sure sign that it is a true, and not a false spirit.* Here Edwards argues, if the spirit that is at work, directs our minds away from all that the world could offer us – the pleasures, profits, and honors, along with a pursuit after them – and instead directs us to concern ourselves with our future state and eternal happiness which the gospel reveals. And causes us to earnestly seek the kingdom of God and His righteousness, then we may be sure it is of the Spirit of God.

Edwards argues, for us to judge a spirit that is working to oppose Satan to be of satanic origin would be tantamount to the devil casting out the devil (Mt 12:25-26). Edwards states: "therefore, if we see persons made sensible of the dreadful nature of sin, and of the displeasure of God against it; of their own miserable condition as they are in themselves, by reason of sin, and earnestly concerned for their eternal salvation – and sensible of their need of God's pity and help, and engaged to seek it in the use of the means that God has appointed – we may certainly conclude that it is from the Spirit of God."[112]

Defending the legitimacy of the revival, Edwards stated the overall positive effects of the Great Awakening in his *Some Thoughts Concerning the Present Revival of Religion,* which he published in 1743. Edwards states that:

Whatever imprudences there have been, and whatever sinful irregularities; whatever vehemence of the passions, and heats of the imagination, transports, and ecstasies: whatever error in judgment,

---

[112] Edwards, Distinguishing Marks of a Work of the Spirit of God, Section II.

Chapter 9: Biblical Evangelism

and indiscreet zeal; and whatever outcries, faintings, and agitations of body; yet, it is manifest and notorious, that there has been of late a very uncommon influence upon the minds of a very great part of the inhabitants of New England, attended with the best effects...**Now, through the greatest part of New England, the holy Bible is in much greater esteem and use than before...Multitudes in New England have lately been brought to a new and great conviction of the truth and certainty of the things of the gospel; to a firm persuasion that Christ Jesus is the Son of God, and the great and only Saviour of the world**; and that the great doctrines of the gospel touching reconciliation by his blood, and acceptance in his righteousness, and eternal life and salvation through him are matters of undoubted truth.

And now let us consider: **Is it not strange that in a Christian country, and such a land of light as this is, there are many at a loss to conclude whose work this is, whether the work of God or the work of the devil? Is it not a shame to New England that such a work should be much doubted of here?** We need not say, Who shall ascend into heaven, to bring us down something whereby to judge of this work? Nor does God send us beyond the seas, nor into past ages, to obtain a rule near at hand, a sacred book that God himself has put into our hands, with clear and infallible marks, sufficient to resolve us in things of this nature; **which book I think we must reject,** not only in some particular passages, but in the substance of it, **if we reject such a work as has now been described, as not being the work of God.** The whole tenor of the gospel proves it; all the notion of religion that the Scripture gives us confirms it (emphasis added).[113]

In these words, Edwards demonstrates the true fruit of revival – the renewal of God's people and the regeneration of sinners. In the last analysis, Edwards states very candidly, that the Holy Spirit is sovereign in His operations. He writes, *"What the church has been used to, is not a rule by which we are to judge; because there may be new and extraordinary works of God, and he has heretofore evidently wrought in an extraordinary manner. He has brought to pass new things, strange works; and has wrought in such a manner as to surprise both men and angels. And as God has done thus in*

---

[113] Edwards, Some Thoughts Concerning the Present Revival of Religion, Part I, Section IV.

435

Chapter 9: Biblical Evangelism

times past, so we have no reason to think but that he will do so still."[114]

Further, Edwards admonishes us to not reject or discard all spiritual activity without making a distinction – to not believe every spirit, but test the spirits, whether they are of God (1 Jn 4:1). There is much we may learn from Edwards. Regarding revival, we would do well to heed his counsel and consider these questions he poses for us: Why would we limit God where He has not limited Himself?[115] And, why should God carefully hide His power?[116]

The Old Gospel

What this country desperately needs right now is the old gospel. The pitiable Savior and the pathetic God of modern pulpits are unknown to the old gospel. The old gospel tells men that they need God, but not that God needs them (a modern falsehood); it does not exhort them to pity Christ, but announces that Christ has pitied them, though pity was the last thing they deserved. It never loses sight of the divine majesty and sovereign power of the Christ whom it proclaims, but rejects flatly all representations of him which would obscure his free omnipotence.[117]

Today, in many pulpits, what is proclaimed in the place of the message of the cross is a weak, man-centered, ethical and social idealism borne by a faith not in Christ alone, but in progress, and the pursuit of the American dream. And this message dares to call itself Christian. What America desperately needs is the old gospel. The fiery flame of eternal truths that once poured from the mouths of men like Boice, Edwards, Kennedy, Moody, Tennent, Whitefield and Wesley must be thundered forth again in the pulpits across the land.

Truths that were basic to the former generations must be reasserted to this generation of Americans, who, in their confusion and agitation, know not the God of Joseph. "The harvest truly is plentiful, but the laborers are few. Therefore

---

[114] Edwards, Distinguishing Marks, Section I.
[115] Ibid.
[116] Edwards, Religious Affections, 37.
[117] Owen, The Death of Death in the Death of Christ, 17.

pray the Lord of the harvest to send out laborers into His harvest" (Mt 9:37-38).

> We've a story to tell to the nations,
> That shall turn their hearts to the right,
> A story of truth and mercy,
> A story of peace and light,
> A story of peace and light.
> For the darkness shall turn to dawning,
> And the dawning to noonday bright,
> And Christ's great kingdom shall come on earth,
> The kingdom of love and light.[118]

---

[118] Nichol, We've a Story to Tell.

Chapter 9: Biblical Evangelism

Recommended Further Reading

1. John Piper, *Let the Nations be Glad.*
2. J.I. Packer, *Evangelism and the Sovereignty of God.*
3. Sam Storms, *Signs of the Spirit.*
4. Jonathan Edwards, *Religious Affections.*
5. Tom Wells, *A Vision for Missions.*

Chapter 9 Review Questions

1. What does it mean to be born again?
2. Does the Great Commission apply to all Christians? Or just ordained ministers?
3. Can a person be saved without Christ?
4. Has the Great Commission been fulfilled?
5. How should Christians interact with culture?
6. Are there any distinguishing marks of the Spirit?
7. How should the gospel be presented?
8. What is revival? Can we have it whenever we desire?
9. Can true believers fall away from grace?
10. Why is God's final judgment delayed?

10 Then I heard a loud voice saying in heaven, "Now salvation, and strength, and the kingdom of our God, and the power of His Christ have come, for the accuser of our brethren, who accused them before our God day and night, has been cast down. 11 And they overcame him by the blood of the Lamb and by the word of their testimony, and they did not love their lives to the death. 12 Therefore rejoice, O heavens, and you who dwell in them! Woe to the inhabitants of the earth and the sea! For the devil has come down to you, having great wrath, because he knows that he has a short time." (Rev 12:10-12).

Chapter 10: Soli Deo Gloria

Saints shall look down upon the burning lake, and in the sense of their own happiness, and in the approbation of God's just proceedings, they shall rejoice and sing, "Thou art righteous, O Lord! Who was, art, and shalt be, because thou hast judged thus."[1] This is Richard Baxter's way of describing how Christ's return to save His people is also His return to render vengeance to His enemies (1 Thess 1:10; 2 Thess 1:7-10). The title of this chapter is *Soli Deo Gloria* which is Latin meaning, "For the glory of God alone." *Soli Deo Gloria* means that everything that is done is for God's glory and not mankind's vain self-glory.

---

[1] Baxter, Saints Everlasting Rest, 97.

Chapter 10: Soli Deo Gloria

In this chapter, we will seek to probe into the problem of suffering and evil. We will, however, not find a complete solution for the problem of suffering. Nevertheless, we will endeavor to offer a more complete picture. To use the analogy of a reconnaissance, we will reconnoiter the problem of suffering from various vantage points, filling information gaps to gain an operational picture of the thorny issue in question. And though much will go unanswered, the desired endstate is to provide a manageable framework that will bring the comfort of hope.

Calamity has a way of not only bringing to the fore a person's true judgment regarding anything, but serves as a litmus test as to whether or not it will stand up to scrutiny. Calamity causes us to search for answers. It moves us to query how a good God can exist alongside evil. To respond to questions like, "Where was God when terrorists flew our airplanes full of our people into the World Trade towers, the Pentagon, and into the Pennsylvanian countryside? Where was God when my baby died? Why does God allow Christians to suffer? Where is God when the innocent are slaughtered? Not to mention natural disasters? In this chapter we will consider the following topics:

- The Sovereignty of God and Evil.
- The Delayed Judgment of God.
- The Sovereignty of God and Spiritual Warfare.
- Delayed Vindication.

The Sovereignty of God and Evil

The ancient philosopher Epicurus (341-270 BC) posed the following puzzle: God either wishes to take evils away or is unable; or He is able, and is unwilling; or He is neither willing nor able; or He is both willing and able. If He is willing and unable, He is feeble, which does not agree with the character of God; If He is able and unwilling, he is malicious, which is equally at odds with God; If He is neither willing nor able, He is both malicious and feeble and therefore not God; If He is both willing and able, which is alone suitable for God, from what source then comes evil? Or why does He not remove them? As you can see this is a thorny issue. Augustine said, "I sought whence evil comes and there was no solution."[1] So, how do we face such an argument termed by atheists as the Achilles heel of Christianity?

To begin with, when facing the problem of evil we must affirm some fundamental biblical truths: (1) God is sovereign, so nothing is outside His control. God is omniscient, omnipotent, and omnipresent; (2) God is perfect, holy, wise, just, and good. He is omnibenevolent, and in Him is no darkness at all; and (3) yet evil is real.

One of the devil's tricks is to redefine terms to not only make it harder to communicate but to transvaluate terms right out of existence. Here we need to discuss three significant terms we will use during this chapter: sovereignty, evil, and suffering. First, the sovereignty of God is the exercise of His power and superiority. Arthur Pink writes,

> The sovereignty of God may be defined as the exercise of His supremacy. Being infinitely elevated above the highest creature, He is the most High, maker of heaven and earth. Subject to none, influenced by none; God does as He pleases, only as He pleases always as He pleases. None can thwart Him, none can hinder Him. So His own Word expressly declares: "My counsel shall stand, and I will do all My pleasure" (Is 46:10).[2]

Christ is sovereign and is presently on His throne upholding all things by the Word of His power (Col 1:17; Heb 1:3). Jesus Christ is the King of kings and Lord of lords, the Almighty and only sovereign (1 Tim 6:15; Rev 19:16). Sovereignty means that God controls and directs everything.

Second, we need to define evil. What is it? Evil is morally bad wills in action. Bad people doing bad things. It also means the waste of good potential which arises from human badness on one hand and tragic accidents on the other. Evil is good somehow gone wrong. Evil is not an entity in itself. Evil is a bad condition of that which was originally good. Mankind was created good, and righteous, in God's image but lost his original righteousness and goodness. All the evils under which

---

[1] Augustine, Confessions, Book VII, Chapter 7.11, 124.
[2] Pink, The Attributes of God, 40.

men suffer and which they commit are manifestations of mankind's fallen nature – the city of man.

As we shall see, evil seems to carry on in the world unchecked. This is instanced in Psalm 73, where the wicked are prospering despite the fact that they're wicked. The psalmist laments the seemingly scandalous fact that the wicked are prospering while they are ill-treating and disregarding others. The psalmist says he was nearly thrown off balance in his faith as he contemplated this evil until he went into the house of God and began to think about eternal values and his peace of mind was restored.

Third, we need to define suffering. Suffering is a condition in which one experiences mental, physical or spiritual pain. Suffering is the direct result of sin in the world. If there was no sin then suffering would not exist. Suffering and its synonyms – affliction, pressure, pain, agony, etc. may be categorized in three ways: (1) suffering due to adversity (hostile people); (2) suffering due to bad health; and (3) suffering due to catastrophes (floods, hurricanes, and other acts of God). Additionally, there are sufferings which elude categories. However, suffering involves all manner of pain that we may experience either as a victim or as a result of our own intentional or unintentional doings. For Christians, I believe suffering refers to all pain and persecution we meet with on our way to heaven and endure by trusting Jesus.

There have been many famous explanations for the problem of evil, which is also referred to as a theodicy, from the Greek Theos "God" + dike "justice." Theodicy is one's undertaking to explain how an all-powerful, perfectly good and loving God can exist simultaneously in a world full of real evil. Proposed solutions interact with Epicurus' *horns of the trilemma* and seek to resolve the issue by removing or lessening one or all of the three biblical presuppositions.

It will prove valuable for us to survey several intellectual options, making our way through the debris of failed solutions, and arriving at a workable biblical solution.

Chapter 10: Soli Deo Gloria

Here are several salient intellectual options:

- Dualism
- Hegel
- Christian Science
- Universalism
- Open Theism and Process Theology
- Leibnizian Theodicy

Dualism

Marcion of Sinope, famously proposed that there were two gods of the Bible. Hippolytus informs us Marcion was the son of the bishop of Sinope in Pontus, Asia Minor, and that he had developed unorthodox views on Christianity for which he was put out of the church.[3] Marcion developed a dualism to reconcile the teachings of Jesus with what he perceived as the incompatible activities of an evil blood-thirsty *demiurge* of the Old Testament. To Marcion, the loving God revealed Himself only in Jesus Christ. What Marcion believed he was doing was extricating the wrathful God of justice revealed in the Old Testament from the God of mercy and love in the New Testament – at least in the parts of it that remained after his textual criticism.[4]

---

[3] Philip Schaff writes, "Marcion was the most earnest, the most practical, and the most dangerous among the Gnostics, full of energy and zeal for reforming, but restless rough and eccentric. But he was utterly destitute of historical sense, and put Christianity into a radical conflict with all previous revelations of God; as if God had neglected the world for thousands of years until he suddenly appeared in Christ. He represents an extreme anti-Jewish and pseudo-Pauline tendency, and a magical supranaturalism, which, in fanatical zeal for a pure primitive Christianity, nullifies all history, and turns the gospel into an abrupt, unnatural, phantomlike appearance. Marcion was the son of a bishop of Sinope in Pontus, and gave in his first fervor his property to the church, but was excommunicated by his own father, probably on account of his heretical opinions and contempt of authority. He betook himself, about the middle of the second century, to Rome (140–155), which originated none of the Gnostic systems, but attracted them all. There he joined the Syrian Gnostic, Cerdo." History of the Christian Church, Volume II: Ante-Nicene Christianity.

[4] Marcion compiled a Bible consisting mainly of Paul's letters and Luke's Gospel.

Chapter 10: Soli Deo Gloria

Regarding this, Tertullian tells us, this shipmaster of Pontus tampers with the cargo before it's even delivered. Describing Marcion's gospel, Tertullian writes, "a better god has been discovered, one who is neither offended nor angry nor inflicts punishment, who has no fire warming up in hell, and no outer darkness wherein there is shuddering and gnashing of teeth: he is merely kind. Of course he forbids you to sin – but only in writing."[5] Marcion sought to remove all severity from God.

How often do people think of God in this way? They imagine a loving Father in the sky, who issues commands but takes no offense at sin and only wishes for people to be happy and get along – to be "a good person." Tertullian asks, "To what purpose does he lay down commands if he will not require performance, or prohibit transgressions if he is not to exact penalties, if he is incapable of judgment, a stranger to all emotions of severity and reproof?"[6]

Similarly, Zoroastrianism posits two equally powerful forces of good and evil, with the later trying to destroy the creation of the good god Ahura Mazda. While this approach is patently wrong, there is only one true God, it rightly accounts for evil as from satanic origin. Further, it fails to explain why the devil is allowed to do evil, that is, why God allows Satan to do evil.

The Scripture does acknowledge that Satan is the god of this world (2 Cor 4:4) in one sense, and that he has immense power, but this approach fails to explain why God allows satanic evil to exist. In order to solve the problem of evil, dualism offers us a less than omnipotent God. This is the view espoused in Harold Kushner's *When Bad Things Happen to Good People*. Kushner, a rabbi, lost his son and determined that God was unable to prevent his son's death. He says, "I can worship a God who hates suffering but cannot eliminate it, more easily than I can worship a God who chooses to make children suffer and die."[7]

However, Dualism is wrong because Christ has already conquered death, hell, and the devil, therefore everything, to include Satan, is already under His feet (1 Cor 15:25-27; Eph

---

[5] Tertullian, Against Marcion 1.27.
[6] Ibid, 1.25-26.
[7] Kushner, When Bad Things Happen to Good People, 134.

1:22; Heb 2:8; 10:12-13). Additionally, dualism is wrong because it constructs a false dichotomy between Gods' love and His wrath. God is Love as well as Judge. Love and judgment are not mutually exclusive (Rom 12:19; 1 Jn 4:7-8). J.I. Packer raises an important issue here when he writes, "The fact is that the subject of divine wrath has become taboo in modern society, and Christians by and large have accepted the taboo and conditioned themselves never to raise the matter."[8]

Furthermore, dualism fails to answer why God allows the devil any power now after the Cross. Besides, the Scripture tells us that "For I know that the Lord is great, and our Lord is above all gods. Whatever the Lord pleases He does, in heaven and in earth" (Ps 135:6).

Hegel

The Enlightenment approached the problem of evil as being simply a problem of the mind. This was Hegel's solution. Hegel was, if not a pantheist, a panentheist. Hegel was a German thinker that had a tremendous influence on Western philosophy. He was a very cloudy writer and one isn't always sure how he is conceiving the relation between God and the world if in fact he even made one. According to Hegel, God is pure mind. And in the beginning, since God was alone, He attempted to think about Himself. But the thought of pure Being is an impossible thought, therefore when God attempted to think Being, He thought nothing.[9] This is what Hegel referred to as God's Self-alienation – Satan's falling away from God.[10] Hegel regarded evil as part of a good process because in his view it's going to produce a good state of affairs in the end. This can be found by way of his dialectical process: of thesis-antithesis-synthesis.

The Enlightenment was in fact a new arrogance, and whereas pre-Enlightenment thought involved a supernatural view of the world, the Enlightenment, however, proposed a

---

[8] Packer, Knowing God, 164.

[9] Palmer, Looking at Philosophy, 226-227.

[10] Hegel, The Phenomenology of Spirit, 776. Although Hegel considered himself a good Lutheran, he conceived of the devil as part of a kind of quaternity within the Godhead – a decidedly unchristian view.

more natural way of looking at the world, in what we would call today deism. Deism conceives the world as a closed system, that is, God created it, set rules in motion and doesn't intervene. As D. A. Carson puts it, "The deist thinks of god as the creator who set this universe on its present course, establishing its order and laws, and then let it go on its way, in much the same way a watchmaker takes care to produce a well-designed and working mechanism but has no interest or control in his product once it has left his hand."[11]

Not only does this line of thinking exclude the reality of miracles, it elevates human reason to the measure of all things (Kant); the mind of man becomes the standard by which we would judge whether something was true or could take place. Thus reason became the autonomous standard and the Bible become just another book. As a consequence of this, the Bible ceased to be viewed as the inspired revelation of God and was approached like any other book. With the Enlightenment came the elevation of man's reason, which presumed to soar above the dictates of Scripture. However, Scripture provides us with presuppositions which are to govern our reasoning.

Besides, God's Word communicates truths which cannot be discovered by reason alone (2 Tim 3:7). Further, deism is wrong not only because it fails to view God as a Person who is personally active in the world He created, but it presents us with a god who is less than omnibenevolent. Thus, the Enlightenment and Hegel are miserable comforters who offer us no hope and no answers to the problem of evil and suffering.

Christian Science

Christian Science maintains that evil is simply not real, and you must simply think it away. According to Walter Martin, Christian Science would like to present itself as a benign "quiet faith that gives its people peace with God without any of the unappealing aspects of traditional Christianity, such as the existence of hell, the doctrine of the Trinity, or the

---

[11] Carson, How Long, O Lord? Reflections on Suffering and Evil, 30.

Chapter 10: Soli Deo Gloria

incarnation, resurrection, and atonement of Jesus Christ."[12] Further, Martin describes Christian Science as, "an ingenious mixture of first-century Gnostic theology, eighteenth-century Hegelian philosophy, and nineteenth-century idealism."[13]

Additionally, Christian Science rejects a belief in a material physical universe – hence no literal resurrection, and rejects the reality of sin, evil, pain, the devil, hell, and heaven. These are all states of mind. To the Christian Scientist, God (the Father-Mother) is a principle known as the 'divine mind.' It has no personhood and no personality. In their philosophy, God is all that exists, and what we perceive as matter is an interpretation of the divine mind. Since God is love, it means that sin and suffering are only errors of interpreting the divine mind and have no true reality.[14]

According to the Christian Science bible, *Science and Health with a Key to the Scriptures*, Evil is the belief in evil. God is all that is real and God is completely good; therefore, good is real and evil is an illusion. The only power evil has is to destroy itself and create its own hell. Not realizing one's true nature as spirit results in selfishness, which can lead to error and disharmony.[15] When Mrs. Mary Baker Eddy spoke of evil, she did, first of all mean pain, specifically bodily pain, which she was very much accustomed to because of her many ailments. Pain, according to Mrs. Eddy, is an illusion. And you must think it away. The ridiculousness of this line of thinking is encapsulated in the following poem:

> A Christian Scientist of Deal
> Once said, although pain isn't real
> When I sit on a pin and it punctures my skin
> I dislike what I fancy I feel.

The Christian Science option seeks to remove the problem of evil by pronouncing it as unreal. This view is decidedly un-Christian as it is unrealistic. Besides, pain is very real. As C.S. Lewis put it, "God whispers to us in our pleasures, speaks in

---

[12] Martin, The Kingdom of the Cults, 149.
[13] Ibid, 45.
[14] Eddy, Science and Health, 330:25-274; 470:9-14.
[15] Ibid, 34, 253

our conscience, but shouts in our pains: it is His megaphone to rouse a deaf world."[16] As we will see, God isn't trying to distance Himself from the fact that He has a purpose for suffering.

Universalism

Universalism says all will be saved. According to Harnack, "Origen believed that all spirits will be finally rescued and glorified."[17] A modern proponent of this idea was John Hick. He believed that moral evil is inescapable and is part of the growing and maturing process of human beings. This view is similar to that of Irenaeus, which postulated that God permitted evil so as to morally develop mankind. However, Irenaeus was no Universalist. He believed hell was reserved for those who rejected the gospel.

Universalism envisions that God will finally bring everyone to full moral maturity, in goodness, uprightness, and in godliness in worlds to come. Hick even imagined further worlds that God would create in order to bring this about. Hick argued, if universal salvation were not true, then nothing could justify the amount of evil God lets happen in this world. It would be too much to bare. Hick says, it's alright because God is going to save everyone in the end. And when that happens, the pain and grief, and immorality which has marked people's paths as they move towards the point of salvation, it will be forgotten because it will seem in retrospect worthwhile because of where it got them in the end. Hick's view is an apparent synthesis of Origen, Irenaeus, and Hegel.

Open Theism and Process Theology

The views of open theism and process theology offer us a solution to the problem of evil that lessons God's omniscience and omnipotence. For instance, John Sanders writes, "God foresaw the evil that would happen in the world but would not rescind the liberty He had granted at creation."[18] In order to

---

[16] Lewis, The Problem of Pain, 91.
[17] Harnack, The History of Dogma, Volume II, 377.
[18] Sanders, The God Who Risks, 239.

escape the trilemma, open theism envisions God limiting His own sovereignty over creation in order to allow for the free exercise of His creatures. For example, process theology states that God is finite and developing but at each stage He is struggling and doing His best. His goodness consists in the fact that He is doing His best, at imposing His will and love on a rebellious universe.

These views are unbiblical because they regard evil as no more a perplexity because God simply hasn't the power to do anything about it. This view envisions a weak god who asks us to help him in the task of spreading goodness and light throughout the world where people are sinful and choose to dwell in moral darkness. However, the Scripture tells us, that God's "dominion is an everlasting dominion, and His kingdom is from generation to generation. All the inhabitants of the earth are reputed as nothing; He does according to His will in the army of heaven and among the inhabitants of the earth. No one can restrain His hand or say to Him, "What have You done" (Dan 4:34-35)?

None of these intellectual hypotheses to the problem of evil are successful because we have to live in the confidence that God orders everything for His glory and the good of His people. If we were like the ancient Greek pagans who believed in a multiplicity of gods, and you remember how capricious and lecherous those gods were, we wouldn't have a problem with evil and suffering because they were neither moral nor loving. They were responsible for villainous acts.

The gods of Greece and Rome, and I might add the rest of the world, won't require you to live holy lives, they simply require you to perform a ritual of some sort. A pinch of incense was to be offered to Jupiter or Neptune (or bowing five times a day to Allah). In fact, ancient Rome didn't care how you lived as long as you performed the ritual ascribing genius to Caesar as lord, the so-called savior of mankind. In short, none of these so-called gods are ever called love incarnate as our God is.

We have been considering theodicy, which is an attempt to explain how an omniscient, omnipotent, omnibenevolent God can exist simultaneously with evil and suffering in the world. However, this wasn't a consideration in the ancient pagan world since the gods behaved as bad as or worse than the humans that worshipped them. People tend to think if we understood why there was evil we could bare it more easily. But because God is love and morally perfect and suffering exists, a tension remains. This, as we have seen, has led to much cognitive dissonance whereby either one or all three fundamental truths: (1) God is sovereign; (2) God is omnibenevolent; and (3) evil is real – are jettisoned for the expediency of removing the tension; but the tension must remain.

In the Parable of the Workers in the Vineyard, Jesus asks, "Is it not lawful for me to do what I wish with my own things?" Regarding this Spurgeon has rightfully said,

There is no attribute more comforting to His children than that of God's Sovereignty. Under the most adverse circumstances, in the most severe trials, they believe that Sovereignty has ordained their afflictions, that Sovereignty overrules them, and that Sovereignty will sanctify them all. There is nothing for which the children ought more earnestly to contend than the doctrine of their Master over all creation—the Kingship of God over all the works of His own hands—the Throne of God and His right to sit upon that Throne. On the other hand, there is no doctrine more hated by worldings, no truth of which they have made such a football, as the great, stupendous, but yet most certain doctrine of the Sovereignty of the infinite Jehovah. Men will allow God to be everywhere except on His throne. They will allow Him to be in His workshop to fashion worlds and make stars. They will allow Him to be in His almonry to dispense His alms and bestow His bounties. They will allow Him to sustain the earth and bear up the pillars thereof, or light the lamps of heaven, or rule the waves of the ever-moving ocean; but when God ascends His throne, His creatures then gnash their teeth, and we proclaim an enthroned God, and His right to do as He wills with His own, to dispose of His creatures as He thinks well, without consulting them in the matter; then it is that we are hissed and execrated, and then it is that men turn a deaf ear to us, for God on His throne is not the God they love. But it is God upon the throne that we love to preach. It is God upon His throne whom we trust.[19]

---

[19] Spurgeon, Sermon No. 77, Matthew 20:15, delivered on Sabbath Morning, May 4, 1856.

Chapter 10: Soli Deo Gloria

The Christian faith is one of balance. And the Bible holds many seemingly paradoxical truths simultaneously. The existence of evil and suffering alongside a perfectly good Sovereign God who loves us is one of those paradoxes we must accept without lessoning the dissonance by removing what seems to be contradictory; as Mrs. Eddy did when she said all pain is an illusion; or the open theists and processed theologians do when they sacrifice God's omniscience upon the altar of cognitive dissonance. The Christian faith is one of balance. And although at present, we can't see that God is working all things for His glory and our good, we accept that fact by faith and not sight. We live in the confidence that in heaven we shall see that this is so when faith passes into sight although we cannot demonstrate that here on earth.

Leibniz

One of the best known theodicies comes to us from the German philosopher Gottfried Wilhelm von Leibniz. I believe it goes without saying that Leibniz's solution to the problem of evil is one of the better theodicies available to us. As we approach a workable solution to the problem of evil, I would like to use Leibniz's theodicy as a sounding board for a further, if I may say, more biblical option.

Often enough, a view comes to be known through the work of a person's detractors. As such, Leibniz's approach to the problem of evil became known to many readers through Voltaire's play *Candide*. The problem of evil, the standard argument for atheism, contends that God and evil are incompatible, and given that evil clearly exists, God cannot.

That the problem of evil disquieted Leibniz more than anything else is evidenced by the fact that his first and the last book-length works he authored, *the Philosopher's Confession* (1672) and *Theodicy* (1710) confronted this issue head on. In *Theodicy*, Leibniz presents us with a powerful synthesis of Christian doctrine and philosophy, of human free will and fate.

In his youth, Leibniz regarded the prevalent Scholastic "privation view," as "a manifest illusion, a leftover from a visionary philosophy of the past; a subterfuge with which no

451

reasonable person will ever be satisfied."[20] He added that the original limitation position is "so lame that a defense attorney with similar arguments before a reasonable judge would be ashamed."[21] Leibniz believed that the Scholastic theory of privation was invented to prove that God was not the author of sin and that sinful creatures could be the efficient causes of evil without requiring the immediate causal contribution of God.

What Leibniz was reacting to was the perceived failure of the Scholastics, viz., the Platonists, St. Augustine, and Aquinas, who supposed that God, provides the substances of all action, albeit not the evil, but were unable to explain how it is that the evil does not result from the act. However, the aged Leibniz reversed his position, and siding somewhat closer to the traditional Scholastic privation view wrote, "Evil is therefore like darkness, and not only ignorance but also error and malice consisting formally in a certain kind of privation."[22]

In short, Leibniz's position on the origin of evil, according to his *Theodicy* is that God is the cause of the material aspect of evil, which consists in positive reality, and not in the formal aspect, which consists in privation. In other words, the root of evil is in nothingness, that is to say, it has no ontological existence. It is a parasitic privation of good. God contributes only the positive, real perfections, whereas creatures contribute limitation.

Augustine said that this world was not what God had intended but was corrupted by the entrance of sin; Adam's original sin bringing his posterity under the divine curse and death. Leibniz, however, disagreed with Augustine, and believed that this world was good and had been since God created it. Albeit, Leibniz did agree with Augustine's view that God permitted evil in order to bring about the greater good, and wrote "an imperfection in the part may be required for a greater perfection in the whole."[23]

---

[20] Leibniz, Philosopher's Confession, 211.
[21] Ibid, 23.
[22] Leibniz, Theodicy, 143
[23] Ibid, 378.

Chapter 10: Soli Deo Gloria

Augustine had said nearly the same when he wrote "God permitted evil in order to derive from it a good, that is to say, a greater good." Similarly, Aquinas wrote that "the permission of evil tends towards the good of the universe." Therefore, Leibniz viewed evil as the privation of good, and imperfection that brings greater perfection. His theory of evil led him to categorize it in three ways: (1) metaphysical evil, (2) physical evil and (3) moral evil. He states metaphysical evil consists in mere imperfection, physical evil in suffering, and moral evil in sin. Leibniz proceeds on the premise that although these forms of evil exist, albeit by divine privation, evil is not good but it is good there is evil, so as to bring about God's will, that is 'a greater perfection in the whole.'

The Nature of the Providence of God

To understand Leibniz's system we must look at his idea of providence. The Christian doctrine of providence states that God orchestrates all history for His glory and the good of the Church.[24] He presents us with three various understandings of fate: (1) *Fatum Mahometanum* Islamic fate, (2) *Fatum Stoicum* Stoic fate, and (3) *Fatum Christianum* Christian fate. Leibniz uses the term "fate" for the Christian view but goes on to describe it in terms more respective of providence. These three fates of Leibniz involve different effective responses to necessity. In contrast to the others, Leibniz's preferred version of fate is a loving response that has been freely chosen by a God who knows what is best, a God who chooses according to 'the principle of the best.'

Leibniz reasons that it's consistent with order and the general good for God to grant to certain of his creatures the opportunity to exercise their freedom, even when He foresees that they would turn to evil. "For," as he says, "God could easily correct the evil."[25] God, says Leibniz, does not will

---

[24] God, the great Creator of all things, doth uphold, direct, dispose, and govern all creatures, actions, and things, from the greatest even to the least, by his most wise and holy providence, according to his infallible foreknowledge, and the free and immutable counsel of his own will, to the praise of the glory of his wisdom, power, justice, goodness, and mercy (WCF 5.1 Providence).

[25] Leibniz, Theodicy, 378.

these evils, but is willing to permit them for a greater good. This he calls God's *consequent* will, which, being a Leibnizian type of "second causes," is consequent from His *antecedent* will, which is God's first cause, the inclination to do something in proportion to the good it contains.[26] In other words, God wills for humanity to be presented with evil so as to be further sanctified by choosing the good or the evil and incur God's wrath.

Leibniz says metaphysical evil gives rise to physical evil which together brings to pass moral evil. His understanding of evil plays a major role, understandably so, to his overall defense of God's justice in light of the presence of evil. Leibniz concludes that God wills all good in Himself antecedently, and wills the best consequently as an end. He adds that God permits physical evil sometimes as a means, but only permits moral evil as a hypothetical necessity which connects it with the best. Therefore the consequent will of God, which has sin for its object, is only permissive. One of the perplexities in Leibniz's system is that he fails to answer the question, what is the origin of metaphysical evil? In typical Christian parlance he states that the devil is the author of sin but he says, "The origin of sin comes from farther away, its source is in the original imperfection of creatures." This is the rub.

According to Leibniz, there is no logical incompatibility between God and suffering in the world. God has morally sufficient reasons for permitting it and incorporates, according to the principle of the best, not only what human beings will freely do but also the operations of His healing grace in response to these evil acts. For God's 'best of all possible worlds,' creation, being incomplete, must fully develop. And evil exists as a type of anvil, serving to further refine mankind.

Leibniz writes, "Even though there were no co-operation by God in evil actions, one could not help finding difficulty in the fact that he foresees them and that, being able to prevent them

---

[26] Although in relation to the foreknowledge and decree of God, the first cause, all things come to pass immutably and infallibly, yet, by the same providence, he ordereth them to fall out according to the nature of second causes, either necessarily, freely, or contingently (WCF 5.2). Second causes are the actions of mankind.

through his omnipotence, he yet permits them."[27] Therefore, according to Leibniz, God wills the good in Himself antecedently and the best consequently as an end. Further, God wills what is indifferent, and physical evil, sometimes as a means, but that He will only permit moral evil as the *sine quo non* or as a hypothetical necessity which connects it with the best. Therefore the consequent will of God, which has sin for its object, is only permissive.

The Nature of Human Freedom

The supreme law of God's conduct, he writes, is "the happy and flourishing state of His empire that consists in the greatest possible happiness of its inhabitants." Perhaps the greatest paradox in the Leibnizian theodicy is his simultaneous position holding to both divine sovereignty and human freewill. These two truths, as we shall see later in this chapter, are presented throughout the Bible on equal footing. According to Leibniz, God actualizes 'the best of all possible worlds' since He chose this world out of all possibilities. And this, best possible world would have the most good and the least evil. One of the reasons for Leibniz's essay was to answer the Socinians who claimed that God was a more limited being, not omniscient who could neither account for nor eliminate all evil.

Even though there were no co-operation by God in evil actions, one could not help finding difficulty in the fact that He foresees them and that, being able to prevent them through his omnipotence, He yet permits them.[28] Leibniz argues that if there weren't determining factors in our choices, we wouldn't choose anything at all (like Buridan's ass, who wants the grass on both meadows and starves to death because there's nothing making him want to go to one instead of the other). Leibniz opts for a kind of 'middle position' between Molinistic middle knowledge and Calvinistic providence by saying, "I am for the Molinists in the first point (first cause), I am for the predeterminators in the second (second cause)."[29]

---

[27] Leibniz, Theodicy, 58.
[28] Ibid, 32.
[29] Ibid, 88.

Chapter 10: Soli Deo Gloria

The Best of All Possible Worlds?

Leibniz's system was worked out in good faith and reverence. His formula stated, that this is "the best of all possible worlds." Leibniz portrays this "best of all possible worlds" as one in which God, desiring our love and worship, has created and sustained it in such a way that it's possible for things to go wrong, and that evil is a necessary component of such a world. According to Leibniz, God wants us to mature morally. God permits evil to exist but reduces it and makes it serve a higher purpose. Leibniz would have Christians attend to the counsel of the psalmist in Psalm 73, and disregard the appearances of injustice which we see in this "small portion of his Kingdom that is exposed to our gaze." He writes, "Here on earth we see apparent injustice, and we believe and even know the truth of the hidden justice of God; but we shall see that justice when at last the Sun of Justice shall show himself as he is."[30]

It is cliché, almost axiomatic today for people to claim the problem of evil as Christianity's biggest hurdle. And that if Christianity offered a better solution to this problem then it would be acceptable. However, the problem of evil hasn't posed an obstacle for Christians for the last twenty centuries because Christians understand that at the beginning of human history, humankind brought evil on themselves by rebelling against God, breaking a commandment which they were free and able to obey, provoking His judgment. Christians have always believed in the chimerical taint of Adam's sin, which has flawed this world, which will continue to be flawed until Christ returns and remakes it (2 Thess 1:6-8; 2 Pet 3:7).

Christians have always believed that life was never promised to be a rose garden (Jn 16:33). And because Christians think of God in terms of holiness and justice, no less than in terms of love and mercy, they recognize the sufferings of this world, the experience of evil working itself out, is what God in His Word has led us to expect.

When facing the problem of evil, we must affirm some fundamental truths: (1) God is sovereign, so nothing is outside

---

[30] Leibniz, Theodicy, 120.

Chapter 10: Soli Deo Gloria

His control, (2) God is love, perfect, holy, wise, just, and good. In Him is no darkness at all, and (3) evil is real. Likewise, Leibniz affirmed these three propositions, however, in the last analysis he says, evil is not good but it is good there is evil, how else could the best of all possible worlds come about? Leibniz concludes his *Theodicy* by answering Epicurus' famous triadic question,

Either God wishes to banish evils and cannot contrive to do so, in which case he would be weak; or he can abolish them, and will not, which would be a sign of malignity in him; or again he lacks power and also will, which would make him appear both weak and jealous; or finally he can and will, but in this case it will be asked why he then does not banish evil, if he exists? I should have preferred to say that he can banish evil, but that he does not wish to do so absolutely, and rightly so, because he would then banish good at the same time, and he would banish more good than evil.[31]

What is particularly curious is Leibniz's wording here, viz., "He (God) can banish evil, but that he does not wish to do so absolutely, and rightly so, because he would then banish good at the same time, and he would banish more good than evil," is that he is drawing from a kingdom principle found in one of the Lord's parables, namely the Parable of the Wheat and the Tares. In the parable, the Son of Man commands for the wheat to grow alongside the tares until the time of the end. At which time He will charge His holy angels to gather out of His kingdom all causes of evil. The point being that good and evil exist together in the field of the world until Christ's Second Coming. We will return to this important point later, but in passing let's say that Leibniz is on to the heart of what I believe is the workable solution to the problem of evil – delayed judgment.

Christians have long struggled with what appears to be God's inactivity with regards to evil, viz., the wicked are prospering despite the fact that they're wicked (Ps 73). The psalmist laments this seemingly scandalous fact. The wicked are prospering while they are ill-treating and disregarding others. However, all this was a non-issue for Leibniz as he was

---

[31] Leibniz, Theodicy, 416.

the consummate optimist. The question is, was Leibniz's optimist theodicy rooted in the Scriptures?

Leibniz's *Theodicy,* though lampooned by Voltaire and dismissed by many others, remains one of the truly distinctive philosophical responses to the problem of evil to date. However, where I believe Leibniz falls short is he says nothing regarding the principle of divine judgment that is operating at present in the world in the way that the Bible says it does. Thus, he sounds rather too optimistic. And that is what Voltaire ridiculed him for. In the play *Candide,* everything goes wrong for the hero and Doctor Pangloss tells him at every turn that everything is for the best.

Overall, it is believed that Leibniz's theodicy fails to be compelling for two main reasons: (1) he failed to account for the prevailing stain of Adam's sin which has infected the whole human race (Leibniz viewed the earth as remaining in the state of unfallen perfection); and (2) he failed to account for the wrath of God for sin. Leibniz, one may fairly say, was looking in the right direction but he fell short. Namely because he failed to see this world as being in a fallen and depraved state, but rather 'the best of all possible worlds.' Leibniz says that creation is incomplete because humans are developing by way of experiencing evil and suffering. And for this end, mankind makes free moral choices, so as to experience the consequences of their own actions; natural evil existing to provide such choices.

In the last analysis it seems Leibniz simply failed to consider the fact that all mankind are already under the curse of death (Jn 3:36). And as far as I can tell, Leibniz fails to address man's depravity and the wrath of God for sin. Topics one would presuppose to frame a theodicy. These topics formed the basis for our discussion in chapter two. There we said that although man is fallen in Adam's physical and spiritual death (death being the judicial sentence of God for sin), by grace through faith are raised in Christ's resurrection, first spiritually, and then at Christ's Second Coming physically. Everyone who exercises faith in Christ is saved through judgment.

Leibniz, one may fairly say, was looking in the right direction but he fell short in his statement of the truth about

Chapter 10: Soli Deo Gloria

this world. Therefore, what we need to do is strengthen the line of thought that he started rather than turn our back on it and look for another. That is the intent of the theodicy that will be presented in this book. Before we go further, what we need to do is discuss a reality that has up to this point either not been fully developed (although to be fair to Leibniz he does in fact discuss God's sovereignty in depth, we simply don't have the space to cover it), or has been completely or partially dismissed, as in the case of dualism, open theism and process theology, and that reality is God's sovereignty.

God is Sovereign

In the following we make no attempt to offer a detailed exposition, however, what is desired is to highlight several weighty texts of Scripture which undoubtedly demonstrate God's 'sovereign sway and masterdom' over the universe. These texts concretely show God's sovereignty over all creation, including: (1) Satan and demons; (2) holy angels, (3) all mankind; (4) the cosmos; and (5) all afflictions be they bodily, psychological, emotional, and spiritual, et al.

1. <u>God is sovereign over the Devil and his fallen angels</u>. Satan cannot do anything against the will and consent of God.

- Job 1:12 and 2:6 show us that Satan needs permission to harm Job. God restricts Satan's attack on Job as He does all of His saints (1 Cor 10:13).
- 1 Sam 16:14 reveals how God punished Saul for his disobedience – God sent an evil spirit to torment him.
- 1 Kings 22:22 indicates the way God brings about king Ahab's death, viz., Ahab is persuaded to go into battle by false prophecy; all of which brings about God's prophecy.
- 1 Chron 21:1 demonstrates how God accomplished His purpose in punishing Israel by allowing Satan to plant a wicked thought into David's mind (cf. 2 Sam 24:1).
- Mt 4:10-11 demonstrates Christ's sovereignty over the devil when He says, "Away with you, Satan!
- In Mt 8:31-32, demons, who are being cast out of a man by Jesus, need Jesus' permission to afflict a herd of swine.

459

Chapter 10: Soli Deo Gloria

- In Lk 22:31-32, Satan needs permission from Jesus to sift Peter (and the other apostles) as wheat. This action of Satan led to a refinement of Peter's faith and character (subduing his pride) which strengthened him and prepared him for his apostolic work.
- Heb 2:14 tells us that Christ, by His atoning death conquered Satan, who had the power of death, and triumphed over all his hosts (Col 2:15).

Satan and his demons are immensely powerful, but God is sovereign over them. Satan is God's unwilling servant. Calvin insightfully writes,

It is evident, therefore, that Satan is under the power of God, and is so ruled by his authority, that he must yield obedience to it. Moreover, though we say that Satan resists God, and does works at variance with His works, we at the same time maintain that this contrariety and opposition depend on the permission of God. I now speak not of Satan's will and endeavor, but only of the result. For the disposition of the devil being wicked, he has no inclination whatever to obey the divine will, but, on the contrary, is wholly bent on contumacy and rebellion. This much, therefore, he has of himself, and his own iniquity, that he eagerly, and of set purpose, opposes God, aiming at those things which he deems most contrary to the will of God. But as God holds him bound and fettered by the curb of his power, he executes those things only for which permission has been given him, and thus, however unwilling, obeys his Creator, being forced, whenever he is required, to do Him service.[32]

The devil and his wicked angels can do nothing against the will and consent of God. Satan cannot operate independently of God. Satan is God's agent of wrath and discipline (1 Cor 5:5; 1 Tim 1:20). Likewise he is always under the sovereign control of God.

- Ps 78:49 reveals that the plagues of Egypt were inflicted by God through the agency of wicked angels.
- Ex 12:23 tells us that when God sees the blood He will not allow the destroyer to strike. Whether this 'destroyer'

---

[32] Calvin, Institutes of the Christian Religion, Book 1, Chapter 17, 99-100.

is a holy or wicked angel we are not told, nor does it matter, for all angels, elect or wicked do the will of God.

- The apostle Paul tells the church at Corinth to "deliver such a one to Satan for the destruction of the flesh, that his spirit may be saved in the day of the Lord Jesus (1 Cor 5:5). In this sense, Satan is an agent of discipline for an immoral man in the church.
- Rev 13:7 tells us that God grants the first Beast (from the sea) authority over the whole earth for the purposes of persecuting the saints and to overcome them.[33]

Francis Turretin tells us, "The devil is no more than the servant of God, the keeper of the prison, who has no power over sinners, unless by the just judgment of God."[34] This is not to dismiss the fact that Satan hates and blasphemes God's name, God's tabernacle (the Church militant), and those who dwell in heaven (the Church triumphant). There is felt enmity between the Seed of the woman and the seed of Satan.

2. God is sovereign over the holy angels. The holy angels exist to worship God and do His bidding. "They are the ministers and dispensers of the divine bounty toward us. Accordingly, we are told how they watch for our safety, how they undertake our defense, direct our path, and take heed that no evil befall us."[35] According to Martin Luther, "an angel is a spiritual creature created by God without a body, for the service of Christendom and the Church."[36]

Within this vast topic, for brevity's sake, let's restrict our discussion to the three primary duties of holy angels: (1) they are messengers of God; (2) they protect and deliver God's people; and (3) they are God's agents in judgment. For example:

---

[33] The Beast from the sea, part of the demonic trinity, signifies antichristian government – the perversity of society. Rev 13:8 tells us that all earth dwellers, those who are not saved, do not have their names recorded in the Lamb's Book of Life and will worship the Beast.

[34] Turretin, A Historical Sketch of Opinions on the Atonement.

[35] Calvin, Institutes of the Christian Religion, 1.14.6.

[36] Luther, Table Talk, 339.

Chapter 10: Soli Deo Gloria

- God sent an angel to guide Israel through the wilderness, as Ex 23:20 reveals, "Behold, I sent an Angel before you to keep you in the way and to bring you into the place which I have prepared." *Angels guide the saints.*
- Well-known is the deliverance of Daniel who spent the night in a den full of hungry lions and was supernaturally preserved through the intervention of God's angel (Dan 6:10-23). *Angels preserve the saints.*
- Ps 34:7 tells us "The angel of the Lord encamps all around those who fear Him, and delivers them."
- Ps 91:11 encourages us that "For He shall give His angels charge over you, to keep you in all your ways."
- In Lk 1:30-33, the angel Gabriel announces the salvation that will come to God's people through the Savior Who will be born unto Mary. Likewise, the angels announce the birth of Jesus in Lk 2:14. *Angels proclaim the salvation of God in Christ* (Rev 14:6-7).
- In Acts 5:19-20, an angel of the Lord freed the imprisoned apostles and commanded them to "Go, stand in the temple and speak to the people all the words of this life." *Angels defend the saints.*
- In Acts 27:24, an angel appears to the apostle Paul and strengthens him with a message from God. *Angels encourage the saints.*
- Likewise, angels share our joy when a sinner repents and believes in Jesus Christ (Lk 15:10).

Scripture clearly reveals God's sovereignty over both the holy angels and the fallen angels. The Bible shows that the angels of heaven do God's will and commands, which includes the execution of God's wrath.

- 2 Sam 24:16 reveals that pestilence and death are mediated through angels, particularly in this text – the Angel of the Lord.[37]

---

[37] The Angel of the Lord or the Angel of God appears as a manifestation of Yahweh Himself, one with Yahweh and yet different from Him. See Gen 16:7-14; 18:2-33; 22:11-16; 31:11-13; 32:30; Ex 3:2-4; 23:21; 32:34; 33:14; Num 22:22-38; Josh 5:13-15; 6:2; Jud 2:1-3; 6:11-23; 13:3-22; 1 Kgs 19:5-7;

Chapter 10: Soli Deo Gloria

- In Ex 14:19, the Angel of God, Who is leading the camp of Israel, moves behind to guard them from the Egyptians. And with the "pillar of cloud," became a source of light to the fleeing Israelites but darkness to the pursuing Egyptians (Exodus 14:19-20). "Thus the double nature of the glory of God in salvation and judgment, which later appears so frequently in Scripture, could not have been more graphically depicted."[38]
- Acts 12:23 reveals the cause of Herod's death as resulting from the 'strike' of an angel of God because "he did not give glory to God." Herod was eaten by worms and died.
- In the Parable of the Wheat and the Tares, Jesus reveals that the holy angels will "gather out of His kingdom all things that offend, and those who practice lawlessness, and will cast them into the furnace of fire" (Mt 13:41-42, cf. Is 10:12; Ezek 9, 1 Pet 4:17, Rev 7:1-10; 13:8; 14:1-3).

3. God is sovereign over all mankind.

Contrary to the open theists and process theologians, human freedom cannot involve absolute authority, a sort of *autexousia* – will independent of God's sovereignty. God is sovereign over all mankind as Dan 4:34-35 tells us, "For His dominion is an everlasting dominion, and His kingdom is from generation to generation. All the inhabitants of the earth are reputed as nothing; He does according to His will in the army of heaven and among the inhabitants of the earth. No one can restrain His hand or say to Him, "What have You done?"

Additionally, it must be stated that God is free from evil but uses the evil acts of men for His glory and the good of His people. D.A. Carson insightfully writes,

God stands behind evil in such a way that not even evil takes place outside the bounds of his sovereignty, yet the evil is not morally chargeable to him: it is always chargeable to secondary agents, to secondary causes. On the other hand, God stands behind good in such a way that it not only takes place within the bounds of his

---

Is 63:9; Zech 1:10-13; 3:1-2. Elwell writes: "In the New Testament, there is no mention of the angel of the Lord; the Messiah himself is this person."
[38] Kaiser, Exodus, 389.

sovereignty, but it is always chargeable to him, and only derivatively to secondary agents. In other words, if I sin, I cannot possibly do so outside the bounds of God's sovereignty (or the many texts already cited have no meaning), but I alone am responsible for that sin – or perhaps I and those who tempted me, led me astray, and the like. God is not to be blamed. But if I do good, it is God working in me both to will and to act according to his good pleasure. God's grace has been manifested in my case, and he is to be praised.[39]

As the Bible demonstrates that God is sovereign over the hearts and decisions of mankind, it also reveals that human beings are morally responsible and are held accountable for their sins. This is not to say that God is the source of mankind's sins. For, the Scripture declares "For You are not a God who takes pleasure in wickedness, nor shall evil dwell with You" (Ps 5:4). Rather, God orchestrates the sin already in the heart of men. Yet Scripture declares that man is fully responsible for his sin. The Bible declares, "Let no one say when he is tempted, 'I am tempted by God'; for God cannot be tempted by evil, nor does He Himself tempt anyone. But each one is tempted when he is drawn away by his own desires and enticed" (James 1:13-14).

Perhaps the greatest example in all Scripture is that of Pharaoh. God didn't make Pharaoh a rebellious hater of God, he was already. In the drama of the Exodus, God used the hardness of Pharaoh's heart to demonstrate His glory and His love for His people (Ex 9:16; Rom 9:17-18).[40] And behind it all, God was bringing salvation through judgment. God was redeeming His people out of bondage and executing judgment on the gods of Egypt (Ex 12:12). If the blood of Christ is on you, the plague of destruction will not touch you. This view, known as compatibilism, maintains that in making moral decisions we are free to do what we want to do in a world in which everything is sovereignly determined by God. This is the rub.

Many objections are raised to this. The atheist Richard Dawkins writes, "If God is omniscient, he must already know

---

[39] Carson, How Long, O Lord? : Reflections on Suffering and Evil, 189.

[40] For an excellent treatment of this subject see: Beale, An Exegetical and Theological Consideration of the Hardening of Pharaoh's Heart in Exodus 4-14 and Romans 9, Trinity Journal 5 NS (1984) 129-154.

how he is going to intervene to change the course of history using his omnipotence."[41] Yet, that is precisely what He has done through His Son Jesus Christ. Mankind would be forever dead, defiled, and damned unless God intervened by sending His Son to die for sinners. Now, that's intervention (see chapter two)! However, Dawkins raises a curious point that must be discussed, and that is the correlation between God's omniscience and omnipotence.

We must agree with Leibniz that God is not the author of sin, nor does He excuse it, condone it, or approve of it. God, nonetheless hates it, but uses it to bring about His purpose. This leads to serious questions. Perhaps Louis Berkhof put it best when he wrote, "Problems arise here which have never yet been solved and which are probably incapable of solution by man."[42] Yet, later Berkhof helps us disentangle this knot by saying,

It is customary to speak of the doctrine of God respecting moral evil as permissive. By His decree God rendered the sinful actions of man infallibly certain without deciding to effectuate them by acting immediately upon and in the finite will. This means that God does not work postpositively in man "both to will and to do," when man goes contrary to His revealed will. It should be carefully noted, however, that this permissive decree does not imply a passive permission of something which is not under the control of the divine will. It is a decree which renders the future sinful act absolutely certain, but in which God determines (a) not to hinder the sinful self-determination of the finite will; and (b) to regulate and control the result of this sinful self-determination (Ps 78:29; 106:15; Acts 14:16; 17:30).[43]

This understanding does not, however, remove our liberty or destroy our responsibility for our own actions. Sin and suffering proceed only from secondary causes, that is, God permits them, but not passively as if it was not under His divine control. God orchestrates all events for His glory and for the good of His Church. Consider that our sovereign God declares, "Surely, as I have thought, so it shall come to pass,

---

[41] Dawkins, The God Delusion, 101.
[42] Berkhof, Systematic Theology, 98.
[43] Ibid, 105.

and as I have purposed, so it shall stand" (Is 14:24). Or, "For the Lord of hosts has purposed, and who will annul it? His hand is stretched out, and who will turn it back" (Is 24:27)? Or these Scriptures:

- Pro 16:9 declares that "A man's heart plans his way, but the Lord directs his steps" (cf. Pro 19:21; 20:24; 21:1).
- Gen 20:3-6 declares that God restrained the sin of Abimelech so that he would not come near Sarah, Abraham's wife.
- Pro 16:4 declares that "The Lord works out everything to its proper end—even the wicked for a day of disaster" (NIV).
- Joseph, speaking to his brothers who sold him into slavery, says, "Do not be afraid, for am I in the place of God? But as for you, you meant evil against me; but God meant it for good, in order to bring it about as it is this day, to save many people alive" (Gen 50:19-20).
- In Judges 14:3-4, Samson, who is seeking to marry a pagan woman, rejects his parent's pleas to take a wife from among his people. However, the Scripture reveals that it is God who is orchestrating these events to bring a confrontation with the Philistines; for they were ruling over them at the time. This fact did not negate Samson's guilt, but it shows how God providentially overrules human folly and brings His will to pass in spite of it
- Acts 4:28 tells us that, although Jesus was betrayed by Judas who handed Him over to the Sanhedrin, so He could be crucified by Roman soldiers by the order of Pilate, these all did "whatever Your hand and Your purpose determined before to be done" (cf. Mt 26:24; Lk 22:22; Acts 2:23).

We are now considering human freedom. And as we saw in chapter two, we cannot discuss it without reference to the fall. For before the fall mankind was *posse non peccare* – able to not sin, however, since the fall, mankind is *non posse non peccare* – not able to not sin.[44] The topic of human freedom

---

[44] See page 126.

Chapter 10: Soli Deo Gloria

normally encompasses a discussion on election. A great summary statement of election is as follows:

Election is the gracious purpose of God, according to which He regenerates, justifies, sanctifies, and glorifies sinners. It is consistent with the free agency of man, and comprehends all the means in connection with the end. It is the glorious display of God's sovereign goodness, and is infinitely wise, holy, and unchangeable. It excludes boasting and promotes humility.[45]

I think Charles Spurgeon put it best when he said, "A man is not saved against his will, but he is made willing by the operation of the Holy Ghost. A mighty grace which he does not wish to resist enters into the man, disarms him, makes a new creature of him, and he is saved."[46] Man is dead, defiled, and damned and will remain so unless Christ saves him.

In this vein, Augustine resounds, "You called, You cried, You shattered my deafness, You sparkled, You blazed, You drove away my blindness, You shed Your fragrance, and I drew in my breath, and I pant for You."[47] And in a sermon on John 6:44 Spurgeon cogently states, "We declare, upon Scriptural authority, that the human will is so desperately set on mischief, so depraved, and so inclined to everything that is evil, and so disinclined to everything that is good, that without the powerful, supernatural, irresistible influence of the Holy Spirit, no human will ever be constrained towards Christ."

In the same breath we may unreservedly state that God has commanded all men to repent and believe in Jesus Christ (Mk 1:15). For example, when eighteen people were killed when the tower in Siloam fell, Jesus said, "Unless you repent you will all likewise perish" (Lk 13:4-5). *Hell is not filled with people who repent.* Further, Acts 17:30 declares, "Truly, these times of ignorance God overlooked, but now commands all men everywhere to repent." This led Augustine to say, "My whole hope is only in Thy exceeding great mercy. Give what Thou commandest, and command what Thou wilt."[48] In other words, give me a repentant heart O Lord and I will repent.

---

[45] Baptist Faith and Message, V. God's Purpose of Grace, 12.
[46] Spurgeon, Sermons, 10.309.
[47] Augustine, Confessions, 10.27.
[48] Ibid, 29.40.

Chapter 10: Soli Deo Gloria

Give me the gift of faith and I will believe. "For you will certainly carry out God's purpose," C.S. Lewis writes, "however you act, but it makes a difference to you whether you serve like Judas or like John."[49]

Much could be said regarding the mystery of these two seeming contradictory truths: Divine sovereignty and human freedom; in fact, much ink has been spent already. However, as John Currid states, "God sovereignty and mankind's responsibility for sin and suffering are simply and clearly expounded in the Scriptures. They are both true, but how they exist together and at the same time are a mystery."[50] This is the rub. The point here is to draw our attention to the fact that God uses even the evil deeds of mankind for His glory and the Church's good (Rom 8:28). And God holds human agents responsible for the evil deed they've committed.

This is a great mystery but as Carson tells us, "The mystery of providence defies our attempt to tame it by reason. I do not mean it is illogical; I mean that we do not know enough to be able to unpack it and domesticate it."[51] There is a pronounced felt tension between the truth regarding Divine sovereignty and human responsibility. We get into trouble when we attempt to remove the tension. We do best to let the tension remain.

4. God is sovereign over the cosmos.

God not only created the universe, He sits enthroned over it and orchestrates all events, bringing them to their consummate end (Ecc 3:11).

- Mt 10:29 famously shows God's sovereignty of all animal life; "Not one of them falls to the ground apart from your Father's will."
- The Book of Jonah reveals that God is sovereign over a great fish (1:17; 2:10), a vine (4:6), and a worm (4:7). This is not to mention the storm God sent into which the sailors toss Jonah (1:4).

---

[49] Lewis, The Problem of Pain, 111.
[50] Currid, Why Do I Suffer? : Suffering and the Sovereignty of God, 45.
[51] Carson, How Long, O Lord? : Reflections on Suffering and Evil, 201.

468

Chapter 10: Soli Deo Gloria

- When one reads Job chapters 38-41 it would be hard not to see God's sovereignty over all of nature.
- God is said to withhold rain to discipline a nation (1 Kgs 17:1; Amos 4:7-10).
- Most famously, God may send rain to inflict His wrath, as Genesis chapters 6-9 so aptly demonstrate.

God is sovereign over all things! This 'all things' includes: the fall of sparrows (Mt 10:29), the rolling of dice (Pro 16:33), the slaughter of his people (Ps 44:11), the decisions of kings (Pro 21:1), the failing of sight (Ex 4:11), the sickness of children (2 Sam 12:15), the loss and gain of money (1 Sam 2:7), the suffering of saints (1 Pet 4:19), the completion of travel plans (Jas 4:15), the persecution of Christians (Heb 12:4–7), the repentance of souls (2 Tim 2:25), the gift of faith (Phil 1:29), the pursuit of holiness (Phil 3:12–13), the growth of believers (Heb 6:3), the giving and taking of life (1 Sam 2:6), not to mention draughts (Lev 26:19-20; Dt 28:24; 2 Sam 24:1; Hos 13:15), hail (Ex 9:23-29; Josh 10:11; Rev 16:21), thunder (1 Sam 7:10; 12:18), even the waves of the sea (Job 38:11), and of course, the crucifixion of his Son (Acts 4:27–28) for our salvation.

Additionally, Christ our Savior and Lord is sovereign. The Gospel of John declares in seven ways that Jesus Christ is sovereign over: *creation* – He turned water into wine (Jn 2:1); *time and space* – He healed a nobleman's son from miles away (Jn 4:46-54); *infirmity* – He healed a lame man (Jn 5:1-9); *hunger* – He fed 5,000 (Jn 6:1-14); *natural laws* – He walked on the water (Jn 6:15-21); *blindness* – He healed a blind man (Jn 9:1-12); and *death* – He raised Lazarus from the dead (Jn 11:1-44). God is sovereign over everything that may cause us suffering – nothing escapes His control.

As Safe in Battle as in Bed

God orchestrates all events for His glory and for the good of His people. For example, in 2006, while serving in Iraq as a member of a Special Forces team, I was shot during a close quarters battle. This occurred during a spiritual highpoint in my career as a soldier. My unit was operating out of Baghdad and we had been there for about three months and things were going well. To top it all off, I was empowered by my chaplain (Mike) to lead Christian services since he was unable to minister to us during our deployment.

I vividly recall all the details of the day I was shot. It was a Sunday and we had the day off. That morning I preached a sermon on Daniel chapter three – the great contest of faith for Daniel's three friends: Shadrach, Meshach, and Abed-Nego. It would be quite fitting for the ordeal I would soon face. If you remember from Sunday school, because the three men would not bow to an idol, they were thrown into a fiery furnace. The Bible tells us that the furnace was so hot that it killed the men who delivered them to the flame (Dan 3:22). The one biblical point that I repeatedly stressed in that message was that God tests our faith in fiery trials, and that He employs these trials at times to purge away the dross of our self-reliance, thereby grounding our faith more on His promises.

That night we set off on a routine raid. I say routine because we had conducted many such raids by the third month in theater. It was all very surgical; in and out. Our unit consisted of men who had done this sort of thing before and they were good at it. As they say, it was not their first rodeo, and for that I had the utmost confidence in the men I was privileged to serve with. After all, close combat was our bread and butter. As we approached the target, I said the Lord's Prayer and considered well the words of Robert Dabney's funeral sermon for Stonewall Jackson:

As to physical security, the child of God is not taught what the special will of God is; he has no revelation as to the security of his person. Nor does he presume to predict the particular end God will grant to the cause in which he is bound. But he knows that, whatever may come, it will be wise, just, and good. Whether the arrows of death shall strike him or pass him by, he knows no more than the unbelieving sinner; but he knows that neither event can happen to him without the purpose and will of his Heavenly Father. And that will, be it whichever it may, is guided by divine wisdom and love. Should the event prove to be the very place, and hour, for life to end; then he accepts it with calm submission; for are not the time and

Chapter 10: Soli Deo Gloria

place chosen for him by the Omniscient, who loves him from eternity?[52]

Having a dangerous occupation leads one to consider a lot, and of all men, the soldier has the strongest reason to become a Christian. During a mission, there is no time for philosophy or deep contemplation, only a ready mind with a heightened sense of awareness. Though a Christian, I could still feel a twinge of fear – those butterflies in your guts that seem to help keep you on edge and ready to pounce. I never asked the other men of my team how they mentally prepared for a mission but as for me, knowing my soul was safe in the hands of Christ, I always felt as safe in battle as in bed.

It seemed like a traditional Iraqi house. There was really nothing particular that would set it apart from the millions of others like it – a two story white plastered block building with a flat roof. We had hit many like this before. By the time we approached the target building it was just after midnight, and after our stealthy approach, we paused and poised for the assault. Then the countdown came, five, four, three, two, booom! The door charges belched their explosive residue into the night air and we were in. We cleared our way through the house and entered the next to the last room, and that's when it happened. I had no sooner stopped moving when it felt like somebody hit me in the head with a mallet. I was down. The sound of the bullet reverberated between my ears. I had been shot in the throat just above the body armor but it felt like I got shot in the head. In fact, for some time I imagined that I had no head.

I vividly remember examining the ceiling of all things. I couldn't move my head. I felt like I was waiting for the man who shot me to finish me off. It seemed like it would happen at any second, I would look up and see a gun barrel in my face. Then I remember a very comforting presence come over me. God was with me and I had no fear of death. I knew that when I died, which seemed like seconds away, I would pass from this life into the next – a seamless transition. I then went unconscious.

---

[52] Robert Dabney, True Courage, A Funeral Sermon for Thomas Jackson.

Chapter 10: Soli Deo Gloria

The truly remarkable part of this story is the path of the bullet. It entered my tracheal notch, clipped my collar bone, passed through my shoulder and out my right shoulder blade. Normally, getting shot in the throat is a done deal especially from a few feet away. At about nine hundred feet per second, the bullet entered my throat head on but was somehow redirected to about a forty-five degree angle where it continued on until exiting at my right shoulder. In the words of the Army surgeon at Walter Reed who spoke to my mother, "The bullet's path, could in no way be recreated even with the most modern sophisticated equipment. I don't believe in God, but He surely delivered your son."

I have never seen or even heard of anyone have a bullet pass through their trachea and esophagus and walk, let alone live, and still retain all functionality. A wicked man shot me but God guided the bullet in such a way that it was redirected, missing all my vital arteries and my spine! God has used that experience to grow me spiritually and more importantly, He has used it as a powerful testimony to His amazing power and grace. The biblical point being made here is God may supernaturally preserve life in order to demonstrate His sovereignty. It is God's prerogative to preserve or take life as He sees fit. There is no such thing as chance or luck.

Regarding this John Currid writes, "The Bible flatly contradicts the view of many today that adversity occurs randomly. In fact, to claim that suffering happens by chance is to deny the all-pervasive biblical doctrine of the sovereignty of God."[53] *The Scriptures teach us that while God is neither the author of evil nor the doer of evil, He most certainly is the orchestrator of evil events for His glory and for the good of His people* (Gen 45:5; 50:20; Pro 16:4; Is 45:7; Acts 4:28: Rev 17:17). Yet, God doesn't sin or condone sin, nor does He cause anyone to sin. So, why does God allow sin to persist? This we hope to answer later in this chapter.[54]

For now, we need to see that God doesn't owe us anything, much less an explanation for why or how He is orchestrating His universe. Additionally, as we will see, God is not trying to

---

[53] Currid, Why Do I Suffer? : Suffering and the Sovereignty of God, 29.
[54] See the section entitled *Delayed Judgment*.

remove Himself from the fact that He has a plan for evil. Christians who object to that should consider Acts 4:28 which informs us that all of the people who gathered together to murder Jesus Christ only did, "whatever Your hand and Your purpose determined before to be done." As Spurgeon has aptly said, "There is no attribute more comforting to His children than that of God's sovereignty." *We are not to judge God's love according to the bad we're experiencing.*

We may not fully comprehend the correlation between God's sovereignty and human freedom or God's sovereignty and the existence of evil and suffering as I admit I cannot, but this should not lead us to despair, because we know that the Judge of all the earth will do right (Gen 18:25; Acts 17:30-31). For certain, if we don't know Christ as Savior, we will know Him as Judge. This should, however, lead us to trust in the One whose wisdom and knowledge are deep and rich beyond measure, whose judgments are unsearchable, and whose ways are past finding out (Rom 11:33). Hence, doctrine ought to lead to doxology.

The fact that God has chosen not to reveal everything human beings want to know should result in our holding Him in awe and glorifying Him. Perhaps J.I. Packer reasons best when he writes, "The safest way in theodicy is to leave God's permission of sin and moral evil as a mystery, and to reason from the good achieved in redemption."[55] This is prudent as it is sage, however, we will consider further points in our discussion on the problem of suffering and the goodness and sovereignty of God.

Why do Christians Suffer?

We have made an effort to cover in depth the doctrine of God's sovereignty but a question remains: why do Christians suffer? I put it this way because God causes sufferings and trials to come upon believers and unbelievers for different reasons. In this section we will tackle the issue of why God causes Christians to suffer and will discuss the purpose of sufferings for unbelievers in the next. Again, we make no

---

[55] Packer, Doctrines Christians Should Believe, 168.

attempt to offer a detailed exposition here. *What we need to bear in mind is that God's priority is holiness for us in this life and happiness in the next.* With this in mind, there are at least ten ways that God uses suffering for Christians:

1. *Suffering is part and parcel of living in a fallen world that is under the sentence of death* (Gen 3:15-24; Rom 5:12-21; 8:18-20). The wrath of God is death and condemnation. We must remember that death signifies God's judgment. Carson helps us remember this fact when we think we are all entitled to seventy years on this planet. He writes, "For the believer, the time of death becomes far less daunting a factor when seen in the light of eternity...Although death remains an enemy, an outrage, a sign of judgment, a reminder of sin, and a formidable opponent, it is, from another perspective, the portal through which we pass to consummated life."[56]

It's important to remember, that as Christians, we have hope even in death because Christ has already conquered Satan, death and hell, and those who are alive in Jesus Christ will never see death but will pass from this life seamlessly into the next (1 Thess 4:15). Death is therefore a defeated enemy that we will face in the confidence that Christ already has the victory (Jn 11:25-26; 1 Cor 11:25-26; 2 Cor 5:8; Rev 1:5, 18). For the Christian, death is an entrance into glory.

2. *God uses suffering to separate His people from the false contentment of the world* (Dt 8:3; Mt 10:34-37; 13:21). The Bible tells us in Dt 8:2-5,

And you shall remember that the Lord your God led you all the way these forty years in the wilderness, **to humble you and test you,** to know what was in your heart, whether you would keep His commandments or not. 3 **So He humbled you, allowed you to hunger**, and fed you with manna which you did not know nor did your fathers know, that He might make you know that man shall not live by bread alone; but man lives by every word that proceeds from the mouth of the Lord. 4 Your garments did not wear out on you, nor did your foot swell these forty years. 5 **You should know in your**

---

[56] Carson, How Long, O Lord? : Reflections on Suffering and Evil, 133.

heart that as a man chastens his son, so the Lord your God chastens you (emphasis added).

God uses suffering to sever our allegiance and bondage to the world. Watson puts it this way, "God would have the world hang as a loose tooth which, being twitched away does not much trouble us."[57] In order to keep His saints from finding their way in the world, or the world from finding its way in the saint, God employs various trials enabling us to keep our eye on the prize. C.S. Lewis writes, "Prosperity knits a man to the world. He feels that he is finding his place in it, while really it is finding its place in him."[58] God doesn't want His saints to grow too comfortable in this world and so He will employ suffering to release our grip on it. For, God has said in His Word, "Do not love the world or the things in the world. If anyone loves the world, the love of the Father is not in him" (1 Jn 2:15).

God desires His people to turn away from the world and look to Him for everything, and He will employ suffering to bring it about. John Piper writes, "For us there is the need, not only to have our obedience tested and proven but also to be purified from all remnants of self-reliance and entanglements with the world."[59] When we suffer trials, God allows us to see how odious sin is and how miserable we are without Him. Describing this further, Richard Sibbes writes,

These depths are left to us, to make us more desirous of heaven; else great men, that are compassed about with earthly comforts, alas, with what zeal they could pray, 'Thy kingdom come,' etc.? No; with Peter they would rather say, 'Master, it is good for us to be here,' Mk 9:5; and therefore, it is God's usual dealing with great men, to suffer them to fall into spiritual desertions, to smoke them out of the world, whether they will or not.[60]

3. *God employs suffering as a means of disciplining us so that we will avoid future opportunities to sin.* (Ps107:17; 119:67, 71; Pro 3:11-12; Heb 12:5-11; Rev 2:9-10). God scourges

---

[57] Watson, All Things For Good, 29.
[58] Lewis, Screwtape Letters
[59] Piper, Let the Nations Be Glad, 108.
[60] Sibbes, Complete Works, VI, 162.

every son He receives (Heb 12:6). "Every print of the rod is a badge of honor."[61] God creates patience in us so we may endure His chastening love. It's as Carson puts it, "Be patient; it is better to be a chastened saint than a carefree sinner."[62] Likewise, William Gurnall writes, "An impatient soul in affliction is a bedlam in chains, yea, too like the devil in his chains, who rages against God, while he is fettered by Him."[63] David says, "Let the bones that you have broken rejoice" (Ps 51:8), and Psalm 119:67 declares, "Before I was afflicted I went astray, but now I keep Your word."

John Currid rightly sees the suffering associated with God's discipline as preparation. He writes,

It is like a vaccination for smallpox or some other disease. The inoculation itself is unpleasant, and the side effects are uncomfortable, and the reality is that one is given a minor dose of the disease. However, when confronted with the disease itself, one's immune system is able to fight it because of growing immunity. Thus, one's system is trained and prepared. That is like the Christian life.[64]

As has been said earlier, God brings temporal judgments upon Christians so that we will not be condemned along with the world (1 Cor 11:32, cf. Rev 2:22). Christ corrects us as He is our Lord. And this correction shows that we are His legitimate children (Heb 12:11).

4. *God allows suffering so we will rely more on Him and not ourselves* (2 Cor 1:9; 12:9; 1 Pet 5:6-7). This is one of the many ways God proves our faith. Afflictions shatter the myth of our self-sufficiency. We clearly see our weaknesses when we suffer. In 2 Cor 1:8-9, the apostle Paul tells us, the reason why God appoints sufferings is so that we would not trust in ourselves but in God who raises the dead.

Likewise, John Currid writes, "By means of adversity, God then restores believers to proper creaturely dependence upon Himself. This is to say that God frequently afflicts Christians

---

[61] Watson, All Things For Good, 30.

[62] Carson, How Long, O Lord? : Reflections on Suffering and Evil, 150.

[63] Gurnall, The Christian in Complete Armour, 60.

[64] Currid, Why Do I Suffer? : Suffering and the Sovereignty of God, 73.

that they would again realize their hope, joy, and sufficiency lies in Him alone. God is thus being gracious in adversity, and uprooting the Christian from the world."[65]

5. *God uses suffering to forge Christ's character in us* (Ps 119:66-67, 71; Pro 27:17; Rom 5:1-5; Heb 2:10; 5:8). God's refining process is so that His Son will be more clearly displayed in us. Suffering teaches us that the greatest good of the Christian life is not absence of pain but Christ-likeness. Suffering is one of the means God uses to sanctify us. As has been said, God's refining process is an expression of his love, never His wrath. His judgment begins with his own people, and then consumes unbelievers (1 Pet 4:17). And only the man who can endure the refining fire of God's holy presence can remain in God's house forever (Jn 8:35).

God, as it were, pours Christ's character into us, forming iron in our souls, and works the rough edges out on His anvil of the world (Is 54:16). Watson insightfully writes,

God's rod is a pencil to draw Christ's image more lively upon us. It is good that there should be symmetry between the Head and the members. Would we be parts of Christ's mystical body, and not be like Him? His life, as Calvin says, was a series of sufferings, 'a man of sorrows, and acquainted with grief' (Is 53:3). He wept and bled. Was His head crowned with thorns, and do we think to be crowned with roses? It is good to be like Christ, though it be true He drank the poison in the cup (the wrath of God), yet there is some wormwood in the cup left, which the saints must drink: only here is the difference between Christ's sufferings and ours; He were satisfactory (that is, to pay the price for sins), ours are castigatory (that is, in order to amend and correct).[66]

I would only add to what Watson has said by saying that Christ's sufferings are unto propitiation (salvation) and Christian sufferings are unto propagation, that is, a means of grace. We will discuss this aspect of Christian suffering in the next section.

---

[65] Watson, All Things For Good, 66.
[66] Ibid, 28-29.

Chapter 10: Soli Deo Gloria

6. *God uses suffering to create in us staying power to faithfully endure persecution* (Jam 1:2-8). God prepares His saints for trouble by causing them to experience suffering. However, this is not just for sufferings sake, but because God's wisdom is as manifold as it is infinite, He causes us to grow in grace, mirroring Christ's image, thereby creating staying power in us, while He prunes us of our sinful proclivities (Jn 15:1-8). As we have seen, the Christian's continuing loyalty to Christ despite trouble serves to define our character and produces staying power. When I say staying power I refer to what the Bible calls *patient-endurance*.

Patient-endurance can only be acquired through testing, and suffering definitely tests our faith. For example, the apostle Paul tells us in Rom 5:3-4, "We also glory in tribulations, knowing that tribulation produces perseverance; and perseverance, character; and character, hope." What character is the apostle Paul talking about? The very character of Christ, Who Himself is forming Himself within us. This doesn't mean, of course, that we have only a hope of future joys, we can be full of joy here and now even in our trials and troubles. Taken in the right spirit these very things will give us patient endurance; this in turn will develop a mature character. A character of this sort produces a steady hope, a hope that will never disappoint us because if we are born again, already we have some experience of the love of God flooding through our hearts by the Holy Spirit given to us. Sufferings temper Christians and is part of God's discipline. This point will be developed further in the next section.

7. *Suffering is the result of a Christian's battle against the three enemies of the kingdom of God – our sin nature, the unbelieving world, and Satan.* When we mortify our flesh, crucify our sin nature, and say no to the desires of the flesh, we carry around in our body the suffering and death of the Lord Jesus (2 Cor 4:11-12). When we take a stand for Christ we will suffer demonic attack and incur the world's enmity, not to mention the fact that our sin nature will hate it, but this will result in the glory of God (Mt 5:9; Heb 12:4-13; Ps 27:12; Ps 37:14-15; 2 Thess 1:5; 2 Tim 2:8-9; 1 Pet 2:19; Rev 1:9 Acts 5:41; 1 Pet 4:14).

478

8. *Suffering affords Christians the opportunity to witness the saving power of Christ* (2 Cor 4:10-11; Col 1:24-29; 1 Pet 2:19-20). Suffering furnishes on opportunity for Christians to testify of the saving power of Christ's Cross, and thereby suffer for His sake, for which there will be two ends: a hardening obstinacy for some, and a means of grace for others. God uses Christian suffering to fill up what is lacking in Christ's sufferings (Col 1:24). Let us understand that Paul is not saying that Christ's afflictions are lacking in their atoning efficacy. For they are sufficient for everyone that believes in Him. Everyone that looks to the Son and believes will be saved.

However, as said earlier, Christ's sufferings are unto propitiation (salvation) and Christian sufferings are unto propagation, that is, Christ's sufferings for the salvation of all who believe in Him are made known to others by way of the verbal witness as well as sufferings of Christians. Rather than being bitter or upset when justice doesn't come swiftly, we can say along with John Bunyan, "Therefore, I bind these lies and slanderous accusations to my person as an ornament; it belongs to my Christian profession to be vilified, slandered, reproached and reviled, and since all this is nothing but that, as God and my conscience testify, I rejoice in being reproached for Christ's sake."[67] Again, this point will be further developed under the section entitled delayed judgment.

9. *Suffering affords God the opportunity to manifest His grace.* Tribulation arises on account of the worship of God, the gospel message, and holy living. Lives like Job's are an indictment to lawlessness. It's important for us to remember that when Job was afflicted he didn't say, the Lord has given and Satan has taken away, no; he said, "The Lord gave, and the Lord has taken away; blessed be the name of the Lord" (Job 1:21). And the Bible, ascribing Job's response as correct says, "In all this Job did not sin *nor charge God with wrong*" (Job 1:22, emphasis added). Job was not suffering for his sins.

---

[67] Bunyan, The Complete Works, Part IV, 69. See more on John Bunyan footnote on page 15.

He suffered so that God might demonstrate to Satan, and the world, that Job would retain his integrity in spite of all of his afflictions. Hence, "The greater the trouble, the greater the deliverance."[68]

This thought is corollary to the one above in which we said that Christian suffering fills up what is lacking in Christ's suffering. The short answer is we are the body of Christ, and in all our sufferings God suffers, as Is 63:8-9 makes known, "So He became their Savior. In all their affliction He was afflicted, and the Angel of His Presence saved them; in His love and in His pity He redeemed them; and He bore them and carried them all the days of old." So, when Saul, who was wreaking havoc on the Church, was confronted by the risen Christ, he asked "Who are you Lord?" The Lord said, "I am Jesus, whom you are persecuting" (Acts 9:5). In this way we may understand how Christian suffering fills up what is lacking in Christ's suffering (Col 1:29).

10. *Suffering is the price for winning the lost for Christ – to fulfill the Great Commission* (Mt 24:9-14; 28:18-20; 2 Tim 2:8-10; 4:5-6). As we have said, Jesus gives us the express purpose of preaching – a witness to all nations (Mt 24:14).[69] The goal of preaching the "gospel of the kingdom" is for "every tribe and tongue and people and nation" to hear the glorious saving power of Christ's cross; and suffering is the cost of fulfilling the Great Commission. Jesus said, "They will deliver you up to tribulation and kill you, and you will be hated by all nations for My name's sake." This is the cost for the completion of the Great Commission (Mt 24:9). Likewise, "He who endures to the end shall be saved," is the confidence which a perfect atonement secures (Mt 24:13; Rom 8:28-39). As Christians, we are enabled to do this because we have been crucified with Christ, Who now dwells in our hearts by faith. Christ, Who has rooted and grounded Himself to us in love, compels us to minister the gospel to see the lost saved (Phil 1:8).

---

[68] Sibbes, Complete Works, VI, 162.
[69] See Chapter 9.

Chapter 10: Soli Deo Gloria

Like Joseph, we may suffer at the hands of even our own family members, but God, working graciously behind the scenes, can bring about a great deliverance out of a great tragedy (Mt 10:34-39). Joseph was a type of Christ; when he suffered, it wasn't because he was a sinner, it was because God was going to use his life to save His people. God takes ordinary people like you and I, and through us accomplishes extraordinary things. God orchestrated events so that the young lad Joseph would end up delivering a nation from certain destruction; Joseph's suffering was the price of it all. The Bible tells us that Joseph spent roughly thirteen years as either a slave or a prisoner (Gen 37:1; 41:46) but was preparing him for the extraordinary tasks. Thus, as Joseph's suffering brought about deliverance for others so does Christian sufferings for the gospel.

This thought not only serves to preface the following section, it encapsulates the part and parcel of the thesis for this chapter which is: Christians will patiently-endure suffering, through the power God supplies, in order to fulfill the Great Commission and hasten the Second Coming of Christ. But before we move on, it's important to note that, as Christians, not all suffering seems to fit neatly into one of the above categories we have made.

On the Lord's Day, February 6, 1870, the reverend George Mueller's wife Mary died of rheumatic fever. They had been married 39 years. The Lord gave him the strength to preach at her memorial service. He said, "I miss her in numberless ways, and shall miss her yet more and more. But as a child of God, and as a servant of the Lord Jesus, I bow, I am satisfied with the will of my Heavenly Father, I seek by perfect submission to His holy will to glorify Him, and I kiss continually the hand that has thus afflicted me." Suffering doesn't always make sense, but as Christians we have a hope that's beyond death. Our hope is in the One Who has conquered death and lives forever; Who always lives to intercede for us, is preparing a place for us, and will take us to our heavenly home (Heb 7:25).

Chapter 10: Soli Deo Gloria

Delayed Judgment of God

An eschatological (end time) judgment will occur at the end of history, notwithstanding, sometimes that judgment intrudes into this age. This may come in the form of warnings and prejudgment for non-believers or range from chastening to suffering with Christ for believers. The final judgment is delayed until the full number of God's people are saved (Mt 1:21; Rom 11:25-26; 2 Pet 3:9). Christ has the keys to death and hell: He has the power over both and can release one from under its control.

As we further consider how to reconcile the problem of suffering and the goodness and sovereignty of God, I want to enumerate for us three biblical truths: First, God delays His final judgment until the full number of those who will believe in Him are saved; Second, God gives staying power to His Church while the full number comes in; and, Third, the very attitude of the Church during this time of testing and suffering is important.

As we look to the first biblical proposition, *God delays His final judgment until the full number of those who will believe in Him are saved*; let us consider where we would be if, say for instance, Christ's Second Coming was in the lifetime of our great grandfather, that is before we were born. Where would that put us? Rational creatures that we are, we would have to say that if Christ returned that long ago we simply would have never existed.

For God to have not brought an end to history before you and I were born, and more importantly, before He could reach us with the gospel of Jesus Christ, is a demonstration of God's great mercy and patience. As I hope to demonstrate, God delays His final judgment until the full number of those who will believe in Him are saved. As we have said, the first coming of Jesus Christ ushered in the acceptable year of the Lord – that is a space of time for salvation not judgment.[70] The apostle Paul says in 2 Cor 6:2, "Behold, now is the acceptable time; behold, now is the day of salvation."

---

[70] See page 364.

482

Chapter 10: Soli Deo Gloria

The Grace of Patience

While this acceptable year lasts, God graciously withholds final judgment, patiently offering full amnesty through the cross of Christ, and suffering occurs because the judgment is delayed until the full number of God's people have come in. The time we currently live in is a day of God's gracious patience. In order for us to fully consider our first premise: *God delays His final judgment until the full number of those who will believe in Him are saved*, it's important for us to consider the grace of patience. There are at least eight ways in which we may consider the grace of patience:

1. It is a fruit of the Spirit.
2. It is essential to steadfastness.
3. It can only be acquired through testing.
4. It is given at the appropriate time.
5. It is ultimately what saved the world.
6. It is akin to grace.
7. It is rooted in the wisdom of God.
8. It is the very nature of God.

At the grammatical level, patience in the original Greek is *makrathumia*, which is often translated long-suffering. And is formed from the two words *makras* meaning long or far to denote time and space, and *thumia* which means passion or anger. In the biblical sense it can mean waiting for a sufficient time before expressing our anger while avoiding the premature use of force or retaliation. The words endurance and patience are co-referentially used in Scripture.[71]

F.F. Bruce writes, "If in English we had an adjective 'long-tempered' as a counterpart to 'short-tempered,' then *makrathumia* could be called the quality of being 'long-tempered.' Thus, as Bruce says, *makrathumia* is a quality of

---

[71] For example, see Lk 8:18; 21:19; Rom 2:7; 5:3-4; 8:25; 15:4-5; 2 Cor 1:6; 6:4; 12:12; Col 1:11; 1 Thess 1;3; 2 Thess 1:4; 3:5; 1 Tim 6:11; 2 Tim 3:10; Tit 2:2; Heb 10:36; 12:1; Jam 1:3-4; 5:11; 2 Pet 1:6; Rev 1:9; 2:2-3; 2:19; 3:10; 13:10; 14:12.

Chapter 10: Soli Deo Gloria

God.[72] With this in mind, J.B. Lightfoot tells us while endurance is the temper or attitude of the mind that does not easily succumb to sufferings, patience is the self-restraint that does not hastily retaliate a wrong. The one is opposed to cowardice or despondency, the other to wrath or revenge. While endurance is closely allied to hope (1 Thess 1:3), patience is often connected with mercy (Ex 34:6).[73] Thus, we see that endurance is opposed to cowardice and patience to revenge.

1. *Patience is a fruit of the Spirit.* Patience is the fourth of nine communicable attributes of God that are enumerated for us in Gal 5:22. These fruit proceed from a heart that is made purified in Christ. As the author of Hebrews tells us, we are disciplined by God so that we may be partakers of His holiness, namely patience. This is the peaceable fruit of righteousness that we have been and will be trained by (cf. Heb 12:9-11).

2. *Patience is essential to steadfastness.* Steadfastness is the fruit of patience as patience is the fruit of the Spirit. We cannot endure without the grace of patience, as Jesus declares, "By your patience possess your souls" (Lk 21:19). Throughout the history of the church, what tormenters have resolved to take from Christians is their steadfastness – the staying power of the saints. When they tortured the martyrs, it was their steadfastness they desired to deprive them of. It simply wasn't enough to take their lives, it goes beyond that. What they hated so much was their ability to endure all that was vented, wanting above all, to hear them beg for their lives, abandoning Christ.

Thomas Brooks tells us, "Perseverance will make a man hold up and hold on in the work and ways of the Lord, in the face of all impediments, discouragements, temptations, tribulations, and persecutions."[74] Steadfastness (perseverance) ensures that Christians will endure persecution. For, while John baptized with water, the One that came after him brought

---

[72] Bruce, Commentary on Galatians, 253.
[73] Lightfoot, Commentary on Colossians and Philemon, 67-68.
[74] Brooks, Complete Works, Volume 2, 503.

an eschatological deluge of Spirit and fire.[75] Satan asked to sift Peter like wheat, but it was Jesus who prayed so that his faith would not fail (Lk 22:31).

3. *Patience can only be acquired through testing.* As we have considered thus far, patience is a grace we receive through testing and suffering. Bunyan writes, "Temptations, when we meet them at first, are as the lion that roared upon Samson; but if we overcome them, the next time we see them we shall find a nest of honey within them."[76] Again, Bunyan writes, "The Lord uses His flail of tribulation to separate the chaff from the wheat. In times of affliction we commonly meet with the sweetest experiences of the love of God."[77]

We cannot be like Christ except by the testing of our faith. As we have said, God's refining fire is an expression of his love, never His wrath, and only the man who can endure the refining fire of God's holy presence can remain in God's house forever (Jn 8:35). As JC Ryle put it, "The golden Word of God is poured into earthen vessels that undergo fiery preparation."[78]

4. *Patience is given at the appropriate time.* This is our second propositional truth we began with: God gives staying power to His Church while the full number comes in. We need not worry if we can stand up under pressure for God gives patience at just the right time – just when we need it. The Bible tells us so in Luke,

12 But before all these things, they will lay their hands on you and persecute you, delivering you up to the synagogues and prisons. You will be brought before kings and rulers for My name's sake. 13 But it will turn out for you as an occasion for testimony. 14 Therefore settle it in your hearts not to meditate beforehand on what you will answer; 15 for I will give you a mouth and wisdom which all your adversaries will not be able to contradict or resist (Lk 21:12-15).

---

[75] Longman, God is a Warrior, 95.
[76] Bunyan, Grace Abounding to the Chief of Sinners, 2.
[77] Bunyan, Complete Works, 79.
[78] Ryle, Holiness, 115.

Chapter 10: Soli Deo Gloria

Friends, we have great promises from the Scriptures that the Lord will not abandon us in time of need, but will give us in that very hour the patience that we need. Corrie Ten Boom was a great woman of God who suffered as a Christian under the Nazi regime. During the Second World War, the Ten Boom home became a refuge, a hiding place, for fugitives and those hunted by the Nazis. By protecting these people, Casper Ten Boom and his daughters, Corrie and Betsie, risked their lives. This non-violent resistance against the Nazi-oppressors was the Ten Booms' way of living out their Christian faith. This faith led them to hide Jews, students who refused to cooperate with the Nazis, and members of the Dutch underground resistance movement.

During 1943 and into 1944, the Ten Boom's sheltered six to seven people in their home. Knowing that the Gestapo could burst into their home at any moment gave the young Corrie much trepidation but not her father. So, Corrie said to her father, "Daddy, I am afraid that I will never be strong enough to be a martyr for Jesus Christ." And her father replied, "'Tell me, when you take a train trip from Harlem to Amsterdam, when do I give you the money for the ticket? Three weeks before?' "'No, Daddy, you give the money for the ticket just before we get on the train.' "'That's right, and so it is with God's strength. Our wise Father in heaven knows when you are going to need things too. Today you do not need the strength to be a martyr; but as soon as you are called upon for the honor of facing death for Jesus, He will supply the strength you need – just in time.'"[79]

Later, the Nazis raided the Ten Boom house and the entire family was arrested and sent to Scheveningen prison. Her two brothers and a cousin were released but her father died ten days later. Then Corrie and Betsie were sent to the Ravensbrück concentration camp in Germany. There Betsie died. As Betsie was dying she said, "We must tell the people what we have learned here. We must tell them that there is no pit so deep that God is not deeper still."[80] The patience that's required to say this can only be acquired through testing. *God*

---

[79] Ten Boom, Tramp for the Lord, 125.
[80] Ten Boom, The Hiding Place, 277.

Chapter 10: Soli Deo Gloria

gives staying power to His Church while the full number comes in.

5. *Patience is what ultimately saved the world.* As Christians we understand that God's patience has led to our salvation and will ultimately save a world full of people that surrender to Jesus Christ. The Puritan Stephen Charnock, defining divine patience writes,

It is part of the divine goodness and mercy, yet differs from both. God being the greatest goodness, hath the greatest mildness. Mildness is always the true companion of true goodness, and the great the goodness the greater the mildness. Who so holy as Christ, and who so meek? God's slowness to anger is branch or slip (a means of restraint) from His mercy, "The Lord is full of compassion, slow to anger" (Ps 145:8). It (divine patience) differs from mercy in the formal consideration of the object; mercy respects the creature as miserable, patience respects the creature as criminal; mercy pities him in his misery, and patience bears with the sin which engendered that misery, and is giving birth to more. Again, mercy is one end of patience; his long-suffering is partly to glorifying His grace: so it was in Paul (1 Tim 1:16). As slowness to anger springs from goodness, so it makes mercy the butt and mark of its operations: "He waits that He may be gracious" (Is 30:18). Goodness sets God upon the exercise of patience, and patience sets many a sinner on running into the arms of mercy. That mercy which makes God ready to embrace returning sinners, makes him willing to bear with them in their sins, and wait their return.[81]

Likewise, Arthur Pink writes, "Personally we would define the Divine patience as that power of control which God exercises over Himself, causing Him to bear with the wicked and forebear so long in punishing them."[82] *God is slow to anger because He is great in power!* He has no less power over Himself than He does His creatures (Charnock). This is patience – the power of self-restraint. If we are sinners saved by grace, saved through eternal judgment, saved from eternal destruction then we most certainly understand the ultimate patience that God has manifested in saving us by the blood of

---

[81] Charnock, Discourses Upon the Existence and Attributes of God, 478-479.
[82] Pink, The Attributes of God, 79.

His Son Jesus. God's goodness and patience are meant to lead us to repentance (Rom 2:4).

Yet, the church by and large is sinning by denying the inerrancy of His Word, which has given way to countless acts of infidelity on the part of His bride. It is amazing to me that God doesn't instantly strike with death those who are so brazenly defying Him (Rev 2:18-29). The church today sins in haste and repents at leisure. Are we trying to anger God? Are we trying to find out how patient God really is? Wouldn't we rather come to the foot of the Cross and confess our sin?

6. *Patience is akin to grace*. The patience we display in suffering can be a means of grace. In the last section we discussed the biblical truth that suffering affords Christians the opportunity to witness the saving power of Christ. When Christians live righteous lives and suffer for it, the Bible says that it can be a way that God uses to save others. The apostle Peter writes in 1 Peter 4:19-23

19 For this is a gracious thing, when, mindful of God, one endures sorrows while suffering unjustly. 20 For what credit is it if, when you sin and are beaten for it, you endure? *But if when you do good and suffer for it you endure, this is a gracious thing in the sight of God. 21 For to this you have been called, because Christ also suffered for you, leaving you an example, so that you might follow in his steps.* 22 He committed no sin, neither was deceit found in his mouth. 23 When he was reviled, he did not revile in return; when he suffered, he did not threaten, but continued entrusting himself to him who judges justly (1 Pet 4:19-23, ESV, emphasis added).

Peter says it's a gracious thing when we endure sorrows while suffering unjustly (1 Pet 2:19), that is, it's a means of grace, a channel of God's grace for Him to save His people and further sanctify them. The apologist Justin Martyr, motivated by witnessing Christians willing to die rather than recant their faith in Christ, was moved from being a follower of Greek philosophers to a follower of Christ. For Justin, the sufferings of Christians was a means a grace. Surely this is what the apostle Paul meant when he said, "I now rejoice in my sufferings for you, and fill up in my flesh what is lacking in the afflictions of Christ, for the sake of His body, which is the church" (Col 1:24).[83]

Christians who live godly lives will most certainly suffer for Christ's sake (2 Tim 3:12). The early Christians rejoiced that they were counted worthy to suffer for the name of Christ (Acts 5:41). When Paul learned that the saints at Philippi were being persecuted he wrote to them, "For to you it has been granted on behalf of Christ, not only to believe in Him, but also to suffer for His sake" (Phil 1:29). In this way, we may understand the expression 'patience is a means of grace.' Edger Allen Poe once said, "Never to suffer would never to have been blessed." If I may redeem this phrase – never to have suffered for the sake of Christ is to have never been blessed. Isn't this what Jesus means when He says, "Blessed are you when they revile and persecute you, and say all kinds of evil against you falsely for My sake. Rejoice and be exceedingly glad, for great is your reward in heaven, for so they persecuted the prophets who were before you" (Mt 5:11-12)? Suffering is the price for winning the lost for Christ – to fulfill the Great Commission (Mt 24:9-14; 28:18-20; 2 Tim 2:8-10; 4:5-6). Likewise, Christians must patiently-endure suffering, only through the power God supplies, in order to fulfill the Great Commission and hasten the Second Coming of Christ.

7. *Patience is rooted in the wisdom of God.* This leads us to our third propositional truth we began with: *the very attitude of the Church during the time of testing and suffering is important.* How we react to suffering matters, because God demonstrates to the world in the lives of His saints, through both His patience and grace, His mighty power for all who come to Him through His Son Jesus Christ. In us, God manifests His superlative power to save, transform, and keep all who come to Christ in faith. The world is to see Christ in us, as our witness is to point away from ourselves to His power. "For we who live are always being delivered over to death for Jesus' sake, so that the life of Jesus also may be

---

[83] An excellent book which exposits this text is John Piper's *Filling Up the Afflictions of Christ.*

manifested in our mortal flesh" (2 Cor 4:11). "We live as chastened, and yet not killed; as sorrowful, yet always rejoicing" (2 Cor 6:9-10).

How important is our attitude when we are suffering? Peter tells us, it's a gracious thing when we endure sorrows while suffering unjustly" (1 Pet 2:19). Our attitude can be and should be gracious in that they should point us away from what we are suffering at the time, namely to Christ, our heavenly home, and the resurrected glorious bodies we will receive when Christ returns. When suffering comes our way our attitude is very important.

As the Roman poet Lucretius once wrote, "So it is more useful to watch a man in times of peril, and in adversity to discern what kind of man he is; for then at last words of truth are drawn from the depths of his heart, and the mask is torn off, reality remains."[84] The apostle Paul in Romans tells us, "We wait eagerly for adoption as sons, the redemption of our bodies. For in this hope we were saved. Now hope that is seen is not hope. For who hopes for what he sees? But if we hope for what we do not see, we wait for it with patience" (Rom 8:23-25).

This hope is based upon Christ, who is its object. Therefore the hope of the Christian persists in spite of delay and discouraging hardships. It persists in spite of injustice, and lawlessness. Calvin writes, "To hope he assigns patience, as it is always conjoined with it, for what we hope for, we in patience wait for."[85] In other words, what we hope for, we patiently wait for. We wait for the resurrection with staying power – the power God supplies, and the continuing loyalty to Christ despite persecution serves to define our character and produces patient-endurance by which we may hope large in our inheritance, which is God Himself at the coming resurrection with the personal physical visible return of Christ.

8. *Patience is the very nature of God.* The Bible tells us Christ's sufferings were unto death. They were not momentary. He never begged for His life. He never retaliated

---

[84] Lucretius, On the Nature of Things, Book III, line 55-58.
[85] Calvin, Exposition of Romans 8:24.

in anger. He never sought to punish those who were punishing Him. Instead, those who were inflicting punishment upon Him unjustly He interceded for by (and us) by saying, "Father, forgive them. For they know not what they do" (Lk 23:34). The prophet Isaiah, foretelling Christ's sufferings, tells us,

4 *Surely He has borne our griefs and carried our sorrows*; yet we esteemed Him stricken, smitten by God, and afflicted. 5 But He was wounded for our transgressions, He was bruised for our iniquities; *The chastisement for our peace was upon Him, and by His stripes we are healed.* 6 All we like sheep have gone astray; we have turned, every one, to his own way; and the Lord has laid on Him the iniquity of us all. 7 *He was oppressed and He was afflicted, yet He opened not His mouth; He was led as a lamb to the slaughter, and as a sheep before its shearers is silent, so He opened not His mouth.* 8 He was taken from prison and from judgment, and who will declare His generation? For He was cut off from the land of the living; for the transgressions of My people He was stricken. 9 And they made His grave with the wicked – but with the rich at His death, because He had done no violence, nor was any deceit in His mouth. 10 *Yet it pleased the Lord to bruise Him; He has put Him to grief.* When You make His soul an offering for sin, He shall see His seed, He shall prolong His days, and the pleasure of the Lord shall prosper in His hand. 11 He shall see the labor of His soul, and be satisfied. By His knowledge My righteous Servant shall justify many, for He shall bear their iniquities. 12 Therefore I will divide Him a portion with the great, and He shall divide the spoil with the strong, because He poured out His soul unto death, and He was numbered with the transgressors, and *He bore the sin of many, and made intercession for the transgressors* (Is 53:4-12, emphasis added).

God is slow to anger because He is great in power! His goodness and patience lead us to repentance. And because Jesus suffered so greatly He is able to comfort so greatly. When you face suffering, Christ will give you His patience that was tested in the fiery trial of Calvary. Our perseverance (patient-endurance) in suffering is evidence of our faith in God. We have to be mentally prepared to suffer as Christ suffered, and not retaliate. The health, wealth, prosperity gospel is simply not the gospel! We must settle this in our minds and entrust our souls to a faithful Creator while doing good (1 Pet 4:19).

Chapter 10: Soli Deo Gloria

Suffering for Unbelievers

God regularly employs various means to bring unbelievers to the knowledge of Jesus Christ. At times He employs suffering. At other times He will simply say "Follow Me" (Mk 1:19-20), and still at other times He employs a firm and steady conviction. For example, the intellectual giant C.S. Lewis was an atheist who was converted by what he would term *intellectual* means.

Lewis writes, "In the Trinity term of 1929 I gave in, and admitted that God is god, and knelt and prayed: perhaps, that night, the most dejected and reluctant convert in all England. I did not see what is now the most shining and obvious thing; the Divine humility which will accept a convert even on such terms. The Prodigal Son at least walked home on his own feet. But who can duly adore that Love which will open the high gates to a prodigal who is brought in kicking, struggling, resentful, and darting his eyes in every direction for a chance of escape?"[86] I thought there could be no personal relationship with God, thought Lewis. And he mused, "I didn't think I could know God personally, any more than Hamlet knew Shakespeare."

Some are converted by God with more radical means. Most famously in the case of Saul (Acts 9), and in a similar manner, the slave trader John Newton.[87] Newton was a proud, blaspheming slave trader. Newton's ship the *Greyhound* was struck by a violent storm while at sea, and began to sink. It was during this storm when Newton was sure he would die that he first found the words, "What mercy can there be for me?" He began praying and found a Bible. Then he repented and believed on the Lord Jesus Christ.

Newton was quite aware how God uses suffering to bring about salvation. The Book of Job tells us:

---

[86] Lewis, Surprised By Joy: The Shape of My Early Life, 229.
[87] John Newton (1725-1807) was an English sailor and evangelical Anglican cleric who was the author of many hymns, including *Amazing Grace* and *Glorious Things of Thee are Spoken.*

492

Chapter 10: Soli Deo Gloria

And if they are bound in chains and caught in the cords of affliction, 9 then he declares to them their work and their transgressions, that they are behaving arrogantly. 10 **He opens their ears to instruction and commands that they return from iniquity.** 11 If they listen and serve him, they complete their days in prosperity, and their years in pleasantness. 12 **But if they do not listen, they perish by the sword and die without knowledge.** 13 "The godless in heart cherish anger; they do not cry for help when he binds them. 14 **They die in youth, and their life ends among the cult prostitutes.** 15 *He delivers the afflicted by their affliction and opens their ear by adversity* (Job 36:8-15, emphasis added).

Likewise, Job 33:29-30 declares, "Behold, God works all these things, twice, in fact, three times with a man, to bring back his soul from the Pit, that he may be enlightened with the light of life." Thus, God uses suffering as a warning of the final judgment, as well as the means to save. Newton knew he was a brand plucked from the fire and that God had placed him in the furnace of affliction to become one of His own.[88] Conversely, for those who rejects the gospel until their dying breath, it may be said, that their sufferings constitute a prejudgment. This sense is brought out in question and answer 83 of the Larger Catechism:

Q. 83. What is the communion in glory with Christ which the members of the invisible church enjoy in this life?
 A. The members of the invisible church have communicated to them in this life the firstfruits of glory with Christ, as they are members of him their head, and so in him are interested in that glory which he is fully possessed of; and, as an earnest thereof, enjoy the sense of God's love, peace of conscience, joy in the Holy Ghost, and hope of glory; as, **on the contrary, sense of God's revenging wrath, horror of conscience, and a fearful expectation of judgment, are to the wicked the beginning of their torments which they shall endure after death** (emphasis added).

Why does God allow war?

No theodicy can be fully orbed without a discussion on war. Namely why God allows war? In short, if there were no sin, there would be no war. Clausewitz tells us war is indeed an

---

[88] Currid, Why Do I Suffer?, 120.

Chapter 10: Soli Deo Gloria

extension of politics by other means.[89] However true this Clausewitzian dictum is, war is also an expression of fallen man's nature. A question we must ask is: why does God permit war to continue, if it brings untold misery and pain? In the Scripture I find four reasons why God allows war to persist:

1. God allows war so as to reveal our sin nature.
2. God allows war in order that men might bear the consequences of their sins as punishment.
3. Third, God allows war so He may recover prodigals.
4. Fourth, God allows war to open the way for the gospel.

The Bible declares that this world has been plunged into the darkness of sin and suffering, from which it will not be released until the end of the age (Rom 8:18-25). As we discussed in chapter two, death is God's just punishment for sin. By mankind's disobedience, the world as we know it is in a fallen and depraved state. Death is a sign of God's judgment, and suffering is part and parcel of living in a fallen world that is under the sentence of death. Therefore, God, having given mankind over to a depraved state, permits man to discover the utter folly of his nature and reap sin's wages (Jer 17:9; Rom 1:28; 6:23; 2 Cor 4:3-4; Eph 2:2-3). James tells us that the ultimate cause of war is lust and desire – the result of sin (Jam 4:1).

Further, God allows war in order that men might bear the consequences of their sin as punishment. As has been said, a final judgment will occur at the end of history, notwithstanding, sometimes that judgment intrudes into this age. Punishment for sin is not altogether postponed until then. A look into the history of Israel will readily declare this truth. For example, Jeremiah declares that the destruction that will be brought against sinful Judah by the hand of the Babylonians is God's work (Jer 1:15; 7:14; 50:25). It is for this very reason that Nebuchadnezzar is called God's servant (Jer 25:9; 26:7).

---

[89] Clausewitz, On War, Book I, Chapter 24, 99.

Chapter 10: Soli Deo Gloria

Likewise, God calls the Assyrian 'the rod of His anger' (Is 10:5). The death of Eli's son's at the hands of the Philistines was because God sought to put them to death for their wickedness (1 Sam 2:25). In this vein, Augustine writes,

Thus also the durations of wars are determined by Him (God) as He may see meet, according to His righteous will, and pleasure, and mercy, to afflict or to console the human race, so that they are sometimes of longer, sometimes of shorter duration.[90]

At this point, someone may raise an objection to this line of thinking, and ask: Why do the innocent suffer? The short answer is no one is innocent, we were all sold under sin, and no one is righteous, and all are guilty (Rom 3:9-18). All mankind are sinners. The longer answer is, as Lloyd-Jones states:

We clearly have to reap the consequences not only of our own personal sins, but also of the sins of the entire race; and, on a smaller scale, the sins of our particular country or group. We are, at one and the same time, individuals, and members of the state and of the entire race. The Gospel saves us as individuals; but that does not mean that we cease to be members of the state and part and parcel of the entire human race. We share the same sun and rain as other people, and we are exposed to the same illnesses and diseases. We are subject to the same trials by way of industrial depression and other causes of unhappiness, including war. Thus it comes to pass that the innocent may have to bear part of the punishment for sins for which they are not directly responsible.[91]

Further, God allows war so He may recover prodigals. We have discussed some negative aspects of war. However, God brings positive aspects out of war as well. Stories of soldiers who come to faith in Christ during war abound. Moreover, stories of soldiers whose faith is deepened by facing death at every turn abound all the more. As a retired soldier, I can readily testify to this fact. God has a way of getting our attention when death is on the line.

---

[90] Augustine, City of God, Book V, Chapter 22, 175.
[91] Lloyd-Jones, Why Does God Allow War?, 98.

Chapter 10: Soli Deo Gloria

Lastly, God allows war to open the way for the gospel. Now, we may clearly see this demonstrated by the way the gospel in recent years has had a freer course in the nations of Iraq and Afghanistan, et al. My father, David LeFavor, served as a U.S. Navy chaplain for over twenty years. Once, while he was assigned to 3rd Battalion, 4th Marines, he was deployed to Operation Just Cause. They say there are no atheists in foxholes. My father can attest to this fact, as combat has a way of bringing the big picture home to you. War certainly makes you reflect of where you will spend eternity. And during that conflict in Panama, my father was able to win many souls to the Lord. In that way, war opened a way for the gospel.

Reverend Harold Voelkel had spent many years as a missionary in Korea. When the war came in 1950, he and his family fled to Japan only to return as a chaplain in the U.S. Army. He was assigned to a 150,000 man prisoner of war camp. Out of the 150,000 North Korean soldiers that chaplain Voelkel evangelized, it is estimated that 15,000 came to Christ. Chaplain Voelkel had made such an impact with the gospel that some 60,000 men decided to remain in South Korea, many joining or founding churches after the war. Some of the men Voelkel reached went onto pastor churches and become missionaries themselves. Now that's an impact![92]

Christians who know their Bible, and who live by its teaching, are not to be worried and perplexed by the problem of war in its relation to God. Likewise, Christian men serving in war have peace in the midst of hell. There are many accounts of harrowing ordeals as Christians are delivered from certain death in combat. Bob Oyler, a U.S. Army officer, whose career spanned over twenty-five years, from the 6th Special Forces Group to the 307th Medical Battalion, recounts one such ordeal. Oyler writes, "We were to perform in-flight rigging for the jump into combat. I said a prayer for safekeeping for myself and all the other jumpers. The jump doors were lifted at 0205. It was early morning on the 20th of December, 1989, and it was 96 degrees with 100% humidity.

I heard what sounded like ricochets hitting the hull of the C-141 we were jumping from. I found out later that the jumper

---

[92] Voelkel, Behind Barbed Wire in Korea.

<cient# Chapter 10: Soli Deo Gloria

behind me was shot in the leg while we were standing in the door. We exited at 500 feet AGL (above ground level) onto Torreos-Tecumen Airfield. The air was so thick that it took forever to land (about fifty seconds). While I was descending, there were green tracers coming up at me from three different directions. I was later informed that there were seventeen bullet holes in my canopy.

As it turned out I landed two kilometers north of where we were supposed to assemble. As I made my way toward the assembly area, I narrowly avoided an enemy patrol. As I laid low, they walked into a Ranger ambush who let loose a hail of machine gun and rifle fire. I thought to myself, "Well, I'm not going that way." After a good walk, I arrived at the assembly area, and when they found out I was a PA (physician's assistant), I was immediately directed to some airborne troopers who had been injured during the jump.

As I was attending to the injured soldiers, the ground to my right and left began disintegrating in gunfire. There were three enemy soldiers firing at us from fifty-feet away. I felt like my guardian angel was working overtime keeping me from harm! Then, the paratrooper I was working on took aim and gave each enemy soldier a three-round burst, killing them instantly.

Bob Oyler certainly understood what the Bible means when it says, that angels are ministering spirits sent forth to minister for those who will inherit salvation (Heb 1:14).[93] Christians who know their Bible, and who live by its teaching, are not worried and perplexed by the problem of war in its relation to God. And why is this? Because men who know their Bible understand that there will be wars and rumors of wars until the end of the age (Mt 24:6-8).

The real question that should be asked is not why does God allow war? But rather, why does God restrain evil and sin, setting a limit to it (Job 38:11)? We have seen how God's patience suffers long with the inhabitants of this world while the lost are saved. That in itself is truly perplexing, not why God allows war to persist. To those to whom this all seems harsh would do well to consider that these matters are clearly

---

[93] Sasser's *God in the Foxhole* outlines copious amounts of harrowing ordeals of Christian men in harm's way who are supernaturally delivered from evil.

taught by Scripture. Besides, if these truths were not useful to be known, then why did God order His prophets and apostles to teach them? Our true wisdom is to embrace with meek docility, and without reservation, whatever the Holy Scriptures have delivered.[94]

As Augustine said, "I sought whence evil comes and there was no solution. But Thou didst not allow me to be carried away from the faith by these fluctuations of thought."[95] As a further response, we would do well to remember the mysterious prophecies of the Book of Revelation which delve into these very murky waters.

The Sovereignty of God and Spiritual Warfare

The Church has believed and taught for twenty centuries that the devil and his angels were created by God naturally good, but they became evil by their own doing (Is 14:12-15).[96] Scripture reveals that these angels sinned by radically and irrevocably rejecting God and His reign (2 Pet 2:4). Further, when our parents sinned by disobeying God, behind it all lurked a seductive demonic voice, opposed to God, tempting them into death (Gen 3:6-7).

The Bible reveals to us that there is a spiritual war raging behind historical events. In this war the stakes are very high, they are eternal! The Bible reveals, that as Christians, we are at war with the powers of darkness (Eph 6:12). The devil and his angels, who abhor God, are dead set on the destruction of His Church. Nowhere else in the Bible is the cosmic battle between Satan and the Church more clearly portrayed than in the twelfth chapter of the Book of Revelation. Rev 12:1-6 tells us,

12 Now a great sign appeared in heaven: a woman clothed with the sun, with the moon under her feet, and on her head a garland of twelve stars. 2 Then being with child, she cried out in labor and in pain to give birth. 3 And another sign appeared in heaven: behold, a great, fiery red dragon having seven heads and ten horns, and seven

---

[94] Calvin, Institutes of the Christian Religion, Book 1, Chapter 18, 141.
[95] Augustine, Confessions, Book VII, Chapter 7.11, 124.
[96] Fourth Lateran Council: 1215, Confession of Faith.

diadems on his heads. 4 His tail drew a third of the stars of heaven and threw them to the earth. And the dragon stood before the woman who was ready to give birth, to devour her Child as soon as it was born. 5 *She bore a male Child who was to rule all nations with a rod of iron. And her Child was caught up to God and His throne.* 6 Then the woman fled into the wilderness, where she has a place prepared by God, that they should feed her there one thousand two hundred and sixty days (emphasis added).

Short of a full exposition of this chapter, it will be beneficial to highlight several weighty texts. Revelation chapter 12 reveals the cosmic war that is behind history. The woman who is clothed with glory is the messianic community, the bride of God (Eph 31-32; Rev 22:17; 21:2, 9).[97] And although the mother of Jesus may be secondarily in mind, the woman represents the people of God living both before and after Christ's coming. This is because, as we will see, after the woman Israel gives birth to the Christ, she is persecuted, and flees into the desert, has other children who are described as faithful Christians (Rev 12:13-17). This woman is the bride of God and of Christ, as the apostle Paul declares "the Jerusalem above is free, which is the mother of us all" (Gal 4:26); and which the prophet Isaiah so frequently refers to (Is 52:2; 54:1-6; 61:10; 62:1-5, 11; 66:7-13, cf. Is 26:16-19).

The woman's birth pangs in verse two represent the afflictions of the covenant community, and particularly the messianic line, leading up to Christ's birth. The dragon of verse three, represents the devil, who, working his will by means of demonic forces, galvanizes the evil kingdoms of the earth to persecute God's people (Rev 17:3-6). Verse four summarizes all of the devil's efforts to exterminate the Seed of the woman (Gen 3:15); from His birth (Lk 4:28-30), to His ministry and finally at the Cross. Verse five is a clear reference to Christ: "She bore a male Child who was to rule all nations with a rod of iron. And her Child was caught up to God and His throne." This is the fulfillment of Psalm 2:7-9 which declares, "I will declare the decree: the Lord has said to

---

[97] The woman's glorious brightness denotes the heavenly purity and beauty of the people of God. The true mother of the incarnate Son of God is the messianic community – the faithful remnant (Kiddle, Revelation, 217, 223).

Chapter 10: Soli Deo Gloria

Me, 'You are My Son, today I have begotten You. Ask of Me, and I will give You the nations for Your inheritance, and the ends of the earth for Your possession. You shall break them with a rod of iron; You shall dash them to pieces like a potter's vessel'" (cf. Is 9:6).

The Bible declares that Jesus Christ is the "Firstborn of the dead, and the ruler of the kings of the earth" (Rev 1:5); the present reigning King of all kings (Rev 19:16). Christ has conquered Satan in the cross (Col 2:15), and presently reigns "far above all principality and power and might and dominion, and every name that is named, not only in this age but also in that which is to come" (Eph 1:21). Jesus Christ is our present reigning King, and His reign must and will continue until every enemy has been conquered (1 Cor 15:25).

Additionally, as we will see, the seed of the woman is not only Christ but also the covenant community of believers. Thus, Greg Beale writes, "The primary purpose of the abbreviation and the portrayal of Christ as a child is to identify him with the wider perspective of the church's historical life."[98] Then, in verse six, the woman is depicted as beginning to experience both the spiritual protection of God as well as tribulation in the world. The woman is protected from the dragon for one thousand two hundred and sixty days, which is the same time period given in Rev 11:2-3. This duration of time, also represented as forty-two months, signifies the period of time between Christ's Ascension and Second Coming (Rev 11:2-3; 12:6, 14; 13:5).[99] The duration between Christ's inauguration and consummation of His kingdom. This time period is also associated with the testing of believers, and the predominance of evil (Dan 7:25; 12:7). Thus, the wilderness (desert) is both a place of persecution as well as preservation; God, making use of means, works to purify His saints.[100]

---

[98] Beale, The Book of Revelation, 639.

[99] So also Augustine, *City of God*, Book XX, Chapter 9; Beale, *The Book of Revelation*, 565-568; Farrer, *Revelation*, 132-136; Hendriksen, *More Than Conquerors*, 143; Kiddle, *The Revelation of St. John*, 230; Storms, *Kingdom Come*, 484.

[100] The Exodus motif, which is explicitly inferred in verse six - the 1,260 days or 42 months - corresponds to the 42 encampments during the wilderness

Chapter 10: Soli Deo Gloria

What we should clearly see in Revelation 12 is that the conflict between the Church and the world is but a manifestation of the war between Christ and the devil. This truth is revealed in the next section of Revelation chapter 12:7-12:

7 And war broke out in heaven: Michael and his angels fought with the dragon; and the dragon and his angels fought, 8 but they did not prevail, nor was a place found for them in heaven any longer. 9 So the great dragon was cast out, that serpent of old, called the Devil and Satan, who *deceives the whole world*; he was cast to the earth, and his angels were cast out with him. 10 Then I heard a loud voice saying in heaven, "Now salvation, and strength, and the kingdom of our God, and the power of His Christ have come, for the accuser of our brethren, who accused them before our God day and night, has been cast down. 11 **And they overcame him by the blood of the Lamb and by the word of their testimony, and they did not love their lives to the death.** 12 Therefore rejoice, O heavens, and you who dwell in them! Woe to the inhabitants of the earth and the sea! For the devil has come down to you, having great wrath, because he knows that he has a short time" (emphasis added).

We are not to think of the war in heaven in verse seven as the fall of Satan at the time of creation. What we are to see is the defeat of Satan which occurred in the crucifixion and resurrection of Jesus Christ. These verses are a narration of the defeat the devil and his angels suffered by Michael and his angels in heavenly combat. Thus, verses 7-12 are the heavenly counterpart to the events of verses 1-6.

After the Fall, the devil and his angels began to do on a world-wide scale what they did in the garden of Eden (Gen 6:5-7). The devil has been a slanderer from the beginning. He is called the adversary, and the deceiver. In the Book of Job we learn that God permitted the devil to lobby complaints and accuse His people (Job 1:6-11; 2:1-6, cf. Zech 3:1-2). The devil is seen to be both the deceiver and the accuser of God's people (Rev 12:9). The Old Testament portrays Satan accusing the saints of being unfaithful, and undeserving of God's salvation. Greg Beale poignantly writes,

---

wanderings of the Hebrews before reaching the Promised Land. These are recorded in Numbers 33:1-39.

501

Chapter 10: Soli Deo Gloria

Implicit also in the accusations was the charge that God's own character was corrupt. For example, Satan says to God in Job 1 that Job would not have been so faithful if God had not prospered or bribed him so much. In the light of Rev 12:11, the accusations of verse 10 appear to be directed against the illegitimacy of the saints' participation in salvation. The devil's accusation is based on the correct presupposition that the penalty of sin necessitates a judgment of spiritual death and not salvific reward. The charges are aimed against all saints who do not receive the deserved punishment. Until the death of Christ, it could appear that the devil had a good case, since God ushered all deceased OT saints into his saving presence without exacting the penalty of their sin. Satan was allowed to lodge these complaints because there was a degree of truth in them. But the devil's case was unjust even before the death of Christ, since the sins about which he was accusing and for which he wanted to punish people were instigated by his own deceptions.[101]

Christ's redemptive work has made it impossible for the devil to come before God to accuse the saints (Rom 8:1). Regarding this the apostle Paul declares, "Who shall bring a charge against God's elect? It is Christ who justifies. Who is he who condemns" (Rom 8:33-34)? The devil was cast out of heaven because his charges had become groundless. Thus, Christ's redemptive work not only loosed God's people from the penalty of their sins, but protects them spiritually from the damning accusations of the devil. This is what led Job to declare even in the pit of his suffering, "Even now, behold, my witness is in heaven, and he who testifies for me is on high" (Job 16:19). The only one who can bring a charge against you and I is the One against you and I have sinned; but in Christ, our sins are removed from us as far as the east is from the west (Ps 103:12).

Before the throne of God above I have a strong and perfect plea:
A great High Priest, whose name is Love, Who ever lives and pleads for me.
My name is graven on His hands, my name is written on His heart;
I know that while in heaven He stands no tongue can bid me thence depart
No tongue can bid me thence depart.

When Satan tempts me to despair, and tells me of the guilt within,

---

[101] Beale, The Book of Revelation, 659.

Chapter 10: Soli Deo Gloria

Upward I look, and see Him there Who made an end to all my sin.
Because the sinless Savior died, my sinful soul is counted free;
For God the just is satisfied to look on Him and pardon me
To look on Him and pardon me.

Behold Him there, the Risen Lamb, my perfect, spotless righteousness,
The great unchangeable I am, the King of glory and of grace!
One with Himself I cannot die, my soul is purchased by His blood
My life is hid with Christ on high, with Christ, my Savior and my God
With Christ, my Savior and my God.[102]

The emphasis of chapter 12 in the Book of Revelation is the protection of God's people against Satan because Jesus Christ has defeated Satan and the powers of darkness through his death and resurrection. Armed with this truth, Christians are to courageously persevere in their witness despite persecution. And that is what the song in Rev 12:11 is all about. The saints can be assured that their suffering is not only part of God's plan but also part of Christ's victory (Rev 6:11; 12:11). The cosmic victory of Christ on earth and of the archangel Michael in heaven is the basis for the victory that suffering Christians on earth win over the devil throughout history.[103] We will need to bring out more of the meaning behind verse 11 later.

Looking further in this chapter, we may observe that Satan has been "cast out" of heaven, and in "great wrath" he pursues the woman "because he knows that he has a short time" (Rev 12:12). The expression "short time" indicates that the expected consummation of Christ's kingdom and Satan's final defeat are immanent (Mt 24:36; Phil 4:5). In this section of Scripture we see the defeated dragon venting his rage on the woman who bore the Seed which brought his doom (Rev 12:13). The dragon's focus is on wreaking as much havoc as he can during this short time. Rev 12:13-17 states:

13 And when the dragon saw that he had been thrown down to the earth, he pursued the woman who had given birth to the male child. 14 But the woman was given the two wings of the great eagle so that she might fly from the serpent into the wilderness, to the place where she is to be nourished for a time, and times, and half a time. 15 **The serpent poured water like a river out of his mouth after the**

---

[102] Charitie Lees Smith, The Advocate (Before the Throne of God Above).
[103] Beale, The Book of Revelation, 663.

woman, to sweep her away with a flood. 16 But the earth came to the help of the woman, and the earth opened its mouth and swallowed the river that the dragon had poured from his mouth. 17 Then the dragon became furious with the woman and went off to make war on the rest of her offspring, on those who keep the commandments of God and hold to the testimony of Jesus. And he stood on the sand of the sea (ESV, emphasis mine).

As we have seen, the Bible likens Satan to a despot who has conquered the whole world, holding mankind hostage as slaves to do his bidding. But the Son of God invades the strong man's occupied territory, and plunders his house (Mt 12:29), setting the captives free (Lk 4:18-19). Satan now wars against the seed of the woman (Rev 12:17). Believers will suffer because of the devil's great rage is directed against them, and they will be caught up in this battle until the Return of Christ. Further, we see the devil's attack against the woman in verse 15 takes the form of a flood. Satan's purpose is to sweep the Church away with a deluge of deception, debauchery and dilution. Satan's scheme is to infiltrate the Church with false teachers to deceive her and compromisers to water-down the gospel to contribute to her downfall and to hold the world in blindness (Mt 13: 25, 39;1 Tim 4:1; 5:15; 2 Tim 2:23-26; Rev 2:14-22; 3:15-17).

As we have said, Christ Himself builds His church (Mt 16:18), and all the powers of darkness cannot overpower it. His church pushes back the domain of spiritual death, rescuing redeemed prisoners, and exercising the power of the keys (Mt 16:19). And because Christ builds His Church in the very precincts of the gates of hell, we are to expect nothing less than the utmost hostility and persecution. What we need to remember in all of this is, Satan, as evil and powerful as he might be, is under the restraint of God, and can only vent his rage as far as God will permit him to. Additionally, although many Christians will suffer, be persecuted and even die in this struggle, we must remember that Satan will never achieve his ultimate victory he desires – the destruction of the city of God, because Christ's victory at Calvary has already assured us of our victory now.

The biblical point being made here is: as Christians we have to face the reality of spiritual warfare and persecution. The conflict between the Church and the world is really a manifestation of the war between Christ and the devil. For as "he who was born according to the flesh then persecuted him who was born according to the Spirit, even so it is now" (Gal 4:26). As believers we spiritually fulfill the same office as Christ in this age by following Christ's model, especially by being faithful witnesses. A witnessing church will always be a persecuted church. Christians are to courageously persevere in their witness despite persecution, because in Christ we have already conquered the world and faithful endurance through tribulation is the means by which we reign in the present with Jesus (1 Jn 5:4; Rev 2:7; 2:11; 2:17; 2:25; 3:5; 3:12; 3:21).

Further, we will endure while the lost are saved by God's established means of grace (Acts 2:41). For, God delays His final judgment until the full number of those who will believe in Christ are saved (Mt 24:14; Rom 11:25-26). To ensure this, God gives patient-endurance to the saints while the full number is brought in. And in this world, Jesus said, we will have persecution, but take heart He said, for I have conquered the world (Jn 16:33). Regarding this Augustine writes,

Thus in this world, in these evil days, not only from the time of the bodily presence of Christ and His apostles, but even from that of Abel, whom first his wicked brother slew because he was righteous (1 Jn 3:12), and thenceforth even to the end of this world, the Church has gone forward on pilgrimage amid the persecutions of the world and the consolations of God.[104]

We will endure while the full number of God's people come in, for which we are in labor (Is 26:17-19; 54:1-8; Jn 16:20-22; Rom 8:22-25; Gal 4:26-27; Rev 12:13-17); and these are the pangs of birth not death. William Van Gemeren, in his book *The Progress of Redemption* writes, "Christianity inherited from the Jewish Diaspora the concern over how to adapt to the world. Jews had to learn how to apply the Scriptures to a changing world, both to Hellenism and to the Roman Empire. Christianity faced first the matter of Gentile membership. Next, the church had to adjust to the growing separation from the synagogue and Judaism. Third, Christians

---

[104] Augustine, City of God, 663.

had to cope with the pressures of Rome and paganism. As the church began to stand on her own, she was continually faced with the problem of living as Christians in a hostile world." And Van Gemeren goes on to say, the early Christians "eagerness to speak about their faith was matched by their readiness to die for Christ."[105] As the church grew throughout the Roman Empire, it was besought with violent persecution from time to time.

As we have said previously, the Book of Revelation is meant to shock Christians into the reality of their faith by giving a heavenly perspective of the cosmic spiritual conflict of which the church finds herself in, thereby heightening their sense of awareness. In the Bible, the sea represents chaos, the traditional abode of evil. As the Book of Daniel depicts the world empires rising out of the sea (Dan 7:1-8), Revelation depicts Daniel's four beasts as one composite beast. Rev 13:5-10 tells us:

5 **And the beast was given a mouth uttering haughty and blasphemous words, and it was allowed to exercise authority for forty-two months.** 6 It opened its mouth to utter blasphemies against God, blaspheming his name and his dwelling, that is, those who dwell in heaven. 7 **Also it was allowed to make war on the saints and to conquer them.** And authority was given it over every tribe and people and language and nation, 8 and all who dwell on earth will worship it, everyone whose name has not been written before the foundation of the world in the book of life of the Lamb who was slain. 9 If anyone has an ear, let him hear: 10 If anyone is to be taken captive, to captivity he goes; if anyone is to be slain with the sword, with the sword must he be slain. **Here is a call for the endurance and faith of the saints** (emphasis added).

God's Sovereignty in Persecution

As we have seen, persecution will inevitably result when the gospel is presented. For, the cross is the peace of Christ, but it's also a sword God wields on the earth (Mt 10:34). Jesus told us, "You will indeed drink the cup that I drink, and with the baptism I am baptized with you will be baptized (Mk 10:39). Persecution is the baptism of fire that the church is to

---

[105] Van Gemeren, The Progress of Redemption, 415.

Chapter 10: Soli Deo Gloria

go through in order to be made white and clean. Looking back at the evil figure of verse 5, we see that the beast rises out of the sea of fallen man. The beast of the sea is the embodiment of the dragon. The beast, the personification of godless politics, is summoned forth from the hellish waters by the dragon, who authorizes the beast to persecute the Church. The beast is a trans-cultural, trans-temporal symbol for all individual and collective, satanically inspired, opposition to Jesus and His people.[106]

Today, all manner of strategies are employed by Christians to attract new people into the church: big bands, coffee bars, guest charismatic speakers, even restaurants. But the early church grew without any of these; in the midst of persecution. Early Christians were persecuted for their faith at the hands of both Jews and the Roman Empire. In the Early Church there were ten great persecutions. These persecutions occurred under the reigns of ten Roman emperors, and are reckoned as the persecutions under: Nero (64-67 AD), Domitian (81-97 AD), Trajan (108 AD), Marcus Aurelius (161-180 AD), Severus (192 AD), Maximus (235 AD), Decius (249 AD), Valerian (257 AD), Aurelian (274 AD), and Diocletian (303 AD).[107]

Persecution at Lyons

In the beginning of the Christian era, in 177 AD, during the reign of Marcus Aurelius in the south of what is now France, there arose a severe persecution against the churches of Vienna and Lugdunum (now Vienne and Lyons). A letter that has come down to us, surviving in fragments, is quoted by Eusebius thus:

The greatness of the tribulation in this region, and the fury of the heathen against the saints, and the sufferings of the blessed witnesses, we cannot recount accurately, nor indeed could they possibly be recorded. For with all his might the adversary fell upon us, giving us a foretaste of his unbridled activity at his future coming. He

---

[106] Storms, Kingdom Come, 488.
[107] Foxe, Foxe's Book of Martyrs, 8-21. So Augustine, City of God, XVIII, 52, but he mentions Antoninus for Marcus Aurelius.

endeavored in every manner to practice and exercise his servants against the servants of God, not only shutting us out from houses and baths and markets, but forbidding any of us to be seen in any place whatever. But the grace of God led the conflict against him, and delivered the weak, and set them as firm pillars, able through patience to endure all the wrath of the Evil One. And they joined battle with him, undergoing all kinds of shame and injury; and regarding their great sufferings as little, they hastened to Christ, manifesting truly that 'the sufferings of this present time are not worthy to be compared with the glory which shall be revealed to us-ward' (Rom 8:18).[108]

The persecutions of Christians under the Caesars was now well into its tenth decade. Philip Schaff, describing how the persecutions came writes, "The policy of the Roman government, the fanaticism of the superstitious, and the desires of the pagan priests conspired together for the persecution of a religion which threatened to demolish the tottering fabric of idolatry; and they left no expedients of legislation, violence, or wickedness untried, in order to blot out Christianity from the earth."[109]

Among the victims of the persecution at Lyon was the bishop Pothinus, who was ninety years old at the time, and had just recovered from an illness. This elicited no sympathy from the persecutors who threw him into a dungeon where he died within two days. Another victim of this madness was the fifteen year old slave girl Blandina. She demonstrated such patient-endurance under the cruelest torture that her tormentors could devise and muster, that she wore her

---

[108] Eusebius, Ecclesiastical History, Book V, Chapter 1.

[109] Schaff, History of the Christian Church, Volume 2, 40. Schaff goes on to state that the Roman government was in a measure tolerant. The ancient religions of the conquered races were tolerated as far as they did not interfere with the interests of the state. Christianity was regarded by Rome as a mere sect of Judaism. Providence had so ordered it that Christianity had already taken root in the leading cities of the empire before its true character was understood. The heathen statesmen and authors considered the Christian religion as a vulgar superstition, hardly worthy of the notice. But it was far too important a phenomenon, and made far too rapid progress to be long thus ignored or despised. So soon as it was understood as a *new* religion, and as, in fact, claiming universal validity and acceptance, it was set down as unlawful and treasonable, a *religio illicita*; therefore the constant reproach of the Christians was: "You have no right to exist" (Tertullian, Apology, 4).

persecutors out. Through it all she declared, "I am a Christian. No wickedness is carried on by us."

The desire of the persecutors was to conquer the indomitable spirit of those they martyred. And perhaps they vent their rage the most severe against Sanctus, who maintained his confession: "I am a Christian." They finally fastened red-hot brazen plates to the tenderest parts of his body, and as these were burned, but he continued unyielding, and firm in his confession. Sanctus nearly lost the form of a man but his tormentors did not cease, intending if possible to conquer his patient-endurance. Eusebius tells us, "And his body was a witness of his sufferings, being one complete wound and bruise, drawn out of shape, and altogether unlike a human form. Christ, suffering in him, manifested his glory, delivering him from his adversary, *and making him an example for the others, showing that nothing is fearful where the love of the Father is, and nothing painful where there is the glory of Christ"* (emphasis added).[110]

In the end of it all, the bodies of the Lyons martyrs after being abused in every possible manner, were burned and reduced to ashes by those wretches, and finally cast into the Rhone that flows nearby. Surely, this is what the apostle Paul was referring to when he said, "I now rejoice in my sufferings for you, and fill up in my flesh what is lacking in the afflictions of Christ, for the sake of His body, which is the church" (Col 1:24). This is what led Tertullian to say "the blood of the martyrs is seed."[111]

What Tertullian meant was the willing sacrifice of Christian martyrs fertilizes the soil of Christ's Kingdom leading to the conversion of others, thus, suffering for Christ is a means of grace. Bonhoeffer writes, "According to the will of God, the church is a scattered people, scattered like seed 'to all the kingdoms of the earth' (Dt 28:25). That is the curse and its promise. God's people must live in distant lands among unbelievers, but they will be the seed of the kingdom of God in the world."[112] Surely this is what Christ means when He says, "Unless a grain of wheat falls into the ground and dies, it

---

[110] Eusebius, Ecclesiastical History, Book V, Chapter 1

[111] Tertullian, Apology, 50.

[112] Bonhoeffer, Life Together, 28.

remains alone; but if it dies, it produces much grain" (Jn 12:24). This is why Augustine writes,

But that grief which arises in the hearts of the pious, who are persecuted by the manners of bad or false Christians, is profitable to the sufferers, because it proceeds from the charity in which they do not wish them either to perish or to hinder the salvation of others.[113]

The apostle Peter reminds us when the fiery trial comes upon us to test us, that we should not be surprised as though something strange were happening to us, but we should rejoice in so far as we are sharing Christ's sufferings (1 Pet 4:12). Thomas Brooks tells us the story of Vincentius who served as a deacon of the Church at Saragossa in Roman Spain. Brooks writes, "God, makes their *patience and constancy invincible*, as it did Vincentius, who by his patience and constancy maddened his tormentors; wherefore they stripped him stark naked, whipped his body all over to a gore blood, sprinkled salt and vinegar over all his wounds, set his feet on burning coals, then cast him naked into a loathsome dungeon, the pavement whereof was sharp shells, and his bed to lie on a bundle of thorns. All which this blessed martyr received, without so much as a groan, breathing out his spirit in these words, "Vincentius is my name, and by the grace of God I will be still Vincentius, in spite of all your torments."[114] What's most interesting to note is the name *Vincentius* in Latin means *prevailing*. Endurance in trial, even unto to death can be a means of grace. When persecuted for Christ, we must, like Vincentius, "Consider him who endured from sinners such hostility against himself, so that you may not grow weary or fainthearted" (Heb 12:3). For, John came baptizing with water unto repentance but He that came after him brought a baptism of Spirit and fire.

Philip Schaff recounts, "The long and bloody war of heathen Rome against the church, which is built upon a rock, utterly failed. It began in Rome under Nero, it ended near Rome at the Milvian Bridge, under Constantine. Aiming to

---

[113] Augustine, City of God, 663.
[114] Brooks, Complete Works, Volume 2, 356.

exterminate, it purified."[115] And what more shall I say? For the time would fail me to tell of how Christians like Polycarp conquered in death by refusing to say Caesar is lord. As we have said, endurance is the temper or attitude of the mind which does not easily succumb under suffering, and patience is the self-restraint which does not hastily retaliate a wrong. The glory outstrips the sufferings! We learn endurance in the school of holy experience. The cross before the crown! Besides, as J.I. Packer tells us, "Your faith will not fail while God sustains it; you are not strong enough to fall away while God is resolved to hold you."[116] Christians will patiently-endure suffering, through the power God supplies, in order to fulfill the Great Commission and hasten the Second Coming of Christ (Mt 24:9-14).

Persecution Today

In light of the reality of spiritual warfare, how is the American God-honoring man to respond? What are soldiers to do, when they must acquiesce to immoral policies? What are soldiers to do when they face disciplinary measures if they raise a moral objection to such immoral policies? There is an undercurrent of persecution underway in America; one in which evangelical Christian service members face daily, the growing hostility toward their faith. What is the projected end? As has been said, religious persecution is currently underway under the auspices of upholding the rights of others.

What is important to be mindful in this is, as Christians, being under the lordship of Jesus Christ, we are to render to Caesar that which is Caesar's and to God that which is God's (Mk 12:13-17; Rom 13:1-2; Tit 3:1). This is not an option but an obligation. As we have said, the believer is both a citizen of the state and the kingdom of God. Christians live in both the city of man and the city of God. However, the state's authority over the believer is limited to the authority God has delegated to the state (Rom 13:1-7).

---

[115] Schaff, History of the Christian Church, Volume 2, 34.
[116] Packer, Knowing God, 275.

Chapter 10: Soli Deo Gloria

In light of Scripture, how should Christians respond to the laws of the state, particularly those laws which require Christians to either break God's commands or prevent them from obeying them? When the state commands what God forbids, or forbids what God commands, we are to obey God rather than men (Acts 5:29), and suffer the consequences for the glory of God. Additionally, it must be remembered that God has delegated the power of the sword to the governments of the world, as Romans 13:1 declares, "Let every soul be subject to the governing authorities. For there is no authority except from God, and the authorities that exist are appointed by God." However, as history shows, Caesar misuses the power of sword, and instead of maintaining justice, he turns it on the body of Christ – as the history of the Church declares.[117]

In the Book of Revelation, the government of the city of man is depicted as a beast (Rev 13:1). The beast of the sea is the embodiment of the dragon. And, although the beast receives the dragon's power, throne, and authority (Rev 13:2), to overcome the saints and receive the worship, the ultimate source of the beast's authority is God. As we have seen Rev 13:5-8 declares:

5 And he was given a mouth speaking great things and blasphemies, **and he was given authority to continue for forty-two months.** 6 Then he opened his mouth in blasphemy against God, to blaspheme His name, His tabernacle, and those who dwell in heaven. 7 **It was granted to him to make war with the saints and to overcome them. And authority was given him over every tribe, tongue, and nation** (cf. Dan 7:21, emphasis added).

Rome, the fourth beast, is given authority over the whole earth (Rev 13:7) for the same duration of time, represented as forty-two months, that signifies the period of time between Christ's Ascension and Second Coming, which is also duration between Christ's inauguration and consummation of His kingdom (Rev 11:2-3; 12:6, 14; 13:5). Further, the time period of the beast's authority is also associated with the

---

[117] In addition to what has been said about persecution, the reader is directed to Eusebius, *Ecclesiastical History* and Foxe, *Foxe's Book of Martyrs.*

testing of believers, and the predominance of evil (Dan 7:25; 12:7). Thus, even though Rome fell, she lives on. Additionally, it appears that the Beast may find a final embodiment in the Antichrist at the end of history.[118]

We may look at this a different way. Why does the sequence of historical kingdoms in this vision extend no farther than the Roman (the fourth beast) whereas we know that many developments came after the Roman Empire and have continued to come before the judgment? Herbert C. Leupold answers by writing,

It may be correctly argued that the pattern of empire development adopted by the Romans has been followed by practically all the succeeding world powers. Roman law is said still to be the pattern of jurisprudence. Roman classic literature dominates the literature produced since that time. In fact, the powers that can be said to have anything like world dominion, are segments of the old Roman Empire, and so the fourth beast is still in a sense alive though Rome was overthrown. It flatters our vanity but little that the Bible does not seem to deem our modern achievements, inventions, and forms of progress in sciences and arts worthy of separate mention. They are really something that was latent in Roman achievement and are now coming to the surface.[119]

The biblical point being made here is, although America was founded on Christian values, directly from the Bible, which has brought enormous blessings to the people of this land, America is still the city of man, and our loyalties lie ultimately with the city of God; Rome lives on in America. What this means practically for Christians is, although we love our country, and serve to protect her from all enemies, our loyalty ultimately lies with Christ and His kingdom. As a soldier, I have fought to defend this great country, and I would have willingly laid down my life in the service of America, however, my ultimate loyalty lies not in this world.

Will Christians in America ever experience the fiery trial that was the lot for the Christians of ancient times? Will Christians in America ever suffer like the Christian do today throughout the world? The Church in tribulation today suffers

---

[118] See Beale, The Book of Revelation, 682-694; 868-876.
[119] Leupold, The Book of Daniel, 314.

Chapter 10: Soli Deo Gloria

fiery persecution as the message of the gospel goes forth (Mt 24:9-14). It is estimated that more Christians were martyred in the 20th century (approx. 171,000), than in all previous centuries combined.[120] Christians in Indonesia, Nigeria, Iraq, Sudan, as well as other parts of the world, suffer every day at the hands of Islamic extremists. Christians in Orissa, India are persecuted daily, and tens of thousands are forced from their homes. The Church in Iran has been nearly wiped out by persecution. The Church in China faces varying degrees of persecution ranging from harassment, imprisonment, and torture. Yet, like the Hebrews in Egypt, "the more they afflicted them, the more they multiplied and grew" (Ex 1:12).

These afflictions are like those of old, of which Tertullian writes,

We are assaulted and betrayed every day. Our meetings are often attacked... No one considers how great a loss it is to the Empire, what an injury to the state, when people as virtuous as we are put to death in such numbers, and so many of the truly good suffer the ultimate penalty... It is our battle to be summoned to your courts and, in fear of execution, to fight there for the truth. But the battle is won when the goal of the struggle is reached. This victory of ours gives us the glory of pleasing God, and the spoil of eternal life. But, you say, we are vanquished. Yes, when we have obtained our wishes. Therefore we conquer in dying; we seize the victory in the very moment that we are overcome. Bound to a stake, we are burned on a heap of wood. This is the attitude in which we conquer, it is our victory robe, it is our triumphal entry. This attitude does not please those whom we overcome. [121]

These little paragraphs can hardy do justice to the amount of suffering the persecuted Church has undergone for the sake of Christ. And what more shall I say? For the time would fail me to tell of Richard Wurmbrand, as Romanian pastor, who suffered terribly at the hands of the Communists, spending some twelve years in prison for his evangelistic efforts, in which many were saved. Wurmbrand in his book Tortured for Christ, "It was strictly forbidden to preach to other prisoners, as it is in captive nations today. It was understood that

---

[120] International Journal of Missionary Research.
[121] Tertullian, Apology, 7, 44, 50.

whoever was caught doing this received a severe beating. A number of us decided to pay the price for the privilege of preaching, so we accepted their (the communists') terms. It was a deal: we preached and they beat us. We were happy preaching; they were happy beating us, so everyone was happy."[122]

Richard Wurmbrand states that, "God will judge us not according to how much we endured, but how much we could love."[123] This is not to neglect mentioning the terrible persecutions Christians in Cuba, Ethiopia, North Korea, and Vietnam continue to suffer. "Others were tortured, not accepting deliverance, that they might obtain a better resurrection. Still others had trial of mockings and scourgings, yes, and of chains and imprisonment. They were stoned, they were sawn in two, were tempted, were slain with the sword. They wandered about in sheepskins and goatskins, being destitute, afflicted, tormented – *of whom the world was not worthy*" (Heb 11:35-38, emphasis added). Let's not forget, the word martyr means witness (Lk 24:48; Acts 1:8; Rev 17:6).

Enchanted Ground

The Church, after its triumph over paganism, forgot the hard lessons it learned in the fiery school of persecution. If Satan cannot get us to neglect our mission responsibility by way of persecution, then he will most certainly employ other strategies of rendering our witness innocuous. For these he employs more subtle tactics. The first takes the form of a flood of false teaching to destroy doctrinal purity, which is what the Churches at Pergamum and Thyatira, as well as others were facing (Rev 2:6, 15, 20; 3:9). The other takes the form of an alluring sleep of false spiritual security, which is the form of demonic attack employed against the Church at Laodicea, resulting in their spiritual torpidity (Rev 3:15). With the first tactic, Satan's purpose being to drown the Christian's witness, he tempts Christians to water down the message of the gospel,

---

[122] Wurmbrand, Tortured For Christ, 41.
[123] Ibid, 39.

515

lobbing off the rough edges of doctrine, thereby making them easier to swallow and remove the offence.

Reciprocal to the satanic allurement of *man-pleasing*, the devil's tactic here is to drown the Christian's witness with a flood of condemning accusations regarding the believer's worthlessness, hypocrisy, and unqualified status, in attempts to leave the Christian feeling like a dejected fake, that the graces they have received from Christ are counterfeit. When Martin Luther sat at the Wartburg Castle translating the Bible, the devil attempted to discontinue this sacred work by tempting Luther in this way. Luther grabbed the ink pot from which he was writing, and threw it at the devil's head. The devil sought to discourage Luther by making him feel guilty, through rehearsing a list of his sins. When the devil had finished, Luther said, "Think harder: you must have forgotten some." And the devil did think, and he listed more sins. When he was done enumerating the sins, Luther said, "Now, with a red pen write over that list, "The blood of Jesus Christ, God's Son, cleanses us from all sin." And the devil had nothing more to say. As Luther would say whole heartedly, believers are saved because Jesus paid their penalty and unbelievers suffer the wrath Jesus bore. They refuse to believe in Jesus so they pay their own penalty.

With regards to the second tactic, an alluring sleep of false spiritual security, Archibald Alexander writes, "Christians are more injured in this warfare, by the insidious and secret influence of their enemies lulling them into the sleep of carnal security, than by all their open and violent assaults."[124] As pilgrims on the road to the city of God we must pray and watch so we don't fall into temptation (Mt 26:41). There is a portion of the road which leads from the city of man to the city of God which is more dangerous than any other. Spurgeon tells us, "It does not abound with lions; there are no dragons in it; it hath no dark woods, and no deep pitfalls; yet more seeming pilgrims have been destroyed in that portion of the road than anywhere else."[125]

---

[124] Alexander, Thoughts on Religious Experience, 158.
[125] Spurgeon, Sermons, Volume 1, The Enchanted Ground, 344.

Chapter 10: Soli Deo Gloria

How do Christians fall into a sleep of carnal security? Spurgeon giving us four reasons: (1) by a state of insensibility; (2) by a state in which we are subject to various delusions; (3) by a state of inaction; and (4) by a state of insecurity.

Additionally, Spurgeon reasons that the Christian is most likely to fall asleep spiritually when: *his temporal circumstances are all right.* He says, "Easy roads tend to make us slumber. Few sleep in a storm; many sleep on a calm night." This immediately brings to mind the parable of the rich fool (Lk 12:13-21). Next, the Christian is most likely to fall asleep spiritually when: *all goes well in spiritual matters.* He writes:

You never read that Christian went to sleep when there were lions in the way; he never slept when he was going through the river Death, or when he was in Giant Despair's castle, or when he was fighting with Apollyon. Poor creature! He almost wished he could sleep then. But when he had got half-way up the Hill of Difficulty, and came to a pretty arbor, then he went, and sat down, and began to read his roll. O, how he rested himself! How he unstrapped his sandals and rubbed his weary feet! Very soon his mouth was open, his arms hung down, and he was fast asleep. Again, the enchanted ground was a very easy, smooth place, and liable to send the pilgrim to sleep.[126]

Lastly, the Christian is most likely to fall asleep spiritually when: *we get near our journey's end.* The enchanted ground is nigh to Beulah, and Bunyan gives the reason why. Again, Spurgeon writes, "For this enchanted ground is one of the last refuges that the enemy to pilgrims has; wherefore it is, as you see, placed almost at the end of the way, and so it standeth against us with the more advantage."[127]

So far we have seen that God brings trials, temptations, and afflictions on His people for various reasons. The question is, can we choose God's will even if it means we will suffer? Sufferings and persecution for the sake of Christ is the inevitable result for those who obey the gospel. What we have tried to make abundantly clear up to this point is: it's God's will for everyone who looks to the Son and believes in Him to not only have eternal life, by grace alone through faith in Jesus

---

[126] Spurgeon, Sermons, Volume 1, The Enchanted Ground, 357.
[127] Ibid, 358.

Christ alone, but to be further sanctified unto purifying holiness and to endure to the end in the power He supplies (Jn 6:39-40; 1 Thess 4:3; 5:16). Thus, God, making use of means, works to purify His saints. Further, God delays His final judgment until the full number of those who will believe in Christ are saved (Rom 11:25-26). To ensure this, God gives staying power to His believers while the full number comes in; their very attitude during this time of testing and suffering being important as it serves a means of grace (1 Pet 2:19).

Delayed Vindication

For God's kingdom to come may mean the destruction of God's enemies, but it may also mean the conversion of God's enemies through the preaching of the gospel.[128] The salvation of the full number of God's people coincides with the destruction of the wicked. The background for this truth is demonstrating in God's covenant with Israel which He inaugurated with Abraham in Gen 15:1-6. God declares that His deliverance of Abraham's offspring will coincide with the destruction of the pagan nations, as Genesis 15:13-16 states:

13 Then He said to Abram: "Know certainly that your descendants will be strangers in a land that is not theirs, and will serve them, and they will afflict them four hundred years. 14 And also the nation whom they serve I will judge; afterward they shall come out with great possessions. 15 Now as for you, you shall go to your fathers in peace; you shall be buried at a good old age. 16 But in the fourth generation they shall return here, for the iniquity of the Amorites is not yet complete" (Gen 15:13-16).

God declares that He will save His people out of a land that is not theirs, where they will serve as slaves. Likewise, when God announces that he will take vengeance on the Egyptians, He will in the same manner render to all the enemies of His people, who are in fact His enemies (Zech 2:8). This is expressly stated in the Song of Moses, where the enemies of God are extended to the pagan nations of the world (Dt 32, cf. Is 30:27-33; 34:1-6; Jer 9:25). *An attack on God's people is an*

---

[128] Belcher, The Messiah and the Psalms, 81.

Chapter 10: Soli Deo Gloria

attack on God. The salvation of the full number of God's people coincides with the destruction of the wicked. The Bible depicts an adumbration of this theme when God destroyed the firstborn of Egypt, and saved Israel His firstborn. God drowned the Egyptians in the Red sea, when the Israelites passed safely through it. The destruction of the former makes way for the salvation of the latter, and so it is said to be a ransom (Pro 11:8; Is 43:3). These judgments of God on the wicked serve as types of the final judgment which befall the wicked at the end of the age (Mt 22:13; 23:33; 25:30, 46).

Commenting on Gen 15:16, Calvin tells us that the wicked cast themselves out by their own wickedness. For, "by polluting the place of their habitation, they in a certain sense tear away the boundaries fixed by the hand of God, which would otherwise have remained immovable. Moreover, the Lord here commends his own longsuffering. Even then the Amorites had become unworthy to occupy the land, yet the Lord not only bore with them for a short time, but granted them four centuries for repentance. And hence it appears, that he does not, without reason, so frequently declare how slow he is to anger. But the more graciously he waits for men, if, at length, instead of repenting they remain obstinate, the more severely does he avenge such great ingratitude."[129]

Thus, the wicked fill up the measure of their iniquity, bringing the wrath of God upon themselves, as the unbelieving Jews did when they refused Jesus Christ (Mt 23:32-33), saying: "His blood be on us and on our children" (Mt 27:25), and further persecuted the messianic community. In the Song of Moses, God solemnly swears that He will deliver His people and fully avenge Himself upon all His enemies which He used as rods to scourge His people (Is 33:1). As we have seen, evil will succeed in this life only for a season, not forever. It rises quickly, dominates for a brief time but collapses just as quickly. Evil will not prevail, God will.

The world's evil kingdom will grow, but so will the Kingdom of God. God's sending of his Son is for those who believe – deliverance from judgment; for the wicked – a sentence of eternal destruction. God delays His final judgment

---

[129] Calvin, Commentary on Genesis 15:16.

until the full number of those who will believe in Christ are saved (Rom 11:25-26). And on the part of the saints, this is a cause for much suffering, for God has yet more faithful witnesses to be martyred, who should die for the same faith and profession (Rev 6:11). When this number of martyrs is complete, by God's word, then He will avenge their blood upon their enemies (Rev 8:3-5).

As we considered, for God to have not brought an end to history before you and I were born, and more importantly, before He could reach us with the gospel of Jesus Christ, is a demonstration of God's great mercy and patience. What if God had heeded the prayers of our ancestors, who, due to the prevalence of lawlessness and injustice, prayed for the world to end with the coming of Christ? My great grandfather, Arthur LeFavor, did in fact often pray the Lord's Prayer on his many trips as a conductor on the Boston and Maine (B & M) Railway network.

What if back in the 1920s God had heeded my great-grandfather's plea to end suffering and misery, bring an end to all war, and consummate the kingdom of God with His return? For that is precisely what we are praying for in the Lord's Prayer. What If God hadn't a purpose in mind – the salvation of the full number of His people – then, like the servants in the parable of the wheat and the tares suggested, He would have immediately "gathered out of His kingdom all things that offend, and those who practice lawlessness," thereby ending history, and ushering in the consummation of His kingdom (Mt 13:24-30; 36-43). For this is certainly the hope we have when we pray the Lord's Prayer.

"Our Father in heaven, hallowed be Your name. Your kingdom come. Your will be done on earth as it is in heaven. Give us this day our daily bread. And forgive us our debts, as we forgive our debtors. And do not lead us into temptation, but deliver us from the evil one. For Yours is the kingdom and the power and the glory forever. Amen" (Mt 6:8-13).

As we faithfully pray the Lord's Prayer, we are reminded that for God's kingdom to come may mean the destruction of God's enemies, but it may also mean the conversion of God's enemies through the preaching of the gospel. As we have said,

Chapter 10: Soli Deo Gloria

God delays His final judgment until the full number of those who will believe in Him are saved. The vindication of God's people awaits Christ's return (Is 54:17). Here is a call for the endurance and faith of the saints (Rev 13:10). Perhaps the clearest demonstration of this, at least to my knowledge, is found in the Parable of the Wheat and Tares.

24 Another parable He put forth to them, saying: "The kingdom of heaven is like a man who sowed good seed in his field; 25 **but while men slept, his enemy came and sowed tares among the wheat and went his way.** 26 But when the grain had sprouted and produced a crop, then the tares also appeared. 27 So the servants of the owner came and said to him, 'Sir, did you not sow good seed in your field? How then does it have tares?' 28 He said to them, 'An enemy has done this.' **The servants said to him, 'Do you want us then to go and gather them up?' 29 But he said, 'No, lest while you gather up the tares you also uproot the wheat with them. 30 Let both grow together until the harvest, and at the time of harvest I will say to the reapers, "First gather together the tares and bind them in bundles to burn them, but gather the wheat into my barn"** (Mt 13:24-30, emphasis added).

This parable teaches that in the end good will triumph over evil (Mt 13:41-43). Like the servants in the parable who question the source of evil, we too are offered only the simple answer: 'An enemy has done this.' And like the servants in the parable, who, instead of venting their anger against the enemy, turn their attention on the weeds, so overzealous Christians have often caused undue damage to the Church. At first sight, we are left with the impression that there are two kinds of people in the world – the good and the bad. However, this is not quite correct. Scripture does not teach that God creates good men and Satan creates bad men.[130]

The truth is that God creates every man, but as we have seen this world is fallen, and men are born under sin, and as such are slaves of the devil, as Christ in explanation of the parable in Mt 13:38 explains. Further, all men will remain fallen, and sold under sin, and so, deserving of hell until Christ in His grace saves them, and they are regenerated (Jn 3:3; Eph 2:1-3). What is at the very heart of this parable is the theodicy,

---

[130] Kistemaker, The Parables of Jesus, 42.

in that, God's long-suffering is magnificently demonstrated in the way He has endured for centuries, with much patience, the vessels of wrath prepared for destruction (Rom 9:22). Yet, God bears long with the wicked so that "He might make known the riches of His glory on the vessels of mercy, which He had prepared beforehand for glory, even us whom He called, not of the Jews only, but also of the Gentiles" (Rom 9:23)? "Or do you despise the riches of His goodness, forbearance, and *longsuffering*, not knowing that the goodness of God leads you to repentance" (Rom 2:4)?

Yet, God's commands, counsels, and invitations continue to be despised. Therefore, what can be more just than this? "Because I have called and you refused, I have stretched out my hand and no one regarded, because you disdained all my counsel, and would have none of my rebuke, I also will laugh at your calamity; I will mock when your terror comes, when your terror comes like a storm, and your destruction comes like a whirlwind, when distress and anguish come upon you" (Pro 1:24-27).

From another perspective, we should understand that grace doesn't run in the blood, that is, I can't get to heaven on the coat tails of my great grandfather. My father's faith won't save me. We have to have our own faith. No man will see God or experience the joys and peace of the eternal Sabbath without a personal, saving faith in Jesus Christ. So, if the analogy of my great grandfather holds, the field of the world must fully mature, until, in God's time, the sons of God will be revealed (Rom 8:19). The tares won't be uprooted until the end because they grow alongside the wheat (Mt 13:29). And the final judgment is delayed until the full revealing of all the sons of God (Rom 8:19).

Until that time, God's witnesses are told to patiently endure suffering (Rev 6:11), for although, vindication is delayed, it is assured (Is 54:17). Then, as Jesus reveals to us in the interpretation of the parable, "As the tares are gathered and burned in the fire, so it will be at the end of this age. The Son of Man will send out His angels, and they will **gather out of His kingdom** all things that offend, and those who practice lawlessness, and will cast them into the furnace of fire. There will be wailing and gnashing of teeth. Then the righteous will shine forth as the sun in the kingdom of their Father. He who has ears to hear, let him hear (Mt 13:40-43, emphasis added)! Thus, the salvation of the full number of God's people coincides with the destruction of the wicked.

Let us not lose sight of the fact that, at the cross, God's great wrath was poured out on Jesus for the sins of the world (Jn 3:16). The judgment that fell upon Jesus at the cross propitiated the Father and purchased our salvation. Christ obeyed where we should have obeyed, and Christ was punished where we should have been punished. God's judgment for sin is true and righteous, and is a necessary part of salvation. Thus, believers are saved because Jesus paid their penalty, and unbelievers will justly suffer the wrath Jesus bore. They refused God, so they pay their own penalty.

Talionic Justice

As we have said, Christ's return to save His people is also His return to render vengeance to His enemies (Mt 25:31-46; 1 Thess 1:10; 2 Thess 1:7-10). The Scripture declares, "When the Son of Man comes in His glory, and all the holy angels with Him, then He will sit on the throne of His glory. All the nations will be gathered before Him, and He will separate them one from another, as a shepherd divides his sheep from the goats" (Mt 25:31-32). The Final Judgment at the end of history will consummate Christ's kingdom and result in the final separation of the righteous and the wicked as Mt 25:33 states, "And He will set the sheep on His right hand, but the goats on the left" (Mt 25:33, cf. Mt 13:40-43). The wicked will be judged while the righteous are openly acquitted.

The basis for the judgment of the wicked is first and foremost their rejection of Christ, and secondarily their treatment of Christ's followers – Christ's own body. The sentence against Christ's enemies is determined according to the *lex talionis* – the law of retaliation. The wicked will reap the reward for their labor – the second death, which is eternal, as Rev 20:14-15 states, "Then Death and Hades were cast into the lake of fire. This is the second death. And anyone not found written in the Book of Life was cast into the lake of

Chapter 10: Soli Deo Gloria

fire." For the wicked, God is applying talionic justice. Joshua Owen explains,

The justice that is celebrated in the consummation of the kingdom of Christ is measured according to the *lex talionis* as both compensation and punishment. In terms of compensation, the servants of God are rewarded, at least in part, with vindication for the unjust condemnation they endured by their persecutors. In terms of judgment, the persecutors of the church receive precisely what they inflicted—wrath and destruction.[131]

Now, as soon as any discussion declares God's wrath for sin is brought up these days, people immediately recoil. However, there is no true love without wrath, for the opposite of love is not wrath but indifference; just as a husband, who failed to respond to his wife's infidelity with jealous anger would demonstrate a lack of love for her. This is precisely how God demonstrates His love for His bride, as Exodus 34:14 makes known, "For you shall worship no other god, for the Lord, whose name is Jealous, is a jealous God" (cf. 2 Cor 11:2). God declares, for His people to enter into a covenant with unbelievers, that is, be "unequally yoked," viz., to have fellowship, communion, accord, a part, an agreement with the unbelieving world is tantamount to spiritual adultery, to harlotry (2 Cor 6:14-7:1; cf. Jer 3:1-10).

God jealously guards His Spirit in the hearts of His own people (Jam 4:5). This is why God is spoken of as a husband who gets angry when someone else competes for the heart of his wife or when His bride's heart goes after other lovers (Jer 3:20). Therefore, God's wrath is an expression of His love.

In Psalm 141, David calls for God to judge the deeds of the wicked, just as a victorious army of old would throw their victims from cliffs to their destruction (Ps 141:6).[132] He prays, I take refuge in the Rock that will be my enemies doom, they will be crushed against the Rock while I will be delivered safely, albeit through my apparent defeat (Ps 141:7; Mic 7:8).

---

[131] Owen, Martyrdom as an Impetus for Divine Retribution in the Book of Revelation, 118.

[132] This is reminiscent of the Army of Judah's destruction of 10,000 Edomites following the Battle of the Valley of Salt (2 Chronicles 25:11-12).

Chapter 10: Soli Deo Gloria

David is conscious of the fact that his very words may bring his enemies to their destruction (Ps 141:3-4).[133] His enemies will learn of the forceful truthfulness of his words on the day they are brought low. When their judges, that is for David immediately, Saul and his officers, who judged and condemned him, are overthrown in stony places, cast down into utter destruction, "they shall hear my words; for they are sweet" (Ps 141:6). Salvation through judgment, the major theme of the Psalms, may be seen as a practical working out of the Song of Moses (Dt 32). Psalm 141 is therefore a model prayer for the church militant which calls upon God to defend the honor of His justice by judging the prosecutors of His people. Thus the saints, viewing trampled justice are to call upon God for vindication and mediate judgment (Ps 50:14-15; 91:15; Jer 33:3; Rev 6:10). This is referred to as imprecation.

Christians, responding properly to persecution, are continually called to seek reconciliation and to practice long-suffering, forgiveness, and kindness after the pattern of God (Rom 2:4). For the saving power of the gospel is to be ever in view. Regarding imprecation Calvin writes,

As we cannot distinguish between the elect and the reprobate, it is our duty to pray for all who trouble us; to desire the salvation of all men; and even to be careful for the welfare of every individual. At the same time, if our hearts are pure and peaceful, this will not prevent us from freely appealing to God's judgment that he may cut off finally the impenitent.[134]

In this vein Belcher writes, "As the gospel goes forth there is the real possibility of the conversion of God's enemies, not just condemnation or destruction. Both aspects are in view in the phrase of the Lord's Prayer, 'thy kingdom come.' For God's kingdom to come may mean the destruction of God's enemies, but it may also mean the conversion of God's enemies through the preaching of the gospel."[135] And Day reminds us, there comes a point at which justice must be enacted whether from God directly or through His

---

[133] Belcher, The Messiah and the Psalms, 81.

[134] Calvin, Commentary on Psalm 4, 283.

[135] Belcher, The Messiah and the Psalms, 81.

525

representatives, such as the state and its judicial system.[136] Thus, when God's people pray for deliverance from their enemies, in response to injustice, they are essentially praying for Christ to come and consummate His Kingdom (Mt 6:8-13).

Whereas the people of God may appear as defeated as dried bones scattered at the mouth of Sheol (Ps 141:7), sufferings, afflictions, trials, tribulation, and persecution works to manifest the grace of endurance. Likewise, for all believers, though the world may hold our lives in contempt saying, why should he be allowed to live any longer? Our enemies will see our deliverance while they are carried off to the king of terrors (Job 18:14).

Whatever may be the cause pressing us to pray, we may rest assured like David that our prayers constitute both God's means of not only bringing us into His gracious presence but the channel for which God brings talionic mediate judgment. We must realize our need for God, and let God the Holy Spirit move us to earnest, consistent prayer. God's desire is for His people to seek holiness, to mortify their sin nature, and to cry to Him for deliverance.

Much like David, God presses a need upon His people to cry out to Him for sanctifying grace, deliverance, and justice. By these prayers, God not only delivers His people from their enemies, but works to further purify them, either by malevolent or benevolent agents, while mediating through their prayers His judgment on an obdurate world (Ps 141:6, 10; Rev 6:10; 8:1-5).

In John's vision of the martyrs in Revelation 6:9-11 and 8:1-5, incense is offered up with prayer; actualizing both God's preserving presence as well as His talionic judgment on unbelievers. In Revelation 5:8, as John is in the throne room of Heaven, where the Lamb will shortly begin opening the seven-sealed scroll and executing God's plan for the ages, we read this, "And when he had taken the scroll, the four living creatures and the twenty-four elders fell down before the Lamb, each holding a harp, and golden bowls full of incense, which are the prayers of the saints." The prayers of the saints

---

[136] Day, Crying for Justice: What the Psalms Teach Us About Mercy and Vengeance in an Age of Terrorism, 115.

are pictured as incense in the throne room of Heaven, they cry out with a loud voice, "O Sovereign Lord, holy and true, how long before you will judge and avenge our blood on those who dwell on the earth (Rev 6:10)?"

This call for vengeance does not arise from malicious intent, but from a desire to see God's justice vindicated (Ps 37:6; 79:10-12; Is 26:21; 54:17; Rev 11:18). "The saints do not cry out for a personal vendetta," as Joshua Owens explains, "but for a demonstration of the righteousness of God that restores order to chaos."[137] The basis for the final judgment will correspond to one's relation to Christ. Whether one has experienced saving faith in Christ or has rejected God's overtures of love through Him (2 Cor 5:20-21). Consequently, judgment will reflect the manner in which one has treated Christ by way of His followers, as the parable of the sheep and goats reveals (Ps 69:9; 79:12; Mt 25:31-46, cf. Acts 7:51-53; 9:4).

Regarding God's retributive justice, Joshua Owen further explains,

The lex talionis was instituted by God to insure that justice was required equally at every level of society. It prevented the wealthy and powerful from buying their way out of suits brought by the underprivileged people they may have abused. It also set limits on the compensation that could be demanded when the roles were reversed. When such laws were not observed judicial inequities abounded against those who belonged to the lower classes. According to Scripture, this latter situation existed quite often. The wicked prospered at the expense of the righteous; and no authority advocated the cause of the oppressed. The only comfort that pertained during these times was that God, the righteous Judge, promised to contend for the oppressed. All of creation rejoiced at the prospect of his coming, because he would restore peace, punishing evil doers and rewarding the righteous. Such was part of the hope of the Apocalypse. This was particularly the case for the martyrs of Jesus.[138]

In the Apocalypse, the lex talionis is still the operative principle of God's justice. This standard of justice is a warning to those tempted

---

[137] Owen, Martyrdom as an Impetus for Divine Retribution in the Book of Revelation, 135.
[138] Ibid, 131.

to compromise with the world, and a comfort to those who find no justice from the courts of men. Ironically, because of the principle of equivalent punishment, the persecutors of the church guarantee a death penalty for themselves by murdering Christ's witnesses. Martyrdom determines the sentence against the persecutors of the church.[139]

Thus, God delays the Church's vindication. God has heard the prayers of His people and is now acting to judge the world that oppresses believers in order to make the kingdom of this world into the kingdom of the Lord and of his Christ (Ex 3:7; Ps 141:6, 10; Rev 16:17-21). Belcher writes, "We pray for the conversion of our enemies, but it is also legitimate that we pray for the destruction of those who violently oppose the kingdom of Christ. In this way it is appropriate for God's people today to use the psalms of imprecation, not for personal revenge, but as part of our prayer for the establishment of the cause of Christ."[140] When we interact with the transcendent, sovereign, personal, God, our purpose in prayer is not to inform God or change His plan in some way but our purpose in prayer is to be a channel through which His ordained plan comes to pass (Ps 141:2; Rev 5:8-11; 6:10; 8:1-5).

We pray to align ourselves with God's will and we pray because God has ordained prayer as one of the means by which he will accomplish his plan. God has received these prayers which have been met with divine acceptance and power which is signified by the incense. God is effectively working by the Spirit through the lives of His saints to consummate His Kingdom; draw out of it all causes of evil (Ps 141:5b-6, 10; Mt 13:41). And he is doing it in answer to those prayers. Pray for the deliverance that God has promised will come at the end of this age. Pray with confidence for Christ to come. Your prayers will arise as incense to the throne room of Heaven, and at the appointed time, God will answer. Thus, the final reality of a pure Kingdom waits on the eschatological separation (Mt 13:30, 40-42).

Count the Cost

---

[139] Ibid, 154.
[140] Belcher, The Messiah and the Psalms, 83.

Chapter 10: Soli Deo Gloria

As Clausewitz states, we should not take the first step without considering the last.[141] God's concern is not for our lives to be prolonged here on earth, to be entitled to our seventy years, rather that we should enter a right relationship with Him in Christ, and begin to experience the joys of the life to come, living lives here that will glorify God. As Baxter tells us, although in this life we may have neither health, wealth, nor prosperity, we do have a lasting comfort, a Sabbath rest that we may begin to enjoy now in Christ.

As the church militant, we reign and feast with Christ even in the presence of our enemies (Ps 23:5). Bonhoeffer wrote, "Jesus Christ lived in the midst of his enemies. In the end all His disciples abandoned Him. On the cross He was all alone, surrounded by criminals and the jeering crowds. He had come for the express purpose of bringing peace to the enemies of God. So Christians, too, belong not in the seclusion of a cloistered life but in the midst of enemies. There they find their mission and work: 'To rule in the midst of your enemies.' And whoever will not suffer this does not want to be part of the rule of Christ."[142] We are at war!

In his classic treatise on spiritual warfare, William Gurnall summarizes this war as follows: "The stage whereon this war is fought is every man's soul. Here is no neuter in this war. The whole world is engaged in the quarrel, either for God against Satan, or for Satan against God." He says, this war is such a bloody one, "that the cruelest which was ever fought by men will be found but sport and child's play to this." Further, as to the duration of this war, Gurnall writes, it embraces "the entire course of the Christian life on earth."[143]

The Armor of God

The Christian is at war; but we are not alone, and we can't win the war alone. Suffering for Christ's sake enables believers to persevere in the proclamation of the Word.[144] That

---

[141] Clausewitz, On War, Book VIII, Chapter 3, 706.

[142] Bonhoeffer, Life Together, 27.

[143] Gurnall, The Christian in Complete Armour, v.

[144] Hendriksen, More Than Conquerors, 125.

is why we must have Christian fellowship. As we have tried to make abundantly clear, Christians forsake the fellowship of the body of Christ to their own hurt (Heb 10:25). Likewise, we must persevere in the means of grace (Acts 2:41). We must put on the whole armor of God as Eph 6:10-18 outlines:

10 Finally, my brethren, be strong in the Lord and in the power of His might. 11 **Put on the whole armor of God, that you may be able to stand against the wiles of the devil.** 12 **For we do not wrestle against flesh and blood, but against principalities, against powers, against the rulers of the darkness of this age, against spiritual hosts of wickedness in the heavenly places.** 13 Therefore take up the whole armor of God, that you may be able to withstand in the evil day, and having done all, to stand. 14 Stand therefore, *having girded your waist with truth,* having put on the *breastplate of righteousness,* 15 and h*aving shod your feet with the preparation of the gospel of peace;* 16 above all, taking the *shield of faith* with which you will be able to quench all the fiery darts of the wicked one. 17 And take the *helmet of salvation,* and the *sword of the Spirit,* which is the word of God; 18 praying always with all prayer and supplication in the Spirit, being watchful to this end with all perseverance and supplication for all the saints (emphasis added).

We must stand firm in the power Christ supplies, wear the armor of God, and pray without ceasing. Here is an inventory of the armor of God which defeats Satan and liberates his captives:

1. Belt of Truth – The Biblical Gospel.
2. Breastplate of Righteousness – The integrity of an honest (clean) conscience.
3. Gospel Shoes – Firmness of stance / assurance of salvation.
4. Shield of Faith – Active trust in Christ and His promises.
5. Helmet of Salvation – Confidence in Christ's keeping power.
6. The Sword of the Spirit – The offensive weapon of the saint.

Regarding the armor of God, it is remarkable that the apostle Paul's inventory of Christian armor includes nothing to protect the back. We are given no promise of protection if we run away, but we are promised victory every time we stand and give battle.[145] Perspective pilgrims on the road to the city

---

[145] Packer, God's Word's.

Chapter 10: Soli Deo Gloria

of God are required to count the cost of discipleship. Jesus says, "For which of you, intending to build a tower, does not sit down first and *count the cost*, whether he has enough to finish it - lest, after he has laid the foundation, and is not able to finish, all who see it begin to mock him, saying, 'This man began to build and was not able to finish'(Lk 14:28-30)?

The Christian is at war! In this war, no breathing space or armistice or truce is given. As J.C. Ryle states:

On weekdays as well as on Sundays, in private as well as in public, at home by the family fireside as well as abroad, in little things, like management of the tongue and temper, as well as great ones, like government of kingdoms, the Christian's warfare must unceasingly go on. The foe we have to do with keeps no holidays, never slumbers and never sleeps. So long as we have breath in our bodies we must keep on our armour and remember we are on an enemy's ground. "Even on the brink of Jordan," said a dying saint, "I find Satan nibbling at my heels." We must fight till we die. Let us consider well these propositions. Let us take care that our own personal religion is real, genuine and true. The saddest symptom about so-called Christians is the utter absence of anything like conflict and fight in their Christianity. They eat, they drink, they dress, they work, they amuse themselves, they get money, they spend money, they go through a scanty round of formal religious services once or twice every week. But of the great spiritual warfare – its watchings and strugglings, its agonies and anxieties, its battles and contests – of all this they appear to know nothing at all. Let us take care that this case it not our own. The worst state of the soul is "when the strong man armed keepeth the house, and his goods are at peace" – when he leads men and women "captive at his will," and they make no resistance. The worst chains are those which are neither felt nor seen by the prisoner (Lk 11:21; 2 Tim 2:26).

We may take comfort about our souls if we know anything of an inward fight and conflict. It is the invariable companion of genuine Christian holiness...Do we find in our heart of hearts a spiritual struggle? Do we feel anything of the flesh lusting against the spirit and the spirit against the flesh, so that we cannot do the things we would (Gal 5:17)? Are we conscious of two principles within us, contending for the mastery? Do we feel anything of war in our inward man? Well, let us thank God for it! It is a good sign. It is strongly probable evidence of the great work of sanctification. All true saints are soldiers...We are evidently no friends of Satan. Like the kings of this world, he wars not against his own subjects. **The**

very fact that he assaults us should fill our minds with hope (emphasis added).[146]

A spiritual struggle therefore is a sign of life not death. Cowards die many times before their deaths, the valiant taste of death but once. The fearful are those that march for hell; the violent and valiant are they which take heaven by force: cowards never won heaven (Mt 11:12). Say not thou hast royal blood running in thy veins, and art begotten of God, except thou canst prove thy pedigree by his heroic spirit, to dare to be holy in spite of men and devils.[147] We must stand firm and resist the devil. The song of the redeemed is ours: "And they overcame him by the blood of the Lamb and by the word of their testimony, and they did not love their lives to the death" (Rev 12:11). Christians conquer Satan by the blood of the Lamb – our *worship*; and by the word of our testimony – our *witness*; and we don't love our lives even unto death – and our *worthy* (holy) living.

As we have sought to make clear in previous chapters, as Christ's servants, we have been given the keys to the kingdom which He intends for us to use zealously (Mt 16:18-19). We are called to go forth in the power of the Spirit, suited with God's armor, into the enemy's territory to "set at liberty" the prisoners of Satan, who sit in gloomy dungeons (Is 29:18). Through us, God is making His appeal of justice, the announcement of the Day of salvation, to those in whom the Spirit is working (2 Cor 5:20-21). Through us, the very precincts of hades is invaded and loses ground as we push back darkness. And Christ in us, like a sword, cuts a swath into the devil's territory, and like a "threshing sledge," harvests souls at His threshing floor (Is 41:15-16, cf. Dan 2:34-35; Is 27:12; 30:24).

Into the Enemies Camp

Up to this point we have considered the fact that the Great Commission has yet to be completed. And that in order to do so it will cost the church in blood. But our confidence is

---

[146] Ryle, Holiness, 36.
[147] Gurnall, The Christian in Complete Armour, 16.

Chapter 10: Soli Deo Gloria

unwavering because we have the double assurance of Christ's promise: "All authority has been given to Me in heaven and on earth," and "lo, I am with you always, even to the end of the age" (Mt 28:18-20). As we go forth to preach the gospel in all the world as a witness to all the nations, we will encounter not only the hatred of the world but the powers of darkness. We are at war!

On a missionary trip to India, my family and I had come to a village my pastor friend and I were led to evangelize. As soon as we arrived, my wife and I felt like we were going to die there. We had both heard the voice of the enemy, telling us to leave or we were going to be killed. As we entered the center of the village, I sensed a prevailing evil. I couldn't miss seeing the many demonic images that stood out in front of the numerous temples we had set up right in the middle of.

As we approached a table that had been set up for our "street evangelism," the voice of the enemy and his evil presence grew with every step. I kept praying that God would do a mighty work there. We had prayed all day for this meeting. Earlier, God seemed so near, but once we arrived at the village, He seemed to withdrawal Himself. Then, after my pastor friend introduced my family and I, the time came for me to speak. A thin sheet was stretched behind where we sat. And as I got up, with Bible in hand, I looked back at my wife and daughters. My wife and daughters were smiling encouragingly, but I felt like any moment we would be attacked, perhaps through the sheet, and my family and I would die there in rural India, in the presence of evil.

Then I opened my Bible, and the presence of God flooded the place where I stood. It was as though the very ground itself became like that of heaven. Then I remember saying "surely the presence of the Lord is in this place." And with that the evil voice disappeared, and the gospel was preached in that desolate part of India, where the enemy had made quite a stronghold. We left feeling that God had accomplished a mighty breakthrough there among the people.

Later, when we discussed the matter, everyone recounted how they had heard the evil voice and felt that perhaps we would all die there. I believe God was doing a lot that night. He was bringing a sword into the enemy's camp to set at

533

liberty the captives. He called men and women out of darkness and brought them into the kingdom of Christ. He also withdrew Himself from us to test us, if I would stand in the power He supplied or not, as He did to His people in the wilderness wanderings (Dt 8:2-3). God did this also to king Hezekiah as the Scripture reveals, "God withdrew from him, in order to test him, that He might know all that was in his heart" (2 Chron 32:31).

We had entered the enemy's territory fully armored, we had prayed for the success of the gospel, and God wanted us to remove any uncertainty to the fact that we conquer the enemy only in His Spirit; as the Scripture declares: "Not by might nor by power, but by My Spirit,' says the Lord of hosts. 'Who are you, O great mountain? Before Zerubbabel you shall become a plain (Zech 4:6-7). Jesus declares to us, "If you say to this mountain, 'Be removed and be cast into the sea,' it will be done. And whatever things you ask in prayer, believing, you will receive" (Mt 21:21-22).

> Expect Great things from God;
> Attempt Great Things for God

Fully armed with God's Spirit, we enter the enemy's territory, into the very precincts of hades, pushing back darkness, liberating prisoners, to the glory of God. God says, fulfill the Great Commission, "Enlarge the place of your tent, and let them stretch out the curtains of your dwellings; do not spare; lengthen your cords, and strengthen your stakes. For you shall expand to the right and to the left, and your descendants will inherit the nations, and make the desolate cities inhabited" (Is 54:2-3). This was the text William Carey chose for his sermon that inspire much missionary enterprise, and gave to missions for all time the inspiring motto, "Expect great things from God: attempt great things for God."

William Carey, an English Baptist pastor, was appalled at the indifference the church of his day had for reaching the lost. "It is related, probably with some embellishment," writes James Culross, "that at a meeting of ministers the elder Ryland called on the younger men around him to propose a subject for discussion at their next gathering, when Carey rose and suggested, 'The duty of Christians to attempt the spread of the gospel among the heathen nations.'"[148] Springing to his feet, astonished and shocked, the older man ordered him to sit down, and said "Young man, when God is pleased to convert the heathen, He will do it Himself."

Many in the church of Carey's day, such as hyper-Calvinists, looked on such efforts as an interference with God's sovereignty; a 'profane outstretching of the hand to help the ark of God.'[149] There were many objections: the means were not available; the distances too far; the dangers too great. Besides, they argued, the Great Commission was only for the first apostles. However, Carey argued the Great Commission is the command of the Risen Christ for every Christian to seek the conversion of the lost. Carey expected great things from God and attempted great things for God. He became the father of modern missions.

Carey departed for India in 1793 with his family and a medical missionary co-worker, John Thomas. Their first year was rough. They soon ran out of funds and found themselves destitute in Calcutta. Through an acquaintance of Thomas, Carey was able to take a job managing an indigo factory near Madras, where he worked for six years. This job proved to be a godsend, as Carey was able to begin work for which he was well suited – Bible translation. However, when Thomas' missionary zeal waned, he was left alone while he labored at translating the Bible into Bengali amidst the hostility of the British East India Company who opposed his efforts at every turn.

When sorrows come, they come not single spies but in battalions. And matters grew worse for the Carey's when William's son Peter died of dysentery and his wife Dorothy suffered a mental breakdown from which she never recovered. Later, on March 11, 1812, while Carey was in Calcutta teaching, a fire broke out in his printing room, and the building which housed Carey's entire library, his completed Sanskrit dictionary, part of his Bengal dictionary, two grammar books, and ten translations of the Bible were lost.

---

[148] Culross, William Carey, 39.
[149] Ibid.

Chapter 10: Soli Deo Gloria

The fire also claimed the type sets for printing fourteen different languages. When Carey returned to Serampore and surveyed the scene, he wept and said, "In one short evening the labors of years are consumed. How unsearchable are the ways of God. I had lately brought some things to the utmost perfection of which they seemed capable, and contemplated the missionary establishment with perhaps too much self-congratulation. The Lord has laid me low, that I may look more simply to him."[150]

It was another devastating blow to Carey, but with a great resiliency he wrote, "The loss is heavy, but as traveling a road the second time is usually done with greater ease than the first time, so I trust the work will lose nothing of real value. We are not discouraged; indeed the work is already begun again in every language. We are cast down but not in despair."[151]

Carey resolved to trust the Lord for provision and within a few months he had another printing press set up. God's providence meets our deepest needs in the wisest ways. And unbeknownst to Carey, the fire generated much support for the gospel cause in India. Funds were being raised in Britain. In fact, so much money was coming in that Andrew Fuller, a great Baptist preacher and friend of Carey's, told his committee when he returned from a fund-raising trip, "We must stop the contributions."[152] Additionally, the incident provoked much missionary zeal and resulted in a flood of volunteers.

"Enlarge the place of your tent" is the command to transform the world; to fill the city of man with the living. Carey dedicated his life to spreading the gospel in India. He served the Lord there from 1793 until his death in 1834, during which time published complete Bibles or portions of the Bible in forty-four languages and dialects. The legacy of William Carey calls for us to "Expect great things from God: attempt great things for God." The Great Commission is not yet fulfilled. Christ is calling for His church to be His saving instrument in the world. For, "this gospel of the kingdom will

---

[150] Belcher, William Carey: A Biography, 168. Carey's printing press in Serampore was the first printing press to be established in India.
[151] Ibid, 170.
[152] Rusten, The One Year Christian History, 142-143.

be preached in all the world as a witness to all the nations, and then the end will come" (Mt 24:14). *God is sovereign to save, the church is obligated to preach, and fallen humanity is responsible to respond.*[153]

We will endure to the end as the lost are saved for the glory of God – *Soli Deo Gloria*. This truth led Charles Spurgeon to write, "It is impossible that any ill should happen to the man who is beloved of the Lord. Ill to him is no ill, but only good in a mysterious form. Losses enrich him, sickness is his medicine, reproach is his honor, death is his gain."[154] We are to seek the city where we have been exiled (Jer 29: 5-7). For, in its peace we will find ours. Here we have no lasting city, but we seek the city that is to come (Heb 13:14). As you go out of the building in which you are reading this book, you are entering the mission field, and the fields are ripe for harvest (Lk 10:2; Jn 4:35). Remember the words of Jesus when he commissioned us (Mt 28:18-20). We have the double assurance: All authority has been given to Jesus Christ, and He will be with us always: now and forever!!!

In light of suffering, persecution, evil, and death, our only comfort in life and death, is that both our body and soul, both in life and death, belong to none other than our faithful Savior Jesus Christ. Who, with his precious blood, has made full satisfaction for all our sins, has delivered us from all the power of the devil; and so preserves us that without the will of our heavenly Father, not a hair can fall from our heads. Further, we understand that all things are working for our salvation, and therefore, by his Holy Spirit, He also assures us of eternal life, and makes us sincerely willing and ready, from now on, to live for Him.[155]

No Guilt in Life, No Fear in Death

At the conclusion of Bunyan's *Pilgrim's Progress*, the two main characters, Christian and Hope are about to cross the river of death in order to enter the celestial city – the City of

---

[153] Shaw, Ten Great Ideas from Church History: A Decision-Maker's Guide to Shaping Your Church, 155.
[154] Spurgeon, The Treasury of David, Vol II, 235.
[155] Heidelberg Catechism, Question and Answer 1.

Chapter 10: Soli Deo Gloria

God (heaven). Relating the Christian's conflict at the hour of death, Bunyan writes,

They then addressed themselves to the water and, entering, *Christian began to sink, and crying out to his good friend Hopeful, he said, I sink in deep waters; the billows go over my head, all his waves go over me!* Selah. *Then said the other, be of good cheer, my brother, I feel the bottom, and it is good.* Then said Christian, Ah! My friend, the sorrows of death hath compassed me about; I shall not see the land that flows with milk and honey; and with that a great darkness and horror fell upon Christian, so that he could not see before him.

Also here he in great measure lost his senses, so that he could neither remember nor orderly talk of any of those sweet refreshments that he had met with in the way of his pilgrimage. But all the words that he spake still tended to discover that he had horror of mind, and heart fears that he should die in that river, and never obtain entrance in at the gate. *Here also, as they that stood by perceived, he was much in the troublesome thoughts of the sins that he had committed, both since and before he began to be a pilgrim.* It was also observed that he was troubled with apparitions of hobgoblins and evil spirits, for ever and anon he would intimate so much by words. *Hopeful, therefore, here had much ado to keep his brother's head above water;* yea, sometimes he would be quite gone down, and then, ere a while, he would rise up again half dead. *Hopeful also would endeavor to comfort him, saying, Brother, I see the gate, and men standing by to receive us:* but Christian would answer, It is you, it is you they wait for; you have been Hopeful ever since I knew you. And so have you, said he to Christian. Ah! brother! said he, surely if I was right he would now arise to help me; but for my sins he hath brought me into the snare, and hath left me. Then said Hopeful, My brother, you have quite forgot the text, where it is said of the wicked, "There are no bands in their death, but their strength is firm. They are not in trouble as other men, neither are they plagued like other men (Ps 73:4-5). *These troubles and distresses that you go through in these waters are no sign that God hath forsaken you; but are sent to try you, whether you will call to mind that which heretofore you have received of his goodness, and live upon him in your distresses.*[156]

As Christians, we will all face troubles, afflictions, trials, persecution and the like. When we go through this various trials, it doesn't mean that God has forsaken us, it means He is

---

[156] Bunyan, The Pilgrim's Progress, 390-392.

Chapter 10: Soli Deo Gloria

trying us to see if we will be mindful of all His goodness and mercy beforehand. Later, Bunyan writes,

Then I saw in my dream, that Christian was as in a muse a while. To whom also Hopeful added this word, Be of good cheer, Jesus Christ maketh thee whole; and with that Christian brake out with a loud voice, Oh, I see him again! And he tells me, "When thou passest through the waters, I will be with thee, and through the rivers, they shall not overflow thee" (Is 43:2). Then they both took courage, and the enemy was after that as still as a stone, until they were gone over. *Christian therefore presently found ground to stand upon, and so it followed that the rest of the river was but shallow.* Thus they got over. Now, upon the bank of the river, on the other side, they saw the two shining men again, who there waited for them; wherefore, being come out of the river, they saluted them, saying, we are ministering spirits, sent forth to minister for those that shall be heirs of salvation. Thus they went along towards the gate.[157]

Now I saw in my dream that these two men went in at the gate: and lo, as they entered, they were transfigured, and they had raiment put on that shone like gold. There was also that met them with harps and crowns, and gave them to them--the harps to praise withal, and the crowns in token of honour. Then I heard in my dream that all the bells in the city rang again for joy, and that it was said unto them, "Enter Ye into the joy of the Lord." I also heard the men themselves, that they sang with a loud voice, saying, "Blessing and honor, and glory, and power, be unto Him who sitteth upon the throne, and unto the Lamb, forever and ever" (Rev 5:13).

Now, just as the gates were opened to let in the men, I looked in after them, and, behold, the City shone like the sun; the streets also were paved with gold, and in them walked many men, with crowns on their heads, palms in their hands, and golden harps to sing praises withal. There were also of them that had wings, and they answered one another without intermission, saying, "Holy, holy, holy is the Lord" (Rev. 4:8). And after that they shut up the gates; which, when I had seen, I wished myself among them.

Now while I was gazing upon all these things, I turned my head to look back, and saw Ignorance come up to the river side; but he soon got over, and that without half that difficulty which the other two men met with. For it happened that there was then in that place, one

---

[157] Bunyan, The Pilgrim's Progress, 393.

Chapter 10: Soli Deo Gloria

Vain-hope, a ferryman, that with his boat helped him over; so he, as the other I saw, did ascend the hill, to come up to the gate, only he came alone; neither did any man meet him with the least encouragement. When he was come up to the gate, he looked up to the writing that was above, and then began to knock, supposing that entrance should have been quickly administered to him; but he was asked by the men that looked over the top of the gate, Whence came you, and what would you have? He answered, I have eat and drank in the presence of the King, and he has taught in our streets. Then they asked him for his certificate, that they might go in and show it to the King; so he fumbled in his bosom for one, and found none. Then said they, Have you none? But the man answered never a word. So they told the King, but he would not come down to see him, but commanded the two Shining Ones that conducted Christian and Hopeful to the City, to go out and take Ignorance, and bind him hand and foot, and have him away. Then they took him up, and carried him through the air to the door that I saw in the side of the hill, and put him in there. Then I saw that there was a way to hell, even from the gates of heaven, as well as from the City of Destruction. So I awoke, and behold it was a dream.[158]

We conquer by being lampstands of witness. Shakespeare likened the world to a stage and men and women merely actors on it. Whereas, in his analysis, the lives of these "players," confused and agitated as they are merely light the way, for those who follow, to dusty death, those who have found in Christ true riches, as lampstands of witness, confidently travel the Calvary Road, are ever joyous and even in defeat and in death are conquering. Toward the end of his life, C.S. Lewis replying to a child's letter wrote, "If you continue to love Jesus, nothing much can go wrong with you, and I hope you may always do so." The promise of inheriting the earth is tied exclusively to reigning as co-heirs with Christ – the art of living courageously for Him.

We shall inherit the earth (Ps 37:11; Rev 21:7) Our inheritance, as God tells us Gen 15:1 is God Himself, of which the possession of the Holy Spirit is the guarantee (Eph 1:14). We conquer though we die. This is the security a perfect atonement secures (Rom 8:31-39)! My desire is for you, who

---

[158] Bunyan, The Pilgrim's Progress, 400-403.

are reading this book, to come to faith in Jesus Christ, and say: *My search is over, You have found me Lord.*

Famous Last Words

Our last words speak volumes. They intimate in many ways what we have pursued in life and what we expect in the life to come. Our last words, in a way encapsulate the quintessence of the life we lived, and what we stood for. The Puritan John Flavel tells us, "death separates all other relations, but the soul's union with Christ is not dissolved in the grave. Indeed, the day of a believer's death is his marriage day, the day of his fullest enjoyment of Christ."[159] But for the wicked, even what he has – borrowed breath – will be taken from him (Mt 25:29).

For the saints, death is the final hurdle between them and glory. Solely because of Christ's victory in the Cross, death has lost its sting (1 Cor 15:55), and in the divine grip, the saints pass seamlessly into the joys of their Master in heaven. Because Christ is the Life of the saints; to live is Christ, to die is gain (Phil 1:21). As Milton put it, "Death is the great key that opens the palace of eternity." Death serves as a vehicle to usher the saints into the presence of God and reunite them with righteous friends and family, where in the absence of pain, they experience the eternal joys of God's glory. For the wicked, death begins an eternity of suffering. At death, those who lived a life of rebellion to God are bound like Ignorance and are cast into outer darkness, where they enter a realm of eternal pain (Dan. 12:2; Mt. 22:13; 25:46; Mk. 9:48; Lk. 16:24; 2 Thes. 1:9; Rev. 20:10).

In death, the righteous are as bold as a lion (Heb 2:14-15). When threatened with beasts and fire, the martyr Polycarp courageously replied, "You threaten me with fire which burns for an hour, and after a little is extinguished, but are ignorant of the fire of the coming judgment and of eternal punishment, reserved for the ungodly. But why do you tarry? Bring forth what you will." In a kindred spirit stood the Czech Reformer, Jan Huss. He was falsely accused of heresy and burned in Constance, Germany in 1415. What was his crime? Preaching

---

[159] Flavel, Sermon on Song of Songs 5:16.

the doctrines of grace. Huss would not renounce the true gospel, and as his body was being consumed by fire, he sang in a clear melodious voice, "Jesus, Thou Son of David have mercy on me."

When Bloody Mary came to the throne of England, Hugh Latimer, the English Reformer, was arrested, tried for heresy, and burned together with his friend Nicholas Ridley. His crime? Preaching the doctrines of grace. His last words at the stake were: "Be of good cheer, Master Ridley, and play the man, for we shall this day light such a candle in England as I trust by God's grace shall never be put out."

Death cannot conquer the saints, who by their inseparable union with Christ have already conquered death (1 Cor 15:55). Even the thralls of death could not diminish the Puritan John Owen's theological precision. As he died, he said, "I am going to Him whom my soul loveth, or rather who has loved me with an everlasting love, which is the sole ground of all my consolation."

George Whitefield, one of the Lord's greatest evangelists, worked tirelessly for the Christ's sake. It is estimated that he preached some 30,000 sermons on both sides of the Atlantic from Scotland to Georgia. Doubtless, many thousands came to faith through his preaching. Yet, with his dying breath, he exclaimed, "Lord Jesus, I am weary in thy work, but not of thy work. If I have not yet finished my course, let me go and speak for Thee once more in the fields, seal the truth, and come home to die."

The saints are as bold as a lion in death. Before he was hanged by the British, the last words of American patriot Nathan Hale were: "I only regret that I have but one life to lose for my country." As General Thomas "Stonewall" Jackson, Lee's 'right arm' lay dying he said, "I see from the number of physicians that you think my condition dangerous, but I thank God, if it is His will, that I am ready to go. It is the Lord's Day; my wish is fulfilled. I have always desired to die on Sunday." Then in delirium he exclaimed. "Order A.P. Hill to prepare for action! Pass the infantry to the front rapidly! Tell Major Hawks...," but stopped, leaving the sentence unfinished. Then a smile of sweetness spread itself over his pale face, and he said quietly with an expression, as if of

Chapter 10: Soli Deo Gloria

relief, "Let us cross the river and rest under the shade of the tree."[160]

For the saints, death is an entrance into glory. C.S. Lewis paints a vivid picture in *Screwtape Letters* of the moment a saint 'shuffles off this mortal coil.' The man who has been afflicted by the demon Wormwood dies, and Wormwood's uncle Screwtape says, "You have let a soul slip through your fingers...How well I know what happened at the instant when they snatched him from you! There was a sudden clearing of his eyes (was there not?) as he saw you for the first time, and recognized the part you had had in him and knew that you had it no longer. Just think (and let it be the beginning of your agony) what he felt at that moment; as if a scab had fallen from an old sore, as if he were emerging from a hideous, shell-like tetter, as if he shuffled off for good and all a defiled, wet, clinging garment.[161]

As for the wicked, death is an entrance to eternal punishment. In Christopher Marlowe's *Doctor Faustus*, the main character of the story, is a professor of divinity. Doctor Faustus, unsatisfied with the limitations of human knowledge, and feeling as though he has plumbed the depths of what he has studied, begins to dabble in the occult. The devil comes to him in the person of Mephistopheles and offers him a remarkable offer: "Sell your soul to me for eternity and I will give you twenty-four years of earthly knowledge and power."

Faustus wrestles with this bargain, perhaps thinking rather lightly of the existence of hell, and driven by his lust for knowledge and power, accepts the devil's offer and sells his soul. In the next twenty-four years, much to his delight, Doctor Faustus obtains, fame, knowledge, power and all the riches this world can offer through his devil-servant, Mephistopheles. But eventually his time runs out, and Faustus realizes he has made a devil's bargain. And as the clock announces his final moment of life, Faustus in agonizing desperation laments "O, it strikes, it strikes! Now, body, turn to air, Or Lucifer will bear thee quick to hell! O soul, be changed into little water-drops, and fall into the ocean, ne'er

---

[160] Cooke, Stonewall Jackson: a Military Biography, 485.
[161] Lewis, The Screwtape Letters, 146.

be found!" But Faustus cannot escape the sting of death, and the devils carry him to hell.

For the wicked, death has a sting, because the sting of death is sin. When the English philosopher Thomas Hobbes died, in horror of conscience he exclaimed, "I'm about to take my last voyage, a great leap into the dark." For Hobbes there was more than he ever dreamed of in his philosophy.

Edward Gibbon, the English Historian deprecated Christianity for its perceived weakness of the providing hope of a better life existed after death. In Gibbon's estimation this fostered an indifference to the present life thereby sapping one's benefit to the state. Christianity to Gibbon was unpatriotic and disloyal to the nation. Gibbon despised Christianity. Just before he died, he cried, "All is now lost. All is dark and doubtful. I know not where I'm going!" At his death Gibbon entered outer darkness.

History tells us that before Madame Du Barry was executed, she exclaimed, "One more moment, Mr. Executioner, I beg you!" For the wicked, all they have is borrowed breath and what they seek to hold on to is only more of this life. "But the eyes of the wicked will fail, and escape will elude them; their hope will become a dying gasp" (Job 11:20).

The renowned atheist, Voltaire, one of the most aggressive antagonists of Christianity that ever lived, wrote much to undermine the church. He once said of Jesus Christ, "Curse the wretch. In 20 years, Christianity will be no more. My single hand will destroy the edifice it took 12 apostles to rear." Needless to say, Voltaire was less than successful. And on his deathbed, a nurse who attended him was reported to have said, "For all the wealth in Europe, I would not see another atheist die."

When a priest asked Voltaire to renounce Satan, he replied, "Now, now, my good man, this is no time for making enemies." And Dr. Trochin, waiting up with Voltaire at his death, said that he cried out with utter desperation, "I am abandoned by God and man. I will give you half of what I am worth if you will give me six more months of life. And the doctor rightly said, "That cannot be done." Voltaire answered, "Then I shall go to hell and you will go with me." And with his dying breath, he exclaimed, "Oh, Christ!" And he died. Trying to hold on to this life – his hope was a dying gasp. For those who reject Christ, what characterizes their passing is anguishing, fear, and despair.

For the righteous, the love of Christ outstrips the pain. The last words of Stephen, who was being stoned to death for the gospel, were, "Lord Jesus, receive my spirit." Then as the Scripture tells us he fell on his knees and cried out, "Lord, do not hold this sin against them." When he had said this, he fell asleep. (Acts 7:59-60).

In the power of Christ, we hope in the resurrection, and meet death not only with equanimity but with undaunted courage that stems from the security Christ's perfect atonement secures (Rom 8:28-39). For John Bunyan the 31st of August 1688, marked the day of his crossing of the river of death and his entrance into the city of God. As he passed into eternity he said peacefully, "Take me, for I come to thee."

For the wicked, "Their end is destruction, their god is their belly, and they glory in their shame, with minds set on earthly things. But our citizenship is in heaven, and from it we await a Savior, the Lord Jesus Christ, who will transform our lowly body to be like his glorious body, by the power that enables him even to subject all things to himself" (Phil 3:19-21). This truth is what lead John Newton to confidently say in death, "I am in the land of the dying, and I am soon going to the land of the living." Likewise, D.L. Moody, the great evangelist, on his deathbed, said, "I see Earth receding and heaven is opening. God is calling me." This beatific vision led Henry Ward Beecher with his last breath to say, "Now comes the mystery."

The Seven Last Words from the Cross

The most precious last words of all are those of Jesus. These words of Jesus are not the ordinary last words of men. The seven last words of Jesus on the cross are gathered from the accounts of Christ's crucifixion on Good Friday. They are a wonderful commentary in His own words of reconciliation, salvation, love, atonement, suffering, victory and security. The Cross is the revelation of man's sin and God's love. His last words provide us with an opportunity to focus on the cross and how Jesus expressed His sacrifice of dying for our sins. The seven last words of Christ are:

1. The word of forgiveness: "Father, forgive them they know not what they do" (Lk 23:34; Is 53:12). The whole world, the Bible tells us, is under the power of the evil one (1 Jn 5:19). The Bible characterizes Satan as the god of this world and this age whose object it is to keep men under his control by holding mankind in darkness and unbelief. Christ's death was God's way of appeasing His wrath for sin. "For there is no difference; for all have sinned and fall short of the glory of God" (Rom 3:22-23). Because Jesus paid it all, He was able to stand in our place and ask for the Father to forgive us.

2. The word of assurance: "Today you shall be with me in paradise" (Lk 23:43; Is 53:10-11). In the moment of the dying thief's repentance and faith Jesus accepted him into His kingdom. Christ's word to penitent criminals gives us the assurance of salvation for as long as it is called today (Heb 3:13; 4:7)! "Therefore, having been justified by faith, we have peace with God through our Lord Jesus Christ" (Rom 5:1). Can you appropriate Christ's promise to yourself?

3. The word of comfort: "Woman behold your son, son behold your mother" (Jn 19:26). When Jesus commits his mother to John's care, he is showing us how our needs will be met when we leave everything to follow him. Even from the cross Jesus fulfills the law of God (Ex 20:12). If Jesus could provide for the needs of His own mother in a moment of His deepest weakness and humiliation, how much more can he provide for your need in His present power and exaltation!

4. The word of desolation: "My God, My God, why have you forsaken Me" (Mt 27:46; Ps 22:1). This was Christ's way of expressing the spiritual agony that was beyond measure. "But God demonstrates His own love toward us, in that while we were still sinners, Christ died for us. Much more then, having now been justified by His blood, we shall be saved from wrath through Him" (Rom 5:8-9). This was the cup He had spoken of in the garden of Gethsemane. The cup represents the wrath

546

of God for sin, it represents God's hatred for sin that He now drank to the dregs; becoming sin for us (2 Cor 5:21).

5. The word of suffering: "I thirst" (Jn 19:28; Is 69:21). This word points to Christ's completion of His redeeming work. He offered Himself up for us and willingly suffered excruciating pain in His body. "For the wages of sin is death, but the gift of God is eternal life in Christ Jesus our Lord" (Rom 6:23). Christ Jesus suffered the wrath that was due for our sins.

6. The word of triumph: "It is finished" (Jn 19:30; Ps 22:31)! In the original language of the NT this is one word: *tetelestai* finished, completed, done! This one word "finished," summarizes all of Jesus Christ's life and ministry. When Jesus said it is finished He meant: sin is finished, Satan is finished, and the separation of death is finished. The devil's dominion was invaded by the Son of God. Now those the devil holds under his power are released every time the gospel is heard with the ears of faith. "If you confess with your mouth the Lord Jesus and believe in your heart that God has raised Him from the dead, you will be saved" (Rom 10:9).

7. The word of committal: "Father, into Thy hands I commit my spirit" (Lk 23:46; Ps 31:5). Jesus made His soul an offering for sin, to give His life as a ransom for many (Mt 26:28; Is 53:12). With the words, "Father, into Thine hands I commit my spirit," He offered up Himself as the sacrifice. *The last word of Jesus teaches us how to die in committal.* It's impossible for death to take us out of the hands of our heavenly Father (Jn 10:25-30). The last word is the word of confidence in this accomplished work. "There is therefore now no condemnation to those who are in Christ Jesus" (Rom 8:1).

> Nothing in my hands I bring,
> Simply to Thy cross I cling:
> Naked, come to Thee for dress,
> Helpless, look to Thee for grace.
> Foul, I to the fountain fly,
> Wash me, Savior, or I die.[162]

---

[162] Toplady, Rock of Ages.

Chapter 10: Soli Deo Gloria

Love of God, Country and truth, lived out in steadfast faith, duteous selfless service, confidence, and undaunted courage, with no thought of personal advancement, ambition or applause; this ranks as the hallmarks of the God-honoring American man; thus unsung, unheard, yet indispensable to life, liberty and the pursuit of happiness. This is a full life, however long, untrammeled by consequence, in full assurance of faith.

Brothers, in the service of Christ we cannot loose. There is but one life to live, that will soon be past; and only what is done for Christ will last. Spend it well.

Friends, as I close this volume, let me say. God has already done everything necessary for us to be reconciled to Him. All we need do is repent of our sins and believe in the Lord Jesus Christ and be saved! As the humble servant of Christ, I plead with you: be reconciled to God (2 Cor 5:20).

Now, in the spirit of Augustine, let me say, I think now that I have by God's help, discharged my obligation in writing this large work. Let those who think I have said too little, or those who think I have said too much, forgive me; and let those who think I have said just enough join me in giving thanks to God. Amen.

> No guilt in life, no power in death; this is the power of Christ in me.
> From life's first cry to final breath, Jesus commands my destiny.
> No power of hell, no scheme of man, can ever pluck me from His hand;
> Til He returns or calls me home, here in the power of Christ I'll stand.[163]

---

[163] Getty, In Christ Alone.

Chapter 10: Soli Deo Gloria

"All the inhabitants of Canaan will melt away. Fear and dread will fall on them; by the greatness of Your arm they will be as still as a stone, *till Your people pass over*, O Lord, *till the people pass over whom You have purchased.* You will bring them in and plant *them in the mountain of Your inheritance*, in the place, O Lord, which You have made for Your own dwelling, the sanctuary, O Lord, which Your hands have established. The Lord shall reign forever and ever" (Ex 15:15-18, emphasis added).

"But you have come to Mount Zion and to *the city of the living God,* the heavenly Jerusalem, to an innumerable company of angels, to the general assembly and church of the firstborn who are registered in heaven, to God the Judge of all, to the spirits of just men made perfect, to Jesus the Mediator of the new covenant, and to the blood of sprinkling that speaks better things than that of Abel" (Heb 12:22-24).

Christian and Hopeful cross the river death to reach the city of God.

Chapter 10: Soli Deo Gloria

Recommended Further Reading

1. Watson, Thomas *All Things for Good.*
2. Sproul, R.C. *The Last Days According to Jesus.*
3. Donnelly, Edward *Biblical Teaching on the Doctrines of Heaven and Hell.*
4. Carson, D.A. *How Long, O Lord?*
5. Longman, Tremper *God is a Warrior.*

Chapter 10 Review Questions

1. Why do Christians get depressed?
2. Why does God allow some people to get caught up in evil?
3. Why does God heal some and not others?
4. How could David be a "man after God's own heart" and yet do the wicked deeds he did?
5. Why does God allow pain that doesn't seem to refine Christians?
6. Why does God allow suffering and evil to go on in the world?
7. What is your view of martyrdom?
8. How are Christians to respond to persecution?
9. If you died today, where would you spend eternity?
10. Do you know Christ as Savior?

Endless Sabbath – Eternal Rest

In boundless age His Eternal decreed
Foreordained works His body dressed:
Quickening birth in His rising
Endless Sabbath – eternal rest.

Apollyon's brood light's countenance withheld
Er fleeting, nr seeing, nr wise:
Confused agitation twice death
Consigned oblivion – pride's demise.

From God-hewn Rock the kingdom upward grows
Course timed faith's reckoned innocence:
Never tasting death's damned sting
Played out course – divine providence.

From First Born of death all brethren numbered
Elect's surety, purchase effected:
At week's ending history's ceasing
Body redeemed – same body perfected.

God's breath and Spirit instantly gathered
His covered, hidden from wrath's might:
Patient endure their soul's possessed
Fullness of time – the Day's full light.

Fallen men and angels ante thronum [1]
Abraham's seed acquitted joyous:
Death's defeat impious to doom
Extra Ecclesium – nulla salus.[2]

Chosen broken vessels haply extol
Effectually drawn, winnowed, and blessed:
At length God's golden City descends
Endless Sabbath – eternal rest.

---

[1] Latin for 'before the throne.'
[2] Outside the Church there is no salvation.

551

Poetic Epilogue

The Destruction of Sennacherib
By Lord Byron

The Assyrian came down like the wolf on the fold,
And his cohorts were gleaming in purple and gold;
And the sheen of their spears was like stars on the sea,
When the blue wave rolls nightly on deep Galilee.
Like the leaves of the forest when Summer is green,
That host with their banners at sunset were seen:
Like the leaves of the forest when Autumn hath blown,
That host on the morrow lay withered and strown.

For the Angel of Death spread his wings on the blast,
And breathed in the face of the foe as he pass'd,
And the eyes of the sleepers wax'd deadly and chill,
And their hearts but once heaved, and forever grew still!
And there lay the steed with his nostril all wide,
But through it there roll'd not the breath of his pride;
And the foam of his gasping lay white on the turf,
And cold as the spray of the rock-beating surf.

And there lay the rider distorted and pale,
With the dew on his brow, and the rust on his mail:
And the tents were all silent, the banners alone,
The lances unlifted, the trumpets unblown.
And the widows of Ashur are loud in their wail,
And the idols are broke in the temple of Baal;
And the might of the Gentile, unsmote by the sword,
Hath melted like snow in the glance of the Lord!

Poetic Epilogue

A Mighty Fortress [3]
By Martin Luther

A mighty fortress is our God, a bulwark never failing;
Our helper he amid the flood of mortal ills prevailing.
For still our ancient foe doth seek to work us woe;
His craft and power are great, and armed with cruel hate,
On earth is not his equal.

Did we in our own strength confide, our striving would be losing,
Were not the right man on our side, the man of God's own choosing.
Dost ask who that may be? Christ Jesus, it is he;
Lord Sabaoth, his name, from age to age the same,
And he must win the battle.

And though this world, with devils filled, should threaten to undo us,
We will not fear, for God hath willed his truth to triumph through us.
The Prince of Darkness grim, we tremble not for him;
His rage we can endure, for lo, his doom is sure;
One little word shall fell him.

That word above all earthly powers, no thanks to them, abideth;
The Spirit and the gifts are ours, thru him who with us sideth.
Let goods and kindred go, this mortal life also;
The body they may kill; God's truth abideth still;
His kingdom is forever.

---

[3] Martin Luther (1483-1546), the Magisterial Reformer, composed this hymn between the years 1527-1529.

Poetic Epilogue

May the Mind of Christ, My Savior [4]

May the mind of Christ, my Savior,
Live in me from day to day,
By His love and power controlling
All I do and say.

May the Word of God dwell richly
In my heart from hour to hour,
So that all may see I triumph
Only through His power.

May the peace of God my Father
Rule my life in everything,
That I may be calm to comfort
Sick and sorrowing.

May the love of Jesus fill me
As the waters fill the sea;
Him exalting, self-abasing,
This is victory.

May I run the race before me,
Strong and brave to face the foe,
Looking only unto Jesus
As I onward go.

May His beauty rest upon me,
As I seek the lost to win,
And may they forget the channel,
Seeing only Him.

---

[4] Kate Barclay Wilkinson (1859-1928).

Appendix 1: Creeds of Christendom

"The Bible is the Word of God to man; the Creed is man's answer to God." – Philip Schaff

The Apostle's Creed [1]

I believe in God, the Father Almighty, the Creator of heaven and earth, and in Jesus Christ, His only Son, our Lord: Who was conceived of the Holy Spirit, born of the Virgin Mary, suffered under Pontius Pilate, was crucified, died, and was buried.

He descended into hell. [1] The third day He arose again from the dead. He ascended into heaven and sits at the right hand of God the Father Almighty, whence He shall come to judge the living and the dead. I believe in the Holy Spirit, the holy catholic [2] church, the communion of saints, the forgiveness of sins, the resurrection of the body, and life everlasting. Amen.

End Notes:

1. "Descended into hell" does not refer to literally going down into the bowels of hell itself to be subject to the devil. Rather, it is a poetic way of stating that Christ truly and assuredly died on the cross, and His body remained under the power of death for three days.
2. The word "catholic" refers not to the Roman Catholic Church, but to the universal church of the Lord Jesus Christ. Catholic *katholikos* means universal in Greek.

---

[1] The Apostles' Creed was not written by the Biblical Disciples. The name is deemed this as a sum and substance of the early Apostolic teaching which the disciples would have held to. Earliest version found is A.D. 215. The current version is circa 542 A.D.

Appendix 1: Creeds of Christendom

The Nicene Creed
381 A.D. [1]

I believe in one God, the Father Almighty, maker of heaven and earth, and of all things visible and invisible; And in one Lord Jesus Christ, the only begotten Son of God, begotten of his Father before all worlds, God of God, Light of Light, very God of very God, begotten, not made, being of one substance with the Father; by whom all things were made; who for us men and for our salvation came down from heaven, and was incarnate by the Holy Ghost of the Virgin Mary, and was made man; and was crucified also for us under Pontius Pilate; he suffered and was buried; and the third day he rose again according to the Scriptures, and ascended into heaven, and sitteth on the right hand of the Father; and he shall come again, with glory, to judge both the quick and the dead; whose kingdom shall have no end.

And I believe in the Holy Ghost, the Lord, and Giver of Life, who proceedeth from the Father and the Son; who with the Father and the Son together is worshipped and glorified; who spake by the Prophets. And I believe one holy Catholic and Apostolic Church; I acknowledge one baptism for the remission of sins; and I look for the resurrection of the dead, and the life of the world to come. Amen.

End Notes:

1. The Nicene Creed is formed on the basis of the Apostles' Creed. The clauses relating to the consubstantial divinity of Christ were contributed by the great Council held in Nicaea in A.D. 325; those relating to the divinity and personality of the Holy Ghost added by the Second Ecumenical Council, held at Constantinople in A.D.381.
2. The filioque clause, "and the Son," was added by the Council of the Western Church held at Toledo, Spain in A.D. 569.

---

[1] In its present form it is the Creed of the whole Christian Church, the Greek Church (Orthodox) rejecting only the last added clause. A. A. Hodge, A Short History of Creeds and Confessions, 4

Appendix 1: Creeds of Christendom

The Definition of Chalcedon [2]
Oct 22, 451 AD

We, then, following the holy Fathers, all with one consent, teach men to confess one and the same Son, our Lord Jesus Christ, the same perfect in Godhead and also perfect in manhood; truly God and truly man, of a reasonable [rational] soul and body; consubstantial [coessential] with the Father according to the Godhead, and consubstantial with us according to the Manhood; in all things like unto us, without sin; begotten before all ages of the Father according to the Godhead, and in these latter days, for us and for our salvation, born of the Virgin Mary, the Mother of God, according to the Manhood; one and the same Christ, Son, Lord, **Only-begotten**, to be acknowledged in two natures, *inconfusedly, unchangeably, indivisibly, inseparably;* the distinction of natures being by no means taken away by the union, but rather the property of each nature being preserved, and concurring in one Person and one Subsistence, not parted or divided into two persons, but one and the same Son, and only begotten, God the Word, the Lord Jesus Christ, as the prophets from the beginning [have declared] concerning him, and the Lord Jesus Christ himself has taught us, and the Creed of the holy Fathers has handed down to us.

Μονογενῆ, ἐκ δύο φύσεων [ἐν δύο φύσεσιν] ,*ἀσυγχύτως*, *ἀτρέπτως* , *ἀδιαιρέτως, ἀχωρίστως*

---

[2] The Chalcedonian Definition, repudiated the notion of a single nature in Christ, and declared that He has two natures in one person and hypostasis; it also insists on the completeness of his two natures: Godhead and manhood.

Appendix 2: Declaration of Independence

IN CONGRESS, July 4, 1776.

The unanimous Declaration of the thirteen united States of America,

When in the Course of human events, it becomes necessary for one people to dissolve the political bands which have connected them with another, and to assume among the powers of the earth, the separate and equal station to which the Laws of Nature and of Nature's God entitle them, a decent respect to the opinions of mankind requires that they should declare the causes which impel them to the separation.

We hold these truths to be self-evident, that all men are created equal, that they are endowed by their Creator with certain unalienable Rights, that among these are Life, Liberty and the pursuit of Happiness. That to secure these rights, Governments are instituted among Men, deriving their just powers from the consent of the governed, --That whenever any Form of Government becomes destructive of these ends, it is the Right of the People to alter or to abolish it, and to institute new Government, laying its foundation on such principles and organizing its powers in such form, as to them shall seem most likely to effect their Safety and Happiness. Prudence, indeed, will dictate that Governments long established should not be changed for light and transient causes; and accordingly all experience hath shewn, that mankind are more disposed to suffer, while evils are sufferable, than to right themselves by abolishing the forms to which they are accustomed. But when a long train of abuses and usurpations, pursuing invariably the same Object evinces a design to reduce them under absolute Despotism, it is their right, it is their duty, to throw off such Government, and to provide new Guards for their future security.--Such has been the patient sufferance of these Colonies; and such is now the necessity which constrains them to alter their former Systems of Government. The history of the present King of Great Britain is a history of repeated injuries and usurpations, all having in direct object the establishment of an absolute Tyranny over these States. To prove this, let Facts be submitted to a candid world.

He has refused his Assent to Laws, the most wholesome and necessary for the public good.

He has forbidden his Governors to pass Laws of immediate and pressing importance, unless suspended in their operation till his Assent should be obtained; and when so suspended, he has utterly neglected to attend to them.

He has refused to pass other Laws for the accommodation of large districts of people, unless those people would relinquish the right of

Appendix 2: Declaration of Independence

Representation in the Legislature, a right inestimable to them and formidable to tyrants only.

He has called together legislative bodies at places unusual, uncomfortable, and distant from the depository of their public Records, for the sole purpose of fatiguing them into compliance with his measures.

He has dissolved Representative Houses repeatedly, for opposing with manly firmness his invasions on the rights of the people.

He has refused for a long time, after such dissolutions, to cause others to be elected; whereby the Legislative powers, incapable of Annihilation, have returned to the People at large for their exercise; the State remaining in the mean time exposed to all the dangers of invasion from without, and convulsions within.

He has endeavoured to prevent the population of these States; for that purpose obstructing the Laws for Naturalization of Foreigners; refusing to pass others to encourage their migrations hither, and raising the conditions of new Appropriations of Lands.

He has obstructed the Administration of Justice, by refusing his Assent to Laws for establishing Judiciary powers.

He has made Judges dependent on his Will alone, for the tenure of their offices, and the amount and payment of their salaries.

He has erected a multitude of New Offices, and sent hither swarms of Officers to harrass our people, and eat out their substance.

He has kept among us, in times of peace, Standing Armies without the Consent of our legislatures.

He has affected to render the Military independent of and superior to the Civil power.

He has combined with others to subject us to a jurisdiction foreign to our constitution, and unacknowledged by our laws; giving his Assent to their Acts of pretended Legislation:

For Quartering large bodies of armed troops among us:

For protecting them, by a mock Trial, from punishment for any Murders which they should commit on the Inhabitants of these States:

For cutting off our Trade with all parts of the world:

For imposing Taxes on us without our Consent:

For depriving us in many cases, of the benefits of Trial by Jury:

For transporting us beyond Seas to be tried for pretended offences

For abolishing the free System of English Laws in a neighbouring Province, establishing therein an Arbitrary government, and enlarging its Boundaries so as to render it at once an example and fit instrument for introducing the same absolute rule into these Colonies:

For taking away our Charters, abolishing our most valuable Laws, and altering fundamentally the Forms of our Governments:

For suspending our own Legislatures, and declaring themselves invested with power to legislate for us in all cases whatsoever.

Appendix 2: Declaration of Independence

He has abdicated Government here, by declaring us out of his Protection and waging War against us.

He has plundered our seas, ravaged our Coasts, burnt our towns, and destroyed the lives of our people.

He is at this time transporting large Armies of foreign Mercenaries to compleat the works of death, desolation and tyranny, already begun with circumstances of Cruelty & perfidy scarcely paralleled in the most barbarous ages, and totally unworthy the Head of a civilized nation.

He has constrained our fellow Citizens taken Captive on the high Seas to bear Arms against their Country, to become the executioners of their friends and Brethren, or to fall themselves by their Hands.

He has excited domestic insurrections amongst us, and has endeavoured to bring on the inhabitants of our frontiers, the merciless Indian Savages, whose known rule of warfare, is an undistinguished destruction of all ages, sexes and conditions.

In every stage of these Oppressions We have Petitioned for Redress in the most humble terms: Our repeated Petitions have been answered only by repeated injury. A Prince whose character is thus marked by every act which may define a Tyrant, is unfit to be the ruler of a free people.

Nor have We been wanting in attentions to our Brittish brethren. We have warned them from time to time of attempts by their legislature to extend an unwarrantable jurisdiction over us. We have reminded them of the circumstances of our emigration and settlement here. We have appealed to their native justice and magnanimity, and we have conjured them by the ties of our common kindred to disavow these usurpations, which, would inevitably interrupt our connections and correspondence. They too have been deaf to the voice of justice and of consanguinity. We must, therefore, acquiesce in the necessity, which denounces our Separation, and hold them, as we hold the rest of mankind, Enemies in War, in Peace Friends.

We, therefore, the Representatives of the united States of America, in General Congress, Assembled, appealing to the Supreme Judge of the world for the rectitude of our intentions, do, in the Name, and by Authority of the good People of these Colonies, solemnly publish and declare, That these United Colonies are, and of Right ought to be Free and Independent States; that they are Absolved from all Allegiance to the British Crown, and that all political connection between them and the State of Great Britain, is and ought to be totally dissolved; and that as Free and Independent States, they have full Power to levy War, conclude Peace, contract Alliances, establish Commerce, and to do all other Acts and Things which Independent States may of right do. And for the support of this Declaration, with a

Appendix 2: Declaration of Independence

firm reliance on the protection of divine Providence, we mutually pledge to each other our Lives, our Fortunes and our sacred Honor.

The 56 signatures on the Declaration appear in the positions indicated:

Column 1
Georgia:
  Button Gwinnett
  Lyman Hall
  George Walton

Column 2
North Carolina:
  William Hooper
  Joseph Hewes
  John Penn

Column 2 (Cont.)
South Carolina:
  Edward Rutledge
  Thomas Heyward, Jr.
  Thomas Lynch, Jr.
  Arthur Middleton

Column 3
Massachusetts:
  John Hancock

Maryland:
  Samuel Chase
  William Paca
  Thomas Stone
  Charles Carroll

Virginia:
  George Wythe
  Richard Henry Lee
  Thomas Jefferson
  Benjamin Harrison
  Thomas Nelson, Jr.
  Francis Lightfoot Lee
  Carter Braxton

Column 4
Pennsylvania:
  Robert Morris
  Benjamin Rush
  Benjamin Franklin
  John Morton
  George Clymer
  James Smith
  George Taylor
  James Wilson
  George Ross

Delaware:
  Caesar Rodney
  George Read
  Thomas McKean

Column 5
New York:
  William Floyd
  Philip Livingston
  Francis Lewis
  Lewis Morris

New Jersey:
  Richard Stockton
  John Witherspoon
  Francis Hopkinson
  John Hart
  Abraham Clark

Column 6
New Hampshire:
  Josiah Bartlett
  William Whipple

Massachusetts:
  Samuel Adams
  John Adams
  Robert Treat Paine
  Elbridge Gerry

Column 6 (Cont.)
Rhode Island:
  Stephen Hopkins
  William Ellery

Connecticut:
  Roger Sherman
  Samuel Huntington
  William Williams
  Oliver Wolcott

Column 6 (Cont.)
New Hampshire:
  Matthew Thornton

Appendix 3: Constitution of the United States

Preamble

We the People of the United States, in Order to form a more perfect Union, establish Justice, insure domestic Tranquility, provide for the common defence, promote the general Welfare, and secure the Blessings of Liberty to ourselves and our Posterity, do ordain and establish this Constitution for the United States of America.

Article. I. - The Legislative Branch

Section 1 - The Legislature

All legislative Powers herein granted shall be vested in a Congress of the United States, which shall consist of a Senate and House of Representatives.

Section 2 - The House

The House of Representatives shall be composed of Members chosen every second Year by the People of the several States, and the Electors in each State shall have the Qualifications requisite for Electors of the most numerous Branch of the State Legislature.

No Person shall be a Representative who shall not have attained to the Age of twenty five Years, and been seven Years a Citizen of the United States, and who shall not, when elected, be an Inhabitant of that State in which he shall be chosen.

(Representatives and direct Taxes shall be apportioned among the several States which may be included within this Union, according to their respective Numbers, which shall be determined by adding to the whole Number of free Persons, including those bound to Service for a Term of Years, and excluding Indians not taxed, three fifths of all other Persons.) (The previous sentence in parentheses was modified by the 14th Amendment, section 2.) The actual Enumeration shall be made within three Years after the first Meeting of the Congress of the United States, and within every subsequent Term of ten Years, in such Manner as they shall by Law direct. The Number of Representatives shall not exceed one for every thirty Thousand, but each State shall have at Least one Representative; and until such enumeration shall be made, the State of New Hampshire shall be entitled to chuse three, Massachusetts eight, Rhode Island and Providence Plantations one, Connecticut five, New York six, New Jersey four, Pennsylvania eight, Delaware one, Maryland six, Virginia ten, North Carolina five, South Carolina five and Georgia three.

When vacancies happen in the Representation from any State, the Executive Authority thereof shall issue Writs of Election to fill such Vacancies.

The House of Representatives shall chuse their Speaker and other Officers; and shall have the sole Power of Impeachment.

562

Appendix 3: Constitution of the United States

Section 3 - The Senate

The Senate of the United States shall be composed of two Senators from each State, (chosen by the Legislature thereof,) (The preceding words in parentheses superseded by 17th Amendment, section 1.) for six Years; and each Senator shall have one Vote.

Immediately after they shall be assembled in Consequence of the first Election, they shall be divided as equally as may be into three Classes. The Seats of the Senators of the first Class shall be vacated at the Expiration of the second Year, of the second Class at the Expiration of the fourth Year, and of the third Class at the Expiration of the sixth Year, so that one third may be chosen every second Year; (and if Vacancies happen by Resignation, or otherwise, during the Recess of the Legislature of any State, the Executive thereof may make temporary Appointments until the next Meeting of the Legislature, which shall then fill such Vacancies.) (The preceding words in parentheses were superseded by the 17th Amendment, section 2.)

No person shall be a Senator who shall not have attained to the Age of thirty Years, and been nine Years a Citizen of the United States, and who shall not, when elected, be an Inhabitant of that State for which he shall be chosen.

The Vice President of the United States shall be President of the Senate, but shall have no Vote, unless they be equally divided.

The Senate shall chuse their other Officers, and also a President pro tempore, in the absence of the Vice President, or when he shall exercise the Office of President of the United States.

The Senate shall have the sole Power to try all Impeachments. When sitting for that Purpose, they shall be on Oath or Affirmation. When the President of the United States is tried, the Chief Justice shall preside: And no Person shall be convicted without the Concurrence of two thirds of the Members present.

Judgment in Cases of Impeachment shall not extend further than to removal from Office, and disqualification to hold and enjoy any Office of honor, Trust or Profit under the United States: but the Party convicted shall nevertheless be liable and subject to Indictment, Trial, Judgment and Punishment, according to Law.

Section 4 - Elections, Meetings

The Times, Places and Manner of holding Elections for Senators and Representatives, shall be prescribed in each State by the Legislature thereof; but the Congress may at any time by Law make or alter such Regulations, except as to the Place of Chusing Senators.

The Congress shall assemble at least once in every Year, and such Meeting shall (be on the first Monday in December,) (The preceding words in

Appendix 3: Constitution of the United States

parentheses were superseded by the 20th Amendment, section 2.) unless they shall by Law appoint a different Day.

Section 5 - Membership, Rules, Journals, Adjournment

Each House shall be the Judge of the Elections, Returns and Qualifications of its own Members, and a Majority of each shall constitute a Quorum to do Business; but a smaller number may adjourn from day to day, and may be authorized to compel the Attendance of absent Members, in such Manner, and under such Penalties as each House may provide.

Each House may determine the Rules of its Proceedings, punish its Members for disorderly Behavior, and, with the Concurrence of two-thirds, expel a Member.

Each House shall keep a Journal of its Proceedings, and from time to time publish the same, excepting such Parts as may in their Judgment require Secrecy; and the Yeas and Nays of the Members of either House on any question shall, at the Desire of one fifth of those Present, be entered on the Journal.

Neither House, during the Session of Congress, shall, without the Consent of the other, adjourn for more than three days, nor to any other Place than that in which the two Houses shall be sitting.

Section 6 - Compensation

(The Senators and Representatives shall receive a Compensation for their Services, to be ascertained by Law, and paid out of the Treasury of the United States.) (The preceding words in parentheses were modified by the 27th Amendment.) They shall in all Cases, except Treason, Felony and Breach of the Peace, be privileged from Arrest during their Attendance at the Session of their respective Houses, and in going to and returning from the same; and for any Speech or Debate in either House, they shall not be questioned in any other Place.

No Senator or Representative shall, during the Time for which he was elected, be appointed to any civil Office under the Authority of the United States which shall have been created, or the Emoluments whereof shall have been increased during such time; and no Person holding any Office under the United States, shall be a Member of either House during his Continuance in Office.

Section 7 - Revenue Bills, Legislative Process, Presidential Veto

All bills for raising Revenue shall originate in the House of Representatives; but the Senate may propose or concur with Amendments as on other Bills.

Every Bill which shall have passed the House of Representatives and the Senate, shall, before it become a Law, be presented to the President of the

Appendix 3: Constitution of the United States

United States; If he approve he shall sign it, but if not he shall return it, with his Objections to that House in which it shall have originated, who shall enter the Objections at large on their Journal, and proceed to reconsider it. If after such Reconsideration two thirds of that House shall agree to pass the Bill, it shall be sent, together with the Objections, to the other House, by which it shall likewise be reconsidered, and if approved by two thirds of that House, it shall become a Law. But in all such Cases the Votes of both Houses shall be determined by Yeas and Nays, and the Names of the Persons voting for and against the Bill shall be entered on the Journal of each House respectively. If any Bill shall not be returned by the President within ten Days (Sundays excepted) after it shall have been presented to him, the Same shall be a Law, in like Manner as if he had signed it, unless the Congress by their Adjournment prevent its Return, in which Case it shall not be a Law.

Every Order, Resolution, or Vote to which the Concurrence of the Senate and House of Representatives may be necessary (except on a question of Adjournment) shall be presented to the President of the United States; and before the Same shall take Effect, shall be approved by him, or being disapproved by him, shall be repassed by two thirds of the Senate and House of Representatives, according to the Rules and Limitations prescribed in the Case of a Bill.

Section 8 - Powers of Congress

The Congress shall have Power To lay and collect Taxes, Duties, Imposts and Excises, to pay the Debts and provide for the common Defence and general Welfare of the United States; but all Duties, Imposts and Excises shall be uniform throughout the United States;
To borrow money on the credit of the United States;
To regulate Commerce with foreign Nations, and among the several States, and with the Indian Tribes;
To establish an uniform Rule of Naturalization, and uniform Laws on the subject of Bankruptcies throughout the United States;
To coin Money, regulate the Value thereof, and of foreign Coin, and fix the Standard of Weights and Measures;
To provide for the Punishment of counterfeiting the Securities and current Coin of the United States;
To establish Post Offices and Post Roads;
To promote the Progress of Science and useful Arts, by securing for limited Times to Authors and Inventors the exclusive Right to their respective Writings and Discoveries;
To constitute Tribunals inferior to the supreme Court;
To define and punish Piracies and Felonies committed on the high Seas, and Offenses against the Law of Nations;
To declare War, grant Letters of Marque and Reprisal, and make Rules concerning Captures on Land and Water;
To raise and support Armies, but no Appropriation of Money to that Use shall be for a longer Term than two Years;
To provide and maintain a Navy;

Appendix 3: Constitution of the United States

To make Rules for the Government and Regulation of the land and naval Forces;

To provide for calling forth the Militia to execute the Laws of the Union, suppress Insurrections and repel Invasions;

To provide for organizing, arming, and disciplining the Militia, and for governing such Part of them as may be employed in the Service of the United States, reserving to the States respectively, the Appointment of the Officers, and the Authority of training the Militia according to the discipline prescribed by Congress;

To exercise exclusive Legislation in all Cases whatsoever, over such District (not exceeding ten Miles square) as may, by Cession of particular States, and the acceptance of Congress, become the Seat of the Government of the United States, and to exercise like Authority over all Places purchased by the Consent of the Legislature of the State in which the Same shall be, for the Erection of Forts, Magazines, Arsenals, dock-Yards, and other needful Buildings; And

To make all Laws which shall be necessary and proper for carrying into Execution the foregoing Powers, and all other Powers vested by this Constitution in the Government of the United States, or in any Department or Officer thereof.

Section 9 - Limits on Congress

The Migration or Importation of such Persons as any of the States now existing shall think proper to admit, shall not be prohibited by the Congress prior to the Year one thousand eight hundred and eight, but a tax or duty may be imposed on such Importation, not exceeding ten dollars for each Person.

The privilege of the Writ of Habeas Corpus shall not be suspended, unless when in Cases of Rebellion or Invasion the public Safety may require it.

No Bill of Attainder or ex post facto Law shall be passed.

(No capitation, or other direct, Tax shall be laid, unless in Proportion to the Census or Enumeration herein before directed to be taken.) (Section in parentheses clarified by the 16th Amendment.)

No Tax or Duty shall be laid on Articles exported from any State.

No Preference shall be given by any Regulation of Commerce or Revenue to the Ports of one State over those of another: nor shall Vessels bound to, or from, one State, be obliged to enter, clear, or pay Duties in another.

No Money shall be drawn from the Treasury, but in Consequence of Appropriations made by Law; and a regular Statement and Account of the Receipts and Expenditures of all public Money shall be published from time to time.

No Title of Nobility shall be granted by the United States: And no Person holding any Office of Profit or Trust under them, shall, without the Consent of the Congress, accept of any present, Emolument, Office, or Title, of any kind whatever, from any King, Prince or foreign State.

Appendix 3: Constitution of the United States

Section 10 - Powers prohibited of States

No State shall enter into any Treaty, Alliance, or Confederation; grant Letters of Marque and Reprisal; coin Money; emit Bills of Credit; make any Thing but gold and silver Coin a Tender in Payment of Debts; pass any Bill of Attainder, ex post facto Law, or Law impairing the Obligation of Contracts, or grant any Title of Nobility.

No State shall, without the Consent of the Congress, lay any Imposts or Duties on Imports or Exports, except what may be absolutely necessary for executing it's inspection Laws: and the net Produce of all Duties and Imposts, laid by any State on Imports or Exports, shall be for the Use of the Treasury of the United States; and all such Laws shall be subject to the Revision and Controul of the Congress.

No State shall, without the Consent of Congress, lay any duty of Tonnage, keep Troops, or Ships of War in time of Peace, enter into any Agreement or Compact with another State, or with a foreign Power, or engage in War, unless actually invaded, or in such imminent Danger as will not admit of delay.

Article. II. - The Executive Branch

Section 1 - The President

The executive Power shall be vested in a President of the United States of America. He shall hold his Office during the Term of four Years, and, together with the Vice-President chosen for the same Term, be elected, as follows:
Each State shall appoint, in such Manner as the Legislature thereof may direct, a Number of Electors, equal to the whole Number of Senators and Representatives to which the State may be entitled in the Congress: but no Senator or Representative, or Person holding an Office of Trust or Profit under the United States, shall be appointed an Elector.

(The Electors shall meet in their respective States, and vote by Ballot for two persons, of whom one at least shall not lie an Inhabitant of the same State with themselves. And they shall make a List of all the Persons voted for, and of the Number of Votes for each; which List they shall sign and certify, and transmit sealed to the Seat of the Government of the United States, directed to the President of the Senate. The President of the Senate shall, in the Presence of the Senate and House of Representatives, open all the Certificates, and the Votes shall then be counted. The Person having the greatest Number of Votes shall be the President, if such Number be a Majority of the whole Number of Electors appointed; and if there be more than one who have such Majority, and have an equal Number of Votes, then the House of Representatives shall immediately chuse by Ballot one of them for President; and if no Person have a Majority, then from the five highest on the List the said House shall in like Manner chuse the President. But in chusing the President, the Votes shall be taken by States, the Representation from each State having one Vote; a

Appendix 3: Constitution of the United States

quorum for this Purpose shall consist of a Member or Members from two-thirds of the States, and a Majority of all the States shall be necessary to a Choice. In every Case, after the Choice of the President, the Person having the greatest Number of Votes of the Electors shall be the Vice President. But if there should remain two or more who have equal Votes, the Senate shall chuse from them by Ballot the Vice-President.) (This clause in parentheses was superseded by the 12th Amendment.)

The Congress may determine the Time of chusing the Electors, and the Day on which they shall give their Votes; which Day shall be the same throughout the United States.

No person except a natural born Citizen, or a Citizen of the United States, at the time of the Adoption of this Constitution, shall be eligible to the Office of President; neither shall any Person be eligible to that Office who shall not have attained to the Age of thirty-five Years, and been fourteen Years a Resident within the United States.

(In Case of the Removal of the President from Office, or of his Death, Resignation, or Inability to discharge the Powers and Duties of the said Office, the same shall devolve on the Vice President, and the Congress may by Law provide for the Case of Removal, Death, Resignation or Inability, both of the President and Vice President, declaring what Officer shall then act as President, and such Officer shall act accordingly, until the Disability be removed, or a President shall be elected.) (This clause in parentheses has been modified by the 20th and 25th Amendments.)

The President shall, at stated Times, receive for his Services, a Compensation, which shall neither be increased nor diminished during the Period for which he shall have been elected, and he shall not receive within that Period any other Emolument from the United States, or any of them.
Before he enter on the Execution of his Office, he shall take the following Oath or Affirmation:

"I do solemnly swear (or affirm) that I will faithfully execute the Office of President of the United States, and will to the best of my Ability, preserve, protect and defend the Constitution of the United States."

Section 2 - Civilian Power over Military, Cabinet, Pardon Power, Appointments

The President shall be Commander in Chief of the Army and Navy of the United States, and of the Militia of the several States, when called into the actual Service of the United States; he may require the Opinion, in writing, of the principal Officer in each of the executive Departments, upon any subject relating to the Duties of their respective Offices, and he shall have Power to Grant Reprieves and Pardons for Offenses against the United States, except in Cases of Impeachment.

Appendix 3: Constitution of the United States

He shall have Power, by and with the Advice and Consent of the Senate, to make Treaties, provided two thirds of the Senators present concur; and he shall nominate, and by and with the Advice and Consent of the Senate, shall appoint Ambassadors, other public Ministers and Consuls, Judges of the supreme Court, and all other Officers of the United States, whose Appointments are not herein otherwise provided for, and which shall be established by Law: but the Congress may by Law vest the Appointment of such inferior Officers, as they think proper, in the President alone, in the Courts of Law, or in the Heads of Departments.

The President shall have Power to fill up all Vacancies that may happen during the Recess of the Senate, by granting Commissions which shall expire at the End of their next Session.

Section 3 - State of the Union, Convening Congress

He shall from time to time give to the Congress Information of the State of the Union, and recommend to their Consideration such Measures as he shall judge necessary and expedient; he may, on extraordinary Occasions, convene both Houses, or either of them, and in Case of Disagreement between them, with Respect to the Time of Adjournment, he may adjourn them to such Time as he shall think proper; he shall receive Ambassadors and other public Ministers; he shall take Care that the Laws be faithfully executed, and shall Commission all the Officers of the United States.

Section 4 - Disqualification

The President, Vice President and all civil Officers of the United States, shall be removed from Office on Impeachment for, and Conviction of, Treason, Bribery, or other high Crimes and Misdemeanors.

Article III. - The Judicial Branch

Section 1 - Judicial powers

The judicial Power of the United States, shall be vested in one supreme Court, and in such inferior Courts as the Congress may from time to time ordain and establish. The Judges, both of the supreme and inferior Courts, shall hold their Offices during good Behavior, and shall, at stated Times, receive for their Services a Compensation which shall not be diminished during their Continuance in Office.

Section 2 - Trial by Jury, Original Jurisdiction, Jury Trials

(The judicial Power shall extend to all Cases, in Law and Equity, arising under this Constitution, the Laws of the United States, and Treaties made, or which shall be made, under their Authority; to all Cases affecting Ambassadors, other public Ministers and Consuls; to all Cases of admiralty and maritime Jurisdiction; to Controversies to which the United States shall be a Party; to Controversies between two or more States; between a State and

Appendix 3: Constitution of the United States

Citizens of another State; between Citizens of different States; between Citizens of the same State claiming Lands under Grants of different States, and between a State, or the Citizens thereof, and foreign States, Citizens or Subjects.) (This section in parentheses is modified by the 11th Amendment.)

In all Cases affecting Ambassadors, other public Ministers and Consuls, and those in which a State shall be Party, the supreme Court shall have original Jurisdiction. In all the other Cases before mentioned, the supreme Court shall have appellate Jurisdiction, both as to Law and Fact, with such Exceptions, and under such Regulations as the Congress shall make.

The Trial of all Crimes, except in Cases of Impeachment, shall be by Jury; and such Trial shall be held in the State where the said Crimes shall have been committed; but when not committed within any State, the Trial shall be at such Place or Places as the Congress may by Law have directed.

Section 3 - Treason

Treason against the United States, shall consist only in levying War against them, or in adhering to their Enemies, giving them Aid and Comfort. No Person shall be convicted of Treason unless on the Testimony of two Witnesses to the same overt Act, or on Confession in open Court.

The Congress shall have power to declare the Punishment of Treason, but no Attainder of Treason shall work Corruption of Blood, or Forfeiture except during the Life of the Person attainted.

Article. IV. - The States

Section 1 - Each State to Honor all others

Full Faith and Credit shall be given in each State to the public Acts, Records, and judicial Proceedings of every other State. And the Congress may by general Laws prescribe the Manner in which such Acts, Records and Proceedings shall be proved, and the Effect thereof.

Section 2 - State citizens, Extradition

The Citizens of each State shall be entitled to all Privileges and Immunities of Citizens in the several States.

A Person charged in any State with Treason, Felony, or other Crime, who shall flee from Justice, and be found in another State, shall on demand of the executive Authority of the State from which he fled, be delivered up, to be removed to the State having Jurisdiction of the Crime.

(No Person held to Service or Labour in one State, under the Laws thereof, escaping into another, shall, in Consequence of any Law or Regulation therein, be discharged from such Service or Labour, But shall be delivered up

570

Appendix 3: Constitution of the United States

on Claim of the Party to whom such Service or Labour may be due.) (This clause in parentheses is superseded by the 13th Amendment.)

Section 3 - New States

New States may be admitted by the Congress into this Union; but no new States shall be formed or erected within the Jurisdiction of any other State; nor any State be formed by the Junction of two or more States, or parts of States, without the Consent of the Legislatures of the States concerned as well as of the Congress.

The Congress shall have Power to dispose of and make all needful Rules and Regulations respecting the Territory or other Property belonging to the United States; and nothing in this Constitution shall be so construed as to Prejudice any Claims of the United States, or of any particular State.

Section 4 - Republican government

The United States shall guarantee to every State in this Union a Republican Form of Government, and shall protect each of them against Invasion; and on Application of the Legislature, or of the Executive (when the Legislature cannot be convened) against domestic Violence.

Article. V. - Amendment

The Congress, whenever two thirds of both Houses shall deem it necessary, shall propose Amendments to this Constitution, or, on the Application of the Legislatures of two thirds of the several States, shall call a Convention for proposing Amendments, which, in either Case, shall be valid to all Intents and Purposes, as part of this Constitution, when ratified by the Legislatures of three fourths of the several States, or by Conventions in three fourths thereof, as the one or the other Mode of Ratification may be proposed by the Congress; Provided that no Amendment which may be made prior to the Year One thousand eight hundred and eight shall in any Manner affect the first and fourth Clauses in the Ninth Section of the first Article; and that no State, without its Consent, shall be deprived of its equal Suffrage in the Senate.

Article. VI. - Debts, Supremacy, Oaths

All Debts contracted and Engagements entered into, before the Adoption of this Constitution, shall be as valid against the United States under this Constitution, as under the Confederation.

This Constitution, and the Laws of the United States which shall be made in Pursuance thereof; and all Treaties made, or which shall be made, under the Authority of the United States, shall be the supreme Law of the Land; and the Judges in every State shall be bound thereby, any Thing in the Constitution or Laws of any State to the Contrary notwithstanding.

Appendix 3: Constitution of the United States

The Senators and Representatives before mentioned, and the Members of the several State Legislatures, and all executive and judicial Officers, both of the United States and of the several States, shall be bound by Oath or Affirmation, to support this Constitution; but no religious Test shall ever be required as a Qualification to any Office or public Trust under the United States.

Article. VII. - Ratification

The Ratification of the Conventions of nine States, shall be sufficient for the Establishment of this Constitution between the States so ratifying the Same.
Done in Convention by the Unanimous Consent of the States present the Seventeenth Day of September in the Year of our Lord one thousand seven hundred and Eighty seven and of the Independence of the United States of America the Twelfth. In Witness whereof We have hereunto subscribed our Names.

Go Washington - President and deputy from Virginia
New Hampshire - John Langdon, Nicholas Gilman
Massachusetts - Nathaniel Gorham, Rufus King
Connecticut - Wm Saml Johnson, Roger Sherman
New York - Alexander Hamilton
New Jersey - Wil Livingston, David Brearley, Wm Paterson, Jona. Dayton
Pensylvania - B Franklin, Thomas Mifflin, Robt Morris, Geo. Clymer, Thos FitzSimons, Jared Ingersoll, James Wilson, Gouv Morris
Delaware - Geo. Read, Gunning Bedford jun, John Dickinson, Richard Bassett, Jaco. Broom
Maryland - James McHenry, Dan of St Tho Jenifer, Danl Carroll
Virginia - John Blair, James Madison Jr.
North Carolina - Wm Blount, Richd Dobbs Spaight, Hu Williamson
South Carolina - J. Rutledge, Charles Cotesworth Pinckney, Charles Pinckney, Pierce Butler
Georgia - William Few, Abr Baldwin
Attest: William Jackson, Secretary

The Amendments

The following are the Amendments to the Constitution. The first ten Amendments collectively are commonly known as the Bill of Rights.

Amendment 1 - Freedom of Religion, Press, Expression. Ratified 12/15/1791.

Congress shall make no law respecting an establishment of religion, or prohibiting the free exercise thereof; or abridging the freedom of speech, or of the press; or the right of the people peaceably to assemble, and to petition the Government for a redress of grievances.

Amendment 2 - Right to Bear Arms. Ratified 12/15/1791.

A well regulated Militia, being necessary to the security of a free State, the right of the people to keep and bear Arms, shall not be infringed.

Appendix 3: Constitution of the United States

Amendment 3 - Quartering of Soldiers. Ratified 12/15/1791.

No Soldier shall, in time of peace be quartered in any house, without the consent of the Owner, nor in time of war, but in a manner to be prescribed by law.

Amendment 4 - Search and Seizure. Ratified 12/15/1791.

The right of the people to be secure in their persons, houses, papers, and effects, against unreasonable searches and seizures, shall not be violated, and no Warrants shall issue, but upon probable cause, supported by Oath or affirmation, and particularly describing the place to be searched, and the persons or things to be seized.

Amendment 5 - Trial and Punishment, Compensation for Takings. Ratified 12/15/1791.

No person shall be held to answer for a capital, or otherwise infamous crime, unless on a presentment or indictment of a Grand Jury, except in cases arising in the land or naval forces, or in the Militia, when in actual service in time of War or public danger; nor shall any person be subject for the same offense to be twice put in jeopardy of life or limb; nor shall be compelled in any criminal case to be a witness against himself, nor be deprived of life, liberty, or property, without due process of law; nor shall private property be taken for public use, without just compensation.

Amendment 6 - Right to Speedy Trial, Confrontation of Witnesses. Ratified 12/15/1791.

In all criminal prosecutions, the accused shall enjoy the right to a speedy and public trial, by an impartial jury of the State and district wherein the crime shall have been committed, which district shall have been previously ascertained by law, and to be informed of the nature and cause of the accusation; to be confronted with the witnesses against him; to have compulsory process for obtaining witnesses in his favor, and to have the Assistance of Counsel for his defence.

Amendment 7 - Trial by Jury in Civil Cases. Ratified 12/15/1791.

In Suits at common law, where the value in controversy shall exceed twenty dollars, the right of trial by jury shall be preserved, and no fact tried by a jury, shall be otherwise re- examined in any Court of the United States, than according to the rules of the common law.

Amendment 8 - Cruel and Unusual Punishment. Ratified 12/15/1791.

Excessive bail shall not be required, nor excessive fines imposed, nor cruel and unusual punishments inflicted.

Appendix 3: Constitution of the United States

Amendment 9 - Construction of Constitution. Ratified 12/15/1791.

The enumeration in the Constitution, of certain rights, shall not be construed to deny or disparage others retained by the people.

Amendment 10 - Powers of the States and People. Ratified 12/15/1791.

The powers not delegated to the United States by the Constitution, nor prohibited by it to the States, are reserved to the States respectively, or to the people.

Amendment 11 - Judicial Limits. Ratified 2/7/1795.

The Judicial power of the United States shall not be construed to extend to any suit in law or equity, commenced or prosecuted against one of the United States by Citizens of another State, or by Citizens or Subjects of any Foreign State.

Amendment 12 - Choosing the President, Vice-President. Ratified 6/15/1804.

The Electors shall meet in their respective states, and vote by ballot for President and Vice-President, one of whom, at least, shall not be an inhabitant of the same state with themselves; they shall name in their ballots the person voted for as President, and in distinct ballots the person voted for as Vice-President, and they shall make distinct lists of all persons voted for as President, and of all persons voted for as Vice-President and of the number of votes for each, which lists they shall sign and certify, and transmit sealed to the seat of the government of the United States, directed to the President of the Senate;
The President of the Senate shall, in the presence of the Senate and House of Representatives, open all the certificates and the votes shall then be counted;
The person having the greatest Number of votes for President, shall be the President, if such number be a majority of the whole number of Electors appointed; and if no person have such majority, then from the persons having the highest numbers not exceeding three on the list of those voted for as President, the House of Representatives shall choose immediately, by ballot, the President. But in choosing the President, the votes shall be taken by states, the representation from each state having one vote; a quorum for this purpose shall consist of a member or members from two-thirds of the states, and a majority of all the states shall be necessary to a choice. And if the House of Representatives shall not choose a President whenever the right of choice shall devolve upon them, before the fourth day of March next following, then the Vice-President shall act as President, as in the case of the death or other constitutional disability of the President.

The person having the greatest number of votes as Vice-President, shall be the Vice- President, if such number be a majority of the whole number of Electors appointed, and if no person have a majority, then from the two highest numbers on the list, the Senate shall choose the Vice-President; a quorum for the purpose shall consist of two-thirds of the whole number of Senators, and a

574

majority of the whole number shall be necessary to a choice. But no person constitutionally ineligible to the office of President shall be eligible to that of Vice-President of the United States.

Amendment 13 - Slavery Abolished. Ratified 12/6/1865.

1. Neither slavery nor involuntary servitude, except as a punishment for crime whereof the party shall have been duly convicted, shall exist within the United States, or any place subject to their jurisdiction.
2. Congress shall have power to enforce this article by appropriate legislation.

Amendment 14 - Citizenship Rights. Ratified 7/9/1868.

1. All persons born or naturalized in the United States, and subject to the jurisdiction thereof, are citizens of the United States and of the State wherein they reside. No State shall make or enforce any law which shall abridge the privileges or immunities of citizens of the United States; nor shall any State deprive any person of life, liberty, or property, without due process of law; nor deny to any person within its jurisdiction the equal protection of the laws.
2. Representatives shall be apportioned among the several States according to their respective numbers, counting the whole number of persons in each State, excluding Indians not taxed. But when the right to vote at any election for the choice of electors for President and Vice-President of the United States, Representatives in Congress, the Executive and Judicial officers of a State, or the members of the Legislature thereof, is denied to any of the male inhabitants of such State, being twenty-one years of age, and citizens of the United States, or in any way abridged, except for participation in rebellion, or other crime, the basis of representation therein shall be reduced in the proportion which the number of such male citizens shall bear to the whole number of male citizens twenty-one years of age in such State.
3. No person shall be a Senator or Representative in Congress, or elector of President and Vice-President, or hold any office, civil or military, under the United States, or under any State, who, having previously taken an oath, as a member of Congress, or as an officer of the United States, or as a member of any State legislature, or as an executive or judicial officer of any State, to support the Constitution of the United States, shall have engaged in insurrection or rebellion against the same, or given aid or comfort to the enemies thereof. But Congress may by a vote of two-thirds of each House, remove such disability.
4. The validity of the public debt of the United States, authorized by law, including debts incurred for payment of pensions and bounties for services in suppressing insurrection or rebellion, shall not be questioned. But neither the United States nor any State shall assume or pay any debt or obligation incurred in aid of insurrection or rebellion against the United States, or any claim for the loss or emancipation of any slave; but all such debts, obligations and claims shall be held illegal and void.
5. The Congress shall have power to enforce, by appropriate legislation, the provisions of this article.

Appendix 3: Constitution of the United States

Amendment 15 - Race No Bar to Vote. Ratified 2/3/1870.

1. The right of citizens of the United States to vote shall not be denied or abridged by the United States or by any State on account of race, color, or previous condition of servitude.
2. The Congress shall have power to enforce this article by appropriate legislation.

Amendment 16 - Status of Income Tax Clarified. Ratified 2/3/1913.

The Congress shall have power to lay and collect taxes on incomes, from whatever source derived, without apportionment among the several States, and without regard to any census or enumeration.

Amendment 17 - Senators Elected by Popular Vote. Ratified 4/8/1913.

The Senate of the United States shall be composed of two Senators from each State, elected by the people thereof, for six years; and each Senator shall have one vote. The electors in each State shall have the qualifications requisite for electors of the most numerous branch of the State legislatures.

When vacancies happen in the representation of any State in the Senate, the executive authority of such State shall issue writs of election to fill such vacancies: Provided, That the legislature of any State may empower the executive thereof to make temporary appointments until the people fill the vacancies by election as the legislature may direct.

This amendment shall not be so construed as to affect the election or term of any Senator chosen before it becomes valid as part of the Constitution.

Amendment 18 - Liquor Abolished. Ratified 1/16/1919. Repealed by Amendment 21, 12/5/1933.

1. After one year from the ratification of this article the manufacture, sale, or transportation of intoxicating liquors within, the importation thereof into, or the exportation thereof from the United States and all territory subject to the jurisdiction thereof for beverage purposes is hereby prohibited.
2. The Congress and the several States shall have concurrent power to enforce this article by appropriate legislation.
3. This article shall be inoperative unless it shall have been ratified as an amendment to the Constitution by the legislatures of the several States, as provided in the Constitution, within seven years from the date of the submission hereof to the States by the Congress.

Amendment 19 - Women's Suffrage. Ratified 8/18/1920.

The right of citizens of the United States to vote shall not be denied or abridged by the United States or by any State on account of sex.
Congress shall have power to enforce this article by appropriate legislation.

Appendix 3: Constitution of the United States

Amendment 20 - Presidential, Congressional Terms. Ratified 1/23/1933.

1. The terms of the President and Vice President shall end at noon on the 20th day of January, and the terms of Senators and Representatives at noon on the 3d day of January, of the years in which such terms would have ended if this article had not been ratified; and the terms of their successors shall then begin.
2. The Congress shall assemble at least once in every year, and such meeting shall begin at noon on the 3d day of January, unless they shall by law appoint a different day.
3. If, at the time fixed for the beginning of the term of the President, the President elect shall have died, the Vice President elect shall become President. If a President shall not have been chosen before the time fixed for the beginning of his term, or if the President elect shall have failed to qualify, then the Vice President elect shall act as President until a President shall have qualified; and the Congress may by law provide for the case wherein neither a President elect nor a Vice President elect shall have qualified, declaring who shall then act as President, or the manner in which one who is to act shall be selected, and such person shall act accordingly until a President or Vice President shall have qualified.
4. The Congress may by law provide for the case of the death of any of the persons from whom the House of Representatives may choose a President whenever the right of choice shall have devolved upon them, and for the case of the death of any of the persons from whom the Senate may choose a Vice President whenever the right of choice shall have devolved upon them.
5. Sections 1 and 2 shall take effect on the 15th day of October following the ratification of this article.
6. This article shall be inoperative unless it shall have been ratified as an amendment to the Constitution by the legislatures of three-fourths of the several States within seven years from the date of its submission.

Amendment 21 - Amendment 18 Repealed. Ratified 12/5/1933.

1. The eighteenth article of amendment to the Constitution of the United States is hereby repealed.
2. The transportation or importation into any State, Territory, or possession of the United States for delivery or use therein of intoxicating liquors, in violation of the laws thereof, is hereby prohibited.
3. The article shall be inoperative unless it shall have been ratified as an amendment to the Constitution by conventions in the several States, as provided in the Constitution, within seven years from the date of the submission hereof to the States by the Congress.

Amendment 22 - Presidential Term Limits. Ratified 2/27/1951.

1. No person shall be elected to the office of the President more than twice, and no person who has held the office of President, or acted as President, for more than two years of a term to which some other person was elected President shall be elected to the office of the President more than once. But this Article shall not apply to any person holding the office of President, when this Article was proposed by the Congress, and shall not prevent any person

Appendix 3: Constitution of the United States

who may be holding the office of President, or acting as President, during the term within which this Article becomes operative from holding the office of President or acting as President during the remainder of such term.

2. This article shall be inoperative unless it shall have been ratified as an amendment to the Constitution by the legislatures of three-fourths of the several States within seven years from the date of its submission to the States by the Congress.

Amendment 23 - Presidential Vote for District of Columbia. Ratified 3/29/1961.

1. The District constituting the seat of Government of the United States shall appoint in such manner as the Congress may direct: A number of electors of President and Vice President equal to the whole number of Senators and Representatives in Congress to which the District would be entitled if it were a State, but in no event more than the least populous State; they shall be in addition to those appointed by the States, but they shall be considered, for the purposes of the election of President and Vice President, to be electors appointed by a State; and they shall meet in the District and perform such duties as provided by the twelfth article of amendment.

2. The Congress shall have power to enforce this article by appropriate legislation.

Amendment 24 - Poll Tax Barred. Ratified 1/23/1964.

1. The right of citizens of the United States to vote in any primary or other election for President or Vice President, for electors for President or Vice President, or for Senator or

Representative in Congress, shall not be denied or abridged by the United States or any State by reason of failure to pay any poll tax or other tax.

2. The Congress shall have power to enforce this article by appropriate legislation.

Amendment 25 - Presidential Disability and Succession. Ratified 2/10/1967.

1. In case of the removal of the President from office or of his death or resignation, the Vice President shall become President.

2. Whenever there is a vacancy in the office of the Vice President, the President shall nominate a Vice President who shall take office upon confirmation by a majority vote of both Houses of Congress.

3. Whenever the President transmits to the President pro tempore of the Senate and the Speaker of the House of Representatives his written declaration that he is unable to discharge the powers and duties of his office, and until he transmits to them a written declaration to the contrary, such powers and duties shall be discharged by the Vice President as Acting President.

4. Whenever the Vice President and a majority of either the principal officers of the executive departments or of such other body as Congress may by law provide, transmit to the President pro tempore of the Senate and the Speaker of the House of Representatives their written declaration that the President is

Appendix 3: Constitution of the United States

unable to discharge the powers and duties of his office, the Vice President shall immediately assume the powers and duties of the office as Acting President.

Thereafter, when the President transmits to the President pro tempore of the Senate and the Speaker of the House of Representatives his written declaration that no inability exists, he shall resume the powers and duties of his office unless the Vice President and a majority of either the principal officers of the executive department or of such other body as Congress may by law provide, transmit within four days to the President pro tempore of the Senate and the Speaker of the House of Representatives their written declaration that the President is unable to discharge the powers and duties of his office. Thereupon Congress shall decide the issue, assembling within forty eight hours for that purpose if not in session. If the Congress, within twenty one days after receipt of the latter written declaration, or, if Congress is not in session, within twenty one days after Congress is required to assemble, determines by two thirds vote of both Houses that the President is unable to discharge the powers and duties of his office, the Vice President shall continue to discharge the same as Acting President; otherwise, the President shall resume the powers and duties of his office.

Amendment 26 - Voting Age Set to 18 Years. Ratified 7/1/1971.

1. The right of citizens of the United States, who are eighteen years of age or older, to vote shall not be denied or abridged by the United States or by any State on account of age.
2. The Congress shall have power to enforce this article by appropriate legislation.

Amendment 27 - Limiting Congressional Pay Increases. Ratified 5/7/1992.

No law, varying the compensation for the services of the Senators and Representatives, shall take effect, until an election of Representatives shall have intervened.

Appendix 4: The Code of Conduct

Article I: I am an American, fighting in the armed forces which guard my country and our way of life. I am prepared to give my life in their defense.

Article II: I will never surrender of my own free will. If in command I will never surrender the members of my command while they still have the means to resist.

Article III: If I am captured, I will continue to resist by all means available. I will make every effort to escape and aid others to escape. I will accept neither parole nor special favors from the enemy.

Article IV: If I become a prisoner of war, I will keep faith with my fellow prisoners. I will give no information nor take part in any action which might be harmful to my comrades. If I am senior, I will take command. If not, I will obey the lawful orders of those appointed over me and will back them up in every way.

Article V: When questioned, should I become a prisoner of war, I am required to give name, rank, service, number, and date of birth. I will evade answering further questions to the utmost of my ability. I will make no oral or written statements disloyal to my country and its allies or harmful to their cause.

Article VI: I will never forget that I am an American, responsible for my actions, and dedicated to the principles which made my country free. I will trust in my God and in the United States of America.

Glossary of Christian Quotations

Assurance

"When life has been well spent; when there is a conscience without reproach; when there is faith in the Saviour; when there is a well-founded hope of heaven, there can be nothing that should disquiet us." – Albert Barnes

"There is nothing in the world that works such satanic, profound, God-defiant pride as false assurance; nothing works such utter humility, or brings to such utter self-emptiness, as the child-like spirit of true assurance." – A.A. Hodge

"Assurance encourages us in our combat; it delivers us not from it." – John Owen

"Faith may be strongest, when assurance is weakest. The woman of Canaan had no assurance, but she had glorious faith." – Thomas Watson

Bible

"The Bible was composed in such a way that as beginners mature, its meaning grows with them." – Augustine

"The Bible is very easy to understand. But we Christians are a bunch of scheming swindlers. We pretend to be unable to understand it because we know very well that the minute we understand, we are obliged to act accordingly."— Søren Kierkegaard

"The primary purpose of reading the Bible is not to know the Bible but to know God."— James Merritt

"In the divine Scriptures, there are shallows and there are deeps; shallows where the lamb may wade, and deeps where the elephant may swim." – John Owen

"Within the covers of the Bible are the answers for all the problems men face."— Ronald Reagan

"A Bible that's falling apart usually belongs to someone who isn't." – C.H. Spurgeon

"Nobody ever outgrows Scripture; the Book widens and deepens with our years." – C.H. Spurgeon

Glossary of Christian Quotations

Christ

The peace of Jesus is the cross. But the cross is the sword God wields on earth." – Dietrich Bonhoeffer

"When Christ calls a man, he bids him come and die." – Dietrich Bonhoeffer

"Jesus was not merely a messenger of revelation from God (like all the other prophets), but was himself the source of revelation from God. Rather than saying, as all the Old Testament prophets did, "Thus says the LORD," Jesus could begin divinely authoritative teaching with the amazing statement, "But I say unto you" (Matt. 5:22; et al.)." – Wayne Grudem

"In the total expanse of human life there is not a single square inch of which the Christ, who alone is sovereign, does not declare, 'That is mine!'" – Abraham Kuyper

"All heroes are shadows of Christ" – John Piper

"Christ is the most cheap physician, he takes no fee. He desires us to bring nothing to him but broken hearts; and when he has cured us he desires us to bestow nothing on him but our love." – Thomas Watson

"Jesus was God and man in one person, that God and man might be happy together again." – George Whitefield

Christian Unity

"In essentials unity, in non-essentials liberty, and in all things charity." – Augustine

"Though the terror upon our adversary would be greater if we all were more uniform, we follow the same colors. And though not clothed alike, and differing in things less significant, against the common enemy, Christians march as soldiers all under the same Captain." – Jeremiah Burroughs

Church

"Christianity without discipleship is always Christianity without Christ." – Dietrich Bonhoeffer

Glossary of Christian Quotations

"The purpose of the church is to make the invisible kingdom visible through faithful Christian living and witness-bearing." – J.I. Packer

"The day we find the perfect church, it becomes imperfect the moment we join it." – C.H. Spurgeon

"That very church which the world likes best is sure to be that which God abhors." – C.H. Spurgeon

"God's Church is the apple of his eye. The eyelid of his providence daily covers and defends it." – Thomas Watson

"Holy solitaries' is a phrase no more consistent with the Gospel than holy adulterers. The Gospel of Christ knows no religion but social; no holiness, but social holiness." – John Wesley

"Mere heathen morality, and not Jesus Christ, is preached in most of our churches." – George Whitefield

Conscience

"The conscience is a man's judgment of himself according to God's judgment of him." – William Ames

"It is when a people forget God that tyrants forge their chains. A vitiated state of morals, a corrupted public conscience, is incompatible with freedom." – Patrick Henry

Discipline

"No voluntary act of spiritual discipline is ever to become an occasion for self-promotion. Otherwise, any value to the act is utterly vitiated." – D.A. Carson

"If you really want to be a rebel get a job, cut your grass, read your Bible, and shut up. Because no one is doing that."— Mark Driscoll

"There is no purpose in having a basis or a confession of faith unless it is applied. So we must assert the element of discipline as being essential to the true life of the church. And what calls itself a church which does not believe in discipline, and does not use it and apply it, is therefore not a true church." – David M. Lloyd-Jones

"We must face the fact that many today are notoriously careless in their living. This attitude finds its way into the church. We have liberty, we have money, we live in comparative luxury. As a result, discipline practically has disappeared. What would a violin solo sound like if the strings on the musician's instrument were all hanging loose, not stretched tight, not 'disciplined'?" – A.W. Tozer

"God's rod is a pencil to draw Christ's image more distinctly upon us." – Thomas Watson

Death

"He whose head is in heaven need not fear to put his feet into the grave." – Matthew Henry

"Death is like my car. It takes me where I want to go." – John Piper

"We have brought nothing into the world, so we cannot take anything out of it either.' There are no U-Hauls behind hearses." – John Piper

"Take care of your life and the Lord will take care of your death." – George Whitefield

Evangelism

"Expect great things from God, attempt great things for God." – William Carey

"If sinners be damned, at least let them leap to Hell over our bodies. If they will perish, let them perish with our arms about their knees. Let no one go there unwarned and unprayed for." – C.H. Spurgeon

"God forbid that I should travel with anybody a quarter of an hour without speaking of Christ to them." – George Whitefield

Faith

"He that has doctrinal knowledge and speculation only, without affection, never is engaged in the business of religion." – Jonathan Edwards

"We are saved by faith alone, but the faith that saves is never alone." – Martin Luther

"By faith we began, by hope we continue, and by revelation we shall obtain the whole." – Martin Luther

Glossary of Christian Quotations

"No man shall ever behold the glory of Christ by sight hereafter who does not in some measure behold it here by faith." – John Owen

"Your faith will not fail while God sustains it; you are not strong enough to fall away while God is resolved to hold you." – J.I. Packer

"A little faith will bring your soul to heaven; a great faith will bring heaven to your soul." – C.H. Spurgeon

"Faith goes up the stairs that love has built and looks out the windows which hope has opened." – C.H. Spurgeon

"The Christian should work as if all depended upon him, and pray as if it all depended upon God." – C.H. Spurgeon

"Faith knows there are no impossibilities with God, and will trust his heart, when it cannot trace his hand." – Thomas Watson

"Faith is the key that unlocks the cabinet of God's promises, and empties out their treasures into the soul." – Thomas Watson

"Fight the good fight of faith, and God will give you spiritual mercies." – George Whitefield

Fear

"Without the fear of God, men do not even observe justice and charity among themselves." – John Calvin

"We fear men so much, because we fear God so little." – William Gurnall

God

"O God, who is ever at work and ever at rest. May I be ever at work and ever at rest." – Augustine

"To deny there is a God, is a sort of atheism that is not to be found in hell." – Thomas Brooks

"A man can no more diminish God's glory by refusing to worship Him than a lunatic can put out the sun by scribbling the word 'darkness' on the walls of his cell." – C.S. Lewis.

Glossary of Christian Quotations

"We want not so much a Father but a grandfather in heaven, a God who said of anything we happened to like doing, 'What does it matter so long as they are contented?'" – C.S. Lewis.

"Happy the soul that has been awed by a view of God's majesty." – A.W. Pink

"God is most glorified in us when we are most satisfied in Him." – John Piper

Gospel

"Saying 'Preach the Gospel Daily, use words if necessary' is like saying 'Feed the hungry, use food if necessary.'"- Ligon Duncan

"The gospel cannot be truly preached without offense and tumult." – Martin Luther

"God writes the gospel not in the Bible alone, but on trees and flowers and clouds and stars." – Martin Luther

"If the Word does not dwell with power in us it will not pass with power from us." – John Owen

Grace

"There is no inconsistency when God raises up those who have fallen prostrate." – John Calvin

"Grace is the seed of glory, the dawning of glory in the heart, and therefore grace is the earnest of the future inheritance." – Jonathan Edwards

"God creates out of nothing. Wonderful you say. Yes, to be sure, but he does what is still more wonderful: he makes saints out of sinners." – Søren Kierkegaard

"To suppose that whatever God requires of us that we have power of ourselves to do, is to make the cross and grace of Jesus Christ of none effect." – John Owen

"Grace is the life of God in the soul of man." – Henry Scougal

"God grant that I may never live to be useless!" – John Wesley

Glossary of Christian Quotations

"What! Get to heaven on your own strength? Why, you might as well try to climb to the moon on a rope of sand!" – George Whitefield

"Lord, help me to begin to begin." – George Whitefield

Heaven

"God destines us for an end beyond the grasp of reason." – Thomas Aquinas

"When the Christians, upon these occasions, received martyrdom, they were ornamented, and crowned with garlands of flowers; for which they, in heaven, received eternal crowns of glory." – John Foxe

"If we do not have some knowledge by faith of the glory of Christ here and now, it means that we have no real desire for His presence in heaven." – John Owen

"What could an unsanctified man do in Heaven, if by any chance he got there? No man can possibly be happy in a place where he is not in his element, and where all around him is not congenial to his tastes, habits, and character." – J.C. Ryle

Hell

"Unconverted men walk over the pit of hell on a rotten covering." – Jonathan Edwards

"The national anthem of hell is, 'I Did It My Way.'" – Peter Kreeft

"There are theologians in the bottom of hell who are more interested in their own thoughts about God than in God himself." – C.S. Lewis

"The safest road to hell is the gradual one - the gentle slope, soft underfoot, without sudden turnings, without milestones, without signposts." – C.S. Lewis

Holy Spirit

"Revivals begin with God's own people; the Holy Spirit touches their heart anew, and gives them new fervor and compassion, and zeal, new light and life, and when He has thus come to you, He next goes forth to the valley of dry bones." – Andrew Bonar

Glossary of Christian Quotations

"Christian holiness is not a matter of painstaking conformity to the individual precepts of an external law code; it is rather a question of the Holy Spirit's producing His fruit in the life, reproducing those graces which were seen in perfection in the life of Christ." – F.F. Bruce

"If the spiritual life be healthy, under the full power of the Holy Spirit, praying without ceasing will be natural." – Andrew Murray

"Trying to do the Lord's work in your own strength is the most confusing, exhausting, and tedious of all work. But when you are filled with the Holy Spirit, then the ministry of Jesus just flows out of you." – Corrie Ten Boom

Hope

"Hope is a passion for the possible." – Søren Kierkegaard

"Everything that is done in this world is done by hope." – Martin Luther

"The hope of heaven under troubles is like wind and sails to the soul." – Samuel Rutherford

"Hope itself is like a star- not to be seen in the sunshine of prosperity, and only to be discovered in the night of adversity." – C.H. Spurgeon

Idolatry

"Man's nature, so to speak, is a perpetual factory of idols." – John Calvin

"Whatever your heart clings to and confides in, that is really your God, your functional savior." – Martin Luther

Justification

"Justification is away beyond anything that a human court of justice ever realizes. It is putting the sinner in the condition before God as if he had never sinned at all. It is giving him a standing in the merit of Jesus Christ of absolute innocency before God." – A.C. Dixon

"Faith is like a channel through which the benefits of Christ flow to us. We are not justified on account of faith; we are justified through

Glossary of Christian Quotations

faith. It is the work of Christ, not our faith, which is the foundation of justification. Faith itself is a gift of God." – Alistair McGrath

"We shall grow in grace, but we shall never be more completely pardoned then when we first believed." – C.H. Spurgeon

"Any church which puts in the place of justification by faith in Christ another method of salvation is a harlot church." – C.H. Spurgeon

Kingdom of God

"We want to reach the kingdom of God, but we don't want to travel by way of death. And yet there stands Necessity saying: 'This way, please.' Do not hesitate, man, to go this way, when this is the way that God came to you." – Augustine

"Jesus' message of the Kingdom of God is the announcement by word and deed that God is acting and manifesting dynamically his redemptive will in history." – George E. Ladd

"The coming of the kingdom brings deliverance, not only for the soul, but also for the body. It embraces nothing less than the re-creation of heaven and earth." – Herman Ridderbos

Knowledge

"There is no knowing that does not begin with knowing God." – John Calvin

"A man may be theologically knowing and spiritually ignorant." – Stephen Charnock

Law of God

"The Law dispels all self-illusions. It puts the fear of God in a man. Without this fear there can be no thirst for God's mercy. God accordingly uses the Law for a hammer to break up the illusion of self-righteousness that we should despair of our own strength and efforts at self-justification." – Martin Luther

"The law of God is what we must do; the gospel is what God will give." – Martin Luther

Glossary of Christian Quotations

"The law breaks the hard heart, but the gospel melts it. A stone duly broken, may be still a hard stone; but the gospel melts." – Ralph Erskine

"For a work to be considered good it must not only conform outwardly to the law of God, but it must be motivated inwardly by a sincere love for God." – R.C. Sproul

Living

"Life can only be understood backwards; but it must be lived forwards." - Søren Kierkegaard

"A Christian is a perfectly free lord of all, subject to none. A Christian is a perfectly dutiful servant of all, subject of all, subject to all." – Martin Luther

"Peace if possible. Truth at all costs." – Martin Luther

"Life is wasted if we do not grasp the glory of the cross, cherish it for the treasure that it is, and cleave to it as the highest price of every pleasure and the deepest comfort in every pain." – John Piper

"Do all the good you can. By all the means you can. In all the ways you can. In all the places you can. At all the times you can. To all the people you can. As long as ever you can." – John Wesley

Love

"Love, in its own nature, demands the perfecting of the beloved." – C.S. Lewis

"The love of God is a delightful and affectionate sense of the divine perfections, which makes the soul resign and sacrifice itself completely unto Him, desiring above all things to please Him, and delights in nothing so much as in fellowship and communion with Him, and being ready to do or suffer anything for His sake, or at His pleasure." – Henry Scougal

"Love takes possession of Heaven – but faith gives a title to it. Love is the crowning grace in Heaven – but faith is the conquering grace on earth." – Thomas Watson

"Humility and patience are the surest proofs of the increase of love." – John Wesley

Glossary of Christian Quotations

Man

"For what am I to myself without You, but a guide to my own downfall?" – Augustine

"Man is to be understood only in his relation to God." – C.S. Lewis

"For it pleased God, after He had made all things by the word of His power, to create man after His own image." – George Whitefield

Obedience

"Resolution One: I will live for God. Resolution Two: If no one else does, I still will." – Jonathan Edwards

"You are not only responsible for what you say, but also for what you do not say." – Martin Luther

"Do you mortify; do you make it your daily work; be always at it while you live; cease not a day from this work; be killing sin or it will be killing you." – John Owen

"We are only living truly human lives just so far as we are laboring to keep God's commandments; no further." – J.I. Packer

"It is better to lose your life than to waste it." – John Piper

"Our obedience is God's pleasure when it proves that God is our treasure." – John Piper

"What one generation tolerates, the next generation will embrace." – John Wesley

Patience

"Patience is the companion of wisdom." – Augustine

"Prayer is the midwife by which faith, the mother, brings forth patience in the heart." – Thomas Goodwin

"Thy peace shall be in much patience." – Thomas a Kempis

"There are three indispensable requirements for a missionary: 1. Patience 2. Patience 3. Patience." – Hudson Taylor

Glossary of Christian Quotations

Perseverance

"Prayer unaccompanied by perseverance leads to no result." – John Calvin

"By perseverance the snail reached the ark." – C.H. Spurgeon

"Our Father refreshes us on the journey with some pleasant inns, but will not encourage us to mistake them for home."- C.S. Lewis

"We are immortal till our work is done." – George Whitefield

Prayer

"Though a man's heart be much indisposed to prayer, yet, if he can but fall into a meditation of God, and the things of God, his heart will soon come off to prayer. Meditation lies so near to prayer, that in the Hebrew, the word that signifies to pray, signifies to meditate."- William Bridge

"Prayers will never reach God unless they are founded on free mercy." – John Calvin

"God loves importunate prayer so much that He will not give us much blessing without it." – Adoniram Judson

"There, in the "grinding of the wheels of providence," they are somehow being used to activate the eternal decrees of God in space-time history." – Douglas Kelly

"The function of prayer is not to influence God, but rather to change the nature of the one who prays." – Søren Kierkegaard

"I have so much to do that I shall spend the first three hours in prayer." – Martin Luther

"All who call on God in true faith, earnestly from the heart, will certainly be heard, and will receive what they have asked and desired." – Martin Luther

"Prayer is reaching out after the unseen; fasting is letting go of all that is seen and temporal. Fasting helps express, deepen, confirm the resolution that we are ready to sacrifice anything, even ourselves to attain what we seek for the kingdom of God." – Andrew Murray

Glossary of Christian Quotations

"He who prays as he ought will endeavor to live as he prays." – John Owen

"What we do every time we pray is to confess our impotence and God's sovereignty." – J.I. Packer

"Prayer is not so much an act as it is an attitude - an attitude of dependency, dependency upon God." – A.W. Pink

"Thanksgiving is inseparable from true prayer; it is almost essentially connected with it. One who always prays is ever giving praise, whether in ease or pain, both for prosperity and for the greatest adversity." – John Wesley

Resurrection

"Our flesh will be renewed by being exempt from decay, just as our soul is renewed by faith." – Augustine

"Let us consider this settled, that no one has made progress in the school of Christ who does not joyfully await the day of death and final resurrection." – John Calvin

"The truth of the resurrection gives life to every other area of gospel truth. The resurrection is the pivot on which all of Christianity turns and without which none of the other truths would much matter. Without the resurrection, Christianity would be so much wishful thinking, taking its place alongside all other human philosophy and religious speculation." – John MacArthur

Revival

"Revival begins by Christians getting right first and then spills over into the world." – C.H. Spurgeon

"Christians in revival are accordingly found living in God's presence (Coram Deo), attending to His Word, feeling acute concern about sin and righteousness, rejoicing in the assurance of Christ's love and their own salvation, spontaneously constant in worship, and tirelessly active in witness and service, fueling these activities by praise and prayer." – J.I. Packer

"Give me one hundred preachers who fear nothing but sin, and desire nothing but God, and I care not a straw whether they be clergymen or laymen; such alone will shake the gates of hell and set up the kingdom of heaven on Earth." – John Wesley

Salvation

"Thou hast made us for thyself, O Lord, and our heart is restless until it finds its rest in thee." – Augustine

"In seeking Him they find Him, and in finding they will praise Him." – Augustine

"To be assured of our salvation is no arrogant stoutness. It is faith. It is devotion. It is not presumption. It is God's promise." – Augustine

"God has promised forgiveness to your repentance, but He has not promised tomorrow to your procrastination." – Augustine

"The universal witness of the New Testament is that apostasy if persisted in not only damns but shows that salvation was never real in the first place. The New Testament reveals how close one may come to the kingdom - tasting, touching, perceiving, understanding. And it also shows that to come this far and reject the truth is unforgivable." – D.A. Carson

"A church has no right to make anything a condition of membership which Christ has not made a condition of salvation." – A.A. Hodge

"For a small reward, a man will hurry away on a long journey; while for eternal life, many will hardly take a single step." – Thomas a Kempis

"Salvation comes through a cross and a crucified Christ." – Andrew Murray

"In contradistinction to the Gospel of Christ, the gospel of Satan teaches salvation by works." – A.W. Pink

"The greatest enemy to human souls is the self-righteous spirit which makes men look to themselves for salvation." – C.H. Spurgeon

"Hearing the word is the devout receiving of the will of God." – William Ames

Glossary of Christian Quotations

Sanctification

"Most of God's people are contented to be saved from the hell that is without; they are not so anxious to be saved from the hell that is within." – Robert Murray M'Cheyne

"Holiness is nothing but the implanting, writing and living out the gospel in our souls." – John Owen

"Without holiness on earth we shall never be prepared to enjoy heaven. Heaven is a holy place. The Lord of heaven is a holy Being. The angels are holy creatures. Holiness is written on everything in heaven... How shall we ever be at home and happy in heaven if we die unholy?" – J.C. Ryle

"If you are renewed by grace, and were to meet your old self, I am sure you would be very anxious to get out of his company." – C.H. Spurgeon

"We should be rigorous in judging ourselves and gracious in judging others." – John Wesley

Sin

"Sin is the dare of God's justice, the rape of His mercy, the jeer of His patience, the slight of His power, and the contempt of His love." – John Bunyan

"Within each of us exists the image of God, however disfigured and corrupted by sin it may presently be. God is able to recover this image through grace as we are conformed to Christ." – Alistair McGrath

"One great power of sin is that it blinds men so that they do not recognize its true character." – Andrew Murray

Spiritual Warfare, Suffering and Trials

"In heaven we shall appear, not in armor, but in robes of glory. But here these are to be worn night and day; we must walk, work, and sleep in them, or else we are not true soldiers of Christ." – William Gurnall

"Suffering, then, is the badge of true discipleship." – Dietrich Bonhoeffer

Glossary of Christian Quotations

"Afflictions make the heart more deep, more experimental, more knowing and profound, and so, more able to hold, to contain, and beat more." – Bunyan.

"Sometimes God chooses to bless us and make us people of integrity in the midst of abominable circumstances, rather than change our circumstances." – D.A. Carson

"The real problem is not why some humble, pious, believing people suffer, but why some do not." – C.S. Lewis

"The servant of Christ must never be surprised if he has to drink of the same cup with His Lord." – J.C. Ryle

"God has never promised a charter of exemption from trouble — but he has promised to be with us in trouble." – Thomas Watson

"The Christian must trust in a withdrawing God." – William Gurnall

"Fiery trials make golden Christians." – Thomas Watson

Truth

"Truth is the agreement of our ideas with the ideas of God." – Jonathan Edwards

"Truth is reality as God sees it." – R.C. Sproul

Worship

"You cannot find excellent corporate worship until you stop trying to find excellent corporate worship and pursue God himself." – D.A. Carson

"Worship is our innermost being responding with praise for all that God is, through our attitudes, actions, thoughts, and words, based on the truth of God as He has revealed Himself." – John MacArthur

"Praising God is one of the highest and purest acts of religion. In prayer we act like men; in praise we act like angels." – Thomas Watson

Recommended Reading List

1. Alcorn, Randy *The Treasure Principle.*
2. Augustine *The City of God.*
3. Augustine, *Confessions.*
4. Baxter, Richard *The Godly Home.*
5. Beale, Greg *The Temple and the Church's Mission.*
6. Beale, Greg *We Become What We Worship.*
7. Boice, James M. *Foundations of the Christian Faith.*
8. Bonhoeffer, Dietrich *The Cost of Discipleship.*
9. Bonhoeffer, Dietrich *Life Together.*
10. Boykin, Jerry *Never Surrender.*
11. Bridge, William *A Lifting Up for the Downcast.*
12. Brooks, Thomas *Precious Remedies against Satan's Devices.*
13. Bunyan, John *Pilgrims Progress.*
14. Bunyan, John *The Holy War.*
15. Calvin, John *Institutes of the Christian Religion.*
16. Carson, D.A. *How Long, O Lord?*
17. Clowney, Edmund *The Church.*
18. De Mar, Gary *America's Christian History.*
19. Donnelly, Edward *Biblical Teaching on the Doctrines of Heaven and Hell.*
20. Edwards, Jonathan *Religious Affections.*
21. Lewis, C.S. *Mere Christianity.*
22. Lewis, C.S. *The Problem of Pain.*
23. Lewis, C.S. *The Screwtape Letters.*
24. Lloyd-Jones, David M. *Preaching and Preachers.*
25. Longman, Tremper *God is a Warrior.*
26. MacArthur, John *The Master's Plan for the Church.*
27. Murray, Andrew *With Christ in the School of Prayer.*
28. Owen, John *The Mortification of Sin in Believers.*
29. Packer, J.I. *Evangelism and the Sovereignty of God.*
30. Packer, J.I. *God's Words.*
31. Packer, J.I. *Knowing God.*
32. Piper, John *The Future of Justification.*
33. Piper, John *Let the Nations be Glad.*
34. Piper, John *Seeing and Savoring Jesus Christ.*
35. Piper, John *What Jesus Demands from the World.*
36. Piper and Grudem, *Recovering Biblical Manhood and Womanhood.*
37. Ryle, J.C. *Holiness.*
38. Ryle, J.C. *Thoughts for Young Men.*
39. Sanders, J. Oswald *Spiritual Leadership.*
40. Sproul, R.C. *The Last Days According to Jesus.*
41. Spurgeon, Charles H. *Lectures to My Students.*
42. Storms, Sam *Signs of the Spirit.*
43. VanGemeren, Willhem *The Progress of Redemption.*
44. Watson, Thomas *All Things For Good.*
45. Weber, Stu *The Christian Husband.*
46. Weber, Stu *Locking Arms: God's Design for Masculine Friendships.*
47. Wells, David F. *God in the Wasteland.*
48. Wells, Tom *A Vision for Missions.*
49. White, John *The Fight: A Practical Handbook for Christian Living.*
50. Wilson, Carl W. *Our Dance Has Turned to Death.*

Scripture Index

598

Scripture Index

Scripture Index

Scripture Index

Scripture Index

Scripture Index

Scripture Index

604

Scripture Index

Scripture Index

Scripture Index

Scripture Index

Scripture Index

Scripture Index

Scripture Index

Scripture Index

Scripture Index

Scripture Index

Scripture Index

Scripture Index

Scripture Index

General Index

General Index

General Index

General Index

General Index

General Index

Author Index

Author Index

Author Index

"And they overcame him by the blood of the Lamb and by the word of their testimony, and they did not love their lives to the death" (Rev 12:11).

CPSIA information can be obtained at www.ICGtesting.com
Printed in the USA
BVOW08s2228150115

383217BV00002B/2/P